IRA L. REISS
University of Minnesota

Readings
on the
Family System

KLAUS THEILE

HOLT, RINEHART AND WINSTON, INC.

*New York   Chicago   San Francisco   Atlanta   Dallas
Montreal   Toronto   London   Sydney*

TO MY GRANDPARENTS:
Eva and Philip Jacobs
Rachel and Simon Reiss

PREFACE

The justification of a book of readings is a product of three key variables: (1) the quality of the selections, (2) the convenience added by the collection, and (3) the integration provided by the editor's introductory materials and organization. I believe that each of these dimensions provides something significant to this anthology.

The readings were selected after an exhaustive search of the literature. The Family Study Center at the University of Minnesota is fortunate in having the Inventory of Research in Marriage and the Family. This inventory indexes all publications throughout the world from 1900 to the present. I concentrated on the most recent material available. Only two of the readings were published before 1960 and the vast majority were published after 1965. Thus the selection is timely and unlikely to go out of date for several years. The coverage is quite broad. Twelve journals and seven books were used as sources. In addition, I wrote an article especially for this reader. Over fifty different authors were involved. Because the readings are drawn from such a wide array, the anthology does a service by presenting them in one place. It would be extremely difficult to duplicate this range of articles even in a large university library.

It should be clear, however, that any anthology such as this involves compromises. There were many excellent articles that could not be included and many very close decisions that had to be made. My choice of what I feel to be the best does not imply that I have exhausted the excellent.

The difficulty of the articles has been kept to the undergraduate level. I have taught courses in the family area for the past 19 years and thereby gained some knowledge of the level of material students can handle. However, the articles include a variety of levels of complexity, and the instructor can elaborate upon them to the extent he desires.

The topical coverage is broad. The Prologue provides a general understanding of courtship, marital, and family institutions and their current trends. Section I introduces the reader to the cross cultural perspective on the family. Sections II, III, and IV focus on the courtship institution in our society and its various sexual and affectional aspects. Sections V through XI deal with marital and family institutions, with particular emphasis on the present-day urban and industrial scene and the relevance of such issues as women's role, black equality, population pressure, and marital dissolution. The final section focuses on deviant behavior and changing social norms in the areas of homosexuality, mate exchange, illegitimacy, and communes.

In addition to the Prologue I have written brief introductions to each of the twelve sections and an Epilogue. In the introductions I make occasional reference to other articles and books for the interested reader. However, it should be clear that I am giving selected rather than comprehensive references. The readings themselves have further references. My purpose in the introductions is to help integrate the articles so that the reader will gain a coherent overall conception of current social-scientific knowledge of the family. The wide range of selections allows the professor the choice of emphasizing those segments of interest to his course. Although the sociological and social-psychological approaches receive primary stress, the readings should prove of value also to those who are teaching courses in the family from a problem or applied perspective. Many of the articles are directly relevant to those interested in social problems as related to the family. Increasing attention is being given to a common approach to the family area, wherein the research done by sociologists and social psychologists is of prime concern regardless of what other emphases may be present in the family course. In this sense, the selections are useful to a very wide range of family courses. The book closes with an Epilogue in which I attempt to extricate some basic themes from the 39 articles.

The process of selecting articles and book chapters for this anthology has left me with an even deeper respect for the quality of work in the family field. Going over the literature again I became even more aware of the improved quality of research and theory that has been put into print, particularly in the past ten years. I believe the area of the sociology of the family has come of age and today represents some of our finest social scientific work. After reading this book, I believe the reader will agree.

ACKNOWLEDGMENTS

My greatest debt is to the thousands of students who have taken my courses on the family. The major way I have learned the sociology of the family area is by trying to meet the challenge of clarifying and integrating different aspects of the family system to my students. When one tries to present his ideas to others, he has the opportunity of seeing his contradictions, lack of information, and lack of organization much more clearly than if he never has had to communicate his ideas in public. In this way teaching forces one, if he is to be successful, to clarify and organize his thinking. Writing does the same thing—perhaps even more rigorously because ideas are down in black and white and can therefore be more easily analyzed. Students afford a most worthwhile service by their frank analytical reactions to their teacher's ideas, and for that I am most grateful. They may not always have the answers but they can recognize flaws and they challenge one to gain the ability to inform, to excite, and to understand.

Many other people besides my students contributed to this book. Kay Michael Troost, my former research assistant, was of considerable aid to me in my choice of articles. He worked with me in amassing the large bibliography from which my final selections were made. My current research assistant, Al Banwart, has also helped a great deal in the preparation of this book. The basic research resources and assistance for locating studies on the family came from Nancy Dahl, the Director of the Inventory of Research in Marriage and the Family, and from her assistant Mary Arnold. The vast amount of detail work, typing, and xeroxing was done by my secretarial staff, consisting of Mary Ann Ellingson, my executive secretary, and her assistants, Margaret Johnson, Sandra Peterson, Phyllis Dehler, Cathy Hicks, Chris Johansen, and Penny Bergeson, who performed these tasks admirably.

I.L.R.

Minneapolis
April 1972

CONTENTS

Prologue: The Family System and Its Probable Future

The 1970s are likely to be to the second half of the twentieth century what the 1920s were to the first half. The 1920s established the form of our family system for a society that had just passed the 50 percent urban residency line and a nation that had only recently taken its place as one of the major powers in the Western world. The older courtship, marriage, and family norms had been transformed radically in the decades preceding the 1920s, and the 1920s consolidated and generalized those changes. Divorce rates grew at an unprecedented rate between 1914 and 1920, premarital intercourse rates for women who started to date in 1915 and shortly thereafter doubled, and full legitimization of a courtship system wherein young people selected their own mates was well established. In these and many other ways the 1920s saw the culmination of the change to a modern urban, industrial society. The 1970s are the culmination of those changes leading to the postindustrial society. I use the term postindustrial to refer to a state wherein the major problems are not the production of goods and services but the fair and equitable distribution and control of such goods and services. The social problems in such a society become defined in terms of such concerns as equity and pollution. Changes in our family system today are in conformity with values held by many generations in our society; values such as equalitarianism, individualism, hedonism, and the pursuit of happiness. We are today embodying these values in our family system in ways integrated with a postindustrial society. Before we analyze further the present-day situation and trends, let us discuss what we mean by the term "family system."

NATURE OF THE FAMILY SYSTEM

The thesis of this book is that in any society the *family system* consists of three interrelated institutions: (1) the courtship institution, (2) the marriage

1

institution, and (3) the family institution. A full development of this idea can be found in the author's recent book, *The Family System in America*. The reader should be clear that I am here discussing the universally required features of the family system and not the specifics of our American variety. I will briefly elaborate my thinking.

The *courtship institution* has the universal societal function of mate selection and accomplishes this by patterns of interaction involving parents and their children. In America we stress the power of free mate-choice by young people, but parents have many indirect influences on such a choice. Parents pass on their basic values to their youngsters in many intended and unintended ways. The reading by Barry and his colleagues (3) shows that there is a general tendency throughout all cultures to teach males to be self-reliant and females to be nurturant and obedient. The subtle ways in which parents influence the values of their children is also brought out in the Heilbrun reading (4), which shows the importance of parental behavior in creating the male–female differences that Barry reports. Parents control the courtship of their older children by sending them to certain schools, moving into preferred types of neighborhoods, and joining special religious groups. Goode's research (10) has led him to conclude that such parental control of mate selection (even in a society like our own) is especially common at the higher socio-economic levels. In almost all societies, at upper class levels, parents are more concerned than are those of lower class levels with the relevance of their childrens' matings to their own economic and social standing in the community. Of course the young people in many societies have considerable power in the mate-selection process, but that point does not need to be stressed in a society such as ours.

The *marital institution* has the universal function of legitimizing parenthood and does this by means of a socially sanctioned union involving two or more people. Looking cross-culturally we can see that such unions can vary tremendously. Middleton (2) for example, points out that during the period of the Roman occupation of Egypt, brother-sister marriage among commoners was quite prevalent. This historical finding smashes some of our notions regarding incest and expands our conception of potential marriage mates in various societies. Among the Nuer in Africa there is a form of marriage involving two women, one of whom plays the father-husband role and one of whom plays the mother-wife role.[1] But all of the varied structures in different cultures have the common function of legitimizing certain people as potential parents. Even in those societies where premarital coitus is widely accepted, children born out of wedlock are more or less unaccepted.

The variety of types of marital relationships in the Western world alone is well brought out by Cuber and Harroff (19) in their discussion of five types of marital relationships, and by Rodman (18) in his comparison of marital power in American marriages with marital power in other Western cultures. Yet in all these systems, one key function prevails and that is the social legitimization of parenthood. In other words, the marital institution, like the courtship institution, is present in all societies, and seems to be fulfilling a universal requirement of human society.

The third interrelated institution within the family *system* is the *family in-*

[1] Evans-Pritchard, E. E., *Kinship and Marriage among the Nuer*. London: Oxford University Press, 1951.

stitution. I have included the courtship and marital institutions as part of the family system for they are functionally essential to the family institution. There must be some system of mate-selection and legitimization if a society is to set the stage for the nurturance of children. It is this nurturance of the newborn that makes up the essential universal function of the family institution. By nurturance I mean the giving of emotional response and support. This function is universally accomplished by some sort of small, kinship-structured group. A kinship-structured group is simply a group wherein people feel they are descended from each other. For example, people who are kin feel that they have descended from some older people in the society (parent–child kinship) or feel they have descended from the same person and thus are kin (brother–sister kinship). Descent is at the heart of the feeling of kinship. This descent need not be biological—it can, for example, be by adoption. It is a socially defined relation. I have developed this notion regarding the family institution in the first reading.

In the family institution, as in the marital and courtship institutions, there are many structural variations that accomplish its key function. Melvin Kohn (22) points out differences in the way white-collar and blue-collar parents rear their children. The white-collar parents stress the value of self-reliance and the blue-collar stress more the value of obedience. It is interesting to note that these class differences in values are very similar to the differences Barry (3) noted between males and females. In our society and in most others, a group that is taught obedience is surely at a disadvantage in competing with a group that is taught self-reliance. Thus, much of our present-day efforts to equalize social class and sex groups may well depend on the degree with which we succeed in altering this type of differential value inculcation. Other articles in Section VIII delineate further the social class and racial differences in families. These articles also point out how the type of family is important in terms of one's occupational position.

Families that stress obedience and those that stress self-reliance are both meeting our functional requirement of nurturing their offspring. Thus, one's preference for one or another type of family cannot solely be based upon discovering what is universally required in the family. Such universal information does inform one of the societal limits on one's choice for a particular type of family. What is essential to all societies must be present, but one still needs a set of values to proceed to choose one of the many structures that will fulfill that essential function.

The above discussion of the family system is oriented to the universal nature of the three institutions involved. I have defined each of the three institutions of the family system in terms of what I believe to be its universally essential structure and function. Any human society should display these institutions in accord with our definitions. This frame of reference can help the reader to integrate conceptually the diverse readings in this book. However, it should be clear that all societies will have family systems that possess other attributes besides these essential structures and functions. But none of these additional characteristics are considered to be universal requirements of the family system.

THE FAMILY SYSTEM IN THE OVERALL SOCIETY

Sociologists have speculated for decades regarding the ways in which the overall family system (courtship, marital, and family institutions) operates in the urban-industrial setting of countries like America. I will here only briefly touch on three areas of concern to those interested in the modern family. These three areas can help show the reader some of the broad outlines that are filled in by many of the readings. They are a sample of what is covered.

The Family and Economic System

Japan, like America, is highly urbanized and industrialized, and yet her family system is quite different from the American family.[2] Thus, it seems that a variety of family forms can exist in an urban-industrial society. In addition, the importance of kinship ties even in modern societies like our own is borne out by Litwak (28) and Adams (29) in Section IX. Our rapid means of communication and transportation have made it possible for kinship ties to be maintained over thousands of miles. It is interesting to note, as some writers point out, that female kin ties, despite the tradition of male dominance, seem to be maintained more closely and powerfully than male kin ties in modern western societies.[3] Goode (10) feels such kin ties are strongest in the upper classes.

The Family and Population Pressure

The importance of the family is nowhere more obvious than when we consider population pressure. Overpopulation and resultant pollution is a major concern in all parts of the world. Davis (30) raises the provocative point that contraceptive control may not be enough to prevent overpopulation, for most women want 3 children and will not limit births below that level. Hill (31) points out how the communication patterns in the family predict whether contraception will be used, by whom, and how effectively. Research in the area of the family is therefore important for those wishing to understand the present population crises in both developed and developing countries.

Marital Dissolution

Another area of concern to Americans is the dissolution of our family system. Our divorce rate has increased since 1963 more rapidly than it has over the past 25 years. In fact, since 1967 the rate of increase in divorce has accelerated even further. Is the family becoming obsolete—is it breaking down at such a rate that it will destroy our society? I think the answer is no. I believe the divorce rate will level off in a few years. More importantly, the speed with which divorced people remarry has recently increased. About half of those who remarry do so within 2 or 3 years after the divorce. Further, about 80 percent of the divorced will remarry and such second marriages do generally last.

Such a dynamic divorce and remarriage system could mean that our existing marriages are on the average happier than our marriages were generations ago

[2] See for example: Wilkinson, Thomas O., "Family Structure and Industrialization in Japan." *American Sociological Review* 27 (October, 1962), 678–682.
    [3] Sweetser, Dorrian Apple, "Intergenerational Ties in Finnish Urban Families." *American Sociological Review* 33 (April, 1968), 236–246.

when unhappy people were more likely to stay married for "the sake of the children." The Rosenberg article (34) affords us some insights into the costs in self-esteem involved for children in broken families. The wide variation in break-age rates for different racial and occupational groups is adequately portrayed in several readings in Section VIII. In Section XI Komarovsky (32) enlarges the portrait for the blue-collar worker in the excerpt from her insightful book. In addition, the readings in this section should enable the reader to understand the way in which our divorce situation is part and parcel of the wider social system in which the family exists. A high divorce rate is not a sign of the demise of the family—particularly when it is accompanied by a high remarriage rate.

FUTURE CHANGES IN THE FAMILY SYSTEM

No one using this collection of readings can avoid the question of the likely changes in the family in the last three decades of this century. I will here merely touch on a few aspects of this question. What new forms of court-ship, marriage, and the family will appear? Will these institutions be replaced? I do believe that we are evolving new forms but these new forms still fit the universal conception of the family system that I gave above. As I have described the family system in this prologue, it is essential to any human society. My basic argument is developed in the first reading, but I can say here that the entire process of getting people together to nurture the newborn infants who make up the next generation is an essential task for any society which wishes to survive. There are broad structural limits within which such tasks can be accom-plished. For example, if most couples instead of getting legally married decided simply to inform their friends that they were now living together, would marriage then cease to exist? No, such a situation could develop into a more informal type of marital system. As long as such sharing of a room was the socially accepted way for couples to live who were to become parents, then it would be the socially accepted way of legitimizing parenthood and that fits our definition of the marital institution. There would still likely be other ways of mating that were not socially accepted. One may morally object to such a way of fulfilling the marital function but that is a separate level of discussion. If the question were asked whether such a system could be a marriage system, the answer is "Yes." In fact some of the Israeli kibbutzim have just such a marital system.[4] The couple that wishes to establish a marital relation that includes the possibility of parenthood, simply asks for a common room. The entire question of parenthood and legitimacy is a fascinating one cross-culturally and the article by Rodman (38) in Section XII, is most relevant to that issue. The question of illegitimacy is vital to any understanding of the marital institution.

The article by Bartell (35) raises another question regarding social change—this in the area of sexual relationships. There is a well-publicized but small minority of couples in America today—both married and unmarried—who par-ticipate in group sex practices in which partners are exchanged, and at times sexual acts occur in public. I think the proper sociological perspective on such practices is that they are not incompatible with a family system, for they are

[4] Spiro, Melford E., *Kibbutz: Venture in Utopia*. Cambridge, Mass.: Harvard University Press, 1956.

present in other cultures in the world. However, the more interesting question for a social scientist is whether such practices are compatible with what Cuber and Harroff (19) call a "total marital relationship." Can one sexually share one's mate with other individuals in a casual fashion and be able to prevent this from interfering with sharing one's complete life experiences in an emotionally meaningful way with that partner? Does such "swapping" alter the significance of the relationship in ways that make full sharing less likely? What about monogamous marriages in a commune setting—what limits does such a setting place on human relations?

Regardless of the answers to these questions, an even more fundamental question would be: Do young Americans want a total, holistic and exclusive type of relationship with each other or do they want a relationship that is more highly compartmentalized and thus would allow for more private worlds of experience? My own feelings would be that most Americans are still socialized into wanting the total type of relationship but that a great many settle for a more segmented relationship in their own marriages. In such relationships, mate exchange probably can more easily be psychologically accepted. However, one must remember here that in such segmented relationships, sexual affairs of any kind with other people are more likely. The swapping arrangement is simply a more equalitarian and open version of old-fashioned adultery. Since our society is more open and more equalitarian about sex, it is not surprising that this new form of adultery has arisen. But I think it is a minority form at present, and although it may grow, it is unlikely to be for many a sought-after goal but rather an adjustment to the stresses of one's overall psychological and sexual existence. Bartell's research helps one understand this new form of adultery.

One other direction of change that is of interest is concerned with the rights of women and blacks. I think it is undoubtedly true that both women and blacks are influenced by an increase in equalitarianism in America and that this will continue for the rest of the century. However, I do think that support for this movement today is not strong enough to lead to full racial and sexual equality even by the end of this century. Prejudice dies slowly and discrimination will probably make it difficult for the low-ranking groups of today to develop the needed power and skills in order to gain full equality. Many women still regard the wife-mother role as primary, and as the early readings (Sections I and II) indicate, the differences in self-reliance between the sexes are rooted in very early socialization. It will take considerable time to change this and, more importantly, it will take a commitment on the part of women and men to a radically changed sex-role conception. As Rossi (36) indicates, in order for sexual equality to occur in terms of economic and political opportunity, the female tie to the home and to children would have to be lessened while the male tie is increased. We will make strides in this direction, but I doubt that we will achieve full equality in the next three decades.

SUMMARY AND CONCLUSIONS

The functions of mate selection, legitimization of parenthood, and nurturance of the newborn are considered to be essential to the survival of human society. These functions, with some very broad structural limitations upon ways of achieving them, are considered to comprise the family system in our society and in every other. The specific makeup of our family system can be further delineated by looking at the ways in which infants are reared, the attitudes toward love and sex, the relation of the family system to the occupational and political system, the ways in which personal choice and desires operate, and the overall global pressure toward social and cultural change.

Let us now turn to the individual selections and further specify the nature of this universally required part of human society called the family system.

I | Cross-Cultural Perspective on the Family

Introduction to Section I

One of the signs of maturity in the sociological study of the family is the rapid increase in cross-cultural studies and in the awareness of the value of such a perspective. To study the family only in our own society runs the risk of provincialism—of believing that the way our family system operates is the way all family systems operate. Whether one's personal tastes favor the status quo or some other system, it is important to know what the range of possible choices are and what the "costs" of each choice are. A cross-cultural perspective enables one to start answering just such queries.

By examining the family cross-culturally one can discern what elements seem essential to any human society and what elements can be varied. For example, the first reading points out that the universally required aspects of the family institution are a small kinship-structured group that will provide nurturance of the newborn. There are a multitude of ways in which nurturant socialization can be performed. The range of choice is clarified by a cross-cultural examination. If one is building his utopia, such an examination can supply one with outlines of the features that must be present. There is a long-standing discussion in the social sciences concerning the universal aspects of the family. The reader will be introduced to the classic statement of George Peter Murdock and to other views in the first reading.[1]

One of the surprising results of cross-cultural examination of the family system is that revealed by Russell Middleton (2). For many decades it had been generally agreed that no society had ever accepted incest except among its royalty (Hawaiian, Incan, and Egyptian) or on very rare occasions. Middleton's historical research indicates otherwise. He finds a large proportion of marriages of commoners during the Roman occupation of Egypt were between brothers and

[1] Murdock, G. P., *Social Structure*. New York: Macmillan, 1949.

9

sisters. This sort of finding reshapes our conceptions of the range of possible marital forms.

In Section XII we will discuss some recent trends, such as the increased emphasis on equality of the sexes stressed by the women's liberation movement. The cross-cultural study of Barry and his colleagues in this opening section (3) is of direct relevance to this movement. Barry investigates the cross-cultural differences in child-rearing and reports that after infancy females are reared to be more nurturant, responsible, and obedient, and males are reared to be more self-reliant and achievement-oriented. Although there may be biological factors related to such differences, Barry and his colleagues conclude that since many cultures provide exceptions to this finding, the behavior cannot be fully biologically based but must be culturally learned. This conclusion supports the arguments of those who favor rearing male and female children in equalitarian ways, for it shows that despite current differences such a change seems possible. Of course, the evidence is not sufficient in itself to settle the nature-vs.-nurture controversy on this point.

One additional insight that a cross-cultural approach yields is that every form of society that one can imagine has a price tag upon it. For example, if one wants a society where men and women are treated more equally in the occupational system, then the price one will have to pay is a de-emphasis of the wife–mother role in favor of the occupational role for women. This would mean that the tasks usually a part of wife–mother roles would have to be more or less taken over by males or be collectively carried out by day-care centers or the like. In any case, it would be a significant change that would provide rewards and costs according to one's personal values. A cross-cultural perspective helps throw light on such key factors in the nature of social and cultural choices.

1 The Universality of the Family: A Conceptual Analysis

IRA L. REISS

During the last few decades, a revived interest in the question of the universality of the family has occurred. One key reason for this was the 1949 publication of George Peter Murdock's book *Social Structure*.[1] In that book, Murdock postulated that the nuclear family was universal and that it had four essential functions which it always and everywhere fulfilled. These four functions were: (1) socialization, (2) economic cooperation, (3) reproduction, and (4) sexual relations. Even in polygamous and extended family systems, the nuclear families within these larger family types were viewed as separate entities which each performed these four functions.

The simplicity and specificity of Murdock's position make it an excellent starting point for an investigation of the universal functions of the human family. Since Murdock's position has gained support in many quarters, it should be examined carefully.[2] Brief comments on Murdock's position appear in the literature, and some authors, such as Levy and Fallers, have elaborated their opposition.[3] The present paper attempts to go somewhat further, not only in testing Murdock's notion but in proposing and giving evidence for a substitute position. However, it should be clear that Murdock's position is being used merely as an illustration; our main concern is with delineating what, if anything, is universal about the human family.

The four functions of the nuclear family are "functional prerequisites" of human society, to use David Aberle's term from his classic article on the

[1] George P. Murdock, *Social Structure*, New York: Macmillan, 1949.

[2] Many of the textbooks in the family field fail to really cope with this issue and either ignore the question or accept a position arbitrarily. The Census definition also ignores this issue: "A group of two persons or more related by blood, marriage, or adoption and residing together." The recently published *Dictionary of the Social Sciences*, ed. by Julius Gould and William Kolb, Glencoe, Ill.: Free Press, 1964, defines the nuclear family as universal. See pp. 257–259. Parsons, Bales, Bell and Vogel are among those who also seem to accept Murdock's position. See: Talcott Parsons and Robert F. Bales, *Family, Socialization and Interaction Process*, Glencoe, Ill.: Free Press, 1955; Talcott Parsons, "The Incest Taboo in Relation to Social Structure and the Socialization of the Child," *British Journal of Sociology*, 5 (January, 1954), 101–117; *A Modern Introduction to the Family*, ed. by Norman Bell and Ezra Vogel, Glencoe, Ill.: Free Press, 1960.

[3] Marion J. Levy, Jr. and L. A. Fallers, "The Family: Some Comparative Considerations," *American Anthropologist*, 61 (August, 1959), 647–651.

The author is grateful to his colleagues David Andrews, June Helm, and David Plath, all of whom read this article and gave the benefits of their comments.

Reprinted from the *Journal of Marriage and the Family*, 27 (November, 1965), 443–453, by permission of the National Council on Family Relations.

topic.[4] This means that these functions must somehow occur for human society to exist. If the nuclear family everywhere fulfills these functions, it follows that this family should be a "structural prerequisite" of human society, i.e., a universally necessary part of society.[5] The basic question being investigated is not whether these four functions are functional pre-requisites of human society—almost all social scientists would accept this—but whether these four functions are necessarily carried out by the nuclear family. If these functions are not everywhere carried out by the nuclear family, then are there any functional prerequisites of society which the nu-clear family or any family form does fulfill? Is the family a universal insti-tution in the sense that it always fulfills some functional prerequisite of society? Also, what, if any, are the universal structural features of the family? These are the ultimate questions of importance that this examination of Murdock's position is moving toward.

Murdock's contention that the nuclear family is a structural prerequisite of human society since it fulfills four functional prerequisites of human society is relatively easy to test. If a structure is essential, then finding one society where the structure does not exist or where one or more of the four functions are not fulfilled by this structure is sufficient to refute the theory. Thus, a crucial test could best be made by focusing on societies with rather atypical family systems to see whether the nuclear family was present and was fulfilling these four functions. The more typical family systems will also be discussed. A proper test can be made by using only groups which are societies. This limitation is necessary so as not to test Murdock unfairly with such subsocietal groups as celibate priests. For pur-poses of this paper, the author accepts the definition of society developed by Aberle and his associates:

> A society is a group of human beings sharing a self-sufficient system of action which is capable of existing longer than the life-span of an indi-vidual, the group being recruited at least in part by the sexual repro-duction of the members.[6]

A TEST OF MURDOCK'S THESIS

One of the cultures chosen for the test of Murdock's thesis is from his own original sample of 250 cultures—the Nayar of the Malabar Coast of India. In his book, Murdock rejected Ralph Linton's view that the Nayar lacked the nuclear family.[7] Since that time, the work of Kathleen Gough has supported Linton's position, and Murdock has accordingly changed his own position.[8] In letters to the author dated April 3, 1963 and January 20, 1964,

[4] David F. Aberle et al., "The Functional Prerequisites of a Society," *Ethics*, 60 (January, 1950), 100–111.
[5] Ibid.
[6] Ibid., p. 101.
[7] Murdock, op. cit., p. 3.
[8] For a brief account of the Nayar, see: E. Kathleen Gough, "Is the Family Universal: The Nayar Case," pp. 76–92 in *A Modern Introduction to the Family*,

Murdock took the position that the Nayar are merely the old Warrior Caste of the Kerala Society and thus not a total society and are more comparable to a celibate group of priests. No such doubt about the societal status of the Nayar can be found in his book. Murdock rejects the Nayar only after he is forced to admit that they lack the nuclear family. In terms of the definition of society adopted above, the Nayar seem to be a society even if they, like many other societies, do have close connections with other groups.

The matrilineage is particularly strong among the Nayar, and a mother with the help of her matrilineage brings up her children. Her husband and "lovers" do not assist her in the raising of her children. Her brother typically assists her when male assistance is needed. Assistance from the linked lineages where most of her lovers come from also substitutes for the weak husband role. Since many Nayar women change lovers rather frequently, there may not even be any very stable male-female relation present. The male is frequently away fighting. The male makes it physiologically possible for the female to have offspring, but he is not an essential part of the family unit that will raise his biological children. In this sense, sex and reproduction are somewhat external to the family unit among the Nayar. Very little in the way of economic cooperation between husband and wife occurs. Thus, virtually all of Murdock's functions are outside of the nuclear family. However, it should be noted that the socialization of offspring function is present in the maternal extended family system. Here, then, is a society that seems to lack the nuclear family and, of necessity, therefore, the four functions of this unit. Even if we accept Gough's view that the "lovers" are husbands and that there really is a form of group marriage, it is still apparent that the separate husband-wife-child units formed by such a group marriage do not here comprise separately functioning nuclear families.

One does not have to rely on just the Nayar as a test of Murdock. Harold E. Driver, in his study of North American Indians, concludes that in matrilocal extended family systems with matrilineal descent, the husband role and the nuclear family are often insignificant.[9] It therefore seems that the relative absence of the nuclear family in the Nayar is approached particularly in other similar matrilineal societies. Thus, the Nayar do not seem to be so unique. They apparently demonstrate a type of family system that is common in lesser degree.

A somewhat similar situation seems to occur in many parts of the Caribbean. Judith Blake described a matrifocal family structure in which the hus-

---

op. cit. It is interesting to note that Bell and Vogel, in their preface to Gough's article on the Nayar, contend that she supports Murdock's position on the universality of the nuclear family. In point of fact, Gough on page 84 rejects Murdock and actually deals primarily with the marital and not the family institution. See also: *Matrilineal Kinship*, ed. by David M. Schneider and Kathleen Gough, Berkeley: University of California Press, 1961, Chaps. 6 and 7. A. R. Radcliffe-Brown was one of the first to note that the Nayar lacked the nuclear family. See his: *African Systems of Kinship and Marriage*, New York: Oxford University Press, 1959, p. 73.

  [9] Harold H. Driver, *Indians of North America*, Chicago: University of Chicago Press, 1961, pp. 291–292.

band and father roles are quite often absent or seriously modified.[10] Sexual relations are often performed with transitory males who have little relation to the raising of the resultant offspring. Thus, in Jamaica one can also question whether the nuclear family exists and performs the four functions Murdock ascribed to it. Socialization of offspring is often performed by the mother's family without any husband, common law or legal, being present. Naturally, if the husband is absent, the economic cooperation between husband and wife cannot occur. Also, if the male involved is not the husband but a short-term partner, sex and reproduction are also occurring outside the nuclear family.

The above societies are all "mother-centered" systems. A family system which is not mother-centered is the Israeli Kibbutz family system as described by Melford Spiro.[11] Here the husband and wife live together in a communal agricultural society. The children are raised communally and do not live with their parents. Although the Kibbutzim are only a small part of the total Israeli culture, they have a distinct culture and can be considered a separate society by the Aberle definition cited above. They have been in existence since 1909 and thus have shown that they can survive for several generations and that they have a self-sufficient system of action. The function which is most clearly missing in the Kibbutz family is that of economic cooperation between husband and wife. In this communal society, almost all work is done for the total Kibbutz, and the rewards are relatively equally distributed regardless of whether one is married or not. There is practically no division of labor between husbands and wives as such. Meals are eaten communally, and residence is in one room which requires little in the way of housekeeping.

Here, too, Murdock denies that this is a real exception and, in the letters to the author referred to above, contends that the Kibbutzim could not be considered a society. Murdock's objection notwithstanding, a group which has existed for over half a century and has developed a self-sufficient system of action covering all major aspects of existence indeed seems to be a society by almost all definitions. There is nothing in the experience of the Kibbutzim that makes it difficult to conceive of such groups existing in many regions of the world or, for that matter, existing by themselves in a world devoid of other people. They are analogous to some of the Indian groups living in American society in the sense that they have a coherent way of life that differs considerably from the dominant culture. Thus, they are not the same as an average community which is merely a part of the dominant culture.

Melford Spiro concludes that Murdock's nuclear family is not present in the Kibbutz he and his wife studied. He suggests several alterations in Murdock's definition which would be required to make it better fit the Kib-

[10] Judith Blake, *Family Structure in Jamaica*, Glencoe, Ill.: Free Press, 1961. Whether Jamaicans actually prefer to marry and have a more typical family system is a controversial point.
[11] Melford E. Spiro, *Kibbutz: Venture in Utopia*, Cambridge, Mass.: Harvard University Press, 1956; and Melford E. Spiro, *Children of the Kibbutz*, Cambridge, Mass.: Harvard University Press, 1958.

butz. The alterations are rather drastic and would still not fit the Nayar and other cultures discussed above.[12]

There are other societies that are less extreme but which still create some difficulty with Murdock's definition of the nuclear family. Malinowski, in his study of the Trobriand Islanders, reports that except for perhaps nurturant socialization, the mother's brother rather than the father is the male who teaches the offspring much of the necessary way of life of the group.[13] Such a situation is certainly common in a matrilineal society, and it does place limits on the socialization function of the nuclear family per se. Further, one must at least qualify the economic function in the Trobriand case. The mother's brother here takes a large share of the economic burden and supplies his sister's family with half the food they require. The rigidity of Murdock's definition in light of such instances is apparent. These examples also make it reasonable that other societies may well exist which carry a little further such modifications of the nuclear family. For example, we find such more extreme societies when we look at the Nayar and the Kibbutz.

Some writers, like Nicholas Timasheff, have argued that the Russian experience with the family evidences the universality of the nuclear family.[14] While it is true that the Communists in Russia failed to abolish as much of the old family system as they wanted to, it does not follow that this demonstrates the impossibility of abolishing the family.[15] In point of fact, the family system of the Israeli Kibbutz is virtually identical with the system the Russian Communists desired, and thus we must admit that it is possible for at least some groups to achieve such a system. Also, the Communists did not want to do away with the family in toto. Rather, they wanted to do away

[12] Spiro suggests that "reference residence" be used in place of actual common residence. The Kibbutz children do speak of their parents' room as "home." He suggests further that responsibility for education and economic cooperation be substituted for the actual doing of these functions by the parents. The parents could be viewed as responsible for the education of their children, but since nothing changes in economic terms when one marries, it is difficult to understand just what Spiro means by responsibility for economic cooperation being part of the family. Spiro also would alter Murdock's definition of marriage so as to make emotional intimacy the key element.

[13] Bronislaw Malinowski, *The Sexual Life of Savages in North-Western Melanesia*, New York: Harvest Books, 1929.

[14] Nicholas S. Timasheff, "The Attempt to Abolish the Family in Russia," pp. 55–63 in Bell and Vogel, op. cit.

[15] Timasheff refers to the family as "that pillar of society." But nothing in the way of convincing evidence is presented to support this view. The argument is largely that since disorganization followed the attempt to do away with the family, it was a result of that attempt. This may well be an example of a *post hoc ergo propter hoc* fallacy. Also, it should be noted that the love-based union of parents that the early communists wanted might well be called a family, and thus that the very title of Timasheff's article implies a rather narrow image of the family. For a recent account of the Soviet family see: David and Vera Mace, *The Soviet Family*, New York: Doubleday, 1963; and Ray Bauer et al., *How the Soviet System Works*, Cambridge, Mass.: Harvard University Press, 1959.

with the patriarchal aspects of the family, to have marriage based on love, easy divorce, and communal upbringing of children. They ceased in much of this effort during the 1930's when a falling birth rate, rising delinquency and divorce rates, and the depression caused them to question the wisdom of their endeavors. However, it has never been demonstrated that these symptoms were consequences of the efforts to change the family. They may well have simply been results of a rapidly changing social order that would have occurred regardless of the family program. Therefore, the Russian experience is really not evidence pro or con Murdock's position.

The Chinese society deserves some brief mention here. Marion Levy contends that this is an exception to Murdock's thesis because in the extended Chinese family, the nuclear family was a rather unimportant unit, and it was the patrilineal extended family which performed the key functions of which Murdock speaks.[16] Regarding present day Communist China, it should be noted that the popular reports to the effect that the Chinese Communes either aimed at or actually did do away with the nuclear family are not supported by evidence. The best information indicates that the Chinese Communists never intended to do away with the nuclear family as such; rather, what they wanted was the typical communist family system which the Israeli Kibbutzim possess.[17] The Communists in China did not intend to do away with the identification of a child with a particular set of parents or vice-versa. If the Israeli Kibbutz is any indication, it would seem that a communal upbringing system goes quite well with a strong emphasis on affectionate ties between parent and child.[18] However, it is well to note that the type of communal family system toward which the Chinese are striving and have to some extent already achieved, clashes with Murdock's conception of the nuclear family and its functions in just the same way as the Kibbutz family does.

Overall, it appears that a reasonable man looking at the evidence presented above would conclude that Murdock's position is seriously in doubt. As Levy and Fallers have said, Murdock's approach is too simplistic in viewing a particular structure such as the nuclear family as always, in all cultural contexts, having the same four functions.[19] Robert Merton has said that such a view of a very specific structure as indispensable involves the erroneous "postulate of indispensability."[20] Certainly it seems rather rash to say that one very specific social structure such as the nuclear family will always have the same consequences regardless of the context in which it is placed. Surely this is not true of specific structures in other institutions such as the political, religious, or economic. The consequences of a particular social structure vary with the socio-cultural context of that structure.

[16] Levy and Fallers, op. cit., pp. 649–650.

[17] Felix Greene, *Awakened China*, New York: Doubleday, 1961, esp. pp. 142–144. Philip Jones and Thomas Poleman, "Communes and the Agricultural Crises in Communist China," *Food Research Institute Studies*, 3 (February, 1962), 1–22. Maurice Freedman, "The Family in China, Past and Present," *Pacific Affairs*, 34 (Winter, 1961–2), 323–336.

[18] Spiro, op. cit.

[19] Levy and Fallers, op. cit.

[20] Robert K. Merton, *Social Theory and Social Structure*, Glencoe, Ill.: Free Press, 1957, p. 32.

Accordingly, a democratic bicameral legislative structure in a new African nation will function differently than in America; the Reform Jewish Denomination has different consequences in Israel than in America; government control of the economy functions differently in England than in Russia.

The remarkable thing about the family institution is that in so many diverse contexts, one can find such similar structures and functions. To this extent, Murdock has made his point and has demonstrated that the nuclear family with these four functions is a surprisingly common social fact. But this is quite different from demonstrating that this is always the case or necessarily the case. It should be perfectly clear that the author feels Murdock's work has contributed greatly to the advancement of our knowledge of the family. Murdock is used here because he is the best known proponent of the view being examined, not because he should be particularly criticized.

A safer approach to take toward the family is to look for functional prerequisites of society which the family fulfills and search for the full range of structures which may fulfill these functional prerequisites. At this stage of our knowledge, it seems more valuable to talk of the whole range of family structures and to seek for a common function that is performed and that may be essential to human society. What we need now is a broad, basic, parsimonious definition that would have utility in both single and cross-cultural comparisons.[21] We have a good deal of empirical data on family systems and a variety of definitions—it is time we strove for a universal definition that would clarify the essential features of this institution and help us locate the family in any cultural setting.

Looking over the four functions that Murdock associates with the nuclear family, one sees that three of them can be found to be absent in some cultures. The Nayar perhaps best illustrate the possibility of placing sex and reproduction outside the nuclear family. Also, it certainly seems within the realm of possibility that a "Brave New World" type of society could operate by scientifically mating sperm and egg and presenting married couples with state-produced offspring of certain types when they desired children.[22] Furthermore, the raising of children by other than their biological parents is widespread in many societies where adoption and rearing by friends and relatives is common.[23] Thus, it seems that sex and reproduction may not be inexorably tied to the nuclear family.[24]

[21] Zelditch attempted to see if the husband-wife roles would be differentiated in the same way in all cultures, with males being instrumental and females expressive. He found general support, but some exceptions were noted, particularly in societies wherein the nuclear family was embedded in a larger kinship system. Morris Zelditch, Jr., "Role Differentiation in the Nuclear Family: A Comparative Study," in Parsons and Bales, op. cit. The Kibbutz would represent another exception since both mother and father play expressive roles in relation to their offspring.

[22] Aldous Huxley, *Brave New World*, New York: Harper and Bros., 1950.

[23] See: *Six Cultures: Studies in Child Rearing*, ed. by Beatrice B. Whiting, New York: John Wiley, 1963. Margaret Mead reports exchange of children in *Coming of Age in Samoa*, New York: Mentor Books, 1949. Similar customs in Puerto Rico are reported in David Landy, *Tropical Childhood*, Chapel Hill: University of North Carolina Press, 1959.

[24] Robert Winch, in his recent textbook, defines the family as a nuclear family with the basic function of "the replacement of dying members." In line

The third function of Murdock's which seems possible to take out of the nuclear family is that of economic cooperation. The Kibbutz is the prime example of this. Furthermore, it seems that many other communal-type societies approximate the situation in the Kibbutz.

The fourth function is that of socialization. Many aspects of this function have been taken away from the family in various societies. For example, the Kibbutz parents, according to Spiro, are not so heavily involved in the inculcation of values or the disciplinary and care-taking aspects of socialization. Neverthless, the Kibbutz parents are heavily involved in nurturant socialization, i.e., the giving of positive emotional response to infants and young children. A recent book by Stephens also reports a seemingly universal presence of nurturance of infants.[25] It should be emphasized that this paper uses "nurturance" to mean not the physical, but the emotional care of the infant. Clearly, the two are not fully separable. This use of the term nurturant is similar to what is meant by "expressive" role.[26] Interestingly enough, in the Kibbutz both the mother and father are equally involved in giving their children nurturant socialization. All of the societies referred to above have a family institution with the function of nurturant socialization of children. This was true even for the extreme case of the Nayar.

The conception of the family institution being developed here has in common with some other family definitions an emphasis on socialization of offspring. The difference is that all other functions have been ruled out as unessential and that only the nurturant type of socialization is the universal function of the family institution. This paper presents empirical evidence to support its contention. It is important to be more specific than were Levy and Fallers regarding the type of socialization the family achieves since all societies have socialization occurring outside the family as well as within. It should be noted that this author, unlike Murdock, is talking of *any* form of family institution and not just the nuclear family.

As far as a universal structure of the family to fulfill the function of nurturant socialization is concerned, it seems possible to set only very broad limits, and even these involve some speculation. First, it may be said that the structure of the family will always be that of a primary group. Basically, this position rests on the assumption that nurturant socialization is a process which cannot be adequately carried out in an impersonal setting and which thus requires a primary type of relation.[27] The author would not specify the biological mother as the socializer or even a female, or even

---

with the present author's arguments, it seems that the actual biological production of infants can be removed from the family. In fact, Winch agrees that the Nayar lack the family as he defined it because they lack a permanent father role in the nuclear family. See: *The Modern Family*, New York: Holt, 1963, pp. 16, 31, and 750.

[25] William N. Stephens, *The Family in Cross-Cultural Perspective*, New York: Holt, Rinehart and Winston, 1963, p. 357. Stephens discusses the universality of the family in this book but does not take a definite position on the issue. See Chapter 1.

[26] Zelditch, op. cit., pp. 307–353.

[27] The key importance of primary groups was long ago pointed out by Charles Horton Cooley, *Social Organization*, New York: Scribners, 1929.

more than one person or the age of the person. If one is trying to state what the family must be like in a minimal sense in any society—what its universally required structure and function is—one cannot be too specific. However, we can go one step farther in specifying the structure of the family group we are defining. The family is here viewed as an institution, as an integrated set of norms and relationships which are socially defined and internalized by the members of a society. In every society in the world, the institutional structure which contains the roles related to the nurturant function is a small kinship structured group.[28] Thus, we can say that the primary group which fulfills the nurturant function is a kinship structure. Kinship refers to descent—it involves rights of possession among those who are kin. It is a genealogical reckoning, and people with real or fictive biological connections are kin.[29]

This specification of structure helps to distinguish from the family institution those nonkin primary groups that may in a few instances perform nurturant functions. For example, a nurse-child relation or a governess-child relation could, if carried far enough, involve the bulk of nurturant socialization for that child. But such a relationship would be a quasi-family at best, for it clearly is not part of the kinship structure. There are no rights of "possession" given to the nurse or the child in such cases, and there is no socially accepted, institutionalized, system of child-rearing involving nurses and children. In addition, such supervisory help usually assumes more of a caretaking and disciplinary aspect, with the parents themselves still maintaining the nurturant relation.

Talcott Parsons has argued, in agreement with the author's position, that on a societal level, only kinship groups can perform the socialization function.[30] He believes that socialization in a kin group predisposes the child to assume marital and parental roles himself when he matures and affords a needed stable setting for socialization. Clearly other groups may at times perform part of the nurturant function. No institution in human society has an exclusive franchise on its characteristic function. However, no society exists in which any group other than a kinship group performs the dominant share of the nurturant function. Even in the Israeli Kibbutz with communal upbringing, it is the parents who dominate in this area.

Should a society develop wherein nonkin primary groups became the predominant means of raising children, the author would argue that these nonkin groups would tend to evolve in the direction of becoming kin groups. The primary quality of the adult-child relation would encourage the notion of descent and possession. Kin groups would evolve as roles and statuses in the nonkin system became defined in terms of accepted male-female and adult-child relationships and thereby became institutionalized. Once these nonkin groups had institutionalized their sex roles and adult-child (descent) roles, we would in effect have a kinship-type system, for kinship results from the recognition of a social relationship between "parents" and children. It seems that there would be much pressure toward institutionalization of

---

[28] The structural definition is similar to Levy and Fallers, op. cit.
[29] Radcliffe-Brown, op. cit.
[30] Parsons, op. cit.

roles in any primary group child-rearing system, if for no other reason than clarity and efficiency. The failure of any one generation to supply adequate role models and adequate nurturance means that the next generation will not know these skills, and persistence of such a society is questionable. The importance of this task makes institutionalization quite likely and kinship groups quite essential. To avoid kinship groups, it seems that children would have to be nurtured in a formal secondary group setting. The author will present evidence below for his belief that the raising of children in a secondary group setting is unworkable.

In summation then, following is the universal definition of the family institution: *The family institution is a small kinship structured group with the key function of nurturant socialization of the newborn.* How many years such nurturant socialization must last is hard to specify. There are numerous societies in which children six or seven years old are given a good deal of responsibility in terms of care of other children and other tasks. It seems that childhood in the West has been greatly extended to older ages in recent centuries.[31] The proposed definition focuses on what are assumed to be the structural and functional prerequisites of society which the family institution fulfills. The precise structure of the kinship group can vary quite radically among societies, and even within one society it may well be that more than one small kinship group will be involved in nurturant socialization. The definition seeks to avoid the "error" of positing the indispensability of any *particular* family form by this approach. Rather, it says that any type of kinship group can achieve this function and that the limitation is merely that it be a kinship group. This degree of specification helps one delimit and identify the institution which one is describing. Some writers have spelled out more specifically the key structural forms in this area.[32] Adams has posited two key dyads: the maternal dyad and the conjugal dyad. When these two join, a nuclear family is formed, but these dyads are, Adams believes, more fundamental than the nuclear family.

There are always other functions besides nurturant socialization performed by the kinship group. Murdock's four functions are certainly quite frequently performed by some type of family group, although often not by the nuclear family. In addition, there are some linkages between the family kinship group and a larger kinship system. But this is not the place to pursue these interconnections. Instead, an examination follows of evidence relevant to this proposed universal definition of the family institution.

EVIDENCE ON REVISED CONCEPTION

The evidence to be examined here relates to the question of whether the definition proposed actually fits all human family institutions. Three types of evidence are relevant to test the universality of the proposed definition of the family. The first source of evidence comes from a cross-cultural examination

[31] Phillippe Aries, *Centuries of Childhood*, New York: Knopf, 1962.
[32] Richard N. Adams, "An Inquiry into the Nature of the Family," pp. 30–49 in *Essays in the Science of Culture in Honor of Leslie A. White*, ed. by Gertrude E. Dole and Robert L. Carneiro, New York: Crowell, 1960.

such as that of this article. All of the cultures that were discussed were fulfilling the proposed functional prerequisite of nurturant socialization, and they all had some sort of small kinship group structure to accomplish nurturant socialization. The author also examined numerous reports on other cultures and found no exception to the proposed definition. Of course, other functions of these family groups were present in all instances, but no other specific universally present functions appeared. However, the author hesitates to say that these data confirm his position because it is quite possible that such a cross-cultural examination will reveal some function or structure to be universally *present* but still not universally *required*. Rather, it could merely be universally present by chance or because it is difficult but not impossible to do away with. As an example of this, one may cite the incest taboo. The evidence recently presented by Russell Middleton on incest among commoners in Ptolemaic Egypt throws doubt on the thesis that incest taboos are functional prerequisites of human society.[33] We need some concept of functional "importance," for surely the incest taboo has great functional importance even if it is not a prerequisite of society. The same may be true of the functional importance of Murdock's view of the nuclear family.

If being universally present is but a necessary and not a sufficient condition for a functional prerequisite of society, then it is important to present other evidence. One source of such evidence lies in the studies of rhesus monkeys done by Harry Harlow.[34] Harlow separated monkeys from their natural mothers and raised them with surrogate "cloth" and "wire" mother dolls. In some trials, the wire mother surrogate was equipped with milk while the cloth mother was not. Even so, the monkeys preferred the cloth mother to the wire mother in several ways. The monkeys showed their preference by running more to the cloth mother when threatened and by exerting themselves more to press a lever to see her. Thus, it seemed that the monkeys "loved" the cloth mother more than the wire mother. This was supposedly due to the softer contact and comfort afforded by the cloth mother. One might speculatively argue that the contact desire of the monkeys is indicative of at least a passive, rudimentary nurturance need. Yerkes has also reported similar "needs" in his study of chimpanzees.[35]

Further investigation of these monkeys revealed some important findings. The monkeys raised by the surrogate mothers became emotionally disturbed and were unable to relate to other monkeys or to have sexual relations. This result was produced irreversibly in about six months. One could interpret this to mean that the surrogate mothers, both cloth and wire, were inadequate

[33] Russell Middleton, "Brother-Sister and Father-Daughter Marriage in Ancient Egypt," *American Sociological Review*, 27 (October, 1962), 603–611.

[34] See the following articles, all by Harry F. Harlow: "The Nature of Love," *American Psychologist*, 13 (December, 1958), 673–685; "The Heterosexual Affection System in Monkeys," *American Psychologist*, 17 (January, 1962), 1–9; (with Margaret K. Harlow), "Social Deprivation in Monkeys," *Scientific American*, 206 (November, 1962), 1–10.

[35] Robert M. Yerkes, *Chimpanzees*, New Haven: Yale University Press, 1943, esp. pp. 43, 68, 257–258; and Robert M. Yerkes and Ada W. Yerkes, *The Great Apes*, New Haven: Yale University Press, 1929, passim.

in that they gave no emotional response to the infant monkeys. Although contact with the cloth mother seemed important, response seemingly was even more important. Those laboratory-raised females who did become pregnant became very ineffective mothers and were lacking in ability to give nurturance.

Harlow found that when monkeys were raised without mothers but with siblings present, the results were quite different. To date, these monkeys have shown emotional stability and sexual competence. In growing up, they clung to each other just as the other monkeys had clung to the cloth mother, but in addition they were able to obtain the type of emotional response or nurturance from each other which they needed.

Harlow's evidence on monkeys is surely not conclusive evidence for the thesis that nurturant socialization is a fundamental prerequisite of human society. There is need for much more precise testing and evidence on both human and nonhuman groups. Despite the fact that human beings and monkeys are both primates, there is quite a bit of difference in human and monkey infants. For one thing, the human infant is far more helpless and far less aware of its environment during the first few months of its life. Thus, it is doubtful if placing a group of helpless, relatively unaware human infants together would produce the same results as occurred when monkeys were raised with siblings. The human infant requires someone older and more aware of the environment to be present. In a very real sense, it seems that the existence of human society is testimony to the concern of humans for each other. Unless older humans care for the newborn, the society will cease to exist. Every adult member of society is alive only because some other member of society took the time and effort to raise him. One may argue that this care need be only minimal and of a physical nature, e.g., food, clothing, and shelter. The author believes that such minimal care is insufficient for societal survival and will try to present additional evidence here to bear this out.

One type of evidence that is relevant concerns the effect of maternal separation or institutional upbringing on human infants. To afford a precise test, we should look for a situation in which nurturant socialization was quite low or absent. Although the Kibbutzim have institutional upbringing, the Kibbutz parents and children are very much emotionally attached to each other. In fact, both the mother and father have expressive roles in the Kibbutz family, and there is a strong emphasis on parent-child relations of a nurturant sort in the few hours a day the family is together.

A better place to look would be at studies of children who were raised in formal institutions or who were in other ways separated from their mothers. Leon J. Yarrow has recently published an excellent summary of over one hundred such studies.[36] For over 50 years now, there have been reports supporting the view that maternal separation has deleterious effects on the child. The first such reports came from pediatricians pointing out physical and psychological deterioration in hospitalized infants. In 1951,

[36] Leon J. Yarrow, "Separation from Parents During Early Childhood," pp. 89–136 in *Review of Child Development*, ed. by Martin L. Hoffman and Lois W. Hoffman, New York: Russell Sage Foundation, 1964, Vol. 1.

Bowlby reviewed the literature in this area for the World Health Organization and arrived at similar conclusions.[37] More recent and careful studies have made us aware of the importance of distinguishing the effects of maternal separation from the effects of institutionalization. Certainly the type of institutional care afforded the child is quite important. Further, the previous relation of the child with the mother before institutionalization and the age of the child are important variables. In addition, one must look at the length of time separation endured and whether there were reunions with the mother at a later date. Yarrow's view is that while there is this tendency toward disturbance in mother separation, the occurrence can best be understood when we learn more about the precise conditions under which it occurs and cease to think of it as inevitable under any conditions. In this regard, recent evidence shows that children separated from mothers with whom they had poor relationships displayed less disturbance than other children. Further, infants who were provided with adequate mother-substitutes of a personal sort showed much less severe reactions. In line with the findings on the Kibbutz, children who were in an all-day nursery gave no evidence of serious disturbance.

Many studies in the area of institutionalization show the importance of the structural characteristics of the institutional environment. When care is impersonal and inadequate, there is evidence of language retardation, impairment of motor functions, and limited emotional responses toward other people and objects.[38] Interestingly, the same types of characteristics are found among children living in deprived family environments.[39] One of the key factors in avoiding such negative results is the presence of a stable mother-figure in the institution for the child. Individualized care and attention seem to be capable of reversing or preventing the impairments mentioned. Without such care, there is evidence that ability to form close interpersonal relations later in life is greatly weakened.[40] As Yarrow concludes in his review of this area:

> It is clear from the studies on institutionalization that permanent intellectual and personality damage may be avoided if following separation there is a substitute mother-figure who develops a personalized relationship with the child and who responds sensitively to his individualized needs.[41]

The evidence in this area indicates that some sort of emotionally nurturant relationship between the child in the first few years of life and some other individual is rather vital in the child's development. Disease and death rates have been reported to rise sharply in children deprived of nurturance. The author is not rash enough to take this evidence as conclusive support for his contention that nurturant socialization is a functional prerequisite of

[37] John Bowlby, *Maternal Care and Mental Health*, Geneva: World Health Organization, 1951.
[38] Yarrow, op. cit., p. 100.
[39] Ibid., p. 101–102.
[40] Ibid., p. 106.
[41] Ibid., pp. 124–125.

human society which the family performs. Nevertheless, he does believe that this evidence lends some support to this thesis and throws doubt on the survival of a society that rears its children without nurturance. In addition, it seems to support the position that some sort of kin-type group relationship is the structural prerequisite of the nurturant function. Indeed, it seemed that the closer the institution approximated a stable, personal kinship type of relationship of the child and a nurse, the more successful it was in achieving emotional nurturance and avoiding impairments of functions.

SUMMARY AND CONCLUSIONS

A check of several cultures revealed that the four nuclear family functions that Murdock states are universally present were often missing. The nuclear family itself seems either absent or unimportant in some cultures. An alternate definition of the family in terms of one functional prerequisite of human society and in terms of a broad structural prerequisite was put forth. The family was defined as a small kinship structured group with the key function of nurturant socialization of the newborn. The nurturant function directly supports the personality system and enables the individual to become a contributing member of society. Thus, by making adult role performance possible, nurturant socialization becomes a functional prerequisite of society.

Three sources of evidence were examined: (1) cross-cultural data, (2) studies of other primates, and (3) studies of effects on children of maternal separation. Although the evidence did tend to fit with and support the universality of the new definition, it must be noted that much more support is needed before any firm conclusion can be reached.

There is both a structural and a functional part to the definition. It is theoretically possible that a society could bring up its entire newborn population in a formal institutional setting and give them nurturance through mechanical devices that would reassure the child, afford contact, and perhaps even verbally respond to the child. In such a case, the family as defined here would cease to exist, and an alternate structure for fulfilling the functional requirement of nurturant socialization would be established. Although it is dubious whether humans could ever tolerate or achieve such a means of bringing up their children, this logical possibility must be recognized. In fact, since the evidence is not conclusive, one would also have to say that it is possible that a society could bring up its offspring without nurturance, and in such a case also, the family institution as defined here would cease to exist. The author has argued against this possibility by contending that nurturance of the newborn is a functional prerequisite of human society and therefore could never be done away with. However, despite a strong conviction to the contrary, he must also admit that this position may be in error and that it is possible that the family as defined here is not a universally required institution. There are those, like Barrington Moore, Jr., who feel that it is largely a middle-class sentimentality that makes social scientists believe that the family is universal.[42] It is certainly crucial to test further the universality

[42] Barrington Moore, Jr., *Political Power and Social Theory*, Cambridge, Mass.: Harvard University Press, 1958, Chap. 5.

of both the structural and functional parts of this definition and their inter-relation.

The definition proposed seems to fit the existing data somewhat more closely than Murdock's definition. It also has the advantage of simplicity. It affords one a definition that can be used in comparative studies of human society. Further, it helps make one aware of the possibilities of change in a society or an institution if we know which functions and structures can or cannot be done away with. In this way, we come closer to the knowledge of what Goldenweiser called the "limited possibilities" of human society.[43] If nurturance in kin groups is a functional and structural prerequisite of society, we have deepened our knowledge of the nature of human society for we can see how, despite our constant warfare with each other, our conflicts and internal strife, each human society persists only so long as it meets the minimal nurturant requirements of its new members. This is not to deny the functions of social conflict that Coser and others have pointed out, but merely to assert the importance of nurturance.[44]

In terms of substantive theory, such a definition as the one proposed can be of considerable utility. If one views the marital institution, as Malinowski, Gough, Davis, Radcliffe-Brown, and others did, as having the key function of legitimization of offspring, then the tie between the marital and family institution becomes clear.[45] The marital institution affords a social definition of who is eligible to perform the nurturant function of the family institution.[46]

. . . There may be other universally required functions of the family institution. Dorthy Blitsten suggests universal family contributions to the social order.[47] Kingsley Davis posits several universal functions, such as social placement, which are worth investigating further.[48]

[43] Alexander A. Goldenweiser, *History, Psychology, and Culture*, New York: Knopf, 1933, esp. pp. 45–49.

[44] Lewis Coser, *The Functions of Social Conflict*, Glencoe, Ill.: Free Press, 1956.

[45] See Gough, op. cit.; Kingsley Davis, "Illegitimacy and the Social Structure," *American Journal of Sociology*, 45 (September, 1939), 215–233; A. R. Radcliffe-Brown, op. cit., p. 5. The structure of the marital institution is not specified in terms of number or sex, for there are cultures in which two women may marry and raise a family. See: B. E. Evans Pritchard, *Kinship and Marriage Among the Nuer*, London: Oxford University Press, 1951, pp. 108–109. It is well to note here that Murdock stressed a somewhat different view of marriage. He focused on sexual and economic functions, and the woman-woman marriage found in the Nuer would not fit this definition. Morris Zelditch recently has used this legitimacy function as the key aspect of his definition of the family rather than marriage. Such a usage would, it seems, confuse the traditional distinction between these two institutions. See p. 682 in *Handbook of Modern Sociology*, ed. by Robert Faris, New York: Rand-McNally, 1964.

[46] Blake, op. cit.

[47] Dorothy R. Blitsten, *The World of the Family*, New York: Random House, 1963, esp. Chap. I.

[48] Kingsley Davis, *Human Society*, New York: Macmillan, 1950, p. 395. Davis lists reproduction, maintenance, placement, and socialization of the young as universal family functions. Social placement is the only function that differs from Murdock's list. One could conceive of this function as part of the marital rather than the family institution.

One major value of the approach of this paper is that it has the potentiality of contributing to our ability to deal cross-culturally with the family. Surely it is useful to theory building to ascertain the essential or more essential features of an institution. Such work enables us to locate, identify, and compare this institution in various cultural settings and to discover its fundamental characteristics. In this respect, Murdock has contributed to the search for a cross-cultural view of the family by his work in this area, even though the author has taken issue with some of his conclusions. It should be clear that this "universal, cross-cultural" approach is not at all presented as the only approach to an understanding of the family. Rather, it is viewed as but one essential approach. Research dealing with important but not universal functions is just as vital, as is empirical work within one culture.

Also of crucial importance is the relation of the family institution to the general kinship structure. It does seem that every society has other people linked by affinal or consanguineal ties to the nurturant person or persons. It remains for these aspects to be further tested. The family typologies now in existence are adequate to cover the proposed definition of the family, although a new typology built around the nurturant function and the type of kin who perform it could be quite useful.

The interrelations of the marital, family, and courtship institutions with such institutions as the political, economic, and religious in terms of both important and essential functions and structures is another vital avenue of exploration. One way that such exploration can be made is in terms of what, if any, are the functional and structural prerequisites of these institutions and how they interrelate. It is hoped that such comparative research and theory may be aided by a universal definition of the family such as that proposed in this paper.

2   Brother-Sister and Father-Daughter Marriage in Ancient Egypt

RUSSELL MIDDLETON

Almost every sociologist and anthropologist in the last thirty years who has written on the general subject of incest prohibitions has proclaimed the universality of the taboo upon the marriage of brothers and sisters and

I am deeply indebted to the following Egyptologists who have given me the benefit of their advice and encouragement: William F. Edgerton, Rudolf Anthes, Jaroslav Černý, Claire Préaux, William C. Hayes, William Kelly Simpson, Elizabeth Riefstahl, and Alan Samuel. I am further indebted to the Research Council of Florida State University which provided financial help for this study.

Reprinted from *American Sociological Review*, 27, No. 5 (October, 1962), 603–611, by permission of The American Sociological Association.

of parents and children. Most of them hasten to add that there are a few exceptions to this "universal" principle—the cases of brother-sister marriage among the Incas, the Hawaiians, and the ancient Egyptians being most frequently cited. They usually maintain, however, that these exceptions were sanctioned only for the royalty and never for commoners. The marriage of brothers and sisters, they argue, functioned "to preserve the purity of the royal blood line," "to keep privilege and rank rigidly within the group," and to set the divine rulers apart from their mundane subjects, who were required to observe the taboos. Ordinarily the authors do not recognize any cases of parent-child marriage, though a few do cite the case of father-daughter marriage among the Azande kings and the case of orgiastic father-daughter incest among the Thonga.

That the kings of ancient Egypt sometimes married their sisters or half sisters is widely recognized by sociologists and social anthropologists today. Yet they remain almost totally unaware of the evidence painstakingly uncovered by Egyptologists regarding father-daughter marriage among the kings and brother-sister marriage among the commoners. This paper attempts to summarize the present state of knowledge concerning the marriage of near kin among both royalty and commoners in three periods in ancient Egypt: Pharaonic period (prior to 332 B.C.), Ptolemaic period (323–30 B.C.), and Roman period (30 B.C.–324 A.D.).

PHARAONIC PERIOD

Although instances of Pharaohs who married their own sisters or half sisters have been reported from several of the dynasties, the greatest concentration of cases appears to be in the 18th and 19th Dynasties. Indeed, probably a majority of 18th Dynasty kings (1570–1397 B.C.) married their sisters or half sisters: Tao II, Ahmose, Amenhotep I, Thutmose I, Thutmose II, Thutmose III, Amenhotep II, and Thutmose IV.[1] In the 19th Dynasty, Rameses II (1290–1223 B.C.) and Merneptah (1223–1211 B.C.) probably married sisters or half sisters.[2] Some authorities maintain that there are no well established cases among the Pharaohs of the marriage of full brothers and sisters; no more than a half-sibling relationship can be proved.

Documented cases of father-daughter marriage among the Egyptian kings are less numerous and more controversial. De Rougé first called

[1] Marc Armand Ruffer, "On the Physical Effects of Consanguineous Marriages in the Royal Families of Ancient Egypt," in *Studies in the Palaeopathology of Egypt*, Chicago: University of Chicago Press, 1921, pp. 325–337; Adolf Erman, *Life in Ancient Egypt*, London: Macmillan, 1894, p. 154; W. M. Flinders Petrie, *A History of Egypt*, 6th ed., London: Methuen and Co., 1917, Vol. 2, pp. 1, 40; W. C. Hayes, *The Scepter of Egypt*, Cambridge: Harvard University Press, 1959, Vol. 2, p. 44; and Alan Gardiner, *Egypt of the Pharaohs*, Oxford: Clarendon Press, 1961, pp. 172–173. There is, however, some dispute among the authorities with regard to some of the kings.

[2] Alfred Wiedemann, *Aegyptische Geschichte*, Gotha: F. A. Perthes, 1884, Vol. 2, p. 466; Ernest A. Wallis Budge, *Egypt Under Rameses the Great*, London: K. Paul, Trench, Trübner and Co., 1902, p. 69; Ruffer, op. cit., pp. 337–340.

attention to evidence that Rameses II married not only two of his sisters, but also at least two of his daughters.[3] Erman, in a footnote in *Aegypten und Aegyptisches Leben im Altertum* published in 1885, denied this, arguing that the title of "Royal Wife," ascribed to the daughters was of mere ceremonial significance and was bestowed upon royal princesses even in infancy. More recent scholarship, however, has demonstrated that Erman was mistaken, and Ranke rightly omitted the footnote in his revision of the work.[4] Many authorities believe that Rameses II was married to three of his daughters: Banutanta, Merytamen, and Nebttaui.[5] There is some doubt about Nebttaui, for she apparently had a daughter, Astemakh, who was not a child of the king. Petrie suggests that she may have been married to a subject after the death of the king—though this is not likely, since she would have been over forty at the time—or Astemakh may have been the daughter not of Nebttaui but of princess Nebta, daughter of Amenhotep.[6]

. A second example of father-daughter marriage that is generally accepted by most Egyptologists involves Amenhotep III (1397–1360 B.C.), who was probably married to his daughter Satamon[7] and possibly to another daughter as well.[8]

Three alleged cases of father-daughter marriage which were accepted earlier, however, have now generally been discarded. Brunner concluded from a fragmentary inscription that Amenhotep IV or Akhenaton (1370–1353 B.C.) was married to his daughter Ankes-en-pa-Aton and had a daughter by her who bore the same name as her mother.[9] Most scholars regard his interpretation as highly subjective, for the inscription nowhere says that Ankes-en-pa-Aton was married to her father.[10] Wiedemann had stated that Psamtik I of the 26th Dynasty (663–609 B.C.) married his daughter Nitocrisis,[11] but

[3] Emmanuel de Rougé, *Recherches sur les Monuments qu'on Peut Attribuer aux Six Premières Dynasties de Manéthon*, Paris: Imprimerie Impériale, 1866.

[4] Adolf Erman, *Aegypten und Aegyptisches Leben im Altertum*, revised by Hermann Ranke, Tübingen: J. C. B. Mohr, 1923, pp. 180–181.

[5] Gaston Maspéro, *The Struggle of the Nations*, New York: D. Appleton and Co., 1897, Vol. 2, p. 424; Wiedemann, op. cit., Vol. 2, p. 466; Budge, op. cit., pp. 69–70. Gardiner also concurs with regard to one of the daughters, Banutanta, and Kees says that it is certain that Rameses II married two of his daughters, if not more. See Gardiner, op. cit., p. 267 and Hermann Kees, "Aegypten," in A. Alt and others, *Kulturgeschichte des Alten Orients*, München: C. H. Beck, 1933, p. 77.

[6] Petrie, op. cit., vol. 3, p. 88.

[7] Alexandre Varille, "Toutankhamon Est-il Fils d'Aménophis III et de Satamon?" *Annales du Service des Antiquités de l'Égypte*, 40 (1941), pp. 655–656; S. R. K. Glanville, "Amenophis III and His Successors in the XVIIIth Dynasty," in *Great Ones of Ancient Egypt*, New York: Charles Scribner's Sons, 1930, pp. 122–123; Gardiner, op. cit., p. 212.

[8] Percy E. Newberry, "King Ay, the Successor of Tutankhamun," *Journal of Egyptian Archeology*, 18 (1932), 51.

[9] Hellmut Brunner, "Eine neue Amarna-Prinzessin," *Zeitschrift für Ägyptische Sprache und Altertumskunde*, 74 (1938), 104–108.

[10] Gardiner, op. cit., p. 236.

[11] Wiedemann, op. cit., vol. 2, p. 622.

Breasted has published texts which show that this was not the case.[12] Sethe argued on the basis of an inscription found above the false door of a tomb that Snefru of the 4th Dynasty (2614–2591 B.C.) was married to his eldest daughter, Nefertkauw and that they had a son named Neferma'at.[13] The Harvard-Boston Expedition in 1926, however, found another inscription which Reisner maintains clears up ambiguities in the earlier text and shows that Neferma'at was the grandson rather than the son of Snefru.[14] This interpretation is now accepted by most Egyptologists, though some remain unconvinced.

Evidence of brother-sister marriage among commoners in Pharaonic times is meager. Černý has examined records of 490 marriages among commoners, but the names of both sets of parents are given for only four of the couples.[15] In each case they are different. The names of the mothers are given for 97, however, and the names are the same in two instances. These two cases, which have a Middle Kingdom date (c. 2052–1786 B.C.) suggest the possibility of the marriage of at least half brothers and sisters, but the names were common during that period and different individuals of the same name may have been involved. In the 20th Dynasty (1181–1075 B.C.) we also have a census list for a village of workmen, and there is no evidence of consanguineous marriages in the village.[16]

One must be cautious of literal interpretations of Egyptian terms of relationship, for in love songs and other inscriptions a lover or spouse is often referred to as "my brother" or "my sister."[17] Černý argues, however, that the custom of calling one's wife "sister" had its origin in the reign of Thutmose III and thus did not develop prior to the 18th Dynasty.[18] If this conclusion is accepted, there are, then, two probable cases of brother-sister marriage in the Middle Kingdom (c. 12th–13th Dynasties).[19] In the first, the reporter of the Vizier Senwosret was married to a woman called both sister and wife. In the second, the priest Efnaierson was married to a woman named Bob, who was either his sister by the same mother or his niece.

Fischer has recently called attention to another possible case of

[12] James Henry Breasted, *Ancient Records of Egypt*, Chicago: University of Chicago Press, 1906, vol. 4, pp. 477–491.

[13] Kurt Heinrich Sethe, "Das Fehlen des Begriffes der Blutschande bei den Alten Ägyptern," *Zeitschrift für Ägyptische Sprache und Altertumskunde*, 50 (1912), p. 57; Kurt Heinrich Sethe, "Zum Inzest des Sneferu," *Zeitschrift für Ägyptische Sprache und Altertumskunde*, 54 (1916), 54.

[14] George Reisner, "Nefertkauw, the Eldest Daughter of Sneferuw," *Zeitschrift für Ägyptische Sprache und Altertumskunde*, 64 (1929), 97–99.

[15] Jaroslav Černý, "Consanguineous Marriages in Pharaonic Egypt," *Journal of Egyptian Archeology*, 40 (December, 1954), 27.

[16] Ibid., pp. 28–29.

[17] Erman, *Life in Ancient Egypt*, p. 154; Gaston Maspéro, *The Dawn of Civilization: Egypt and Chaldaea*, 2nd ed., London: Society for Promoting Christian Knowledge, 1896, p. 50. Gardiner points out that kinship terms were sometimes used loosely in other circumstances too. Gardiner, op. cit., p. 178.

[18] Černý, op. cit., p. 25.

[19] Ibid., pp. 25–26.

brother-sister marriage among commoners in the Middle Kingdom.[20] Two stelae deal with the family of a keeper of the chamber of the daily watch. On one, Mr is called "his sister" and Dng.t is named with her in such a manner as to suggest that she is a sister too. On the second Dng.t is called "his wife," but Mr's relationship is not mentioned. Although the wife Dng.t is not explicitly identified as a sister, there is circumstantial evidence that she is. The one fairly certain case of the marriage of a commoner to his sister in the Pharaonic period, however, occurs in the 22nd Dynasty during the reign of Sheshonk III (823–772 B.C.).[21] The genealogy of the Libyan commander Pediese is given on a votive stela, which indicates that he is married to his sister Tere and has two sons by her. He and his wife have the same father, but the stela does not contain evidence regarding their mothers.

Murray has published eleven genealogies of small officials in the Middle Kingdom which she maintains contain several cases of mother-son marriage, several of father-daughter marriage, and one of brother-sister marriage.[22] Murray assumes, however, that different examples of the same name on the same stela, and even on different stelae, necessarily refer to one and the same individual, even though the names were very common at the time. If one discards unwarranted assumptions and establishes the genealogies properly, there is no substantial evidence in the genealogies of marriages occurring within the nuclear family, and Egyptologists today do not take these cases seriously.

PTOLEMAIC PERIOD

Upon the death of Alexander the Great in 323 B.C., Ptolemy, one of Alexander's generals, established a new dynasty of Macedonian kings in Egypt. The Ptolemaic kings apparently found it prudent to adopt many of the customs of their royal predecessors, including brother-sister marriage. Greek law probably permitted the marriage of paternal half brothers and half sisters, but it certainly prohibited the union of full brothers and sisters.[23] Ptolemy II, nevertheless, married his full sister Arsinoe. If we may judge by a story told by Athenaeus, who lived in Egypt at the end of the second century A.D., this act probably was regarded as scandalous by the Hellenistic elements of the population. According to Athenaeus, Sotades, a popular Greek writer of obscene verses, described the marriage in a coarse line as incestuous. He was forced to flee Alexandria immediately, but he was caught

[20] Henry George Fischer, "A God and a General of the Oasis on a Stela of the Late Middle Kingdom," *Journal of Near Eastern Studies*, 16 (October, 1957), 231.

[21] Breasted, op. cit., vol. 4, p. 386.

[22] Margaret A. Murray, "Notes on Some Genealogies of the Middle Kingdom," *Ancient Egypt*, (June, 1927), pp. 45–51.

[23] See Philo Judaeus, "On the Special Laws," in *Philo*, Vol. 7, translated by F. H. Colson, Cambridge: Harvard University Press, 1937, book 3, paragraph 4; Plutarch, *Plutarch's Lives*, translated by Bernadotte Perrin, London: William Heinemann, 1948, pp. 87–89.

by the king's general, Patroclus, and thrown into the sea in a leaden jar.[24]

The descendants of Ptolemy II tended to follow his example, marrying half sisters or full sisters. Of the thirteen Ptolemies who came to the throne, seven contracted such marriages. Ptolemy VIII was married to two of his sisters, and both Ptolemy XII and Ptolemy XIII were married to their sister, the famous Cleopatra VI.[25]

Brother-sister marriage during the Greek period in Egypt seems to have been restricted to the royalty, for there is no evidence of its practice among commoners, either Egyptian or Hellenistic.

ROMAN PERIOD

During the period of Roman rule in Egypt there is, for the first time, an abundance of papyrus documents and records which give evidence that commoners often practiced brother-sister marriage. These documents are of several kinds: personal letters, marriage contracts, other types of contracts, petitions and documents addressed to the administrative authorities, and census documents carrying genealogical information. Unlike some of the earlier types of evidence which may be subject to differing interpretations, these documents of a technical character have an "indisputable precision."[26]

Egyptologists have been aware of this evidence at least since 1883, when Wilcken concluded from his study of some papyri that marriage between brothers and sisters occurred often during the Roman period.[27] Among the marriages recorded in the fragments which he examined, marriages between brother and sister were in an absolute majority. Moreover, most of the marriages were with full sisters, not half sisters. One of the papyri, for example, speaks of "his wife, being his sister by the same father and the same mother."[28]

Grenfell and Hunt published in 1901 the text of an application from a woman named Demetria asking that her son Artemon might be admitted to a group with special tax privileges, on the grounds that he was a descendant

[24] Athenaeus, *The Deipnosophists*, translated by C. B. Gulick, Cambridge: Harvard University Press, 1951, book 14, paragraph 621.

[25] Edwyn Bevan, *A History of Egypt under the Ptolemaic Dynasty*, London: Methuen, 1927, p. 60; J. P. Mahaffy, "Cleopatra VI," *Journal of Egyptian Archeology*, 2 (1915), 1–4; Arthur Weigall, *The Life and Times of Cleopatra: Queen of Egypt*, rev. ed., New York: Putnam, 1924, pp. 44, 65; Franz V. M. Cumont, *L'Égypte des Astrologues*, Brussels: La Fondation Égyptologique, 1937, pp. 177–179; Ruffer, op. cit., pp. 341–356.

[26] Marcel Hombert and Claire Préaux, "Les Mariages Consanguins dans l'Égypte Romaine," in *Collection Latomus: Hommages à Joseph Bidez et à Franz Cumont*, Bruxelles: Latomus, 1949, Vol. 2, p. 138.

[27] U. Wilcken, "Arsinoitische Steuerprofessionen aus dem Jahre 189 n. Chr. und verwandte Urkunden," *Sitzungsberichte der Königlich Preussischen Akademie der Wissenschaft zu Berlin*, (1883), 903.

[28] Ibid.

of members of the group.[29] The papyrus gives the genealogy for five generations. Although there are no consanguineous marriages on the father's side, during a period extending from about 50 to 120 A.D., Demetria's father, grandfather, and great-grandfather were all married to their full sisters. About the same time Wessely published genealogies of four well-to-do Egyptian families in which marriages between brothers and sisters were in a majority.[30] Only a little later Mitteis and Wilcken published a text dating from the third century A.D. of a card of invitation issued by a mother for the marriage together of her son and daughter.[31]

Approximately 150 papyri have been found dealing with a man named Apollonius, who was the civil administrator of the nome of Apollonopolis Heptakomia (c. 117 A.D.).[32] The papyri show clearly that he was married to his sister Aline and that they were deeply attached to each other. "During the Jewish war Aline writes to him begging him to put the burden of the work on to his subordinates as other strategi did and not to run into unnecessary danger; when he went away, she says, she could taste neither food nor drink, nor could she sleep."[33] Romans were not permitted to contract marriages with their sisters, but there was apparently little or no social stigma attached to the custom, for Appollonius had many Roman friends.

Calderini in 1923 examined 122 fragments of papyri from the fourteen-yearly census conducted by the Roman administrators between 6 and 310 A.D.[34] In eleven of the papyri he found evidence of thirteen cases of consanguineous marriages, including eight in which husband and wife had both parents in common. Three of the cases are found in the census year 173–4 A.D. and six in 187–8 A.D. The concentration of cases at these dates, however, is due in large part to the greater number of fragments available for these censuses.

All available evidence of the marriage of brothers and sisters among commoners in Roman Egypt has recently been summarized by Hombert and Préaux as follows:[35]

[29] Bernard P. Grenfell and Arthur S. Hunt, *The Amherst Papyri*, London: H. Frowde, 1901, part 2, pp. 90–91.

[30] Carl Wessely, *Karanis und Soknopaiu Nesos*, Vienna: Carl Gerold's Sohn, 1902, pp. 23–24.

[31] Ludwig Mitteis and U. Wilcken, *Grundzüge und Chrestomathie der Papyruskunde*, Leipzig: B. G. Teubner, 1912, vol. 1, p. 568.

[32] Johannes Nietzold, *Die Ehe in Ägypten zur Ptolemäisch-Römischen Zeit*, Leipzig: Verlag von Veit and Co., 1903, p. 13; C. H. Roberts, "The Greek Papyri," in S. R. K. Glanville, ed., *The Legacy of Egypt*, Oxford: Clarendon Press, 1942, pp. 276–279.

[33] Ibid., pp. 278–279.

[34] Aristide Calderini, *La Composizione della Famiglia Secondo le Schede di Censimento dell' Egitto Romano*, Milan: Società Editrice "Vita e Pensiero," 1923.

[35] Marcel Hombert and Claire Préaux, *Recherches sur le Recensement dans l'Égypte Romaine, Papyrologica Lugduno-Batava*, Leiden: E. J. Brill, 1952, Vol. 5, p. 151.

Place	Consanguine Marriages	Other Marriages
Arsinoe	20	32
Villages of Fayoum	9	39
Oxyrhynchus	0	7
Hermoupolis	5	14
Others	4	32
Total	38	124

Some of these cases involve merely half brothers and sisters, but the majority are full brothers and sisters. Though it is hazardous to generalize from the small and unrepresentative number of cases, it appears that consanguineous marriages were more common in the cities than in the rural villages. There are no examples of brother-sister marriage occurring after 212 A.D., but Diocletian's issuance of an edict in 295 condemning such marriages suggests that they were still occasionally practiced.[36]

A further source of evidence concerning marriage customs in Egypt is in the writings of Greek and Roman observers. The Greeks were notoriously ethnocentric and their accounts of the customs of "barbarians" are often suspect, but when these accounts are taken in conjunction with other evidence, they provide additional corroboration. Diodorus of Sicily, a Greek historian of the first century B.C., who drew heavily on the historical romance of Hecataeus of Abdera, wrote, "The Egyptians also made a law, they say, contrary to the general custom of mankind, permitting men to marry their sisters, this being due to the success attained by Isis in this respect; for she had married her brother Osiris. . . ."[37] The Hellenistic Jewish philosopher Philo Judaeus, who lived in Alexandria (20 B.C.–c. 50 A.D.), made the following statement: "But the lawgiver of the Egyptians poured scorn upon the cautiousness of both [Athenians and Lacedaemonians], and, holding that the course which they enjoined stopped halfway, produced a fine crop of lewdness. With a lavish hand he bestowed on bodies and souls the poisonous bane of incontinence and gave full liberty to marry sisters of every degree whether they belonged to one of their brother's parents or to both, and not only if they were younger than their brothers but also if they were older or of the same age."[38] The Roman philosopher Seneca (c. 4 B.C.–65 A.D.) commented similarly with regard to the marriage of brothers and sisters: *Athenis dimidium licet, Alexandriae totum.*[39] Claudius Ptolemy, a Greek mathematician, astronomer, and geographer living in Alexandria (c. 127–151 A.D.) commented that Egypt, because of the conjunction of certain planets, was "governed by a man and wife who are own brother and sister."[40] Finally,

[36] Ibid., p. 153.

[37] *Diodorus of Sicily*, translated by C. H. Oldfather, London: William Heinemann, 1946, book 1, section 27, p. 85.

[38] Philo Judaeus, op. cit.

[39] See William Adam, "Consanguinity in Marriage," *Fortnightly Review*, 2 (1865), Vol. 2, p. 714.

[40] Ptolemy, *Tetrabiblos*, translated by F. E. Robbins, Cambridge: Harvard University Press, 1940, book 2, Chap. 3, p. 151.

Pausanias, a Greek traveler and topographer (c. 175 A.D.) wrote, "This Ptolemy fell in love with Arsinoe, his full sister, and married her, violating herein Macedonian custom, but following that of his Egyptian subjects."[41]

CONCLUSION AND DISCUSSION

For the Pharaonic period there is reasonably firm evidence that the Egyptian kings, especially those in the 18th and 19th Dynasties, sometimes married their sisters or half sisters and perhaps on rare occasions their daughters. For the commoners, on the other hand, there is only one fairly certain case of the marriage of brother and sister, though there are several other possible or even probable cases. In no instance, however, is there proof that the individuals were more than half brother and half sister. Bell[42] and Wilcken[43] believed that the relative lack of evidence of brother-sister marriage among the commoners before Roman times was due to the paucity of documents pertaining to commoners rather than to the absence of the custom among them. Nevertheless, on the basis of evidence now available, we must conclude that, although the marriage of brothers and sisters was probably not forbidden to commoners in the Pharaonic period, it was practiced only very rarely.

In the Ptolemaic period the evidence is conclusive that many of the kings married their sisters or half sisters, but there are no reports of such marriages among commoners. During the Roman period, on the other hand, there is an abundance of evidence that points to a fairly high incidence of marriages between brothers and sisters among commoners.

How can the extensive practice of brother-sister marriage in Egypt be explained? This question has stimulated much speculation, but no final answers are possible on the basis of evidence presently available. Some Egyptologists have argued in favor of a diffusion hypothesis, maintaining that the custom was not indigenous but was adopted as a result of the influence of other cultures. Kornemann, for example, believed that the Ptolemies copied the Persian custom and that the Egyptian commoners later began to follow the practices of the royalty.[44] It is a matter of vigorous controversy whether consanguineous marriages were practiced among the ancient Persians,[45] but the fact that such marriages apparently did exist in the contiguous culture of Egypt lends credence to the Persian case. With scanty informa-

[41] Pausanias, *Description of Greece*, translated by W. H. S. Jones, London: William Heinemann, 1918, book 1, section 7, paragraph 1, p. 35.

[42] H. I. Bell, "Brother and Sister Marriage in Graeco-Roman Egypt," *Revue Internationale des Droits de l'Antiquité*, 2 (1949), 84.

[43] Wilcken, op. cit.

[44] E. Kornemann, "Die Geschwisterehe im Altertum," *Mitteilungen der Schlesischen Gesellschaft für Volkskunde*, 24 (1923), 83.

[45] See J. S. Slotkin, "On a Possible Lack of Incest Regulations in Old Iran," *American Anthropologist*, 49 (October–December, 1947), 612–617; Ward H. Goodenough, "Comments on the Question of Incestuous Marriages in Old Iran," *American Anthropologist*, 51 (April–June, 1949), 326–328; and J. S. Slotkin, "Reply to Goodenough," *American Anthropologist*, 51 (July–September, 1949), 531–532.

tion, however, it is difficult to determine the direction of the diffusion process. Moreover, alien cultural elements are not ordinarily adopted by a society unless they have some functional significance in the new setting. Thus the diffusion hypothesis, even if it were possible to establish it firmly, still does not answer the question of why the custom developed in the original host culture or why it was later adopted in a secondary culture.

Several authors, following Diodorus, suggest that the custom of brother-sister marriage in Egypt had its origin in the religious system.[46] The gods Osiris and Set according to legend married their sisters Isis and Nepthys, presumably setting a pattern which was subsequently imitated by their followers. Incestuous origin myths characterize almost every society, however, including those which maintain strict taboos on the marriage of brothers and sisters. Also religious myths tend to be a reflection or popular explanation of more basic cultural elements rather than their source. White, on the other hand, believes that the Ptolemies adopted the practice of marrying their sisters as a means of conciliating the cult of Osiris and of undermining the prestige and authority of the hostile Theban priesthood, who were associated with the rival cult of Amon-Ra.[47]

Another hypothesis that has been advocated by many Egyptologists in the past is that ancient Egypt was in a transitional stage between matrilineal and patrilineal descent systems.[48] The royalty were governed by matrilineal descent with authority handed down through the female line. The king secured his legitimacy only through marriage with the heiress queen. Thus marriages contracted between brothers and sisters were merely an expedient for shifting the succession from the female to the male line. This type of explanation, however, smacks of the now discredited evolutionary schemes of the nineteenth century anthropologists who maintained that a matrilineal stage preceded the "higher" patrilineal stage in most societies at some distant time in the past. Anomalous customs, for which there was no readily perceived functional explanation, were seized upon as "survivals" and evidences of the earlier period. The bulk of the evidence for Egypt suggests that kingship was not inherited primarily through the female line but through the male line. In the absence of a male heir able to assert his rights effectively, however, it frequently happened that a son-in-law of the king became the new king.

The First Story of Sethon Khamwese, which, as Griffith remarks, is the only account we possess of an early Egyptian betrothal or marriage that is not of the fairy-tale order, suggests that not only was the marriage of

[46] John Wilkinson, *Manners and Customs of the Ancient Egyptians*, rev. ed., New York: Dodd, Mead, 1878, Vol. 3, p. 113; Ernest A. Wallis Budge, *The Dwellers on the Nile*, London: Religious Tract Society, 1926, p. 23; and Ruffer, op. cit., pp. 323–324.

[47] Rachel Evelyn White, "Women in Ptolemaic Egypt," *Journal of Hellenic Studies*, 18 (1898), 238–239.

[48] Petrie, op. cit., vol. 2, p. 183; White, op. cit.; Kornemann, op. cit.; Margaret Murray, "Royal Marriages and Matrilineal Descent," *Journal of the Royal Anthropological Institute*, 45 (1915), 307–325; and Margaret Murray, *The Splendour that Was Egypt*, London: Sidgwick and Jackson, 1949, pp. 100–102, 321–323.

brothers and sisters not necessary for the succession, but it tended to endanger it:[49]

> . . . . The ancient Pharaoh's argument about his son Neferkeptah and his daughter Ahure seems to be that it would be impolitic, when there were only two children in the royal family, to risk the succession by marrying them together. His preference, following a family custom, would be to marry them to a son and a daughter of two of his generals in order to enlarge his family. At a banquet he questioned Ahure, and was won over by her wishes to the other plan; thereupon he commanded his chief steward to take the princess to her brother's house that same night with all necessary things. . . .

It is often stated that the Egyptian kings, like the Incas or the kings of Hawaii, married their sisters or daughters in order to maintain the purity of the royal blood. The frequency with which kings married commoners or even slaves, however, belies this explanation. The offspring of these unions frequently acceded to the throne. Moreover, neither this, nor the preceding explanation that the king had to seek legitimacy by marrying the heiress to the throne, can account for the existence of brother-sister marriage among the commoners. One might argue that the royal custom was established first and that it was gradually adopted by the commoners through a filtering-down process. But again, a custom is not likely to be adopted unless it has some functional significance within the social system or subsystem.

The most plausible explanation that has been advanced for the marriage of brothers and sisters in Egypt is that it served to maintain the property of the family intact and to prevent the splintering of the estate through the operation of the laws of inheritance.[50] Since daughters usually inherited a share of the estate,[51] the device of brother-sister marriage would have served to preserve intact the material resources of the family as a unit. That marriages of brothers and sisters were probably more common in the cities than in the rural communities during Roman times is consistent with this explanation, for there was a greater concentration of wealth among the urban residents. Other societies have, of course, used other means of dealing with the problem of fractionalism—primogeniture, ultimogeniture, or unilineal inheritance through an extended family system. The reason for the Egyptian adoption of the more unusual alternative remains obscure, particularly since the marriage of brothers and sisters could ordinarily be expected to have dysfunctional consequences.[52]

[49] F. L. Griffith, "Marriage (Egyptian)," in J. Hastings, ed., *Encyclopaedia of Religion and Ethics*, New York: C. Scribner's Sons, 1955, Vol. 8, p. 444.
[50] See Nietzold, op. cit., p. 13; Budge, op. cit., p. 23.
[51] Gaston Maspéro, *Life in Ancient Egypt*, London: Chapman and Hall, 1892, p. 11.
[52] See Bronislaw Malinowski, "Culture," *Encyclopedia of the Social Sciences*, New York: Macmillan Co., 1930, Vol. 4, pp. 629–630; Bronislaw Malinowski, *Sex and Repression in Savage Society*, London: Kegan Paul,

There is also a suggestion in the Roman laws that their Egyptian subjects may have employed consanguine marriages as marriages of convenience for the transmission of property that otherwise would have fallen to the state. Roman citizens in Egypt, on the other hand, were specifically enjoined from marrying their sisters, and when a brother married a sister, the state confiscated the property.[53]

In conclusion, the evidence from ancient Egypt, particularly from the Roman period, casts doubt upon the universality of the taboo upon the marriage of brothers and sisters. Apparently brother-sister marriage can be institutionalized for commoners as well as for royalty and it may be practiced on a fairly wide scale. What are the implications of this finding for the theoretical problems which revolve around the incest taboo? First, there is further evidence, if further evidence were needed, of the social nature and origins of incest prohibitions. Second, and more important, it is clear that unicausal explanations of the "universality" of the brother-sister taboo are inadequate. Firth has written perceptively, "I am prepared to see it shown that the incest situation varies according to the social structure of each community, that it has little to do with the prevention of sex relations as such, but that its real correlation is to be found in the maintenance of institutional forms in the society as a whole, and of the specific interest of groups in particular. Where these latter demand it for the preservation of their privileges, the union permitted between kin may be the closest possible."[54] Although the need to maintain clearly differentiated roles within the nuclear family or the need to establish cooperative alliances with other

---

Trench, Trubner, and Co., 1927, pp. 244–251; E. B. Tylor, "On a Method of Investigating the Development of Institutions; Applied to Laws of Marriage and Descent," *Journal of the Anthropological Institute*, 18 (1888), 266–267; Leslie A. White, "The Definition and Prohibition of Incest," *American Anthropologist*, 50 (July–Sept., 1948), 422–426; Brenda Z. Seligman, "The Incest Barrier: Its Role in Social Organization," *British Journal of Psychology*, 22 (January, 1932), 274–276; and Talcott Parsons, "Social Structure and the Development of Personality: Freud's Contribution to the Integration of Psychology and Sociology," *Psychiatry*, 21 (November, 1958), 332–336.

[53] See Papyrus 206 in A. S. Hunt and C. C. Edgar, *Select Papyri*, Cambridge: Harvard University Press, 1934, Vol. 2, p. 47.

[54] Raymond W. Firth, *We, the Tikopia*, London: G. Allen and Unwin, 1936, p. 340. Parsons has commented in a similar vein: ". . . Anything so general as the incest taboo seems likely to be a resultant of a constellation of different factors which are deeply involved in the foundations of human societies. Analysis in terms of the balance of forces in the social system rather than of one or two specific 'factors' seems much more promising." Talcott Parsons, "The Incest Taboo in Relation to Social Structure and the Socialization of the Child," *British Journal of Sociology*, 5 (June, 1954), 101. Parsons, however, was misled by Murdock's sweeping statement—based upon the analysis of only 250 societies—that "in no known society is it conventional or even permissible for father and daughter, mother and son, or brother and sister to have sexual intercourse or to marry." George P. Murdock, *Social Structure*, New York: Macmillan Co., 1949, p. 12. Consequently, Parsons fails to recognize that the "balance of forces in the social system" may in some cases be such that marriages between brother and sister or even parent and child are permitted.

families may serve as the foundation for incest prohibitions in the great majority of societies, these needs may in some cases be offset by other functional requirements of overriding importance. This has long been recognized in connection with small ruling elites, but not with regard to general institutions which may be applicable to the whole society.

Although it is probably the most significant example, the Egyptian case does not stand alone as an exception to the universality of the brother-sister incest taboo. Wilson has recently reported that forty-two members of a community on a Caribbean island have been carrying on incestuous relations for the past thirty years, including relations between mothers and sons, fathers and daughters, and brothers and sisters.[55] This, however, apparently is an aberrant situation which developed because of special circumstances, and the original normative standards are now beginning to be reasserted. At any rate, this does not represent a long-term institutionalized pattern persisting for hundreds of years, as was the case in ancient Egypt.

There is also evidence, however, that societies which have sanctioned unions between brothers and sisters or between parents and children have not been nearly as rare as has been generally supposed in recent years. In dust-covered volumes, which for the most part have been left unopened and unread on the library shelves by the current generation of social scientists,[56] there are many instances of such cases reported by travelers, government officials, missionaries, ethnographers, and archeologists.[57] Although many of the several dozen reports are of doubtful authenticity, there probably remains a substantial number of societies which are deserving of greater attention. It is important not only that we test the validity of our empirical generalizations, but also that we seek to discover in greater detail the various conditions which may impinge upon the structure of the nuclear family.

[55] Peter J. Wilson, "Incest—A Case Study," paper presented at 60th Annual Meeting of the American Anthropological Association, Philadelphia, November, 1961.

[56] Earlier social scientists, on the other hand, such as Spencer, Sumner, Frazer, Westermarck, Briffault, Letourneau, and Howard, were aware of many of the reports and called attention to them. Since their works also remain largely unread today, most of the cases have long since been forgotten.

[57] I am currently completing a survey of these reports and plan to publish a summary of this material shortly.

3 | A Cross-Cultural Survey of Some Sex Differences in Socialization

HERBERT BARRY III, MARGARET K. BACON, and
IRVIN L. CHILD

In our society, certain differences may be observed between the typical personality characteristics of the two sexes. These sex differences in personality are generally believed to result in part from differences in the way boys and girls are reared. To the extent that personality differences between the sexes are thus of cultural rather than biological origin, they seem potentially susceptible to change. But how readily susceptible to change? In the differential rearing of the sexes does our society make an arbitrary imposition on an infinitely plastic biological base, or is this cultural imposition found uniformly in all societies as an adjustment to the real biological differences between the sexes? This paper reports one attempt to deal with this problem.

DATA AND PROCEDURES

The data used were ethnographic reports, available in the anthropological literature, about socialization practices of various cultures. One hundred and ten cultures, mostly nonliterate, were studied. They were selected primarily in terms of the existence of adequate ethnographic reports of socialization practices and secondarily so as to obtain a wide and reasonably balanced geographical distribution. Various aspects of socialization of infants and children were rated on a 7-point scale by two judges (Mrs. Bacon and Mr. Barry). Where the ethnographic reports permitted, separate ratings were made for the socialization of boys and girls. Each rating was indicated as either confident or doubtful; with still greater uncertainty, or with complete lack of evidence, the particular rating was of course not made at all. We shall restrict the report of sex difference ratings to cases in which both judges made a confident rating. Also omitted is the one instance where the two judges reported a sex difference in opposite directions, as it demonstrates only unreliability of judgment. The number of cultures that meet these criteria is much smaller than the total of 110; for the several variables to be considered, the number varies from 31 to 84.

The aspects of socialization on which ratings were made included:

This research is part of a project for which financial support was provided by the Social Science Research Council and the Ford Foundation. We are greatly indebted to G. P. Murdock for supplying us with certain data, as indicated below, and to him and Thomas W. Maretzki for suggestions that have been used in this paper.

From *Journal of Abnormal and Social Psychology*, 55 (November, 1957), 327–332, by permission of the American Psychological Association.

1. Several criteria of attention and indulgence toward infants.

2. Strength of socialization from age 4 or 5 years until shortly before puberty, with respect to five systems of behavior; strength of socialization was defined as the combination of positive pressure (rewards for the behavior) plus negative pressure (punishments for lack of the behavior). The variables were:

(a) Responsibility or dutifulness training. (The data were such that training in the performance of chores in the productive or domestic economy was necessarily the principal source of information here; however, training in the performance of other duties was also taken into account when information was available.)

(b) Nurturance training, i.e., training the child to be nurturant or helpful toward younger siblings and other dependent people.

(c) Obedience training.

(d) Self-reliance training.

(e) Achievement training, i.e., training the child to orient his behavior toward standards of excellence in performance, and to seek to achieve as excellent a performance as possible.

Where the term "no sex difference" is used here, it may mean any of three things: (a) the judge found separate evidence about the training of boys and girls on this particular variable, and judged it to be identical; (b) the judge found a difference between the training of boys and girls, but not great enough for the sexes to be rated a whole point apart on a 7-point scale; (c) the judge found evidence only about the training of "children" on this variable, the ethnographer not reporting separately about boys and girls.

SEX DIFFERENCES IN SOCIALIZATION

On the various aspects of attention and indulgence toward infants, the judges almost always agreed in finding no sex difference. Out of 96 cultures for which the ratings included the infancy period, 88 (92%) were rated with no sex difference by either judge for any of those variables. This result is consistent with the point sometimes made by anthropologists that "baby" generally is a single status undifferentiated by sex, even though "boy" and "girl" are distinct statuses.

TABLE 1 Ratings of Cultures for Sex Differences on Five Variables of Childhood Socialization Pressure

Variable	Number of Cultures	Both Judges Agree in Rating the Variable Higher in		One Judge Rates No Difference, One Rates the Variable Higher in		Percentage of Cultures with Evidence of Sex Difference in Direction of		
		Girls	Boys	Girls	Boys	Girls	Boys	Neither
Nurturance	33	17	0	10	0	82%	0%	18%
Obedience	69	6	0	18	2	35%	3%	62%
Responsibility	84	25	2	26	7	61%	11%	28%
Achievement	31	0	17	1	10	3%	87%	10%
Self-reliance	82	0	64	0	6	0%	85%	15%

On the variables of childhood socialization, on the other hand, a rating of no sex difference by both judges was much less common. This finding of no sex difference varied in frequency from 10% of the cultures for the achievement variable up to 62% of the cultures for the obedience variable, as shown in the last column of Table 1. Where a sex difference is reported, by either one or both judges, the difference tends strongly to be in a particular direction, as shown in the earlier columns of the same table. Pressure toward nurturance, obedience, and responsibility is most often stronger for girls, whereas pressure toward achievement and self-reliance is most often stronger for boys.

For nurturance and for self-reliance, all the sex differences are in the same direction. For achievement there is only one exception to the usual direction of difference, and for obedience only two; but for responsibility there are nine. What do these exceptions mean? We have reexamined all these cases. In most of them, only one judge had rated the sexes as differently treated (sometimes one judge, sometimes the other), and in the majority of these cases both judges were now inclined to agree that there was no convincing evidence of a real difference. There were exceptions, however, especially in cases where a more formal or systematic training of boys seemed to imply greater pressure on them toward responsibility. The most convincing cases were the Masai and Swazi, where both judges had originally agreed in rating responsibility pressures greater in boys than in girls. In comparing the five aspects of socialization we may conclude that responsibility shows by far the strongest evidence of real variation in the direction of sex difference, and obedience much the most frequently shows evidence of no sex difference at all.

In subsequent discussion we shall be assuming that the obtained sex differences in the socialization ratings reflect true sex differences in the cultural practices. We should consider here two other possible sources of these rated differences.

1. The ethnographers could have been biased in favor of seeing the same pattern of sex differences as in our culture. However, most anthropologists readily perceive and eagerly report novel and startling cultural features, so we may expect them to have reported unusual sex differences where they existed. The distinction between matrilineal and patrilineal, and between matrilocal and patrilocal cultures, given prominence in many ethnographic reports, shows an awareness of possible variations in the significance of sex differences from culture to culture.

2. The two judges could have expected to find in other cultures the sex roles which are familiar in our culture and inferred them from the material on the cultures. However, we have reported only confident ratings, and such a bias seems less likely here than for doubtful ratings. It might be argued, moreover, that bias has more opportunity in the cases ambiguous enough so that only one judge reported a sex difference, and less opportunity in the cases where the evidence is so clear that both judges agree. Yet in general, as may be seen in Table 1, the deviant cases are somewhat more frequent among the cultures where only one judge reported a sex difference.

The observed differences in the socialization of boys and girls are consistent with certain universal tendencies in the differentiation of adult sex role. In the economic sphere, men are more frequently allotted tasks that involve leaving home and engaging in activities where a high level of skill yields important returns; hunting is a prime example. Emphasis on training in self-reliance and achievement for boys would function as preparation for such an economic role. Women, on the other hand, are more frequently allotted tasks at or near home that minister most immediately to the needs of others (such as cooking and water carrying); these activities have a nurturant character, and in their pursuit a responsible carrying out of established routines is likely to be more important than the development of an especially high order of skill. Thus training in nurturance, responsibility, and, less clearly, obedience may contribute to preparation for this economic role. These consistencies with adult role go beyond the economic sphere, of course. Participation in warfare, as a male prerogative, calls for self-reliance and a high order of skill where survival or death is the immediate issue. The childbearing which is biologically assigned to women, and the child care which is socially assigned primarily to them, lead to nurturant behavior and often call for a more continuous responsibility than do the tasks carried out by men. Most of these distinctions in adult role are not inevitable, but the biological differences between the sexes strongly predispose the distinction of role, if made, to be in a uniform direction.[1]

The relevant biological sex differences are conspicuous in adulthood but generally not in childhood. If each generation were left entirely to its own devices, therefore, without even an older generation to copy, sex differences in role would presumably be almost absent in childhood and would have to be developed after puberty at the expense of considerable relearning on the part of one or both sexes. Hence, a pattern of child training which foreshadows adult differences can serve the useful function of minimizing what Benedict termed "discontinuities in cultural conditioning" (1).

The differences in socialization between the sexes in our society, then, are no arbitrary custom of our society, but a very widespread adaptation of culture to the biological substratum of human life.

VARIATIONS IN DEGREE OF SEX DIFFERENTIATION

While demonstrating near-universal tendencies in direction of difference between the socialization of boys and girls, our data do not show perfect uniformity. A study of the variations in our data may allow us to see some of the conditions which are associated with, and perhaps give rise to, a greater or smaller degree of this difference. For this purpose, we classified cultures as having relatively large or small sex difference by two different methods, one more inclusive and the other more selective. In both methods the ratings were at first considered separately for each of the five variables. A sex difference rating was made only if both judges made a rating on this variable and at least one judge's rating was confident.

In the more inclusive method the ratings were dichotomized, separately for each variable, as close as possible to the median into those showing a

[1] For data and interpretations supporting various arguments of this paragraph, see Mead (2), Murdock (3), and Scheinfeld (6).

large and those showing a small sex difference. Thus, for each society a large or a small sex difference was recorded for each of the five variables on which a sex difference rating was available. A society was given an over-all classification of large or small sex difference if it had a sex difference rating on at least three variables and if a majority of these ratings agreed in being large, or agreed in being small. This method permitted classification of a large number of cultures, but the grounds for classification were capricious in many cases, as a difference of only one point in the rating of a single variable might change the over-all classification of sex difference for a culture from large to small.

In the more selective method, we again began by dichotomizing each variable as close as possible to the median; but a society was now classified as having a large or small sex difference on the variable only if it was at least one step away from the scores immediately adjacent to the median. Thus only the more decisive ratings of sex difference were used. A culture was classified as having an over-all large or small sex difference only if it was given a sex difference rating which met this criterion on at least two variables, and only if all such ratings agreed in being large, or agreed in being small.

We then tested the relation of each of these dichotomies to 24 aspects of culture on which Murdock has categorized the customs of most of these societies[2] and which seemed of possible significance for sex differentiation. The aspects of culture covered include type of economy, residence pattern, marriage and incest rules, political integration, and social organization. For each aspect of culture, we grouped Murdock's categories to make a dichotomous contrast (sometimes omitting certain categories as irrelevant to the contrast). In the case of some aspects of culture, two or more separate contrasts were made (e.g., under form of marriage we contrasted monogamy with polygyny, and also contrasted sororal with nonsororal polygyny). For each of 40 comparisons thus formed, we prepared a 2×2 frequency table to determine relation to each of our sex-difference dichotomies. A significant relation was found for 6 of these 40 aspects of culture with the more selective dichotomization of over-all sex difference. In four of these comparisons, the relation to the more inclusive dichotomization was also significant. These relationships are all given in Table 2, in the form of phi coefficients, along with the outcome of testing significance by the use of χ^2 or Fisher's exact test. In trying to interpret these findings, we have also considered the non-significant correlations with other variables, looking for consistency and inconsistency with the general implications of the significant findings. We have arrived at the following formulation of results:

1. Large sex difference in socialization is associated with an economy that places a high premium on the superior strength, and superior development of motor skills requiring strength, which characterize the male. Four of the correlations reported in Table 2 clearly point to this generalization: the correlations of large sex difference with the hunting of large animals, with grain rather than root crops, with the keeping of large rather than small domestic animals, and with nomadic rather than sedentary residence. The correlation with the unimportance of fishing may also be consistent with

---

[2] These data were supplied to us directly by Professor Murdock.

TABLE 2   Culture Variables Correlated with Large Sex Difference in Socialization, Separately for Two Types of Sample

Variable	More Selective Sample		More Inclusive Sample	
	ϕ	N	ϕ	N
Large animals are hunted	.48*	(34)	.28*	(72)
Grain rather than root crops are grown	.82**	(20)	.62**	(43)
Large or milking animals rather than small animals are kept	.65*	(19)	.43*	(35)
Fishing unimportant or absent	.42*	(31)	.19	(69)
Nomadic rather than sedentary residence	.61**	(34)	.15	(71)
Polygyny rather than monogamy	.51*	(28)	.38**	(64)

*$p < .05.$
**$p < .01.$
Note: The variables have been so phrased that all correlations are positive. The phi coefficient is shown, and in parentheses, the number of cases on which the comparison was based. Significance level was determined by χ^2, or Fisher's exact test where applicable, using in all cases a two-tailed test.

this generalization, but the argument is not clear.[3] Other correlations consistent with the generalization, though not statistically significant, are with large game hunting rather than gathering, with the hunting of large game rather than small game, and with the general importance of all hunting and gathering.

2. Large sex difference in socialization appears to be correlated with customs that make for a large family group with high cooperative interaction. The only statistically significant correlation relevant here is that with polygyny rather than monogamy. This generalization is, however, supported by several substantial correlations that fall only a little short of being statistically significant. One of these is a correlation with sororal rather than nonsororal polygyny; Murdock and Whiting (4) have presented indirect evidence that co-wives generally show smoother cooperative interaction if they are sisters. Correlations are also found with the presence of either an extended

[3] Looking (with the more inclusive sample) into the possibility that this correlation might result from the correlation between fishing and sedentary residence, a complicated interaction between these variables was found. The correlation of sex differentiation with absence of fishing is found only in nomadic societies, where fishing is likely to involve cooperative activity of the two sexes, and its absence is likely to mean dependence upon the male for large game hunting or herding large animals (whereas in sedentary societies the alternatives to fishing do not so uniformly require special emphasis on male strength). The correlation of sex differentiation with nomadism is found only in nonfishing societies; here nomadism is likely to imply large game hunting or herding large animals, whereas in fishing societies nomadism evidently implies no such special dependence upon male strength. Maximum sex differentiation is found in nomadic nonfishing societies (15 with large difference and only 2 with small) and minimum sex differentiation in nomadic fishing societies (2 with large difference and 7 with small difference). These findings further strengthen the argument for a conspicuous influence of the economy upon sex differentiation.

or a polygynous family rather than the nuclear family only; with the presence of an extended family; and with the extreme contrast between maximal extension and no extension of the family. The generalization is also to some extent supported by small correlations with wide extension of incest taboos, if we may presume that an incest taboo makes for effective unthreatening cooperation within the extended family. The only possible exception to this generalization, among substantial correlations, is a near-significant correlation with an extended or polygynous family's occupying a cluster of dwellings rather than a single dwelling.[4]

In seeking to understand this second generalization, we feel that the degree of social isolation of the nuclear family may perhaps be the crucial underlying variable. To the extent that the nuclear family must stand alone, the man must be prepared to take the woman's role when she is absent or incapacitated, and vice versa. Thus the sex differentiation cannot afford to be too great. But to the extent that the nuclear family is steadily interdependent with other nuclear families, the female role in the household economy can be temporarily taken over by another woman, or the male role by another man, so that sharp differentiation of sex role is no handicap.

The first generalization, which concerns the economy, cannot be viewed as dealing with material completely independent of the ratings of socialization. The training of children in their economic role was often an important part of the data used in rating socialization variables, and would naturally vary according to the general economy of the society. We would stress, however, that we were by no means using the identical data on the two sides of our comparison; we were on the one hand judging data on the socialization of children and on the other hand using Murdock's judgments on the economy of the adult culture. In the case of the second generalization, it seems to us that there was little opportunity for information on family and social structure to have influenced the judges in making the socialization ratings.

Both of these generalizations contribute to understanding the social background of the relatively small difference in socialization of boys and girls which we believe characterizes our society at the present time. Our mechanized economy is perhaps less dependent than any previous economy upon the superior average strength of the male. The nuclear family in our society is often so isolated that husband and wife must each be prepared at times to take over or help in the household tasks normally assigned to the other. It is also significant that the conditions favoring low sex differ-

---

[4] We think the reverse of this correlation would be more consistent with our generalization here. But perhaps it may reasonably be argued that the various nuclear families composing an extended or polygynous family are less likely to develop antagonisms which hinder cooperation if they are able to maintain some physical separation. On the other hand, this variable may be more relevant to the first generalization than to the second. Occupation of a cluster of dwellings is highly correlated with presence of herding and with herding of large rather than small animals, and these economic variables in turn are correlated with large sex difference in socialization. Occupation of a cluster of dwellings is also correlated with polygyny rather than monogamy and shows no correlation with sororal vs. nonsororal polygyny.

entiation appear to be more characteristic of the upper segments of our society, in socioeconomic and educational status, than of lower segments. This observation may be relevant to the tendency toward smaller sex differences in personality in higher status groups (cf. Terman and Miles, 8).

The increase in our society of conditions favoring small sex difference has led some people to advocate a virtual elimination of sex differences in socialization. This course seems likely to be dysfunctional even in our society. Parsons, Bales, et al. (5) argue that a differentiation of role similar to the universal pattern of sex difference is an important and perhaps inevitable development in any social group, such as the nuclear family. If we add to their argument the point that biological differences between the sexes make most appropriate the usual division of those roles between the sexes, we have compelling reasons to expect that the decrease in differentiation of adult sex role will not continue to the vanishing point. In our training of children, there may now be less differentiation in sex role than characterizes adult life—so little, indeed, as to provide inadequate preparation for adulthood. This state of affairs is likely to be especially true of formal education, which is more subject to conscious influence by an ideology than is informal socialization at home. With child training being more oriented toward the male than the female role in adulthood, many of the adjustment problems of women in our society today may be partly traced to conflicts growing out of inadequate childhood preparation for their adult role. This argument is nicely supported in extreme form by Spiro's analysis of sex roles in an Israeli kibbutz (7). The ideology of the founders of the kibbutz included the objective of greatly reducing differences in sex role. But the economy of the kibbutz is a largely nonmechanized one in which the superior average strength of men is badly needed in many jobs. The result is that, despite the ideology and many attempts to implement it, women continue to be assigned primarily to traditional "women's work," and the incompatibility between upbringing or ideology and adult role is an important source of conflict for women.

Note on Regional Distribution

There is marked variation among regions of the world in typical size of sex difference in socialization. In our sample, societies in North America and Africa tend to have large sex difference, and societies in Oceania to have small sex difference. Less confidently, because of the smaller number of cases, we can report a tendency toward small sex differences in Asia and South America as well. Since most of the variables with which we find the sex difference to be significantly correlated have a similar regional distribution, the question arises whether the correlations might better be ascribed to some quite different source having to do with large regional similarities, rather than to the functional dependence we have suggested. As a partial check, we have tried to determine whether the correlations we report in Table 2 tend also to be found strictly within regions. For each of the three regions for which we have sizable samples (North America, Africa, and Oceania) we have separately plotted 2×2 tables corresponding to each of the 6 relationships reported in Table 2. (We did this only for the more inclusive sample, since for the more selective sample the number of cases within a region would have been extremely small.) Out of the 18 correlations thus determined, 11 are positive and only 3 are negative (the other 4 being exactly zero). This result clearly suggests a general tendency for these correlations to hold true within regions as well as between regions, and may lend further support to our functional interpretation.

SUMMARY

A survey of certain aspects of socialization in 110 cultures shows that differentiation of the sexes is unimportant in infancy, but that in childhood there is, as in our society, a widespread pattern of greater pressure toward nurturance, obedience, and responsibility in girls, and toward self-reliance and achievement striving in boys. There are a few reversals of sex difference, and many instances of no detectable sex difference; these facts tend to confirm the cultural rather than directly biological nature of the differences. Cultures vary in the degree to which these differentiations are made; correlational analysis suggests some of the social conditions influencing these variations, and helps in understanding why our society has relatively small sex differentiation.

REFERENCES

1. Benedict, Ruth, Continuities and discontinuities in cultural conditioning. *Psychiatry*, 1 (1938), 161–167.
2. Mead, Margaret, *Male and female.* New York: Morrow, 1949.
3. Murdock, G. P., Comparative data on the division of labor by sex. *Social Forces*, 15 (1937), 551–553.
4. Murdock, G. P., & Whiting, J. W. M., Cultural determination of parental attitudes: The relationship between the social structure, particularly family structure and parental behavior. In M. J. E. Senn (Ed.), *Problems of infancy and childhood: Transactions of the Fourth Conference*, March 6–7, 1950. New York: Josiah Macy, Jr. Foundation, 1951. Pp. 13–34.
5. Parsons, T., Bales, R. F., et al., *Family, socialization and interaction process.* Glencoe, Ill.: Free Press, 1955.
6. Scheinfeld, A., *Women and men.* New York: Harcourt, Brace, 1944.
7. Spiro, M. E., *Kibbutz: Venture in Utopia.* Cambridge: Harvard University Press, 1956.
8. Terman, L. M., & Miles, Catherine C., *Sex and personality.* New York: McGraw-Hill, 1936.

II | Learning Male and Female Sex Roles

Introduction to Section II

The question of male and female role differences, which I touched upon in my introductory comments to Section I, comes up again in the readings in this section. It appears that as early as the first year of life parents behave differently toward female and male infants.[1] However, such data do not conclusively settle the question of infant predisposition. It is still possible that parents respond differently to male and female infants because the infants themselves are behaving differently. This is a fascinating area of study that begs for additional careful research. There is a renewed interest in this area today due to the concern with issues of the new sexual freedom and of women's liberation. What limits exist to possible changes in male and female societal roles? To what degree can men and women share specific motivations and skills?

Related to this area of sex-role learning is the question of parental identification. Do we learn our sex role by identification with the parent of the same sex? Is the mother or the father more important in such sex-role differentiation? Alfred Heilbrun (4) examines Miriam Johnson's iconoclastic theory that it is the father who distinguishes most sharply the male and female sex roles of his children and thus identification with him is the determinant of a clear sex-role conception for both male and female children. A very interesting test supports this conception and Heilbrun brings out further implications of this for the theories of Talcott Parsons and other social scientists.

The great importance of sex-role behavior of parents is brought out in the Heilbrun article. The mechanisms by which we learn our sex roles are of tremendous importance in understanding our courtship, marital, and family attitudes and behaviors. We are just on the threshold of learning how certain groups

[1] Goldberg, Susan, and Michael Lewis, "Play Behavior of the Year Old Infant: Early Sex Differences." *Child Development* 40 (March, 1969), 21–31.

49

promote different conceptions of sex roles and relatedly how certain parents influence the sex roles of their children.

The Broderick research (5) provides a very clear appreciation of the systematic, cumulative aspects of sex-role learning. Broderick's study of 10–17 year olds shows the steplike quality involved in the heterosexual dimension of sex-role learning. Let me be clear, however, that learning to be masculine or feminine is a very broad, complex thing and that heterosexuality is but one part of it. As we saw in the Barry study in Section I, the female sex role typically involves elements of obedience, responsibility, and nurturance and the male sex role has elements of achievement and self-reliance. Heterosexuality is one aspect of the sex role that cultures also teach, although some cultures teach youngsters how to be homosexual as well as heterosexual (Siwans in Africa, for example).[2] It is important to realize that evidence indicates that most male homosexuals in our society do not think of themselves as feminine—they rather think of themselves as masculine, just as most men who are low on self-reliance think of themselves as masculine. Missing one aspect of the generally expected sex role does not usually cause one to change his sex identity. This point will appear again in the Simon and Gagnon article on homosexuality (37) in Section XII.

The steplike development of heterosexuality is shown by Broderick in terms of choice of cross-sex friends, enjoying love scenes in movies, liking to get married someday, kissing, dating, and falling in love. These and other elements gradually build up from the age of 10 to 17 to produce a heterosexually oriented individual. From the other studies in this section, one will gain some idea of how males and females start very early along different sex-role paths. Broderick maps the heterosexual path for certain key years. We need more work on the earlier roots of this heterosexual development and more research on how heterosexual development relates to other aspects of masculine and feminine roles. There are a few such studies underway today by men such as Floyd Martinson at Gustavus Adolphus College and others which may well greatly increase our understanding here. Some of the readings on love and sex in Sections III and IV should also help the reader fill in his awareness of the ways in which males and females are socialized in our society. It is interesting to note that in viewing sexually stimulating slides and movies females respond in many ways much closer to males than our past conceptions would have led us to suspect. The Schmidt and Sigusch article (14) in Section IV details this finding. Such findings bear directly on questions of current and future male and female sex-role changes, and thus relate to the articles in Section II.

[2] Ford, Clellan S., and Frank A. Beach. *Patterns of Sexual Behavior.* New York: Harper & Row, 1951, Chap. 7.

4 An Empirical Test of the Modeling Theory of Sex-Role Learning

ALFRED B. HEILBRUN, JR.

Johnson (1955) has recently proposed that the crucial factor in learning the masculine sex role for males *and* the feminine sex role for females is identification with the father. She bases her reasoning upon certain basic premises adopted from Parsons' role theory (Parsons, 1958; Parsons & Bales, 1955). First, Parsons considers identification as encompassing the behaviors a child learns in the context of a social role with a parent (i.e., the internalization of a reciprocal-role relationship). Accordingly, the learned behaviors need not be those which are typical of the adult but rather are those which are systematically elicited and reinforced in the course of the child's interaction with the adult. The child is presumed to make a series of successive identifications, both boys and girls making an initial identification with the mother which is not sex typed. The following identification with the father, in which he forms differentiated role relationships with the son and the daughter, provides the basis for sex-role learning in offspring of both sexes.

Second, Parsons regards the essence of masculinity and femininity to be a difference in instrumental and expressive orientation. The feminine-expressive role is distinguished by an orientation of giving rewarding responses in order to receive rewarding responses. Johnson states, "The expressive role player is oriented toward the relationships among the actors within a system. He is primarily oriented to the attitudes and feelings of those actors toward himself and toward each other. . . . By being solicitious, appealing, and 'understanding,' a woman seeks to get a pleasurable response by giving pleasure" (1963, pp. 320–321). The instrumental (masculine) role, in contrast, is defined as a behavioral orientation toward goals which transcend the immediate interactional situation. Since the interaction is viewed primarily as a means to an end, the instrumental-role player cannot be primarily oriented to the immediate emotional responses of others to him. Rather than soliciting positive responses from others like the expressive person, instrumental-role-playing requires an ability to tolerate the hostility which it will very likely elicit.

It is further proposed that the father (but not the mother) is capable of engaging in both instrumental and expressive roles. This follows from the assumption that the early relationship of both boys and girls with their mothers mediates learning of expressive behavior and that later boys, but not girls, learn a new orientation, instrumentalness, so they can deal effectively with the non-familial environment. Thus, boys retain the capacity to respond in either an expressive or instrumental manner, whereas girls can behave only expressively. Ten studies are cited by Johnson (1963, pp. 323–327) that support the conclusion that fathers differentiate their own sex-role behavior toward male and female offspring more than mothers do.

Reprinted from *Child Development*, 36, No. 3 (September, 1965), 789–799, by permission of The Society for Research in Child Development.

Johnson summarized her hypothesis as follows: "The mother is predominantly expressive toward children of both sexes and uses, intentionally or not, 'love-oriented' techniques of control on both. It is in this first identification of both male and female children with the mother in a love-dependency relationship that the basic superego is laid down. Sex-role differentiation then follows the initial mother identification and results from the identification of both sexes with the father in differentiated role relationships. The father adds the specifically feminine element to the female's initial expressiveness by rewarding her, by his appreciative attitude, not simply for being 'good' but for being 'attractive.' With his son as with his daughter the father is solidary, but with his son he is also demanding, thus giving the extra push that instrumentalness requires" (1963, p. 324).

Although Johnson presents a cogent argument for a reciprocal-role interpretation of sex-role learning, there is no reason, in principle, why a single mode of transmitting sex-role attributes from parents to children must be posited. For example, modeling theory (Sears, Maccoby, & Levin, 1957, pp. 368–376) would predict that sex-typed behaviors that are observed in the repertories of the parents and are modeled after by children represent an important basis for appropriate sex-typing. The major question pursued in the present investigation was whether modeling principles would also prove useful in predicting the sex-role behavior of children, granting that fathers are more capable of sex-role differentiation than mothers and that the instrumental-expressive distinction represents a useful basis for defining the masculine and feminine sex roles. The present study did not compare the relative usefulness of the reciprocal-role and the modeling hypotheses, however, since no evidence relevant to the former was collected.

Even though the father typically assumes the instrumental role within the nuclear family, it must be assumed that individual differences in masculinity occur, since many fathers have not learned instrumentalness in the course of their own social development. On the other hand, a very high proportion of fathers have at least been exposed to the conditions under which expressive qualities are presumably learned (early mother-child interaction). The observation that there are at least two classes of fathers—those who are primarily instrumental but retain the capacity for expressive behavior (i.e., can differentiate their roles) and a smaller proportion who are primarily expressive but lack the capacity for instrumental behavior (i.e., are less capable of differentiating their roles)—seems accurate. A similar case can be made for mothers; although most mothers may be regarded as expressive in orientation, some, at least, will have learned instrumental behaviors in their social development. When these four classes of parent-model types are employed, the following prediction would follow from a modeling hypothesis of sex-role learning:

The greatest sex-role disparity between males and females, commonly identified with a single parent type, will be mediated by identification with (modeling after) the instrumental father. This parent, more than any other single type, is capable of providing an instrumental model for his son and an expressive model for his daughter.

Two logical assumptions implicit in this prediction should be emphasized. First, it is reasonable to maintain that a father's behavior is of a generally instrumental character even though he may behave expressively under
special conditions, one such condition being interaction with a female child.
Second, the parental behavior that is most likely to be modeled after by a
child is the behavior that occurs in the context of the parent's interaction
with him.

The first of these assumptions allows for the possibility that a girl
whose father is legitimately classified as masculine based upon the preponderance of his behavior may still be directly exposed to an expressive model
in his dealings with her. This avoids the seeming paradox of a finding that
modeling after a masculine parent mediates feminine qualities in a girl. The
second assumption is equally crucial to interpretation of father-daughter results. If the masculine father engages in expressive behaviors only in the exceptional circumstance of father-daughter interaction, it must be assumed
that the father's behavior at these times has a greater potency to elicit
modeling from the daughter than do the more frequently emitted instrumental behaviors that the daughter observes as a bystander and in direct dealings with the father. Since many of the father's expressive behaviors which
occur in interaction with the daughter can be described as nurturant in
character, the findings of Bandura and Huston (1961) strengthen the second
assumption. They found that children imitate the behavior of more nurturant
adult models more readily than they imitate that of their less nurturant
counterparts. Thus, the instrumental father should be especially effective as
a model when he directly interacts with the daughter.

METHOD

Subjects

A total of 279 undergraduates at the State University of Iowa, 139
males and 140 females, were employed in this study. These groups were
further divided by the particular parent with whom they made their primary identification and the relative instrumental-expressive orientation of
that parent. The resultant group sizes were: males identified with instrumental fathers $(N = 47)$, with instrumental mothers $(N = 27)$, with expressive fathers $(N = 20)$, with expressive mothers $(N = 45)$; females
identified with instrumental fathers $(N = 42)$, with instrumental mothers
$(N = 31)$, with expressive fathers $(N = 21)$, with expressive mothers
$(N = 46)$.

Measures of Developmental Variables

The parental object of identification was indicated by a scale that reflects the relative similarity between the child and his two parents as
perceived by the child. Norms for the identification scale have been developed for college students so that a score of $T = 50$ indicates the average

similarity between the son or daughter and the same-sex parent along 15 personality dimensions (e.g., nurturance, dominance, aggression). A score of $T > 50$ was used to define identification with the same-sex parent, whereas $T \leq 50$ indicated a cross-sex identification. A detailed description and validity evidence pertaining to this scale are available elsewhere (Heilbrun, 1965).

Instrumental-expressive orientation of the parents was estimated from behavioral descriptions rated by the subjects and used as part of the identification measure. Each was asked to judge whether certain types of behaviors were descriptive more of his mother or of his father. Nine of the 15 behaviors so rated had been found to be sex-typed based upon the ratings of 400 college students (Heilbrun, in press). In this earlier study fathers were rated as more need-achieving, autonomous, and dominant and as showing greater endurance; whereas mothers were judged to be more deferent, affiliative, succorant, abasing, and nurturant. The instrumental character of the "father" traits and the expressive nature of the "mother" traits are clearly evident. In the present study the appropriateness of the parents' sex roles was determined by counting the number of times the appropriate parent was rated as better described by the prescribed instrumental or expressive behavior. A score of 6 or greater was selected as a cutting point for defining instrumental fathers and expressive mothers; 5 or less defined the sex-role reversed, expressive fathers and instrumental mothers. These particular cutting scores resulted in classifying about 66 per cent of the male Ss' parents and about 63 per cent of the female Ss' parents as appropriately instrumental or expressive in orientation.[1]

The Personality Measure

The Adjective Check List (ACL) (Gough & Heilbrun, 1965) was used as the personality test in this study. Included in the ACL are 300 behavioral adjectives from which the person is asked to select those which are most self-characteristic. There are a large number of studies (see Gough & Heilbrun, 1965 that demonstrate that ACL self-descriptions obtained from normally functioning persons afford valid predictions of their actual social behaviors.

RESULTS

The ACL self-descriptions of the four sets of male and female comparison groups were analyzed by chi square procedures. Differential endorsement of any ACL adjective as self-descriptive was defined as $p < .05$. The 1,200 χ^2 values were obtained by computer analysis which included Yates' correction for continuity.

[1] We recognize that the measurement of instrumental or expressive character of parental behaviors employed here represents but one of many possible approaches and involves the same risks as any personal evaluation by a single, ego-involved judge. The congruence between ratings obtained in this fashion and expectancies based upon Parsons' theory, however, makes us confident that their use is justified.

TABLE 1 Instrumental and Expressive Behavior Differences between Males and Females who Identified with Sex-Role Appropriate Parents

Instrumental Fathers		Expressive Mothers	
Males More:	*Females More:*	*Males More:*	*Females More:*
Aggressive[a]	Appreciative[b]	Aggressive[a]	Adaptable
Cruel[a]	Artistic[b]	Conservative	Attractive[b]
Enterprising[a]	Curious	Enterprising[a]	Contented[b]
Forceful[a]	Effeminate	Handsome	Fearful[b]
Foresighted[a]	Emotional[b]	Inventive[a]	Feminine
Frank[a]	Excitable[b]	Masculine	Flirtatious
Handsome	Fearful[b]	Quiet	Frivolous
Hardheaded[a]	Fickle	Shrewd[a]	Mannerly
Logical[a]	Reliable[a]	Strong[a]	Outgoing[b]
Masculine	Self-pitying[b]	Tough[a]	Pleasant[b]
Opportunistic[a]	Sentimental[b]		Poised
Progressive[a]	Sincere[b]		Praising[b]
Reckless[a]	Sympathetic[b]		Selfish
Sharp-witted[a]	Warm[b]		Sympathetic[b]
Shrewd[a]	Wholesome[b]		Talkative
Stern[a]			Unaffected[a]
Strong[a]			Understanding[b]
Tough[a]			Wholesome[b]
Unscrupulous [a]			
Vindictive[a]			

[a]Behaviors judged to be instrumental.
[b]Behaviors judged to be expressive.

Although the χ^2 analysis provided a basis for establishing patterns of behavior differences between sex groups, evaluation of whether these patterns reflect instrumental versus expressive orientation differences was still necessary. This was accomplished by using the judgments of four clinical psychologists at the University of California as the basis for defining ACL adjectives as instrumental (I) or expressive (E) in character. All discriminating ACL adjectives were rated as I, E, or indeterminate based upon definitions provided by Johnson (1963). Interjudge agreement was high when only I and E ratings of the four judges are considered; some 93 per cent of these ratings were in accord. Final acceptance of an adjective as I or E required the agreement of at least two judges with no contrary (E or I) judgment ($N = 13$), the agreement of three judges as I or E ($N = 15$), or the agreement of four judges ($N = 16$).

The test of the prediction that the clearest instrumental vs. expressive sex-role distinctions would be evidenced by males and females identified with instrumental fathers was based upon data presented in Tables 1 and 2. These four patterns of behavior differences provide rather striking support for the prediction. Comparison of male and female offspring who identified with instrumental fathers provided 35 differences in behavior, 29 of which were judged to be appropriately instrumental or expressive. This proportion for the remaining three conditions were: expressive-mother identified, 15 of 28; instrumental-mother identified, 7 of 17; and expressive-father identified, 6 of 16. Chi square comparison of these proportions (not con-

TABLE 2 Instrumental and Expressive Behavior Differences between Males and Females Identified with Sex-Role Inappropriate Parents

Expressive Fathers		Instrumental Mothers	
Identified Males More:	*Identified Females More:*	*Identified Males More:*	*Identified Females More:*
Aggressive[a]	Awkward	Calm	Feminine
Anxious	Confused	Insightful	Mischievous
Deliberate[a]	Feminine	Masculine	
Faultfinding[a]	Outgoing[b]	Mild	
Handsome	Selfish	Opportunistic[a]	
Masculine	Sympathetic[b]	Original	
Opportunistic[a]	Unaffected[a]	Peculiar	
Self-denying[b]		Relaxed[b]	
Self-punishing		Resourceful[a]	
		Robust[a]	
		Sharp-witted[a]	
		Shrewd[a]	
		Silent	
		Steady[a]	
		Tough[a]	

[a]Behaviors judged to be instrumental.
[b]Behaviors judged to be expressive.

sidering "masculine," "feminine," and "effeminate")[2] showed them to be significantly different ($\chi^2 = 13.34$ for 3 df; $p < .01$).

One inferential limitation of a χ^2 statistical analysis such as that reported above is that finding male and female offspring who describe themselves as more similar to instrumental fathers are most distinct in their instrumental and expressive role behaviors could be the result of comparing extremely masculine males with females who are not particularly feminine. That is, the distinct instrumental-expressive patterns could be accounted for by extreme instrumentality in the males without assuming expressive qualities in the females. One additional set of comparisons would allow greater clarity here. The ACL indorsement patterns of girls identified with instrumental fathers could be compared with those obtained from girls identified with expressive mothers; boys identified with these two types of models could similarly be compared. The extent and quality of difference patterns which emerged would tell us something of the deviance of instrumental-father identified females from what is presumably the most expressive group of girls and the deviance of expressive-mother identified boys from their highly instrumental counterparts, males identified with instrumental fathers. These comparisons (Table 3) indicate that relatively few differences appear between the two female groups. Those differences which were found suggest that instrumental-father identified females do not assume blatant instrumental qualities relative to very expressive females but rather maintain an expressive orientation which lacks the passive character of extreme expressiveness. The male pattern indicates that more extensive

[2] The adjectives "masculine," "feminine," and "effeminate" were not rated because of their similarity in meaning to "instrumental" and "expressive."

TABLE 3   Behavior Differences between Instrumental-Father and Expressive-Mother Identified Males and Females

Males		Females	
Instrumental-Father Identified More: *	*Expressive-Mother Identified More:*	*Instrumental-Father Identified More:*	*Expressive-Mother Identified More:*
Adaptable	Appreciative	Self-confident	Considerate
Assertive	Cautious		Fearful
Capable	Conservative		Gentle
Confident	Dependent		Obliging
Dominant	Excitable		Silent
Egotistical	Meek		Submissive
Forceful	Peaceable		Trusting
Frank	Quiet		
Hard-headed	Shy		
Opinionated	Slipshod		
Outgoing	Timid		
Outspoken			
Self-confident			
Self-seeking			

*All adjectives on this table discriminated at the $p < 0.05$ level.

personality differences appear as a function of the attributes of the primary parent model than is the case for females. The differentiating behaviors suggest both the strong instrumental qualities of a masculine-father identification and the passive-dependent expressiveness of a feminine-mother identification. Summarily, this additional analysis suggests that the distinct instrumental-expressive behavior differences found when instrumental-father identified males and females were compared can be attributed to the presence of both instrumental qualities in the sons and expressive (but not passive) qualities in the daughter.

DISCUSSION

Males and females who are identified in a modeling (similarity) sense with instrumental fathers show the most extensive and appropriate sex-role differences in personality. Sex-role differences for males and females identified with expressive mothers are somewhat less extensive and appropriate, while male and female differences under the condition of identification with a sex-role reversed instrumental mother or expressive father were restricted and even less aprropriate to sex role. These empirical findings suggest that identification with (role-modeling after) the instrumental father is associated with enhanced masculinity in the son and femininity in the daughter, the same relationships predicted by Johnson (1963) from Parsons' reciprocal-role hypothesis.

Since the same sex-role outcomes are predictable from two apparently different hypotheses of sex-role "identification," one is led to wonder whether the differences are not semantic. The importance of reciprocal-role practice to the strengthening of sex-role behavior can be granted without abandoning modeling principles of identification-learning. Even though the expressive behaviors of the mother as a model may provide the initial opportunity and instigation for the girl to learn components of the expressive role, the amount of reinforced practice of these behaviors offered by the father or any other person should strengthen the expressive orientation of the girl. If the term "identification" were used to encompass any learning experience that contributed toward the sex-role adoption of the child, such sex-role practice would be legitimately included. However, to broaden the definition of identification to this extent would require inclusion of such divergent experiences as athletic activities and military service for males and dating behaviors and marriage for both sexes. It seems more useful to accept a more restricted conception of parental identification (i.e., as role-modeling behavior) but to consider it as but one contributor to the adult sex-role identity of the person.

It was noted earlier that fathers are presumed by Parsons to be more capable than are mothers of differentiating their sex role. That is, fathers are more capable of responding expressively than mothers are of acting instrumentally. It was also assumed that fathers systematically vary their sex role as they relate to male and female offspring. These suppositions bear considerable explanatory weight in interpreting the present results within the scope of a modeling theory, since the data suggest that employing the generally instrumental father as a model for identification mediates expressive behaviors in the daughter. Data collected from University of Iowa students for a previous study (Heilbrun, 1964) and some currently unpublished data obtained from males at the University of California allow some further light to be shed on these assumptions. Ratings of the degree of parental nurturance provided by instrumental and by expressive fathers were obtained

TABLE 4   Perceived Nurturance of Instrumental and Expressive Fathers

Sex of Child	Instrumental Fathers[a]			Expressive Fathers[b]			
	N	Mean Nurturance	SD	N	Mean Nurturance	SD	t
Male:							
Iowa	38	25.2	5.8	18	28.4	5.2	2.00*
California	46	25.1	6.5	18	28.4	6.7	1.79*
Female:							
Iowa	38	30.7	5.3	22	30.4	7.3	. . .

[a]Ratings on Parental Description Survey 6 or more.
[b]Rating on Parental Description Survey 5 or less.
*$p < .05$ (one-tailed test).

from college males and females, and those data (Table 4) corroborate the proposed tendency of fathers to relate in an equally expressive manner toward daughters whether the father was regarded as more expressive or more instrumental in his general sex-role orientation. Thus, an instrumental father as a model does seem to provide expressive qualities for the daughter to emulate. The relationship of fathers to sons, as rated by the sons in both samples, demonstrates the expected difference between instrumental and expressive fathers. Instrumental fathers are, as a group, significantly less nurturant than are expressive fathers.

Since the present study provided identification and sex-role learning results which were interpreted as consonant with a modeling theory, a final point of discussion is called for. How can the trend of parental identification research findings (see Johnson, 1963, pp. 324–331) be accounted for within a modeling framework? Specifically, the trend suggests that father-son identification relationships are clearly established, with stronger father identification being associated with better adjustment and more masculine sex-role behavior of the son. In contrast, the female results are almost without exception more equivocal than those for males (Sopchak, 1952; Helper, 1955; Johnson, 1955; Osgood, Suci, & Tannenbaum, 1957; Emmerich, 1959; Gray, 1959; Mussen & Distler, 1959), usually reported as "not significant but . . ."! Heilbrun has also reported a similar set of findings (1962); maladjusted males were significantly less identified with their fathers than were their adjusted counterparts, but two samples of maladjusted girls demonstrated less clear tendencies to be more identified with their mothers than did adjusted girls. The equivocal findings for females suggest that *additional* variables (perhaps of an interactive nature) must be considered before the relationships among the identification, sex-role, and adjustment variables for females will come into clearer focus. One such variable treated in the present study, but for some reason largely ignored in others, are individual differences in the sex-role behavior of the parents. Despite numerous investigations showing individual differences in sex-role adoption among children of the same biological sex, both fathers and mothers have usually been treated as homogeneous classes as far as their sex-role identity is concerned.

REFERENCES

Bandura, A., & Huston, A. C. Identification as a process of incidental learning. *Journal of Abnormal and Social Psychology*, 63, (1961), 311–318.

Emmerich, W. Parental identification in young children. *Genetic Psychology Monographs*, 60, (1959), 257–308.

Gough, H. G., & Heilbrun, A. B. *Joint manual for the Adjective Check List and the need scales for the ACL.* Palo Alto, Calif.: Consulting Psychologists Press, 1965.

Gray, S. W. Perceived similarity to parents and adjustment. *Child Development*, 30, (1959), 91–107.

Heilbrun, A. B. Parental identification and college adjustment. *Psychological Reports*, 10, (1962), 853–854.

Heilbrun, A. B. Parent model attributes, nurturant reinforcement, and consistency of behavior in adolescents. *Child Development*, 35, (1964), 151–167.

Heilbrun, A. B. The measurement of identification. *Child Development*, (1965).

Heilbrun, A. B. Perceived maternal attitudes, masculinity-femininity of the maternal model, and identification as related to incipient psychopathology in adolescent girls. *Journal of General Psychology*, in press.

Helper, M. M. Learning theory and the self-concept. *Journal of Abnormal and Social Psychology*, 51, (1955), 184–194.

Johnson, Miriam M. Instrumental and expressive components in the personalities of women. Unpublished doctoral dissertation, Radcliffe, 1955.

Johnson, M. M. Sex role learning in the nuclear family. *Child Development*, 34, (1963), 319–333.

Mussen, P., & Distler, L. Masculinity, identification, and father-son relationships. *Journal of Abnormal and Social Psychology*, 59, (1959), 350–356.

Osgood, C., Suci, G., & Tannenbaum, P. H. *The Measurement of meaning.* Urbana: University of Illinois Press, 1957.

Parsons, T. Social structure and the development of personality: Freud's contribution to the integration of psychology and sociology. *Psychiatry*, 21, (1958), 321–340.

Parsons, T., & Bales, R. F. *Family, socialization and interaction process.* Glencoe, Ill.: Free Press, 1955.

Sears, R. R., Maccoby, E. E., & Levin, H. *Patterns of child rearing.* New York: Row, Peterson, 1957.

Sopchak, A. L. Parental "identification" and "tendency toward disorders" as measured by the MMPI. *Journal of Abnormal and Social Psychology*, 47, (1952), 159–165.

5 | Socio-Sexual Development in a Suburban Community

CARLFRED B. BRODERICK

For many years the standard sequence of events leading up to full adult heterosexuality has been set forth as including the following: (1) a period of initial heterosexual orientation in which basic sex identification and social and emotional skills are established through experiences within the family; (2) a period of sexual latency and segregation during which sex itself and particularly the opposite sex are of little or no importance; and (3) the period of adolescence when sex and the opposite sex begin to assume a position of focal importance.

Recent studies by Lewis (1958, pp. 30–31), by Broderick and Fowler (1961) and by Kanous, Dougherty, and Cohn (1962), however, have indicated that children who are theoretically in the "latency" period (ages 9–12) may

This study was supported by a grant, MH-4974, from the National Institute of Mental Health and by the Pennsylvania State University. Acknowledgments are made to Stanley Fowler, Mary Harrison, Jay Richardson, and Robert Hobaugh for their extensive help in the design and execution of this study, and to Flora Ann Norris for her assistance in the preparation of this manuscript.

Reprinted from *The Journal of Sex Research*, 2, No. 1 (April, 1966), 1–24, by permission of The Society for the Scientific Study of Sex.

have substantial heterosexual involvements. Further exploration of this phenomenon has led me to the belief that current theories of socio-sexual
development do not sufficiently appreciate the essential continuity between
the preadolescent and adolescent stages of development. As this paper will
attempt to show, the heterosexual activities and attitudes typical of adolescents may also be well developed among younger children. The dramatic
physiological, psychological and social changes which have everywhere been
noted at puberty may be most accurately described as a simple quickening
of tempo in a process that has continuous roots back into early childhood.

The present paper, however, is based on the findings of a preliminary
cross-sectional study of children aged 10 to 17 in a suburban community in
Pennsylvania. Its primary purpose is to provide documentation for the general
point of view indicated above. A secondary purpose is to provide more adequate descriptive material on socio-sexual development in this type of
community than is presently available. Thirdly, it is hoped that this study
will produce hypotheses for a subsequent longitudinal study. Where relevant,
comparison will be made with the levels of heterosexual involvement found
in a middle class, white Georgia community previously studied (Broderick
and Fowler, 1961), and with data collected from Pennsylvania urban and
rural communities in another phase of the project. Comparisons will also be
made with the findings of other researchers.

The setting for the present report was an upper middle-class suburb
of a medium-sized city. Sixty per cent of the fathers' occupations were professional or managerial. About 30% of the mothers worked, largely at professional or clerical jobs. Eighty per cent of the graduates of the high school
went on to college. Only 7% of the parental marriages had been broken by
death, divorce, or desertion.

The data were collected by means of questionnaires administered to the
children by members of the research team. The study included virtually
every child present in the 7th through 12th grades. Data were also collected
from the 5th and 6th grades in three of the four elementary schools in the
district.

For the purposes of this paper the children were divided into sex and

TABLE 1 Total Number in Each Age-Sex Group

Age	Boys	Girls	Total
10-11	98	90	188
12-13	106	115	221
14-15	172	159	331
16-17	96	110	206
Total	472	474	946

age-categories. The distribution of subjects is presented in Table 1. Differences between the sexes or between ages were tested by chi square. The
.05 level of significance is used throughout.

For each age level three basic questions were asked: (1) What was the
level of social prejudice against the opposite sex? (2) What was the attitude
toward romantic (as contrasted to merely social) relationships with the

opposite sex in general? (3) What experience had there been with members of the opposite sex in a romantic context?

THE 10–11 YEAR OLDS

Social Prejudice

The work of Kanous et al. (1962), and also our own earlier findings in Georgia, had both indicated that the almost total social segregation of the sexes reported in earlier studies was beginning to break down. The fact is, however, that despite considerable romantic involvement which will be noted later, the level of cross-sex social interaction was not very high among these 10–11 year olds.

The basic social unit at this age was the reciprocal friendship pair or triangle, and almost without exception these units were monosexual in their composition. Interconnecting these basic units was a web of less intimate, nonreciprocal relationships. It was among the latter—on the fringe, so to speak—that the large majority of heterosexual friendships were found. Among the five friends that the questionnaire permitted subjects to list, 30% of the boys and 38% of the girls listed at least one member of the opposite sex (Item 1, Table 2). It was indicative of the peripheral nature of these relationships that despite this sizeable percentage of cross-sex choices only about 3% of the whole sample were involved in reciprocal cross-sex friendships. Girls are more likely at this age, as at all ages, to choose a boy among their friends than boys are to choose a girl.

As in the case of racial prejudice, prejudice against the opposite sex is exhibited in different degrees depending on the situation. In order to check this, the subjects were asked to rank the desirability of having a companion

TABLE 2 Heterosexual Attitudes and Activities of 10–11 Year-Olds

Item	Boy %	Girl %
1. Chooses one or more cross-sex friends	30	38
2. Prefers cross-sex companion when		
Eating in school cafeteria	8	17
Taking a walk	8	31*
Going to the movies	27	37
3. Approves love scene in movie	30	57*
4. Would like to get married someday	61	79*
5. Has played kissing games		
Ever	33	46
This year	15	23
6. Has kissed, when it meant "something special"	15	14
7. Has begun to date	28	28
8. Has a girlfriend (boyfriend)	58	78*
9. Has gone steady	20	20
Is now going steady	8*	2
10. Has been in love	49	50

*The difference between the sexes is significant beyond the .05 level using chi square with 1 degree of freedom.

of the opposite sex, a companion of the same sex or being alone in each of three different situations: eating in the school cafeteria, taking a walk, and going to the movies. Item 2, Table 2 shows the percentage of boys and of girls of this age who ranked as their first choice a companion of the opposite sex in each setting. Prejudice against the opposite sex was greatest in the cafeteria situation where only 8% of the boys and 17% of the girls preferred a cross-sex companion and least in the movie situation where 27% of the boys and 37% of the girls prefer to go with a member of the opposite sex.

It is probable that there are at least two features that discriminate these two settings. First, the level of visibility is different in the two cases. If there are negative sanctions against socializing with girls at this age, one could scarcely find a setting more sure to evoke them than the school cafeteria. Secondly, it seems likely that the sanctions themselves would be more permissive in the case of the movie because of the vastly different symbolism of the two acts.

Eating together has always been a symbol of fraternal acceptance and social solidarity, and therefore social prejudices of every variety are always most evident in this type of situation. In this case the in-group whose solidarity is at stake is the monosexual clique and it is not surprising that few children wanted to break ranks in order to sit next to a member of the out-group, whatever his personal attractiveness might be. Heterosexual pairing in private is much less of a threat to group solidarity than defection in the public lunch room. Moreover, in our culture going to the movies is very often associated with dating and with the romantic status that goes with it.

This also applies to some extent to taking a walk, which, at all other ages, evoked less prejudice than the cafeteria setting, but more than the movie setting. Among these 10–11 year-old boys walking with a girl was as firmly rejected as eating with one.

Girls were twice as ready as boys to cross the sex barrier in the school lunch room and four times as ready to walk with a boy as boys were to walk with a girl.

Attitudes Toward Romantic Heterosexual Relationships

The data reviewed this far clearly establish the existence of social prejudice against the opposite sex at ages 10–11, but they also suggest that these prejudices may exist side by side with some romantic interest. The latter point was emphasized by the responses to two further items on the questionnaire. The first item showed a picture of children watching a love scene in a movie. The subjects were asked how the children of their own sex felt about what they were seeing. Assuming that the subjects' own feelings correspond to those imputed to the children in the picture, this item provided some index of the attitudes which these 10–11 year-olds had toward adult romantic behavior. These data appear in Item 3, Table 2 and indicate that a majority of girls and nearly a third of the boys responded positively to a movie love scene even at this age.

A second item asked directly whether they would like to get married some day. In Item 4, Table 2 the percentage reporting *Yes* are shown. It is apparent that marriage was considered desirable by the large majority of 10–11 year-old children of both sexes, but especially by girls.

Romantic Experience

A wide range of items might be classified under the heading of romantic experience.

Kissing One of the things which became clear in the pretesting stage of this study was that there are two basically different social settings for kissing which have quite different meanings for children. Kissing in kissing games is essentially exploratory without interpersonal implications. For this reason our data were divided into information on kissing games and information on kissing when "it means something special." Forty-six per cent of the girls had at some time played kissing games, but only half that many had done so within the last year. It would seem that some of the boys involved in these games must have come from an older age group, since only one-third of the 10–11 year-old boys had ever played, and only 15% within the last year. This interpretation was supported by the figures for the 12–13 year-olds which showed an excess of boys who played kissing games during these years.

All of the kissing in the present sample was not done in games, however. Fifteen per cent of the boys and fourteen per cent of the girls report having "seriously kissed" a member of the opposite sex.

Dating A few years ago a discussion of dating at ages 10 and 11 would have seemed inappropriate. Previous studies which have included these ages at all have reported only about 5% of this age group as dating (Michigan Univ. Survey 1957, Smith 1952). However, the earlier Georgia study found that approximately 40% of this age group claimed to have had at least one date, which indicated the presence, in some communities at least, of new norms. The children in the present sample were not so precocious as this, but in answer to the question "have you ever had a date?", 28% of the boys and an equal proportion of girls did claim to have begun dating. This was a considerably larger percentage of 10–11 year-olds than in any of the other Pennsylvania communities we studied. These differences were consistent with Lowrie's 1961 finding that more dating occurs among children whose parents are middle and upper class than among children whose parents were in the blue-collar class.

In order to find out more about dating at each age, those who had begun to date were asked a series of probe questions: How old had they been on their first date? How often did they go out? How many different people had they actually dated? Did they prefer single-, or double-, or group-dating? What time did they think children their age should have to be in after a date? The answers to these questions begin to provide some idea of what dating at ages 10–11 is like.

As we might have guessed, dating was a recent development for nearly all of these children. In fact, only 15% of the daters (4% of the whole sample of 10–11 year olds) had dated before the age of 10. Most of them (about two-thirds) went out only occasionally, once a month or less often. A few, however, did claim fairly high frequencies. Two boys (2% of all 10–11 year-old boys and 8% of those who dated) claimed to go out at least once every week; and five girls (6% of all 10–11 year-old girls and 20% of those who dated) claimed a similar frequency.

Among those who had begun to date, most (about three-fourths) had had only one or two dating partners. With regard to type of date, most boys (60%) preferred the single-date over any other arrangement at this age, as at most subsequent ages. Next in preference was the double-date (28%) and finally the group-date (12%). Girls were much less certain than boys about single-dating although it received more votes than any other type (44%). They were more comfortable than boys with the group-date which was their second choice (36%). Only 20% preferred double-dating at this age, but at every subsequent age it was the first choice among girls.

Boys felt that they should be home after a date by 9:00 or 10:00, and girls thought 9:00 or 9:30 were the most appropriate times.

When non-daters were asked when they would like to begin dating, one-third of the boys and one-half of the girls wanted to begin within the next two years. The desire to begin dating at early ages was far more common in this school than in either the industrial or rural settings we studied.

Girlfriend-Boyfriend One of the surprising findings of the Georgia study was that 86% of the boys and 96% of the girls of this age claimed to have a girlfriend or boyfriend. The present data supported these earlier findings to the extent that a majority did report a "sweetheart," but the majority was much reduced from the level of the Georgia sample. Fifty-eight per cent of the boys and girls and 78% of the girls, reported having a sweetheart. The sex difference was statistically significant and was consistent with the higher level of girls' romantic interest reported in several parts of the study.

The questionnaire, furthermore, included several probes phrased here as they appeared on the boys' schedules: "Does she know you like her? Do your friends know how you feel about her? Do your parents know how you feel about her?" About 40% of these relationships appear to have been wholly secret in that not even the other party knew about it. Girls were more likely than boys to confide their feelings to friends and parents. Both boys and girls were more likely to confide in friends than in parents. Both tendencies were statistically significant.

About 40% of these children felt certain that the other person reciprocated their feelings. The majority were unsure. Actually, even the 40% were over-sanguine in many cases. Of those for whom actual reciprocation could be checked (namely, for those who chose sweethearts from within the sample) only about 21% had their choices reciprocated.

It has been noted earlier in this paper that some 10–11 year-old girls are interested in older boys. This is supported by our analysis of the ages of the chosen sweethearts. Of those 10–11 year olds who had sweethearts, only about 16% of either sex had sweethearts younger than themselves; but 25% of the boys and 42% of the girls claimed sweethearts older than themselves.

Going Steady   Going steady is an institution most typical among high school students, but it was imitated by some of the elementary school children in the 10–11 age bracket. Twenty per cent claimed to have gone steady, although several of these children had never had a date. Informal interviews indicated that going steady at these ages might involve the exchange of tokens (inexpensive rings and pins) and a sort of proprietory relationship which was acknowledged by the couple and their classmates. It might involve little or no contact outside of school. At the time of the study only 8% of the boys and 2% of the girls in this age group described their relationship to their sweetheart as "going steady." The discrepancy between 8% and 2% suggests some degree of nonconsensus between boys and girls as to whether or not a relationship could be called "going steady."

Love   As kissing games provide an emotionally safe training ground for developing competence, there seems to be a kind of practice emotion in the area of love—the "crush." Crushes on movie, TV, and recording "personalities" are surely the safest form of love. One can wish, yearn, dream, without the slightest risk of being rejected. Familiar adults such as school teachers or attractive married neighbors can also provide objects of affection almost as safe and somewhat more rewarding. Ages 10–11 seem to be the last ages that any great number of boys permit themselves the luxury of such emotions. At this age about one-fourth of the boys reported having had a crush on a famous person and an equal proportion, on a familiar adult. At subsequent ages, all but a few boys deny ever having had such a feeling. Girls, on the other hand, indulged in this romantic fantasy in larger numbers and for a longer period. At 10–11, 57% reported a crush on a famous personality and 33% on a familiar adult.

Children themselves made a distinction between these crushes and "love." As can be seen in Item 10, Table 2, approximately half of the 10–11 year-olds felt that they had been in love at least once. A comparison of these percentages with those reported at later ages (See Item 10 in Tables 3, 4, and 5) reveals a curious thing: unlike the behavioral measures in this study (such as kissing or dating), the cumulative number who had been in love did not increase systematically from age to age but fluctuated uncertainly. Moreover, if one checks the data (not included in these tables) on when the individual reported he was first in love, one discovers that at virtually every age the large majority had first found love within the last year. From these two facts one may deduce that at each age there was a redefinition of what love is. It seems that old loves were systematically explained away as something less than love and only the more recent attachments were admitted. How much of this process was due to the discovery at each age of new facets of relationships which made earlier attachments seem shallower, and how much was simple rationalization, cannot be determined. Whatever the explanation, there seemed to be at each age and for each sex a large and relatively stable proportion of young people who claimed to have fallen in love for the first time within the last year. This phenomenon was already apparent at ages 10 and 11.

Summary of 10–11 Year-Olds

In summary it can be said that the 10 and 11 year-old children in this community live in a world dominated by monosexual associations, but already leavened with heterosexual interest and activity. The foundations of future social and romantic relationships have already been laid in the general appreciation of adult romance, in the acceptance of marriage as a desirable eventuality, in the prevalence of special attachment to a member of the opposite sex, and in the crushes on relatively safe adults. At these ages kissing games become a fairly common pastime at parties. Over one quarter of these boys and girls have had their first date, and more wish they had.

Now let us see what changes occur in the next two years, which include the onset of puberty for most of the girls and for many of the boys.

THE 12–13 YEAR-OLDS

Social Prejudice

In our discussion of the 10–11 year-olds we noted that the social separation of the sexes was substantial but that elements of budding romantic interest and involvement were also evident. Paradoxically, both the social segregation and the romantic interest increased in the 12–13 year-old group. Twelve years of age has traditionally been held as the age of greatest sociometric cleavage between the sexes, and this was fully substantiated by our data. If each age is examined separately, age 12 was characterized by the fewest cross-sex friendship choices among both boys and girls. It is true that comparisons with similar data from earlier generations show that the degree of sexual segregation is not as great as formerly—at least in this type of community—but there can be no doubt about the continuance of the traditional withdrawal pattern.

The paradoxical entrenchment of social segregation at the same time that romantic heterosexual contacts were increasing is well illustrated by the items showing the frequency of preference for a cross-sex companion in three different situations (Item 2, Table 3). The data showed that in the essentially fraternal act of eating together, mixed company was still very unpopular, while in the potentially more romantic situations of taking a walk and going to the movies, the preference for cross-sex companions was well up from the 10–11 year-old level. In fact, preferences for a cross-sex companion in these activities were expressed by over 40% of the children in each case. With one exception (girls in the movie situation), these levels were significantly different from 10–11 levels and also they were significantly different in each case from the eating situation.

There were no significant differences between boys and girls in their response to these items at this age.

Attitudes Toward Romantic Heterosexual Relationships

A further reinforcement of our observation that romantic interest increases at this age despite the sociometric withdrawal, came from the data

TABLE 3 Heterosexual Attitudes and Activities of 12–13 Year-Olds

Item	Boy %	Girl %
1. Chooses one or more cross-sex friends	25	24†
2. Prefers cross-sex companion when		
Eating in school cafeteria	13	10
Taking a walk	41†	45
Going to the movies	50†	47
3. Approves love scene in movie	44†	63*
4. Would like to get married someday	66	94*
5. Has played kissing games		
Ever	58	54
This year	33†	20
6. Has kissed, when it meant "something special"	23	29†
7. Has begun to date	60	64†
8. Has a girlfriend (boyfriend)	55	79*
9. Has gone steady	24	19
Is now going steady	7	5
10. Has been in love	53	45

*The difference between the sexes is significant beyond the .05 level using chi square with 1 degree of freedom.

†The difference from the previous age is significant beyond the .05 level using chi square with 1 degree of freedom.

on attitude toward the romantic scene in the movie. Comparison with the same Item in Table 2 shows a dramatic shift in the attitudes of boys. At 10–11, only 30% enjoyed the scene. At 12–13 the percentage who enjoyed it was up to 44%. The girls, a majority of whom had approved and enjoyed the scene at 10–11, shifted even further in the direction of approval. The difference between boys and girls remained substantial and was statistically significant.

Attitudes toward marriage provide one more evidence of a shift toward a more positive view of the opposite sex in the romantic context. An examination of Item 4 in Table 2 and in Table 3 permits a comparison between this age and the previous one. There has been a slight increase in the proportion of boys who wanted to get married (from 61% to 66%). For girls, however, the shift was dramatic. At 12–13 girls jumped from the 79% of the 10–11 to 94%—a level similar to that of girls at each subsequent age. This corresponds exactly with the findings of a national study of young girls, which also found that 94% of the girls in this age group wanted unreservedly to get married someday (Michigan Univ. Surv. 1957).

Romantic Experience

Kissing Kissing games rose to new heights of popularity at 12–13. One out of three boys and one out of five girls had played kissing games during the year. This was the peak year for this activity for boys, just as 10–11 was for girls. A gradually decreasing number of children played kissing games at each subsequent age. By the end of the 12–13 period over half of the children had been involved in this activity at some time in their lives.

In answer to the question "Have you ever seriously kissed a girl (boy)?" 23% of the boys and 29% of the girls answered "Yes," a considerable increase over the 15% and 14% levels of the previous period.

Dating At twelve 48% of the boys and 57% of the girls were dating. At thirteen the figures were 69% for both. These levels were almost twice as high as those found in the rural and urban districts of Pennsylvania which we sampled. They were two or three times higher than the levels reported by Smith (1952) and in the Girl Scout study.

Typically boys and girls dated only a few times a year. Sixty per cent of the daters (about one-third of the entire age group) went out once per month or less. Only 15% of the dating boys and 10% of the girls went out as often as once per week. Thus it can be seen that although the percentage of children who dated was much higher at this age than at 10–11, the frequency of activity for children who dated had scarcely changed at all.

In the typical case a child in the dating column had been out with only 2 or 3 different persons in his whole dating career, but this was up from the previous period.

Preference for single-dating reached its low point at this age. Boys retreated from the strong preference for the single-date which they showed at other ages to the extent that only 44% preferred it at 12–13. Among girls this age only 24% prefer this more adventurous dating pattern. As interest in single-dating waned, interest in double-dating rose to its highest point (45% of the boys and 57% of the girls). The even greater safety of group-dating was preferred by 11% of the boys and 19% of the girls, but for the boys at least, this was the last age at which this alternative appealed to any appreciable number.

The majority of both sexes felt that a reasonable hour to return home from a date was 10 P.M. or possibly 11:00. Boys were more inclined toward the later hour.

As at the earlier age, those who did not date hoped to begin within the next year or two.

Girlfriend-Boyfriend One of the interesting features about girlfriend and boyfriend choices is that the percentage making these choices remained relatively constant at each age. But if the proportion of sweethearts chosen did not change, there was some evidence that the nature of the relationship did. Expected reciprocation had moved up to 48% and the actual reciprocation to 35%. It would seem that this reflects an important step toward real romantic relationships with the opposite sex and away from the largely imaginary character of earlier relationships.

Children of this age were somewhat more willing to reveal their romantic attachments than at earlier ages. The biggest increase was in the girls' communication with their friends. At this age and at subsequent ages girls were more likely to let their friends know how they felt (71%) than they were to let the boyfriend himself know (66%). Girls seemed to have acquired more confidence in their parents also, since the percentage who knew about their daughter's boyfriend jumped from 46% to 64%. Despite this increase, parents still trailed friends considerably.

Boys increased their confidences to friends and parents too, but not so dramatically as girls. For 62% of the boys their sweetheart knew, for 53% their friends knew, and for 40% their parents knew. It is clear that for boys particularly, a great deal of secretiveness was still a part of the sweetheart picture.

The tendency for girls to choose boyfriends older than themselves and for boys to choose girlfriends younger than themselves was accentuated at this age. Forty-seven per cent of the girls as compared to only 17% of the boys reported sweethearts one of more years older than themselves while 23% of the boys and only 14% of the girls reported sweethearts younger than themselves.

Going Steady   There was no important increase in the percentage of children who claimed they had ever gone steady. Nineteen per cent of the girls and 24% of the boys reported having gone steady at least once. Approximately 5% of both sexes were currently going steady at the time of the survey. It appears that steady-dating at this age remained something of an anomaly. While with respect to early casual-dating this suburban community was far in advance of the rural and urban communities sampled, early steady-dating was far more popular in the urban than suburban setting. Even the generally more conservative rural groups were not much behind the suburban sample where going steady was concerned.

Love   The age of crushes on teachers and other familiar adults and also on famous entertainers had passed for boys by 12–13. From this age and onward we found that fewer than 15% of the boys admitted ever having had such feelings. This probably does not mean that these boys had fewer crushes than the 10–11 year-olds in our sample, but that having had crushes was seen as being a little ridiculous and juvenile and was therefore denied by older boys.

Unlike the boys, a large proportion of girls (about half) continued to report having had such crushes. Unfortunately our data did not permit us to be certain that these crushes were current, but our own feeling is that denial of this activity is probably a fairly reliable indication of the social stigma surrounding it for any age group. That this denial did not occur among 12–13 year-old girls, seems to indicate the acceptability in this group of crushes on adults.

As for "love" itself, as has been noted the pattern did not vary much from age to age. At 12–13 most of the loves which were claimed by 10–11 year-olds had been repudiated as something less than love. Approximately half reported having been in love at sometime, but in most cases it was within the last two years. Typically, students reported having had only one, or at most two, such loves in their whole experience.

Summary of 12–13 Year-Olds

This age group continues to show little inclination to form close social attachments to members of the opposite sex whether it be on a friendship or on a steady-dating basis. In contrast to this social rejection, interest in the opposite sex as an object of romantic attraction increases significantly.

The stage is set for the major shift toward heterosexual social involvement which comes with fully established adolescence.

THE 14–15 YEAR-OLDS

Social Prejudice

The withdrawal of the two sexes into separate groups which was such a notable part of the social world of 12–13 year-olds was beginning to diminish at 14–15. The percentage of boys who chose at least one girl among their

TABLE 4   Heterosexual Attitudes and Activities of 14–15 Year-Olds

Item	Boy %	Girl %
1. Chooses one or more cross-sex friends	39†	50†
2. Prefers cross-sex companion when		
Eating in school cafeteria	21	22†
Taking a walk	41	75*†
Going to the movies	65†	74†
3. Enjoys love scene in movie	72†	77†
4. Like to get married someday	73	91*
5. Has played kissing games		
Ever	70	78†
This year	21†	18†
6. Kissed, when it meant "something special"	49†	54†
7. Has begun to date	84†	84†
8. Has a girlfriend (boyfriend)	45	68*†
9. Has gone steady	41†	45†
Is now going steady	9	16†
10. Has been in love	64*	42

*The difference between the sexes is significant beyond the .05 level using chi square with 1 degree of freedom.
†The difference from the previous age is significant beyond the .05 level using chi square with 1 degree of freedom.

friends rose from 25% to 39% (Item 1, Table 4). For girls, who are usually the more precocious in such matters, the percentage rose from 24% to 50%. An increasing proportion of girls reported not one, but two, members of the opposite sex among their friends, thus foreshadowing a basic change in the nature of the sociometric network at the next age. All of these data on cross-sex friendship contrasted with the findings of Gordon (1957) that in his entire tenth-grade sample not one person made a cross-sex friendship choice.

Preference for a companion of the opposite sex in various situations also increased. Both boys and girls continued to be rather conservative when choosing a companion in the school cafeteria situation. Out of every five boys and girls only one felt that he would actually prefer a member of the opposite sex.

For girls this age marked a big increase in their preference for a male companion in walking and movie situations. The percentage preferring boys was up from about 45% at 12–13 to a solid 75% at 14–15. For boys the level of cross-sex preference in the walking situation remained at 41%. In the movie situation the percentage preferring girls was up from 50 to 65.

Attitude Toward Romantic Heterosexual Relationships

The impression that attitudes toward romance had taken a decisive up-turn was reinforced by the responses of these young people to the romantic movie scene. Three out of four 14–15 year-old boys and girls enjoyed and approved such scenes.

Boys' attitude toward marriage improved still further at this age. Seventy-three per cent were sure they wanted to marry. The comparable figure for the girls was 91%.

Romantic Experience

Kissing   An analysis of Item 5 in Tables 2, 3, 4, and 5 indicates that at each age from 10 through 15 a new wave of young people discovered kissing games, played them at their parties off and on for a year or two, and then passed on to other activities. It appears also that the 14–15 group was the last among whom kissing games had a place for any significant number. Even at this age, although the large majority had at some time played kissing games, most of them had not participated within the last year. But if most 14–15 year-olds had passed on from kissing games to other pursuits, it is clear from Item 6 in Table 4 that one of these pursuits was kissing on a private enterprise basis. Actually in this instance the grouping of 14 and 15 year-olds together obscures an important development. At age fourteen 36% of the boys and girls had "seriously" kissed someone outside of kissing games. By 15 the percentages were 60 for boys and 69 for girls. If 12–13 was the big age for kissing games, it is clear that 15 was the age at which private kissing became a major phenomenon in this suburban community.

Consistent with this big increase in "serious" kissing we found an increase in the total number of kissing partners reported. Thus the majority of 14 year-olds who had kissed any one at all had only kissed one to three persons, but for 15 year-olds two to six partners was a more typical range.

Dating   As previously stated, most children in this community had begun to date by the age of 13; however, an additional 15% joined the ranks of daters in the present age-period to bring the totals to 84% for both boys and girls.

Among those who dated there was some increase in frequency. For boys the per cent who claimed they went out at least once per week increased from 15% at ages 12–13 to 24% at 14–15. For girls the increase was from 10% to 34%. It remained true, however, that the majority of boys (53%) and a substantial number of girls (42%) who had begun to date went out only once per month or less.

The typical dater had been out with four or more different persons.

Girls were more likely than boys to have dated this broadly. (Seventy per cent of the girls versus 56% of the boys.) The difference was statistically significant.

Double-dating remained the most popular type of date for girls; 51% preferred it to 39% who preferred single-dating. Boys swung back to a preference for the single-date with 52% preferring this arrangement against 42% for the double-date. Group-dating retained very few advocates at this age: only 7% of the boys and 10% of the girls.

In the opinion of these young people 11:00 or 12:00 was the appropriate hour to come home after a date. Girls favored the earlier hours, and boys were about evenly divided.

Girlfriend-Boyfriend At 14–15 the definition of a "girlfriend" is sharply revised. At 14–15, only 45% did. At earlier ages 78% to 79% of the girls claimed to have a boyfriend. At 14–15, only 68% did. Some insight can be gained into the meaning of this downward turn in the extension of sweetheart choices by noting that at this age two out of three children expected reciprocation (compared to about half at 12–13). Actual reciprocation also rose sharply from the 35% levels of the previous age to about 55%. It appears that girlfriend-boyfriend relationships were becoming far more real.

This impression is reinforced by an examination of the relationship between friendship choices and sweetheart choices. Near the beginning of the questionnaire, before the cross-sex focus of the study was apparent, each subject was asked to list his best friend and then four other persons he liked almost as well. Near the end of the questionnaire he was asked the name of his special girlfriend if he had one. By comparing names it was possible to determine whether a boy's girlfriend was listed also as his best friend or, failing that, as one of his other four close friends. This comparison showed that the 14–15 year-old boy was significantly more likely than younger boys to list his sweetheart as a friend. Girls showed a similar pattern but the difference between this age and earlier ones was not statistically significant. For both, the big amalgamation of sweetheart and friend came at 16–17, but the movement in this direction at 14–15 was a further indication of the increasing social reality of the sweetheart relationship.

This point was further documented by the increased openness in communication about the relationship. At this age 85% of the boys and 74% of the girls were sure that the other person knew how they felt. Eighty-one per cent of the boys' friends and 77% of the girls' friends knew about it, and 67% of the boys' parents compared to 61% of the girls' parents. Parents lagged about 15 percentage points behind friends as confidantes.

The spread between the ages of sweethearts continued to increase at this age as more boys chose younger girls and more girls chose older boys. Fourteen to 15 year-old girls were more likely to choose up the age scale than their masculine contemporaries were to choose downward. For the first time a clear majority of girls (63%) reported boyfriends one or more years older than themselves.

Going Steady Young people of 14 and 15, particularly the girls, began to show some indications of a greater interest in this social arrangement.

At the time of the study 9% of the boys and 16% of the girls were currently going steady. The proportion who claimed that they had at some time gone steady at least once was about double the proportion reported at the earlier age, with 41% of the boys and 45% of the girls putting themselves in the experienced column. The big boom in steady dating lay ahead in the 16–17 age group, but the beginnings of this movement were already apparent About one in ten of the total sample of 14–15 year-old boys and a similar percentage of the girls claimed to have gone steady three or more times.

Love   This age period was distinguished by having the largest percentage of boys who felt that they had ever been in love (64%) and the smallest percentage of girls (42%). The sex difference was statistically significant. Some further light is cast on this difference by noting a related difference between the sexes at this age. As at all ages, the majority of subjects reported that they first experienced love within the last year. However, the percentage for boys was only 56% compared to 71% for the girls. Although not significant, this difference probably helped to account for the higher percentage of boys who reported ever being in love. It seems that these girls were more systematic than the boys in their repudiation of past loves and thus fewer appeared to have ever been in love. Boys, by contrast, were more prone to accept earlier attachments as being love and thus reported more loves. This interpretation is supported further by the fact that many more boys than girls claimed to have been in love two or more times.

Summary of the 14–15 Year-Olds

This is indeed an age of transition. The monosexual cliques of earlier ages have begun to open up to the opposite sex. In some situations, such as taking a walk and especially going to the movies, the preference for an opposite sex companion is general. Girls seem to be more advanced than boys of their own age, and the majority of them seek older boys as boyfriends while the boys are left to seek younger girls. The "secret love" is largely replaced by the publicly acknowledged girlfriend, and steady-dating begins to be more popular—especially among girls. Social interaction with the opposite sex has pushed forward on every front. Yet, as the next section shows, all of this is but prologue to the thoroughgoing heterosexuality of the social world of the 16–17 year-olds.

THE 16–17 YEAR-OLDS

Social Prejudice

In this community, 16–17 marks the passing of any substantial social sex prejudice. In fact the data suggests a basic restructuring of clique composition. Of those who chose five friends, 54% of the boys and 76% of the girls chose one or more members of the opposite sex among them (Item 1, Table 5). Among the girls, more chose two than chose only one cross-sex friend. This second cross-sex friend tended to be a close friend's sweetheart.

TABLE 5 Heterosexual Attitudes and Activities of 16–17 Year-Olds

Item	Boy %	Girl %
1. Chooses one or more cross-sex friends	54†	76*†
2. Prefers cross-sex companion when		
Eating in school cafeteria	34†	27
Taking a walk	55†	74*
Going to the movies	79†	93*†
3. Enjoys love scene in movie	69	79
4. Like to get married someday	75	94*
5. Played kissing games		
Ever	69	81*
This year	13*	5†
6. Kissed, when it meant "something special"	73†	82†
7. Has begun to date	96†	97†
8. Has a girlfriend (boyfriend)	59†	72*
9. Has gone steady	65†	73†
Is now going steady	29†	35†
10. Has been in love	59	60†

*Sex difference significant beyond the .05 level using chi square with 1 degree of freedom.
†The difference from the previous age is significant beyond the .05 level using chi square with 1 degree of freedom.

It is our impression that among an important segment of the 16–17 year-olds in this community, the basic unit of the clique had become not the individual but the boy-girl pair.

By this age there was a great degree of consensus about the desirability of a cross-sex companion when going to the movies, with 79% of the boys and 93% of the girls favoring this arrangement. As at other ages, walking was the situation in which a cross-sex companion was next most desirable. These young people were still quite conservative in their choice of table mates. It appears that even at this age cafeteria social life involved segregation by sexes although there was some relaxing of this principle as compared with earlier ages. The differences between movies and walking and between walking and eating were significant for both boys and girls.

Attitudes Toward Romantic Heterosexual Relationships

The high level of appreciation for romantic movies continued virtually unchanged into the present period. Attitudes toward marriage also continued unchanged from the previous age.

Romantic Experience

Kissing For the 16–17 year-olds kissing games were outmoded. As Item 5, Table 5 shows, only 13% of the boys and 5% of the girls played kissing games within the last year. Serious kissing, on the other hand, rose to new heights. At 16, 60% of the boys had kissed and at 17 it had jumped to 87%. Thus by 17 the boys had caught up with the girls, 82% of whom had kissed at 16 and 83% at 17. Most of these had kissed between four and ten different persons.

Dating   By this age nearly everyone had begun to date. Only 4% of the boys and 3% of the girls had never dated. This unanimity was not observed in other communities. In the rural schools, for example, about 25% of the boys and about 15% of the girls were still not dating at this age.

Four out of five of the daters had gone out with at least four different persons. The frequency of dating was also up. Fifty-eight per cent of the girls now went out regularly, at least once per week, compared to only 34% at 14–15. The boys were only a little behind, with 44% dating weekly.

Single-dating increased in popularity with both boys (62%) and girls (44%), but more girls (49%) still preferred double-dating. Only 5% of the boys and 6% of the girls preferred group-dating at this age. Both boys and girls believed that midnight was the most reasonable hour for returning home after a date, with some boys pushing for 1 A.M.

Despite all of this increase, dating was reserved for weekends.

Girlfriend-Boyfriend   The tendency toward a more open and consequential sweetheart choice developed much more fully at this age. About the same proportion of children made sweetheart choices as at 10–11 or 12–13; namely, 59% for boys and 72% for girls. Only one in ten had any doubts about recip- rocation, which is a big change from the one in three who were unsure at 14–15. Moreover, the actual reciprocation rate calculated for sweethearts who were in the sample rose to about 85%. In other words, the gap between expected and received reciprocation nearly disappeared at this age. Girls were more communicative about their boyfriends than previously. There re- mained, it is true, a small handful who were uncertain of the boy's feelings, uncertain as to whether he knew of their interest, and uncommunicative about their own feelings, but the very large majority were involved in an open, reciprocal relationship. It was known to their friends and parents and, we might add, approved of by their parents in most (92%) of the cases.

The boys differed from the girls only in that they were a good deal less communicative about the relationship to friends and to parents.

Increasingly boys and girls of this age listed their sweethearts among their close friends. Nearly one-third of the boys named their sweetheart as their best friend compared to 8% at 14–15. When those who listed the sweetheart among their "other" friends were added to these, the total overlap between sweetheart and friend was about 50%. Only 21% of the girls listed their sweethearts as their best friend, but so many listed him among their "other" friends that sweetheart and friend overlapped in about two-thirds of the cases. This observation adds materially to the impression that by 16–17 the once secretive sweetheart choice had become a social relationship of some substance.

Among girls the preference for older boyfriends leveled off somewhat, however, the majority of girls continued to date older boys. Since these girls were juniors and seniors, many of them found their boyfriends outside the high school (56%).

Steady Dating This was the first age at which the majority of young people reported having gone steady at some time, with 65% of the boys and 73% of the girls reporting this activity. This age also showed by far the highest rate of current steady-dating. Twenty-nine per cent of the boys and 35% of the girls reported going steady at the time of the study. These levels were two or three times as high as among 14–15 year-olds.

In connection with our observations of the newly developing pattern of mixed cliques, it seems likely that steady pairs formed the nuclei of these social groupings. A further evidence of the social meaning of going steady at this age is revealed by the answers of each age group to the question "Do you have to be in love to go steady?" Whereas at earlier ages the idea of romantic love as a prerequisite to going steady was held by 40% to 50% of the subjects, at 16–17 only 20% subscribed to this view. The other 80% apparently held that going steady was a desirable social arrangement that need not involve any deep emotional attachment. Certainly this view is consistent with the social realities of the world of 16–17 year-olds. By 17 years of age 36% of the boys and 40% of the girls had gone steady at least twice. These figures included about one in ten who had gone steady four or more different times.

Love It has been seen that love was not generally held to be a prerequisite for going steady. Nevertheless about 60% of the subjects reported having been in love. As at every other age most of these had experienced love for the "first time" within the last year.

Summary of 16–17 Year-Olds

In many ways the growing tendency toward heterosexual interaction which we have noted at earlier ages comes to fruition at 16–17. The data suggests a social network in which mixed pairs play a key role. Young people increasingly go steady for pragmatic social reasons.

The processes of socio-sexual development in this community seem to be functioning smoothly, leading on toward the future stages of courtship, marriage and parenthood.

CONCLUSIONS

Although the longitudinal data necessary for a definitive test are not yet available, these cross-sectional data suggest a real continuity between pre-pubertal attitudes and experience and those of adolescence. For an important segment of the population studied, the years from 10 through 13 represented a period of preparation for later heterosexual involvement. It was a period marked by relative social isolation from the opposite sex but with all kinds of mechanisms for rehearsing the skills and feelings appropriate to the later relationships. Gradually, in a process of continual redefinition which appears to extend throughout the period of adolescence, these relationships became progressively more real, more open, more reciprocal, more consequential. Inevitably they also became less idealized and more practical.

Much work remains to be done in tracing the patterns of socio-sexual development in our culture, but even these preliminary findings suggest that we may need to modify our traditional points of view.

REFERENCES

Broderick, C. B., and Fowler, S. E., New patterns of relationships between the sexes among preadolescents. *Marriage and Family Living*, 23, (1961), 27–30.

Cameron, W. J., and Kenkel, W. F., High school dating: a study in variation. *Marriage and Family Living*, 22, (1960), 74–6.

Gordon, W. C., *The social system of the high school*. New York: Free Press of Glencoe, 1957.

Heiss, J. S., Variations in courtship progress among high school students. *Marriage and Family Living*, 22, (1960), 165–70.

Kanous, L. E., Dougherty, R. A., and Cohn, T. S., Relation between heterosexual friendship choices and socio-economic level. *Child Development*, 33, (1962), 251–5.

Landis, P. H., Research on teen-age dating. *Marriage and Family Living*, 22, (1960), 266–7.

Lewis, G. M., *Educating children in grades four, five, and six*. Washington, D. C., U. S. Office of Education, 1958.

Lowrie, S. H., Factors involved in the frequency of dating. *Marriage and Family Living*, 18, (1956), 46–51.

Lowrie, S. H., Early and late dating: some conditions associated with them. *Marriage and Family Living*, 23, (1961), 284–91.

Michigan Univ. Surv. Res. Center, *Adolescent girls*. Ann Arbor: Author, 1957.

Schnepp, G. P., Survey of going steady and other dating practices. *American Catholic Sociological Revue*, 20, (1960), 238–50.

Smith, W. A., Rating and dating: a restudy. *Marriage and Family Living*, 14, (1952), 312–17.

Sutton-Smith, B., Rosenberg, B. G., and Morgan, F. F., Jr., Development of sex differences as in play choices during preadolescence. *Child Development*, 34, (1963), 119–26.

III Love and Mate Selection

Introduction to Section III

Not long ago it was thought sophisticated to comment that outside of the Western world, premarital, heterosexual love relationships were unknown. The sociological study of love before marriage has given us new understanding and we now believe that love is a psychological potential that members of all human societies possess and are aware of. The variations seem to be, as Goode points out (10), in the way in which societies control such premarital love relationships. Even in a society like ours, love relationships are controlled by "outsiders" such as parents. This point was elaborated upon in my prologue.

My own contribution to this section of the book (6) points out that love is fundamentally one type of primary relationship and it is as likely to occur, therefore, as are friendship relationships. I elaborate the general processes by means of which love develops. The controversy that Winch and others involve themselves with concerns more specific details of this process of falling in love. My general description of that process fits with Winch and also with his critics' views, for I do not spell out whether opposite needs or similar needs are the key to falling in love. The article by Winch (7) reflects his more recent conception of this controversy over needs.

Another important research into how people select their marital mates was done by Kerckhoff and Davis (8). They formulate an explanation of their findings that accepts Winch's complementary-needs notion as the final "filter" in the mate-selection process but they present two other "filters" that they believe operate earlier in the process. These two filters refer to common social background and consensus on values. The Kerckhoff and Davis study utilizes a longitudinal design by tracing progress to marriage over a six-month period. They used a sample of students at Duke University. However, more recent studies by men such as George Levinger show that many questions are still unanswered.[1]

Precise measures of the degree of love are hard to find. In addition, measures of degree of "liking" that are distinguishable from those of degree of love are indeed rare. Zick Rubin's selection (9) provides the reader with his recently developed measures of love and liking. This research was carried out as part of his doctoral requirements and is a valuable addition to the scientific understanding of love. Rubin's findings indicate only a weak relationship between loving someone and liking them. The article provides the reader with a simple scale one can use to analyze one's own dating relationship.

The serious student can indeed have a most stimulating time trying to integrate the various notions of mate selection, and the readings in this section should help in our thinking. For example, Talmon (11) presents data from three Israeli Kibbutzim that show how institutional arrangements, such as the location of high schools and the requirement of military service, are key factors in determining who marries whom. Such institutional arrangements increase the chances of meeting certain types of people and thus unintentionally affect mate choice. On the motivational level, the desire for individuality in a collective Kibbutz setting may encourage marrying outside of one's own Kibbutz. In these and other illustrations Talmon does a brilliant job of outlining the basic elements of mate selection. Her approach shows the importance of understanding the broad social system in order to grasp the private, personal process of mate selection. For additional cross-cultural perspectives on love, the study done by Theodorson[2] should prove instructive as well as the work by Goode (10).

The area of mate selection has long been involved with questions of "posing" or "faking." Do girls pretend that they are submissive in order to attract men? The work of sociologists such as Mirra Komarovsky and Jerold Heiss would support a positive answer to this question.[3] Although we have no readings that deal directly with this question, I would like to pose it for the reader's consideration. Many sociologists have suggested that behavior is a better index of social reality than attitudes. Yet although girls behave submissively, their equalitarian attitudes can lead them to change such behavior once they become more committed to marriage and are more intimate with their boyfriends. Once again one sees that social forms such as serious vs. casual dating can be predictive of some very private behavior such as the degree of "posing." Is this situation changing today? Is there more or less posing among young people today than a decade or two ago? Does such posing actually help the relationship lead to marriage or is it unnecessary?

[1] Levinger, G. et al., "Progress Toward Permanence in Courtship: A Test of the Kerckhoff-Davis Hypothesis." *Sociometry* 33 (December, 1970), 427–433.

[2] Theodorson, G. A., "Romanticism and the Motivation to Marry in U.S., Singapore, Burma, and India." *Social Forces* 44 (September, 1965), 17–27.

[3] Heiss, J. S., "Degree of Intimacy and Male-Female Interaction," *Sociometry* 25 (June, 1962), 197–208; Komarovsky, M., "Cultural Contradictions and Sex Roles," *The American Journal of Sociology* 52 (September, 1946), 184–189.

6 | Toward a Sociology of the Heterosexual Love Relationship

IRA L. REISS

The heterosexual love relationship is one of the most vital and one of the most neglected aspects of courtship behavior. Recently the author examined the sociological literature, in particular the marriage and family textbooks, to discern the type of analysis present. In addition preliminary research was conducted on a new approach toward analyzing the love relationship. The purpose of this article is to put forth the basic findings of the above studies and, thereby, to propose a new direction for the sociological study of the heterosexual love relationship.

TEXTBOOK TREATMENT OF THE LOVE RELATIONSHIP

An examination of twenty-six textbooks in marriage and the family revealed that twenty of these books took a rather limited or restricted approach to the heterosexual love relationship—that is, they most often focused on one type of love, which was usually described as the "best," "real," or "true" type.[1] Other types, besides the preferred type, would commonly be viewed as

[1] The 26 books examined represent the author's total collection over the years from teaching in this field. They comprise almost all of the widely used books in this area. The following 20 books of the 26 examined were found to have a "restricted" approach. Specific page numbers indicate the most relevant portions. Ray B. Baber, *Marriage and the Family*, New York: McGraw-Hill, 1953, p. 137; Howard Becker and Reuben Hill, eds. *Family Marriage and Parenthood*, selection by J. K. Folsom, Boston: D. C. Heath, 1955, pp. 212, 221; Henry A. Bowman, *Marriage For Moderns*, New York: Crowell, 1953, p. 403; Ruth S. Cavan, *The American Family*, New York: Crowell, 1953, p. 403; Evelyn M. Duvall, *Family Development*, New York: Lippincott, 1957, p. 355; Evelyn M. Duvall and Reuben Hill, *When You Marry*, New York: D. C. Heath, 1953, p. 32; Morris Fishbein, M.D., and Ruby Jo Reeves Kennedy, eds. *Modern Marriage and Family Living*, selection by H. Bowman, New York: Oxford, 1957, pp. 135, 139; Norman E. Himes and Donald L. Taylor, *Your Marriage*, New York: Rinehart, 1955, pp. 22–23; J. L. Hirning and Alma L. Hirning, *Marriage Adjustment*, New York: American, 1956, pp. 122, 123, 125; John J. Kane, *Marriage and the Family*, New York: Dryden, 1954, pp. 79–81; Earl Lomon Koos, *Marriage*, New York: Holt, 1957, pp. 106, 109, 110; Judson T. Landis and Mary G. Landis, *Building a Successful Marriage*, Englewood Cliffs, New Jersey: Prentice-Hall, 1958, pp. 166–169; Paul H. Landis, *Making the Most of Marriage*, New York: Appleton-Century-Crofts, 1955, p. 105; E. E. LeMasters,

For a full development of this area, see the author's book, *Premarital Sexual Standards in America*, New York: The Free Press, Macmillan, 1960.
Reprinted from the *Journal of Marriage and Family Living*, 22, No. 2 (May, 1960), 139–155, by permission of the National Council on Family Relations.

not real forms of love or as inferior in quality to the true type of love. The following are several quotations from these marriage and the family textbooks which illustrate this restricted approach:

Although one may fall precipitously into a condition of violent infatuation, it takes time for real love to develop. . . . Genuine love is centered on one person only.[2]

Love at first sight is actually impossible, because love between two individuals is always a product of intimate and complex interaction, which depends upon varied types of experiences.[3]

. . . love never makes the individual less effective, less fully functioning; rather it promotes growth and increases awareness of meanings, needs and opportunities in the world about one.[4]

We can admit that young couples may be, and usually are, "terribly infatuated" or "awfully thrilled" with each other, but we hesitate to apply the word "love" to such untested relationships. [untested by many years of marriage][5]

Genuine love is possible only when couples know each other well. . . . Is it actually possible to "fall in love at first sight"? The answer is "no". . . . If a person has serious doubts as to whether or not he is in love, obviously he is not.[6]

These textbook authors appear to have accepted one of our cultural beliefs; namely, that a "marriage type love" is the real form of love, and that such love is to be preferred over other emotional states such as romantic

Modern Courtship and Marriage, New York: Macmillan, 1957, p. 61; Alexander F. Magoun, *Love and Marriage*, New York: Harper, 1956, p. 7; Meyer F. Nimkoff, *Marriage and the Family*, New York: Houghton Mifflin, 1947, p. 376; James A. Peterson, *Education for Marriage*, New York: Scribner's, 1956, p. 15; Rex A. Skidmore and Anthron S. Cannon, *Building Your Marriage*, New York: Harper, 1951, pp. 57–61; Willard Waller and Reuben Hill, *The Family*, New York: Dryden, 1951, pp. 114, 128; Robert F. Winch and Robert McGinnis, eds. *Marriage and the Family*, selection by J. K. Folsom, New York: Holt, 1953, p. 359. The following six books did not spend much time on love, and others took a more comprehensive approach: Ernest W. Burgess and Harvey J. Locke, *The Family*, New York: American, 1953; Robert Geib Foster, *Marriage and Family Relationships*, New York: Macmillan, 1950; Clifford Kirkpatrick, *The Family*, New York: Ronald, 1955; Judson T. Landis and Mary G. Landis, eds. *Readings In Marriage and the Family*, New York: Prentice-Hall, 1952; Arthur R. Olsen, Emily H. Mudd, and Hugo Bourdeau, eds. *Marriage and Family Relations*, Harrisburg: Stackpole, 1953; Andrew Truxal and Francis E. Merrill, *Marriage and The Family in American Culture*, New York: Prentice-Hall, 1953.
  [2] Bowman, op. cit., pp. 32–37.
  [3] Hirning and Hirning, op. cit., p. 125.
  [4] Landis and Landis, op. cit., p. 169.
  [5] LeMasters, op. cit., p. 61.
  [6] Skidmore and Cannon, op. cit., pp. 57–61.

love or "infatuation."[7] Although this restriction of analysis by a preferred type of love may afford insight into this preferred type, it does limit the objective investigation of other cultural forms of love in American society. In short, to the extent that this more restricted approach is emphasized, a more comprehensive sociological approach is minimized.[8]

OTHER CONCEPTUALIZATIONS

Even when we step outside the "textbook" area, this restricted approach is still operative. For example, this is how one sociologist defines love in an article in Psychiatry: "Love is that relationship between one person and another which is most conducive to the optimal development of both."[9] Here, too, one finds a particular kind of love as the center of focus rather than an objective analysis of all cultural types of love.

Winch's work on love relationships has been quite suggestive.[10] However, his efforts so far seem to be more fully in the realm of psychology than in sociology. Heavy reliance on psychoanalytic concepts in his analysis of love relationships, focusing on the individual relationship, and emphasis on the complementary needs of the particular couple without reference to possible cultural sources, all indicate greater concern with what the personality system has to contribute to love relationships rather than what the social or cultural systems may have to contribute to such relationships. Nevertheless, Winch does not by any means totally ignore the cultural background. He brings it in partly when he mentions that his theory applies only to societies where marriages are for love. He also makes up four major types of complementariness but he fails causally to relate these types to any cultural variables.[11]

Winch's effort is of importance to sociologists, but unless he brings the

[7] Much of the doubt individuals display concerning their love affairs is not about whether they are experiencing some kind of love relationship but rather about whether they are experiencing a particular type of love, one capable of being the basis for marriage. The textbooks emphasize this type of love as the only type and make many people anxious and confused. These people do not see love as existing on a continuum but rather as an all-or-none state most difficult to discover and constantly subject to doubts.

[8] Whenever a controversial or highly emotional issue such as love or sex is involved, the danger of provincial approaches increases. One tends not to recognize as valid cultural forms, those beliefs which one feels to be in error. This seems to be the case concerning forms of love beliefs such as romantic love. For a criticism of some of the marriage and family textbooks for their restricted treatment of premarital coitus see Ira L. Reiss, "The Treatment of Pre-Marital Coitus in 'Marriage and the Family' Texts," Social Problems, 4 (April, 1957), 334–338.

[9] Nelson N. Foote, "Love," Psychiatry, 16 (August, 1953), 247. Work on love, such as that by Fromm and Reik, will not be dealt with here since it is clearly not within the sociological frame of reference. See Erich Fromm, The Art of Loving, New York: Harper, 1956; and Theodor Reik, A Psychologist Looks at Love, New York: Rinehart, 1944.

[10] For the most recent statement of Winch's work see Robert F. Winch, Mate Selection, A Study of Complementary Needs, New York: Harper, 1958.

[11] See Winch, op. cit., Chapters 7–10 and 14.

social and cultural system into more central focus, there will be a serious gap in the sociological approach to the heterosexual love relationship.[12] As sociologists we must know what kinds of social and cultural factors are related to particular types of love relationships. Whether the personality needs that individuals are satisfying are complementary or homogamous does not seem to be as important in a sociological analysis as the discernment of the socio-cultural factors which are causally related to these personality needs.[13]

In addition to Winch's formulations the work of Burgess and Wallin is important for a sociological conception of love.[14] In particular their efforts in dealing with homogamy seem quite relevant, for here the emphasis is on common cultural factors, such as religion and education, which are to be found in love relationships.[15] Burgess and Wallin also deal with personality needs, but they, like Winch, fail to tie this level to relevant causal background factors in the social and cultural systems.[16] Even when dealing with homogamy, no complete effort is made to show why such background factors as religion and education are similar in many love relationships. In short, a correlational rather than a causal approach is taken. Thus, although Winch and Burgess and Wallin have contributed to our sociological knowledge of the love relationship, none of these individuals has related the personality-need level of the love relationship to its cultural sources—to put it another way, we are lacking a basic framework for a sociological theory of love.

There are interesting works on the love relationship, such as those by Caplow, Kirkpatrick, Ellis and others.[17] However, these works, though valuable,

[12] The classic statement by Durkheim on the level of sociological analysis, "A social fact must be explained by another social fact," is relevant here. See Emile Durkheim, *Rules of Sociological Method*, Glencoe, Illinois: The Free Press, 1938. One does not have to be a full "Durkheimian" in order to insist that this level of analysis be at least included in any sociological conceptualization. Much of the textbook literature on love has a strong psychological aspect, also, in its explanation of the child's love development. Frequently the Freudian conception of narcissistic, homosexual and other stages of love is accepted. For Freud's view see Sigmund Freud, *Group Psychology and the Analysis of the Ego*, London: Hogarth, 1922.

[13] The author will develop this point in detail in a later article.

[14] Ernest W. Burgess and Paul Wallin, *Engagement and Marriage*, New York: Lippincott, 1953. Especially Chapters 6 and 7.

[15] Ibid., Chapter 6.

[16] One of the earliest writers on personality needs and love was Anselm Strauss. However, here too, the connection between personality needs and their cultural sources was not fully developed. See Anselm Strauss, "Personality Needs and Marital Choice," *Social Forces*, 25 (March, 1947), 332–335.

[17] Included here are some of the classic researches into the love relationship: Clifford Kirkpatrick and Theodore Caplow, "Courtship in a Group of Minnesota Students," *The American Journal of Sociology*, 55 (May, 1950), 550–558. See also the interesting study of romantic love notions in our communication media: Albert Ellis, *The American Sexual Tragedy*, New York: Twayne, 1954, Chap. 5 especially. There are other important researches in this area going on at the present time, e.g., Pitirim Sorokin's work on altruistic love, which is broader than just heterosexual love. The recent work of William J. Goode is also at point here and will be referred to later.

are not directly relevant to the question of a basic over-all sociological approach to the love relationship; rather they are researches dealing with specific aspects of such relationships.

A SOCIOLOGICAL THEORY OF LOVE

The above examination of the literature gives one the impression that what is needed in our approach to love is a frame of reference which is more fully on the sociological level. As a step toward this goal, a general theoretical approach to the heterosexual love relationship has been formulated which, it is believed, takes account of the psychological level but brings into central focus the social and cultural levels. As will be shown, this formulation is in accord with the research evidence in this area, and interviews of numerous students also seem to support this conceptualization.[18] The following theory is put forth only as a first attempt to formulate the broad outlines of a sociological theory of the heterosexual love relationship.

First, it is important to describe the processes through which it is proposed all of our major cultural types of love develop. In American society young people meet under a variety of informal conditions such as at a party, a dance, or in school. After meeting, these two people became aware of the presence or lack of a feeling of rapport.[19] That is, they may feel quite at ease and relaxed and be willing and desirous to talk about themselves and learn more about the other person, or they may feel quite ill at ease and watch the clock until the evening ends. To the sociologist the vital question is *not* just whether such a couple feels rapport because they complement each other or are similar to each other in their personality needs. Such information certainly can be valuable, as Winch has shown; but the crucial sociological question is: What are the social and cultural background factors which make this type of couple capable of feeling rapport—what social and cultural variables are related to particular personality needs? Certainly, if cultural backgrounds differ too sharply the people involved would be unable to communicate at all. However, if cultural backgrounds differ in some particular ways they may still be compatible; while the same amount of difference in other directions makes compatibility most unlikely.

Thus, it is one of the sociologist's tasks to discern what role cultural background plays in heterosexual love relationships. This can be done on a more precise level than just seeing if the two people are of the same religion or

[18] The author has interviewed dozens of individuals over the past several years concerning the development of their love relationships. However, these interviews can only be suggestive and not conclusive evidence for the theory of love to be presented here. Other, more systematic research is referred to elsewhere.

[19] There are articles relevant to the study of dyadic rapport, such as Howard Becker and Ruth H. Useem, "Sociological Analysis of the Dyad," *American Sociological Review*, 7 (February, 1942), 13–26; Leonard S. Cottrell, Jr. and Rosalind F. Dymond, "The Empathic Responses," *Psychiatry*, 12 (November, 1949), 355–359.

education group. The latter has been done for us by Burgess and Wallin—but one must also see what cultural factors made these two particular people, who are of the same religious and education group, feel rapport for each other. The specific way each views and defines his social roles may be a fruitful area to examine.[20] For example, within the same religious, educational, and income group there are divisions regarding how equalitarian the female role should be, and those people whose definitions of the female role are alike may well be more apt to feel rapport for each other. As a preliminary testing of this approach, seventy-four students were asked to select from ten personality needs which ones they felt to be the most important in their best love relationship. Table I shows some of the results of this pilot study.

TABLE I   Personality Needs Which College Students Consider to Be Most Important in Their Best Love Relationship*

Personality Needs for Someone:	Boys %	Girls %
1. Who loves me	87	95
2. To confide in	60	65
3. Who shows me a lot of affection	40	53
4. Who respects my ideals	50	74
5. Who appreciates what I want to achieve	32	28
6. Who understands my moods	36	23
7. Who helps me in making important decisions	16	28
8. To stimulate my ambition	16	7
9. I can look up to very much	22	70
10. Who gives me self-confidence in my relations with people	32	19

*Each student was allowed to check as many of the ten as he thought were "most important." These ten needs are the same as Anselm Strauss used; see "Personality Needs and Marital Choice," *Social Forces,* 25 (March, 1947), 332–335. The questionnaire was administered by R. Wayne Kernodle and the author in 1958 to 74 of our "marriage" students (43 girls, 31 boys). A more rigorous testing is planned for the future.

These results are surely not conclusive but they are suggestive. In need number 9, for example, only 22 per cent of the boys stated that they felt it most important in their love relationship to have "someone to look up to." Seventy per cent of the girls checked this response. This large difference seems to reflect the double standard in our society which brings girls up with more of an orientation to want to love someone they can "look up to."[21] A girl who felt this need would, it seems, blend well with a boy who did *not* feel this need, and both of these attitudes are traceable to our double-standard culture. This is one way in which we may connect personality needs with cultural background. Other needs in Table I suggest cultural variables,

[20] Burgess and Wallin do include role conceptions in their analysis of homogamy. However, they do so in the sense of showing correlations and not fully in the sense of showing what, if any, causal relations underlie such correlations.

[21] For an analysis of the double standard see: Ira L. Reiss, "The Double Standard in Premarital Sexual Intercourse: A Neglected Concept," *Social Forces*, 34 (March, 1956), 224–230.

e.g., the higher percentage of men who need their ambition stimulated and the higher percentage of girls who need help in decisions.[22]

It should be emphasized that this is but a pilot study and much further work is needed to refine this method of analysis and test some of the above interpretations. The effort here is merely aimed at showing that one can analyze the rapport aspect of a relationship in terms of the cultural background which makes such rapport possible.[23]

The feeling of rapport seems to be the first step in the development of heterosexual love relationships. Concomitant with such rapport is a second process which may be labeled "self-revelation." When one feels at ease in a social relationship he is more likely to reveal intimate aspects of his existence. He is, under such conditions, more likely to tell of his hopes, desires, fears, and ambitions. He is also more likely to engage in sexual activities, according to recent studies on college students.[24] Here, too, the sociologist need not focus on the psychological aspects—he can, instead, look at the cultural backgrounds of the participants. The cultural background of each person should help determine what he feels is proper to reveal, i.e., whether petting is acceptable, whether talking about one's personal ambitions is proper, or whether discussing religion is right. The person's cultural background will define what and how much one should reveal when a certain amount of rapport is present.

The above process of self-revelation is vital to the development of love, and it is through this that a third process occurs; namely, the development of mutual dependencies, or, more technically put, of interdependent habit systems. One becomes dependent on the other person to fulfill one's own habits: e.g., one needs the other person to tell one's ideas or feelings; one needs the other person to joke with; one needs the other person to fulfill one's sexual desires. When such habitual expectations are not fulfilled, loneliness and frustration are experienced. Thus, such habits tend to perpetuate a relationship. The type of habits which are established are culturally determined, in large measure, for these habits are outgrowths of the revelations, and the type of revelation is culturally regulated.

Finally, a fourth process is involved, and that is personality need fulfill-

[22] Another interesting point was that most of the girls who checked need No. 4 (someone who respects my ideals), also checked need No. 9 (someone I can look up to very much), showing that although the double standard may be modified to the point where girls want to have their ideals respected, the same girls want a boy whom they can "look up to." This relationship between No. 4 and No. 9 did not hold for the boys.

[23] The oft asked question "Why did this particular person fall in love with this other particular person?" can be answered by sociologists in terms of our approach. From our point of view, the love object could have been a number of people with similar socio-cultural characteristics. Chance factors led to it being this particular person. Thus, even here an "individualistic" explanation is not needed.

[24] Winston Ehrmann's study of students at the University of Florida is the source of this statement. Ehrmann found that coitus was three times as likely to occur when love was involved. Winston Ehrmann, *Premarital Dating Behavior*, New York: Holt, 1959.

ment. The needs referred to here are needs such as the basic needs in Table I, which were examined in relation to feelings of rapport. As has been shown, these needs seem to vary with cultural background. These four processes are in a sense really one process, for when one feels rapport, he reveals himself and becomes dependent, thereby fulfilling his personality needs. The circularity is most clearly seen in that the needs being fulfilled were the original reason for feeling rapport. In summary, then, the cultural background produces certain types of personality needs in particular groups of people, and when these people meet other groups which have similar or complementary backgrounds they feel rapport, reveal themselves, become dependent, and thereby fulfill these personality needs.

Since these four processes turn one into the other and are constantly occurring, the above formulation concerning the development of love will be called the "Wheel Theory." This is, of course, merely a label for the above four processes—one which was chosen because the term has explanatory value and helps emphasize the circularity and unity of these four processes. As has been mentioned, the key interest for the sociologist would be in the cultural and social factors underlying these four processes as they occur between various types of young people. The following diagram is a graphic representation of this theory:

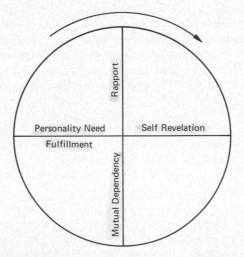

Figure 1   Graphic presentation of the wheel theory of the development of love.

Of course, the "wheel" can turn in a negative direction and "unwind"; that is, the relationship can weaken when an argument or competing interest, or such, occur. Such an event can lessen rapport and that, in turn, decrease self-revelation, mutual dependency, and need fulfillment. This decrease further lessens rapport and can thus continue to "unwind" the relationship. The wheel can also continue to turn indefinitely in a positive direction as long as the four processes continue to be activated. In this fashion the rapport, revelation, dependency and fulfillment processes can continue to "turn" for as long and as intensely as the cultural backgrounds of the people involved will allow.

Upon inspection it can be seen that the four spokes of the wheel are processes which universally occur in any primary relationship, i.e., the general description would apply to the development of a friendship relationship or a parent-child relationship. The four wheel processes would be involved in a primary relationship in Samoa as well as in New York. Thus, heterosexual love in America is the cultural development and elaboration of *one* type of primary relationship.

We give a specific meaning and content to this type of heterosexual love relation that distinguishes it from all other types of primary relations. For the last thousand years the Western world has singled out the heterosexual type of primary relationship for special attention.[25] Many other cultures have people who fall in love, but usually they do not use such love feelings as the basis for marriage. Such feelings most often develop after marriage and they lack the "romantic" aura ours possess. Goode has recently put forth evidence on the relative potentiality and actuality of love relationships in other cultures.[26]

Love in America is culturally defined regarding how intense the feelings should be before one calls it "love," and how one should behave when he believes he is in love. Although such cultural definitions are widely shared there still are some people who will apply the label "love" to a relationship quite freely, and some others who require so much that they may never believe a relationship is intense enough to be love. There may possibly be variation by social classes as to what is required before using the term "love" to describe a heterosexual primary relationship.

The symptoms which go along with love vary from the Hollywood variety of walking into doors and losing one's appetite to the more "rational" type of symptoms which involve knowing the person thoroughly and wanting to be with him. These symptoms are learned in much the same way we learn other cultural forms. The kind of symptoms one displays depends in large measure on the type of love one accepts. The author's studies of college love affairs indicate that love in American culture may be hypothetically classified into several types, which have varying degrees of support in our society: (1) ultra romantic love at first sight, (2) sexual love where the sexual factor is dominant, (3) rational love where the intellectual appraisal of the affair is important, and (4) probably several other mixed varieties. Much more research is needed to verify and extend this typology.

[25] For a brief discussion of the development of romantic love see Hugo Beigel, "Romantic Love," *American Sociological Review*, 16 (June, 1951), 326–334. Dr. Beigel is planning to publish a book on romantic love later this year. See also Dennis De Rougemont, *Love in the Western World*, New York: Harcourt Brace, 1940.

[26] William J. Goode, "The Theoretical Importance of Love," *American Sociological Review*, 24 (February, 1959), 37–48. Our explanation of love as a type of primary relationship fits in with Goode's findings that heterosexual love is more common than once thought and that many cultures set up specific controls to prevent its occurrence. For if heterosexual love develops as do other primary relationships, then it is more of an ever-present possibility, and one would expect to find it more widespread or to find specific controls set up against it. This is precisely what Goode found.

All of these types of love can be explained theoretically as developing via the wheel processes of rapport, revelation, dependency, and fulfillment. The romantic variety just goes through these processes in rapid order and one feels he knows the person fully—he feels the rapport, reveals himself, becomes dependent and feels fulfilled, all sometimes in the course of one evening! The sexual type of love merely emphasizes one way around the wheel—one way of revealing oneself.[27] The rational type of love emphasizes the need to know each other under a variety of circumstances and to evaluate the relationship before allowing oneself to become too involved. This type of love seems to be increasingly popular among college students.[28] It involves a larger number of rapport, revelation, dependency, and fulfillment factors than do the other love types.

FINAL COMMENTS

With the Wheel Theory, one can distinguish and describe the development and maintenance of the major types of love relationships. Love, thus, can be viewed as a type of primary relationship which our culture has singled out for special attention. The problem becomes to discern what cultural forms have been given to this primary relationship and what cultural backgrounds tend to promote the possibility of this type of primary relationship. In this fashion one can avoid the more restricted approaches referred to above. Instead one can analyze the characteristics and consequences of each type of love in various segments of our culture and society. Goode's recent analysis suggests that love attitudes may differ considerably by social class.[29] The Wheel Theory thus affords a broad over-all conception which can encompass all the heterosexual love relationships.

Furthermore, the Wheel Theory does not depend on the truth or falsity of the complementary needs or homogamy conceptions. Rather, if one desires he may incorporate Winch's notion of complementary mating as well as the homogamy and personality-need views of Burgess and Wallin and Strauss.[30] Such explanations are compatible with the Wheel Theory and future research can resolve any competing conceptions which exist among these explanations.

[27] One important area of love is its relation to sexual standards and behavior. This relation is developed at length in a book by the author: *Premarital Sexual Standards in America*, New York: The Free Press, 1960.

[28] Burgess and Wallin, op. cit., p. 170. Over two-thirds of the engaged couples in this study refused to call their relationship, "head-over-heels in love" because that phrase smacked too much of ultra romantic love notions. The author's interviews with college students also tends to support this popularity of a "rational" type love. However, there are quite strong emotional attachments to some of the older romantic love notions, even among those who are intellectually "liberated."

[29] Goode, op. cit., p. 46.

[30] Burgess and Wallin do not speak of homogamy alone—they emphasize personality need fulfillment as vital in love. Even though they do not stress the necessity for getting behind personality needs to their social and cultural correlates, their approach is still quite compatible with the Wheel Theory. See Burgess and Wallin, op. cit., pp. 202–204, 212.

In addition the Wheel Theory seems to be capable of accounting for and integrating much of the available specific field research evidence on love relationships. For example, some of the key findings in this area by Strauss show that 100 per cent personality need fulfillment is had by only a minority of the couples in his sample (18 per cent); Burgess and Wallin in their study of 1000 engaged couples showed how very common doubt and conflict were in engaged love relationships; Ellis in his study of 500 college girls points out that about a quarter of them had experienced simultaneous loves.[31] These are representative findings and they all are explainable by the Wheel Theory: e.g., if love does develop through the culturally directed processes of a primary relationship involving rapport, revelation, dependency, and need fulfillment, then one would expect that there would be wide differences in the amount of needs which were fulfilled in any one relationship; that the very common failure to fully satisfy one's needs might well make one have some doubts and conflicts concerning the value of the relationship; and it also follows that although one has fulfilled some of his needs in one love relationship, he may fall simultaneously in love with another person who is capable of fulfilling different combinations of needs.

Of course, the fact that the Wheel Theory is compatible with the major theoretical approaches and research findings in this area is not in itself conclusive evidence of its worth. The analysis here should serve mainly as a spur to further research testing of the Wheel Theory. It is believed that a new direction for study of the love relationship is needed. This paper is put forth only as a step toward filling the gaps in the sociological conceptualization of the heterosexual love relationship in America.

[31] Strauss, op. cit., p. 333. Burgess and Wallin, op. cit., pp. 179–182, 247; Albert Ellis, "A Study of Human Love Relationships," *The Journal of Genetic Psychology*, 75 (September, 1949), 61–71.

7	*Another Look at the Theory of Complementary Needs in Mate-Selection*
	ROBERT F. WINCH

INTRODUCTION

The purpose of this paper is to review the theory of complementary needs in mate-selection and to indicate the direction in which the theory has recently been developing.

From 1954 through 1958 the writer and his associates published several

Reprinted from the *Journal of Marriage and the Family*, 29, No. 4 (November, 1967), 756–762, by permission of the National Council on Family Relations.

papers and a book on the theory of complementary needs in mate-selection.[1] Very simply, the theory begins with the observation that in the United States mate-selection has been shown to be largely homogamous with respect to age, race, religion, social class, education, location of previous residence, and previous marital status. It has been proposed that these variables define for each individual a field of eligible spouse-candidates and that there remains the task of accounting for mate-selection within the field of eligibles. Toward this objective the theory of complementary needs offers the following hypothesis: In mate-selection each individual seeks within his or her field of eligibles for that person who gives the greatest promise of providing him or her with maximum need gratification.

THE ORIGINAL TEST OF THE THEORY

In 1950, 25 young married couples served as test subjects for the theory. At the time of testing, one or both members of each couple were undergraduate students. In 1950 a considerable number of veterans of World War II were still completing their education, and a considerable number of the husbands in this study were veterans. An effort was made to obtain couples as soon after marriage as possible.[2] No couple had been married more than

[1] The theory and the immediately relevant data were presented in a series of three articles in the *American Sociological Review:* Robert F. Winch, Thomas Ktsanes, and Virginia Ktsanes, "The Theory of Complementary Needs in Mate-Selection: An Analytic and Descriptive Study," 19 (1954), 241–249; Robert F. Winch, "The Theory of Complementary Needs in Mate-Selection: A Test of One Kind of Complementariness," 20 (1955), 52–56; and Robert F. Winch, "The Theory of Complementary Needs in Mate-Selection: Final Results on the Test of the General Hypothesis," 20 (1955), 552–555. Further consideration of the data by means of multivariate analysis appears in two articles: Thomas Ktsanes, "Mate Selection on the Basis of Personality Type: A Study Utilizing an Empirical Typology of Personality," *American Sociological Review*, 20 (1955), 547–551; and Robert F. Winch, Thomas Ktsanes, and Virginia Ktsanes, "Empirical Elaboration of the Theory of Complementary Needs in Mate-Selection," *Journal of Abnormal and Social Psychology*, 51 (1955), 508–513. In addition there were two articles on methodological features of the study: Robert F. Winch and Douglas M. More, "Quantitative Analysis of Qualitative Data in the Assessment of Motivation: Reliability, Congruence, and Validity," *American Journal of Sociology*, 61 (1956), 445–452; and Robert F. Winch and Douglas M. More, "Does TAT Add Information to Interviews? Statistical Analysis of the Increment," *Journal of Clinical Psychology*, 12 (1956), 316–321. The most general treatment of the theory appears in Robert F. Winch, *Mate-Selection: A Study of Complementary Needs*, New York: Harper, 1958.

[2] That is, the decision was made (a) to study only those who had already selected mates and (b) those who had selected their mates as recently as possible. With respect to criterion (a), it was reasoned that among dating and even engaged couples there would be some who would not marry, and at least some of these broken relationships would result from non-complementariness of needs. With respect to criterion (b), it was not assumed that a couple would necessarily remain complementary all their lives; changes in

two years; the median couple had been married for one. At the time of being interviewed no couple had children.

The data-gathering procedure employed two interviews and a projective test. The main interview (called a "need interview") was based on nearly 50 open-ended questions. Each question was designed to elicit information on the intensity of one of the needs or traits, i.e., to give an indication as to the strength of the need in the person being interviewed and the manner in which that person went about obtaining gratification for the need or expressing the trait. For example, to elicit information about the subject's hostile need (n Hos), he was asked the following:

Let us suppose that you have entered a crowded restaurant, have stepped in line, have waited your turn, and presently someone enters and steps in front of you in line. What would you do? Has this ever happened to you? When was the last time this happened? Tell me about it.

A second interview sought to uncover the subject's perceptions concerning the salient relationships in his life and how he saw these as being related to his psychic and social development. In particular, he was asked to recount from his earliest memories the history of his relationships with his parents and siblings, as well as those in school and peer group. The third procedure was an abridged (ten-card) version of the Thematic Apperception Test, wherein a person is presented with a somewhat ambiguous picture concerning which he is asked to tell a story.

From each of these three sets of information a separate set of ratings was developed. For each instrument at least two raters were employed.

The theory was interpreted as predicting two types of complementariness:

Type I: The same need is gratified in both person *A* and person *B* but at very different levels of intensity. A negative interspousal correlation is hypothesized. For example, it is hypothesized that if one spouse is highly dominant, the other will be very low on that need.

Type II: Different needs are gratified in *A* and *B*. The interspousal correlation may be hypothesized to be either positive or negative, contingent upon the pair of needs involved. For example, it is hypothesized that if one spouse is highly nurturant, the other will be found to be high on the succorant (or dependent) need.

Statistical analysis of the results came out in the hypothesized direction, and the data were interpreted as providing adequate, though not overwhelming, support for the theory of complementary needs in mate-selection.[3]

Qualitative analysis of the same 50 persons suggested that there were two principal psychological dimensions underlying the various needs: (1) nurturance-receptivity, or a disposition to give versus a disposition to receive, and (2) dominance-submissiveness. On the basis of these dimensions, the following types of complementariness were induced:

---

their roles, especially in their occupational and familial roles, might modify their need-patterns with the consequence that they would become less complementary.

[3] See the first three papers listed in footnote 1.

Dominent-Submissive Dimension	Nurturant-Receptive Dimension	
	Husband Nurturant Wife Receptive	Husband Receptive Wife Nurturant
Husband Dominant Wife Submissive	Ibsenian*	Master-Servant Girl
Husband Submissive Wife Dominant	Thurberian**	Mother-Son

*After *A Doll's House.*
**After James Thurber's conception of the relation (battle?) between the sexes.

SUBSEQUENT EFFORTS BY OTHERS TO TEST THE THEORY

Unfortunately no one has ever replicated the original study. For a time the literature bristled with articles purporting to be tests of the theory, and it seemed that the more categorical the claims of the authors in this regard, the less directly their results actually bore on the theory.

There is one probably very significant difference between the original study and all subsequent studies of complementary needs in mate-selection of which the author is aware. In the original study each test subject was interviewed about his need-pattern and then his answers were assessed by two or more trained analysts, whereas all subsequent studies of which the author is aware used some paper-and-pencil test in which the subject assessed himself. Some critics of the original study have made the seemingly absurd observation that the analysts on the mate-selection study were probably more subjective in their ratings (and hence less valid) than would have been the subjects themselves. How can it be reasoned that the analysts would be more concerned whether Subject 17, whom they did not know, was rated high or low on need dominance, say, than Subject 17 himself? It is this author's view that the frequently observed disposition of test subjects (like human beings generally) to portray themselves in a favorable light biases their responses.

In 1954 Allen Edwards published the Personal Preference Schedule (PPS), a paper-and-pencil test designed to measure fifteen of the needs that had been postulated and nominally defined by Murray. By name ten of the fifteen needs in the PPS were similar with or cognate to those used in the Winch study. Presumably this fact encouraged a considerable number of social scientists to think that an easy way to duplicate the Winch study was to use the PPS. The fact is that no evidence was presented to show that the Edwards test was valid either by means of a behavioral or a peer-rating criterion. Undaunted by this fact, a very considerable number of studies have purported to have tested the theory of complementary needs by means of the PPS.

Other ways in which subsequent studies have failed to be true replications include: extraneous variables (when all of the variables of the PPS are used, more than half of the resulting matrix of correlations involves variables not even proposed by name in the original study), incomplete concept of complementariness (a good many studies have ignored what is designated above as type II complementariness), and inappropriate subjects (instead of a sample of newly married couples selected in order to have complementariness at its presumed maximum, various studies used dating couples, couples married ten to thirty years, couples belonging to one unspecified church, and couples selected in such a way that they could be called only a "grab" sample).

Perhaps one should expect that if the theory were a really good one, then even with poor samples and even with a very questionable instrument the results should support the theory. In the original study, the support was visible though not overwhelmingly strong. In the subsequent studies, the general result was to show no correlation between members of couples and such correlation as did appear was more often in the direction of similarity than of complementarity.

CRITICISMS OF THE THEORY

Several thoughtful critiques of the theory have been published. Irving Rosow is the author of the first of these to come to this writer's attention.[4] Beginning with the observation that the theory had applicability to other social groups as well as to marital dyads,[5] Rosow went on to point out that Winch's statement of the theory did not make clear at what level the needs were hypothesized to be functioning, i.e., whether at the overt or behavioral level or at some covert or perhaps even unconscious level. The locus of gratification he saw as another problem; by this is meant the question of what happens to the expression of a need within the marriage if the person is obtaining gratification of that need outside the marriage, or if the gratification of that need is being frustrated outside the marriage. Perhaps Rosow's most important criticism of the theory is that it does not provide criteria for determining which needs are complementary; a further difficulty, he says, is that in many cases similarity of need may be as compatible and as functional as complementarity.

Levinger has proposed some remedies for the difficulties posed by Rosow. The former writer has suggested an operation that he believes removes the conceptual ambiguity between complementarity and similarity of needs. He advocates having the testing procedure concentrate on gratification derived from within the marital relationship in order to remove the problem about the locus of gratification, and he sees the formulation of needs by Schutz as clarifying the idea of complementarity by offering the more limited idea of compatibility.[6] Another proposal, about which more will be said below, is that of Tharp, who advocates substituting the sociological concept of role for the psychological concept of need.[7]

[4] Irving Rosow, "Issues in the Concept of Need-Complementarity," *Sociometry*, 20 (1957), 216–233.

[5] An example of such an application is: Rudolf H. Moos and Joseph C. Speisman, "Group Compatibility and Productivity," *Journal of Abnormal and Social Psychology*, 65 (1962), 190–196.

[6] George Levinger, "Note on Need Complementarity in Marriage," *Psychological Bulletin*, 61 (1964), 153–157. Cf. also William C. Schutz, *FIRO: A Three-Dimensional Theory of Interpersonal Behavior*, New York: Rinehart, 1958.

[7] Roland G. Tharp, "Reply to Levinger's Note," *Psychological Bulletin*, 61 (1964), 158–160.

DEVELOPMENTS BEARING ON A REFORMULATION OF THE THEORY

Two studies have contributed to the development and refinement of the theory of complementary needs. Kerckhoff and Davis have studied a sample of undergraduates who were "engaged, pinned or 'seriously attached' " and concluded that there was a sequence of filtering factors such that first individuals sort out each other by characteristics of social background (social class, religion, etc.), later by consensus on familial values (place in the community, having healthy and happy children, etc.), and still later by need complementarity.[8] It is perhaps worth noting that this is the first time the theory of complementary needs received support from a study using a paper-and-pencil test; that test was not the Edwards PPS but Schutz's FIRO-B, each scale of which deals with the desire of the respondent to act toward others with respect to inclusion, control, and affection and also to have the others act toward him with respect to the same three variables.

A very interesting development comes from an application of the theory of complementary needs in a context other than that of mate-selection. Bermann has been studying the stability of dyadic relationships among female students at the University of Michigan.[9] He dealt with three categories of undergraduate women: student nurses, women residents of a cooperative house, and residents of a sorority house. He determined that membership in each category involved a set of norms distinctive from each of the others. That is, his investigation revealed that a nursing student is expected to be friendly, gregarious, affiliative, abasing, to suppress concern about any bodily ailments she might experience, and to be low on dependent needs as well as needs for recognition. This set of norms may be regarded as defining part of the role of the student nurse. Normative traits contributing to a definition of the role of the resident of the cooperative house were that she should be politically progressive and active, rebellious, sorority-shunning, avoid the constraints of conventional dormitories, and be a member of a religious or ethnic minority, of urban residence, highly intellectual, achieving, autonomous, nondeferent, aggressive, nonabasing, and individualistic. The only norm Bermann lists as pertaining to the role of the sorority girl is that of emitting highly dominant behavior.

Bermann reports on a study of 44 pairs of roommates in a dormitory for nursing students. Of these, 22 pairs were rated by themselves and by peers as highly stable pairs, whereas the other 22 were rated as being of low

[8] Alan Kerckhoff and Keith E. Davis, "Value Consensus and Need Complementarity in Mate Selection," *American Sociological Review*, 27 (1962), 295–303. The idea of a sequence of selective procedures is present in the earlier formulations of the field of eligibles and of homogamy with respect to interests and attitudes. Kerckhoff and Davis have provided empirical support for the proposition that such a sequence exists and have proposed the useful term "filtering" to denote the process.

[9] Eric A. Bermann, "Compatibility and Stability in the Dyad," paper presented before the American Psychological Association, New York, September, 1966.

stability. As in Winch's study, interviews provided the basis for assessing the needs of the subjects; the questions designed to elicit data about needs were open-ended. The protocols of the interviews were coded for nine needs: dominance, deference, exhibition, aggression, abasement, nurturance, succorance, achievement, and affiliation.

Bermann sought to predict the stability of pairs of roommates on the basis of the relationship between the pattern of needs of one girl in each pair to the pattern of her roommate. To do this, he used role theory and the theory of complementary needs to generate competing hypotheses. Using role theory, he reasoned that if both roommates were close to the ideal specified by the appropriate set of norms—in the case of student nurses, if both were friendly, abasing, etc.—each would serve the other as an object of identification with a resulting solidarity that would bind the two roommates into a stable relationship. From this reasoning he inferred, e.g., that, if both should be low on the need to dominate, the pair should be stable (since low dominance was found to be an element in the definition of the role of student nurse). Using the theory of complementary needs, however, Bermann reasoned, as was done in Winch's study of mate-selection, that a more solidary relationship should exist where one was high and the other low on dominance (type I complementariness).[10] More formally, Bermann hypothesized (1) that compatibility with respect to role is predictive of stability, (2) that complementariness of needs is predictive of stability, and (3) that both of these predictors considered together predict stability better than either does when taken separately. Generally, Bermann's data supported all of these propositions. Need complementarity predicted stability, but role compatibility predicted it better. Bermann's index of total compatibility, which is a combination of need complementarity and role compatibility, was the most effective predictor of stability.

SOME THOUGHTS ON A REFORMULATION OF THE THEORY

The theory of complementary needs is a psychological theory in that it refers to the actor's personality, conceived as the organization of a set of needs and traits. Role theory is a sociological theory in that its referent is a role, which is the product of the consensus of some collectivity. What Bermann has done is to show that the psychological *plus* the sociological theory is better than either of these standing alone.[11]

Before attempting to integrate the significance of these findings and formulations, it may be useful to distinguish a bit more explicitly between role

[10] It may be recalled that Rosow had made the point that the theory of complementary needs might be generalizable beyond the marital dyad, a point made also by Winch in *Mate-Selection*, pp. 305–309.

[11] Students of social thought may note that this outcome seems pragmatically to give the lie to the stricture of Durkheim to the effect that the explanation of a "social fact" must be another social fact, or in our language, that it is intellectually illegitimate and logically indefensible to combine the two levels of explanation (psychological and sociological) in a single problem. Cf. Emile Durkheim, *The Rules of Sociological Method*, trans. by Sarah Solovay and John H. Mueller, Chicago: University of Chicago Press, 1938.

and personality. Very simply, the distinction is seen as follows. Role directs our attention to behaviors and attitudes that are appropriate to a situation, irrespective of the actor, whereas personality directs our attention to behaviors and attitudes that are characteristic of the actor, irrespective of the situation. As Bermann has shown, both role and personality may be stated in terms of needs.

How can Bermann's results, obtained from studying pairs of girls rooming together, bear on the marital dyad? In the general statement of the theory of complementary needs, the sex of the actor is not significant; the gender of the actor became significant in Winch's study because he placed the test of the theory in the context of mate-selection.

This writer would argue that the theoretically significant feature is not whether the members of the dyad are of the same or different sexes but whether their roles are or are not differentiated. The student nurses were enacting identical roles; there is always some difference between the familial roles of men and women because of the fact that women bear and nurse children. The degree to which roles of the sexes are differentiated beyond this inescapable consideration varies from one societal and cultural context to another. Elsewhere the present writer has argued that the degree of differentiation of sex roles varies inversely with the use of nonhuman power.[12]

Beyond the point of initial attraction, at which differences between the sexes tend to be emphasized,[13] the Kerckhoff-Davis study shows that during the filtering process prospective mates are selecting each other as they find that they participate in the same subculture. After that, according to Kerckhoff and Davis, selection occurs on the basis of complementarity. But is this complementarity of personality or of role or of both?

Before trying to answer the foregoing question, the writer must pause for a slight detour. It has been noted above that the study of complementary needs concluded with the proposal that there were two underlying dimensions of complementariness: nurturance-receptivity and dominance-submissiveness. Subsequent reflection leads the writer to the view that those same data revealed a third dimension that was not quite as well determined as the other two but seems, nevertheless, to be conceptually distinct from them. This dimension may be called "achievement-vicariousness." In the theory of complementary needs, it will be recalled, it makes no difference which spouse is high on needs pertaining to which end of any of these three dimensions—if one spouse is high on one, e.g., nurturance, the other spouse is predicted to be low on that need and to be high on its complement, in this case, receptivity.[14]

[12] Robert F. Winch, *The Modern Family*, New York: Holt, Rinehart and Winston, rev. ed., 1963, pp. 399–401.
[13] The qualifying phrase "tend to" seems warranted by the fad of self-presentation during the latter 1960's in a manner that seems to minimize such differences.
[14] Actually, the name used to designate the need is "succorance." In Table 7 of Winch, *Mate-Selection*, op. cit., p. 125, evidence of type I and type II complementariness for these dimensions may be noted for the following pairs of variables: nurturance and succorance (the nurturance-receptivity dimen-

As we try to incorporate role theory into the above formulation, the first question is whether or not any of these variables enters into the specification of the role of husband or of wife. If so, what bearing would this have? It seems justified to assert that the traditional public image of the husband-father in the American middle class represents him as the dominant member of the family and as being strongly oriented to achievement. The wife-mother is traditionally portrayed as nurturant but as having the children as the objects of her nurturance; also she is traditionally seen as deriving vicarious gratification from the achievements of her husband.

If these statements of role-specification are correct (or to the extent that they are correct), it does follow that the variables of Winch's study of mate-selection can be related to roles that are familial, including marital. At this point it is useful to recall that roles, through what Gross et al.[15] call the "norm-senders," put a strain on personality to conform to the specifications of the roles. To the extent that one sees that one's need-pattern (personality) is consistent with present and prospective roles, one can feel comfortable and adjusted. But where personality is inconsistent with role(s)—e.g., the succorant or submissive or non-achievement-oriented husband—there is room for regarding oneself a misfit and for developing intrapsychic conflict. Placed in the present context, the Bermann study suggests a hypothesis:

> A pair of spouses who are attracted to each other on the basis of complementary needs will be a less stable pair if the complementariness is counter to role-specification than if it is consistent with role-specification.

The point here is that, where personality and role are mutually consistent, this state of affairs should not generate intrapsychic conflict, while the pair of actors should find that their relationship is given normative support. On the other hand, where personality is in conflict with role, each actor is put in a situation to suffer intrapsychic conflict (unless each accepts a self-definition as a deviant) and the marital relationship is open to criticism on normative grounds.

Perhaps an example is in order. Let us assume there are two persons, A and B, in a dyadic relationship. A is high on dominance and low on submissiveness; B has the opposite need-pattern. At this point we do not specify which is male, which is female. With respect to needs they are complementary on this dimension. Accordingly, the theory of complementary needs predicts they are more likely to select each other as mates than a pair in which both are dominant or both are submissive. (And of course the theory of complementary needs purports to predict only mate-selection, not marital happiness

---

sion); dominance and abasement (the dominance-submissiveness dimension); and achievement and vicariousness (the achievement-vicariousness dimension). Of the 12 cells (3 dimensions × 2 variables in each dimension × 2 spouses) referred to in that table, there is only one cell that fails to support the theory: with respect to the interspousal correlation on the traits of vicariousness, the data show no relationship instead of the predicted negative correlation.

[15] Neal Gross, Ward S. Mason, and Alexander W. McEachern, *Explorations in Role Analysis*, New York: John Wiley, 1958.

nor marital stability.) With respect to role what is the situation? If we are given the information that they are members of a society wherein the male role is defined as dominant and the female role submissive, then we are part of the way home. If, in addition, we learn that *A* is the male and *B* the female, we conclude that their need-complementariness on the dominance-submissiveness dimension is consistent with their role-specifications. Then, on the basis of the hypothesis derived from the Bermann study, we might predict that this relationship would be a relatively stable one. Of course if we were told that *B* was the man and *A* the woman, the prediction about their being attracted to each other would still stand but the prediction about the stability of their marriage would be reversed.[16] This case has been oversimplified for heuristic purposes; one would not be justified in predicting either mate-selection or marital stability on only this narrow view of the two parties.

The next step in the prediction of mate-selection and marital stability would seem to be the further analysis of marital and other familial roles. It is not clear whether or not it is desirable to continue working with the needs and traits used by Winch and by Bermann. The latter has shown that, to a limited extent at least, such variables may be used as elements of both personality and of role and thus can be used to integrate the two kinds of theory. It is in contemplating further, even exhaustive, analysis of marital and other familial roles where there arises some uncertainty as to just how adequately such an analysis can be made in terms of, or translated into, needs and traits. Some idea of the task can be seen from the following examples taken from a list of components of marital roles derived from a middle-class sample by Hurvitz[17]: performer of domestic chores; companion of spouse; friend, teacher, and guide of offspring; sexual partner; and model for offspring. The present author has previously published the following list of conceptually derived components or marital subroles:[18]

progenitor or progenitrix
father or mother (nurturer, disciplinarian, socializer, model)
position conferrer (provider of position in society for self, spouse, offspring)
emotional gratifier
sexual partner

[16] In practice, such a prediction would have to be made contingent on the pair having an opportunity to get well acquainted. It appears that initially men and women tend to create images of their ideal mates in terms of normative definitions. At this stage they are disposed to reject as spouse-candidates those who complement their need-patterns if, at the same time, they deviate from the normative standards (i.e., from role-specifications). Later some discard normatively defined ideals after experience convinces them that a better fit results from one who complements their idiosyncratic need-patterns. Case materials supporting this point can be seen in chapters 7-13 of Winch, *Mate-Selection*, op. cit., and in Winch, *The Modern Family*, op. cit. See also the discussion of the cultural ideal and the psychic ideal in *The Modern Family*.

[17] Nathan Hurvitz, "The Components of Marital Roles," *Sociology and Social Research*, 45 (1961), 301–309.

[18] This set appears in Winch, *The Modern Family*, op. cit., p. 664.

The list of five subroles shown just above is intended to be universal, or culture-free, although precisely how they are defined is of course specified in each culture. For the specific setting of the American middle class, the following might be added:

host or hostess
home manager
companion in leisure

Presumably the task of translating such subroles into needs is to analyze (a) how the spouses complement each other with respect to these subroles and (b) the needs involved in such complementariness.

There are two further ideas to be taken into account in suggesting a possible direction for the analysis of marital roles. First, there will be variation from one society to another and from one segment to another within even moderately differentiated societies as to the number and nature of the subroles relating spouses to each other. In general, the more functional the nuclear family is, the greater will be the number of such subroles. Second, the importance of complementary needs as a mate-selective criterion appears to vary inversely with the functionality of the extended family.[19] It may be surmised that the relevance of complementary needs to marital stability is also inversely related to the functionality of both the nuclear and extended family forms. In other words, in societal contexts where the family—extended and/or nuclear—is highly functional, the resulting subroles are important; it should follow that the more important such subroles are, the less importance the culture will give to the idiosyncratic needs of the individual. In middle-class America, where the extended family appears to be relatively nonfunctional and where the functions of the nuclear family also tend toward the low end, love can exist as a criterion for mate-selection and its absence as a criterion for marital dissolution. Hence it is reasoned that complementariness of needs, as a basis for such love, tends to assume importance with respect to both mate-selection and marital stability in family systems of low functionality, whereas role compatibility tends to assume importance for both the selection and retention of mates in more functional family systems.

One final consideration not to be lost sight of is that with the passage of time very significant changes take place in roles and in gratifications and frustrations, and quite possibly in need-patterns. As we follow a couple from their period of engagement into early marriage with its concomitants of occupational demands for the man and domestic demands for the wife-mother into middle and later years when their offspring have been launched and the breadwinner retires, it is obvious that the roles are modified and energy-levels changed and aspirations modified.

SUMMARY

Twenty-five recently married young couples were examined by means of two lengthy interviews and a projective technique in order to provide a test

[19] Ibid., pp. 41–43 and 318–320.

of the theory of complementary needs in mate-selection. The data were interpreted as providing some support of the theory. Originally two dimensions of
complementariness were induced from the data: nurturance-receptiveness and
dominance-submissiveness. Subsequently a third has been proposed: achievement-vicariousness. A spate of non-replicative tests based on the PPS has
provided no support for the theory; however, Kerckhoff and Davis' study based
on Schutz's FIRO-B has shown a culturally homogenizing filtering process
followed by mate-selection on the basis of complementary needs. Whether
or not replication of the study of mate-selection would provide additional
support of the theory remains an unanswered question.

In a study of roommates in a dormitory of nursing students, Bermann has
strongly suggested the advisability of adding the concept of role compatibility
to that of need complementarity; he showed that the stability of pairs of roommates could be predicted better by using both concepts together than by using
either singly.

8 | Value Consensus and Need Complementarity in Mate Selection

ALAN C. KERCKHOFF and KEITH E. DAVIS

One of the continuing interests in family research has been the attempt to
define the factors which lead to a lasting relationship between a man and
a woman. The two major concerns in such research have been with the process through which mates are chosen and the characteristics of mates which
are predictive of "success" in the marital relationship. A considerable body
of knowledge has been assembled based on data gathered in both the premarital and postmarital periods.[1] Although there have been somewhat incon-

[1] Relevant studies involving subjects in the premarital period are C. E.
Bowerman and B. R. Day, "A Test of the Theory of Complementary Needs as
Applied to Couples During Courtship," *American Sociological Review*, 21
(October, 1956), 602–605; Joseph S. Himes, Jr., "Value Consensus in Mate

The research was supported by a Faculty Research Grant from the Duke
University Research Council to the first-named author. Helpful counsel was
received from Kurt Back, Glenn McCann, Joel Smith and Herman Turk, and we
gratefully acknowledge their assistance. The present paper is a revision of a
briefer report given at the meeting of the American Sociological Association,
St. Louis, August 31, 1961.
Reprinted from the *American Sociological Review*, 27, No. 3 (June, 1962)
295–303, by permission of the American Sociological Association.

sistent results at times, the most general conclusion suggested by these data is that individuals who are similar to each other are most likely to choose each other as mates and are most likely to be successful in the relationship. Similarities have been noted in a large number of characteristics such as area of residence, socioeconomic level, religious affiliation and activity, and many kinds of attitudes and values. This tendency toward homogamy in mate selection, however, is not the only tendency noted in the literature. A strong case has been made, for instance, for the proposition that heterogamy or complementarity of personality needs is an important prin-

---

Selection Among Negroes," *Marriage and Family Living*, 14 (November, 1952), 317–321.

Studies utilizing married couples only are R. J. Corsini, "Understanding and Similarity in Marriage," *Journal of Abnormal and Social Psychology*, 52 (May, 1956), 327–332; A. B. Hollingshead, "Cultural Factors in the Selection of Marriage Mates," *American Sociological Review*, 15 (October, 1950), 619–627; I. Katz, S. Glucksberg, and R. Krauss, "Need Satisfaction and Edwards PPS Scores in Married Couples," *Journal of Consulting Psychology*, 24 (June, 1960), 205–208; E. L. Kelly, "Consistency of the Adult Personality," *American Psychologist*, 10 (November, 1955), 659–681; T. Ktsanes, "Mate Selection on the Basis of Personality Type: A Study Utilizing an Empirical Typology of Personality," *American Sociological Review*, 20 (October, 1955), 547–551; R. F. Winch, T. Ktsanes, and V. Ktsanes, "A Theory of Complementary Needs in Mate Selection: An Analytic and Descriptive Study," *American Sociological Review*, 19 (June, 1954), 241–249; R. F. Winch, "The Theory of Complementary Needs in Mate Selection: Final Results on the Test of the General Hypothesis," *American Sociological Review*, 20 (October, 1955), 552–555; R. F. Winch, *Mate-Selection*, New York: Harper, 1958.

Some studies have employed subjects in both the premarital and married stages of the relationship: J. A. Schellenberg and L. S. Bee, "A Re-Examination of the Theory of Complementary Needs in Mate Selection," *Marriage and Family Living*, 22 (August, 1960) 227–232; J. A. Schellenberg, "Homogamy in Personal Values and the 'Field of Eligibles,'" *Social Forces*, 39 (December, 1960), 157–162; E. W. Burgess and P. Wallin, "Homogamy in Personality Characteristics," *Journal of Abnormal and Social Psychology*, 39 (October, 1944), 475–484.

There are also quite a number of studies bearing on the general issues of factors determining selective association. Among the most relevant of these are: J. Altrocchi, "Dominance as a Factor in Interpersonal Choice and Perception," *Journal of Abnormal and Social Psychology*, 59 (November, 1959), 303–308; L. R. Hoffman, "Similarity in Personality: A Basis for Interpersonal Attraction?" *Sociometry*, 21 (December, 1958), 300–308; C. E. Izard, "Personality Similarity and Friendship," *Journal of Abnormal and Social Psychology*, 51 (July, 1960), 47–51; E. E. Jones and B. N. Daugherty, "Political Orientation and the Perceptual Effect of Anticipated Interaction," *Journal of Abnormal and Social Psychology*, 59 (November, 1959), 340–349; G. Lindzey and J. A. Urdan, "Personality and Social Choice," *Sociometry*, 17 (February, 1954), 47–63; T. M. Newcomb, "Varieties of Interpersonal Attraction," in D. Cartwright and A. Zander, eds., *Group Dynamics*, Evanston, Ill.: Row, Peterson, 1960, pp. 104–119; J. A. Precker, "Similarity of Valuings as a Factor in Selection of Peers and Near-authority Figures," *Journal of Abnormal and Social Psychology*, 47 (April, 1952), 406–414; W. C. Schutz, *FIRO: A Three-*

cipal of selection. Winch[2] has indicated that those variables normally associated with the theory of homogamy in mate selection simply define the "field of eligibles" from which each individual then chooses a mate who is likely to complement himself on the personality level.

The present study is intended as a contribution to this body of knowledge. The major innovation it introduces is a longitudinal perspective during the selection period so that further knowledge of the actual selection process is gained. This is in contrast to most of the earlier studies which have compared a number of cases at a single point in time. The present study attempts to examine the relationship between progress in the mate selection process in the premarital period and measures of homogamy and complementarity.

METHOD

In October, 1959 an attempt was made to enlist the cooperation of a number of women students at Duke University as participants in this study. This was done both through calling a meeting for this purpose and through making the study instruments available in the dormitories. Women who were engaged, pinned or "seriously attached" were asked to participate. The latter term was used to refer to those who were seriously considering marriage even though not actually pinned or engaged. Since the women were told that the man would be asked to take part also, we assume the group was limited to those who were fairly confident of the relationship. The women filled out an extended questionnaire (including materials not reported here) and gave us the names and addresses of their fiancés or boy-friends. The same questionnaire was sent to the men by mail. One hundred and sixteen women filled out the questionnaire, and 103 of their boy-friends returned

Dimensional Theory of Interpersonal Behavior, New York: Rinehart, 1958; H. Zimmer, "Motivational Factors in Dyadic Interaction," Journal of Personality, 24 (March, 1956), 251–262.

In addition to the discussions to be found in the empirical studies, important theoretical analyses relevant to the problem of selective association may be found in A. M. Katz and R. Hill, "Residential Propinquity and Marital Selection: A Review of Theory, Method, and Fact," Marriage and Family Living, 20 (February, 1958), 27–35; I. Rosow, "Issues in the Concept of Need-Complementarity," Sociometry, 20 (September, 1957), 216–223; J. W. Thibaut and H. H. Kelley, The Social Psychology of Groups, New York: John Wiley, 1959, pp. 31–50.

Other relevant studies would include: H. M. Richardson, "Studies of Mental Resemblance between Husbands and Wives and between Friends," Psychological Bulletin, 36 (February, 1939), 104–120; P. F. Lazarsfeld and R. K. Merton, "Friendship as a Social Process," in M. Berger, T. Abel, and C. H. Page, eds., Freedom and Control in Modern Society, New York: Van Nostrand, 1954, 18–66; E. Gross, "Symbiosis and Consensus as Integrative Factors in Small Groups," American Sociological Review, 21 (April, 1956), 174–179; W. Kernodle, "Some Implications of the Homogamy-Complementary Needs Theories of Mate Selection for Sociological Research," Social Forces, 38 (December, 1959), 145–152.

[2] Op. cit., 1958.

completed questionnaires. In May of 1960 both members of the 103 couples on whom we had complete October data were sent another short questionnaire. Data for the present report on 94 couples[3] were derived from these returns.

Four factors were considered in the analysis. The dependent variable was the degree of movement toward a permanent union between October and May. The two independent variables were: (a) the degree of consensus between the man and woman on family values, and (b) the degree of need complementarity. In addition, the length of time the couple had been going together was used as a control variable since it was expected that the relationship of either or both of the independent variables with the dependent variable might differ at different stages of the mate selection process.

Two hypotheses guided the analysis:

(1) Degree of value consensus is positively related to progress toward a permanent union.

(2) Degree of need complementarity is positively related to progress toward a permanent union.

The variables were measured as follows:

Progress Toward a Permanent Union

In May the subjects were asked: "Is the relationship (between you two) different from what it was last fall when you filled out the first questionnaire?" There were three possible responses: "Yes, we are farther from being a permanent couple," "No, it is the same," and "Yes, we are nearer to being a permanent couple." Since only twelve gave the first response, the sample was divided into those who said they were *closer* to being a permanent couple (56 couples) vs. all others (38 couples). This factor will be referred to as "progress toward permanence."[4]

Value Consensus

Bernard Farber's "index of consensus" was used for this purpose. As in Farber's original work, both members of the couple were asked (in October)

---

[3] An examination of the data on the thirteen women whose partners did not respond indicates that no systematic bias was apparent. However, it seems likely that these thirteen men were not as serious about the relationship as were those who did respond. It is also likely that most of the nine couples for whom we do not have complete information in May are cases of "failures," although this could not be clearly predicted from the October data.

[4] Here, as in all other such cases, if the man and woman did not agree, the most conservative choice was made. That is, if one said they were closer to being a permanent couple and the other said the relationship was the same, the couple was recorded as *not* closer to being permanent. Although there were not many such cases, they are an indication of the problems encountered when using individual responses to form a group response. The decision made here was based on the argument that if either of them was in doubt about being closer, it was questionable that they were in fact closer.

TABLE 1   Distribution of Spearman Rank
Correlation Coefficients for Value Consensus

Coefficient	Frequency	
Below −.40	1	
−.21 to −.40	3	
−.01 to −.20	10	Low
.00 to .19	11	
.20 to .39	21	
.40 to .59	25	
.60 to .79	14	High
.80 & above	9	
Total	94	

to rank order ten standards by which family success might be measured.[5] The rank correlation between the two sets of rankings was the index of consensus. The distribution of correlation coefficients is presented in Table 1.

Need Complementarity

William Schutz's FIRO-B scales were used in the October questionnaire.[6] There are six of these scales consisting of nine items each. Each scale is concerned with one of the content variables which Schutz calls "inclusion," "control," and "affection," and each is also concerned with either the desire to have others act in some way toward one's self or the desire to act in some way toward others. These two directions are called "wanted" and "expressed" by Schutz. Before computing the complementarity scores for each couple, the scalability of the six scales was tested. It was found that it was necessary to reduce the size of the scales to five items each in order to arrive at equal-sized scales which met the scaling criteria[7] for both men and women separately.[8] Using the scale scores on the six five-item scales, need complementarity was computed using Schutz's formula for what he calls "reciprocal compatibility." The formula is $rk_{ij} = |e_i - w_j| + |e_j - w_i|$ where

[5] The items are published in: "An Index of Marital Integration," *Sociometry*, 20 (June, 1957), 117–134.

[6] Op. cit., pp. 58–65.

[7] The scaling method used and the criteria applied are those outlined by Robert N. Ford, "A Rapid Scoring Procedure for Scaling Attitude Questions," in Matilda White Riley, John W. Riley, Jr., and Jackson Toby, eds., *Sociological Studies in Scale Analysis*, New Brunswick, New Jersey: Rutgers University Press, 1954.

[8] This reduction was also effected because we were in doubt about the justifiability of including in the same scale two items which differed only in the form of the response categories and the cut points among these categories. For instance, Schutz uses the following as two separate items in the same scale, the slash line indicating the cut point: "I like people to act close toward me: most people, many people, / some people, a few people, one or two people, nobody." "I like people to act close toward me: usually, / often, sometimes, occasionally, rarely, never." All such duplications were left out of the final five-item scales.

e_i and w_i are the expressed and wanted scores of the man and e_j and w_j are the expressed and wanted scores of the woman. A separate rk was computed for each need area (inclusion, control, and affection). Since the scale scores varied from 0 to 5, it was possible for rk to assume values of from 0 to 10,

TABLE 2   Distribution of Need Complementarity Scores by
Content Area

Score	Inclusion	Control	Affection	
0	6	6	2	⎫
1	12	13	12	⎬ High
2	13	18	23	⎭
3	22	20	21	⎫
4	15	12	16	
5	13	11	7	
6	9	10	9	⎬ Low
7	3	3	2	
8	1	1	1	
9	0	0	1	
10	0	0	0	⎭
Total	94	94	94	

lower values indicating greater complementarity.[9] The distribution of these scores is shown in Table 2.

Length of Association

For the purposes of this analysis, couples were divided into approximately equal groups, the "long-term" group having gone together for 18 months or more, the "short-term" group having gone together less than 18 months.

[9] Schutz also offers two other compatibility formulae. One is called "interchange compatibility," the formula for which is: $xk=(e_i+w_i)-(e_j+w_j)$. The second is called "originator compatibility," the formula for which is: $ok=(e_i-w_i)+(e_j-w_j)$. The possible range of the first, using our scales, is 0 to 10, the possible range for the second is −10 to +10. Neither of these measures seems to involve the reasoning normally used in discussions of need complementarity. The first simply takes the overall quantity of a particular need area (wanted *and* expressed) for one person and compares it with the overall quantity for the other person. Thus, for instance, a woman's high need for control by others can be balanced off with the man's high need for control by others, which would be the opposite of what is normally called complementarity. The second formula gives the balance between the *excess* of e or w one person has in an area and the excess of the other person. It includes the confounding factor of balance *within* each individual which is of doubtful utility for our purposes. In contrast, the formula we used seems to be exactly the kind of measure called for by the concept of complementarity. As Winch puts it, two people are complementary "when A's behavior in acting out A's need X is gratifying to B's need Y and B's behavior in acting out B's need Y is gratifying to A's need X." (Op. cit., 1958, p. 93.)

RESULTS

Since the dependent variable was a dichotomy and since the independent variables could not be assumed to be more than ordinal scales, the form of analysis used was the test of significance of the difference in the proportions of couples showing progress toward permanence in the categories defined by the hypotheses. In all tests, the distributions of cases on the independent and control variables were dichotomized as close to the median as possible. One-tailed tests were used.

When the simple relationships between the independent and the dependent variables were tested, only that between value consensus and progress in the relationship proved to be statistically significant at the .05 level or better. Two of the measures of complementarity (inclusion and control) approached this level of significance, however, and the third relationship was in the predicted direction. (These relationships are reported in the "Total" rows of Table 4.) Although these findings lead to the tentative acceptance

TABLE 3 **Proportions of Couples Indicating Progress by Value Consensus and Need Complementarity Combined (Total P = .596)**

(A) Value Consensus and Inclusion Complementarity

	High Consensus	Low Consensus	Groups Compared	Significance of Diff.
High Comp.	.760 (25)	.571 (28)	HH > LL	.01
Low Comp.	.696 (23)	.278 (18)	HH > HL	—
			HH > LH	.10
			HL > LL	.01
			LH > LL	.10

(B) Value Consensus and Control Complementarity

	High Consensus	Low Consensus	Groups Compared	Significance of Diff.
High Comp.	.692 (26)	.636 (11)	HH > LL	.05
Low Comp.	.773 (22)	.400 (35)	*HH < HL	—
			HH > LH	—
			HL > LL	.01
			LH > LL	.10

(C) Value Consensus and Affection Complementarity

	High Consensus	Low Consensus	Groups Compared	Significance of Diff.
High Comp.	.750 (16)	.571 (21)	HH > LL	.01
Low Comp.	.718 (32)	.360 (25)	HH > HL	—
			HH > LH	—
			HL > LL	.01
			LH > LL	.10

Note: The cell frequency is presented in parentheses in each cell. In the cell comparisons the value consensus measure is listed first in all cases. Thus, HL means high consensus, low complementarity.
*The asterisk marks the single reversal of direction of relationship from that predicted.

of the first hypothesis and the rejection of the second, further analysis presents a somewhat different picture.

As we have noted, all four of the differences in the "Totals" rows of Table 4 are in the predicted direction. It may also be argued that *if* the two hypotheses being tested are true, we should find a general pattern of relationships among the categories of couples defined by a combination of the two types of independent variables (homogamy and complementarity). This pattern should be: HH>Mixed>LL. (Since the original hypotheses did not include a statement about the relative importance of the two independent variables, there is no basis for predicting a difference between the HL and LH cases within the Mixed category.) Table 3 indicates that, with one exception, this pattern is found in each of the combinations of value consensus with one of the complementarity measures.

In all three sets of comparisons, the difference between the HH and the LL cases approaches significance.[10] Although this table does not provide unequivocal support for the hypotheses, it does present a rather consistent pattern of relationships which may be derived from those hypotheses.

The introduction of the control variable of length of association provides even more information about the adequacy of the hypotheses. The data relevant here are provided in Table 4. In all four cases, the introduction of the control variable points up a difference in the pattern for short-term and long-term couples. Most interesting is the fact that the pattern is consistently different for value consensus and the three measures of need complementarity.

The relationship between value consensus and progress toward permanence is still significant for the short-term couples as it was for the total sample. However, for the long-term couples, although the direction of the relationship remains the same, the degree of significance falls even below the .10 level. On the other hand, when the relationships between progress toward permanence and the three measures of complementarity are examined, the reverse is true. For the short-term couples there is no hint of a relationship between complementarity and progress toward permanence. But for the long-term couples the relationship is significant at the .02 level in the inclusion area and at the .05 level in the control area. In the affection area the direction of the relationship is the same, but it is not statistically significant.[11]

[10] The consistency of the pattern is of particular note given the fact that the three complementarity values are not highly correlated. The Pearsonian coefficient for Inclusion-Affection is .332, for Inclusion-Control it is −.105, and for Affection-Control it is −.018. Only the first deviates significantly from zero.

[11] It may be worth noting also that both long-term and short-term couples experienced progress toward permanence in about the same proportions. This may seem surprising at first since we would expect that the long-term couples were originally more committed to the relationship and would have less "distance" to move in the seven months. However, when one remembers that the measure of progress is a subjective one, it becomes apparent that, even if the long-term couples were objectively closer to a permanent union in October, their sense of progress would be a function of the expectations for

TABLE 4 Proportions of Couples Indicating Progress by Value Consensus, Need Complementarity and Length of Association (Total P = .596)

(A) Value Consensus

	High Consensus	Low Consensus	Significance of Diff.
Short-term	.783 (23)	.350 (20)	.01
Long-term	.680 (25)	.538 (26)	—
Total	.729 (48)	.457 (46)	.01

(B) Inclusion Complementarity

	High Comp.	Low Comp.	Significance of Diff.
Short-term	.560 (25)	.611 (18)	—
Long-term	.750 (28)	.435 (23)	.02
Total	.660 (53)	.512 (41)	.10

(C) Control Complementarity

	High Comp.	Low Comp.	Significance of Diff.
Short-term	.588 (17)	.577 (26)	—
Long-term	.750 (20)	.516 (31)	.05
Total	.676 (37)	.544 (57)	.10

(D) Affection Complementarity

	High Comp.	Low Comp.	Significance of Diff.
Short-term	.588 (17)	.577 (26)	—
Long-term	.700 (20)	.548 (31)	—
Total	.649 (37)	.561 (57)	—

Note: The *n* on which each proportion is based is presented in parentheses after the proportion.

Although it had originally been considered necessary to control for length of association while examining the relationship between the independent variables, the particular pattern of relationships which was found had not been hypothesized. The original hypotheses simply dealt with the overall relationship between progress toward permanence and value consensus and the three measures of complementarity. Thus, it is not possible to state that the original hypotheses were clearly either confirmed or denied by the data, although value consensus was significantly related to progress toward permanance for the total sample.

DISCUSSION

If we accept the pattern of relationships discussed above as significant for the research enterprise, two further issues remain: (a) How do we in-

---

that stage of the mate selection process. Not only would we expect that objective and subjective "distances" might not be directly comparable, it is also important to remember that the measure is a very crude one differentiating only between progress and no progress rather than between amounts of progress or "distances."

terpret or explain the pattern of relationships noted? (b) How does this research fit into the body of knowledge about the process of mate selection?

Turning to the first question, it is necessary to argue on a somewhat ad hoc basis since the specific pattern of relationships found had not been explicitly predicted. However, the pattern does fit rather well with some earlier work in the field of inquiry. It was noted above that Winch speaks of the "field of eligibles" from which one presumably chooses a spouse who complements one's personality needs. In his discussion of the concept "fields of eligibles" Winch says:

> There is a set of variables upon which homogamy has been shown to function: race, religion, social class, broad occupational grouping, location of residence, income, age, level of education, intelligence, etc. It is my opinion that these variables function to select for each of us the sort of people with whom we shall be most likely to interact, to assure that the people with whom we otherwise associate are more or less like us with respect to that set of variables and also with respect to cultural interests and values.[12]

Although neither this particular passage nor others in Winch's writings make the point explicit, he seems to be lumping social structure variables and attitude and value variables together in his discussion. The expectation that the two kinds of variables would be highly correlated is a reasonable one, but, we would argue, further understanding of the selection process might be gained if we examined the concept "field of eligibles" more closely.

The present study indicates that such a blanket statement concerning the homogamy variables may give a misleading image of the mate selection process. The homogamy variable discussed above is value consensus. However, other measures of homogamy were also made in this study, such as education, religion, and father's occupation. It is of interest to note that such social categories did not discriminate effectively among the couples. That is, the subjects of this study were very homogamous with respect to social attributes.[13] On the other hand, the use of the more individual measure of values reported here led to a much clearer discrimination among

---

[12] Op. cit., p. 14.

[13] The degree of homogamy is evidenced by the following: (a) Seventy per cent of the couples had the same level of education. If we accept as homogamous those cases in which the man has graduated from college and is no longer in school and the woman is still in college, only fourteen remain. Of these fourteen, ten are cases of men in graduate school and women in college and only four are cases of women in college and men who are high school graduates. (b) Eighty-seven per cent of the couples are members of the same religious groups (Protestant, Catholic, Jew). Forty per cent report the same rate of attendance at services and 83 per cent are within one category on a five-point scale ranging from "never attend" to "four or more times a month." (c) Using Hollingshead's seven-category classification of occupations, the fathers of the man and woman are in the same category in 45 per cent of the cases; in 76 per cent of the cases they are in the same or adjacent categories.

the couples, as indicated in Table 1, although even here the degree of homogamy is notable.

Thus, a different kind of homogamy is evidently represented by family value consensus than by similarity in social characteristics. Evidently the couples of the present study had *already* limited their field of eligibles with respect to social characteristics but were far from having limited it with respect to value consensus.

This leads us to the tentative suggestion that there are various "filtering factors" operating during the mate selection period. The social attributes presumably operate at an early stage, but values and needs are more clearly operative later on.

Our data do not fit neatly into the logic of a serial set of filtering factors, however. If they did, and if we assume that social attributes, value consensus, and complementarity operate in that order we would expect a significantly higher proportion of high value consensus couples in the long-term group, since many of the low consensus couples would have broken up (been filtered out) in the early stages of courtship. This is not the case. What we do find is that *if* the couple survives the earlier stages despite having low value consensus, they are more likely than short-term low consensus couples to progress toward permanence, and this greater likelihood is largely explained by the variable of complementarity.

This may be seen in part from the fact (see Table 4) that long-term low consensus couples show progress more often than short-term low consensus couples (.538 vs. .350). If the low consensus couples are sorted according to *both* length of association *and* one measure of complementarity, however,

TABLE 5   Proportions of Low Consensus Couples Showing Progress by Length of Association and Need Complementarity (Total P = .467)

	Inclusion		Control		Affection	
	High	Low	High	Low	High	Low
Short term	.357 (14)	.333 (6)	.400 (5)	.333 (15)	.333 (9)	.364 (11)
Long term	.786 (14)	.250 (12)	.833 (6)	.450 (20)	.750 (12)	.357 (14)

Note: The *n* on which each proportion is based is presented in parentheses after the proportion.

it is even more striking. Table 5 shows this analysis. In the case of each measure of complementarity, there is a negligible difference in the short-term row but a very sizeable difference in the long-term row. Thus, complementarity evidently does have a differential effect in long-term and short-term low consensus couples. What remains unspecified is the mechanism through which some short-term low consensus couples manage to stay together.

However, even if this question were answered adequately, our data raise another question about the order of influence of these filtering factors, namely: How does it happen that the filtering effects of need complementarity are not noticeable until the later stages of courtship? Although our data do not provide a wholly satisfactory answer to this question either, some light may be shed on the issue. One of the measures used in the October questionnaire was the other half of Farber's "Index of Marital Integration," the measure of value consensus being the first half. This second measure involves the rating of one's self and of one's partner on a set of personality characteristics. Some of these characteristics are "negative," such as "irritable," "stubborn," "easily excited," etc. Scores are computed for each person according to the number and intensity of such negative personality traits he attributes to his partner. If we sum the two scores for the couple, we have a measure of negative person perception in the couple or what Farber calls "an index of role tension."

When we analyze these scores according to the length of association, we find that short-term couples have much lower scores than long-term couples. That is, short-term couples were less likely to attribute negative personality characteristics to each other than were long-term couples. Also, there is a greater tendency for the person perception scores of short-term couples to become *more* negative between October and May, even when we hold original scores constant. This seems to be in keeping with the point so often stressed in the literature that couples go through a period of idealization and perception distortion which may lead to disillusionment (or "reality shock") at a later date.

In the light of our other findings, we would interpret this to mean that the short-term couples were likely to be responding to an idealized version of the love object which would make the effectiveness of any personality complementarity less probable. They were responding to a stylized role relationship rather than to another personality. Not until the idealization is destroyed can they interact at the more realistic level of personality, and only then can need complementarity "make a difference" in the relationship.

We may now turn to our other question: How does this research fit into the body of knowledge about the process of mate selection? First, the research gives added support for both the homogamy and complementarity theories, and it provides a tentative statement of the relationship between these two during the selection process.

Second, rather than simply comparing married or engaged couples with a random pairing of other individuals in order to show greater complementarity in the couples, this study attempts to demonstrate that complementarity "makes a difference" in the actual selection process. So far as we know, this is the first time such a longitudinal perspective has been provided.

Third, this is the first study of mate selection in which paper and pencil measures have pointed to a significant contribution of complementarity in the selection process. One of the criticisms of Winch's work has been that his measures were not adequately freed of rater bias.[14] On the other hand, one of Winch's criticisms of other attempts to test the importance of complementarity with paper and pencil instruments has been that such instruments are not sufficiently sensitive to tap the relevant need area.[15] Although there may be some disagreement over the adequacy of our operational definitions of the needs involved, the fact remains that this study has

[14] Cf. H. Zimmer, op. cit.

[15] Winch, op. cit., 1958, p. 83, footnote. Winch is referring to the Edwards Personal Preference Schedule here, but presumably his point is a more general one.

been more successful in showing a contribution of complementarity than any other of its kind.[16]

Finally, although the present study has added to our knowledge, it still leaves many unanswered questions which are also left unanswered by earlier studies. One of the most critical of these is the question of the importance or the salience of the needs being studied. In order for complementarity to make much of a difference in the selection process, one would expect that the needs involved must be of some importance to the individuals. Neither the present study nor the earlier ones has provided a means of determining the salience of the needs. It would be possible with the present measuring devices to use the intensity dimension of Guttman scaling as a measure of salience, but with such a small sample the simultaneous control of another variable in addition to those already included would not be feasible.

SUMMARY

We have reported on the findings of a study in which measures of value consensus and need complementarity have been shown to be related to a sense of progress toward permanence during a seven-month interval in the mate selection period. Although only value consensus was related to progress toward permanence for the sample as a whole, when the sample was divided into long-term and short-term couples, value consensus was related to progress for the short-term couples and two of three measures of complementarity were related to progress for the long-term couples. These findings are interpreted as indicating that a series of "filtering factors" operate in mate selection at different stages of the selection process. Our data generally support the idea that social status variables (class, religion, etc.) operate in the early stages, consensus on values somewhat later, and need complementarity still later. Our interpretation of the delay in the operation of the complementarity factor is that such personality linkages are often precluded by the unrealistic idealization of the loved one in the early stages of courtship.

[16] We have purposely avoided a discussion of the concept "need" in this article. It is defined in so many different ways in the literature that we feel it best to let the operational definition stand on its own feet rather than attempting to add still another definition. Let it suffice to note that Schutz refers to his scales as measures of "interpersonal needs," but they are certainly a very different kind of measure than that provided by the TAT.

9 | Measurement of Romantic Love

ZICK RUBIN

Love is generally regarded to be the deepest and most meaningful of sentiments. It has occupied a preeminent position in the art and literature of
every age, and it is presumably experienced, at least occasionally, by the
vast majority of people. In Western culture, moreover, the association between love and marriage gives it a unique status as a link between the individual and the structure of society.

In view of these considerations, it is surprising to discover that social
psychologists have devoted virtually no attention to love. Although interpersonal attraction has been a major focus of social-psychological theory
and research, workers in this area have not attempted to conceptualize love
as an independent entity. For Heider (1958), for example, "loving" is merely
intense liking—there is no discussion of possible qualitative differences
between the two. Newcomb (1960) does not include love on his list of the
"varieties of interpersonal attraction." Even in experiments directed specifically at "romantic" attraction (e.g., Walster, 1965), the dependent measure is
simply a verbal report of "liking."

The present research was predicated on the assumption that love may
be independently conceptualized and measured. In keeping with a strategy
of construct validation (cf. Cronbach & Meehl, 1955), the attempts to define
love, to measure it, and to assess its relationships to other variables are
seen as parts of a single endeavor. An initial assumption in this enterprise
is that love is an *attitude* held by a person toward a particular other person,
involving predispositions to think, feel, and behave in certain ways toward
that other person. This assumption places love in the mainstream of social-
psychological approaches to interpersonal attraction, alongside such other
varieties of attraction as liking, admiration, and respect (cf. Newcomb,
1960).

The view of love as a multifaceted attitude implies a broader perspective than that held by those theorists who view love as an "emotion,"
a "need," or a set of behaviors. On the other hand, its linkage to a particular

This report is based on a doctoral dissertation submitted to the University of Michigan. The research was supported by a predoctoral fellowship
from the National Institute of Mental Health and by a grant-in-aid from the
Society for the Psychological Study of Social Issues. The author is grateful
to Theodore M. Newcomb, chairman of the dissertation committee, for his
invaluable guidance and support. Mitchell Baris, Cheryl Eisenman, Linda
Muller, Judy Newman, Marlyn Rame, Stuart Katz, Edward Krupat, and Phillip
Shaver served as observers in the experiment, and Mr. Shaver also helped
design and assemble the equipment.

Reprinted from *Journal of Personality and Social Psychology*, 16, No. 2
(October, 1970), 265–273, by permission of the American Psychological
Association.

target implies a more restricted view than that held by those who regard love as an aspect of the individual's personality or experience which transcends particular persons and situations (e.g., Fromm, 1956). As Orlinsky (1970) has suggested, there may well be important common elements among different varieties of "love" (e.g., filial love, marital love, love of God). The focus of the present research, however, was restricted to *romantic love*, which may be defined simply as love between unmarried opposite-sex peers, of the sort which could possibly lead to marriage.

The research had three major phases. First, a paper-and-pencil love scale was developed. Second, the love scale was employed in a questionnaire study of student dating couples. Third, the predictive validity of the love scale was assessed in a laboratory experiment.

DEVELOPING A LOVE SCALE

The development of a love scale was guided by several considerations:

1. Inasmuch as the content of the scale would constitute the initial conceptual definition of romantic love, its items must be grounded in existing theoretical and popular conceptions of love.

2. Responses to these items, if they are tapping a single underlying attitude, must be highly intercorrelated.

3. In order to establish the discriminant validity (cf. Campbell, 1960) of the love scale, it was constructed in conjunction with a parallel scale of liking. The goal was to develop internally consistent scales of love and of liking which would be conceptually distinct from one another and which would, in practice, be only moderately intercorrelated.

The first step in this procedure was the assembling of a large pool of questionnaire items referring to a respondent's attitude toward a particular other person (the "target person"). Half of these items were suggested by a wide range of speculations about the nature of love (e.g., de Rougemont, 1940; Freud, 1955; Fromm, 1956; Goode, 1959; Slater, 1963). These items referred to physical attraction, idealization, a predisposition to help, the desire to share emotions and experiences, feelings of exclusiveness and absorption, felt affiliative and dependent needs, the holding of ambivalent feelings, and the relative unimportance of universalistic norms in the relationship. The other half of the items were suggested by the existing theoretical and empirical literature on interpersonal attraction (or liking: cf. Lindzey & Byrne, 1968). They included references to the desire to affiliate with the target in various settings, evaluation of the target on several dimensions, the salience of norms of responsibility and equity, feelings of respect and trust, and the perception that the target is similar to oneself.

To provide some degree of consensual validation for this initial categorization of items, two successive panels of student and faculty judges sorted the items into love and liking categories, relying simply on their personal understanding of the connotations of the two labels. Following this screening procedure, a revised set of 70 items was administered to 198 introductory psychology students during their regular class sessions. Each respondent completed the items with reference to his girlfriend or boyfriend (if he had one), and also with reference to a nonromantically viewed "platonic friend" of the opposite sex. The scales of love and of liking which were employed in the subsequent phases of the research were arrived at through factor analyses of these responses. Two separate factor analyses were performed—one for responses with reference to boyfriends and girlfriends (or "lovers") and one for responses with reference to platonic friends. In each case, there was a general factor accounting for a large proportion of the total variance. The items loading highest on this general factor, particularly for lovers, were almost exclusively those which had previously been categorized as love items. These high-loading items defined the more circumscribed conception of love adopted. The items forming the liking scale were based on those which loaded highly on the second factor with respect to platonic friends. Details of the scale development procedure are reported in Rubin (1969, Ch. 2).

The items forming the love and liking scales are listed in Table 1. Although it was constructed in such a way as to be factorially unitary, the content of the love scale points to three major components of romantic love:

1. *Affiliative and dependent need*—for example, "If I could never be with ———, I would feel miserable"; "It would be hard for me to get along without ———."

2. *Predisposition to help*—for example, "If ——— were feeling badly, my first duty would be to cheer him (her) up"; "I would do almost anything for ———."

3. *Exclusiveness and absorption*—for example, "I feel very possessive toward ———"; "I feel that I can confide in ——— about virtually everything."

The emerging conception of romantic love, as defined by the content of the scale, has an eclectic flavor. The affiliative and dependent need component evokes both Freud's (1955) view of love as sublimated sexuality and Harlow's (1958) equation of love with attachment behavior. The predisposition to help is congruent with Fromm's (1956) analysis of the components of love, which he identifies as care, responsibility, respect, and knowledge. Absorption in a single other person is the aspect of love which is pointed to most directly by Slater's (1963) analysis of the social-structural implications of dyadic intimacy. The conception of liking, as defined by the liking-scale items, includes components of favorable evaluation and respect for the target person, as well as the perception that the target is similar to oneself. It is in reasonably close accord with measures of "attraction" employed in previous research (cf. Lindzey & Byrne, 1968).

QUESTIONNAIRE STUDY

The 13-item love and liking scales, with their component items interspersed, were included in a questionnaire administered in October 1968 to 158 dating (but non-engaged) couples at the University of Michigan, recruited by means of posters and newspaper ads. In addition to the love and liking

TABLE 1   Means, Standard Deviations, and Correlations with Total Scale Scores of Love-Scale and Liking-Scale Items

	Women				Men			
Love-Scale Items	$\bar{X}$	SD	r^a Love	r Like	$\bar{X}$	SD	r^a Love	r Like
1. If —— were feeling badly, my first duty would be to cheer him (her) up.	7.56	1.79	.393	.335	7.28	1.67	.432	.304
2. I feel that I can confide in —— about virtually everything.	7.77	1.73	.524	.274	7.80	1.65	.425	.408
3. I find it easy to ignore ——'s faults.	5.83	1.90	.184	.436	5.61	2.13	.248	.428
4. I would do almost anything for ——.	7.15	2.03	.630	.341	7.35	1.83	.724	.530
5. I feel very possessive toward ——.	6.26	2.36	.438	−.005	6.24	2.33	.481	.342
6. If I could never be with ——, I would feel miserable.	6.52	2.43	.633	.276	6.58	2.26	.699	.422
7. If I were lonely, my first thought would be to seek —— out.	7.90	1.72	.555	.204	7.75	1.54	.546	.328
8. One of my primary concerns is ——'s welfare.	7.47	1.62	.606	.218	7.59	1.56	.683	.290
9. I would forgive —— for practically anything.	6.77	2.03	.551	.185	6.54	2.05	.394	.237
10. I feel responsible for ——'s well-being.	6.35	2.25	.582	.178	6.67	1.88	.548	.307
11. When I am with ——, I spend a good deal of time just looking at him (her).	5.42	2.36	.271	.137	5.94	2.18	.491	.318
12. I would greatly enjoy being confided in by ——.	8.35	1.14	.498	.292	7.88	1.47	.513	.383
13. It would be hard for me to get along without ——.	6.27	2.54	.676	.254	6.19	2.16	.663	.464

scales, completed first with respect to one's dating partner and later with respect to a close, same-sex friend, the questionnaire contained several personality scales and requests for background information about the dating relationship. Each partner completed the questionnaire individually and was paid $1 for taking part. The modal couple consisted of a junior man and a sophomore or junior woman who had been dating for about 1 year.

Each item on the love and liking scales was responded to on a continuum ranging from "Not at all true; disagree completely" (scored as 1) to "Definitely true; agree completely" (scored as 9), and total scale scores were computed by summing scores on individual items. Table 1 presents the mean scores and standard deviations for the items, together with the correlations between individual items and total scale scores. In several cases an inappropriate pattern of correlations was obtained, such as a love item correlating more highly with the total liking score than with the total love score (minus that item). These inappropriate patterns suggest specific revisions for future versions of the scales. On the whole, however, the pattern of correlations was appropriate. The love scale had high internal consistency (coefficient alpha was .84 for women and .86 for men)[1] and, as desired, was only moderately correlated with the liking scale ($r = .39$ for women and .60 for men). The finding that love and liking were more highly correlated among men

[1] Coefficient alpha of the liking scale was .81 for women, and .83 for men.

	Women				Men			
Liking-Scale Items	$\overline{X}$	SD	r Love	rb Like	$\overline{X}$	SD	r Love	rb Like
1. When I am with ——, we are almost always in the same mood.	5.51	1.72	.163	.270	5.30	1.77	.235	.294
2. I think that —— is unusually well-adjusted.	6.36	2.07	.093	.452	6.04	1.98	.339	.610
3. I would highly recommend —— for a responsible job.	7.87	1.77	.199	.370	7.90	1.55	.281	.422
4. In my opinion, —— is an exceptionally mature person.	6.72	1.93	.190	.559	6.40	2.00	.372	.609
5. I have great confidence in ——'s good judgment.	7.37	1.59	.310	.548	6.68	1.80	.381	.562
6. Most people would react very favorably to —— after a brief acquaintance.	7.08	2.00	.167	.366	7.32	1.73	.202	.287
7. I think that —— and I are quite similar to each other.	6.12	2.24	.292	.410	5.94	2.14	.407	.417
8. I would vote for —— in a class or group election.	7.29	2.00	.057	.381	6.28	2.36	.299	.297
9. I think that —— is one of those people who quickly wins respect.	7.11	1.67	.182	.588	6.71	1.69	.370	.669
10. I feel that —— is an extremely intelligent person.	8.04	1.42	.193	.155	7.48	1.50	.377	.415
11. —— is one of the most likable people I know.	6.99	1.98	.346	.402	7.33	1.63	.438	.514
12. —— is the sort of person whom I would like to be.	5.50	2.00	.253	.340	4.71	2.26	.417	.552
13. It seems to me that it is very easy for —— to gain admiration.	6.71	1.87	.176	.528	6.53	1.64	.345	.519

Note: Based on responses of 158 couples. Scores on individual items can range from 1 to 9, with 9 always indicating the positive end of the continuum.
[a]Correlation between item and love scale total *minus that item.*
[b]Correlation between item and liking scale total *minus that item.*

than among women ($z = 2.48$, $p < .02$) was unexpected. It provides at least suggestive support for the notion that women discriminate more sharply between the two sentiments than men do (cf. Banta & Hetherington, 1963).

Table 2 reveals that the love scores of men (for their girlfriends) and women (for their boyfriends) were almost identical. Women *liked* their boyfriends somewhat more than they were liked in return, however ($t = 2.95$, $df = 157$, $p < .01$). Inspection of the item means in Table 1 indicates that this

TABLE 2 Love and Liking for Dating Partners and Same-Sex Friends

	Women		Men	
Index	$\overline{X}$	SD	$\overline{X}$	SD
Love for partner	89.46	15.54	89.37	15.16
Liking for partner	88.48	13.40	84.65	13.81
Love for friend	65.27	17.84	55.07	16.08
Liking for friend	80.47	16.47	79.10	18.07

Note: Based on responses of 158 couples.

sex difference may be attributed to the higher ratings given by women to their boyfriends on such "task-related" dimensions as intelligence, good judgment, and leadership potential. To the extent that these items accurately represent the construct of liking, men may indeed tend to be more "likable" (but not more "lovable") than women. Table 2 also reveals, however, that there was no such sex difference with respect to the respondents' liking for their same-sex friends. The mean liking-for-friend scores for the two sexes were virtually identical. Thus, the data do not support the conclusion that men are generally more likable than women, but only that they are liked more in the context of the dating relationship.

Table 2 also indicates that women tended to *love* their same-sex friends more than men did ($t = 5.33$, $df = 314$, $p < .01$). This result is in accord with

TABLE 3 Intercorrelations among Indexes of Attraction

Index	1	2	3	4
Women				
1. Love for partner				
2. Liking for partner	.39			
3. "In love"[a]	.59	.28		
4. Marriage probability[b]	.59	.32	.65	
5. Dating length[c]	.16	.01	.27	.46
Men				
1. Love for partner				
2. Liking for partner	.60			
3. "In love"[a]	.52	.35		
4. Marriage probability[b]	.59	.35	.62	
5. Dating length[c]	.04	−.03	.22	38

Note: Based on responses of 158 couples. With an *N* of 158, a correlation of .16 is significant at the .05 level and a correlation of .21 is significant at the .01 level (two-tailed values).
[a]Responses to question, "Would you say that you and —— are in love?" scored on a 3-point scale ("No" = 0, "Uncertain" = 1, "Yes" = 2).
[b]Responses to question, "What is your best estimate of the likelihood that you and —— will marry one another?" Scale ranges from 0 (0–10% probability) to 9 (91–100% probability).
[c]The correlation across couples between the two partners' reports of the length of time they had been dating (in months) was .967. In this table, "dating length" was arbitrarily equated with the woman's estimates.

cultural stereotypes concerning male and female friendships. It is more socially acceptable for female than for male friends to speak of themselves as "loving" one another, and it has been reported that women tend to confide in same-sex friends more than men do (Jourard & Lasakow, 1958). Finally, the means presented in Table 2 show that whereas both women and men *liked* their dating partners only slightly more than they liked their same-sex friends, they *loved* their dating partners much more than their friends.

Further insight into the conceptual distinction between love and liking may be derived from the correlational results presented in Table 3. As expected, love scores were highly correlated both with respondents' reports of whether or not they were "in love" and with their estimates of the likelihood that they would marry their current dating partners. Liking scores were only moderately correlated with these indexes.

Although love scores were highly related to perceived marriage probability, these variables may be distinguished from one another on empirical as well as conceptual grounds. As Table 3 indicates, the length of time that the couple had been dating was unrelated to love scores among men, and only slightly related among women. In contrast, the respondents' perceptions of their closeness to marriage were significantly correlated with length of dating among both men and women. These results are in keeping with the common observations that although love may develop rather quickly, progress toward marriage typically occurs only over a longer period of time.

The construct validity of the love scale was further attested to by the findings that love for one's dating partner was only slightly correlated with love for one's same-sex friend ($r = .18$ for women, and $r = .15$ for men) and was uncorrelated with scores on the Marlowe-Crowne Social Desirability Scale ($r = .01$ for both women and men). These findings are consistent with the assumption that the love scale was tapping an attitude toward a specific other person, rather than more general interpersonal orientations or response tendencies. Finally, the love scores of the two partners tended to be moderately symmetrical. The correlation across couples between the woman's and the man's love was .42. The corresponding intracouple correlation with respect to liking was somewhat lower ($r = .28$). With respect to the partners' estimates of the probability of marriage, on the other hand, the intracouple correlation was considerably higher ($r = .68$).

LABORATORY EXPERIMENT: LOVE AND GAZING

Although the questionnaire results provided evidence for the construct validity of the emerging conception of romantic love, it remained to be determined whether love-scale scores could be used to predict behavior outside the realm of questionnaire responses. The notion that romantic love includes a component of exclusiveness and absorption led to the prediction that in an unstructured laboratory situation, dating partners who loved each other a great deal would gaze into one another's eyes more than would partners who loved each other to a lesser degree.

The test of the prediction involved a comparison between "strong-love" and "weak-love" couples, as categorized by their scores on the love scale. To control for the possibility that "strong" and "weak" lovers differ from one another in their more general interpersonal orientations, additional groups were included in which subjects were paired with opposite-sex strangers. The love scores of subjects in these "apart" groups were equated with those of the subjects who were paired with their own dating partners (the "together" groups). In contrast to the prediction for the together groups, no difference in the amount of eye contact engaged in by the strong-apart and weak-apart groups was expected.

METHOD

Subjects

Two pools of subjects were established from among the couples who completed the questionnaire. Those couples in which both partners scored above the median on the love scale (92 or higher) were designated "strong-love couples," and those in which both partners scored below the median were designated "weak-love couples." Couples in which one partner scored above and the other below the median were not included in the experiment. Within each of the two pools, the couples were divided into two subgroups with approximately equal love scores. One subgroup in each pool was randomly designated as a together group, the other as an apart group. Subjects in the together group were invited to take part in the experiment together with their boyfriends or girlfriends. Subjects in the apart groups were requested to appear at the experimental session individually, where they would be paired with other people's boyfriends or girlfriends. Pairings in the apart conditions were made on the basis of scheduling convenience, with the additional guideline that women should not be paired with men who were younger than themselves. In this way, four experimental groups were created: strong together (19 pairs), weak together (19 pairs), strong apart (21 pairs), and weak apart (20 pairs). Only 5 of the couples contacted (not included in the above cell sizes) refused to participate—2 who had been preassigned to the strong together group, 2 to the weak together group, and 1 to the strong apart group. No changes in the preassignment of subjects to groups were requested or permitted. As desired, none of the pairs of subjects created in the apart groups were previously acquainted. Each subject was paid $1.25 for his participation.

Sessions

When both members of a scheduled pair had arrived at the laboratory, they were seated across a 52-inch table from one another in an observation room. The experimenter, a male graduate student, explained that the experiment was part of a study of communication among dating and unacquainted couples. The subjects were then asked to read a paragraph about "a couple contemplating marriage" (one of the "choice situations" developed by Wallach and Kogan, 1959). They were told that they would subsequently discuss the case, and that their discussion would be tape recorded. The experimenter told the pair that it would take a few minutes for him to set up the tape recorder, and that meanwhile they could talk about anything except the case to be discussed. He then left the room. After 1 minute had elapsed (to allow the subjects to adapt themselves to the situation), their visual behavior was observed for a 3-minute period.[2]

Measurement

The subjects' visual behavior was recorded by two observers stationed behind a one-way mirror, one facing each subject. Each observer pressed a button, which was connected to a cumulative clock, whenever the subject he was watching was looking across the table at his partner's face. The readings

[2] Visual behavior was also observed during a subsequent 3-minute discussion period. The results for this period, which differed from those for the prediscussion waiting period, are reported in Rubin (1969, Chap. 5).

on these clocks provided measures of *individual gazing*. In addition, a third clock was activated whenever the two observers were pressing their buttons simultaneously. The reading on this clock provided a measure of *mutual gazing*. The mean percentage of agreement between pairs of observers in 12 reliability trials, interspersed among the experimental sessions, was 92.8. The observers never knew whether a pair of subjects was in a strong-love or weak-love group. They were sometimes able to infer whether the pair was in the together or the apart condition, however. Each observer's assignment alternated between watching the woman and watching the man in successive sessions.

RESULTS

Table 4 reveals that as predicted, there was a tendency for strong-together couples to engage in more mutual gazing (or "eye contact") than weak-together couples ($t = 1.52$, $p < .07$, one-tailed). Although there was also a tendency for strong-apart couples to make more eye contact than weak-apart couples, it was not a reliable one ($t = .92$).

Another approach toward assessing the couples' visual behavior is to consider the percentage of "total gazing" time (i.e., the amount of time during which at least one of the partners was looking at the other) which was occupied by mutual gazing. This measure, to be referred to as *mutual focus*, differs from mutual gazing in that it specifically takes into account the individual gazing tendencies of the two partners. It is possible, for example, that neither member of a particular pair gazed very much at his partner, but

TABLE 4 Mutual Gazing (in seconds)

Group	n	$\overline{X}$	SD
Strong together	19	56.2	17.1
Weak together	18[a]	44.7	25.0
Strong apart	21	46.7	29.6
Weak apart	20	40.0	17.5

[a]Because of an equipment failure, the mutual-gazing measure was not obtained for one couple in the weak-together group.

that when they did gaze, they did so simultaneously. Such a pair would have a low mutual gazing score, but a high mutual focus score. Within certain limits, the converse of this situation is also possible. Using this measure (see Table 5), the difference between the strong-together and the weak-together groups was more striking than it was in the case of mutual gazing ($t = 2.31$, $p < .02$, one-tailed). The difference between the strong-apart and weak-apart groups was clearly not significant ($t = .72$).

Finally, the individual gazing scores of subjects in the four experimental groups are presented in Table 6. The only significant finding was that in all groups, the women spent much more time looking at the men than the men spent looking at the women ($F = 15.38$, $df = 1/150$, $p < .01$). Although there was a tendency for strong-together subjects of both sexes to look at their partners more than weak-together subjects, these comparisons did not approach significance.

DISCUSSION

The main prediction of the experiment was confirmed. Couples who were strongly in love, as categorized by their scores on the love scale, spent more time gazing into one another's eyes than did couples who were only weakly in love. With respect to the measure of individual gazing, however, the tendency for strong-together subjects to devote more time than the weak-together subjects to looking at their partners was not substantial for either women or men. This finding suggests that the obtained difference in mutual gazing between these two groups must be attributed to differences in the *simultaneousness*, rather than in the sheer quantity, of gazing. This conclusion is bolstered by the fact that the clearest difference between the strong-together and weak-together groups emerged on the percentage measure of mutual focus.

TABLE 5   Mutual Focus

Group	n	$\bar{X}$	SD
Strong together	19	44.0	9.8
Weak together	18	34.7	14.0
Strong apart	21	35.3	14.6
Weak apart	20	32.5	9.4

Note: Mutual focus = $100 \times \dfrac{\text{mutual gazing}}{\text{woman's nonmutual gazing + man's nonmutual gazing + mutual gazing}}$

This pattern of results is in accord with the assumption that gazing is a manifestation of the exclusive and absorptive component of romantic love. Freud (1955) maintained that "The more [two people] are in love, the more completely they suffice for each other [p. 140]." More recently, Slater (1963) has linked Freud's theory of love to the popular concept of "the oblivious lovers, who are 'all wrapped up in each other,' and somewhat careless of their social obligations [p. 349]." One way in which this oblivious absorption may be manifested is through eye contact. As the popular song has it, "Millions of people go by, but they all disappear from view—'cause I only have eyes for you."

Another possible explanation for the findings is that people who are in love (or who complete attitude scales in such a way as to indicate that they are in love) are also the sort of people who are most predisposed to make eye contact with others, regardless of whether or not those others are the people they are in love with. The inclusion of the apart groups helped to rule out this possibility, however. Although there was a slight tendency for strong-apart couples to engage in more eye contact than weak-apart couples (see Table 5), it fell far short of significance. Moreover, when the percentage measure of mutual focus was employed (see Table 6), this difference virtually disappeared. It should be noted that no predictions were made con-

TABLE 6 Individual Gazing (in seconds)

Group	Women			Men		
	n	$\bar{X}$	SD	n	$\bar{X}$	SD
Strong together	19	98.7	23.2	19	83.7	20.2
Weak together	19	87.4	30.4	19	77.7	33.1
Strong apart	21	94.5	39.7	21	75.0	39.3
Weak apart	20	96.8	27.8	20	64.0	25.2

cerning the comparisons between strong-together and strong-apart couples or between weak-together and weak-apart couples. It seemed plausible that unacquainted couples might make use of a relatively large amount of eye contact as a means of getting acquainted. The results indicate, in fact, that subjects in the apart groups typically engaged in as much eye contact as those in the weak-together group, with the strong-together subjects outgazing the other three groups. Future studies which systematically vary the extent to which partners are acquainted would be useful in specifying the acquaintance-seeking functions of eye contact.

The finding that in all experimental groups, women spent more time looking at men than vice versa may reflect the frequently reported tendency of women to specialize in the "social-emotional" aspects of interaction (e.g., Strodtbeck & Mann, 1956). Gazing may serve as a vehicle of emotional expression for women and, in addition, may allow women to obtain cues from their male partners concerning the appropriateness of their behavior. The present result is in accord with earlier findings that women tend to make more eye contact than men in same-sex groups (Exline, 1963) and in an interview situation, regardless of the sex of the interviewer (Exline, Gray, & Schuette, 1965).

CONCLUSION

"So far as love or affection is concerned," Harlow wrote in 1958, "psychologists have failed in their mission. The little we know about love does not transcend simple observation, and the little we write about it has been written better by poets and novelists [p. 673]." The research reported in this paper represents an attempt to improve this situation by introducing and validating a preliminary social-psychological conception of romantic love. A distinction was drawn between love and liking, and its reasonableness was attested to by the results of the questionnaire study. It was found, for example, that respondents' estimates of the likelihood that they would marry their partners were more highly related to their love than to their liking for their partners. In light of the culturally prescribed association between love and marriage (but not necessarily between liking and marriage), this pattern of correlations seems appropriate. Other findings of the questionnaire study, to be reported elsewhere, point to the value of a measurable construct of romantic love as a link between the individual and social-structural levels of analysis of social behavior.

Although the present investigation was aimed at developing a unitary conception of romantic love, a promising direction for future research is the attempt to distinguish among patterns of romantic love relationships. One theoretical basis for such distinctions is the nature of the interpersonal rewards exchanged between partners (cf. Wright, 1969). The attitudes and behaviors of romantic love may differ, for example, depending on whether the most salient rewards exchanged are those of security or those of stimulation (cf. Maslow's discussion of "Deficiency Love" and "Being Love," 1955). Some of the behavioral variables which might be focused on in the attempt to distinguish among such patterns are in the areas of sexual behavior, helping, and self-disclosure.

REFERENCES

Banta, T. J., & Hetherington, M. "Relations between Needs of Friends and Fiancees." *Journal of Abnormal and Social Psychology*, 66, (1963), 401–404.

Campbell, D. T., "Recommendations for APA Test Standards Regarding Construct, Trait, and Discriminant Validity," *American Psychologist*, 15, (1960), 546–553.

Cronbach, L. J., & Meehl, P. E., "Construct Validity in Psychological Tests," *Psychological Bulletin*, 52, (1955), 281–302.

De Rougemont, D., *Love in the Western World*, New York: Harcourt, Brace, 1940.

Exline, R. V., "Explorations in the Process of Person Perception: Visual Interaction in Relation to Competition, Sex, and Need for Affiliation," *Journal of Personality*, 31, (1963), 1–20.

Exline, R., Gray, D., & Schuette, D., "Visual Behavior in a Dyad as Affected by Interview Content and Sex of Respondent," *Journal of Personality and Social Psychology*, 1, (1965), 201–209.

Freud, S., "Group Psychology and the Analysis of the Ego," in, *The Standard Edition of the Complete Psychological Works of Sigmund Freud*, Vol. 18. London: Hogarth, 1955.

Fromm, E., *The Art of Loving*, New York: Harper, 1956.

Goode, W. J., "The Theoretical Importance of Love," *American Sociological Review*, 24, (1959), 38–47.

Harlow, H. F., "The Nature of Love," *American Psychologist*, 13, (1958), 673–685.

Heider, F., *The Psychology of Interpersonal Relations*, New York: Wiley, 1958.

Jourard, S. M., & Lasakow, P., "Some Factors in Self-Disclosure," *Journal of Abnormal and Social Psychology*, 56, (1958), 91–98.

Lindzey, G., & Byrne, D., "Measurement of Social Choice and Interpersonal Attractiveness," in G. Lindzey & Aronson, eds., *Handbook of Social Psychology*. Vol. 2. (2nd ed.), Reading, Mass.: Addison-Wesley, 1968.

Maslow, A. H., "Deficiency Motivation and Growth Motivation," *Nebraska Symposium on Motivation*, 2, 1955.

Newcomb, T. M., "The Varieties of Interpersonal Attraction," in D. Cartwright & A. Zander, eds., *Group Dynamics*, (2nd ed.), Evanston: Row, Peterson, 1960.

Orlinsky, D. E., "Love Relationships in the Life Cycle: A Developmental Inter-
   personal Perspective," unpublished manuscript, University of Chicago, 1970.
Rubin, Z. *The Social Psychology of Romantic Love*, Ann Arbor, Mich.: Uni-
   versity Microfilms, 1969, No. 70–4179.
Slater, P. E., "On Social Regression," *American Sociological Review,* 28,
   (1963), 339–364.
Strodtbeck, F. L., & Mann, R. D., "Sex Role Differentiation in Jury Delibera-
   tions," *Sociometry*, 19, (1956), 3–11.
Wallach, M. A., & Kogan, N., "Sex Differences and Judgment Processes,"
   Journal of Personality, 27, (1959), 555–564.
Walster, E., "The Effect of Self-Esteem on Romantic Liking," *Journal of Experi-
   mental Social Psychology*, 1, (1965), 184–197.
Wright, P. H., "A Model and a Technique for Studies of Friendship,"*Journal of
   Experimental Social Psychology*, 5, (1969), 295–309.

| 10 | *The Theoretical Importance of Love* |

WILLIAM J. GOODE

Because love often determines the intensity of an attraction[1] toward or
away from an intimate relationship with another person, it can become one
element in a decision or action.[2] Nevertheless, serious sociological attention
has only infrequently been given to love. Moreover, analyses of love generally have been confined to mate choice in the Western World, while the
structural importance of love has been for the most part ignored. The present
paper views love in a broad perspective, focusing on the structural patterns

[1] On the psychological level, the motivational power of both love and sex
is intensified by this curious fact (which I have not seen remarked on elsewhere): Love is the most projective of emotions, as sex is the most projective
of drives; only with great difficulty can the attracted person believe that the
object of his love or passion does not and will not reciprocate the feeling
at all. Thus, the person may carry his action quite far, before accepting a
rejection as genuine.

[2] I have treated decision analysis extensively in an unpublished paper by
that title.

This paper was completed under a grant (No. M-2526-S) by the National
Institute of Mental Health.
   Reprinted from the *American Sociological Review*, 24 (February, 1959),
39–47, by permission of the American Sociological Association.

by which societies keep in check the potentially disruptive effect of love relationships on mate choice and stratification systems.

TYPES OF LITERATURE ON LOVE

For obvious reasons, the printed material on love is immense. For our present purposes, it may be classified as follows:

1. Poetic, humanistic, literary, erotic, pornographic: By far the largest body of all literature on love views it as a sweeping experience. The poet arouses our sympathy and empathy. The essayist enjoys, and asks the reader to enjoy, the interplay of people in love. The storyteller—Boccaccio, Chaucer, Dante—pulls back the curtain of human souls and lets the reader watch the intimate lives of others caught in an emotion we all know. Others— Vatsyayana, Ovid, William IX Count of Poitiers and Duke of Aquitaine, Marie de France, Andreas Capellanus—have written how-to-do-it books, that is, how to conduct oneself in love relations, to persuade others to succumb to one's love wishes, or to excite and satisfy one's sex partner.[3]

2. Marital counseling: Many modern sociologists have commented on the importance of romantic love in America and its lesser importance in other societies, and have disparaged it as a poor basis for marriage, or as immaturity. Perhaps the best known of these arguments are those of Ernest R. Mowrer, Ernest W. Burgess, Mabel A. Elliott, Andrew G. Truxal, Francis E. Merrill, and Ernest R. Groves.[4] The antithesis of romantic love, in such analyses, is "conjugal" love; the love between a settled, domestic couple.

A few sociologists, remaining within this same evaluative context, have instead claimed that love also has salutary effects in our society. Thus, for example, William L. Kolb[5] has tried to demonstrate that the marital counselors who attack romantic love are really attacking some fundamental values of our larger society, such as individualism, freedom, and personality growth. Beigel[6] has argued that if the female is sexually repressed, only the psycho-

[3] Vatsyayana, *The Kama Sutra*, Delhi: Rajkamal, 1948; Ovid, "The Loves," and "Remedies of Love," in *The Art of Love*, Cambridge, Mass.: Harvard University Press, 1939; Andreas Capellanus, *The Art of Courtly Love*, translated by John Parry, New York: Columbia University Press, 1941; Paul Tuffrau, ed., *Marie de France: Les Lais de Marie de France*, Paris: L'edition d'Art, 1925; see also Julian Harris, *Marie de France*, New York: Institute of French Studies, 1930, especially Chap. 3. All authors but the first *also* had the goal of writing literature.

[4] Ernest R. Mowrer, *Family Disorganization*, Chicago: The University of Chicago Press, 1927, pp. 158–165; Ernest W. Burgess and Harvey J. Locke, *The Family*, New York: American Book, 1953, pp. 436–437; Mabel A. Elliott and Francis E. Merrill, *Social Disorganization*, New York: Harper, 1950, pp. 366– 384; Andrew G. Truxal and Francis E. Merrill, *The Family in American Culture*, New York: Prentice-Hall, 1947, pp. 120–124, 507–509; Ernest R. Groves and Gladys Hoagland Groves, *The Contemporary American Family*, New York: Lippincott, 1947, pp. 321–324.

[5] William L. Kolb, "Sociologically Established Norms and Democratic Values," *Social Forces*, 26 (May, 1948), 451–456.

[6] Hugo G. Beigel, "Romantic Love," *American Sociological Review*, 16 (June, 1951), pp. 326–334.

therapist or love can help her overcome her inhibitions. He claims further that one influence of love in our society is that it extenuates illicit sexual relations; he goes on to assert: "Seen in proper perspective, [love] has not only done no harm as a prerequisite to marriage, but it has mitigated the impact that a too-fast-moving and unorganized conversion to new socio-economic constellations has had upon our whole culture and it has saved monogamous marriage from complete disorganization."

In addition, there is widespread comment among marriage analysts, that in a rootless society, with few common bases for companionship, romantic love holds a couple together long enough to allow them to begin marriage. That is, it functions to attract people powerfully together, and to hold them through the difficult first months of the marriage, when their different backgrounds would otherwise make an adjustment troublesome.

3. Although the writers cited above concede the structural importance of love implicitly, since they are arguing that it is either harmful or helpful to various values and goals of our society, a third group has given explicit if unsystematic attention to its structural importance. Here, most of the available propositions point to the functions of love, but a few deal with the conditions under which love relationships occur. They include:

(1) An implicit or assumed descriptive proposition is that love as a common prelude to and basis of marriage is rare, perhaps to be found as a pattern only in the United States.

(2) Most explanations of the conditions which create love are psychological, stemming from Freud's notion that love is "aim-inhibited sex."[7] This idea is expressed, for example, by Waller who says that love is an idealized passion which develops from the frustration of sex.[8] This proposition, although rather crudely stated and incorrect as a general explanation, is widely accepted.

(3) Of course, a predisposition to love is created by the socialization experience. Thus some textbooks on the family devote extended discussion to the ways in which our society socializes for love. The child, for example, is told that he or she will grow up to fall in love with some one, and early attempts are made to pair the child with children of the opposite sex. There is much joshing of children about falling in love; myths and stories about love and courtship are heard by children; and so on.

(4) A further proposition (the source of which I have not been able to locate) is that, in a society in which a very close attachment between parent and child prevails, a love complex is necessary in order to motivate the child to free him from his attachment to his parents.

(5) Love is also described as one final or crystallizing element in the decision to marry, which is otherwise structured by factors such as class, ethnic origin, religion, education, and residence.

(6) Parsons has suggested three factors which "underlie the prominence of the romantic context in our culture": (a) the youth culture frees the individual from family attachments, thus permitting him to fall in love; (b) love is

[7] Sigmund Freud, *Group Psychology and the Analysis of the Ego*, London: Hogarth, 1922, p. 72.
[8] Willard Waller, *The Family*, New York: Dryden, 1938, pp. 189–192.

a substitute for the interlocking of kinship roles found in other societies, and thus motivates the individual to conform to proper marital role behavior; and (c) the structural isolation of the family so frees the married partners' affective inclinations that they are able to love one another.[9]

(7) Robert F. Winch has developed a theory of "complementary needs" which essentially states that the underlying dynamic in the process of falling in love is an interaction between (a) the perceived psychological attributes of one individual and (b) the complementary psychological attributes of the person falling in love, such that the needs of the latter are felt to be met by the perceived attributes of the former and vice versa. These needs are derived from Murray's list of personality characteristics. Winch thus does not attempt to solve the problem of why our society has a love complex, but how it is that specific individuals fall in love with each other rather than with someone else.[10]

(8) Winch and others have also analyzed the effect of love upon various institutions or social patterns: Love themes are prominently displayed in the media of entertainment and communication, in consumption patterns, and so on.[11]

4. Finally, there is the cross-cultural work of anthropologists, who in the main have ignored love as a factor of importance in kinship patterns. The implicit understanding seems to be that love as a pattern is found only in the United States, although of course individual cases of love are sometimes recorded. The term "love" is practically never found in indexes of anthropological monographs on specific societies or in general anthropology textbooks. It is perhaps not an exaggeration to say that Lowie's comment of a generation ago would still be accepted by a substantial number of anthropologists:

> But of love among savages? . . . Passion, of course, is taken for granted; affection, which many travelers vouch for, might be conceded; but Love? Well, the romantic sentiment occurs in simpler conditions, as with us— in fiction. . . . So Love exists for the savage as it does for ourselves—in adolescence, in fiction, among the poetically minded.[12]

A still more skeptical opinion is Linton's scathing sneer:

> All societies recognize that there are occasional violent, emotional attachments between persons of opposite sex, but our present American culture is practically the only one which has attempted to capitalize these, and make them the basis for marriage. . . . The hero of the modern American movie is always a romantic lover, just as the hero of the old Arab epic is always an epileptic. A cynic may suspect that in any ordinary

[9] Talcott Parsons, *Essays in Sociological Theory*, Glencoe, Ill.: Free Press, 1949, pp. 187–189.
[10] Robert F. Winch, *Mate Selection*, New York: Harper, 1958.
[11] See, e.g., Robert F. Winch, *The Modern Family*, New York: Holt, 1952, Chap. 14.
[12] Robert H. Lowie, "Sex and Marriage," in John F. McDermott, ed., *The Sex Problem in Modern Society*, New York: Modern Library, 1931, p. 146.

population the percentage of individuals with a capacity for romantic love of the Hollywood type was about as large as that of persons able to throw genuine epileptic fits.[13]

In Murdock's book on kinship and marriage, there is almost no mention, if any, of love.[14] Should we therefore conclude that, cross-culturally, love is not important, and thus cannot be of great importance structurally? If there is only one significant case, perhaps it is safe to view love as generally unimportant in social structure and to concentrate rather on the nature and functions of romantic love within the Western societies in which love is obviously prevalent. As brought out below, however, many anthropologists have in fact described love *patterns*. And one of them, Max Gluckman,[15] has recently subsumed a wide range of observations under the broad principle that love relationships between husband and wife estrange the couple from their kin, who therefore try in various ways to undermine that love. This principle is applicable to many more societies (for example, China and India) than Gluckman himself discusses.

THE PROBLEM AND ITS CONCEPTUAL CLARIFICATION

The preceding propositions (except those denying that love is distributed widely) can be grouped under two main questions: What are the consequences of romantic love in the United States? How is the emotion of love aroused or created in our society? The present paper deals with the first question. For theoretical purposes both questions must be reformulated, however, since they implicitly refer only to our peculiar system of romantic love. Thus: (1) In what ways do various love patterns fit into the social structure, especially into the systems of mate choice and stratification? (2) What are the structural conditions under which a range of love patterns occurs in various societies? These are overlapping questions, but their starting point and assumptions are different. The first assumes that love relationships are a universal psychosocial possibility, and that different social systems make different adjustments to their potential disruptiveness. The second does not take love for granted, and supposes rather that such relationships will be rare unless certain structural factors are present. Since in both cases the analysis need not depend upon the correctness of the assumption, the problem may be chosen arbitrarily. Let us begin with the first.[16]

We face at once the problem of defining "love." Here, love is defined as a strong emotional attachment, a cathexis, between adolescents or adults of opposite sexes, with at least the components of sex desire and tenderness. Verbal definitions of this emotional relationship are notoriously open to attack; this one is no more likely to satisfy critics than others. Agreement

[13] Ralph Linton, *The Study of Man*, New York: Appleton-Century, 1936, p. 175.

[14] George Peter Murdock, *Social Structure*, New York: Macmillan, 1949.

[15] Max Gluckman, *Custom and Conflict in Africa*, Oxford: Basil Blackwell, 1955, Chap. 3.

[16] I hope to deal with the second problem in another paper.

is made difficult by value judgments: one critic would exclude anything but "true" love, another casts out "infatuation," another objects to "puppy love," while others would separate sex desire from love because sex presumably is degrading. Nevertheless, most of us have had the experience of love, just as we have been greedy, or melancholy, or moved by hate (defining "true" hate seems not to be a problem). The experience can be referred to without great ambiguity, and a refined measure of various degrees of intensity or purity of love is unnecessary for the aims of the present analysis.

Since love may be related in diverse ways to the social structure, it is necessary to forego the dichotomy of "romantic love—no romantic love" in favor of a continuum or range between polar types. At one pole, a strong love attraction is socially viewed as a laughable or tragic aberration; at the other, it is mildly shameful to marry without being in love with one's intended spouse. This is a gradation from negative sanction to positive approval, ranging at the same time from low or almost nonexistent institutionalization of love to high institutionalization.

The urban middle classes of contemporary Western society, especially in the United States, are found toward the latter pole. Japan and China, in spite of the important movement toward European patterns, fall toward the pole of low institutionalization. Village and urban India is farther toward the center, for there the ideal relationship has been one which at least generated love after marriage, and sometimes after betrothal, in contrast with the mere respect owed between Japanese and Chinese spouses.[17] Greece after Alexander, Rome of the Empire, and perhaps the later period of the Roman Republic as well, are near the center, but somewhat toward the pole of institutionalization, for love matches appear to have increased in frequency—a trend denounced by moralists.[18]

This conceptual continuum helps to clarify our problem and to interpret the propositions reviewed above. Thus it may be noted, first, that individual love relationships may occur even in societies in which love is viewed as irrelevant to mate choice and excluded from the decision to marry. As Linton conceded, some violent love attachments may be found in any society. In our own, the Song of Solomon, Jacob's love of Rachel, and Michal's love for David are classic tales. The Mahabharata, the great Indian epic, includes love themes. Romantic love appears early in Japanese literature, and the use of Mt. Fuji as a locale for the suicide of star crossed lovers is not a myth invented by editors of tabloids. There is the familiar tragic Chinese

[17] Tribal India, of course, is too heterogeneous to place in any one position on such a continuum. The question would have to be answered for each tribe. Obviously it is of less importance here whether China and Japan, in recent decades, have moved "two points over" toward the opposite pole of high approval of love relationships as a basis for marriage than that both systems as classically described viewed love as generally a tragedy; and love was supposed to be irrelevant to marriage, i.e., noninstitutionalized. The continuum permits us to place a system at some position, once we have the descriptive data.

[18] See Ludwig Friedländer, *Roman Life and Manners under the Early Empire* (7th ed.), translated by A. Magnus, New York: Dutton, 1908, Vol. 1, Chap. 5, "The Position of Women."

story to be found on the traditional "willowplate," with its lovers transformed into doves. And so it goes—individual love relationships seem to occur everywhere. But this fact does not change the position of a society on the continuum.

Second, reading both Linton's and Lowie's comments in this new conceptual context reduces their theoretical importance, for they are both merely saying that people do not *live by* the romantic complex, here or anywhere else. Some few couples in love will brave social pressures, physical dangers, or the gods themselves, but nowhere is this usual. Violent, self-sufficient love is not common anywhere. In this respect, of course, the U.S. is not set apart from other systems.

Third, we can separate a *love pattern* from the romantic love *complex*. Under the former, love is a permissible, expected prelude to marriage, and a usual element of courtship—thus, at about the center of the continuum, but toward the pole of institutionalization. The romantic love complex (one pole of the continuum) includes, in addition, an ideological prescription that falling in love is a highly desirable basis of courtship and marriage; love is strongly institutionalized.[19] In contemporary United States, many individuals would even claim that entering marriage without being in love requires some such rationalization as asserting that one is too old for such romances or that one must "think of practical matters like money." To be sure, both anthropologists and sociologists often exaggerate the American commitment to romance;[20] nevertheless, a behavioral and value complex of this type is found here.

But this complex is rare. Perhaps only the following cultures possess the romantic love value complex: modern urban United States, Northwestern Europe, Polynesia, and the European nobility of the eleventh and twelfth centuries.[21] Certainly, it is to be found in no other major civilization. On the other hand, the *love pattern*, which views love as a basis for the final decision to marry, may be relatively common.

[19] For a discussion of the relation between behavior patterns and the process of institutionalization, see my *After Divorce*, Glencoe, Ill.: Free Press, 1956, Chap. 15.

[20] See Ernest W. Burgess and Paul W. Wallin, *Engagement and Marriage*, New York: Lippincott, 1953, Chap. 7 for the extent to which even the engaged are not blind to the defects of their beloveds. No one has ascertained the degree to which various age and sex groups in our society actually believe in some form of the ideology.

Similarly, Margaret Mead in *Coming of Age in Samoa*, New York: Modern Library, 1953, rates Manu'an love as shallow, and though these Samoans give much attention to love-making, she asserts that they laughed with incredulous contempt at Romeo and Juliet (pp. 155–156). Though the individual sufferer showed jealousy and anger, the Manu'ans believed that a new love would quickly cure a betrayed lover (pp. 105–108). It is possible that Mead failed to understand the shallowness of love in our own society: Romantic love is, "in our civilization, inextricably bound up with ideas of monogamy, exclusiveness, jealousy, and undeviating fidelity" (p. 105). But these are *ideas* and ideology; *behavior* is rather different.

[21] I am preparing an analysis of this case. The relation of "courtly love" to social structure is complicated.

WHY LOVE MUST BE CONTROLLED

Since strong love attachments apparently can occur in any society and since (as we shall show) love is frequently a basis for and prelude to marriage, it must be controlled or channeled in some way. More specifically, the stratification and lineage patterns would be weakened greatly if love's potentially disruptive effects were not kept in check. The importance of this situation may be seen most clearly by considering one of the major functions of the family, status placement, which in every society links the structures of stratification, kinship lines, and mate choice. (To show how the very similar comments which have been made about sex are not quite correct would take us too far afield; in any event, to the extent that they are correct, the succeeding analysis applies equally to the control of sex.)

Both the child's placement in the social structure and choice of mates are socially important because both placement and choice link two kinship lines together. Courtship or mate choice, therefore, cannot be ignored by either family or society. To permit random mating would mean radical change in the existing social structure. If the family as a unit of society is important, then mate choice is too.

Kinfolk or immediate family can disregard the question of who marries whom, only if a marriage is not seen as a link between kin lines, only if no property, power, lineage honor, totemic relationships, and the like are believed to flow from the kin lines through the spouses to their offspring. Universally, however, these are believed to follow kin lines. Mate choice thus has consequences for the social structure. But love may affect mate choice. Both mate choice and love, therefore, are too important to be left to children.

THE CONTROL OF LOVE

Since considerable energy and resources may be required to push youngsters who are in love into proper role behavior, love must be controlled *before* it appears. Love relationships must either be kept to a small number or they must be so directed that they do not run counter to the approved kinship linkages. There are only a few institutional patterns by which this control is achieved.

1. Certainly the simplest, and perhaps the most widely used, structural pattern for coping with this problem is child marriage. If the child is betrothed, married, or both before he has had any opportunity to interact intimately as an adolescent with other children, then he has no resources with which to oppose the marriage. He cannot earn a living, he is physically weak, and is socially dominated by his elders. Moreover, strong love attachments occur only rarely before puberty. An example of this pattern was to be found in India, where the young bride went to live with her husband in a marriage which was not physically consummated until much later, within his father's household.[22]

[22] Frieda M. Das, *Purdah*, New York: Vanguard, 1932; Kingsley Davis, *The Population of India and Pakistan*, Princeton: Princeton University Press, 1951, p. 112. There was a widespread custom of taking one's bride from a village other than one's own.

2. Often, child marriage is linked with a second structural pattern, in which the kinship rules define rather closely a class of eligible future spouses. The marriage is determined by birth within narrow limits. Here, the major decision, which is made by elders, is *when* the marriage is to occur. Thus, among the Murngin, *galle*, the father's sister's child is scheduled to marry *due*, the mother's brother's child.[23] In the case of the "four-class" double-descent system, each individual is a member of *both* a matri-moiety and a patri-moiety and must marry someone who belongs to neither; the four-classes are (1) ego's own class, (2) those whose matri-moiety is the same as ego's but whose patri-moiety is different, (3) those who are in ego's patri-moiety but not in his matri-moiety, and (4) those who are in neither of ego's moieties, that is, who are in the cell diagonally from his own.[24] Problems arise at times under these systems if the appropriate kinship cell—for example, parallel cousin or cross-cousin—is empty.[25] But nowhere, apparently, is the definition so rigid as to exclude some choice and, therefore, some dickering, wrangling, and haggling between the elders of the two families.

3. A society can prevent widespread development of adolescent love relationships by socially isolating young people from potential mates, whether eligible or ineligible as spouses. Under such a pattern, elders can arrange the marriages of either children or adolescents with little likelihood that their plans will be disrupted by love attachments. Obviously, this arrangement cannot operate effectively in most primitive societies, where youngsters see one another rather frequently.[26]

Not only is this pattern more common in civilizations than in primitive societies, but is found more frequently in the upper social strata. *Social segregation* is difficult unless it is supported by physical segregation—the harem of Islam, the zenana of India[27]—or by a large household system with individuals whose duty it is to supervise nubile girls. Social segregation is thus expensive. Perhaps the best known example of simple social segregation was found in China, where youthful marriages took place between

[23] W. Lloyd Warner, *Black Civilization*, New York: Harper, 1937, pp. 82–84. They may also become "sweethearts" at puberty; see pp. 86–89.

[24] See Murdock, op. cit., pp. 53 ff. *et passim* for discussions of double-descent.

[25] One adjustment in Australia was for the individuals to leave the tribe for a while, usually eloping, and then to return "reborn" under a different and now appropriate kinship designation. In any event, these marital prescriptions did not prevent love entirely. As Malinowski shows in his early summary of the Australian family systems, although every one of the tribes used the technique of infant betrothal (and close prescription of mate), no tribe was free of elopements, between either the unmarried or the married, and the "motive of sexual love" was always to be found in marriages by elopement. B. Malinowski. *The Family Among the Australian Aborigines*, London: University of London Press, 1913, p. 83.

[26] This pattern was apparently achieved in Manus, where on first menstruation the girl was removed from her playmates and kept at "home"—on stilts over a lagoon—under the close supervision of elders. The Manus were prudish, and love occurred rarely or never. Margaret Mead, *Growing Up in New Guinea*, in *From the South Seas*, New York: Morrow, 1939, pp. 163–166, 208.

[27] See Das, op. cit.

young people who had not previously met because they lived in different villages; they could not marry fellow-villagers since ideally almost all inhabitants belonged to the same *tsu*.[28]

It should be emphasized that the primary function of physical or social isolation in these cases is to minimize informal or intimate social interaction. Limited social contacts of a highly ritualized or formal type in the presence of elders, as in Japan, have a similar, if less extreme, result.[29]

4. A fourth type of pattern seems to exist, although it is not clear cut; and specific cases shade off toward types three and five. Here, there is close supervision by duennas or close relatives, but not actual social segregation. A high value is placed on female chastity (which perhaps is the case in every major civilization until its "decadence") viewed either as the product of self-restraint, as among the 17th Century Puritans, or as a marketable commodity. Thus love as play is not developed; marriage is supposed to be considered by the young as a duty and a possible family alliance. This pattern falls between types three and five because love is permitted before marriage, but only between eligibles. Ideally, it occurs only between a betrothed couple, and, except as marital love, there is no encouragement for it to appear at all. Family elders largely make the specific choice of mate, whether or not intermediaries carry out the arrangements. In the preliminary stages youngsters engage in courtship under supervision, with the understanding that this will permit the development of affection prior to marriage.

I do not believe that the empirical data show where this pattern is prevalent, outside of Western Civilization. The West is a special case, because of its peculiar relationship to Christianity, in which from its earliest days in Rome there has been a complex tension between asceticism and love. This type of limited love marked French, English, and Italian upper class family life from the 11th to the 14th Centuries, as well as 17th Century Puritanism in England and New England.[30]

5. The fifth type of pattern permits or actually encourages love relation-

[28] For the activities of the *tsu*, see Hsien Chin Hu, *The Common Descent Group in China and Its Functions*, New York: Viking Fund Studies in Anthropology, 10 (1948). For the marriage process, see Marion J. Levy, *The Family Revolution in Modern China*, Cambridge: Harvard University Press, 1949, pp. 87–107. See also Olga Lang, *Chinese Family and Society*, New Haven: Yale University Press, 1946, for comparisons between the old and new systems. In one-half of 62 villages in Ting Hsien Experimental District in Hopei, the largest clan included 50 per cent of the families; in 25 per cent of the villages, the two largest clans held over 90 per cent of the families; I am indebted to Robert M. Marsh who has been carrying out a study of Ching mobility partly under my direction for this reference: F. C. H. Lee, *Ting Hsien, She-hui K'ai-K'uang t'iao-ch'a*, Peiping: Chung-hua p'ing-min Chiao-yu ts'u-chin hui, 1932, p. 54. See also Sidney Gamble, *Ting Hsien: A North China Rural Community*, New York: International Secretariat of the Institute of Pacific Relations, 1954.

[29] For Japan, see Shidzué Ishimoto, *Facing Two Ways*, New York: Farrar and Rinehart, 1935, Chaps. 6, 8; John F. Embree, *Suye Mura*, Chicago: University of Chicago Press, 1950, Chaps. 3, 6.

[30] I do not mean, of course, to restrict this pattern to these times and places, but I am more certain of these. For the Puritans, see Edmund S. Morgan, *The Puritan Family*, Boston: Public Library, 1944. For the somewhat

ships, and love is a commonly expected element in mate choice. Choice in this system is *formally* free. In their 'teens youngsters begin their love play, with or without consummating sexual intercourse, within a group of peers. They may at times choose love partners whom they and others do not consider suitable spouses. Gradually, however, their range of choice is narrowed and eventually their affections center on one individual. This person is likely to be more eligible as a mate according to general social norms, and as judged by peers and parents, than the average individual with whom the youngster formerly indulged in love play.

For reasons that are not yet clear, this pattern is nearly always associated with a strong development of an adolescent peer group system, although the latter may occur without the love pattern. One source of social control, then, is the individual's own 'teen age companions, who persistently rate the present and probable future accomplishments of each individual.[31]

Another source of control lies with the parents of both boy and girl. In our society, parents threaten, cajole, wheedle, bribe, and persuade their children to "go with the right people," during both the early love play and later courtship phases.[32] Primarily, they seek to control love relationships by influencing the informal social contacts of their children: moving to appropriate neighborhoods and schools, giving parties and helping to make out invitation lists, by making their children aware that certain individuals have ineligibility traits (race, religion, manners, tastes, clothing, and so on). Since youngsters fall in love with those with whom they associate, control over informal relationships also controls substantially the focus of affection. The results of such control are well known and are documented in the more than one hundred studies of homogamy in this country: most marriages take place between couples in the same class, religious, racial, and educational levels.

As Robert Wikman has shown in a generally unfamiliar (in the United States) but superb investigation, this pattern was found among 18th Century

---

different practices in New York, see Charles E. Ironside, *The Family in Colonial New York*, New York: Columbia University Press, 1942. See also: A. Abram, *English Life and Manners in the Later Middle Ages*, New York: Dutton, 1913, Chaps. 4, 10; Emily J. Putnam, *The Lady*, New York: Sturgis and Walton, 1910, Chapter 4; James Gairdner, ed., *The Paston Letters, 1422–1509*, 4 vols., London: Arber, 1872–1875; Eileen Power, "The Position of Women," in C. G. Crump and E. F. Jacobs, eds., *The Legacy of the Middle Ages*, Oxford: Clarendon, 1926, pp. 414–416.

[31] For those who believe that the young in the United States are totally deluded by love, or believe that love outranks every other consideration, see: Ernest W. Burgess and Paul W. Wallin, *Engagement and Marriage*, New York: Lippincott, 1953, pp. 217–238. Note Karl Robert V. Wikman, *Die Einleitung Der Ehe. Acta Academiae Aboensis (Humaniora)*, 11 (1937), pp. 127 ff. Not only are reputations known because of close association among peers, but songs and poetry are sometimes composed about the girl or boy. Cf., for the Tikopia, Raymond Firth, *We, the Tikopia*, New York: American Book, 1936, pp. 468 ff.; for the Siuai, Douglas L. Oliver, *Solomon Island Society*, Cambridge: Harvard University Press, 1955, pp. 146 ff. The Manu'ans made love in groups of three or four couples; cf. Mead, *Coming of Age in Samoa*, op. cit., p. 92.

[32] Marvin B. Sussman, "Parental Participation in Mate Selection and Its Effect upon Family Continuity," *Social Forces*, 32 (October, 1953), 76–81.

Swedish farmer adolescents, was widely distributed in other Germanic areas, and extends in time from the 19th Century back to almost certainly the late Middle Ages.[33] In these cases, sexual intercourse was taken for granted, social contact was closely supervised by the peer group, and final consent to marriage was withheld or granted by the parents who owned the land.

Such cases are not confined to Western society. Polynesia exhibits a similar pattern, with some variation from society to society, the best known examples of which are perhaps Mead's Manu'ans and Firth's Tikopia.[34] Probably the most familiar Melanesian cases are the Trobriands and Dobu,[35] where the systems resemble those of the Kiwai Papuans of the Trans-Fly and the Siuai Papuans of the Solomon Islands.[36] Linton found this pattern among the Tanala.[37] Although Radcliffe-Brown holds that the pattern is not common in Africa, it is clearly found among the Nuer, the Kgatla (Tswana-speaking), and the Bavenda (here, without sanctioned sexual intercourse).[38]

A more complete classification, making use of the distinctions suggested in this paper, would show, I believe, that a large minority of known societies exhibit this pattern. I would suggest, moreover, that such a study would reveal that the degree to which love is a usual, expected prelude to marriage is correlated with (1) the degree of free choice of mate permitted in the society and (2) the degree to which husband-wife solidarity is the strategic solidarity of the kinship structure.[39]

[33] Wikman, op. cit.

[34] Mead, *Coming of Age in Samoa*, op. cit., pp. 97–108; and Firth, op. cit., pp. 520 ff.

[35] Thus Malinowski notes in his "Introduction" to Reo F. Fortune's *The Sorcerers of Dobu*, London: Routledge, 1932, p. xxiii, that the Dobu have similar patterns, the same type of courtship by trial and error, with a gradually tightening union.

[36] Gunnar Landtman, *Kiwai Papuans of the Trans-Fly*, London: Macmillan, 1927, pp. 243 ff.; Oliver, op. cit., pp. 153 ff.

[37] The pattern apparently existed among the Marquesans as well, but since Linton never published a complete description of this Polynesian society, I omit it here. His fullest analysis, cluttered with secondary interpretations, is in Abram Kardiner, *Psychological Frontiers of Society*, New York: Columbia University Press, 1945. For the Tanala, see Ralph Linton, *The Tanala*, Chicago: Field Museum, 1933, pp. 300–303.

[38] Thus, Radcliffe-Brown: "The African does not think of marriage as a union based on romantic love, although beauty as well as character and health are sought in the choice of a wife," in his "Introduction" to A. R. Radcliffe-Brown and W. C. Daryll Ford, eds., *African Systems of Kinship and Marriage*, London: Oxford University Press, 1950, p. 46. For the Nuer, see E. E. Evans-Pritchard, *Kinship and Marriage Among the Nuer*, Oxford: Clarendon, 1951, pp. 49–58. For the Kgatla, see I. Schapera, *Married Life in an African Tribe*, New York: Sheridan, 1941, pp. 55 ff. For the Bavenda, although the report seems incomplete, see Hugh A. Stayt, *The Bavenda*, London: Oxford University Press, 1931, pp. 111 ff., 145 ff., 154.

[39] The second correlation is developed from Marion J. Levy, *The Family Revolution in China*, Cambridge: Harvard University Press, 1949, p. 179. Levy's formulation ties "romantic love" to that solidarity, and is of little use because there is only one case, the Western culture complex. As he states it, it is almost so by definition.

LOVE CONTROL AND CLASS

These sociostructural explanations of how love is controlled lead to a subsidiary but important hypothesis: From one society to another, and from one *class* to another within the same society, the sociostructural importance of maintaining kinship lines according to rule will be rated differently by the families within them. Consequently, the degree to which control over mate choice, and therefore over the prevalence of a love pattern among adolescents, will also vary. Since, within any stratified society, this concern with the maintenance of intact and acceptable kin lines will be greater in the upper strata, it follows that noble or upper strata will maintain stricter control over love and courtship behavior than lower strata. The two correlations suggested in the preceding paragraph also apply: husband-wife solidarity is less strategic relative to clan solidarity in the upper than in the lower strata, and there is less free choice of mate.

Thus it is that, although in Polynesia generally most youngsters indulged in considerable love play, princesses were supervised strictly.[40] Similarly, in China lower class youngsters often met their spouses before marriage.[41] In our own society, the "upper upper" class maintains much greater control than the lower strata over the informal social contacts of their nubile young. Even among the Dobu, where there are few controls and little stratification, differences in control exist at the extremes: a child betrothal may be arranged between outstanding gardening families, who try to prevent their youngsters from being entangled with wastrel families.[42] In answer to my query about this pattern among the Nuer, Evans-Pritchard writes:

> You are probably right that a wealthy man has more control over his son's affairs than a poor man. A man with several wives has a more authoritarian position in his home. Also, a man with many cattle is in a position to per-

[40] E.g., Mead, *Coming of Age in Samoa*, op. cit., pp. 79, 92, 97–109. Cf. also Firth, op. cit., pp. 520 ff.

[41] Although one must be cautious about China, this inference seems to be allowable from such comments as the following: "But the old men of China did not succeed in eliminating love from the life of the young women. . . . Poor and middle-class families could not afford to keep men and women in separate quarters, and Chinese also met their cousins. . . . Girls . . . sometimes even served customers in their parents' shops." Olga Lang, op. cit., p. 33. According to Fried, farm girls would work in the fields, and farm girls of ten years and older were sent to the market to sell produce. They were also sent to towns and cities as servants. The peasant or pauper woman was not confined to the home and its immediate environs. Morton H. Fried, *Fabric of Chinese Society*, New York: Praeger, 1953, pp. 59–60. Also, Levy (op. cit., p. 111): "Among peasant girls and among servant girls in gentry households some premarital experience was not uncommon, though certainly frowned upon. The methods of preventing such contact were isolation and chaperonage, both of which, in the 'traditional' picture, were more likely to break down in the two cases named than elsewhere."

[42] Fortune, op. cit., p. 30.

mit or refuse a son to marry, whereas a lad whose father is poor may have to depend on the support of kinsmen. In general, I would say that a Nuer father is not interested in the personal side of things. His son is free to marry any girl he likes and the father does not consider the selection to be his affair until the point is reached when cattle have to be discussed.[43]

The upper strata have much more at stake in the maintenance of the social structure and thus are more strongly motivated to control the courtship and marriage decisions of their young. Correspondingly, their young have much more to lose than lower strata youth, so that upper strata elders *can* wield more power.

CONCLUSION

In this analysis I have attempted to show the integration of love with various types of social structures. As against considerable contemporary opinion among both sociologists and anthropologists, I suggest that love is a universal psychological potential, which is controlled by a range of five structural patterns, all of which are attempts to see to it that youngsters do not make entirely free choices of their future spouses. Only if kin lines are unimportant, and this condition is found in no society as a whole, will entirely free choice be permitted. Some structural arrangements seek to prevent entirely the outbreak of love, while others harness it. Since the kin lines of the upper strata are of greater social importance to them than those of lower strata are to the lower strata members, the former exercise a more effective control over this choice. Even where there is almost a formally free choice of mate—and I have suggested that this pattern is widespread, to be found among a substantial segment of the earth's societies—this choice is guided by peer group and parents toward a mate who will be acceptable to the kin and friend groupings. The theoretical importance of love is thus to be seen in the sociostructural patterns which are developed to keep it from disrupting existing social arrangements.

[43] Personal letter, dated January 9, 1958. However, the Nuer father can still refuse if he believes the demands of the girl's people are unreasonable. In turn, the girl can cajole her parents to demand less.

Mate Selection in Collective Settlements

YONINA TALMON

Sociologists and psychologists who studied the second generation in the Kibbutzim in Israel have all noted that children born and bred in the same Kibbutz do not marry one another as adults. Attempts to account for this phenomenon are usually based on the assumption that it is an exogamous extension of a self-imposed incest taboo generated by the collective system of education. In the Kibbutz, children are brought up together in peer groups which substitute, to a large extent, for their families.[1] Children in the same peer group live in close proximity, interact constantly and share most of their daily experiences from birth to maturity. It is assumed that much like biological siblings, members of the peer group develop an incest taboo that neutralizes their sexual interest in each other, and that this prohibition of sexual relations and marriage within the peer group is somehow extended to all children born

[1] The main features of the collective settlements (Kvutzot or Kibbutzim) are common ownership of property except for a few personal belongings and communal organization of production and consumption. Members' needs are provided for by communal institutions on an equalitarian basis. All income goes into the common treasury; each member gets only a very small annual allowance for personal expenses. The community is run as a single economic unit and as a single household. Husband and wife have independent jobs. Main meals are taken in the communal dining hall. In most Kibbutzim children live apart from their parents and are looked after by members assigned to this task. They spend a few hours every day with their parents and siblings, but from their birth on they sleep, eat and study in special children's houses. Each age group leads its own life and has its autonomous arrangements. The Kibbutz is governed by a general assembly, which convenes as a rule once a week, by a secretariat and by various committees. Each Kibbutz is affiliated to one of the Federations of Collectives. The Federations recruit most of their new members from youth movements that channel their members to settlement Kibbutzim.

This is a revised version of a paper prepared for the International Seminar on Family Research held in Oslo, August, 1963. I owe a special debt of gratitude to my research assistants Uri Avner, Batsheva Bonné and Lea Shamgar who helped me collect the data on patterns of marriage in the Kibbutz and contributed much to the analysis presented in this paper. Erik Cohen assisted me in directing this study and made many useful suggestions. I wish to express my sincere gratitude to Max Gluckman and David M. Schneider for their critical comments on an earlier version of this paper. While rewriting the paper, I profited greatly from the comments made by Daniel J. Levinson, Charlotte Green Schwartz, Morris S. Schwartz and Kurt H. Wolff.
Reprinted from the *American Sociological Review*, 29, No. 4 (August, 1964), 491–508, by permission of the American Sociological Association.

and reared in the same Kibbutz.[2] This explanation, which is based on an analogy to the genesis and extension of the incest taboo in the elementary family, is plausible but tells us very little about the origin of the exogamous tendency or about the mechanisms that maintain and stabilize it. It ignores altogether the structural implications of exogamy and does not deal with its effects on the social system.

Theories of incest and exogamy fall into two major categories: first, those that deal with these mate selection patterns in terms of social system functions and emphasize their effect on intra-group or inter-group solidarity, and second, those of the psychological-genetic variety that deal with this problem primarily on the motivational level. Very few explanations of incest and exogamy attempt to combine the two approaches in a systematic way. The Kibbutz presents us with the rare opportunity to observe exogamy in *statu nascendi* and follow the dynamic process of its initial development and crystallization. Since exogamy in the Kibbutz is not an established and taken-for-granted injunction but an emergent pattern, it enables us to examine closely the intricate interplay between social structure and individual volition. The main purpose of this paper is to relate, coordinate and integrate the two basic perspectives and deal with the problem on both levels of analysis.

SECOND-GENERATION "EXOGAMY"

My analysis of second-generation exogamy is based on the sociological study of mate selection and marriage patterns of the second generation in three long established Kibbutzim. This study is part of a larger research project carried out in a representative sample of 12 of the Kibbutzim affiliated with one of the four Federations of Kibbutzim.[3] The project combined sociological and anthropological field methods. The data obtained from questionnaires, from various types of interviews and from analysis of written material were examined and carefully interpreted by direct observation. The present analysis is based primarily on the special inquiry focused on marriage patterns of the second generation, but the more comprehensive investigation supplied many insights and provided a considerable amount of corroborative evidence.

I shall first sum up the facts revealed by our inquiry:

[2] See for instance Gerald Caplan, *Social Observation on the Emotional Life of Children in the Communal Settlements in Israel*, New York: Josiah Macy Jr. Foundation, 1954; Melford Spiro, *Children of the Kibbutz*, Cambridge: Harvard University Press, 1958, pp. 326–336 and 347–350; see also his "Is the Family Universal?—The Israeli Case" in Norman W. Bell and Ezra F. Vogel (eds.), *A Modern Introduction to the Family*, Glencoe, Ill.: The Free Press, 1960, pp. 59–69; J. R. Fox, "Sibling Incest," *British Journal of Sociology*, 13 (June, 1962), 128–150.

[3] The project was conducted by the Research Seminar of the Sociology Department of the Hebrew University. Rivka Bar-Yoseph took an active part in the initial planning. Amitai Etzioni assisted me in directing the project in its first stage. The other main research assistants were Eli Ron, Moshe Sarell and Joseph Sheffer. Moshe Sarell and Erik Cohen took over from Amitai Etzioni in the second stage. The main research assistants were Uri Avner, Batsheva Bonné, Uri Hurwitz, Ziporah Stup and Rachel Shaco.

1. Among the *125 couples* we examined, there was not one instance in which both mates were reared from birth in the same peer group. In four cases husband and wife were born in the same Kibbutz but reared in different peer groups. In addition we found eight couples in which one mate was born and raised in the Kibbutz while the other entered the educational institutions of the Kibbutz at diverse ages, ranging from three to fifteen. In six of these cases the "outsider" came to the Kibbutz and was subjected to collective education just before or after puberty. Only three of these "outsiders" joined the Kibbutz together with their parents; the others came as "external pupils" while their families continued to reside in town. In seven out of the eight couples the respective mates were reared in different peer groups. The single case of intra-peer group marriage occurred between a native and an "outsider" who was sent to the Kibbutz as an "external pupil" at the age of 15. The love affair between these two started after they left school and after an additional period of separation brought about by service in the army and study in town. In addition, 12 cases of intermarriage occurred between second generation members born and reared in different Kibbutzim.

Thus, in-migrants who undergo only part of their socialization in the Kibbutz and remain semi-outsiders in it and members of the second generation of other Kibbutzim seem to be more acceptable mates than full insiders.

2. Our data on *erotic attachments and sexual relations* are scantier and less reliable than our data on marriage. The pattern of distribution of love affairs, however, seems to parallel closely the pattern of distribution of marriages. We have not come across even one love affair or one instance of publicly known sexual relations between members of the same peer group who were cosocialized from birth or through most of their childhood. A small number of love affairs occurred between members of different peer groups, and a somewhat larger number between a native and an outsider who entered collective institutions at a later age and between second generation members of different Kibbutzim. The very rare cases of intra-group affairs involve an "outsider" who came to the Kibbutz as an "external pupil" long after puberty. These affairs did not occur during the period of study and started only after completion of secondary school.

The tendency to avoid in-group sexual relations and marriage is, then, strongest between members of the same age group. It is somewhat weaker between members of different age groups and between second generation members of different Kibbutzim. Age of entry into the Kibbutz educational system is yet another factor: the tendency toward out-group erotic relationships is strongest among those socialized in the Kibbutz since earliest infancy. In-migrants who undergo only part of their socialization in the Kibbutz are partly outsiders and as such are more desirable than insiders. Our data underline the importance of relations within the peer group, which appear to be at the core of the matter. It should be emphasized, however, that the tendency to avoid intra-second generation erotic relationships is almost as strong as the tendency to avoid intra-peer group erotic relationships. With few exceptions, love affairs and marital unions are extra-second generation.

3. We did not make a full study of the *demographic aspects* of our problem, but we did examine the possibility that the exogamous tendency may be a function of such demographic factors as age, sex and number of available

prospective mates in the second generation.[4] Our data indicate that while the limited number of suitable second-generation candidates is an important factor, it is certainly not the only or even the major factor operative here. The exogamous tendency appears in all Kibbutzim irrespective of the number of available second-generation members of a marriageable age. The unmarried members of the second generation in our sample could have chosen from about 20 to 60 second generation members who were within the acceptable age range, yet almost invariably they by-passed this pool of prospective mates and sought erotic gratification and marriage outside it.

4. A careful analysis of our data led to the conclusion that the tendency to out-group mate selection in the Kibbutz *is an attitudinal and behavioral trend and not an institutionalized normative pattern.* This tendency differs radically from full-fledged incest taboos and exogamic injunctions, which regulate mate selection by means of explicit norms and negative sanctions.

Scrutiny of the literature on incest and exogamy in different societies[5] reveals a great deal of variation as to explicitness of norms, stringency of prohibitions and severity of sanctions. The breach may be defined as sinful and punishment relegated to automatic mystical retribution.[6] It may be defined as criminal and subject to penal sanctions. It is viewed in some cases as merely scandalous and disreputable and subject to diffuse public disapproval and derision.[7] It may invoke extreme rage, horror and revulsion, or merely embarrassment and scorn. This variation should not obscure the fact that infractions of the core taboos and injunctions are hardly ever condoned and almost invariably incur more or less severe negative sanctions.[8]

The second-generation tendency toward out-group mate selection in the Kibbutz is not backed by any formal or informal prescriptions or proscriptions, and it is not buttressed by any institutionalized sanctions or inducements. The rare cases of intra-second generation affairs and marriages attract attention

[4] For an attempt to explain incest and exogamy in demographic-ecological terms, see Mariam Kreiselman Slater, "Ecological Factors in the Origin of Incest," *American Anthropologist*, 61 (December, 1959), 1042–1058.

[5] See George P. Murdock, *Social Structure*, New York: Macmillan, 1949, Chap. 10; see also A. R. Radcliffe-Brown, "Introduction," in A. R. Radcliffe-Brown and W. C. Daryll Ford (eds.), *African Systems of Kinship and Marriage*, London: Oxford University Press, 1950, pp. 60–72; Kathleen E. Gough, "Incest Prohibitions and Rules of Exogamy," *International Archives of Ethnography*, 46 (1952), 81–105; Brenda Seligman, "Incest and Exogamy—A Reconsideration," *American Anthropologist*, 52 (July, 1950), 305–326; Talcott Parsons, "The Incest Taboo," *British Journal of Sociology*, 5 (June, 1954), 101–117; Jack Goody, "A Comparative Approach to Incest and Adultery," *British Journal of Sociology*, 7 (December, 1956), 286–305.

[6] See David M. Schneider, "Political Organization, Supernatural Sanctions and Punishment for Incest on Yap," *American Anthropologist*, 59 (October, 1957), 791–800 and Robert A. Levine, "Gusii Sex Offenses—A Study of Social Control," *American Anthropologist*, 61 (December, 1959), 965–990.

[7] See Meyer Fortes, *The Web of Kinship Among the Tallensi*, London: Oxford University Press, 1949, p. 250.

[8] See J. R. Fox, op. cit. Fox tends to ignore the universality of negative sanctioning of the core taboos and injunctions and to overstress the extent of variation.

and comment but are not considered in any sense illegitimate or irregular. These unions are fully accepted by parents, friends and public opinion, without even a shade of censure or unease. Not only is proscription or negative evaluation of intra-second generation marriage completely absent, but as I shall show later, many of the parents prefer intra-second generation marriage above any other pattern. This difference between a non-normative trend and a fully institutionalized normative pattern is so fundamental that the two phenomena should not be designated by the same term without due reservations. To underline this basic distinction, I have consistently put such terms as "incest," "endogamy" and "exogamy" in quotes when I apply them to mate selection trends in the Kibbutz.

These findings concerning the prevalence, range and significance of the "exogamous" tendency among members of the second generation in the Kibbutz indicate that this is a self-imposed limitation which cannot be accounted for by either demographic or normative pressures. This brings into even sharper relief the twin questions originally posed: What are the social functions of this "exogamous" tendency? What are its sources and its functions at the level of individual personality?

PATTERNS OF MARRIAGE

The tendency of the second generation toward out-group marriage cannot be studied in isolation. Avoidances should be examined in conjunction with preferences and related to the overall distribution of marital choice categories. The first step toward such an analysis is a detailed examination of the group membership of all the spouses in our sample. Classification of these couples in this respect yields an "endogamy"-"exogamy" continuum, a graded series between two polar extremes.

1. *Intra-second generation marriage:* (a) Intra-peer group marriage—marriage between members of the second generation who were brought up in the same peer group. (b) Inter-peer group marriage—intermarriage between members of the second generation who were brought up in different peer groups. Such unions are "exogamous" with respect to the peer group but "endogamous" with respect to the second generation.

2. *Intra-Kibbutz marriage*—Intermarriage between members of the second generation of a given Kibbutz and candidates for membership or members who have joined their Kibbutz at later stages of its development. Such unions are "exogamous" from the point of view of the second generation but "endogamous" from the point of view of membership in the Kibbutz.

3. *Inter-Kibbutz marriage*—Intermarriage between members of the second generation of a given Kibbutz and members of other Kibbutzim. Contacts between the Kibbutzim occur either within the framework of the Federation[9] to which they are affiliated or within the framework of the regional organization that unites all the Kibbutzim in the region.

[9] To simplify this typology, I have disregarded organizational and ideological divisions within the collective movement, so that intra-Federation and inter-Federation marriage patterns are not distinguished.

4. *Intra-movement marriage*—Intermarriage between members of the second generation of a given Kibbutz and members of the youth movements that share the ideology of the Kibbutzim and channel their members to settlement in them. There are many institutionalized contacts between the Kibbutzim and the youth movements from which they recruit most of their new members. The youth movements send groups of prospective settlers to established Kibbutzim for preparatory training; such groups may reside and work in the Kibbutz for periods ranging from a few months to two years. Second-generation members often serve as instructors and organizers in youth groups and nuclei of prospective settlers in town. Such unions are "exogamous" with respect to the Kibbutzim concerned but "endogamous" with respect to the collective movement as a whole.

5. *Extra-movement marriage*—Intermarriage between members of the second generation and outsiders who are not members of the collective movement and do not share its ideology. Such outsiders are either hired professional workers—mostly teachers, but occasionally a resident doctor or an engineer—who reside in the Kibbutz temporarily but are not members and are not committed to its ideology, or outsiders who have no direct contact and no affinity with the Kibbutz ideology and way of life. Members of the second generation meet the latter type of outsiders primarily during the period of compulsory service in the Israeli army.

In our sample of 125 couples the distribution of marriage patterns is as follows:

	Per cent
1. Intra-second generation:	
(a) Intra-peer group	0
(b) Inter-peer group	3
2. Intra-Kibbutz	31
3. Inter-Kibbutz	23
4. Intra-movement	27
5. Extra-movement	16
	100
	(125)

These results are tentative and should be viewed with great caution. In many cases, it was not easy to determine the group membership of the spouse at the time of marriage, especially among couples who left the Kibbutz to join another Kibbutz or left the collective movement altogether. There is, in addition, considerable variation among the Kibbutzim in our sample, and we are by no means certain that our results are representative of other Kibbutzim. Yet, the pattern we found does not seem atypical and may well give a good indication of the major trends.

Most marriages are concentrated in the intermediate range of the typology; 81 per cent are of the intra-Kibbutz, inter-Kibbutz or intra-movement types. Both intra-second generation marriage and extra-movement marriage, the polar extremes, are less prevalent than the intermediate types. Examination of the distribution of the marriage patterns in terms of this typology locates the specific problem in a wider context. Instead of focusing exclusively on the near-absence of type 1 we can examine it as part of the total constellation of marital choice categories.

THE SOCIAL FUNCTIONS OF MARRIAGE PATTERNS

The voluminous literature on the functions of marriage patterns in different societies clearly indicates that these patterns have a crucial effect on the social system.[10] Marriage brings about a rearrangement of the social structure by segregating and interlinking sub-groups within it. It bears directly on the cohesion and continuity of the social system. What, then, are the functions of the extra-second generation marriage patterns from the point of view of any single Kibbutz and from the point of view of the movement as a whole?

Close scrutiny of our data reveals that the extra-second generation marriage patterns have a number of important functions on the *local level.* The intra-Kibbutz pattern is an important mechanism for *reinforcing membership ties by kinship ties.* The nuclei of settlers and the candidates for membership who join the Kibbutz during later stages of its development remain marginal for a long time. Direct confrontation with the realities of life in the Kibbutz has a corrosive effect on their commitment to stay in it. Their absorption is a prolonged and difficult process, and many drop out at first. Marriage to a son or a daughter of an old-timer consolidates the new member's ties to the established Kibbutz and reinforces his identification with it. The marital bond and the newly acquired kinship affiliations turn the newcomer, still a semi-outsider, into an insider and facilitate his adjustment.

Closely related to the function of reinforcing membership ties is the function of *recruiting new members.* The extra-Kibbutz patterns are an important external source of additional members. Both sons and daughters are expected to stay on in their Kibbutz after their marriage and to prevail on their spouses to join them there. The Kibbutzim in our sample have gained a considerable number of additional members through marriage—the ratio of gain to loss is about three to one. Established Kibbutzim suffer from a shortage of manpower, and the flow of new members drawn into it by extra-Kibbutz marriage is very welcome.

Thus, membership and kinship are, in a very important sense, complementary. The Kibbutz, however, is based on the primacy of membership ties

[10] For analysis of the functions of intermarriage see Robert K. Merton, "Intermarriage and the Social Structure," *Psychiatry*, 4 (August, 1941), 361–374; Kingsley Davis, "Intermarriage in Caste Societies," *American Anthropologist*, 43 (July, 1941), 376–395; Meyer Fortes, op. cit.: I. Schapera, "The Tsawana Conception of Incest" and E. E. Evans Pritchard, "Nuer Rules of Exogamy and Incest," both in Meyer Fortes (ed.), *Social Structure*, Oxford: Clarendon Press, 1949, pp. 85–121; E. E. Evans-Pritchard, *Kinship and Marriage among the Nuer,* Oxford: Clarendon Press, 1951; Claude Lévi-Strauss, *Les Structures Elémentaires de la Parenté*, Paris: Presses Universitaires de France, 1949; Talcott Parsons, op. cit., pp. 101–117; and Jack Goody, op. cit. See also William J. Goode, "The Theoretical Importance of Love," *American Sociological Review*, 24 (February, 1959), 38–47.

over kinship affiliations and it cannot afford to let kinship gain an upper hand.[11] All established Kibbutzim face the problem of the gradual re-emergence of wider kinship ties within them. Relatives often form united blocks and conduct a covert struggle for particularistic interests.[12] Occasionally such blocks become quite powerful and exert a considerable influence on communal affairs. Predominance of kinship ties over ties of membership undermines the primacy of collective considerations and engenders internecine strife. The established Kibbutzim have devised many mechanisms to limit the influence of kinship groups. One function of the extra-second generation marriage patterns is *to check the emergence and consolidation of large and powerful kinship groupings within the Kibbutz.* When intermarriage occurs between a member of the second generation and a newcomer or an outsider, only one spouse has his family of orientation and his siblings' families living with him in the same community, while marriage between members of the second generation would proliferate kinship ties within the Kibbutz.

The extra-second generation patterns also *link different subgroups in the Kibbutz;* marrying out *bridges the intergeneration cleavage.* The educational system partly segregates the second generation from the rest of the Kibbutz. The children's society has its autonomous arrangements and children live within this semi-separate framework uninterruptedly throughout the long process of socialization. They share with their age mates most of the formative experiences of infancy, childhood and adolescence; internal relations within the peer group are more frequent and more continuous than relations with outsiders. Members of the second generation are highly conscious of their special position in their Kibbutz and often tend to keep to themselves. Extra-second generation marriage mitigates this intense in-group solidarity after maturity. Marrying out propels members of the second generation outside their group and bolsters their external ties.

Extra-second generation marriage bridges the gap between subgrougs within the Kibbutz in yet another way. *Marrying out checks the consolidation of the emergent stratification system.* The founders of the Kibbutz usually enjoy a privileged position in terms of prestige and power. The kinship ties produced by any considerable number of "endogamous" marriages between their children would reinforce in-group solidarity among them and enhance the consolidation of the old-timers into a separate and dominant group. The extra-second generation patterns counteract this tendency to closure and exclusion. Through their children, the established old-timers are linked to less established and more marginal members. Extra-second generation marriage is thus *an equalizing mechanism* of major importance.

The functions of the prevalent mate selection patterns for the *movement as a whole* are even more evident. The inter-Kibbutz and intra-movement patterns counteract the strong separatist tendencies of the local communities by cutting across the boundaries between them and by strengthening their ties

[11] For a fuller analysis of this problem see Yonina Talmon, "The Family in a Revolutionary Movement" in Meyer Nimkoff (ed.), *Comparative Family Systems*, Boston: Houghton-Mifflin, 1964.

[12] See Yonina Talmon-Garber, "The Family and the Social Placement of the Second Generation in Collective Settlements," *Megamoth*, 8 (1958), 369–392 (in Hebrew).

to the youth movements. The function of inter-Kibbutzim unions as *living links between distinct communities* is particularly noticeable in the cases of inter-collective "adoption." The Federations have recently developed a system whereby each established Kibbutz "adopts" a newly founded Kibbutz and pledges itself to assist it until it is able to manage on its own. Intermarriage links the long-established and newly founded Kibbutzim together and gradually reinforces the pseudo-kinship ties entailed in "adoption." Parents and relatives of members of the second generation who have gone over to new Kibbutzim maintain frequent and close ties with them and eventually come into contact with other members as well. Since the assistance scheme affects the well-being of their close kin, members of the established Kibbutz become personally committed to it and press for a strong alliance between the two communities. Cross-cutting kinship affiliations transform "adoption" into a comprehensive and lasting partnership.[13]

Of similar importance is the *revitalization and renewal of relations with the youth movements*. Established Kibbutzim tend to settle down and lose much of their revolutionary zeal. The sense of belonging to a revolutionary movement becomes less pervasive and less urgent; growing involvement in local affairs brings about a concomitant limitation of the horizons of identification and participation. There is an increasing tendency toward contraction of commitment and withdrawal from the movement. Estrangement occurs also because of the gradual shift in relations between the established Kibbutz and the youth movements. The dependence of the established Kibbutz on the youth movements for new members diminishes and at the same time the movement's claims on it grow manifoldly. The established Kibbutzim realize the importance of supporting the youth movements, yet they cannot help feeling hard-pressed and overburdened when confronted with demands to send more youth leaders to the cities and to participate more actively in the training programs. Intra-movement marriage links the youth movements with the Kibbutzim and emphasizes the unity of the collective movement that encompasses them all.

Finally, intra-movement and extra-movement marriages *bridge the gap between Kibbutzim and other sectors of the society.* In many notable cases, they provide very valuable personal links with other elite groups. Unions contracted between members of the second generation and military, political and intellectual leaders or their close kin cement the manifold ties between the Kibbutzim and both the pivotal and secondary elites of Israeli society. Extra-movement unions curb separatist tendencies and create solidarities that transcend the local units and reinforce wider ranging unities.

So far, I have analyzed only the *positive* functions of the extra-second generation marriage patterns, disregarding the fact that to a lesser or greater degree they all constitute a *threat to local continuity.* Intra-second generation

[13] For a recent restatement and development of the view that the incest taboo and exogamy diffuse attachment and harness it to larger coordinated aggregates, see Philip E. Slater, "On Social Regression," *American Sociological Review*, 28 (June, 1963), 339–364. For an analysis of the way in which estrangement within the group strengthens loyalties to wider ranging unities, see Max Gluckman, *Custom and Conflict in Africa*, Oxford: Basil Blackwell, 1955, Chap. 3.

marriage is the pattern most conducive to local continuity. Both spouses are natives of the Kibbutz and share a common commitment and attachment to it. Their staying on in the Kibbutz after marriage is safeguarded also by the fact that all their close relatives and friends reside there. A new member's ties to the Kibbutz are weaker and more vulnerable—he is much more prone to leave and to draw his spouse out of the Kibbutz.

The threat to local continuity is even more noticeable in the inter-Kibbutz and intra-movement patterns. A union between a member of the second generation and a member of another Kibbutz or a member of a nucleus of prospective settlers engenders a conflict of loyalties. When members of two established Kibbutzim intermarry, they tend to spend a trial period in each community and settle in the one that is more congenial to both spouses. But intermarriage with a member of a new Kibbutz, or with a member of a nucleus of settlers that is about to found its own Kibbutz, creates cross pressures and counter-claims with no institutionalized solution. Members of the second generation are often attracted by the numerous openings offered to them in the new Kibbutz. They also feel that it is their duty to help the newly founded Kibbutz rather than return to the fairly prosperous community established by their parents. In spite of their commitment to their native village and in spite of the pressure put on them by their parents, the conflict is often resolved in favor of the new Kibbutz.

Extra-movement marriages are the grestest hazard from the point of view of continuity. Some of the hired professional workers who marry into the Kibbutz become attached to it and wish to join as members in their own right. This also happens occasionally with outsiders who have had no affinity and no direct contact with the collective movement prior to marriage. Yet more often than not, extra-movement marriages lead to desertion of the Kibbutz and dissociation from the movement. This happens more often when the second-generation member is a woman; in spite of the fact that both sons and daughters are expected to stay in their native Kibbutz, wives follow their husbands more than husbands follow their wives. Linkage of a couple to the Kibbutz through a son is therefore less vulnerable than linkage through a daughter.[14]

The foregoing analysis of *functions and dysfunctions* enables us to weigh the effects of the marriage patterns on the social system. Intra-second genera-tion marriage ensures local continuity, yet if it were prevalent, it would deprive the Kibbutz of important internal and external integrating mechanisms. It would lead to the consolidation of kinship blocks and to the hardening of the line dividing the old-timers from the newcomers and outsiders. It would separate the Kibbutz from the movement and from the society at large. At the other extreme, extra-movement marriage links the Kibbutz to the society at large, but this advantage is counterbalanced by heavy losses in terms of cohe-sion and continuity. *The intermediate marriage patterns combine in-group closure with intergroup linkage, and in this respect are more functional than the two polar types.* The most prevalent marriage patterns are those that safe-

[14] John A. Barnes, "Marriage and Residential Continuity," *American Anthropologist*, 62 (October, 1960), 850–866; see also his "Land Rights and Kinship in Two Bremnes Hamlets," *Journal of the Royal Anthropological Institute*, 87 (1957), 31–56.

guard the cohesion and continuity of the local community, yet at the same time promote the unity and growth of the movement as a whole.

The intermediate patterns provide a functional solution from the point of view of the elementary family as well. Extreme homogamy limits the possibilities of interchanges and complementariness; extreme heterogamy is inherently unstable, since it joins together spouses with conflicting loyalties and incompatible norms and aspirations. The intermediate patterns combine basic homogeneity with manageable differentiation: they enable members of the second generation to marry newcomers and outsiders without disrupting their matrix of interpersonal relations. It seems, then, that the intermediate patterns perform important functions for the social system on all levels.

INSTITUTIONAL MECHANISMS

The preceding analysis indicates that the net effect of the present distribution of marital choices is by and large favorable. This elucidation of functions supplies an indispensable starting point for a causal analysis, yet in and by itself it does not explain differential incidence. To account for the adoption of a certain institution it is not sufficient to show that it is in some sense "good" for society and serves its long-range interests.[15] Listing the beneficial or dire consequences of an institutional pattern from the observer's point of view does not in itself account for the actors' attitudes and behavior. Second-generation members are only partly aware of the considerations outlined above, and even if they do recognize them, that does not mean that they actually choose their mates to suit the best interests of their society. Mate selection is considered a purely personal and private matter and there is a strict ban against meddling in the process of choice. How, then, do the functional considerations impinge on the individuals directly concerned? How does the structure, or the "sake" of the Kibbutz interact, as it were, with individual volition? What are the efficient causes and the immediate determinants of action?

An examination of the social system from the point of view of *differential availability* of categories of prospective mates provides an important connecting link between the functional and causal analyses of marriage patterns. The fact that the Kibbutzim are not closed, self-sufficient communities but interconnected and interdependent units, operating within an active and proselytizing movement, is of utmost importance in this context. The strong separatist tendencies of the local communities are counterbalanced by external ties. There are first of all the federative affiliations based on an ideological-political affinity. Secondly there are the regional schemes that further cooperation between settlements situated in the same district and encompass Kibbutzim affiliated with different federations. Last but not least, we should take into

[15] See George C. Homans and David M. Schneider, *Marriage, Authority and Final Causes*, Glencoe, Ill.: The Free Press, 1955, pp. 3–20; see also Harry C. Bredemeier, "The Methodology of Functionalism," *American Sociological Review*, 20 (April, 1955), 172–180, and Ronald P. Dore, "Function and Cause," *American Sociological Review*, 26 (December, 1961), 843–853.

consideration the manifold ties that connect the Kibbutzim with the overall structure of Israeli society.[16]

The external relations of the Kibbutz impinge directly on its internal organization. The youth movements supply the Kibbutz with reinforcements. The Kibbutz accommodates, in addition, transient members of the youth movements, who stay for varying periods to get their basic training or to lend a hand during the busy season. Many Kibbutzim have developed special institutions for immigrant youth who stay in the Kibbutz for a number of years, combining study and part-time work. In border settlements, units of a special formation of the army combine military duties and work. Even while staying in their native Kibbutz, members of the second generation are brought into institutionalized and more or less prolonged contact with groups of new members, candidates for membership and various kinds of transients, and these out-groups provide a pool of prospective mates. Activity on the regional, federative and national level further extends the range of participation and provides opportunities to develop durable and meaningful ties outside the confines of the local community.[17]

Members of Kibbutzim and especially leaders of the movement are aware of the dangers of closure and separatism, and have devised ingenious mechanisms to link the different groups and different communities affiliated with the movement in common endeavors. Situational exigencies and ideological considerations have led to the expansion of the regional schemes beyond their original, rather limited scope. These schemes curtail local autonomy and have a considerable impact on the economic, social and cultural life of the participating communities. Large scale regional enterprises and institutions create a common meeting ground and bring the members of different Kibbutzim together. Most important, from the point of view of our special problem, are the regional secondary and vocational schools that draw out and bring together the adolescent youth growing up in these Kibbutzim. Several of the inter-Kibbutz marriages in our sample originated in friendships formed during study in such an inter-collective secondary school.

Many of the inter-Kibbutz and intra-movement unions are by-products of the newly developed scheme of federative assistance. A series of serious setbacks in the new settlements and a crisis of recruitment in the youth movements have led the Federations to intensify and widen the scope of federative cooperation. After completing their army service, members of the second generation are drafted for an additional year of service in a newly established Kibbutz or in a youth movement training group. Recruitment is channeled primarily through "adoption," and most recruits serve in the new settlement adopted by their native Kibbutz. In addition, members of the second generation of a number of established Kibbutzim serve in new settlements that require considerable reinforcement to keep them going and consequently find adoption by only one established Kibbutz inadequate. Inter-Kibbutz second-generation teams participate also in maintaining their Federation's outpost in outlying,

[16] See Yonina Talmon and Erik Cohen, "Collective Settlements in the Negev," in Joseph Ben-David (ed.), *Agricultural Planning and the Village Community in Israel*, Paris: Unesco, 1964, pp. 58–95.

[17] For comparative data on the influence of propinquity on mate selection see A. M. Katz and Reuben Hill, "Residential Propinquity and Marital Selection," *Marriage and Family Living*, 20 (February, 1958), 27–35.

uninhabited and arid areas. They are engaged there in experimental cultivation and in preparation of the land for permanent settlement. A certain percentage of the annual quota of recruits serve as instructors and organizers of training groups in the youth movements.

Since service to a common cause and prolonged and close contacts breed affairs and lasting attachments, these schemes create ready opportunities for inter-group unions. The widening of the frameworks of cooperation results in a concomitant widening of the range of available mates. The three to three and one-half years of service in the army and in new settlements are concentrated in the beginning of adulthood, so that young people are taken out of the narrow confines of their Kibbutz at the time they begin to contemplate marriage. Maximal external contacts occur at the most marriageable age.

Influencing mate-choice is not an intended aim of the supplementary institutional mechanisms analyzed above. The established Kibbutzim view the intermarriages brought about by the regional and federative schemes with ambivalence and anxiety. Assistance schemes resulting in permanent settlement of a considerable number of second generation members in the new Kibbutzim evoke covert competition and acute tension. To avoid open conflict, some of the established Kibbutzim have reached an agreement with their adopted settlements that as long as the official ties of adoption last, second generation members will not be allowed to settle in the new Kibbutz or even volunteer for a second term of service in it. The established Kibbutzim press for deferment of the year of service in new Kibbutzim until members of the second generation reach a more mature age and are already married and settled down in their native villages. Most inter-Kibbutz and intra-movement marriages occur as *unintended, unanticipated and even undesired* consequences of organizational arrangements made for other purposes.

At times availability is an outcome of a *more conscious and purposeful design* to channel mate choice. The demographic policy of the Kibbutz is not uninfluenced by considerations of mate selection. Members of the Kibbutz are aware of the intra-second generation avoidance. They realized that intra-Kibbutz marriage is a safeguard against the desertion of the second generation to other communities and that the best way to ensure local continuity is to provide for their adult children a pool of suitable mates within their native village. They are partly aware also of the stabilizing effect that such marriages have on their new members. The timing of stages of demographic expansion by means of absorbing groups of new members, and the selection of such groups, are not unaffected by these considerations.

The Kibbutzim have lately become very concerned about the "undesirable" associations developed by members of the second generation during their army service. Service in the army throws the young recruits into direct and intense contact with all segments of Israeli society and provides them with an opportunity to develop attachments outside the aegis of the Kibbutz and the collective movement. The Kibbutzim try to limit the disruptive effects of these external contacts by channeling a certain quota of their recruits to the agricultural-military formation of the army, which maintains their contacts with the movement throughout the period of service. They make special efforts to keep in touch with members of the second generation who serve in other units and to maintain and strengthen their intra-movement ties.

The need to counteract extra-movement associations has led the Federations to design new inter-Kibbutz and intra-movement frameworks of en-counter and interaction. An important instance of such indirect yet intentional channeling of mate choice is the ideological seminars and refresher courses, which are planned with matchmaking as one of their unofficial, yet tacitly recognized, aims. This gives rise to much bantering during the seminars and figures as a major theme in the humorous skits and songs presented at parties. At times the program of instruction and the lectures serve mainly as a con-venient cover while the main purpose of the seminar is to provide a congenial atmosphere and ready opportunities for forming attachments. The channeling of mate choice is achieved by means of control over the frameworks of formal and informal interaction. *The prevalence of the intermediate patterns stems, at least in part, from institutional arrangements that make certain categories of mates more readily accessible.*

Analysis in terms of differential accessibility supplies an important clue, but not the full answer. Second generation members are more available than any other categories of prospective mates. They interact closely and are within easy reach of each other, yet they do not regard each other as erotically desirable. Our initial question is still unanswered. How can we account for this sexual neutralization on the motivational level? What makes newcomers, out-siders and strangers more desirable? How do these deep-lying tendencies develop during the process of maturation?

MATE SELECTION AND THE PROCESS OF MATURATION

The life of children in the Kibbutz is dominated from the outset by *a divi-sion between the communal sphere represented by the peer group and the private sphere represented by the family*. This division determines the eco-logical patterning and the time rhythm of the child's schedule and is main-tained by the daily shifting from the children's house to the parents' home. The family and the peer group are dominated by different yet complementary principles.[18] Relations between parents and small children are very intimate, intense and highly eroticized. Expressions of love become more restrained and less overt as the children grow up, but the relationship remains warm and affectionate. Throughout the process of socialization the family supplies the child with uncontested love and exclusive personal attention.

[18] For an analysis of the division of functions between the family and the peer groups see Yonina Talmon, "The Family in a Revolutionary Movement," op. cit. and "The Family and Collective Socialization in the Kibbutz," *Niv–Hakvutsah*, 8 (1959), 2–52 (in Hebrew). See also Rivka Bar-Yoseph, "The Pattern of Early Socialization in the Collective Settlements in Israel," *Human Relations*, 12 (1959), 345–360; Elizabeth Irvine, "Observations on the Aims and Methods of Child-Rearing in Communal Settlements in Israel," *Human Rela-tions*, 5 (1952), 247–275; Helen Faigin, "Social Behavior of Young Children in the Kibbutz," *Journal of Abnormal Social Psychology*, 61 (1958), 117–129; A. I. Rabin, "Infants and Children under Conditions of Intermittent Mothering," *American Journal of Orthopsychiatry*, 28 (July, 1958), 577–586, and his "Atti-tudes of Kibbutz Children to Parents and Family," *American Journal of Ortho-psychiatry*, 29 (January, 1959), 172–179.

The atmosphere in the peer group is more neutral, less affectively toned. A certain routine, diffuse general friendliness and overall solidarity is emphasized, rather than love or intimacy. Everything is shared and each child is entitled to the same amount of attention. Relations in the peer group are based on a diffuse and all-embracing internal solidarity that discourages exclusive friendships or love affairs with it.[19] Love is anchored in the specifically personal and private sphere; since it leads to preoccupation with inner emotional states, it competes with involvement with the group and detracts from dedicated commitment to collective goals. Romantic love is in its very nature exclusive; it sets the lovers apart and separates them from the rest of their comrades. The emphasis on commitment to the group discourages dyadic withdrawal; members look askance at intense friendships of any kind, and they occur infrequently.[20] Since the child's personal need for exclusive intimate relations is from the outset provided for outside the peer group rather than within it, the formation of erotic attachments in adolescence and adulthood is inhibited. The "exogamous" tendency should be viewed as one manifestation of the *basic distinction between peers who are comrades and intimates who are "outsiders."*

Data on educational institutions in the Kibbutz enable us to probe a little further *into the ways in which the peer groups neutralize and inhibit sexual attraction between their members.* Relations between the sexes are de-eroticized not by means of strict restrictive norms or enforced segregation, but by dealing with sexual problems in a straightforward, objective and "rational" way and by minimizing the differentiation and distance between the sexes. Children of different sexes share the same living quarters[21] and physical shame is de-emphasized. There is very little differentiation between the sexes in style of dress and demeanor and hardly any sex-differentiated social activities. Interaction between age mates in the peer group is much tighter and all-pervasive than interaction between siblings. Siblings share only activities and experiences in the family, and their participation is age and sex differentiated, but members of the peer groups eat, study, work and play together as a group most hours of the day and sleep together in the same room or in adjoining rooms at night. We encounter here, then, very close propinquity and very intensive interaction between peers of different sexes.

The de-eroticizing mechanisms described above operate throughout the

[19] For analysis of the opposition between dyadic attachment and group solidarity see W. R. Bion, "Experiences in Groups," III, *Human Relations*, 2 (1949), 13–22; see also Slater, op. cit., pp. 348–361.

[20] Shmuel Golan, *Collective Education*, Merchavia: Sifriat Poalim, 1961, 204–214 (in Hebrew).

[21] See Melford Spiro, *Children of the Kibbutz*, op. cit. It should be noted that the Kibbutz described by Spiro is affiliated with a Federation that pursues a much more extreme and more rigorous policy of sexual desegregation than the Federation in which we conducted our research. Kibbutzim affiliated to the orthodox religious Federation practice considerable segregation between sexes. We are engaged now in a cross-Federation comparative study of mate selection which will enable us to examine the relation between intensity of heterosexual contact during the process of socialization and the development of "exogamy."

process of socialization, but the norms regulating relations between the sexes, as well as actual behavior, change during *different phases of maturation*.[22] Attitudes to childhood sexuality are permissive and sexual manifestations in young children are viewed as normal. Living and sleeping quarters are bisexual during this stage. Children of different sexes sleep in the same room, shower together, play and run around in the nude and there is a considerable amount of wrestling, tickling, exploring, soothing and caressing between them. This close contact between the sexes continues until the second or third grade, and then decreases with age. Gradually, a sense of sexual shame emerges, and a growing distance between the sexes. Showers are taken separately. Sleeping arrangements are reshuffled; from the fourth grade on room occupancy is unisexual. All group activities remain bisexual but friendships become unisexual.

The onset of puberty brings about a conspicuous increase in sexual shame and the development of considerable hostility between the sexes. Girls take great pains to hide their nudity when undressing and keep to themselves as much as possible. Members of both sexes insist on sitting separately in the classroom and at all assembles and parties. They declare that they detest each other and are constantly involved in petty quarrels. The girls regard the boys as immature and uncouth and treat them with disdain, and the boys retaliate by annoying the girls and poking fun at them. Much of this tension stems from the differential rate of sexual maturation—girls reach puberty and manifest a renewed interest in sex a few years earlier than boys. This interest is directed to older students and to other young unmarried males in their Kibbutz and not to their peers. The boys react to this development with resentment and aggression. This hostility continues until the age of 14 or 15 and then recedes, as the boys catch up with the girls and the relations between them cease to be highly charged with tension. The intensity of physical shame decreases. Girls and boys conceal their nudity from each other but this is now done without much ado in a calm and matter-of-fact manner. The unity of the peer group is restored and relations between the sexes become easy, unconstrained and friendly. During most of their adolescence age mates interact with each other as asexual peers rather than as potential sex objects.

Attitudes toward adolescent sexuality are more restrictive than attitudes toward childhood sexuality. The educational ideology upheld by both teachers and parents maintains that adolescents should refrain from sexual relations until they finish secondary school. It is felt that preoccupation with sexual matters prevents full concentration on school activities and has a disruptive effect on the peer group and on the student society. The energies of the adolescents are channeled to work, to study and to hectic participation in extra-curricular group and inter-group activities. All social participation is group rather than couple centered.[23] Seductiveness, coquetry and flirtatious-

[22] Ibid., pp. 219–228, 275–283, 326–336.
[23] For comparative data on heterosexual interaction during adolescence see Willard Waller, "The Rating and Dating Complex," *American Sociological Review*, 2 (October, 1937), 727–734; Robert O. Blood, "A Retest of Waller's Rating Complex," *Marriage and Family Living*, 17 (1955), 41–47.

ness are strongly discouraged. Sex does not loom very large in the lives of these adolescents. Shifting relations and indiscriminate experimentation are not common, nor do many couples go steady.[24] There are only few infractions of the injunction against sexual intercourse. Couples who become engrossed in each other and neglect their duties are admonished by their educators and peers to restrain themselves and to "return to the fold."

During this stage interaction cutting across divisions between peer groups increases considerably. Intergroup cooperation is highly organized and much more intensive than in the primary school. The committees elected by the students have jurisdiction over all matters other than the purely academic ones. Interaction between members of different peer groups occurs also in youth movement activities and in the numerous cultural interest and discussion groups. In most established and well-to-do Kibbutzim there are, in addition, a students' choir, a students' orchestra and a students' paper, which require close cooperation among many students. Activity in age-heterogenous groups leads to a student-society solidarity that complements and reinforces peer group solidarity. Students of the senior classes have a strong "generational" consciousness and view themselves as the representatives of the second generation in their Kibbutz.[25]

Another relevant feature of adolescent life is a change in the balance between the communal and family spheres. Young children are deeply dependent on their parents. They gradually outgrow this intense involvement and become attached to their age mates. Adolescents become firmly embedded in their peer group and in the students' society and drift away from their families. Their relations with their parents remain friendly and affectionate but no longer very intense or intimate. The solidarities cultivated by communal education gain an upper hand and partly supersede family solidarity.

After graduation from secondary school, members of the second generation may engage in sexual relations with impunity and are given a free hand with respect to choice of mate. There is no objection to pre-marital sexual relations as long as they are not treated in a frivolous and off-hand way. The prevalent view of sexuality and marriage stresses personal autonomy and genuine intimacy, and it is felt that both sexual relations and marriage should be anchored in spontaneous love. The search for a mate draws members of the second generation away from their peers and away from all other members of the second generation. As noted before, the overwhelming majority of love affairs and marital unions are extra-second generation, and as far as we can judge, relations between adult members of the second generation are friendly and familiar but devoid of any signs of erotic tension.

[24] See Robert D. Herman, "The Going Steady Complex," *Marriage and Family Living*, 17 (1955), 36–40.

[25] On the problem of generations see Karl Manheim's *Essays on the Sociology of Knowledge*, New York: Oxford University Press, 1959, pp. 276–321; see also Shmuel N. Eisenstadt, *From Generation to Generation*, Glencoe, Ill.: The Free Press, 1956, and Bruno Bettleheim, "The Problem of Generations" in Erik H. Erikson (ed.), *Youth: Change and Challenge*, New York: Basic Books, 1963, pp. 64–93.

Members of the second generation view their relations with each other as "sexless" and erotically indifferent.[26]

How do members of the second generation account for their tendency to out-marriage? How does the transition from adolescence to adulthood lead to the emergence of "exogamy"? One of the most frequent reasons given by second generation members for their lack of sexual interest in each other is *overfamiliarity.* They firmly believe that overfamiliarity breeds sexual disinterest and that it is one of the main sources of "exogamy." Our second-generation respondents stressed that they knew each other "inside-out," or more figuratively, "We are like an open book to each other. We have read the story in the book over and over again and know all about it." That this is an important issue with them we learn also from the reasons they give for their interest in newcomers, outsiders and strangers. They refer to the curiosity, excitement and anticipation that unfamiliar people evoke in them and to the exhilarating sense of discovery and triumph they get when they establish a relationship with one of them. They describe the unfolding of an affair as an exchange of confidences and emphasize the importance of relating and comparing different life histories. The affair with the outsider is experienced as an *overcoming of distance between persons* and as a growth of a newly won and unfamiliar sense of intimacy. The most perceptive and introspective among our respondents regard their affairs with unfamiliar persons also as a means of *self-discovery.* The effort to bridge the gap and reach mutual understanding requires self-scrutiny and brings about a heightened sense of self-awareness. To quote one of them "We are all cut from the same mold. We take each other and ourselves for granted. Reaching-out to an outsider has made me conscious of myself. I know now more clearly what I am and what I stand for." The search for self-awareness and genuine intimacy as distinct from mere familiarity is an insistent and recurrent theme in many interviews.

Closely related to the issue of overfamiliarity is *the issue of privacy.* The concern with privacy is very intense.[27] Adolescent couples are very secretive about their relationships. The typical partners give few overt indications of their relationship. They do not appear together in public as a couple nor do they seek each other out informally between classes or at work. All meetings are clandestine. It would be unthinkable to show any physical sign of affection in the presence of other people. This exaggerated secrecy disappears after

[26] Two different psychological hypotheses have been proposed concerning this neutralization of sexual attraction. Spiro bases his analysis on Freudian premises and assumes that sexual attraction between co-socialized children of opposite sex is inhibited and suppressed but persists subconsciously. Fox contructs a neo-Westermarckian model and assumes that intense heterosexual bodily contact before puberty extinguishes desire. Since our research does not supply data on subconscious motivation, I cannot resolve the problem of suppressed versus extinguished sexual attraction. Both hypotheses have only limited explanatory value: as they stand, neither can fully account for the genesis of second generation "exogamy." They explain the neutralization of sexual desire between members of the same peer group but not the generalization of attitudes engendered within the peer group to the second generation as a whole. See Spiro, op. cit., pp. 347–350 and Fox, op. cit., pp. 128–150.

[27] See Spiro, op. cit., pp. 334.

adolescence, but the concern with privacy remains very strong. As one of our respondents put it "In the children's society everything is 'ours.' This affair is mine. It is something of my own that I do not want to share with others. I try to keep it to myself as much as I can." Communal living and constant sharing of daily experiences with peers seems to breed a strong urge to seclude one's personal life and protect it from external intrusion. Maintenance of secrecy is also a mechanism for dealing with stringent group control against dyadic withdrawal.[28] The threat to group cohesion is less evident if the relationship remains subdued and covert.

One of the major advantages of the extra-second generation over the intra-second generation union is that it is *more amenable to segregation and seclusion.* Members of the second generation are part of a highly interconnected network of interpersonal relations. Being the first-born of their Kibbutz they are at the center of public attention. An amorous attachment between members of the second generation attracts immediate notice and incessant comment. The courtship will be conducted with the whole community looking on. It is much easier to keep secrecy or at least to maintain a semblance of privacy when the partner is a newcomer or an outsider who has few or no contacts with the Kibbutz. Members of the second generation take great pains to guard knowledge of their extra-second-generation affairs from public notice.

The aspirations and expectations of second-generation members concerning their mates often reflect the external influence of the ideals of romantic love derived from novels, poems, plays and films.[29] The quest for individuation and genuine intimacy, however, should not be attributed to illicit external influences. These concerns are anchored in the image of love and family life upheld by the Kibbutz and are therefore legitimate. Preoccupation with overfamiliarity and lack of privacy stems from the internal dynamics of the system and reflects the dilemma engendered by the interplay between the communal and private spheres of the Kibbutz.

The social and psychological dynamics engendering this quest for individuation are further clarified by considering the *relation between "exogamy" and the demand for local continuity.* Loyalty to the Kibbutz is defined in localized terms, and members of the second generation are pledged to stay in their native Kibbutz for the rest of their lives. This duty gives rise to serious problems that become particularly acute during the transition from adolescence to adulthood. The Kibbutz is part of a revolutionary movement that puts a premium on discontinuity and creative innovation. Since it still depends on reinforcements from the youth movements, it encourages young people to dissociate themselves from their parents and continues to glorify rebellion. At the same time, it expects its own second generation to stay on in their native villages and continue their parents' lifework there. Inheriting a revolution engenders an inevitable dilemma. The second generation is called upon *to continue and conserve in a movement committed to dis-*

[28] See Slater, op. cit., pp. 348–353.
[29] See Hugo G. Beigel, "Romantic Love," *American Sociological Review*, 16 (June, 1951), 326–334, and Jackson Toby, "Romantic Love" in Harry C. Bredemeier and Jackson Toby (eds.), *Social Problems in America*, New York: John Wiley, 1960, pp. 461–467.

continuity.[30] Most members of the second generation accept responsibility to their heritage and stay on in the Kibbutz, but their attitude toward continuity is very ambivalent.

The duty to stay on in the native village engenders a deep *fear of closure* because it implies blocked mobility and a curtailment of life chances. It imposes a drastic limitation on free choice of domicile, of career, of associates and of friends. The cultivation of external contacts and the period of service outside the Kibbutz mitigate local closure but at the same time accentuate the problems involved in local continuity. Resettlement in the Kibbutz after prolonged service outside it entails a difficult reorientation and readjustment. Many second generation members are loath to sever their external ties and to forego the more variegated opportunities offered by life outside their Kibbutz. Most of them feel cut off and hemmed in. They realize that the course of their lives is set from the outset and that their future is predetermined by membership in their home Kibbutz. The tendency to marry out is an attempt to counteract this limitation. The large majority of extra-second generation mates have been brought up outside the Kibbutz; they come from a different milieu and represent the outside world. "Exogamy" enables second generation members to extend their contacts beyond the narrow confines of the circle of people with whom they have been associated since they were born. It expresses their craving for new experiences and their groping for new contacts. Most important, perhaps, it affords them opportunities to explore on their own, to initiate and experiment. In short, out-group marriage enables the second generation to escape the in-group closure imposed on them by their education and by their commitment to continuity.

The relation between "exogamy" and the commitment to continuity is especially significant in the context of relations between the first and second generations. Parents and children are at cross purposes on this issue. Parents have a strong vested interest in "endogamy." Their major concern is to ensure that the new family will stay on in the Kibbutz. From the point of view of familial and local continuity, intra-second generation marriage is the safest solution, and it is in fact a first preference with many parents. They view with enthusiasm and anticipation any sign of attachment between their children and give them their full blessing. The tendency of their children to marry out is a source of constant anxiety to them, and they watch them with unease until they settle down. Parents are not supposed to have any say whatsoever in the matter, yet they cannot refrain from comments and covert pressure. They openly oppose the decision of their children to move to another Kibbutz and do their utmost to win them back. Their opposition to out-movement "exogamy" is particularly strong and stubborn in cases of extra-movement unions leading to desertion of the Kibbutz and estrangement from the movement.

The "exogamous" tendencies of the children should be examined in conjunction with the "endogamous" preferences of their parents. *In the confrontation between the generations the parents represent the tendency toward in-marriage, while the children represent the tendency toward out-*

[30] For a fuller analysis see Yonina Talmon-Garber, "Social Structure and Family Size," op. cit., pp. 121–146; and Moshe Sarell, "The Second Generation in Collective Settlements," *Megamoth*, 11 (1961), 123–132 (in Hebrew).

marriage. Viewed in this context, "exogamy" is, among other things, an attempt to cut loose from the parents and redefine relations with the first generation. Our material reveals many undertones of resentment and opposition to the parents' generation. Exogamy is often defended in terms of the right of the second generation to self-determination and free choice, irrespective of the wishes of the parents and the Kibbutz. The parents want to hold their children back and to tie them as securely as possible to their Kibbutz. The second generation has a strong urge to break out and explore the more variegated possibilities of the surrounding world. Exogamy is an attempt to dissociate from the first generation as a whole and from the parents. It expresses a quest for a separate and partly independent identity.[31]

This interpretation of "exogamy" throws additional light on the functions of the intermediate marriage patterns. These patterns are compromise solutions that enable members of the second generation to meet the pressures impinging on them half way and to work out the dilemma of continuity versus discontinuity.[32] Our study indicates that in the majority of cases the conflict is resolved in favor of continuity. Most members of the second generation either stay in their native Kibbutz or join another one. Joining a young frontier Kibbutz and starting anew there is essentially a re-enactment of the revolutionary deed of the parent generation. Although it breaks local continuity, it affirms the revolutionary tradition. The individual quest for a separate identity is an aspect of the revolutionary ideology and as such is not without normative support. Only a minority of the second generation marry outside the movement and dissociate themselves from it. Total estrangement is uncommon.

Our material did not allow full examination of the relation between choice of marital partner and degree of identification with the Kibbutz and the movement. Extra-movement unions, however, are more prevalent in less integrated Kibbutzim, in which a rebellious second generation rejects many of the tenets of the collectivist ideology, than in Kibbutzim in which the second generation is more loyal to the Kibbutz and its values. Only 6 per cent of marriages in the most integrated Kibbutz are extra-movement marriages, compared with 27 per cent in the least integrated one. In many cases a decision to marry outside the movement is not an accidental outcome of circumstances, but a culminating step in a long developmental process of dissociation; it reinforces a pre-existing estrangement.[33] *By combining "exogamy" and "endogamy," the second generation reconciles dissociation with identification and maintains a flexible balance between rebellion and loyalty.*

Mate selection is thus a solution to the basic dilemma of individuation. The intermediate patterns make it possible for members of the second

[31] Mate selection is viewed as a resolution of conflicts in the process of identity formation in Maria H. Levinson and Daniel J. Levinson, "Jews Who Intermarry," *Yivo Annual*, 12 (1958/59), 103–129; see also John E. Mayer, *Jewish-Gentile Courtships*, Glencoe, Ill.: The Free Press, 1961.

[32] For a general discussion of the problem of identity and loyalty to a historical heritage, see Erik H. Erikson, "Youth, Fidelity and Diversity," in Erikson (ed.), *Youth: Change and Challenge*, op. cit., pp. 1–23.

[33] For a close analogy see the analysis of the "emancipated" type in Levinson and Levinson, op. cit.

generation to maintain continuity without being totally hemmed in and encapsulated. The compromise between in- and out-marriage enables them to cut loose without losing their roots, to remain within the fold yet achieve distinctiveness.

CONCLUSION

This case study highlights the importance of mate selection patterns as major integrating mechanisms. The thesis that marriage brings about a realignment of the social structure, and that it has a direct bearing on the cohesion and continuity of the social system, has been fully demonstrated with respect to kinship-dominated primitive and traditional societies. The social functions of mate selection are less evident when we turn to non-familistic societies. The decline in the strategic importance of kin lines, which reduces the impact of mate selection on the overall institutional structure, reduces also the need for stringent regulation of mate choice. Young people are given more leeway in their choice of marital partners and the channeling of selection becomes more indirect and covert. Spontaneous love is regarded as the most important basis of marriage, and mate selection is defined as a purely personal matter. Relegation of mate selection to the private sphere obscures its social functions. Small wonder that most theories of mate selection in modern societies deal with it as a process of inter-personal negotiation and minimize its repercussions on the social structure. Great emphasis is put on the "fit" and compatibility between personalities in terms of either complementary or similar character traits.[34]

The present study demonstrates the inadequacy of a purely interpersonal approach to the analysis of mate selection. The Kibbutz is a non-familistic revolutionary society. Kinship affiliations are irrelevant in most institutional spheres and there is no institutionalized normative regulation of mate choice. Yet marriage patterns have a direct impact on the cohesion and continuity of the social system; *they mesh closely with the overall institutional structure and serve as crucial integrating mechanisms even in non-familistic societies.*[35]

Analysis of the intermediate marriage patterns revealed that their main function is to maintain a delicate and flexible balance between in-group closure and intergroup connectedness. *Endogamy is essentially a segregating boundary maintaining mechanism*, safeguarding the internal uniformity and cohesion of the group and ensuring its continuity as a distinctive unit. *Exogamy is an interlinking associative mechanism*, connecting groups and cementing them together as segmental units within wider ranging unities. Ascendancy of endogamy leads to withdrawal from out-group commitments and to separatism. Ascendancy of exogamy leads to over-diffusion of attach-

[34] See, for instance, Robert F. Winch, *Mate Selection*, New York: Harper, 1953; Irving Rosow, "Issues in the Concept of Need Complementarity," *Sociometry*, 20 (September, 1954), pp. 216–223; Reuben Hill and Evelyn M. Duvall, *Family Development*, Chicago: J. B. Lippincott, 1957.

[35] For an analysis of the social functions of love and marriage in modern societies see Goode, op. cit. and Slater, op. cit.

ments and to attenuation and withering of narrower loyalties. It engenders discord and conflicting commitments and threatens continuity. The intermediate patterns reconcile the drawing inward with the thrust outward. The centrifugal tendencies in exogamy are held in check by the centripetal drag of endogamy. *A combination of exogamy and endogamy militates against insulation yet safeguards distinctiveness.*

While I have emphasized the social functions of the patterns of mate selection, I have also examined the ways in which the marriage patterns meet the needs and interests of the individuals directly concerned. Developmental analysis has revealed that the interpersonal "fit" approach is inadequate even with respect to individual motivation. One of the most important conclusions of this study is that mate selection is a way of resolving the conflict between rebellion and loyalty. *The quest for the most intimate role partner is influenced by the way in which collective identification is counterpointed by individual identity.* The development of a lasting commitment to a spouse is intertwined with the process of defining and delimiting one's commitments to the collective.[36] Marriage involves an interplay between the life-stage transition of the individual and social processes. Individual choice has far-reaching repercussions on the social system and conversely, social system determinants channel and direct individual choice.[37]

And last, but perhaps most important, this study has dealt with the more general theoretical problem of *the relation between functional and causal analyses.* Starting from the assumption that elucidation of functions cannot in and by itself account for the distribution of the marriage patterns, I have sought the efficient, operative causes and direct determinants of action and spelled out the institutional mechanisms and devices that channel and influence mate choice. An important connecting link between the two modes of analysis is *purposeful action based on awareness of function.* The anticipation of future outcome contributes to the movement toward a goal so that this goal is, to some extent at least, a cause of its causes.[38] The Kibbutz is a planned society. So far as some of the institutional patterns affecting mate selection directly or indirectly are introduced with reference to their intended consequences, analysis of function leads to analysis of cause.

Another important connecting link between functional and causal analyses

---

[36] See Erikson, op. cit., p. 20; see also his "The Problem of Ego Identity," in *Identity and the Life Cycle, Psychological Issues*, New York: International Universities Press, 1959, Vol. I, No. 1. In terms of Erikson's analysis of critical life stage tasks, our case study indicates that the process of establishing intimacy is closely intertwined with the process of identity formation.

[37] For an attempt to relate social, ideological and personal factors in the process of choice see Alan Kerchoff and Keith E. Davies, "Value Consensus and Need Complementarity in Mate Selection," *American Sociological Review*, 27 (June, 1962), 295–304.

[38] Cf. Dorothy Emmet, *Function, Purpose and Powers*, London: Macmillan, 1958; Carl G. Hempel, "The Logic of Functional Analysis," in Llewellyn Gross (ed.), *Symposium on Sociological Theory*, Evanston, Ill.: Row Peterson, 1959, pp. 271–307; and Harold Fallding, "Functional Analysis in Sociology," *American Sociological Review*, 28 (February, 1963), 5–13.

is *the degree of individual identification with society and its values.* Recognition that an institutional pattern serves the best interests of society would not, in itself, guarantee that it would be adopted and adhered to. Identification with the Kibbutz partially merges personal and collective goals. Hence the considerable congruence between individual needs and aspirations and long range societal interests, which leads to the development of a personal commitment to continuity.

But this is only part of the explanation. Marriage is not regulated by consciously held norms. Moreover, most functions of the marriage patterns are latent. Recognition of the issues involved is partial, vague and unequally distributed within the system. Even leaders and educators, who are more clearly conscious of the effects of mate selection on the social system than those directly concerned, recognized only some of the implications of the problem. Purposeful and conscious indirect control of mate selection is of only secondary importance. Channeling of mate choice occurs primarily as an unintended, unanticipated or even undesired consequences of *institutional arrangements made for other purposes.* The incidence of the marriage patterns is determined mainly by the framework and setting of interaction and by the interpersonal relations engendered by the social structure and by the system of socialization. The processes that influence mate choice stem from the internal dynamics of the system and reflect the *tensions and conflicting interests, the pressures and counter-pressures inherent in it.* Thus, elucidation of functions and examination of causes are partly overlapping yet partly independent modes of analysis.

IV | *Premarital Sexual Relationships*

Introduction to Section IV

Two elements are at the heart of understanding the dynamics of our mate-selection system. One of these is love, and we discussed that in Section III. The other one is sex, and that is discussed in this section. As with other sections of this reader, the ideas developed in one section are integrated with ideas developed in other sections. There are related articles in the last section of the book on illegitimacy, homosexuality, and group sex. There is much more to sexual relations than what occurs premaritally, but in this section the focus is on premarital heterosexuality.

Two basic criticisms of research on premarital sex were that it lacked data on the all-important area of attitudes toward sex in addition to the actual behavior and that the research utilized poor samples. I sought to meet these criticisms in my own work on premarital sex during the 1960s. I focused on the study of premarital sexual attitudes and I utilized a sample chosen so as to represent the nation. This is the only national probability sample used for analysis of premarital sexual relationships. It was published in book form in 1967.[1] The basic question I sought to answer was why some groups were more permissive than other groups. These findings were the first national indications of the increase of premarital sexual permissiveness among the college-educated portion of the American population. As such they indicated the changes that were occurring in social class orientations to premarital sex.

Rather than try to present in detail the many specific findings of my research and that of others such as Kinsey, I have decided that it would be more valuable to give the student an overview of the changes that have been occurring as they are recorded in history and in the several key researches that have been

[1] Reiss, I. L., *The Social Context of Premarital Sexual Permissiveness.* New York: Holt, Rinehart and Winston, 1967.

carried out. With this in mind I have written, especially for this reader, my article (12) in this section and have attempted therein to present a perspective on current developments in premarital sexual relationships. I have tried to write this in a nontechnical style and have appended references that the interested reader can consult.

The textbooks on marriage and the family have for decades had a bias against premarital sexual intercourse. This was gradually corrected in the 1960s, although it is by no means fully eliminated from all texts in use even in the 1970s. One of the basic—and erroneous—assumptions of this approach was that all premarital sexual relationships were of one sort and all led to the same set of consequences. Harold Christensen's research (13) compared attitudes and behavior regarding premarital sex among college students in Denmark, Indiana, and Utah. He found that the Danish students were more acceptant of premarital coitus, that they experienced less guilt, were less likely to rush into marriage if pregnant, less likely to have high divorce rates among the premaritally pregnant couples, and were more equalitarian. The same act of intercourse in Utah was more likely to lead to guilt, and pregnancy was more likely to lead to a hasty marriage and high probability of divorce. Thus, Christensen's data force us to assert that the consequences of premarital coitus vary according to the subcultural group to which one belongs. Any moral judgment of premarital coitus must now take this set of findings into consideration and therefore a stereotypic view of premarital sex is less likely to develop.

One additional—and rare—value of the Christensen article is that it presents data from 1958 that may be compared with more recent data from 1968. There has been a good deal of talk regarding changes in sexual attitudes and behaviors in recent decades. Most of the research evidence from Kinsey and others, however, indicated that the increase in the percentage of nonvirginal females at marriage occurred just before the 1920s, when it increased from about one of every four to one of every two. Since that time the changes seem to be more in the realm of attitudes and public awareness of what was going on. Nevertheless, starting in the late 1960s surveys of college campuses began to report higher rates of nonvirginity. For example, Kinsey reported roughly 20 percent of college girls nonvirginal by the age of 20, whereas more recent studies reported roughly 40 percent nonvirginal at the same age. Christensen's findings in three cultures supports the idea that changes have occurred and spells these out in some detail. Christensen's study and others have encouraged me to accept the position that female nonvirginity rates have changed since the mid-1960s. I indicate by current thinking in article 12 (see especially pp. 179–180).

Ever since the 1970 report of the Commission on Obscenity and Pornography appeared, there has been interest and controversy over the impact of "obscene" materials on young people, particularly over their role in encouraging premarital sexual relationships. The Commission report seemed to indicate that although there was a temporary arousal, pornography predominantly motivated behavior that the individual had already tried, such as masturbation, petting, or coitus. Some of the interesting work on the differential impact of visual material on males and females was done at the Institute for Sexual Research at the University of Hamburg, Germany, by Gunter Schmidt and Volknar Sigusch (14). They found smaller male–female differences than did Kinsey and they speculate as to whether this is a result of freer sex codes or of their particular sample.

12 | Premarital Sexuality: Past, Present and Future

IRA L. REISS

THE PAST: MYTH AND REALITY

One of our most prevalent myths is that in past centuries the typical form of courtship was that of two virgins meeting, falling in love, and doing very little with each other sexually. They then married, learned about sex together in the marital bed, and remained faithful to each other until death separated them. I am certain that some couples did have exactly that type of experience and I would go even further and grant that this happens in some cases today. But the key point is that I am sure it was never the common pattern for the majority of Americans. The evidence for this exists in large part in historical records. We know, for example, that in Massachusetts at a well-known church in the last part of the eighteenth century one in every three women who married confessed fornication to her minister. The major reason for making such a confession would be that the woman was pregnant and if she did not make that confession at her marriage, the baby could not be baptized. Many other girls who were nonvirginal but not pregnant would likely not confess fornication to their minister. This was the time of bundling in New England and many ministers blamed the high premarital pregnancy rates on that custom. It is probable that much of the pregnancy occurred after engagement. Engagements in those days were very seldom broken and thus were more akin to actual marriage. In any case it seems clear that at the time of the formal marriage, the sexual innocence of many couples was questionable.

The Double Standard

If we look at male nonvirginity, the picture becomes even more extreme. Certainly the history of the western frontier was not one of male virginity. In fact it was quite the contrary. The western frontier was settled largely by males and this male-dominated society had a heavy reliance on prostitution. The very term "red light district" comes from the custom of girls in prostitution houses leaving a red lantern in the window so that the cowboys riding into town would know "where the action was." "Gunsmoke" notwithstanding, dance hall girls did more than dance. In the typical case the upstairs rooms were where the girls would entice the customers to take them and then collect a suitable fee for the sexual services rendered.

To further show the mythical quality of our view of the past, let us briefly look back at the 1870's and the women's liberation movement of that time. In New York City we find Victoria Claflin and her sister, "Tennessee," setting up a brokerage business as well as other ventures, including a weekly newspaper. Commodore Vanderbilt took to them favorably and helped considerably in getting them established. Victoria was a left-wing feminist who favored free love. She believed that a woman should live with a man if she loved him and leave him when she no longer loved him. She practiced what she preached and had more than one man living with her in New York City. The more conservative feminists like Harriet Beecher Stowe and Catherine Beecher attacked Victoria regularly and Victoria was annoyed by their statements. The brother of the Beecher sisters, the Reverend Henry Ward Beecher, lived in New York and was one of America's most famous ministers. Victoria tried to persuade the Reverend Beecher to prevail on his sisters to be less critical, but to no avail. Finally, she learned that while she was having an affair with a Mr. Tilton, Mrs. Tilton was having an affair with the Reverend Beecher. She threatened to reveal the adultery in her weekly newspaper if the Beecher girls were not quieted. Either due to inability or lack of effort, the Reverend Beecher did not succeed in quieting his sisters' criticisms of Victoria. True to her word, Victoria publicized the adulterous affair of the Reverend Beecher and Mrs. Tilton in her weekly newspaper on November 2, 1872. Adultery was against the law and a trial ensued. The character of the age was revealed in the outcome of the trial. During the events that followed, the Reverend Beecher was acquitted by a hung jury of the charge of adultery and Mrs. Tilton was charged by a church committee of "indefensible conduct" with the Reverend Beecher. The Victorian era of 100 years ago was surely not an era of the single standard of abstinence. The Beecher-Tilton scandal displayed the nineteenth century's orthodox double standard with its granting of greater sexual privileges to males. Once again the data fail to support the virginal view of our historical past.

One final example that illustrates the sexual orientation of the nineteenth century is afforded by the Philadelphia World's Fair of 1876. The aspect of that fair that echoed around the country was the introduction of the first vulcanized rubber condom for males. This condom was on display at the Fair and created a great deal of interest. Previous to that time condoms were made out of animal skins and a vulcanized rubber condom was a notable advance. But in a culture that was largely practicing abstinence, this contraceptive advance would hardly have received so much notice. However, in a society where prostitution was rampant and where people were concerned with avoiding venereal disease and unwanted pregnancy, such an advance was important. It was about this same time that the diaphragm and the pessary cap were invented. A few decades later, by the time of World War I, knowledge of these contraceptive techniques had spread widely among the wealthier and better educated classes and did create an impact of major importance on their sexual behavior. I will speak of this impact very shortly.

Not only is it mistaken to think of earlier generations of Americans as people who mostly entered marriage virginally, but this view would be erroneous for virtually any society. I have examined the historical and cross-cultural record rather closely and have found no society, at any time in history, in which the majority of even one generation of its males remained virginal on reaching physical maturity—say age twenty or so. This is not an argument against a single standard of abstinence, it is rather a statement of the fact that no society has been able to achieve abstinence for both sexes unless they sanctioned either child marriage or very youthful matings. It is not difficult to understand why no society has been able to produce a generation of virginal males. The reason is very likely that since males are in power in almost all societies, it is unlikely that they would structure that societal system so as to deny themselves access to sexual pleasures before marriage. The major change in premarital sexuality throughout history has been in the partners of men. Societies have differed mainly in the selection of female partners for men. Such partners have at times come from groups such as slaves, prostitutes, lower-class females, or the girl next door. The basic shift in the partners of men in the twentieth century is toward a majority of the women and away from small select groups. In earlier centuries cultures utilized other categories of females and smaller groups of females as the sex partners for males. There have been historical periods wherein women have been temporarily liberated sexually—for example, the Elizabethan period. But the situation in twentieth century America is different in some key respects. First, in past times the sexual liberalization was of a small group, the ruling class or the aristocracy. Such a change then affected only a small proportion of the total female population; and such changes were not as long lived as the current sexual liberalization of women in America. Also, the sexual liberalization was often in extramarital sex and not in premarital sex.

General Trends

According to our best information the majority of American women have been entering marriage nonvirginal for over fifty years. Kinsey's findings indicated that about half the women born in the 1900–1910 decade were nonvirginal at marriage. This proportion rose only slightly until the late 1960's but since then it seems to have risen rapidly. Sometime around the first world war the proportion of nonvirginal women doubled from about 25 to 50 percent and during the late 1960's the proportion probably has risen from about 50 percent to 70 or 75 percent. In the fifty years from World War I to the late 1960's the predominant change was not in the proportion of women nonvirginal but rather in the attitudes of women and men toward premarital sexuality. During that half century, guilt feelings were reduced, the public discussion of sex increased radically, probably the number of partners increased, and the closeness to marriage required for coitus to be acceptable decreased. For males, other changes were occurring. Males were becoming more discriminate; they were beginning to feel that sex with someone they felt affection for, person-centered sex, was much to be preferred to body-centered coitus. The male partners were shifting from the prostitute and the lower-class female to the girl next door. One of the most dramatic decreases that has constantly evidenced itself during the twentieth century is the rapid decline in the proportion of males, particularly college-educated males, who have experienced intercourse with a prostitute. That proportion today is probably only a small percentage.

The basic change then during the past centuries has been from an orthodox double standard ethic of premarital sexuality, which allowed males to copulate but which condemned their partners as "bad" women, to a more modified version of the double standard in which women are allowed to have premarital coitus but not quite with the abandon of men. Of course, this is an oversimplification and with almost 210 million Americans there are many variations in standards. There are those who are fully equalitarian in a permissive direction and also those who are equalitarian in a restrictive direction, and there still are those who are orthodox double standard. But the overall shift is toward less dominance of the sexual scene by males. This by no means indicates full equality of the sexes but rather a lessening of inequality.

Full equality in the sexual sphere is not possible today given the different priorities of family and occupational roles that males and females have. This is a point that present-day Women's Liberation adherents have often made. Regardless of whether one agrees with all the beliefs of Women's Liberation, this particular point seems sociologically well established. If females think that getting married and starting a family is their first priority in life and place occupational ambitions secondary to this, then they will view sex in terms of these goals. This means that they will consider whether copulating with a boy will waste time in their search for a mate; whether this boy will tell others what happened and thus hurt their chances of getting married; whether having intercourse will make a boy more seriously committed to marriage or less; and so forth. These concerns are nowhere near as potent to a male, for he is not so strongly oriented toward marriage as his primary life goal. In the middle class his primary goal will be an occupational career and having premarital intercourse is not very likely to matter one way or the other in terms of that goal. Surely men today are oriented toward marriage but the immediate pressures felt by such a marriage goal are considerably less than those felt by females. A male is not that concerned with the time wasted in an affair, nor is he so worried about the impact of the word getting around that he is having an affair. In fact, in many circles news of such an affair might enhance his image as an exciting date or a romantic interest for females.

The Role of Contraception

One of the key factors that encouraged the sexual liberalization of women, particularly in the middle and upper classes, was the contraceptive revolution of the late nineteenth century. As I noted above, it was almost one hundred years ago that the vulcanized rubber condom, the pessary cap, and the diaphragm made their appearance on the scene. To be sure these methods were known and used predominantly by the upper 20 or 30 percent of the population. There were contraceptive measures available from the biblical method of "withdrawal" to Casanova's method of placing a hollowed out lemon rind over the cervix. What was new about the late nineteenth century methods was that they were extremely effective in preventing pregnancy and they occurred at a time when there was a large group of well-off people with a strong demand for such techniques. Let me briefly elaborate on this.

Ever since Priscilla told John to speak for himself, it has been clear to historians of the family that the American courtship system was to a very high degree run by the participants in it and not directly controlled by parents. By the late nineteenth century this meant that due to the size and complexity of the new urban centers and the fact that even in 1890 almost 4 million women were working, parents could not possibly know the people that their children were dating. This autonomy of dating coupled with the high risk taking and the pleasure emphasis that youth culture has always exhibited meant that the desire for sexual pleasures would be relatively strong. Being alone with an attractive person of the opposite sex for several hours on a date exposed one to high temptation. Yet the upper- and middle-class groups in this country were considerably concerned with having legitimate children. Thus sexual desires were present but so was the inhibitory influence of a strong desire to avoid illegitimate offspring. The development of very effective contraceptive methods that would avoid pregnancy in the late nineteenth century afforded a way out of the dilemma. By the time of the first world war, condoms were available in a variety of places and their usefulness was widely known. The better-off male could use them and have intercourse with relative safety from venereal disease and also with the comfort that he was unlikely to impregnate his partner. This meant that he would be more likely to feel free to copulate with the girl next door. Females, too, became aware that males could avoid impregnating them and this must have had an important impact on their sexual orientations. It was mainly married women who used diaphragms but the attitude that males could prevent pregnancy with condoms and that females too had available methods lessened the view of pregnancy as an uncontrollable consequence.

The lower classes historically had a record of high premarital sexual permissiveness, although much of that record is impressionistically recorded. The lack of knowledge of contraception did not deter the lower classes over the centuries. The probable reason for this was that economic pressures were such as to make marriage to a man who could earn a steady living and support a wife and family not very likely. Thus the alternative of children born out of wedlock, although not desired or preferred, still had to be tolerated. The new middle- and upper-class permissiveness was not based on the difficulty of economically sound marriages, nor on the fatalism or social disorganization that was so common in the lower classes. The new middle- and upper-class permissiveness was based on an ethic of person-centered sexuality that stressed intimacy with those one was in love with. It also stressed a rational control of undesired consequences such as venereal disease and premarital pregnancy. The ethic of freedom of choice, equalitarianism, and pursuit of happiness is stronger in this new middle- and upper-class sexual emancipation. Thus the early thrust of the new sexuality that appeared around World War I was related to contraceptive advances that made possible both sexual pleasure and the avoidance of unwanted pregnancies.

THE CURRENT SCENE

The Impact of the Pill

The topic of contraception affords a bridge into the current situation regarding premarital sexuality. Many people believe that the availability of the pill contraceptive, starting about 1960, has had a major impact on sexual beliefs and behaviors. I think this case has been oversold. As noted above, I do believe that in the past the condom and diaphragm did have such an impact on the middle and upper classes. This was so because these classes wanted to participate in sexual behavior but also wanted desperately to avoid pregnancy. In addition, they had no highly effective techniques readily available. Under such conditions the introduction of effective techniques can have a dramatic impact. The doubling of the female nonvirginity rates around World War I was partially a result of this force. Of course, diversity in norms, changes in religious controls, and urban-industrial development also were important causal variables contributing to the growth of the new permissiveness.

The introduction of the pill in the 1960's was something quite different from the introduction of the condom in the 1870's. In the 1960's there already were highly effective contraceptive techniques and they were widely disseminated to the middle and upper classes. The pill was simply another technique that was highly effective. It is easy to overestimate the pill's effectiveness. It does require a rather routinized, organized, person for it to work. The pill must be taken each day for twenty days a month and any lapses can lead to pregnancy. Also, there are side effects, mostly minor ones such as weight gain and temporary nausea and such, but they too may lead to preference for other methods. Finally, the pill method means that the male will not use a condom and this radically increases the risk of venereal disease for both the male and the female. I am saying all this not to belittle the pill technique but rather to place it in perspective. It is a valuable method of contraception but has its limitations as do all human inventions.

More important than its effectiveness is the fact that the pill places the control of contraception in the hands of the female. Furthermore it does this in a way that still allows the act to occur spontaneously since the pill does not have to be taken in conjunction with the act of coitus. The consequences of this are multiple. For some females the thought of being constantly ready for coitus is not acceptable. They want to be carried away by romantic feelings of the moment and they want the male to be the aggressor and for the male to plan to be ready for coitus. This attitude leads to a high risk of pregnancy and is often heard in unwed mother's homes.

A second result of the contraceptive control being in female hands is that the female comes to value sexuality much more highly than before. Her risks of conception are reduced and her abilities to enjoy the physical aspects of sex and view herself as a sexual creature are increased. This is a slow process and it is reinforced by many other aspects of our type of courtship situation. It is part of the increased similarity of men and women in their view of sexuality. Women today are more likely than before to value sex for its own sake and men are more likely today to value sex with affection. As I have noted above, the sexes still differ in that women are more oriented to affectionate sexuality and men more oriented to body-centered sexuality but each sex has increasingly learned to appreciate the major orientation of the other. In sum then the importance of the pill, in my mind, is not that it is so effective contraceptively but that it places the burden of contraception on the female and therefore forces her to think about her own sexuality.

The Legitimacy of Choice

Probably the major characteristic of the current premarital sex scene is the felt legitimacy of the sexual choice. More than any other characteristic this one epitomizes what has changed in the last half century. It is no longer a secretive choice of sexual codes that is made privately and with great guilt if the choice is not abstinence. There is still an element of privacy and still an element of psychological qualms often present, but the degree of change is vast. Boys have always talked openly about certain aspects of their sexual lives with other males and this continues. However, there is change here, too, in that more males seem willing to admit they have difficulties sexually, in their thinking as well as in their behavior. The mask of the naturalness of sex for males is increasingly being put aside. Furthermore, the affectionate affair is being protected by privacy except from close friends. Here then is a change for males in the area of sexual communication. Conversely, females do talk more about their affairs, although most fully with their very close friends.

I have visited dozens of campuses during the past few years on speaking engagements and over and over I was impressed with the openness of communication regarding sex on the part of females. Very intimate details are kept for close friends but many other aspects of sex, such as attitudes toward premarital coitus, acceptability of oral love, and such, are increasingly discussed. I recall one coed telling me how naive one of her sorority sisters was. This girlfriend was soon to be married and was unaware of the very common role of mouth-genital sex in marriage. The coed looked at her friend as being very poorly informed and lacking experience. Such comments are frequently made and indicate a striving for sophistication in knowledge and somewhat in acceptance and experience on the part of coeds today.

The choice of how to think and behave sexually is now accepted as an important choice for young people to make and they are seriously exploring the full range of possibilities in their conversations with same and opposite sex friends. It is true that there are many parents today who do not accept the legitimacy of such sexual choices and who believe that only abstinence is the proper path. But the majority of young people believe the choice is legitimately theirs in sex as it is in politics, religion, and other personal areas of their existence.

Generation versus Role Changes

My comment above on parent-child differences concerning the legitimacy of the sexual choice might mislead the reader into thinking that the basic change in premarital sex is a generational one. During the early 1960's I selected several samples of high school students, college students, and one national sample that was chosen to represent the nation. The results of this study, the only one to date to utilize a representative national sample for intensive analysis of sexual relationships before marriage, were published in my 1967 book, *The Social Context of Premarital Sexual Permissiveness*. One of our most interesting findings was that the difference between 55-year olds and 25-year olds was not very dramatic. However, the differences between people of the same age who were single, married without children, or married and parents of dating-age children were indeed dramatic. For example, 45-year-old bachelors were highly acceptant of premarital intercourse, whereas 45-year-old married people without children or with little children were much less acceptant, and 45-year-old married people with teenage or older children were the least acceptant of premarital intercourse. People of the same age are of the same generation and yet their differences are much greater than people who are of different ages and generations. Thus it is the specific role we play that is most important in how we feel about premarital sexuality.

The same parents who themselves participated in premarital coitus may well change and become less permissive as they move into the parental role. The reasons for this are not hard to find. The parent does not experience the pleasures of sex that his child is undergoing, nor is he exposed to the temptations of being with an attractive person of the opposite sex on a date. In addition, the parent is held responsible by the community if his daughter becomes pregnant or his child contracts venereal disease. We found that even older siblings were low on sexual permissiveness compared to their younger siblings because as older siblings they were put into parentlike supervisory roles. Thus the roles an individual plays in society are a major factor in determining his level of acceptable premarital activity. It follows then that there are 45-year-old bachelors who are more sexually liberated than some 20-year-olds. Thus young people are not all involved in the new changes in sexuality nor are older people excluded from such changes.

The forces that promote premarital permissiveness on the part of young people in their courtship roles are also not hard to understand. If we were to invite a sociologist from another country to visit our country and examine our courtship system and tell us what he thinks it accomplishes sexually and how it operates, what would he say? He would note that the average young person dates for approximately ten years and that at least during the last five years of that period, the typical pattern of dating involves (1) the use of some sort of drug such as alcohol or pot, (2) the occurrence of dancing with movements that are clearly genital and sexual in meaning, and (3) a period of time at the end of each date when the couple are supposed to be allowed privacy. That privacy is very often supplied by the young person's parents. The living room of the girl is a very common place for the last hour of a date to take place. It is also the most common place for a girl to start having intercourse. Her parents are upstairs usually "trusting her to behave properly." It is not typical for parents to spy on their youngsters and try to catch them copulating. These parents also teach that love is a key justification for behavior and being self-reliant is important. Such values also help to develop an acceptance of sexuality on the part of their children.

Our foreign sociologist would surely look upon this system and note that it is well organized to promote sexual intimacies between young people. I feel sure that if we presented him with the figures showing the majority of females and almost all males entering marriage nonvirginally, his amazement would not be that the figures are so high but, to the contrary, that they are so low. The question that needs answering is not why do so many people have premarital intercourse—that can easily be understood by examining our type of courtship—the key question is why do so few people have premarital intercourse. How does anyone go through years of such an intimacy-promoting type of courtship institution and avoid having intercourse? The answer to this question resides in good measure in the basic emphasis by females, and increasingly also by males, on person-centered coitus. Such coitus stresses the value of close ties to another person and thus puts limits on casual coitus and imposes difficulties in locating proper sex partners. Our marriage-for-love type of system implies that person-centered sexual behavior should be involved in some way in our courtship institution and thus such a development is not surprising. It is these monogamous norms that have much to do with the control of coitus when it occurs. This is especially true for females. Males are still more body centered and therein lies part of the "battle of the sexes."

In a very basic, fundamental sense, all Americans regardless of age are involved in the changes that are occurring in our sexual orientations. How could it be otherwise? Parents of the young people who are involved in premarital sex cannot ignore the greater openness of discussion of sex because much of it occurs right in the home. Also, parents themselves are encouraged by sex education courses in the public schools, by courses in adult education, by articles in the popular press, by the mass media, and in many other ways to think more carefully and fully about the meaning of sex. This is not simply a youth rebellion, it is a cultural change rooted in our rapid movement toward a post-industrial society. Further, it is clear to this writer that the stress on examination of premarital sexuality leads to an examination of marital and extramarital sexuality as well. The stress on variety in marital sexuality and the examination of the conditions under which swinging or old-fashioned secretive adultery may be acceptable are highly visible phenomena in the lives of millions of people in the over-30 generation. In part this spread of sexual dialogue is due to the fact that when the same young people who have examined their sexuality premaritally do marry, they tend to carry over this rational, examining approach. I find many more couples today who are working out agreements on extramarital sex before they marry. Many of these agreements are the conventional one of being faithful but others are agreements regarding under what conditions extramarital sex of various types would be allowed. This is new and shows how extramarital sex has also come under scrutiny.

In good measure it is "situational ethics" that stresses the importance of the particular person and his circumstances as a key causal factor. We are becoming more and more aware of the fact that standards may differ and yet be equally "correct" due to personal and situational differences. The absolutes of this view of ethics can only hold for all those of a certain type in a certain situation and not for all mankind regardless. Thus everyone must find out who he is and what his situation or life style consists of. The stress of our civilization today is increasingly on self-realization, personal fulfillment, and happiness and thus situational ethics is a very compatible philosophy for it allows for a self-designed ethical system. Large segments of Americans at all age levels are involved in this search for self-discovery and for a more personally designed life style. I am sure that America will still have shared patterns of life styles and will not atomize into over 200 million different life styles. But I am equally sure that the variety of tolerated life styles has increased at all age levels. The point I am making is the extensiveness of this search for selfhood.

Social Class Differences in Sexuality

One other important area of change that was discovered in my national research during the 1960's concerns social class differences in premarital sexual attitudes. It has long been believed that the lower classes were the most permissive in both attitude and behavior, and that the upper or college-educated group were the least permissive of the social classes. As a matter of historical fact, I do believe there is good evidence to support this proposition. But sometime during the twentieth century, probably about the time World War II was ending, this situation was no longer so true. When we took our national sample in 1963 and examined it for the expected relation between social class and premarital sexual permissiveness, we found no relationship at all. We also looked at four college samples and two high school samples and found no relation between the social class background of the person and his level of premarital sexual permissiveness. This was one of the most exciting findings and it is reported on in depth in my 1967 book. Let me simply state here that after very elaborate computer checks what we discovered was that there were, in relation to sexual orientation at least, two radically different social class systems. We divided our sample into thirds and labeled each third either "lower," "middle," or "upper" class. If among all the respondents, we looked only at conservative people—that is, people who were conservative in politics, education, and religion—then we would indeed find that the lower-class people in this conservative group were the most permissive. However, if we look only at liberal people—that is, liberal in politics, education, and religion—then we find that the lower-class people are the least permissive and the upper-class (college-educated) people are the most permissive. Thus there are two opposite types of people in each social class level. The aspect of this situation that is new is the presence of a highly permissive group among the upper third of the social class hierarchy. This group, I believe, has emerged gradually but became noticeable only during the past twenty-five years or less. They are members of the largest growing occupational groups—professionals and managers. It was in the professional group particularly that highly permissive individuals were found. This group, I would argue, has been most influenced by the contraceptive revolution begun at the Philadelphia World's Fair of 1876. They have the highest educational level, the highest incomes, and the greatest amount of time to think about things other than food, clothing, and shelter. I believe that the possibility of avoiding consequences like pregnancy and venereal disease led to this group becoming increasingly sexually permissive. Much of the professional group was for a long time politically, educationally, and religiously liberal. The possibility of controlling negative consequences of sex led to their also becoming sexually liberal. In the campus changes of the last few years, many of the student leaders and certainly many of the sympathizers have come from this upper third of the population and from professional parents. It should be clear that there are professionals who are rather low on permissiveness but compared to other groups who fall in the top one third of our status hierarchy, the professional group contains a relatively larger proportion of high sexual permissive individuals.

This growth of a permissive upper class is a very important occurrence;

because if the leaders in this country are permissive in the area of sex, then change in this area through more liberal legislation should be forthcoming. We have already seen radical change in the past five years in the area of abortion laws, contraceptive distribution, and censorship decisions. I believe this trend will continue due to the influence of this powerful professional group. The new sexual orientation is exactly what would be expected from a college-educated group in that it emphasizes control of pregnancy and venereal disease and stresses person-centered sexual encounters. In short, it differs from the older, lower-class permissiveness which had an economic base and a fatalistic philosophy and this difference is in ways that character-ize college-student culture. Thus it is really not surprising to find high levels of the new permissiveness in those with college backgrounds who end up in professional positions.

THE NEXT DECADES: THE LIKELY OUTCOMES

Given the above situation regarding the past and present, what can we say about the future of sex during the balance of this century? First, let us examine the notions of some people that full sexual equality is coming and males and females will be identically oriented to sex. We spoke of this briefly before—we shall pursue it more fully here. The worth of such an outcome is not the issue, merely its likelihood. We have already noted a trend toward greater male-female similarity in sexual orientation. That trend is shown even more specifically by the results of one of the studies done by Gunter Schmidt and his colleagues at the University of Hamburg concern-ing the impact of pornography.

Schmidt conducted a rather ingenious experiment. He used male and female volunteers and measured both their verbal response and their physio-logical response to pornographic materials. The males' verbal responses agreed with their physiological responses and both sources showed arousal from seeing the pornographic materials. The females' verbal responses indicated that they were more likely to be "shocked, irritated, or disgusted." However, their physiological responses were very similar to those of the males! Thus it seems that cultural training inhibits the females from full conscious enjoyment of the erotic materials. I am assuming that there was little cover up by females and that, despite their erotic physiological re-sponse, they at times also responded with feelings of distaste due to their training as females in a double-standard society. The level of similarity and yet the clear difference between males and females in the Schmidt study makes my point precisely. Clearly, there are strong areas of similarity be-tween males and females but equally clear is the fact that even today there still are vast areas of differences. The next few decades should reduce these differences but since they are, as we discussed above, rooted in the primacy given to the home for females, they are not likely to fully vanish.

Possible Limits on Feminist Goals

Alice Rossi and other feminists have suggested that what is needed is perhaps to have 20-hour work weeks for interested people; every husband

and wife would work 20 hours a week and spend another 20 hours per week taking care of the home. There are obvious difficulties in restructuring occupations to a 20-hour work week but the more serious difficulties lie elsewhere. The male group most favorable to this type of proposal consists of the professional and managerial people. We have seen that this group is high on sexual permissiveness and also liberal in other respects. However, it is precisely within this group that the strongest commitment to career lines and the strongest interest and enjoyment in work exists. Thus it is precisely those men who most accept sexual equality in occupation and home who are often too devoted to their own work to make this sort of change.

Lower down the social class hierarchy we note more patriarchal traditions and more opposition to male-female equality. It should be noted, too, that at these lower levels the interest in work outside the home on the part of the female also often decreases. The type of work that blue-collar wives can do is not nearly as challenging or interesting as that available to white-collar wives. Such blue-collar work would involve being a lathe operator, driving a truck, putting fenders on automobiles, and so on. The wealthier woman has ambitions for the professional, managerial, and technical jobs that offer more in money, prestige, and intellectual rewards. Thus there are built-in blocks to any total changeover to a 20-hour work week and a 20-hour home week.

What the feminists will accomplish will be to open up options such as the 20-hour work week as well as similar ones for those couples who can make a go of it. This in itself will be a major change and an important opportunity to those females who want to escape the full-time housewife role. However, I expect most women will still predominate in the home in the year 2000. Finally, although equality will increase over the next few decades, I expect males will still predominate in most areas of high-prestige occupations, although not to the extent they do today. If I am correct, then there will be greater equalization between the sexes in general and in their view of sexuality, but there will still be recognizable differences due to the blocks to full equality mentioned above.

Physiological Differences

It should be clear that there is no physiological barrier to sexual equality. The data we have from the Kinsey studies and also from the Masters and Johnson studies show clearly that there are more women who can achieve multiple orgasms than there are men and that some female rates of orgasm are far beyond what any male can hope to achieve. The lack of representative samples is not so serious a matter in this conclusion for we are certain that no group of males exists that can achieve orgasm every few seconds over and over again as many females do. The high-performing male is capable of about six or seven orgasms an hour and the few cases that exceed this do not even approach the extreme end of the female orgasm curve. If one were to venture a conclusion, the most probable one would be that women's orgasmic ability is greater on both ends of the curve; that is, more women fall in both the nonorgasmic category and the multiple orgasmic category.

Males are more clustered toward the center. Although it is entirely possible that females who are nonorgasmic could be psychologically trained to be orgasmic, it is not very likely that males could ever be trained to be as capable of multiple orgasms as are females. Thus overall, the advantage, orgasmically, would seem to go to the female.

Now, of course, there is more to sex than orgasms. It could still be true that males have some advantages in the ease with which they develop erotic imagery. Kinsey felt the male cortex afforded such an advantage. As a sociologist, I would tend to posit learning as the key factor in determining the sexes' different ability to "turn on" but we cannot be sure at this point. The most important conclusion to draw here is that we know that whatever innate differences exist between the sexes, we can bring up males and females to be relatively equal in their sexual orientation. The evidence for this comes from cross-cultural studies that report societies in which the sexes are relatively equal in their desire for coitus. Also, we know that even within our own society vast differences exist between female groups and these differences would seem to be based on training and experience. In my 1967 book I report on a comparison of samples of females from California and New York. Twice the percentage of females in California accepted premarital coitus as did those in New York. I assume that California girls are no different physiologically but rather that something in their life style is different. I will leave the exact specifications of such differences to future researchers.

Trends in Nonvirginity

What about some of the newer trends? For example, what is likely to be the percent premaritally nonvirginal among females and males in the remaining decades of this century? First, we should note that the percent of nonvirginal males has been about 85 to 90 percent for generations and thus there is little room for change here. Nevertheless, as pointed out earlier, there is change going on in the attitudinal area and in the type of partners with whom males have coitus. In the case of females there was an increase in the World War I period from about 25 percent to about 50 percent non-virginal by the time of marriage. There has been no indication of any change in this proportion except during the period from the late 1960's to date. During this recent period reports of studies showing 30 to 40 percent of the 20-year-old college girls nonvirginal have appeared. The Kinsey data from the 1940's showed only 20 percent of the 20-year-old college girls nonvirginal. These data are not conclusive evidence of a sharp increase in female nonvirginity. For example, if such an increase were occurring, we would expect to see some evidence of the increased female sexuality in an increase in the number of partners of women and in the percentage of women who mastur-bate and the frequency of masturbation. Few such changes have been reported. Thus it is possible that college girls today are copulating sooner and thereby reaching the peak percentage of 50 percent sooner and that they will not exceed that percent nonvirginal. Unless we were to follow a college sample through to marriage, it would be hard to draw definite conclusions. College girls do have a greater likelihood of marrying today than they had in the 1940's and much of a female's coital performance is related to being in love and engaged. Therefore it may be that there is more reported coitus because of an earlier marriage age for college girls and partially because more of them are in the serious courtship process that leads to marriage during their college years. However, the studies by Bell and Christensen and others are so consistent regarding increases in nonvirginity that it is hard to believe that their findings are not valid. Also, if 40 percent of the 20-year-olds are nonvirginal, it is difficult to conclude that by marriage the rate will be only 50 percent. Finally, Bell does find that his more recent sample of coeds had more partners and required less affection than in his older 1958 sample.

In 1960 I published a book entitled, *Premarital Sexual Standards in America* in which I attempted to sum up what the research evidence told us about sexual orientations in America. I predicted then that sometime by the end of the 1960's we would witness a noticeable rise in the percentage of nonvirginal females. It seemed to me that behavior and attitude were coming into balance around 1960 and, according to my interpretation of the evidence, that usually meant that behavior would then move forward again. Until recently I have held to the belief that the expected increase in nonvirginity had not yet occurred. I still feel that the evidence is not fully in, but the data that are coming in are so consistent in their findings of higher nonvirginity rates at specified ages, I am now willing to assert that the change predicted has occurred and that the actual premarital nonvirginity rate is now probably close to 70 percent for females.

The 1970's, I believe, will be to the last few decades of this century what the 1920's were to the decades of the first half of this century. More specifically, this decade will set the pace for the next few decades and afford clear outlines of the emerging life style. In the decade preceding the 1920's the older sexual orientations were attacked from a variety of perspectives. A new urban-industrial life style was then emerging and the developing liberal attitudes toward divorce, sex, and women had taken hold and were to evolve gradually during the next forty years. Then in the 1960's the same process of rapid change that occurred before 1920 was again present. Between 1915 and 1920 the divorce rates doubled and we were in the midst of a major war. Likewise between 1967 and 1972 the divorce rates rose 50% and we were again in the midst of a major war. Many alternative approaches to sex and the family were put forth in the realms of suggestions regarding abortion, life-long unions, living together, swinging, and female sexual orientations. What we are witnessing now is the culmination of the exploration of new life styles in the area of sex. The sixties spelled out many of the new possibilities and the seventies will lead to collective choices and priorities that will define these alternatives and their estimated worth in a way that will likely last a few decades.

Living Together

Situational ethics has made us aware of the variety of choices that may be viewed as legitimate and has moved us away from the view that only one choice is legitimate. The key characteristic of the seventies will be the awareness and toleration of a larger variety of alternative life styles. For example, living together has recently become a much more noticeable and popular custom on college campuses. Some people have reacted to this custom by viewing it as the death knell of marriage. That view is mistaken on two grounds. First, marriage need not be a legal contract. Indeed, most societies in the world lack a legal system and thus could not have legal marriage. Marriage can be celebrated by a meal together as in the Trobriand Islands, by requesting a common room as in some Israeli Kibbutzim, or by an elaborate church wedding as in some segments of American society. If a new custom of marriage came into America in the form of couples living together, that could still be considered marriage. The test of whether a custom symbolizes marriage is whether the custom sanctions parenthood. If living together were accepted as a way for two people to become parents, then it would indeed be a new marriage custom. From the data I have seen from Michael Johnson and others it appears that, as a general rule, living together on American campuses is not a substitute for marriage because most of the couples involved do not want children and are quite careful to avoid them. Most of these couples, however, seem to plan on a legal marriage someday—a marriage that is to take place when they do want children. They seem to be living together as part of a code of honesty and openness in sexual behavior. They reason that it is hypocritical to try to cover up a sexual affair by taking the girl home from a boy's apartment. Why not live with her and acknowledge that a sexual affair is occurring? For such people living together is simply a new form of courtship and not at all a substitute for marriage. I expect living together to become more popular as a courtship form. We seem to be continuing in our greater openness regarding sex and such a custom is integrated with that honesty. I doubt if it will extend to the sanctioning of children in such arrangements. Our type of society with its inheritance laws, social security laws, and other laws is far too complex to encourage parenthood without a legal ceremony. On the other hand, living together before legal marriage as a form of courtship or preparenthood relationship has the advantage of avoiding the possible need for divorce in early marriage. That advantage is often cited by its practitioners. I leave the ethical evaluation of the custom to the individual reader's conscience.

Experimentation in Sex

Actually, a proper perspective for viewing living together is to see it as one of many developments that epitomize the emphasis on the value of experimentation. We can see evidence of this in the use of drugs "just to see what it is like." We see it in the area of sex in the reduced occurrence of quick self-labeling. For example, people are less likely to label themselves as homosexual because of one homosexual experience or as loose women because of one affair. Today young people seem to have more of a "shoppers" attitude toward their sexual lives. They know they will experiment with different kinds of sexual relationships but they also know that they need not continue any kind of sexuality that they find not to their liking. They reduce thereby the stigma of any one type of sexual encounter and increase the importance of experimenting in order to find which sexual life style suits them best. Living together is one outcome of such a philosophy. Other outcomes are the increased openness of the Gay Liberation Movement and the increased attempt at getting societal legitimation for homosexuality. Cases are now in the courts to allow two homosexuals to marry. The economic advantage to homosexuals of such an arrangement is but one motivation for such legal action. My own feeling is that the main motivation is to gain approval in a legal and social sense for homosexuality by public acceptance of the marriage of homosexuals. Homosexuality is thus another one of the avenues that young people may experiment with. It should be clear, however, that the vast majority of young people who have a homosexual experience develop into persons who strongly prefer heterosexuality. The homosexual experimentation for most of these young people is simply a phase in their search for sexual identity.

We can be easily misled into thinking that experimentation with all possible varieties of human sexuality is very widespread in our society. Such a view would be in serious error. Most people in any society have very limited and restricted areas that they feel are open to rational examination. In our own society, technological areas are open to rational examination, for they are viewed as instrumental to important valued goals. Areas of life that embody the basic values or goals are most often not examined. For example, ordinarily the worth of motherhood is not questioned. Even women's liberation groups usually discuss this topic in terms of who will do the mothering, and not *if* mothering of newborn infants is important.

More is open to questioning in the area of sex than formerly. It is now legitimate in the minds of young people to decide if they want to have premarital intercourse. But note what a small range of alternatives is actually being explored. The question of incest is not debated very much. People are not proposing sibling or parent-child coitus as a legitimate way to express sexuality. Further, people are not proposing rape as acceptable nor are they proposing that we legitimize adult-preadolescent coitus, or other so-called sexual "aberrations." In point of fact, a few years ago a Scandinavian doctor, Lars Ullerstram, did make the observation that the homosexual was the most favored of all the so-called sexual deviants. He noted that the other sexual deviants were not tolerated nearly as much and suggested that we try to learn to be good "erotic Samaritans" and wherever possible help out some of these deviants. For example, if one knows that a voyeur is seeking to watch one undress, then one may allow that to happen. Many of the reviews of his book expressed shock at these suggestions.

I offered the illustration above not as an argument for any one moral position but rather to point out the limits of the experimentation with sexuality that exist in America. The debate in America on premarital sex centers heavily on whether premarital sex with or without affection is worth seeking and under what conditions. Incest, rape, pedophilia, and voyeurism are rather minor or rarely discussed segments of the debate. Even homosexuality enters into the dialogue for most people as peripheral—something to be tolerated perhaps but not as something at the heart of their sexual identity. Homosexuality, however, does enter into the dialogue on sex in America more than any other so-called deviant form of sex but, for most people, still not as one of the central issues.

In short, then, we have opened up premarital sexuality for public debate, experimentation, and moral examination to a much greater extent than any previous generation in America. But in terms of the possible areas that such a debate could consider, it is still a rather narrow dialogue. Nevertheless, in order to keep our perspective it is important to add that most European countries have not opened up their debate on sex even to the extent of ours.

Control of the Consequences of Sex

One issue that has been central in the new openness regarding human sexuality is that of abortion. Since the late 1960's the amount of legal change in abortion legislation has been remarkable. Again, I warn the reader that the amount of change is unusual for a society such as ours, not that it is extreme in any logical sense, for after all only sixteen states have changed their abortion laws and in many of these sixteen the change is not to the point of allowing "abortion on demand." It is likely that such changes will continue although I doubt if all states in the union will have open abortion laws such as are found in New York state. However, enough states will have such laws so that the single or married woman who wants an abortion (and it most often is a married woman) will be able to have it with much greater ease than ever before. For college girls, who generally can afford the abortion fee, this means an added feeling of control over the consequences of premarital coitus. Like the pill, the liberalization of abortion laws puts the control of sexuality more in the hands of females and thereby helps in the development of their own sense of sexuality. They are no longer so likely to conceive of sex as something that happens to them and over which they have little control. Females now have control over their own sexuality and its consequences to a degree unmatched in Western history. This situation will continue in the remaining decades of the twentieth century.

A qualification is in order here. The discussion above of the greater control over consequences, greater rationality in choices, and greater experimentation may lead to the view of the current scene as a neat, organized group of clear-thinking young people carefully reasoning out their sexual identities. One recent experience of mine helps put such a conclusion in perspective. A short time ago I visited one of our major universities to participate in a colloquium on sexuality. During my stay there one of the male students told me of a recent sexual experience. He had been dating a coed for about a month and they liked each other a good deal. One night they both got drunk and went up to his room and had sexual intercourse. He felt certain that she would never have done this unless she was on the pill and his girlfriend felt certain that he would never have done this unless he used a condom. They continued to copulate for about five weeks more until they realized that the girl was pregnant. Only then did the fact come out that she was not on the pill and he was not using a condom. I asked him why he never spoke to her about contraceptive measures and he replied that he felt that was too personal to be discussed. This incident reveals how sexual intimacies may well occur before other levels of self-revelation have taken place. Further, it illustrates the nonrational, emotional aspect of human behavior in the sexual realm. We should not expect knowledge of how to avoid unwanted consequences such as pregnancy to guarantee that such knowledge will be properly utilized. The above case is simply one way to illustrate the fallibility of humans and the perpetual limits on human rationality that are documented in many researches.

One other point is illustrated by the above case and that is the potentiality of sex interfering with the full development of a love relationship. Love relationships have high levels of self-revelation. Clearly sex is one level of revelation that is present in courtship relations; but we are still learning how to keep the sexual revelation from blocking other areas of revelation. People in love have often at times found out how to do this but many others have failed. Males, for example, due to a lack of sexual opportunities may focus on "scoring" and not bother to try to get to know the other rewards a particular relationship may possess. Females may stress their sexual attractions to the point where they fail to develop or present other aspects of themselves. Or as in the case cited above, carelessness regarding pregnancy can make an otherwise developing relationship undergo a crisis that may lead to its termination. In many ways sex can act as a block to the growth of a relationship and it should be clear that this can be the case whether the couple is kissing or copulating. This is not an argument against copulation— it is a statement of the fit of any type of sex in a relationship. The focus on sexual attractions is not just present in couples who copulate, it is present in some degree in nearly all couples. Many couples seem able to place sex in perspective and develop other aspects of their relationship and some couples can do this by having intercourse and thereby relieving that tension, whereas others are able to do it by sexual behaviors short of coitus. The point I am making is that this generation seems to value honesty, totalistic types of relationships, and "telling it like it is," and such open relationships can best be achieved if we know how to keep sex from interfering with that growth and, equally important, how to utilize sex to help in developing a totalistic type of relationship.

One indication of our "hang up" regarding sexuality is our "touch inhibition." Our preoccupation with sex is such that when a male touches a female our immediate thought is that such contact implies a sexual advance made by the male. This type of orientation to touch means that many people cannot harmlessly release sexual tension by, say, putting their arm around a person. This further implies that we may well have people who feel they ought to go further once they start to touch because they defined touching as a sexual advance preliminary to full sexual relations. Carolyn Symmonds and others have set up encounter groups in which couples are taught how to touch each other without any necessary implication that coitus will follow. My observation of young people today is that they are more in line with this acceptance of touching than were previous generations and I expect this acceptance to grow over the next few decades. Such a natural attitude toward sexually related activities increases the ability to utilize sex to help develop a relationship rather than allowing it to be the preoccupation of the couple.

CONCLUSIONS

We are entering a new historical phase. We are entering into the post-industrial society just as around World War I we had clearly entered into the modern phase of the industrial society. Note that this entry into the modern type of industrial society occurred in conjunction with a major war. The same sort of situation prevails today. The Viet Nam War has been a major factor in the change to a post-industrial society. It is a very unpopular war and as such it has caused us to bring into question much of our political, religious, economic, and educational systems that support the war. We, as a people, began to examine what sort of society we had built that had led us into this war in Southeast Asia. More than any other single force, then, the war revealed to us what we were and to many Americans the revelation was unpleasant and pressured toward change.

The Post-Industrial Society and Sex

The basic forces moving us toward a post-industrial society were present before the war. By post-industrial society, I mean a society in which the industrial output is no longer problematic and thus the means of increasing productivity become secondary to questions concerning equity in distribution of wealth and power and concern with the quality of our life style. Our concern shifted noticeably in this direction in 1954 with the important racial desegregation decision of the Supreme Court. Civil Rights legislation followed that decision. Legislation demanding equal rights in employment for females was also passed in the early 1960's. The 1960's also witnessed an ever-increasing concern with pollution. All of these issues showed that millions of Americans had shifted their attention from industrial output problems to questions of justice and the good life. Certainly the high level of affluence of the past thirty years has been a major factor in this change.

When most people have no real problem in obtaining food, clothing, and shelter, and even many of the luxuries, then the stage is set for them to devote their energies to more fundamental issues concerning our type of society. Twenty-five centuries ago, this situation prevailed for the very small ruling class in Athens and many of the greatest works of philosophy and literature were produced. The difference today is that our society has found it possible to give the level of affluence necessary for such thinking to per-haps a majority of the population and unlike the Athenians many Americans are not willing to tolerate a slave class to make this life style possible. It is no accident that the leaders of the post-industrial life style are the children of upper middle-class parents. We have discussed before how these upper middle-class parents are often permissive sexually and liberal in general. They are the leaders in the change to a post-industrial society for they are the most involved in the affluence that makes this change possible.

Our sexual customs are changing in accord with the emphasis in the post-industrial society on the quality of human relationships rather than on material things. We can emphasize the human relationship in sex because we are learning very fast how to take care of the disease and pregnancy conse-quences of premarital intercourse and by doing this we have increased the moral quality of the sexual choice. To illustrate, it is hardly a moral act to return a wallet found in front of the police station—for fear of consequences would make us turn it over to the police. However, if a wallet is found and no one else is around, we then have a moral choice, for fear of being found out is minimized. The situation in sex today is analogous. We can most often avoid, if we are careful, the unwanted consequences of sex such as pregnancy and venereal disease and thus we cannot use them as final reasons for our sexual decisions. We must delve deeper into the sexual relationship and decide whether we feel that our personality growth and that of our partner will be helped or hindered by having a sexual relationship of one sort or another. We can examine the potential impact of the relation upon ourselves and the others who are involved. It is just such an examination that has led to the popularity of situational ethics, for it is abundantly clear that for some people having premarital coitus would contribute to the development of responsibility, the ability to relate to people, a sense of integrity, and self-realization; for other people having premarital coitus might lead to exactly the opposite set of consequences. As Alex Comfort, a British physician, put it a few years ago, this is the first generation that Western society has called upon to make a truly moral, intelligent choice of sexual life styles. Other generations were spared the choice by virtue of the social straitjackets they were wearing.

Mental Health and Choice

The question arises regarding the mental health impact in the next few decades of our orientation today toward premarital sexuality. What will be the rewards and the costs? These are, of course, difficult to generalize about. However, it seems that we can already discern a different type of cost. Psychiatrists do report that whereas generations ago people would seek help because they could not get started sexually, today they more and more seek help because they cannot stop sexually. It seems that our type of evolving system is more conducive to getting people started sexually, particularly females. The culture's definition that the individual has the responsibility for determining the specific controls of his sexual life style means that outside societal support is not (particularly for females) as ever present or so narrow as it was for past generations and it is this that leads to control being one of the key personal problems of the current sexual scene.

I believe that in a very few years there will be a noticeable increase in the closure we reach on sexual questions. The 1960's opened up the doors on a wide range of possibilities. The 1970's are going to reach closure on many of the issues raised by this wider range of possible sex behaviors. We will have learned to live with a greater range of choice and we will learn more about the consequences of the newer choices confronting us. Let me illustrate by discussing hard-core pornographic movies. For those who have not seen pornographic movies this experience may be sexually exciting. Nevertheless for most college-educated youngsters I would expect that they would soon tire of the heavy genital focus of such "flicks." I expect more movies to be made that involve explicit scenes of sexual intercourse but that focus on a plot concerning human relationships rather than on the genital aspect of the sex act. These movies would be "turn on" movies and in that sense pornographic but their approach would not be purely genital. I think this newer type of movie will fit more with the emphasis on permissiveness with affection and on sex in the context of a close relationship and thus I think it will represent the wave of the future. The other type of genital pornographic movie will remain as an experience for millions of of curious and as a focus for a small minority of genitally oriented people. The next few years should thus help structure this area of sexuality with the newer "eroticism in context" type of movie. Let me add, however, that the increased freedom of choice also implies that despite the trend toward person-centered sex, there will remain a visible amount of body-centered sex. Such body-centered sex is part of the experimentation process and for some people is a preferred life style.

The new sexuality offers a variety of forms of sexual expression and individualizes choice to a greater extent and this should be a mental health advantage. The older sexual morality was a procrustean bed. If an individual did not fit, the society did not offer alternatives but rather tried to cut that individual down to size. The key advantage of the new sexuality is also its key disadvantage, namely, the increased possibility of choice. The advantages of choice are obvious—a person can choose a sexual life style more suited to himself. The disadvantages of greater freedom of choice is that we run the risk of choosing "fools' gold." In short, we may choose some course of action that yields temporary satisfaction but in the longer run destroys more valuable parts of our life style. For example, we may choose to have a weekend with a sexually attractive person we just met and thereby alienate a person we love. Freedom of choice imposes the responsibility for restraint on the individual. The social restraints must be minimized for the freedom to be more than a facade and this means that the possibility for individual error must be accepted.

In some areas the evidence toward which way to choose is far from in. For example, there are proposals that young people be encouraged to live in mixed sex communes for a year or so before settling down. This is not so radically different from the "junior year in Paris" that only a wealthier segment experienced in years past. Such communal living could be a rite of passage into the outside society; it would be a supportive communal group but one without very narrow structures of relationships and thus it would allow for experimentation to help in personal development. I am not proposing this be accepted, rather I offer it as one of the many doors that the 1960's opened and that the experience of the next few years will help clarify.

Another recent proposal concerns the responsibility of the parent to teach erotic behavior to his children. This proposal states that parents should masturbate their children and teach them as they grow up how to derive erotic satisfactions from their own bodies. These proponents believe that just as parents have a responsibility for the spiritual development and intellectual development of their children they have a responsibility for the erotic development of their children. Most people that I have observed discussing this particular proposal have been opposed to it. Part of the opposition may be due to incestuous taboos, part due to fear of "too much" erotic arousal or "too much" body-centered sexuality. In this case I would feel more certain in predicting that this proposal will be acceptable to a much smaller proportion of the American population than the "temporary commune" proposal. It is this evaluation and ranking of various sexual possibilities that characterizes the present and that makes me predict that the

1970's will witness closure on many of these issues. The various proposals of new sex codes and practices are being evaluated by trial and error and reason and this should lead to the forming of more socially shared conclusions.

Final Summation

We are witnessing the growth of a new, integrated post-industrial type of sexuality. This change has come about gradually and evolutionarily except for two brief periods of time: (1) the period around World War I and (2) the late 1960's. The 1920's contained the major resolution of the changes that led into a full industrial society and the 1970's are witnessing the major resolution of the changes into a full post-industrial society. The key characteristics of the current sexual life styles are the emphasis on personal choice and the greater tolerance for experimentation. More than at any other time in our history we now tolerate a variety of life styles in almost all areas of our sexual existence. We are far too varied and large a nation ever to expect to find one life style best suited to all people. Thus this development toward tolerance of alternative life styles is functional for our society. Tolerance of alternatives does not mean acceptance of all alternatives, nor even acceptance of all alternatives as equally good. Some life styles will still be viewed as beyond the pale and some as not to be preferred, but there will also be a variety of accepted life styles. This examination of alternatives need not weaken our belief in our own ultimate convictions. It can, by the knowledge and understanding it gives, afford us a firmer basis upon which to find ourselves. We shall all be increasingly more aware of this aspect of our post-industrial society as the years tick away in the remaining decades of the twentieth century. As the young people today become parents we will witness the typical change toward less tolerance of risk taking that occurs as people become parents. But I believe there will be less of this sort of parent-child gap than ever before. This should be so because this generation has gone on record as supporting the legitimacy of choice in the area of sex. I believe that we will soon see they not only have made such choices themselves but they will allow the same privileges to their children to a greater extent than any previous generation.

REFERENCES

Bell, Robert R., and Jay B. Chaskes, "Premarital sexual experience among coeds: 1958–1968", *Journal of Marriage and the Family*, 32 (February, 1970), 81–84.

Christensen, Harold T., and Christina Gregg, "Changing sex norms in America and Scandinavia", *Journal of Marriage and the Family*, 32 (November, 1970), 616–627.

Comfort, Alex, *The Anxiety Makers*. London: Nelson, 1967.

Cuber, John F., and Peggy Harroff, *The Significant Americans*. New York: Appleton-Century-Crofts, 1965.

Kinsey, Alfred C., Wardell B. Pomeroy, and Clyde E. Martin, *Sexual Behavior in the Human Male*. Philadelphia: Saunders, 1948.

Kinsey, Alfred C., Wardell B. Pomeroy, Clyde E. Martin, and Paul H. Gebhard, *Sexual Behavior in the Human Female.* Philadelphia: Saunders, 1953.

Johnson, Michael P., Courtship and commitment; A study of cohabitation on a University Campus. Master's Thesis, Unpublished, University of Iowa, 1969.

Masters, William H., and Virginia E. Johnson, *Human Sexual Response.* Boston: Little, Brown, 1966.

Reiss, Ira L., *Premarital Sexual Standards in America.* New York: Macmillan-Free Press, 1960.

Reiss, Ira L., *The Social Context of Premarital Sexual Permissiveness.* New York: Holt, Rinehart and Winston, 1967.

Reiss, Ira L., *The Family System in America.* New York: Holt, Rinehart and Winston, 1971.

Rossi, Alice S., "Sex equality: The beginnings of ideology", in Mary Lou Thompson (Ed.), *Voices of the New Feminism.* Boston: Beacon Press, 1971, 59–74.

Schmidt, Gunter, and Volkmar Sigusch, "Sex differences in responses to psychosexual stimulation by films and slides", *Journal of Sex Research*, 6, (November, 1970), 268–283.

Symonds, Carolyn, "A nude touchy-feely group", *Journal of Sex Research*, 7, (May, 1971), 126–133.

Ullerstram, Lars, *The Erotic Minorities.* New York: Grove, 1966.

13 | Changing Sex Norms in America and Scandinavia

HAROLD T. CHRISTENSEN and CHRISTINA F. GREGG

It has been popular of late to claim that the so-called *Sexual Revolution* which has been sweeping America during the recent fifties and sixties is little more than a liberalization of attitudes: that there has been no real or

The research upon which this paper is based was done in 1958 and again in 1968, permitting a trend analysis. George R. Carpenter assisted with the questionnaire part of the research in 1958. Christina F. Gregg has been responsible for carrying out the midwestern phase of the study in 1968, including the special statistical analyses of the data from that sample. The authors wish to express appreciation to Wayne Gregg, Kathryn Johnsen, Eugene Kanin, Dean Knudsen, and Carolyn C. Perrucci for critical reviews of the manuscript; but assume full responsibility themselves for any imperfections that may remain.

Reprinted from the *Journal of Marriage and the Family*, 32, No. 4 (November, 1970), 616–627, by permission of the National Council on Family Relations.

significant increase in nonmarital sexual behavior. No one disputes the more or less obvious facts of greater tolerance with respect to the sexual behavior of others or of greater freedom and openness in discussion, in dress and manners, in public entertainment, and throughout the mass media. But when it comes to the question of whether premarital coitus—the practice itself—is undergoing much of an increase, there tends to be either uncertainty or the suggestion that it is not. Part of this may be due to wishful thinking, part to a lack of adequate data, and part to a tendency among scholars to overgeneralize from the data available. At any rate, there is need for new data and for a reexamination of the problem.

Terman (1938:320–323) was one of the first to present solid evidence concerning incidence and trends in premarital coitus. He compared persons born in and subsequent to 1910 with persons born before 1890 and reported increases of premarital coitus for both men and women—though at a more rapid rate for the latter, signifying an intersex convergence.

Then came Kinsey. Kinsey and associates (1953:298–302) also compared incidence of premarital coitus by decade of birth and reported virtually no trend for males but a very significant increase for females, which likewise pointed to an intersex convergence. Yet even for females there appeared to be little difference in non-virginity among those born during the first, second and third decades of the present century. But non-virginity was more than twice as great for females born in these three decades after the turn of the century as compared with those born before 1900. Since approximately twenty years are required to reach maturity, the suggestion in this finding is that the big change in the liberalization of female sexual behavior took place during the decade following World War I and that the picture has not altered much since that time. It must be noted, however, that these data are not suitable for measuring trends that may have occurred during the 1950's and 1960's.

Nevertheless, Reiss (1969) and certain other scholars (for example, Bell, 1966; Gagnon and Simon, 1970), after drawing upon the Kinsey data, have moved beyond the reach of these findings by claiming that there has been little if any increase in non-virginity over the past twenty years or so. Reiss explains the widespread *belief* concerning an increase as being due largely to the liberalizing of attitudes, which makes people more willing to talk and so increases their awareness and anxiety. In support of his position of no significant trend in premarital coitus since the 1920's, he cites several studies made during the 1950's and 1960's (Ehrmann, 1959; Freedman, 1965; Kirkendall, 1961; Reiss, 1967; Schofield, 1965) which give somewhat similar incidence percentages as those reported earlier by Kinsey. But there is a question of comparability. Although these more recent studies do not show incidence percentages greatly different from Kinsey's, they each tap different populations and employ differing methodologies—so that the no-trend conclusion may be quite spurious. Furthermore, the reported research by Reiss himself deals almost exclusively with attitudes, largely ignoring behavior. It is to his credit though, that he recognized the tenuous nature of the evidence and because of this, states his position somewhat cautiously. He said simply that the common belief that non-virginity has markedly increased of late "is not supported by the research"; and concluded: "Thus, although the evidence is surely not perfect, it does suggest that there has not been any change in the proportion of non-virginity for the past four or five decades equal to that which occurred during the 1920's" (Reiss, 1969: 110).

But the message that has come across to the public and even some scholars is that research has established that a virtually static level of pre-marital coitus has maintained itself since the early post World War I period. This has been the most usual interpretation given recently in the popular press, by radio and television, and in some high school and college textbooks.

Even so, not everyone has believed it. Some, like the authors of this paper, have held mental reservations, though, until recently, they have been without appropriate data to test it out. A few years ago Leslie (1967:387–392) examined this question by classifying chronologically virtually all studies which had reported incidence of premarital coitus, starting with 1915 and ending with 1965. He observed that for both sexes percentages tend to be higher in the more recent studies. Similarly, Packard (1968:135–204, 491–511, 517–523) took a careful look at the reported findings of over forty studies including one of his own, which elicited student responses from 21 colleges in the United States and five from other countries (Luckey and Nass, 1969). He compared these studies and their findings across time; conceding, of course, the lack of strict comparability due to differing samples and methods. His tentative general conclusion was that ". . . while coital experience of U. S. college males seemed comparable to that of males 15 or 20 years ago, the college females reported a quite significantly higher rate of experience" (Packard, 1968:186).

The very latest information coming to our attention is a report by Bell and Chaskes (1970) wherein the earlier no-evidence-to-support-a-trend position of Bell (1966) is modified with the statement: "The writers believe that change *has* been occurring in the sexual experience of college girls since the mid 1960's" (Bell and Chaskes, 1970:81). These authors report increases in the premarital coitus of coeds between 1958 and 1968: from 10 to 23 percent during the dating relationship, from 15 to 28 percent during the going-steady relationship, and from 31 to 39 percent during the engagement relationship. Since proportionate increase was greatest at the first two dating levels, they conclude that the commitment of engagement has become a less important condition for many coeds participating in premarital coitus. They also report significant reductions at each dating level in the guilt connected with coitus, and point to a suggestion from their data of an increase in promiscuity. Still additional findings—though ones less relevant to our present analysis—were that premarital coitus tends to be associated with non-attendance at church, starting to date at an early age, and dating or going steady with a larger than average number of boys.

The Bell and Chaskes study has an advantage over many of the previous ones in that it taps college students in the same institution with the same measuring instrument at two different points in time, which more clearly enables it to look at *trends*. It nevertheless is limited to females alone on one college campus, and so sees its conclusions as suggestive rather than conclusive of any national change. These authors argue, from what is known about the youth rebellion movement of very recent years, that the increase in the premarital coitus of coeds is a phenomenon of the mid 1960's. It should be noted, however, that there is nothing in their data to establish the change as occurring at that precise point in time as against the early 1960's or even the late 1950's.

Our own research about to be reported has some of the same limitations as certain of the earlier studies (including the small size and non-random character of its samples) but there are added features which we hope will enable us to carry the analysis a little farther. We have involved behavior as well as attitudes, studied males as well as females, .compared three separate cultures against each other, and measured identical phenomena in the same manner in the same poulations at two different points in time. The focus of this report is to be upon the time dimension, or social change. Nevertheless, by seeing change cross-culturally and in the context of male-female interaction and attitude-behavior interrelatedness, it should be possible to better understand what actually is taking place. There is an interplay among these and possibly other factors. We feel that it is important to try to see the premarital sex phenomenon as a network and to look for inter-relationships and then build toward an empirically based theory to explain it all. Our study is but one start in that direction.

The senior author initiated his cross-cultural research on premarital sex back in 1958, at which time questionnaires were administered to college samples in three separate cultures differing on a restrictive-permissive continuum: highly restrictive Mormon culture in the Intermountain region of western United States; moderately restrictive Midwestern culture in central United States; and highly permissive Danish culture which is part of Scandinavia (Christensen, 1960; 1966; 1969; Christensen and Carpenter, 1962a; 1962b). The 1958 study involved both record linkage and questionnaire data, but it is only the latter that are of concern in the present writing. He then repeated the study in 1968, using the same questionnaire administered

TABLE 1   Percentages[a] Taking Liberal Positions on Sex Questions, 1958 and 1968 Compared

Items and Years	Intermountain		Midwestern		Danish	
	Males	Females	Males	Females	Males	Females
I. Opposition to Censorship						
1968	61	58	71	59	99	97
1958	42	54	47	51	77	81
Difference	19	4	24	8	22	16
II. Acceptance of Non-Virginity						
1968	20	26	25	44	92	92
1958	5	11	18	23	61	74
Difference	15	15	7	21	31	18
III. Approval of Pre-marital Coitus						
1968	38	24	55	38	100	100
1958	23	3	47	17	94	81
Difference	15	21	8	21	6	19

[a]Percentages are based on numbers answering the question. The number of cases leaving a question unanswered varied from 0 to 8 in the various groups.

in the same three universities. Every effort was made to achieve comparability across the two years. The unchanged questionnaire was administered in the same way to similar classes in the identical universities. In most instances within both years, social science classes were used; the only real change being in Denmark, where large proportions of medical and psychology students were used in 1958 as against an almost exclusively sociology student sample in 1968. The repeat, of course, was chiefly for the purpose of getting at changes which may have occurred during a period of time popularly described as experiencing a sexual revolution. Although the study dealt with all levels of intimacy—necking, petting, and coitus—this report is to be limited to premarital coitus alone. Furthermore, it is limited to only selected aspects of premarital coitus. This is because our analysis of data has just begun, plus the necessity to restrict the length of a journal article.

Respective sample sizes involved in calculations for the statistics now to be reported were: for the Intermountain, 94 males and 74 females in 1958, and 115 and 105 respectively in 1968; for the Midwestern, 213 males and 142 females in 1958, and 245 and 238 respectively in 1968; for the Danish, 149 males and 86 females in 1958, and 134 and 61 respectively in 1968.

SOME MEASURES OF THE LIBERAL ATTITUDE

Three items from the questionnaire have been selected to illustrate comparisons and trends in the attitudinal component. Table 1 has been constructed to show percentages of respondents holding liberal or permissive views regarding these matters.

Opposing the Censorship of Pornography

Presented first are percentages of respondents who indicated agreement with the statement: "It is best not to try to prohibit erotic and obscene literature and pictures by law, but rather to leave people free to follow their own judgments and tastes in such matters." The three comparisons of interest in this analysis are as follows:

(1) As one moves from left to right—from the restrictive Intermountain culture to the permissive Danish culture—percentages taking the liberal stance by agreeing with the statement are seen to increase. This is true for both sexes and with respect to both sample years (with the single exception of the 1958 female comparison between Intermountain and Midwestern).

(2) More females than males opposed the censorship of pornography in 1958, whereas ten years later the reverse was true. Furthermore, this shift in pattern occurred consistently in each of the three cultures, suggesting that it may be something of a general phenomenon.

(3) The time trend over the decade 1958–68 was consistently in the direction of increasing opposition to this kind of censorship. The trend held for each of the three cultures and for both sexes—although females liberalized on this point in *smaller* degree than did males, which accounts for the shift in the male-female pattern mentioned in the previous paragraph.

Since (as will be shown throughout the remainder of our paper) females generally have liberalized in a proportionately *greater* degree than have males, this contrary finding on censorship requires some attempt at explanation. Our speculation is that females, with their more sheltered life, have been less knowledgeable and realistic regarding pornography and also possibly less attracted by its appeal. This might explain their greater opposition to censorship than males in 1958, not seeing pornography as particularly threatening. But the new openness of recent years undoubtedly has given them greater sophistication in these matters, and they may now better understand the reality of hardcore pornography and its differential appeal to the male; which could explain their lower opposition to censorship than males in 1968.

Accepting the Non-Virginity of a Partner

In the second section of Table 1 are shown percentages of those who indicated *disagreement* with the statement: "I would prefer marrying a virgin, or in other words, someone who has not had previous coitus (sexual intercourse)." As with the statement on pornography, permissive attitudes increased for both sexes and in both sample years from lows in the restrictive Intermountain to highs in the permissive Danish; and increased between 1958 and 1968, for both sexes and in each of the three cultures. These trends are shown to be without exception. The male-female comparisons show *females* to be the most *permissive*, in both sample years and in each of the cultures (with the single exception of 1968 Danish respondents, where they were equal).

Since practically every other measure in our questionnaire—as well as virtually all studies now in the literature—show females to be more conservative than males in sexual matters, one must ask "why this exception?" Two possible reasons occur to us: in the first place, the typical female attitude may represent a realistic acceptance that more males do have premarital sex, making her chances of actually marrying a virgin somewhat smaller; and in addition, some females, with a sheltered upbringing and more limited sexual expression, may feel inadequate and hence welcome an experienced male to help show them the way. In this connection, it is interesting to note also that in the Midwestern sample—which may approximately reflect the overall situation for United States—females moved away from insistence on a virginal partner at a much more rapid rate than did males.

Approving Coitus Among the Unmarried

Finally, Table 1 shows percentages of those approving premarital coitus. Respondents were asked: first, to consider an average or typical courtship "in which there is normal love development and mutual responsibility"; next, to assume that this hypothetical relationship progresses at a uniform rate of six months between the first date and the start of going steady, another six months to an engagement, and still another six months to the wedding (or a total courtship of eighteen months); and then to mark on a scale the earliest time they would approve the start of necking, then of petting, and then of coitus. The percentages shown are restricted to coitus and they represent approval at any point prior to the wedding.

This item on approval of premarital coitus is free of the kinds of irregularities mentioned for the previous two. It shows highly consistent results for all three comparisons: a movement toward greater approval from Intermountain to Midwestern to Danish, for both sexes and in both sample years; greater approval given by males than by females (except for a tie among 1968 Danish respondents where both sexes hit the ceiling), for both sample years and each of the three cultures; and a trend toward greater approval over the 1958–68 decade, for both sexes and in each of the three cultures.

In connection with this last point, it is important to note that in each of the cultures females moved toward approval more strongly than did males, which means a trend toward intersex convergence. Females still have more restrictive attitudes than males but the difference is less than formerly.

An additional observation which should not be missed is that, in both sample years, male-female percentages are closer together in Denmark than in the other two cultures. This suggests that norm permissiveness may operate to reduce differences between the sexes seen in cross-cultural comparisons as well as in liberalizing trends over time.

Trend Comparison with Relevant Variables Controlled

As a double check on this trend pattern—and to at least partially determine whether it is real or merely the result of differing compositions of the two samples drawn ten years apart—we made a supplementary analysis

TABLE 2   Measures of Premarital Coital Approval on Matched and Total Samples, Midwestern Culture, 1958 and 1968 Compared

Measures of Coital Approval	Total Sample		Matched Sample	
	Males	Females	Males	Females
I. Average Score				
1968	8.10	9.02	8.10	9.47
1958	8.58	9.69	8.63	9.67
Difference	−.48	−.67	−.53	−.20
II. Percent Approving				
1968	55.4	37.7	55.1	30.7
1958	46.7	17.4	48.0	21.3
Difference	8.7	20.3	7.1	9.4

of matched data. This was done for the Midwestern culture only (the most representative of American society and the most feasible for matched testing because of the larger sizes of its samples) and was further limited to data on premarital coitus (the most central in our present analysis). The matching occurred on four variables: sex of respondent, cumulative number of years in school, frequency of church attendance, and level of courtship development. This had the effect of controlling these variables across the 1958–68 period, while the time trend was being examined. Successful matching was completed for 202 pairs of respondents (127 pairs were male, 75 female).

In Table 2 we show for the Midwestern culture two measures of premarital coital approval for both matched and total samples. The first consists of average (mean) scores computed from the approval timing scale introduced earlier. The scale had ten divisions, with the first representing time of first date and the last representing time of marriage. Scores ranged from 1 to 10 according to markings on the scale, and it is *average* coital scores (means) that are shown here. The lower the score, the farther from marriage is the approved timing of first coitus. It will be observed that, by this measure, both males and females showed up more permissive in 1968 than they did in 1958 and that the trend held for the matched as well as unmatched comparisons.

The second measure is simply percent approving premarital coitus. Unmatched percentages are shown here in juxtaposition to percentages from the matched cases. But again the picture is very clear: matching has not altered the general trend; in the uncontrolled and the controlled analyses the trend was found to be toward greater approval—which is the permissive stance. And this was true for males and females alike, but for the latter the trend was the stronger.

RELATIONSHIP OF BEHAVIOR TO ATTITUDE

Some might argue that most of our generalizations up to this point are obvious, that everyone accepts the fact that attitudes toward premarital coitus have been liberalizing in recent years. The more controversial ques-

TABLE 3 Percentage[a] with Premarital Coital Experience, Total and Matched Samples

| Samples and Years | Sample Culture | | | | | |
| | Intermountain | | Midwestern | | Danish | |
	Males	Females	Males	Females	Males	Females
I. Total Samples						
1968	37	32	50	34	95	97
1958	39	10	51	21	64	60
Difference	−2	22	−1	13	31	37
II. Matched Samples						
1968			49	32		
1958			55	25		
Difference			−6	7		

[a]Based upon number answering. The number who failed to answer in any one group varied from 0 to 4.

tions have to do with trends in sexual *behavior* and with how these relate to attitude. Has incidence of premartial coitus remained virtually unchanged since the 1920's, with a decline in guilt brought about by an increasing acceptance of the behavior—which is the position arrived at by Reiss (1969), or has behavior changed with attitudes regarding it?

Incidence of Premarital Coitus

As a first approach to the behavioral component, we show percentages of respondents claiming the premarital coital experience (Table 3). Our percentages on incidence of premarital coitus do not, of course, give an accurate picture of total coitus before marriage but only of experience up to the time the questionnaire was administered. This fact should not influence our various comparisons, however, since all the data are the same kind and hence comparable. Percentages are given for males and females separately and for the three cultures and both sample years of our study. An added refinement in testing for a time trend is provided for the Midwestern culture by means of matched cases to control for intervening variables, as was done in the case of attitudes.

Before examining the time-trend data, let it be noted that these incidence figures are (1) higher for males than females and (2) higher for the Midwestern than the Intermountain and for the Danish than the Midwestern. These generalizations are consistent for all comparisons (except the one between 1958–68 Danish males and females) and are the same as our earlier ones regarding approval of premarital coitus. Furthermore, there is, as before, the phenomenon of greater male-female similarity in Denmark than the other two cultures, suggesting that norm permissiveness may induce a leveling of gender differences.

Comparisons of 1968 with 1958 produce three additional generalizations. (1) In the two American samples, male incidence of premarital coitus remained approximately the same. Actually the figures show that it decreased slightly, but our conjecture is that this is no more than random variation. (2) On the other hand, female incidence in the two American samples rose sharply, suggesting that, as with coital approval, there is a trend toward intersex convergence. (3) The Danish sample, while showing a slightly higher rise in premarital coitus for females than for males, demonstrated a sharp rise for *both* sexes. This brought incidence figures for that country close to the ceiling. Approximately 95 percent had engaged in premarital coitus; and it will be recalled that 100 percent of both sexes there approved of such activity. It may be, of course, that at least part of the dramatic liberalization shown for Danish respondents is to be explained by the greater weighting of the 1968 Danish sample with sociology students.

The introduction of controls through matched-sample comparisons in the Midwestern culture made no appreciable change in the outcome (Table 3, part II). Although males decreased their behavior more and females increased theirs less in the matched sample as compared with the total sample, the conclusion of greater female than male liberalization and of intersex convergence during the decade seems inescapable.

The Approval-Experience Ratio

It is important to know how approval of and experience in premarital coitus interrelate: to what extent practice corresponds with precept and what are the directions and magnitudes of discrepancies in this regard. The ratios of Table 4 have been calculated by dividing percentages approving premarital coitus (part III of Table 1 and part II of Table 2) by percentages having experienced it (Table 3). A ratio of 1.00 would mean that approval and experience coincide exactly. Ratios lower than this indicate that experience exceeds approval; and higher, that approval exceeds experience. With the sex drive as strong as it is, one may wonder how the approval-experience ratio could ever be above 1.00: why, if people approve premarital coitus, they don't engage in it. The primary explanation seems to be that the attitude percentages are for approval of coitus occurring *anytime prior to marriage*, and approving respondents may not be close enough to marriage to feel ready for the experience.

TABLE 4 Comparisons of Approval-Experience Ratios, Total and Matched Samples

| Samples and Years | Sample Cultures | | | | | |
| | Intermountain | | Midwestern | | Danish | |
	Males	Females	Males	Females	Males	Females
I. Total Samples						
1968	1.05	.73	1.10	1.10	1.06	1.04
1958	.59	.31	.92	.84	1.48	1.35
Difference	.46	.42	.18	.26	−.42	−.31
II. Matched Samples						
1968			1.13	.96		
1958			.87	.84		
Difference			.26	.12		

The following generalizations seem evident: (1) In 1958, the magnitude of the ratio varies directly with the permissiveness of the culture; which means that restrictive cultures have higher percentages of their offenders who are violating their own standards—though it must be remembered that restrictive cultures have fewer offenders to start with. (2) Except for Midwestern respondents in 1968, females showed up with lower ratios than males, which means that proportionately more of them violate their own standards when they engage in premarital coitus. However, this intersex difference is of large magnitude only within the highly conservative Intermountain culture. (3) The 1958–68 trend was toward a rise in the ratio for both the Intermountain and Midwestern samples, where it previously had been below 1.00, and a lowering of the ratio in Denmark where it previously had been above 1.00. Thus the time trend has been toward a leveling and balancing of the approval-experience ratios, bringing them closer to each other and to the value of 1.00. In 1968, all ratios except for Midwestern males were closer to 1.00 than was true ten years earlier, and Intermountain females represented the only group in the total sample with experience remaining greater than approval (although in the matched sample this was true for Midwestern females also). The evidence suggests that there is less of a gap today between one's values and his behavior; that, regardless of his sex or the culture he is in, a person is more likely now than formerly, to follow his own internalized norms.

Again, the matching procedure has not altered the basic conclusion. With these data, as with the total sample, the trend is seen to be toward a rising ratio. Attitudes have liberalized more rapidly than has behavior, so that the over-all pattern today seems not to be one of violating one's own value systems. Some individuals do, of course, but in terms of group averages the evidence is against it.

Evidences of Value-Behavior Discrepancy

In an earlier article (Christensen and Carpenter, 1962b) the senior author has demonstrated from cross-cultural data for 1958 that—even more than the act itself—it is the discrepency between what one values and what he then does that determines guilt, divorce, and related negative effects. The analysis was based upon both group and individual comparisons between permissiveness scores (measuring attitude) and behavioral percentages (measuring coital experience).

Here we wish to report a slightly different approach applied to the 1958 and 1968 Midwestern samples, first with the total respondents and then with

TABLE 5 Percentages with Premarital Coitus Who Approved Such Experience, Midwestern Culture, 1958 and 1968 Compared

	Total Sample		Matched Sample	
	Males	*Females*	*Males*	*Females*
1968	82	78	76	58
1958	65	41	65	37
Difference	17	37	11	21

the matched cases. In Table 5 are presented percentages of those with pre-marital experience who answered approvingly of coitus before marriage. These percentages, in other words, are based upon *individual* case-by-case comparisons between coitus and coital approval. They show the proportions of cases in which there was *no discrepancy* of this kind. By subtracting any percentage figure from 100.0, the reader can, if he prefers it that way, de-termine the corresponding discrepancy magnitude.

It will be observed that the trend between 1958 and 1968 was toward larger approval percentages (or less value-behavior discrepancy). This is true with respect to both sexes and for the matched as well as the total samples. It supports a similar finding based upon grouped data reported in the previous section. In both instances the evidence suggests that attitudes have been catching up with behavior and that proportionally fewer people today violate their own values when they engage in premarital coitus. Never-theless, some individuals still show this discrepancy—perhaps as many as one-fifth of the males and two-fifths of the females.

It will be observed also that the movement of premarital coital partici-pants toward approving what one does was greater for females than males (consistently shown in both sets of comparisons). Females in 1968 still gave evidence of greater value-behavior discrepancy than did males but the intersex difference in this regard was less than in 1958. And here too, the finding of Table 5 stands in general support of the picture for grouped data shown in Table 4.

Using Attitudes to Predict Behavior

Since the overall evidence is that attitudes have been liberalizing at a greater rate than behavior, which is narrowing the gap between the two, it

TABLE 6 Incidence of Premarital Coitus as Related to Approval of Premarital Coitus, Midwestern Sample

Incidence of Premarital Coitus	Approval of Premarital Coitus					
	Males			Females		
	Yes	No	Total	Yes	No	Total
			1968			
Yes	98	22	120	63	18	81
No	35	83	118	26	128	154
Total	133	105	238	89	146	235
	Gamma = .83			Gamma = .89		
			1958			
Yes	68	37	105	12	17	29
No	30	73	103	12	95	107
Total	98	110	208	24	112	136
	Gamma = .63			Gamma = .69		

might be expected that the predictive power of attitudes is increasing. To test this out, we calculated Gammas on the interaction of two variables: approval of premarital coitus and experience with premarital coitus. The Gammas reported in Table 6 indicate that the expectation was supported: coital approval was a better predictor of coital behavior for males and females at the end of the decade than at the beginning.

THE COMMITMENT PHENOMENON

Reiss (1969), largely from analyses of his attitudinal data, has concluded that America is moving toward the traditional Scandinavian pattern of "permissiveness with affection." This phrase has been used by Reiss and others to also mean *permissiveness with commitment.* Our own data should permit us to check out this claim at the behavioral level.

Two indices of affection-commitment are presented in Table 7: percent-

TABLE 7 Percentage[a] Distributions of Responses to Items Showing a Commitment in the Sexual Relationship

Items and Years	Sample Cultures					
	Intermountain		Midwestern		Danish	
	Males	Females	Males	Females	Males	Females
I. Experience Confined to One Partner						
1968	28.6	43.8	39.0	70.0	20.5	25.0
1958	35.1	57.1	33.7	65.5	40.9	42.9
Difference	−6.5	−13.3	5.3	4.5	−20.4	−17.9
II. First Experience with a Steady of Fiance(e)						
1968	53.8	78.1	52.9	86.3	46.3	55.4
1958	47.2	100.0	42.8	75.9	67.8	74.5
Difference	6.6	−21.9	10.1	10.4	−21.5	−19.1

[a]Based upon number answering. The number failing to answer in any one group varied from 0 to 4.

ages (of those experienced in premarital coitus) who had confined their overall experience to one partner; and percentages whose first experience was with a steady or fiance(e). It will be noted that the cross-cultural, cross-sex, and time-trend comparisons derived from these two measures are remarkably similar. In both cases (with very minor exceptions that become evident upon close inspection) rather consistent patterns show up: more American than Danish respondents, more female than male respondents, and more 1958 than 1968 respondents confined their total premarital coital experience to one partner and *also* had their first coitus in a commitment relationship. The other side of the coin, so to speak, is that Danes appear to be more promiscuous than Americans, males more promiscuous than females, and 1968 respondents more promiscuous than 1958 respondents. The term "promiscuity" is used here in a nonevaluative sense and merely to designate the opposite of "commitment." Our measures of these two concepts are indirect and imperfect, to be sure, but undoubtedly they tell something.

Not only were the Danish generally more promiscuous than the Americans (1958 Danish males being an exception), but the shift toward greater promiscuity during the decade under study was greater for them. Apparently, Denmark may be moving away from its traditional pattern of premarital sex justified by a commitment relationship, and sexual promiscuity is coming in to take its place. But without further testing, this observation must be regarded as highly speculative, since the two Danish samples lack strict comparability.

It also is worth noting that the Danish male-female differences in response to both of these items tended to be smaller than in either of the other two cultures, another example of the possible leveling effect of norm permissiveness.

Intermountain females also moved dramatically in the direction of greater promiscuity as indicated by these two measures, possibly because, being so near the "floor" at the beginning of the decade, there was opportunity for the general trend toward permissiveness to affect them proportionately more. Intermountain males did not change much by either measure and, with them, direction of change was inconsistent.

In two important respects Midwestern respondents stood out from the rest. In the first place, they tended to show higher proportions in a commitment relationship (1958 males being the most noticeable exception); and in the second place, this was the only culture where both sexes on both measures showed *higher* commitment percentages in 1968 than 1958 (1958 Intermountain males did on the item "first coitus with a steady or fiance"). Could it be that a general trend toward sexual freedom, such as has occurred in recent years, encourages the development of promiscuity in *both* the commitment-oriented permissive society (such as Denmark) and the ascetic-oriented restrictive society (such as the Intermountain Mormon): the same trend but for different reasons—in the first, to escape commitment; in the second, to escape repression? The question needs further research.

At any rate, the time trend in our Midwestern culture seems clear. To the extent that our sample is representative and our measures adequate, the Reiss hypothesis is supported there. Although it must be said that the testing of this important phenomenon has only begun, it probably can be tentatively concluded that at least a major current in premarital sex trends within this country is a movement toward permissiveness with commitment.

While the emerging American pattern seems to be toward the traditional Danish norm of premarital sex justified by commitment, the emerging Danish pattern may be away from both commitment and restriction, toward free and promiscuous sex. Furthermore, in this one respect at least, the converging lines of the two cultures seem now to have passed each other. Today the Danes appear to be less committed and more promiscuous in their premarital sexual contacts than do Midwestern Americans.

NEGATIVE ACCOMPANIMENTS OF COITUS

Considerable interest centers around the question of consequences. Does premarital coitus affect everyone the same, or do the norms of the culture and the values which the individual has incorporated into his personality make any difference? Our working hypothesis has been that values are relevant data; and following this, the consequences of premarital sex acts are to some extent relative to the alignment or misalignment of values and behavior, being most negative where the disjuncture is the greatest. In sociological circles this line of reasoning has been labeled "Theory of Cognitive Dissonance" (Festinger, 1957). Applied to the data of our present study, we would predict greater negative effects in America than Denmark, for females than males, and during 1958 as compared with 1968 since these are the categories showing disproportionately high value-behavior discrepancy.

Table 8 presents data for two negative accompaniments of premarital coitus. The first of these—yielding to force or felt obligation—means simply

TABLE 8 Percentage[a] Distributions of Responses to Items that Indicate Negative Feelings Accompanying First Premarital Coitus

| | Sample Cultures | | | | | |
| | Intermountain | | Midwestern | | Danish | |
Items and Years	Males	Females	Males	Females	Males	Females
I. First Experience Either Forced or by Obligation						
1968	2.4	24.2	2.5	23.1	10.0	18.5
1958	13.5	42.9	9.3	37.9	4.4	35.6
Difference	−11.1	−18.7	−6.8	−14.8	5.6	−17.1
II. First Experience Followed Chiefly by Guilt or Remorse						
1968	7.1	9.1	6.6	11.1	1.6	0.0
1958	29.7	28.6	12.1	31.0	4.3	2.0
Difference	−22.6	−19.5	−5.5	−19.9	−2.7	−2.0

[a]In I, the percentages are based upon the number answering; the number failing to answer varying from 0 to 6.
In II, the total number of cases was used as th base of the percents.

that there were pressures other than personal desire which were chiefly responsible for the experience. It will be observed that, in general, results turned out as expected: coitus because of pressure is seen to be higher in restrictive than permissive cultures, higher among females than males, and higher in 1958 than in 1968.

One irregularity in the patterns just noted was introduced by an unexpected increase in pressured coitus among Danish males, which also had the effect of reversing the cross-cultural picture for 1968 males. Reasons for this reverse trend for Danish males are not known, but it will be remembered from Table 7 that it also was Danish males who showed the greatest increase in promiscuous coitus. There is at least the possibility that these two phenomena are connected.

Part II of Table 8 gives percentages of those who specified either guilt or remorse as their predominant feeling the day after first premarital coitus. Here again, the overall patterns were in expected directions: coitus followed by guilt or remorse is seen to be higher in restrictive than permissive cultures (although Midwestern females exceed the Intermountain), higher for females than males (although not uniformly and with Denmark being a major exception), and consistently higher in 1958 than 1968. Whether the exceptions noted represent anything more than random variation cannot be determined from our non-probability samples. But at least the broad patterns seem clear and the consistency between our two measures builds confidence in the general findings.

Thus, whether measured by a feeling of external pressure at the time or a subsequent feeling of guilt or remorse, the negative accompaniments of premarital coitus appear to be greatest where the sex norms are restrictive (and, significantly, also where value-behavior discrepancy is the greatest)— in the American cultures as compared with the Danish, with females as compared with males, and in 1958 as compared with 1968.

CONCLUSION

The design of our investigation has enabled us to compare premarital sexual attitudes and behavior against each other; and to compare them separately and in combination across a restrictive-permissive continuum of cultures, across the differing worlds of males and females, and across the recent decade in time. Although the primary concern of this paper has been with recent social changes in premarital sex values and practices, the additional involvement of intersex and cross-cultural variables has enabled us to see the phenomena in better perspective and to tease out certain meanings that otherwise may have remained obscure. Furthermore, we have been interested in going beyond mere description, to the discovery of relationships; and then to interconnect these relationships with each other and with relevant concepts and propositions, with theory building as the ultimate goal. To establish needed controls, we have in places made supplementary analyses of Midwestern data including the use of matched sampling techniques. Nevertheless, we regard our study as more exploratory than definitive. We feel that some significant leads have been uncovered but at the same time regard our conclusions as tentative—as plausible for the present, perhaps, but as hypotheses for future research.

We call attention to the strong suggestion from our data that values and norms serve as intervening variables *affecting the effects* of behavior. For the explaining of consequences, it would seem that even perhaps more important than the sexual act itself is the degree to which that act lines up or fails to line up with the standards set. Whether the comparisons have been between males and females, across cultures, or over time, we have demonstrated two parallel and probably interrelated patterns: value-behavior discrepancy is associated with sexual restrictiveness; and certain negative effects of premarital intimacy are associated with sexual restrictiveness. The possibility—we think probability—is that it is primarily value-behavior discrepancy that is causing the difficulty. This facet of our theory has been explored at greater length in earlier writing (Christensen, 1966; 1969).

REFERENCES

Bell, Robert R., *Premarital Sex in a Changing Society*, Englewood Cliffs, New Jersey: Prentice-Hall, 1966.

Bell, Robert R. and Jay B. Chaskes, "Premarital Sexual Experience Among Coeds, 1958 and 1968," *Journal of Marriage and the Family*, 32 (February, 1970): 81–84.

Christensen, Harold T., "Cultural Relativism and Premarital Sex Norms," *American Sociological Review*, 25 (February, 1960), 31–39.

———, "Scandinavian and American Sex Norms: Some Comparisons, with Sociological Implications," *Journal of Social Issues*, 22 (April, 1966), 60–75.

———, "Normative Theory Derived from Cross-Cultural Family Research," *Journal of Marriage and the Family*, 31 (May, 1969), 209–222.

Christensen, Harold T. and George R. Carpenter, "Timing Patterns in the Development of Sexual Intimacy," *Marriage and Family Living*, 24 (February, 1962a), 30–35.

———, "Value-Behavior Discrepancies Regarding Premarital Coitus in Three Western Cultures," *American Sociological Review*, 27 (February, 1962b), 66–74.

Ehrmann, Winston W., "Marital and Nonmarital Sexual Behavior," in Harold T. Christensen (ed.), *Handbook of Marriage and the Family*. Chicago: Rand McNally, 1964, 585–622.

———, *Premarital Dating Behavior*, New York: Holt, Rinehart and Winston, 1959.

Festinger, Leon, *A Theory of Cognitive Dissonance*, New York: Harper and Row, 1957.

Freedman, Mervin B., "The Sexual Behavior of American College Women: An Empirical Study and an Historical Survey," *Merrill-Palmer Quarterly of Behavior and Development*, 11 (January, 1965), 33–48.

Gagnon, John H. and William Simon, "Prospects for Change in American Sexual Patterns," *Medical Aspects of Human Sexuality*, 4 (January, 1970), 100–117.

Kinsey, Alfred C., Wardell Pomeroy, Clyde Martin, and Paul Gebhard, *Sexual Behavior in the Human Female*, Philadelphia: Saunders, 1953.

Kirkendall, Lester A., *Premarital Intercourse and Interpersonal Relationships*, New York: Julian, 1961.

Leslie, Gerald R., *The Family in Social Context*, New York: Oxford University Press, 1967.

Luckey, Eleanor B. and Gilbert D. Nass, "A Comparison of Sexual Attitudes and Behavior in an International Sample," *Journal of Marriage and the Family*, 31 (May, 1969), 364–379.

Packard, Vance, *The Sexual Wilderness: the Contemporary Upheaval in Male-Female Relationships*, New York: David McKay, 1968.

Reiss, Ira L., *The Social Context of Premarital Sexual Permissiveness*, New York: Holt, Rinehart and Winston, 1967.

————, "Premarital Sexual Standards," in Carlfred B. Broderick and Jessie Bernard (eds.), *The Individual, Sex, and Society: A Siecus Handbook for Teachers and Counselors*, Baltimore: The Johns Hopkins Press, 1969.

Schofield, Michael, *The Sexual Behavior of Young People*, Boston: Little, Brown, 1965.

Terman, Lewis M., *Psychological Factors in Marital Happiness*, New York: McGraw-Hill, 1938.

14 Sex Differences in Responses to Psychosexual Stimulation by Films and Slides

GUNTER SCHMIDT and VOLKMAR SIGUSCH

In a previous publication we reported on the emotional and physiological-sexual reactions as well as the changes in sexual behavior in men and women when they were confronted with sexual thematic slides (Sigusch, 1970). In contrast to the data of Kinsey (1953), we found relatively few sex-specific differences for the variables we covered. We were not able to establish any sex differences at all for physiological-sexual reactions during the showing of the pictures and for changes in sexual behavior in the 24 hours after the experiment.

In this report, too, emotional and physio-sexual behavior will be described, with a special view on sex specific differences. This time, however, we are using a different set of stimuli, namely films and slides that show petting and coitus. In addition, more variables are isolated and examined.

Translated from the German by Fred Klein, Switzerland.

Reprinted from *The Journal of Sex Research*, 6, No. 4 (November, 1970), 268–283, by permission of the Society for the Scientific Study of Sex.

TABLE 1 Comparison of Background Data: Male and Female Subjects

	Males (N = 128)	Females (N = 128)
Age (Years)		
19-20	9%	41%
21-22	22%	31%
23-24	35%	17%
25-26	27%	7%
27+	7%	4%
	100%	100%
Median	23.5	21.4
Marital Status		
Single	80%	86%
Married	20%	14%
	100%	100%
Denomination		
None	13%	11%
Protestant	76%	81%
Catholic	9%	9%
Others	2%	0%
	100%	101%
Church Attendance		
Never/Seldom	73%	63%
Sometimes/Regular	27%	37%
	100%	100%
Political Attitude*		
Conservative	33%	36%
Liberal	67%	64%
	100%	100%
Premarital Attitude†		
Restrictive	38%	45%
Permissive	62%	55%
	100%	100%
Coitus Experience		
No	26%	27%
Yes	74%	73%
	100%	100%

*According to the Melvin Scale (1955): up to 65 points = conservative; more than 65 points = liberal.
†Restrictive = premarital coitus judged not acceptable or only acceptable with love or being engaged; permissive = premarital coitus acceptable even without love or engagement.

I. METHOD

The sample consisted of 128 male and 128 female students of the Hamburg University who volunteered for the experiment. Table 1 shows some of the important background data. The men are on the average two years older than the women. Since with respect to the other background data such as marital status, denomination and church attendance, political and pre-marital attitudes, and coitus experience there are practically no differences between the sexes, the age difference is unlikely to impair the comparison of the samples.

Our stimulus set consisted of the following four themes:

1. Petting I: Both partners undress to their underwear and pet (manual—genital contacts) without reaching orgasm.
2. Petting II: Both partners undress completely and pet (manual—genital contacts, cunnilingus, and fellatio) reaching orgasm.
3. Coitus I: Foreplay with manual—genital contacts; face to face coitus.
4. Coitus II: Foreplay with manual—genital contacts, cunnilingus, and fellatio; coitus in different positions.

Every one of the themes was presented in color film, black-white film, a color slide series, and a black-white slide series. Our material therefore consisted of altogether 16 stimuli sets. The black-white films were copies of the corresponding color films. The slides were taken by a time-sampling method during the film shooting. Exposure time for films and slide series was ten minutes. Every subject was shown only one of the 16 stimuli sets. Therefore each set was displayed to 8 male and 8 female subjects.

The experiment was divided into three parts:

1. One to two weeks before the actual experiment, background data such as demographic data, religious, political and sexual attitudes, sexual history and personality traits were obtained through questionnaires from groups of subjects (5–15 persons at a time).

2. In individual sessions, a film or slide series was shown to the subjects. The showing of the stimuli ensued automatically so that the experimenter was not present in the room.

Directly after viewing the stimuli, the subjects described their impressions through rating scales. In addition, the subjects judged their emotional reactions by a semantic differential which they already had once before filled out in part 1. By comparing the two semantic differentials it was possible to estimate the emotional changes which were induced through viewing the stimuli.

3. At the end of the second phase a questionnaire in a sealed envelope was given to each subject which was to be read and filled out 24 hours after the experiment. The importance of keeping to this time interval was strongly stressed. The questionnaire contained similar questions regarding sexual behavior and sexual reactions in the 24 hours *after* the viewing of the film or slide series, as well as the 24 hours *before* the viewing. In addition, the subjects stated their emotional and autonomic reactions on the day after the experiment as well as their physiological-sexual reactions *during* the showing of the film or slide series.

For the female subjects a female experimenter carried out the experiment while for the male students a male experimenter was used. The anonymity of all answers was guaranteed.

II. RESULTS

1. Ratings of Sexual Arousal and Favorable-Unfavorable Response

Directly after viewing the film or slide series the subject had to judge on 9 point scales if and how strong he was sexually aroused and whether he considered the stimulus favorable or unfavorable.

TABLE 2   Ratings of Sexual Arousal: Mean and Standard Deviation of 4 Themes

Theme	Males			Females			
	M*	SD	N	M*	SD	N	p-Value†
Petting I	4.4	1.7	32	4.7	2.2	32	ns
Petting II	5.4	2.0	32	4.5	1.9	32	0.05
Coitus I	5.3	1.7	32	5.0	2.5	32	ns
Coitus II	5.6	1.4	32	4.7	2.4	32	0.05
Total	5.2	1.8	128	4.7	2.3	128	0.05

*Low value = low sexual arousal; high value = high sexual arousal.
†According to t-Test (ns = not significant, p > 0.05).

Table 2 shows the mean stimulation ratings of the men and the women for the four themes. The mean ratings for the women lie between 4.5 to 5.0, and for the men 4.4 to 5.6, both being around the category "moderately stimulated." There are no significant differences between the sexes for the themes "Petting I" and "Coitus I." The more intensive and unusual acts of "Petting II" and "Coitus II" were experienced by the men as much more stimulating. The difference, however, is only significant at the 5% level. When the four stimuli are combined there also is a significantly stronger sexual stimulation for the men as compared to the women.

TABLE 3   Ratings of Favorable-Unfavorable Response: Mean and Standard Deviation of 4 Themes

Theme	Males			Females			
	M*	SD	N	M*	SD	N	p-Value†
Petting I	4.7	1.3	32	4.1	1.6	32	ns
Petting II	4.5	2.0	32	5.3	1.6	32	ns
Coitus I	4.3	1.6	32	4.9	1.8	32	ns
Coitus II	3.8	1.2	32	4.9	1.8	32	0.01
Total	4.3	1.6	128	4.8	1.7	128	0.02

*Low value = favorable; high value = unfavorable.
†According to t-Test (ns = not significant, p > .005).

Table 3 shows the mean favorableness ratings. The means of the women vary between 4.1 and 5.3, thus around the category "neutral." For the men, the means are between 3.8 and 4.7, thus being between the categories "neutral" and "somewhat favorable." For the themes "Petting I," "Petting II" and "Coitus I" there are no significant sex specific differences, even though the trend shows that the men judged the last two and the women the first as relatively more favorable. However, for the theme "Coitus II" there is a significant sex difference, the men judging this theme more favorably than the women. When the four themes are combined, the men judged the stimuli as significantly more favorable, too.

Altogether, the men tended to describe the pictures and films as more sexually arousing and more favorable than the women. The difference as a whole, however, is not pronounced; it is only an average tendency with a large individual variability. This becomes very clear when one looks at the frequency distribution of the male and female judgments which show large overlappings: for example 42% of the women regarded the slides or films more arousing and 41% more favorable than did the average (median) man.

2. Mood List (Semantic Differential)

The sexual arousal and the favorable-unfavorable response are obviously not the only emotional reactions brought forth through the viewing of the films or slides. In order to measure other emotional changes, we used a semantic differential which the subjects filled out before (part 1 of the experiment) as well as directly after the exposure to the stimuli. A comparison of the answers gives us information about the spontaneous emotional reactions to the slides and films.

Figure 1 shows the results for the male subjects. They described themselves after the experiment as significantly more: bored, aggressive, gregarious, repelled, excited, shocked, irritated, cheered up, emotional, innerly agitated, and impulsive. These changes as a whole speak for an emotional activation and labilizing effect. However, one must keep in mind that these emotional changes are to be judged only in relation to the previous emotional profile obtained under "normal conditions." Thus for example, after the experiment the subjects felt relatively stronger repulsion as compared to before the experiment, but on the average they still chose the category "attracted" more often than "repelled."

The women in general show a similar picture (Figure 2). After the experiment they described themselves as significantly more: bored, aggressive, excited, shocked, repelled, cheered up, driven, emotional, wild, uninhibited, innerly agitated, jumpy, disgusted, irritated, angered, and dizzy.

In comparing the results on men and women, we see that the women had more items significantly changed; 16 out of 24 characteristics were significantly different (to the 5% level) for the women while the men had 11 items changed. This indicates that the women reacted stronger to a psychosexual stimulation. As a matter of fact, for three items the emotional changes (=differences between the first and second semantic differential) are significantly larger for the women than for the men: women were more shocked, irritated and disgusted. This is shown by analyses of variance (sex × time of filling out the semantic differential [before vs. after the experiment]) for each item; for the 3 items mentioned above, there is a significant interaction between sex and time of completion.

3. Emotional and Autonomic Reactions in the 24 Hours after the Experiment

In addition to the emotional changes which were experienced immediately after the viewing, there were the emotional and autonomic reactions regis-

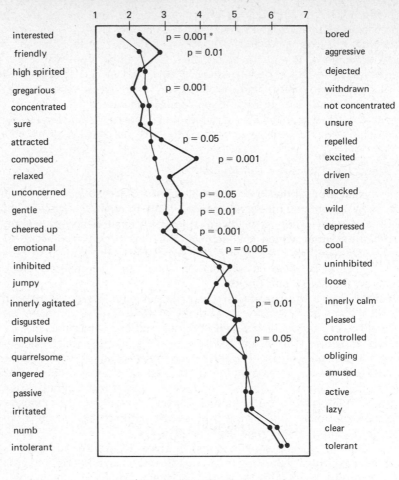

	1	2	3	4	5	6	7	
interested			p = 0.001 *					bored
friendly			p = 0.01					aggressive
high spirited								dejected
gregarious			p = 0.001					withdrawn
concentrated								not concentrated
sure								unsure
attracted			p = 0.05					repelled
composed				p = 0.001				excited
relaxed								driven
unconcerned				p = 0.05				shocked
gentle				p = 0.01				wild
cheered up				p = 0.001				depressed
emotional				p = 0.005				cool
inhibited								uninhibited
jumpy								loose
innerly agitated					p = 0.01			innerly calm
disgusted								pleased
impulsive					p = 0.05			controlled
quarrelsome								obliging
angered								amused
passive								active
irritated								lazy
numb								clear
intolerant								tolerant

*   p-values according to Sign-Test

——   before the experiment

——   after the experiment

Figure 1   Judgments of "Present Feelings on the Semantic Differential: Means for Male Subjects ($N = 128$)

tered by the subjects in the 24 hours after the experiment (as compared to the 24 hours before the experiment).

Table 4 shows the results for both the men and women. Significantly more men reported a stronger (as opposed to a weaker) inner uneasiness for the 24 hours before. Correspondingly, there is a significant reduction of concentration ability and an increase of general activity.

The women showed a significant increase of inner uneasiness, general activity, aggressiveness, and autonomic complaints as well as a decrease of concentration ability. More women also had a more restless sleep the night after the experiment as compared to the night before.

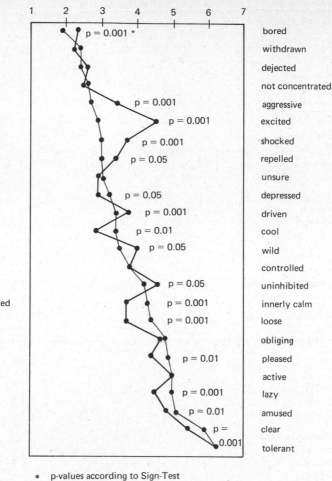

interested	bored
gregarious	withdrawn
high spirited	dejected
concentrated	not concentrated
friendly	aggressive
composed	excited
unconcerned	shocked
attracted	repelled
sure	unsure
cheered up	depressed
relaxed	driven
emotional	cool
gentle	wild
impulsive	controlled
inhibited	uninhibited
innerly agitated	innerly calm
jumpy	loose
quarrelsome	obliging
disgusted	pleased
passive	active
irritated	lazy
angered	amused
numb	clear
intolerant	tolerant

*   p-values according to Sign-Test
─── before the experiment
━━━ after the experiment

Figure 2 Judgments of "Present Feelings" on the Semantic Differential: Means for Female Subjects ($N = 128$)

An emotional labilizing effect and activation is observed therefore not only directly after the experiment but is also seen in the 24 hours afterwards. As with the semantic differential, the day after the experiment shows that women react more strongly than men to pictures and films with sexual themes. Out of seven items, six significant changes were registered by women while men registered only three.

However, it seems important to us to point out that though significant changes were registered, the majority of subjects did not register any changes in the 24 hours after the experiment in the emotional and autonomic areas.

TABLE 4 Emotional and Autonomic Reactions in the 24 Hours After the Experiment for Males (N = 128) and Females (N = 128)

Reaction	Males Per cent	p-Value*	Females Per cent	p-Value*
Inner Uneasiness				
Increased	27		38	
Decreased	6	0.001	2	0.001
No Change	67		60	
Concentration Ability				
Increased	4		9	
Decreased	14	0.01	25	0.001
No Change	82		66	
General Activity				
Increased	18		23	
Decreased	5	0.001	13	0.05
No Change	77		64	
Aggressiveness				
Increased	15		23	
Decreased	10	ns	7	0.001
No Change	75		70	
General Physical Status				
Worse	6		13	
Better	6	ns	9	ns
No Change	88		78	
Sleep				
More Restless	9		18	
Quieter	4	ns	5	0.001
No Change	87		77	
Autonomic Complaints				
Increased	5		14	
Decreased	1	ns	2	0.001
No Change	91		84	

*Significance of the difference between the first two categories (increased-decreased); according to Sign-Test (ns = not significant, p > 0.05).

4. Physio-Sexual Reactions during the Experiment

Table 5 summarizes some physio-sexual reactions during the experiment. The women reported most often sensations in the genital area (65%). The next frequent (28%) reaction named was vaginal lubrication. Sensations in the breasts were registered only by a small number (9%). No woman reached an orgasm during the viewing of the pictures or films.

The most frequent physio-sexual reaction reported by men was erection. Out of a total of 86% of the subjects, 31% reported a full erection and 55% a slight to moderate one. In the majority, the erection lasted less than five minutes (which is less than half of the time of exposition). A fourth of the subjects observed pre-ejaculatory secretion. Four per cent of the men reported an ejaculation during the experiment. These were not spontaneous ejaculations—they were produced through masturbation. About 20% of both

TABLE 5 Physiological-Sexual Reactions During the Showing of the Film/Slides for Males (N = 128) and Females (N = 128)

Males		Females	
Preejaculatory Emission		Vaginal Lubrication	
Don't Know	23%	Don't Know	18%
No	52%	No	54%
Yes	25%	Yes	28%
Erection		Genital Sensations*	
None	14%	Don't know	6%
Slight, Moderate	55%	No	29%
Full	31%	Yes	65%
Duration of Erection		Sensations in the Breasts	
None	14%	Don't Know	7%
To 2'	25%	No	84%
3'–5'	38%	Yes	9%
+6'	23%		
Ejaculation		Orgasm	
No	96%	No	100%
Yes	4%	Yes	0%
Any Reaction†		Any Reaction‡	
No	13%	No	28%
Yes	87%	Yes	72%

*Feelings of warmth, pulsations, "itching."
†Preejaculatory emission and/or erection and/or ejaculation.
‡Vaginal lubrication and/or genital sensations and/or sensations in the breasts and/or orgasm.

the men and the women reported some masturbatory activity during the viewing of the pictures or films.

The above mentioned physio-sexual reactions of men and women can hardly be compared in detail since the anatomical substrates are different. However, it is important to point out that the greater majority of the men as well as the women (87% and 72%) observed some sort of physio-sexual reaction in themselves. This finding says nothing about the possible physio-sexual reactions under psycho-sexual stimulation since reference was made only to reactions localized in the genital area and so pronounced that they could be registered by the subjects themselves.

5. Sexual Behavior and Reactions in the 24 Hours after the Experiment

On the day after the experiment, the subjects were asked about their sexual reactions and behavior in the 24 hours before and in the 24 hours after the experiment. A comparison of the answers for the time before and after the experiment permits us to estimate if and how far the psychosexual stimulation led to sexual activation.

Table 6 shows the results for both male and female subjects. 30% of the men report higher, 11% lower masturbation activity after the experiment. The number of subjects with higher masturbation activity is significantly larger than that with diminished activity. Psychosexual stimulation therefore demonstrably influenced the masturbation behavior of the men. The women too demonstrated a significant activation of masturbatory behavior: 14%

TABLE 6 Sexual Behavior and Sexual Reactions in the 24 Hours Before and in the 24 Hours After the Slowing of the Film/Slides for Males (N = 128) and Females (N = 128)

Behavior/Reaction		Males		Females	
		Per cent	p-Value*	Per cent	p-Value*
Masturbation	+	30		14	
	−	11	0.001	4	0.01
	=	59		82	
Petting	+	5		9	
	−	6	ns	2	0.06
	=	89		89	
Coitus	+	15		14	
	−	9	ns	5	0.02
	=	76		81	
Total Orgasms	+	41		22	
	−	15	0.001	5	0.001
	=	44		73	
Sexual Dreams	+	5		8	
	−	3	ns	9	ns
	=	92		83	
Sexual Phantasies†	+	33		35	
	−	2	0.001	2	0.001
	=	65		63	
Talk about Sex	+	34		47	
	−	18	0.02	14	0.001
	=	48		39	
Sexual Tension	+	32		35	
	−	19	0.05	18	0.01
	=	49		47	
Wish for Sexual Activity	+	41		46	
	−	14	0.001	11	0.001
	=	45		43	

Note: +: In the 24 hours after the showing of the film/slides > in the 24 hours before the showing of the film/slides. −: In the 24 hours after < in the 24 hours before. =: No difference between the 24 hours after and the 24 hours before.
*Significance of the difference between the + and − category; according to Sign-Test (ns = not significant, p > 0.05).
†Phantasies during masturbation, petting, or coitus not included.

reported higher and 4% lower masturbatory activity after the experiment. In order to ascertain if activation is more intense for men or for women, a statistical analysis was made. It showed that there is no significant difference between the sexes in this respect. Psychosexual stimulation leads to an increase of masturbation to the same extent in both men and women.

By comparison, heterosexual behavior as a whole was less influenced. Significant changes in the sense of activation were found only in women. Increase in coitus and petting activity could be observed, it was, however, not large. Similar trends in male subjects did not reach the level of statistical significance.

The total number of all orgasms, on the other hand, was clearly and significantly increased for both sexes in the 24 hours after the experiment. Forty-one per cent of the men and 22% of the women reported that they had more orgasms on the day after the experiment than on the preceding

TABLE 7 The Influence of the Film/Slides on Phantasies and Sexual Techniques During Masturbation and Coitus in the 24 Hours After the Experiment

	Males	Females	p-Value*
Only Subjects Who Masturbated in the 24 Hours After the Experiment:			
Masturbatory phantasies about the shown film/slides			
no	32%	57%	0.05
yes	68%	43%	
	N = 50	N = 23	
Only Subjects Who Had Coitus in the 24 Hours After the Experiment:			
Phantasies during coitus about the shown film/slides			
no	82%	84%	
yes	18%	16%	ns
	N = 28	N = 25	
Previously seldom or never used techniques during coitus foreplay			
no	89%	96%	
seldom used	11%	0%	−†
never used	0%	4%	
	N = 28	N = 25	
Previously seldom or never used coitus positions			
no	82%	96%	
seldom used	14%	0%	−†
never used	4%	4%	
	N = 28	N = 25	

*Significance according to chi-square (ns = not significant, p > 0.05).
†Calculation of chi-square not possible due to too few cases.

day. This finding could suggest a conclusion that under a psychosexual stimulation men put sex into practice more often than women. However, if one again compares among both sexes those subjects who had more orgasms after the experiment in relation to those who had fewer orgasms the difference between the sexes disappears.

Although the experiment had no effect on sexual dreams, phantasy activity was equally intensified in both sexes. The tendency to discuss things of a sexual nature also increased significantly after the experiment. This happened more often with women than with men, however, without statistical significance.

We also asked questions about sexual tension and the wish to have sexual contact. Both were increased significantly for both sexes after the experiment. There was no statistical difference for the sexes in the degree of such increase of sexual desire.

Finally we specially asked those subjects who masturbated or had intercourse in the 24 hours after the experiment about the influence of the film/slides on their sexual behavior. As Table 7 shows, we were able to establish a distinct influence of the psychosexual stimulation on the masturbation phantasies and a slight influence on phantasies during coitus and on coitus techniques. Of those who masturbated on the day after the experiment, 68% of the men and 43% of the women thought about the film or slide series during masturbation. The sex difference is significant, i.e. the men were readier than the women to incorporate the stimuli into their masturbation phantasies. Of the subjects who had coitus on the day after the experiment, only 18% of the men and 16% of the women thought about the film or slides during coitus. This sex difference is not significant. The influence on sexual techniques during coitus foreplay or during coitus itself was small; only one man and one woman reported coitus positions and one woman foreplay techniques they had never practiced before. The resumption of previously seldom performed acts was also established for only a very small percentage and then only for the men. Because of the small number of cases, it is not possible to make any statements regarding statistical significance of sex differences.

III. DISCUSSION

The results of this study confirm our opinion based on a previous experiment (Sigusch, 1970) that the present views regarding marked sex-specific differences in visual arousability through pictures and films must be revised.

It is true that in our experiment, too, women were sexually somewhat less stimulated than men, especially when pictures and films showed more unusual heterosexual practices. The difference, however, is slight and much less than was to be expected from Kinsey's data. This stated difference moreover is only an average tendency. A large percentage of the women (about 40%) reported a stronger sexual arousal through the pictures and films than the "average" man.

If we consider emotional reactions other than sexual stimulation, both sexes show an activation and labilizing effect. These emotional changes are, according to our data, more pronounced for the women. It is therefore quite probable that women allow themselves to be affected somewhat more strongly than men.

As opposed to the slight differences in the emotional area, we could not establish sex-specific differences with respect to physio-sexual reactions and sexual behavior: The majority of the men and women registered such reactions in the genital area. Both sexes were sexually more active in the 24 hours after being confronted with the stimuli as compared to the 24 hours before. This activation was seen above all in an increase of masturbation activity, and to a lesser extent (significant only for the women) in an increase of petting and coitus. Sexual phantasy activity and sexual desire were also increased.

The activation of sexual behavior for both the men and women therefore was approximately of the same strength; one has to assume that women have the same readiness to transpose an induced sexual excitation through pictures and films into an actual sexual activity.

We have already referred to the fact that Kinsey's data (1953) which until now presented the most extensive material regarding sex differences differed considerably from our results. According to Kinsey, men are stimulated through pictures with sexual scenes much more often than women. Two explanations are possible for this discrepancy between Kinsey's statements and our results:

1. It is very difficult to obtain valid results regarding sex-specific differences in psychosexual arousability through such questionnaires as Kinsey used since the stimuli cannot be exactly defined and controlled. The results in the Kinsey study, therefore, possibly reflect much less sex-specific differences in psychosexual arousability than differences in the degree and type of experience with visually offered sexuality. This may be expected since in comparison to men women in our culture have much less opportunity to experience these types of psychosexual stimuli.

2. Kinsey's data were collected 20 to 30 years ago. We know today that the double standard and corresponding differences in sexual behavior (e.g., premarital sex) were then much more marked in the U.S.A. than they are today in the countries of Northwestern Europe (Christensen, 1966; Giese, 1968; Zetterberg, 1969; Israel, 1970; Schmidt, in prep.). It is therefore not surprising that the reaction of the women whom we examined was different from that of the American women whom Kinsey interviewed. The degree of sex differences in psychosexual arousability is obviously a function of the grade of sexual emancipation of women in a social group or a society. From this follows that a larger sex difference than that described by us would be seen if we dealt with women who are less sexually emancipated than those in our sample.

Finally, it's important to touch once more on the question of sexual activation through the experiment. This activation is, even if significant, only slight, especially if one considers that the experiment dealt with films and slides which contained very strong and intensive sexual stimuli. These results agree with the findings which we obtained in previous experiments with 99 men and 50 women with completely different stimulus material (Schmidt, 1969; Sigusch, 1970). Scientifically, these results do not justify the often expressed fear that sexual "disinhibition" is brought about by visual-sexual stimuli or "pornography." Our results absolutely do not point to such a rise in sexual appetite or to such a reduction in effective controlling mechanisms when one is confronted with pictures or films with sexual themes so that a rise in uncontrollable sexual activity could be expected.

REFERENCES

Christensen, H. T., "Scandinavian and American Sex Norms: Some Comparisons with Sociological Implications," *Journal of Social Issues*, 22, No. 2, (1966), 60–75.

Giese, H. und Schmidt, G., *Studenten-Sexualität*, Verhalten und Einstellung, Reinbek: Rowohlt, 1968.

Israel, J., Gustavsson, N., Eliasson, R.-M. und Lindberg, G., "Sexuelle Verhaltensformen der schwedischen Großstadtjugend," in Bergström-Walan, M.-B. et al., *Modellfall Skandinavien? Sexualität und Sexualpolitik in Dänemark und Schweden*, Reinbek: Rowohlt, 1970.

Kinsey, A. C., Pomeroy, W. B., Martin, C. E., and Gebhard, P. H., *Sexual Behavior in the Human Female*, Philadelphia and London: Saunders, 1953.

Melvin, D., "An Experimental and Statistical Study of Two Primary Social Attitudes," Ph.D. Thesis, University London Lib., 1955.

Schmidt, G., Sigusch, V., and Meyberg, U., "Psychosexual Stimulation in Men: Emotional Reactions, Changes of Sex Behavior, and Measures of Conservative Attitudes," *Journal of Sex Research*, 5, (1969), 199–217.

Schmidt, G., Sigusch, V. und Meier, H. T., *Arbeiter-Sexualität*, Eine empirische Untersuchung an jungen Industriearbeitern. Neuweid und Berlin: Luchterhand, 1971.

Sigusch, V., Schmidt, G., Reinfeld, A., and Wiedemann-Sutor, I., "Psychosexual Stimulation: Sex Differences," *Journal of Sex Research*, 6, (1970), 1.

Zetterberg, H. L., *Om Sexuallivet i Sverige.* Stockholm: Statens Offentliga Utredningar, 1969.

|V| Mixed Marriage

Introduction to Section V

One of the surprising results of a so-called free system of mate selection is the high degree of homogamy in marriage: the high proportion of marriages between people with similar educational, religious, and racial backgrounds. Yet despite the high degree of homogamy we have a rising proportion of "mixed marriages." What promotes interfaith and interracial marriages? How well do they fare compared to homogamous marriages? What is the probable trend in terms of these mixed marriages? These are the questions that this section begins to answer.

As is the case so often in social science, we lack complete data to answer many of the questions that interest us. For example, on trends in interfaith marriage we must rely on data showing constant increases in Canada and assume that the same trends hold for America. Due to the objections of a few small groups, the U.S. Bureau of the Census has never included a question concerning religion in its decennial census.

The study by Burchinal and Chancellor (15) is an important one. They are the first to utilize statewide data on intermarriage with breakdowns by occupation of groom and age of bride. The importance of this can be seen in that it is possible that mixed-faith marriages have above average divorce rates simply because they occur more often among poor husbands and young brides. We know that poor husbands and young brides have high divorce rates even if they are not intermarried. It is therefore necessary to look within a particular occupational level of husband and age level of wife and see if the mixed marriages within that level have a yet higher divorce rate. This is precisely what Burchinal and Chancellor did. They found that although mixed religion is still a factor in divorce, occupation of groom and age of bride are more important predictors of divorce. The precise findings and interpretations are well worth careful reading.

Older studies in this area exaggerated the impact of religious mixture on a marriage because they did not separate out factors like "age of bride" and "occupation of groom." Also, older studies presented "failure rates" (for example, 15 percent of mixed marriages fail compared to 5 percent of same-faith marriages). The same findings presented as "success rates" (85 percent succeed versus 95 percent), do not sound so "pessimistic." Burchinal presents his data in terms of success rates. The interested reader should look at other important studies such as that done in New York City by Jerold Heiss.[1] Heiss' study contains valuable findings on the religious and family type background of the intermarried.

Heer's findings on black–white marriage (16) support the hypothesis of the importance of homogamy in mate selection. He finds that intermarriage rates increase when status differences between blacks and whites are reduced. Since in general the status differences are still quite large between blacks and whites, one would predict that although there will be an increase, such marriages will still constitute but a small proportion of total marriages.

[1] Heiss, J., "Premarital Characteristics of the Religiously Intermarried in an Urban Area." *American Sociological Review* 25 (February, 1960), 47–55.

15 | Survival Rates Among Religiously Homogamous and Interreligious Marriages

LEE G. BURCHINAL and LOREN E. CHANCELLOR

Family sociologists long have emphasized the positive relations between religious homogamy and marital success. Earlier studies by Bell, Weeks, and Landis as well as the results of more recent investigations are used to support this generalization.[1] These studies, however, include serious sampling and other methodological limitations such as being based on nonrandom samples or on samples from restricted portions of the married population. Also, controls for variables known to be related to divorce rates have been lacking. The purpose of this report is to present the results of more carefully refined tests of the religious homogamy and marital stability generalization than have been reported previously.

Four sets of results are presented. First, comparisons of marital survival rates are made among homogamous Catholic, homogamous Protestant and Catholic-Protestant marriages. Second, refinements in classifications are made among the Protestant marriages to permit comparisons of marital survival rates among selected types of denominationally homogamous Protestant marriages and denominationally mixed Protestant marriages. Third, comparisons are presented for marital survival rates between homogamous Catholic marriages and selected types of denominationally homogamous Protestant marriages. And fourth, marital survival rate differences are determined for selected types of marriages involving Catholics and persons who claim affiliation with certain Protestant denominations. The first set of comparisons includes retests of previous studies, whereas the last three sets of comparisons include data which have not been previously reported.

[1] Howard W. Bell, *Youth Tell Their Story* (Washington, D.C.: American Council on Education, 1938), p. 21; H. Ashley Weeks, "Differential Divorce Rates by Occupation," *Social Forces*, 21 (March, 1943), 334–337; Judson T. Landis, "Marriages of Mixed and Non-Mixed Religious Faith," *American Sociological Review*, 14 (June, 1949), 401–407; Jerold S. Heiss, "Interfaith Marriage and Marital Outcome," *Marriage and Family Living*, 23 (August, 1961), 228–233; Thomas P. Monahan and William M. Kephart, "Divorces and Desertion by Religious and Mixed-Religious Groups," *The American Journal of Sociology*, 59 (March, 1954), 454–465.

Journal Paper No. J-4364 of the Iowa Agricultural and Home Economics Experiment Station, Project No. 1447, Iowa State University, Ames, Iowa, in cooperation with the Division of Vital Statistics, Iowa State Department of Health. This investigation was supported in part by Public Health Service Research Grant M-3401(A) from the National Institute of Mental Health, Public Health Service.

Reprinted from *Social Forces*, 41 (May, 1963), 353–362, by permission of The University of North Carolina Press.

METHOD

All data used in this study were obtained from the marriage and divorce records maintained by the Iowa Division of Vital Statistics. In this study, data are used for a seven-year period, from 1953 through 1959. Religious identification or affiliation was based on the responses to the religious item on the form. This item simply asks: "Your religion" and is followed by a blank.

The analyses began with the identification of the marital religious types

TABLE 1   Marriage and Divorce Frequencies by Spousal Religious Affiliation Combinations and Seven Marriage Duration Periods for Iowa First Marriages, 1953–1959

Religious Affiliation Types	Marital Duration Periods						
	1	2	3	4	5	6	7
Homogamous Catholic							
Marriages	14,193	11,960	9,898	7,791	5,598	3,413	1,640
Divorces	32	96	139	155	145	121	76
Homogamous Protestant							
Marriages	52,720	44,357	36,209	27,906	19,924	11,997	5,728
Divorces	728	1,468	1,937	2,009	1,774	1,283	758
Catholic-interreligious							
Catholic wife							
Marriages	2,957	2,497	2,043	1,601	1,147	666	307
Divorces	49	112	161	171	145	118	64
Catholic husband							
Marriages	2,615	2,167	1,780	1,384	997	586	294
Divorces	75	136	176	188	160	108	62
Total Catholic-interreligious							
Marriages	5,572	4,664	3,823	2,985	2,144	1,252	601
Divorces	124	248	337	359	305	226	126
Total of all cases							
Marriages	72,485	60,981	49,930	38,682	27,666	16,662	7,969
Divorces	886	1,805	2,410	2,504	2,221	1,630	958

shown in Table 1. The population of marriages for each religious type was limited to first-married white couples, both of whom were Iowa residents at the time of marriage. Because the data were restricted to official records, longitudinal analyses could not be conducted. It was possible, however, to approximate a longitudinal investigation by creating marriage- and divorce-linked cohorts of data. This was done by first obtaining counts for the population of marriages in each religious type for each year. The frequencies of divorces occurring each year were obtained for each religious type. For reasons which are expanded shortly, these divorce frequencies also were determined for seven duration periods. Within these duration periods, the frequencies of divorces were subtracted from the original marriage frequencies for each year of marriage. The resulting numbers then were converted to percentages of the original marriage frequencies for that religious type. These percentages are called the marital survival rates.

It is important to remember two things about the marital survival rates as defined in this investigation. One, these survival rates are based on divorce frequencies only. If separations or other nondivorce marital dissolutions were included, different results might be obtained. The present results, therefore, must be limited to differential divorce proneness among the several religious types. Second, all results represent parameters, not sample estimates. Hence, statistical tests are not needed for the purpose of drawing inferences about population differences. The statistical tests which are reported are used to establish degrees of relationship among certain factors.

A few details should be provided for the matching process of marriage and divorce frequencies for each religious type. All divorces which were granted from 1953 through 1959 but which involved marriages which occurred prior to 1953 were deleted from subsequent analyses. For the remaining divorces, seven duration periods were established; from less than 12 months through to 72-83 months. Divorces granted in a given year which occurred within the first year of marriage were subtracted from the original marriage frequencies for that year of marriage. For instance, divorces granted in 1953 with a duration of less than 12 months were subtracted from the 1953 marriage frequencies. Similarly, divorces granted in 1954 with a duration of less than 12 months were subtracted from the 1954 marriage frequencies. This process was continued through the 1959 marriage and divorce data. Of course, all marriage and divorce comparisons involved the same religious type. Thus, for the marriage survival comparisons based on the less than 12 months duration period, all seven cohorts of marriage- and divorce-linked data were used.

For each succeeding duration period, the data for one marriage cohort was deleted because the divorces occurred among marriages performed before the period of observation used in the present study. For instance, the 1953 divorces which included marriages of 12–23 months duration, the 1954 divorces which included marriages of 24–35 months duration, and so on to the 1959 divorces which included marriages of 84–95 months duration, were deleted from the analyses. Thus, it was possible to develop marital survival rates for the second duration period for six marriage cohorts—those marriages which occurred during 1953 through 1958. Five cohorts of data were available for the third duration period, four for the fourth, three for the fifth, two for the sixth, and finally only one, the 1953 marriage cohort, was available for the seventh duration period.

Complex tables would be necessary for reporting the marriage frequencies for each of the seven years and the corresponding divorce frequencies by duration of marriage for each religious type. These data, as well as a more detailed description of the methodology and its limitations, are available elsewhere.[2] Data are provided in Table 1 to show the sizes of the marriage and divorce populations upon which the survival rates are based for the first set of comparisons.

Use of the marriage and divorce cohort-linked method of estimating sur-

[2] Amy B. Russell, "Comparisons of Divorce Rates by Religious Affiliations of Husbands and Wives," unpublished M. S. thesis, Iowa State University Library, Ames, Iowa, 1961.

TABLE 2 Marital Survival Rates Among Four Types of Religiously Homogamous or Interreligious Marriages by the Ages of Brides and the Status of Husbands at Divorce

Religious Affiliation Types		Ages of Brides									Total on Status of Husbands		
		19 or Younger					20 or Older						
			Status of Husbands					Status of Husbands					
	Total	Total	Low	Middle	High	Total	Low	Middle	High	Total	Low	Middle	High
Homogamous Catholic	96.2		88.3	92.6	97.2	92.9	95.5	97.6	99.4	97.9	92.3	96.0	98.6
Homogamous Protestant	86.2		68.1	81.5	93.2	80.9	83.1	92.0	96.3	92.7	72.7	86.2	94.9
Catholic-interreligious													
Catholic wife	79.8		63.9	74.3	86.7	73.0	77.4	89.4	91.1	86.9	69.2	82.4	89.4
Catholic husband	74.8		56.3	68.3	84.2	67.0	77.7	82.4	91.0	84.5	64.0	75.3	87.9
Total	77.6		60.3	71.2	85.5	70.1	77.6	86.1	91.0	85.8	66.8	79.1	88.7
Total of all cases	87.6		70.0	82.2	93.3	81.8	86.1	93.0	96.7	93.5	75.8	87.5	95.3

vival rates involved limitations associated with movement in and out of the state during the period of observation. The universe of marriages was limited to white, first-married couples where both spouses were Iowa residents. The first two controls were imposed on the divorce cases as well, but residence was not controlled. The residence control was not applied to the divorce data because inclusion of some couples who were married in another state and later divorced in Iowa served to offset the migration and possible later divorce of couples included in the Iowa marriage population. Unfortunately, no controls could be applied to correct family migration out of the state. The lack of control for post-marital migration, however, probably is not too serious. First, there are no theoretical grounds for assuming that family migration is highly selective by marital religious types. Second, the controls on age at marriage and the occupations of husbands (both related to migration) virtually should eliminate any relationship which may have existed between family migration and the religious affiliation types.

Use of the seven rates would have required seven separate sets of comparisons. Such a procedure would not only have been repetitious, but also would have been at least partially spurious because the rates were not independent of one another. With the exception of the first duration period, each survival rate was dependent on all preceding rates. Instead of using the data for each duration period or arbitrarily selecting certain survival periods for testing the hypotheses, data for all duration periods were used to estimate survival rates for the eight-year duration period.[3] Graphs of the survival rates over the seven duration periods indicated that the declines in survival rates were mostly linear. The estimated eighth-year survival rates are used in all survival rate comparisons.

HOMOGAMOUS CATHOLIC, HOMOGAMOUS PROTESTANT AND INTERRELIGIOUS MARRIAGE SURVIVAL RATES

The first set of comparisons, shown in Table 2, are based on the survival rates of the homogamous Catholic, homogamous Protestant and Catholic-Protestant marriages. The meaning of homogamous Catholic marriages should be clear. Homogamous Protestant marriages included marriages among persons who reported any Protestant denominational affiliation or who simply reported themselves as Protestants but who gave no denominational affiliation. Interreligious marriages are limited to Catholic-Protestant combinations. For the latter marriages, however, survival rates were developed for two subtypes based on the sex of the Catholic (or non-Catholic party, if you like) as well as for the total population of interreligious marriages.

Sufficient numbers of cases were available to permit the application of two control variables on the religious affiliation types. These controls, shown in Table 2, were the ages of the brides at marriage and the occupations of the grooms at marriage and at the time of divorce. Survival rates were

[3] George W. Snedecor, *Statistical Methods*, (5th ed.), Ames, Iowa: Iowa State University Press, 1956, pp. 153–156.

developed separately for each religious type within the six age and occupational cells and for the totals shown in Table 2. The control on the occupation of the groom was based on the assumption that the husband's occupational status levels were similar at the time of marriage and at the time of divorce. Some occupational class changes undoubtedly occurred, but these changes in occupational levels during the short period of observation probably would not greatly alter the results.

The occupational trichotomy was based on the 11-point occupational code used by the Iowa Division of Vital Statistics. The high status category included professional men, farm operators and managers, managers, officials, and proprietors; the middle status level included men in the sales, clerical, and craft occupations; and the low status level included operatives, domestic servants, farm laborers, and other laborers. The couples with grooms in the remaining occupational category, the armed forces, were deleted because no further data were available to indicate the status level of the grooms.

The classification of the marital survival rates by the four religious types, the two age levels and the three status levels suggested use of the three-way analysis of variance model for analyzing sources of variance among the survival rates. The relative sizes of the mean squares could be used to compare the magnitudes in variations among the survival rates with each source of variation.

The marital survival rates represent proportions. These proportions were converted by an arc-sign transformation to homogenize their variances and to permit the analysis of variance test. The results of the three-way analysis

TABLE 3   Results for the Three-Way Analysis of Variance of Marital Survival Rates Based on Spousal Religious Affiliation Types, Ages of Brides and Status Levels of Husbands

Source of Variation	Degrees of Freedom	Mean Squares
Religious affiliation types	3	303.579
Ages of brides	1	372.172
Status of husbands	2	342.621
Religious affiliation types by ages of brides	3	2.792
Religious affiliation types by status of husbands	6	6.631
Ages of brides by status of husbands	2	17.256
Religious affiliation types by ages of brides by status of husbands	6	1.169
Total	23	

of variance for the transformed survival rates are given in Table 3. The mean squares associated with the three two-way interactions or the one three-way interaction were small compared with those for the three main effects. The mean squares for the three independent variables were large and relatively similar. It is clear the survival rates were a function of ages at marriage and status levels of husbands as well as of the religious affiliation types.

Inspection of the results in Table 2 reveals the direction of differences in survival rates among the religious types. On the basis of previous research, the homogamous Catholic marriages should have had the highest survival rates. The homogamous Protestant marriages should have been next, fol-

lowed by the interreligious marriages involving Catholic wives and the interreligious marriages involving Catholic husbands should have had the lowest
survival rates. All but the comparisons between the two types of interreligious marriages conformed to this expected pattern. Within the six age and
status cells, the two total age cells or the three total status cells, the survival rates declined from the homogamous Catholic marriages to the homogamous Protestant marriages and then declined further to the two interreligious marriage types. But there were only small and inconsistent differences
between the survival rates of the two types of interreligious marriages.
Hereafter, therefore, no differentiation is made between the interreligious
marriages involving Catholic wives versus those involving Catholic husbands.

The homogamous Catholic marriages and homogamus Protestant marriages had higher survival rates than the interreligious marriages. It is also
apparent from Table 2 that the differences in survival rates among the four
religious types were a function of the age and status control variables. For
instance, the smallest variation among the four sets of survival rates was
observed at the high status level and the greatest variation was observed
at the low status level. Also, greater variation occurred at the younger as
compared with the older age level. Aside from the main objective of the
study, two other generalizations may be drawn from Table 2. In all religious
affiliation types (1) survival rates were greater among the marriages involving the older as compared to the younger brides; and (2) survival rates
increased directly with the occupational status levels.

DENOMINATIONALLY HOMOGAMOUS AND DENOMINATIONALLY MIXED PROTESTANT MARRIAGE SURVIVAL RATES

Sufficient numbers of cases were available for certain Protestant denominations to permit comparisons of survival rates between marriages
involving two persons who reported the same Protestant denominational affiliation and marriages involving persons who reported different Protestant
denominational affiliations. The former marriages are called denominationally
homogamous Protestant marriages and the latter are called denominationally
mixed Protestant marriages. As shown in Table 4, these denominations included Lutheran, Methodist, Presbyterian and Baptist church bodies. Marriages involving all other persons who reported a specific Protestant denominational affiliation are combined in the residual specified Protestant category.
This category is used to differentiate church-affiliated Protestants from
persons who reported themselves to be Protestants only and who failed to
supply any denominational affiliation. Marriages involving the denominationally non-affiliated Protestants are called homogamous or mixed unspecified
Protestant marriages.

Following the method already described, survival rates were calculated
for each of the denominationally homogamous and mixed Protestant marriage
types. Due to the smaller number of cases available for these religious types,
the age and occupation controls were applied separately and not jointly as
in the preceding analyses.

Various arguments used to support the relationship between homogamy

TABLE 4 Marital Survival Rates Among Denominationally Homogamous and Mixed Protestant Marriages by the Ages of Brides and the Status of Husbands at Divorce

| Religious Affiliation Types* | Total | Ages of Brides | | Status of Husbands | | |
		19 or Younger	20 or Older	Low	Middle	High
Homogamous Lutheran	94.1	90.9	97.0	86.6	93.2	97.7
Mixed Lutheran	93.0	90.1	95.9	86.6	93.1	96.5
Homogamous Methodist	91.4	88.3	95.6	83.9	90.2	96.3
Mixed Methodist	92.9	90.0	96.5	87.3	92.3	96.8
Homogamous Presbyterian	91.0	88.3	94.0	83.5	90.2	94.3
Mixed Presbyterian	94.6	92.5	96.6	90.4	92.9	97.2
Homogamous Baptist	89.8	87.1	95.4	83.8	93.5	93.4
Mixed Baptist	90.0	87.5	93.9	83.8	90.7	95.7
Homogamous unspecified Protestant	35.0	16.2	62.6	−0.7	43.0	73.2
Mixed unspecified Protestant	82.7	76.1	91.5	74.8	80.0	93.4
Residual specified Protestant	94.0	92.2	96.6	88.6	92.8	97.9

*Mixed Lutheran, etc., includes marriages of Lutherans (etc.) to persons reporting other Protestant denominational affiliation, but it does not include marriages with Catholics.

and marital stability also should support the hypothesis the marital survival rates for a given denominationally homogamous Protestant marriage type would be greater than those for the corresponding denominationally mixed Protestant marriage type. The data in Table 4, however, do not support this contention. All differences in survival rates between pairs of denominationally homogamous and mixed Protestant marriage types were small and, furthermore, a greater number of differences favored the denominationally mixed Protestant marriages.

The survival rates for the marriages involving the residual specified Protestants approximated those of the homogamous Lutheran marriages.

Survival rates were considerably greater among the mixed unspecified Protestant marriages than among the homogamous unspecific Protestant marriages. There are several reasons for expecting this result which is contrary to that expected for the comparisons between the denominationally homogamous and mixed Protestant marriages. First, in general, Protestants with any denominational affiliation, as contrasted to the denominationally nonaffiliated Protestants, should be expected to adhere more strongly to the norm for marital permanence. On this basis, marriages involving two non-nonaffiliated Protestants might be expected to have lower survival rates than marriages where one partner reported affiliation with some Protestant denomination. Second, there are other conditions which probably influenced the survival rates of the homogamous unspecified Protestant marriages. Except possibly for the high status level, it is doubtful if the survival rates of the homogamous unspecified Protestant marriages actually were as low as those reported in Table 4. In particular, the −0.7 rate for the low status category must, by definition, be incorrect. This rate indicated that there would be more divorces among homogamous unspecified Protestant low status couples in the eighth duration period than there had been marriages for these couples in the first place. The probable explanation for this result is that some persons who reported themselves to be members of a Protestant denomination at the time of marriage reported themselves as unaffiliated Protestants at the time of divorce. Public censure of divorce and the critical view of many Protestant clergymen may influence some members of Protestant churches to feel reluctant to identify their church affiliation at the time of divorce.

HOMOGAMOUS CATHOLIC AND DENOMINATIONALLY HOMOGAMOUS PROTESTANT MARRIAGE SURVIVAL RATES

Previous comparisons showed that the homogamous Catholic marriages had higher survival rates than the homogamous Protestant marriages. As used here, Protestant includes both the denominationally specified and unspecified Protestants. As such, the Protestant category included considerable heterogeneity, even though these were called homogamous Protestant marriages. Therefore, the original comparisons were reconsidered by comparing the survival rates of the homogamous Catholic marriages with those of the denominationally homogamous Protestant marriages. The appropriate data from Tables 2 and 4 are used for these comparisons.

For the total populations of marriages and for each of the two age-level or the three status-level comparisons, the survival rates for the homogamous Catholic marriages exceeded those for any of the denominationally homogamous Protestant marriage types. But the maximum differences between the survival rates of the homogamous Catholic marriages and any of the denominationally homogamous Protestant marriage types were smaller than the original differences observed between the homogamous Catholic marriages and the homogamous Protestant marriages. For instance, a ten percent difference was observed between the survival rates for the total population of homogamous Catholic marriages and the total population of homogamous Protestant marriages. Differences in marital survival rates between the homogamous Catholic marriages and the denominationally homogamous Protestant marriages ranged from two percent (for Lutherans) to six percent (for Baptists). Detailed study of Tables 2 and 4 also generally shows smaller differences between the homogamous Catholic and denominationally homogamous marriages than between the former and the homogamous (really heterogeneous) Protestant marriages in each of the age- or status-level comparisons.

SURVIVAL RATES AMONG INTERRELIGIOUS MARRIAGES WITH PROTESTANT DENOMINATIONS SPECIFIED

Survival rates also were determined for marriages of Catholics with Lutherans, Presbyterians, Methodists, Baptists, unspecified Protestants and the residual specified Protestants. The small numbers of cases prevented age and status subsample comparisons.

The rank order of the survival rates for these interreligious marriages was Catholic-Lutheran, 90.5 percent; Catholic-Presbyterian, 89.8 percent; Catholic-residual specified Protestant, 89.1 percent; Catholic-Methodist, 83.8 percent; Catholic-Baptist, 81.6 percent; and Catholic-unspecified Protestant, 28.7 percent. From Table 2, we can observe that the survival rate of all inter-religious marriages was 77.6 percent. Again, it seemed that the inclusion of the unspecified Protestants lowered the survival rate for all interreligious marriages.

RANK ORDER OF SURVIVAL RATES FOR ALL RELIGIOUS AFFILIATION TYPES

The rank order of survival rates for all religious affiliation types are presented in Table 5. Several observations may be drawn from Table 5. First, the survival rates formed a continuum with no large gaps between the various denominational affiliation types. The only sharp break in survival rates occurred between the total Catholic interreligious marriage survival rate and the survival rate of the homogamous unspecified Protestant marriages or the Catholic-unspecified Protestant marriages. The probable spurious nature of the latter two estimates has been discussed already.

Second, the homogamous Catholic marriages had the highest survival rate. However, the survival rates for mixed Presbyterian, homogamous Lutheran, residual specified Protestant, mixed Lutheran or Methodist, and homogamous Methodist or Presbyterian marriages ranged from 91.0 to 94.6

TABLE 5   Rank Order of Marital Survival Rates for All Religious
Affiliation Types

Religious Affiliation Types	Marital Survival Rates
Homogamous Catholic	96.2
Mixed Presbyterian	94.6
Homogamous Lutheran	94.1
Residual specified Protestant	94.0
Mixed Lutheran	93.0
Mixed Methodist	92.9
Homogamous Methodist	91.4
Homogamous Presbyterian	91.0
Catholic-Lutheran	90.5
Mixed Baptist	90.0
Catholic-Presbyterian	89.8
Homogamous Baptist	89.8
Catholic-residual specified Protestant	89.1
Homogamous Protestant	86.2
Catholic-Methodist	83.8
Mixed unspecified Protestant	82.7
Catholic-Baptist	81.6
Catholic-interreligious	77.6
Homogamous unspecified Protestant	35.0
Catholic-unspecified Protestant	28.7
Total population	87.6

percent and closely approached the 96.2 percent mark which was observed for the homogamous Catholic marriages.

Third, the survival rates for a group of interreligious marriage types as well as religiously homogamous marriage types ranged with one percentage point of another. Survival rates for Catholic-Lutheran, mixed Baptist, Catholic-Presbyterian, homogamous Baptist, and Catholic-residual specified Protestant marriages ranged between 89.1 percent and 90.5 percent.

Fourth, the lower middle segment of Table 5 included homogamous Protestant marriages, the marriages of Catholics with Methodists or Baptists, mixed unspecified Protestant marriages and the total for all interreligious marriages.

And, fifth, at the bottom of the array were the homogamous unspecified Protestant marriages and those of Catholics and unspecified Protestants.

SUMMARY AND DISCUSSION

The results for several of the sets of comparisons require only brief comment. First, there was virtually no difference between the survival rates of the denominationally homogamous Protestant marriage types and the corresponding denominationally mixed Protestant marriage types. More of the differences, however, favored the denominationally mixed marriages.

Second, differences in marital survival rates between the two general types of Catholic-Protestant marriages, based on the sex of the Catholic spouse, were smaller than that reported by Landis.[4] The total difference of five percent in survival rates in favor of the marriages of Catholic wives hardly seemed sufficient to support Landis' argument of the greater strain in the interreligious marriages involving non-Catholic wives as compared with the marriages involving Catholic wives. Also, the two inter-religious marriage types had approximately the same mean length of marriage before divorce, 6.9 years. The number of children born to a couple is generally correlated with the couples' length of marriage. It is not surprising, therefore, that each interreligious marriage type also had approximately the same number of children, 1.3, by the time of divorce. It cannot be said whether the differences in survival rates between the two interreligious marriage types will increase as the duration of marriage increases or whether the differences will approach those reported by Landis for his small samples of interreligiously married parents of college-level students.

Third, two sets of results should be discussed jointly. These are the comparisons involving homogamous Catholic, homogamous Protestant and the denominationally homogamous or mixed Protestant marriages. The homogamous Catholic marriages maintained consistently higher survival rates than the homogamous Protestant marriages, especially when the comparisons involved younger brides and low status or middle status husbands and older brides and low status husbands. For these comparisons, differences in survival rates in favor of homogamous Catholic marriages were 20, 11, and 12 percent, respectively. When the survival rates for the populations of the

---

[4] Landis, op. cit.

denominationally homogamous or mixed Protestant marriages were compared with the survival rate for the population of the homogamous Catholic marriages, the differences in survival rates ranged between two and six percent. The deletion of the denominationally unspecified Protestants from the homogamous Protestant category brought the survival rates of the denominationally specified Protestant marriages closer to those for the homogamous Catholic marriages.

In an absolute sense, the small differences in survival rates between all homogamous Catholic marriages and those of the denominationally homogamous or mixed Protestant marriages supported presently accepted generalizations. In a substantive sense, however, these small differences between survival rates of homogamous Catholic marriages and denominationally homogamous or mixed Protestant marriages cannot be considered as representing important differences in the Iowa populations under study.

The results of the tests for differences in the survival rates between the religiously homogamous and interreligious marriages require more extensive discussion. Survival rates for a variety of religious affiliation types, including those for the homogamous Catholic, homogamous Protestant, total interreligious marriages and the denominationally specified Protestant and Catholic interreligious marriages, are relevant to this discussion.

The data in Table 2 show that the homogamous Catholic or homogamous Protestant marriages had higher survival rates than the interreligious marriages. However, both the homogamous Protestant marriage type and the total interreligious marriage type included couples in which one or both spouses were unspecified Protestants. Previous data revealed the extremely low and probably spurious survival rates among the homogamous unspecified Protestant couples. Additional tests of the hypothesis for differences in survival rates between the homogamous Catholic marriages and interreligious Catholic marriages may be based on comparisons between the survival rates for the former marriages and those for marriages of Catholics with members of specific Protestant denominations.

The results of these more refined comparisons still supported the hypothesis of higher survival rates among homogamous Catholic marriages than among marriages of Catholics and denominationally affiliated Protestants, but the sizes of the differences were reduced considerably. By themselves, the smaller differences hardly justify generalizations of considerably greater marital difficulties facing Catholics who marry outside of their faith, providing the person they marry is identified or affiliated with a Protestant denomination, as compared with Catholics who marry endogamously.

Similar comparisons between the homogamous Protestant marriages and the interreligious marriages must be adjusted for the inclusion of the unspecified Protestants in the general homogamous Protestant marriage type and in the interreligious marriages. The survival rates for the nine denominationally homogamous or mixed Protestant marriage types ranged from 94.6 to 89.8 percent. The median of this array was 92.9 percent and the mean was 92.3 percent. Small differences were observed between either the median survival rate or the mean survival rate for the denominationally homogamous or mixed Protestant marriage types and the survival rates for marriages of Catholics and denominationally affiliated Protestants. These differences ranged from approximately 2 percent for the Catholic-Lutheran marriages to 11 percent for the Catholic-Baptist marriages. These small differences in survival rates between marriages of two church-affiliated Protestants and marriages involving church-affiliated Protestants and Catholics provided only meager support for the expectation of greater divorce rates among denominationally affiliated Protestants who married Catholics or vice versa.

Three sets of observations further reduced the substantive importance of the observed differences in survival rates between the religiously homogamous and interreligious marriages. Two of these observations involved the age and status variables. First, the mean squares for sources of variation in marital survival rates associated with these two variables were greater than the mean square for the religious classification. This observation indicates that the differences in marital survival rates were more a function of either of the two control variables than they were a function of the religious types. Second, the marital survival rates for interreligious marriages in some age and status subsamples exceeded those for religiously homogamous marriages in other age and status subsamples. Careful study of Tables 2 and 4 will disclose these patterns. Third, with the exception of the marriages involving unspecified Protestants, the rank order of marital survival rates for all spousal religious affiliation types formed a pattern of continuous and small variations from one type to the next. Survival rates for some interreligious marriage types were interspersed with the survival rates for denominationally homogamous or mixed Protestant marriages.

One of the important findings of the present investigation is that the lower survival rates of interreligious marriages were derived mainly from the marriages of Catholics with persons who apparently were not affiliated with any Protestant denomination. Apparently, the clash of religious values and beliefs less frequently led to divorce in the interreligious marriages than did circumstances associated with the lack of affiliation or identification with a church by the non-Catholic partner.

This inference suggests many problems for additional research on factors influencing the outcomes of interreligious marriages. What differences exist between Catholics who marry denominationally unaffiliated Protestants as compared with Catholics who marry denominationally affiliated Protestants? What differences exist between the two groups of Protestants? How are either of these sets of differences related to dating patterns, courtship, mate selection, subsequent marital relations, and adherence to the norm of marital permanence, especially in cases of great marital discord?

The present data also permitted retesting the generalizations that marital survival rates are lower among marriages of younger brides as contrasted with older brides and that marital survival rates are directly related to the status of the husbands. Marital survival rates were consistently higher among the marriages involving the older brides. Also, a direct relationship was observed between the status levels of the couples and marital survival rates.

Author's Note: Other publications based on the investigation of interreligious and religiously homogamous marriage and divorce patterns in Iowa include: Lee G. Burchinal and Loren E. Chancellor, "Ages at Marriage, Occupations of Grooms and Interreligious Marriage Rates," *Social Forces*, 40 (May 1962), 348–354; Lee G. Burchinal and Loren E. Chancellor, "Proportions of Catholics, Urbanism, and Mixed-Catholic Marriage Rates Among Iowa Counties," *Social Problems*, 9 (Spring, 1962), 359–365; Lee G. Burchinal, William F. Kenkel and Loren E. Chancellor, "Comparisons of State- and Diocese-Reported Marriage Data for Iowa, 1953–1957," *American Catholic Sociological Review*, 23 (Spring, 1962), 21–29; Loren E. Chancellor and Lee G. Burchinal, "Relations Among Interreligious Marriages, Migratory Marriages and Civil Weddings in Iowa," *Eugenics Quarterly*, 9 (June 1962), 75–83; Lee G. Burchinal and William F. Kenkel, "Religious Identification and Occupational Status of Iowa Grooms, 1953–1957," *American Sociological Review*, 27 (August 1962), 526–532; Lee G. Burchinal and Loren E. Chancellor, *Factors Related to Interreligious Marriages in Iowa, 1953–1957*, Iowa Agricultural and Home Economics Experiment Station, Iowa State University, Ames, Iowa, Research Bulletin R-510, November 1962; Lee G. Burchinal and Loren E. Chancellor, *Survival Rates Among Types of Religiously Homogamous and Interreligious Marriages, Iowa, 1953–1959*, Iowa Agricultural and Home Economics Experiment Station, Iowa State University, Ames, Iowa, Research Bulletin R-512, December 1962; Lee G. Burchinal and Loren E. Chancellor, "Status Levels of Grooms, Religious Affiliations, and Ages of Brides and Grooms, Iowa, 1953–1957," *Marriage and Family Living*, forthcoming.

16 | Negro-White Marriage in the United States

DAVID M. HEER

In the last year or two tremendous popular interest in the United States has been aroused in the subject of Negro-white intermarriage. Fifteen years ago Negro protest leaders soft-pedaled talk of such marriage and claimed they

Revised and expanded version of a paper presented at the 1964 meeting of the American Sociological Association at Montreal, Canada, September 1, 1964. The writer wishes to acknowledge the help given him by Dr. Hugh Carter, Chief, and Dr. Carl Ortmeyer, Statistician, Marriage and Divorce Statistics, Division of Vital Statistics, National Center for Health Statistics, U.S. Public Health Service; Mr. Paul W. Shipley and Miss Jo Ann Wray of the Bureau of Vital Statistics of the Department of Health, State of California; Mr. George Tokuyama, Research Planning and Statistics Office, Department of Health, State of Hawaii; Mr. Robert C. Schmitt, Department of Planning and Economic Development, State of Hawaii; Miss Doris L. Duxbury, Chief, Statistical Methods Section, Michigan Department of Health; and Miss Freda Theis, Director, Bureau of Vital Statistics, Nebraska State Department of Health. The writer also wishes to thank Mrs. Judith Bryden for aid in the computation.

Reprinted from the *Journal of Marriage and the Family*, 28, No. 3 (August, 1966), 262–273, by permission of the National Council of Family Relations.

were interested only in jobs and votes. Conservative whites were comforted by Gunnar Myrdal's report that, although the ban on intermarriage was for them the most important aspect of the caste system, for Negroes it was the least important of the various forms of discrimination they were forced to suffer.[1]

Very recently, however, the attitude of many Negro leaders toward intermarriage has changed. Increasingly such leaders, particularly the younger ones, are asking, "Why not?" The marriage in 1963 to a fellow white student of the first Negro admitted to the University of Georgia shocked many conservative whites. Intransigent whites have also become alarmed by the possibility that in the very near future the United States Supreme Court will decree that state legislation banning interracial marriage is illegal.[2] This possibility arises because the Supreme Court has recently ruled in favor of an interracial couple from Florida convicted for illegal cohabitation under the state's law against miscegenation. A further ruling by the Supreme Court interdicting state bans on racial intermarriage would allow such marriage in the 19 states, mostly but not entirely Southern, where it is now prohibited.[3]

There are several reasons why Negro-white marriage is sociologically important. However, one of these reasons may be singled out for special attention.

INTERMARRIAGE AND NEGRO-WHITE STATUS DIFFERENCE

Most Negro thinking tended earlier to isolate political and economic deprivation from the social deprivation symbolized par excellence by white attitudes toward racial intermarriage. However, restrictions on racial intermarriage may be closely linked to the economic inequality that Negroes in our society endure. Kingsley Davis has identified the main social functions of the family as the reproduction, maintenance, placement, and socialization of the young.[4] Let us focus our attention on the placement function of the family in the contemporary United States, i.e., on the consequences which birth into a given family has for the youngster's future social position. First it is obvious that the transfer of wealth in the United States is largely accomplished by bequeathal from one family member to another. The possession of wealth not only entitles one to receive regular monetary interest; it is also a source of power, credit, and prestige. Secondly, although objectively recognized merit may be the predominant criterion for the matching of job

[1] Gunnar Myrdal, *An American Dilemma*, New York: Harper, 1944, pp. 57–67.

[2] Arthur Krock, "The Debate on Miscegenation," *The New York Times*, September 9, 1963, and Arthur Krock, "In the Nation," *The New York Times*, December 8, 1964.

[3] These 19 states are Alabama, Arkansas, Delaware, Florida, Georgia, Indiana, Idaho, Kentucky, Louisiana, Mississippi, Missouri, North Carolina, Oklahoma, South Carolina, Tennessee, Texas, Virginia, West Virginia, and Wyoming. Since 1944 the following states have eliminated their miscegenation statutes: Arizona, California, Colorado, Maryland, Montana, Nebraska, Nevada, North Dakota, Oregon, South Dakota, and Utah.

[4] Kingsley Davis, *Human Society*, New York: Macmillan, 1949, pp. 394–396.

applicants to job vacancies, influence and family connections are also quite important. In the building trades, for example, jobs cannot be obtained without admittance to the union's apprenticeship program. In many instances it is almost impossible to obtain entrée into the apprenticeship program unless one is a son or other close relative of a union member. Thirdly, entrée into elite positions in modern industrial societies is most easily obtained by those who are born into a family having relatively high status.[5] Birth in a high status family provides the financial means for obtaining advanced education, and it also gives one a sense of familiarity with the activities and functioning of high status society. This familiarity not only reduces the fear of inter-personal contacts in such a society but also increases the motivation to become a full participant.

In summary, being born into one family rather than another is a very important determinant of one's eventual social status. How may this fact affect the relative status of Negroes and whites in the United States? Consider first the pattern of familial inheritance. On a per capita basis white persons hold a far higher share of the nation's wealth than do Negroes. The formal and informal prohibitions on intermarriage serve to perpetuate this pattern of inequality because they make it unlikely for a Negro to inherit wealth from any white person. Secondly, Negroes are by and large excluded from those jobs to which entrance is strongly determined by "connections." This occurs simply because those jobs are usually held only by whites. Thirdly, the lack of close relatives among whites affects the socialization of Negro youth. Specifically, it prevents many of them from having an easy familiarity with the terrain of the social world of white persons and hence makes them afraid to apply for jobs demanding such familiarity even when their technical qualifications are completely satisfactory.

Thus a relaxation of the norms militating against Negro-white marriage should serve to reduce the status gap between Negroes and whites. This is not to say that a substantial increase in Negro-white marriage would necessarily soon bring Negroes into equality with whites. As we shall show later, the present frequency of marriages involving Negro grooms and white brides is considerably greater than the frequency of marriages involving white grooms and Negro brides. Perhaps upward social mobility would be more probable for a male child if he had a white father and a Negro mother rather than the reverse. The father is more likely than the mother to teach the son the terrain of the occupational world of white persons; therefore, if job entrance is determined by particularistic factors, a white father will be of greater advantage than a white mother. Also, children of mixed marriages may encounter discrimination not only from white persons but also from other Negroes, because they are a product of a marriage not generally approved.[6]

[5] Joseph A. Kahl, *The American Class Structure*, New York: Rinehart, 1953, pp. 276–298.

[6] According to the results of a recent Gallup Poll (*Boston Globe*, March 11, 1965) 48 percent of adult Americans approve of laws making interracial marriage a crime. The percentages of various subgroups who approve such laws were as follows: Negroes outside the South, 14 percent; Southern Negroes, 30 percent; whites outside the South, 42 percent; Southern whites, 72 percent.

Furthermore, it is not clear that an increased amount of Negro-white marriage is a necessary prerequisite for the elimination of Negro-white status differences. Americans of Jewish faith, with very low rates of intermarriage, have achieved a socioeconomic status at least as high as the rest of the population despite the fact that most of them are the recent descendants of poor immigrants.[7]

Thus the strength of the link between low frequency of Negro-white marriage and the Negro's inferior socioeconomic status is uncertain. Nevertheless, because the inferior status of the Negro is now of such concern, it is important for sociologists to maintain a close temperature reading concerning data on Negro-white marriage in the United States.

ANALYSIS OF STATE DATA

Unfortunately, current data on this subject are very incomplete. At the present time, there are 31 states in which marriage between whites and Negroes is legal. However, in only three states is there any officially published record of such intermarriages: Hawaii, Michigan, and Nebraska. For selected years prior to 1960 the state of California made public a cross-tabulation of marriages by race of bride and race of groom, but this practice was discontinued in 1960 because of new legislation prohibiting a record of race on marriage licenses.[8]

For the period from 1950 to the time this paper was prepared, the only data on interracial marriages tabulated by state offices of vital statistics were as follows: California for 1955, 1957, 1958, and 1959; Hawaii, 1956-64; Michigan, 1953-63; Nebraska, 1961-64. In this paper we shall analyze these data and compare them with some data for earlier years. We shall not be concerned with other types of interracial marriage, such as between whites and Orientals.[9]

Some readers may question the quality of the official data on Negro-white marriage. On the one hand, it might be argued that social sanctions against such marriages are so severe that the reported number of such marriages would be less than the actual number. The difference between actual and reported numbers would then consist of marriages in which the race of

[7] Data on the current socioeconomic status of American Jews and on Jewish intermarriage patterns can be found in Donald J. Bogue, *The Population of the United States*, New York: The Free Press of Glencoe, 1959, pp. 694–709. Data on the status of immigrant Jews in the late 19th and early 20th centuries are summarized in Oscar and Mary F. Handlin, "A Century of Jewish Immigration to the United States," *American Jewish Yearbook*, 50, (1948–49), 1–84.

[8] Personal communication from Dr. Hugh Carter, Chief, Marriage and Divorce Statistics, Division of Vital Statistics, National Center for Health Statistics, U.S. Public Health Service.

[9] An excellent description of the current California data on interracial marriages of all types is found in Larry D. Barnett, "Interracial Marriage in California," *Marriage and Family Living*, 25, No. 4 (November, 1963), 424–427, and of the recent data for Hawaii in Robert C. Schmitt, "Demographic Correlates of Interracial Marriage in Hawaii," *Demography*, Vol. II, (1965), pp. 463–473. Data on interracial marriage of all types for Los Angeles County, California, are found in John H. Burma, "Interethnic Marriage in Los Angeles, 1948-1959," *Social Forces*, 42 (December, 1963), 156–165.

one partner was consciously misreported on the marriage license. On the other hand, it might be argued that, because the true number of Negro-white marriages is very small, the reported number exceeds the actual number because of accidental misreporting of race for one partner on the marriage license. Since no study has yet been made of the validity of the reported numbers of interracial marriages in any of these states, some caution is warranted in the interpretation of the reported data.[10]

Much of the previous work on interracial marriage has focused on Negro-white marriages as a proportion of all marriages involving Negroes or as a proportion of all Negro brides and grooms to the exclusion of Negro-white marriages as a proportion of all marriages involving whites or of all white brides and grooms. Since a time series of intermarriage rates for which the base is Negro brides and grooms might show an entirely different trend from one in which the intermarriage rates had as their base the number of white brides and grooms, we shall present here intermarriage rates for both whites and Negroes.

In Table 1 we show six sets of reported data: (1) the proportion of white brides and grooms marrying Negroes, (2) the proportion of white grooms with Negro brides, (3) the proportion of white brides with Negro grooms, (4) the proportion of Negro brides and grooms marrying whites, (5) the proportion of Negro grooms with white brides, and (6) the proportion of Negro brides with white grooms.[11] Data are presented for the states and years mentioned

[10] Our data refer only to registered marriages between whites and Negroes. They do not take into account the unknown number of relatively stable sexual unions between whites and Negroes which are not legally registered as marriages. Data on the total number of sexual unions between whites and Negroes might show different patterns from the data on legal unions presented here.

[11] The previous literature on intermarriage is confused by the fact that there are two different ways of computing intermarriage rates. Many studies compute an intermarriage rate in which the numerator is the number of intermarriages and the denominator is the number of marriages in which either bride or groom is from the ingroup. In other studies the numerator is the number of brides and/or grooms intermarrying and the denominator is the number of brides and/or grooms in the ingroup. Intermarriage rates computed by the two different procedures can be quite dissimilar. In this study the second procedure is used. For a further discussion of the two ways of measuring intermarriage see Hyman Rodman, "Technical Note on Two Rates of Mixed Marriage," *American Sociological Review*, 30 (October, 1965), 776–778.

It should also be noted that if for either whites or Negroes the number of brides who intermarry is equal to the number of grooms who intermarry, the proportion of brides and grooms marrying into the other race will be the average of the separate figures for out-marriages of brides and grooms. On the other hand, if for either whites or Negroes the number of brides who intermarry is substantially less or greater than the number of grooms, then the percentage for both sexes will not equal the unweighted average for each sex but will be influenced more heavily by the intermarriage percentage for the sex having the greater proportion intermarrying. In the present case, the percentage of Negro brides and grooms marrying white brides and grooms is more heavily influenced by the percentage of Negro grooms marrying white brides than by the percentage of Negro brides marrying white grooms.

previously, and, for comparison, also for New York State (excluding New York City) for the years 1921-24.[12] All data are tabulated by area in which the marriage license was issued rather than by area of residence of bride or groom prior to marriage. This fact introduces an unknown amount of bias into our data. It is possible, for example, that many couples who live in states where Negro-white marriage is illegal obtain the license for such a marriage in some state where it is legal. No doubt, however, not all of these couples return to live in their former state of residence.

Of the four states with recent data, Hawaii has the highest reported incidence of Negro-white intermarriage. The rank of the remaining states in descending order of Negro-white intermarriage is California, Michigan, and Nebraska. This rank order holds true regardless of which of the six columns of data is examined. For whites of both sexes, the highest reported interracial marriage rate in each of the four states was as follows: Hawaii, 0.38 percent; California, 0.21 percent; Michigan, 0.15 percent; and Nebraska, 0.02 percent. For Negroes of both sexes the highest interracial marriage rate in each of the four states was: Hawaii, 16.16 percent; California, 2.58 percent; Michigan, 1.56 percent; and Nebraska, 0.67 percent. Thus, there is considerable variation among these states in the reported proportions of interracial marriage. In addition to the familiar case of Hawaii, the contrast between Michigan and California is also noteworthy. These are both large industrial states with similar proportions of Negro population. In 1959, the latest year in which data are available for both states, the proportion of Negro-white marriages in California was more than double that in Michigan according to each of the six indices shown in Table 1.

Table 1 also reveals a differential incidence of Negro-white marriage by sex, manifested in previous data on interracial marriage. Specifically, for each of the four states recording Negro-white marriages, marriages between Negro men and white women are much more common than those between white men and Negro women. For example, for California in 1959 the inter-marriage rate of white grooms was 0.09 percent and that of white brides 0.33 percent. Similarly, the interracial marriage rate of Negro grooms was 3.96 percent and of Negro brides 1.16 percent.

Reasons for the differential incidence of interracial marriage by sex have been advanced by Kingsley Davis and Robert Merton.[13] Davis proposed two explanations. First, if, as he believed, marriages between Negro men and white women largely involved Negro males of high social status and white women of low social status, then the groom could trade his class advantage for the racial caste advantage of the bride. This was also Merton's explanation. Secondly, Davis believed that marriages between a white man and a Negro woman would be relatively rare simply because the norms allowed white men to take sexual advantage of Negro women without marrying them. Subsequent research has failed to establish that marriages between Negro

[12] J. V. DePorte, *Marriage Statistics*, Albany: New York State Department of Health, 1928.

[13] Kingsley Davis, "Intermarriage in Caste Societies," *American Anthropologist*, 43 (July–September, 1941), 388–395; and Robert K. Merton, "Intermarriage and the Social Structure: Fact and Theory," *Psychiatry*, 4 (August, 1941), 361–374.

TABLE 1 Negro-White Intermarriage Percentages for Available States and Years (Base for Each Percentage Is in Parentheses)

A. White Brides and Grooms

State and Year	Percentage of: White Brides and Grooms Marrying Negro Brides and Grooms		White Grooms Marrying Negro Brides		White Brides Marrying Negro Grooms	
California						
1955	0.14	(150,770)	0.06	(75,235)	0.21	(75,535)
1957	0.17	(167,926)	0.06	(83,809)	0.28	(84,117)
1958	0.17	(174,211)	0.08	(86,998)	0.26	(87,213)
1959	0.21	(183,563)	0.09	(91,643)	0.33	(91,920)
1955–59	0.17	(676,470)	0.07	(337,685)	0.27	(338,785)
Hawaii						
1956	0.13	(3,127)	0.00	(1,820)	0.31	(1,307)
1957	0.20	(2,994)	0.00	(1,721)	0.47	(1,273)
1958	0.10	(2,898)	0.06	(1,662)	0.16	(1,236)
1959	0.22	(3,201)	0.11	(1,821)	0.36	(1,380)
1960	0.24	(3,387)	0.16	(1,908)	0.34	(1,479)
1961	0.29	(3,429)	0.11	(1,898)	0.52	(1,531)
1962	0.24	(3,811)	0.05	(2,070)	0.46	(1,741)
1963	0.27	(4,004)	0.14	(2,162)	0.43	(1,842)
1964	0.38	(4,230)	0.13	(2,305)	0.68	(1,925)
1956–64	0.24	(31,081)	0.09	(17,367)	0.43	(13,714)
Michigan						
1953	0.07	(97,517)	0.04	(48,748)	0.10	(48,769)
1954	0.06	(94,516)	0.04	(47,246)	0.09	(47,270)
1955	0.08	(101,684)	0.05	(50,858)	0.11	(50,858)
1956	0.09	(103,972)	0.04	(51,971)	0.13	(52,001)
1957	0.07	(100,242)	0.01	(50,091)	0.14	(50,151)
1958	0.09	(100,583)	0.05	(50,269)	0.13	(50,314)
1959	0.10	(106,901)	0.04	(53,420)	0.16	(53,481)
1960	0.10	(111,122)	0.06	(55,544)	0.14	(55,578)
1961	0.11	(115,046)	0.05	(57,487)	0.18	(57,559)
1962	0.12	(118,157)	0.05	(59,044)	0.19	(59,113)
1963	0.15	(124,152)	0.07	(62,027)	0.23	(62,125)
1953–63	0.10	(1,173,892)	0.05	(586,673)	0.15	(587,219)
Nebraska						
1961	0.00	(21,080)	0.00	(10,542)	0.00	(10,538)
1962	0.00	(21,408)	0.00	(10,708)	0.00	(10,700)
1963	0.01	(22,498)	0.01	(11,257)	0.02	(11,241)
1964	0.02	(22,902)	0.01	(11,452)	0.03	(11,450)
1961–64	0.01	(87,888)	0.00	(43,959)	0.01	(43,929)
New York (excluding New York City)						
1921	0.04	(84,027)	0.01	(41,999)	0.06	(42,028)
1922	0.03	(83,782)	0.02	(41,885)	0.05	(41,897)
1923	0.04	(87,164)	0.03	(43,572)	0.06	(43,592)
1924	0.06	(84,769)	0.03	(42,367)	0.10	(42,402)
1921–24	0.04	(339,742)	0.02	(169,823)	0.07	(169,919)

TABLE 1 (continued)

B. Negro Brides and Grooms

State and Year	Percentage of: Negro Brides and Grooms Marrying White Brides and Grooms		Negro Grooms Marrying White Brides		Negro Brides Marrying White Grooms	
California						
1955	2.21	(9,514)	3.36	(4,815)	1.02	(4,699)
1957	2.14	(13,198)	3.47	(6,691)	0.78	(6,507)
1958	2.20	(13,458)	3.35	(6,812)	1.02	(6,646)
1959	2.58	(14,877)	3.96	(7,549)	1.16	(7,328)
1955–59	2.30	(51,047)	3.56	(25,867)	1.00	(25,180)
Hawaii						
1956	6.45	(62)	9.09	(44)	0.00	(18)
1957	9.52	(63)	13.33	(45)	0.00	(18)
1958	4.35	(69)	4.08	(49)	5.00	(20)
1959	9.33	(75)	9.80	(51)	8.33	(24)
1960	13.79	(58)	14.71	(34)	12.50	(24)
1961	13.33	(75)	16.00	(50)	8.00	(25)
1962	13.04	(69)	17.78	(45)	4.17	(24)
1963	12.79	(86)	14.81	(54)	9.38	(32)
1964	16.16	(99)	20.31	(64)	8.57	(35)
1956–64	11.28	(656)	13.53	(436)	6.82	(220)
Michigan						
1953	0.75	(8,929)	1.09	(4,479)	0.40	(4,450)
1954	0.78	(7,818)	1.10	(3,922)	0.46	(3,896)
1955	0.80	(9,578)	1.12	(4,806)	0.48	(4,772)
1956	0.89	(9,979)	1.32	(5,013)	0.46	(4,966)
1957	0.76	(9,837)	1.37	(4,949)	0.14	(4,888)
1958	0.94	(9,573)	1.37	(4,808)	0.50	(4,765)
1959	1.01	(10,566)	1.62	(5,318)	0.40	(5,248)
1960	1.01	(10,877)	1.39	(5,458)	0.63	(5,419)
1961	1.13	(11,368)	1.76	(5,724)	0.48	(5,644)
1962	1.20	(11,625)	1.90	(5,853)	0.49	(5,772)
1963	1.56	(11,972)	2.34	(6,033)	0.77	(5,939)
1953–63	1.01	(112,122)	1.53	(56,363)	0.48	(55,759)
Nebraska						
1961	0.00	(693)	0.00	(346)	0.00	(347)
1962	0.00	(800)	0.00	(401)	0.00	(399)
1963	0.39	(766)	0.52	(384)	0.26	(382)
1964	0.67	(745)	1.07	(374)	0.27	(371)
1961–64	0.27	(3,004)	0.40	(1,505)	0.13	(1,499)
New York (excluding New York City)						
1921	3.21	(936)	5.63	(480)	0.66	(456)
1922	2.52	(1,151)	3.60	(582)	1.40	(569)
1923	2.17	(1,796)	2.87	(905)	1.46	(891)
1924	2.63	(1,974)	4.09	(1,003)	1.13	(971)
1921–24	2.56	(5,857)	3.87	(2,970)	1.21	(2,887)

men and white women most frequently involve a groom of high social class and a bride of low social class.[14] Most such marriages in fact appear to involve spouses from the same class position. Thus further research is necessary to attain a satisfactory explanation for the sex differential in Negro-white marriage.

In view of the interest in the question of whether the trend in interracial marriages is upward or downward, it is unfortunate that, for the four states for which we have recent statistics, we have no data for earlier years. For the areas—mostly cities—for which we have earlier statistics, the recent data are not readily available. Therefore, no valid comparison of the rate of interracial marriage in the contemporary period with that one or two generations back is possible. The best we can do is to compare the recent data in the four states of California, Hawaii, Michigan, and Nebraska with available earlier data from other places. It is apparent from Table 1 that the rate of Negro-white marriage for Negroes in New York State (excluding New York City) in the early 1920's was higher than the recent rates for either Michigan or California. On the other hand, the intermarriage rate for whites is higher in California and Michigan in the recent period than in New York State 40 years ago. As will be explained later in greater detail, this result is attributable to higher proportions of Negroes in the present populations of California and Michigan than in New York State some 40 years ago.

TABLE 2   Measures Indicating the Correlation of Negro-White Intermarriage with Time, for Michigan, 1953-1963

	Whites			Negroes		
	Both Sexes	Males	Females	Both Sexes	Males	Females
Product-moment correlation coefficient	+.909*	+.517	+.937*	+.893*	+.916*	+.505
Slope of regression line (percent per year)	+.007*	+.003	+.009*	+.066*	+.111*	+.025

*Significantly different from 0 at .01 level.

The Negro-white intermarriage rate for Negroes in Hawaii during 1964 was higher than any previously recorded rate for members of that race in any part of the United States during any time period. The closest competitor to Hawaii in this respect is the city of Boston in the period of 1900-1904. For Boston during this period the proportion of Negro grooms marrying white brides was 13.7 percent as compared with 20.3 percent in Hawaii in 1964, and the proportion of Negro brides marrying white grooms was 1.1 percent as compared with 8.6 percent in Hawaii in 1964.

We are on somewhat surer ground when we try to investigate the trend of interracial marriage in the United States within the last few years. The available data shown in Table 1 for the four states of California, Hawaii, Michigan, and Nebraska are certainly not conclusive, but they give a strong indication of the probable trend during recent years. First, we may compare

[14] Joseph Golden, "Characteristics of the Negro-white intermarried in Philadelphia," *American Sociological Review*, 18 (April, 1953), 177–183.

the intermarriage rates during the first and final year in the series for each state according to each of the six indices. For each state the higher interracial marriage rates invariably occur during the final rather than the initial year of the series. Thus for these four states there is an indication of an upward trend in interracial marriage. Because we have not only an 11-year time series but also a large base population for Michigan, a more refined measurement of increase in interracial marriage can be made for that state. The association between interracial marriage and time was investigated for Michigan by means of product-moment correlation analysis. Table 2 presents the coefficients of correlation and the slopes of regression for the six indices of interracial marriage in Michigan. All six indices show an increase of the interracial marriage rate with time, but they vary in the consistency of this increase. For four of the indices, i.e., those for whites of both sexes, white women, Negroes of both sexes, and Negro men, the trend in interracial marriage has been one of very steady rise, as shown by correlation coefficients with time greater than 0.89 ($P < .01$ that rho equals 0). On the other hand, the trends for white men and for Negro women show a less consistent increase over the 11-year interval. The coefficient of correlation for white men is only 0.52 and that for Negro women is 0.51. In Michigan the most pronounced increase in Negro-white marriage has been in those marriages involving Negro men and white women.

The recent data pointing to an upward trend in Negro-white marriage are of enhanced interest because statistics for previous periods in the United States indicated a decreasing trend in such marriages.[15] For example, data are available concerning interracial marriage rates for both whites and Negroes in the city of Boston for the period from 1900-1938. These indicate an almost continuous decline in the intermarriage rate for both whites and Negroes. The most drastic decline occurred between 1900-04 and 1914-18, when the interracial marriage rate per 100 Negro marriages dropped from approximately 14 to approximately 5. Wirth and Goldhamer have attributed this decline in the city of Boston to the fact that in the nineteenth century the city was the center of the abolitionist movement and was "unusually and almost sentimentally receptive to Negroes." As the pro-Negro sentiments fostered during and after the Civil War declined in their intensity, the willingness of whites to marry Negroes declined correspondingly. Data for New York State (exclusive of New York City) also indicated a small decline from 1922-24 to 1934-36 in Negro-white marriages as a proportion of all marriages involving Negroes. No data were provided concerning the trend of interracial marriage for whites during this period.[16]

The sharp decline in Negro-white intermarriage in Boston after the turn of the century was almost entirely due to decline in marriages involving Negro grooms and white brides. The proportion of Negro grooms marrying white brides in Boston declined from 13.7 percent in the period 1900-04 to

[15] The best summary of previous data on Negro-white marriage in the United States is contained in Louis Wirth and Herbert Goldhamer, "The Hybrid and the Problem of Miscegenation," in *Characteristics of the American Negro*, ed. by Otto Klineberg, New York: Harper, 1944.

[16] Ibid., pp. 276–280.

3.2 percent in the period 1914-38. On the other hand, the proportion of Negro brides marrying white grooms declined only from 1.1 percent to 0.7 percent.[17] Together with the recent Michigan experience, these data suggest that the volatile element in Negro-white intermarriage may be the marriage between the Negro male and the white female and the interracial marriage rate between white males and Negro females may remain relatively constant.

NEGRO-WHITE INTERMARRIAGE AND RACIAL DISTRIBUTION

It has been well-established that, for given religious groups, the rate of marriage outside the group varies inversely with the proportion of all potential marriage partners belonging to that group. For example, Locke, Sabagh, and Thomes have shown that for each of the Canadian provinces in 1954 there was a perfect inverse rank order correlation between the percentage of Catholic brides and grooms having interfaith marriages and the percentage of the total population of each province that was Catholic.[18] In addition, Glick has shown for the United States that religious distribution helps to explain the fact that there is a higher proportion of interfaith marriage among couples where at least one spouse is Catholic than among couples where at least one spouse is Protestant.[19]

Religious distribution differences affect the proportion of interfaith marriages in a mechanical fashion: increased availability of marriage partners of differing religion and decreased availability of partners of the same religion cause interfaith marriage to increase, and vice versa. As yet, however, no research has been done to determine if racial distribution affects the proportion of interracial marriage in the same way. Fortunately, it was possible to obtain data on Negro-white marriages for each county in California for the year 1959. Since these counties contain varying proportions of Negro and white population, it was possible to determine the associations between Negro-white intermarriage proportions and racial distribution.

Altogether there are 58 counties in California. Since the counties lying outside of metropolitan areas often have very small populations and in particular very small Negro populations, they have been combined in various ways. Areal correlations were performed using as units the 17 counties lying within a Standard Metropolitan Statistical Area in 1960 and combinations of the remaining counties, using as additional units the nine State Economic Areas,[20] lying wholly outside a Standard Metropolitan Area.[21]

[17] Ibid., p. 282.

[18] Harvey J. Locke, Georges Sabagh, and Mary Margaret Thomes, "Interfaith Marriages," *Social Problems*, 4 (April, 1957), 329–333.

[19] Paul C. Glick, "Intermarriage and Fertility Patterns among Persons in Major Religious Groups," *Eugenics Quarterly*, 7 (March, 1960), p. 31–38.

[20] For a definition of the counties included in each of these nine State Economic Areas, see U.S. Bureau of the Census, *United States Census of Population, 1960*, Final Report PC (3)—1A, "State Economic Areas," Washington, D.C.: U.S. Government Printing Office, 1963, p. 464.

[21] Even with the combination of nonmetropolitan counties into State Economic Areas, the problem of small numbers of Negro brides and grooms was not solved. Three State Economic Areas each had fewer than 50 Negro brides and grooms in 1959. In State Economic Areas 1, 2, and 9 there were respectively 6, 20, and 16 Negro brides and grooms.

Coefficients of correlation were computed between actual Negro-white intermarriage proportions and the proportions which would be expected if marriages took place at random without regard to race. For white grooms the expected proportion was simply that of all brides who were Negro; for white brides it was the proportion of all grooms who were Negro. For white brides and grooms the expected proportion of Negro-white marriage was defined as the weighted sum of the expected proportion of white grooms marrying Negro brides and of white brides marrying Negro grooms, the first term weighted by the proportion of grooms among all white brides and grooms and the second term weighted by the proportion of brides among all white brides and grooms. For Negro grooms the expected proportion was that of all brides who were white; for Negro brides that of all grooms who were white; for Negro brides and grooms the expected proportion was defined as a weighted sum of the expected proportions of Negro grooms marrying white brides and of Negro brides marrying white grooms.[22] Table 3 shows the relevant data for each of the 26 areal units.

The six correlation coefficients show that the relationships between actual white intermarriage proportions and the proportions expected if marriage took place without regard to race are strongly positive and significantly different from 0 at the .01 level. In contrast, the relationships between actual and expected Negro intermarriage proportions are all very low. For white grooms the correlation between actual and expected proportion was $+0.77$, for white brides $+0.79$, and for white brides and grooms $+0.85$. On the other hand, the correlation for Negro grooms was -0.08, for Negro brides $+0.16$, and for Negro brides and grooms $+0.01$. Thus, among these areal units racial distribution is a good predictor of variation in white intermarriage proportions but fails to predict variation in Negro intermarriage proportions.

Why is racial composition a good predictor for whites but not for Negroes in these California areas? The apparent reason is that these areas show very little variation in the proportion of all potential partners who are white. In no area is the proportion of grooms or brides who are white less than 82 percent. Hence for Negroes the expected proportions of Negro-white marriage have only a small variance relative to their mean. On the other hand, for whites the expected proportions of Negro-white marriage display high variability with respect to their mean. If there were as much variability in the proportions of all brides and grooms who were white as in the proportions Negro, the proportions expected on the basis of random choice might be as good predictors of interracial marriage for Negroes as for whites.[23] Thus the low correlations obtained for the Negroes do not disturb the general conclusion that the actual proportion of an ingroup who marry into an outgroup is a direct function of the proportion of all potential partners belonging to that outgroup.

[22] The concept of an expected interracial marriage rate for a given area implies that area is a closed marriage market. To the extent that persons select partners from outside the area or to the extent that both bride and groom obtain the marriage license from an areal jurisdiction in which neither resides, the model of a closed marriage market departs from reality.

[23] For a general discussion of this issue, see H. M. Blalock, *Causal Inferences in Nonexperimental Research*, Chapel Hill: University of North Carolina Press, 1964, pp. 44–52.

TABLE 3 Actual Negro-White Intermarriage Percentages and Expected Percentages According to Racial Distribution for 17 Metropolitan Counties and Nine Non-Metropolitan State Economic Areas of California, 1959

Area	White Grooms			White Brides			Negro Grooms			Negro Brides		
		Percentage Marrying Negro Brides			Percentage Marrying Negro Grooms			Percentage Marrying White Brides			Percentage Marrying White Grooms	
	Number	Actual	Expected	Number	Actual	Expected	Number	Actual	Expected	Number	Actual	Expected
Metropolitan counties:												
Alameda	4,280	0.26	14.13	4,267	0.35	14.32	736	2.04	83.05	726	1.52	83.30
Contra Costa	1,408	0.14	9.21	1,410	0.35	9.47	148	3.38	90.21	144	1.39	90.08
Fresno	2,386	0.00	4.95	2,404	0.42	5.30	136	7.35	93.61	127	0.00	92.91
Kern	1,756	0.00	6.21	1,761	0.00	6.16	116	0.00	93.52	117	0.00	93.26
Los Angeles	34,294	0.12	9.95	34,384	0.40	10.17	3,990	3.41	87.67	3,901	1.03	87.44
Marin	545	0.00	4.84	545	0.18	5.02	29	3.45	94.29	28	0.00	94.29
Orange	3,496	0.06	2.06	3,499	0.06	2.03	73	2.74	97.28	74	2.70	97.19
Riverside	1,946	0.05	4.84	1,953	0.31	5.13	106	5.66	94.44	100	1.00	94.10
Sacramento	2,326	0.09	2.77	2,330	0.30	3.02	74	9.46	94.99	68	2.94	94.82
San Bernardino	2,642	0.04	3.90	2,650	0.19	4.04	112	4.46	95.63	108	0.93	95.34
San Diego	7,098	0.01	4.23	7,119	0.17	4.39	330	3.64	94.65	318	0.31	94.38
San Francisco	5,522	0.22	9.80	5,551	0.90	10.43	691	7.24	83.80	649	1.85	83.36
San Joaquin	1,088	0.00	6.74	1,102	0.54	7.31	89	6.74	90.55	82	0.00	89.40
San Mateo	1,690	0.00	3.78	1,697	0.12	3.89	70	2.86	94.38	68	0.00	93.99
Santa Barbara	1,173	0.09	2.46	1,175	0.17	2.54	31	6.45	96.23	30	3.33	96.07
Santa Clara	3,299	0.03	1.71	3,308	0.12	1.83	63	6.35	96.00	59	1.69	95.73
Solano	568	0.35	14.58	579	1.04	15.16	104	5.77	84.40	100	2.00	82.80
Non-metropolitan State Economic Areas:												
1	1,209	0.00	0.25	1,205	0.00	0.25	3	0.00	99.01	3	0.00	99.34
2	1,075	0.09	0.91	1,078	0.09	0.91	10	10.00	98.45	10	10.00	98.17
3	2,413	0.04	3.54	2,436	0.25	3.77	97	6.19	94.75	91	1.10	93.85
4	1,044	0.10	1.50	1,046	0.10	1.50	16	6.25	97.94	16	6.25	97.75
5	1,511	0.00	2.50	1,517	0.00	2.50	39	0.00	97.24	39	0.00	96.86
6	1,876	0.00	3.73	1,879	0.00	3.73	73	0.00	95.97	73	0.00	95.81
7	1,268	0.00	2.65	1,272	0.24	2.88	38	7.89	96.44	35	0.00	96.13
8	4,536	0.13	7.15	4,560	0.42	7.41	367	5.18	92.08	354	1.69	91.60
9	1,194	0.00	0.66	1,193	0.00	0.66	8	0.00	97.79	8	0.00	97.87

In previous work Paul C. Glick and the present writer have employed the concept of the ratio of actual proportion intermarried to the expected proportion intermarried if marriages took place at random without regard to ingroup-outgroup differences.[24] Variation in the ratio of actual to expected Negro-white intermarriage proportions implies that differences in the proportion of interracial marriages are due to some factor or factors additional to that of racial distribution.

For the California data shown in Table 3, the ratios of actual to expected Negro-white marriages for white grooms are in all cases almost identical to those for Negro brides, and those for white brides to those for Negro grooms. The ratio for whites of one sex will be identical to that for Negroes of the other sex whenever Negroes of one sex have the same tendency to marry persons of other races, such as Chinese, Japanese, Filipinos, and Indians. The white rate for one sex will be lower than the Negro rate for the other sex whenever whites of one sex have a greater tendency than Negroes of the other sex to marry persons of races other than white or Negro; the white rate for one sex will be higher than the Negro rate for the other sex whenever whites of one sex have a lesser tendency than Negroes of the other sex to marry persons neither white nor Negro. Because of the near identity of the California ratios for whites of one sex with those for Negroes of opposite sex, further analysis will be limited to the ratios for whites.

CAUSES OF VARIATION IN RATIOS OF ACTUAL TO EXPECTED INTERMARRIAGE

Differences between California areas in the ratio of actual to expected Negro-white marriage may be caused in part by migratory marriage or by errors in recording. Among other possible explanations, one of the most important may be the residential segregation of Negroes and whites within the area of reference. The ratio of actual to expected Negro-white marriage controls for variation in racial distribution between counties or State Economic Areas, but not for racial distribution within the county or area. Moreover, it is well-known that potential marriage partners tend to be chosen largely from among those living a very small distance away.[25] Hence the residential segregation of whites from Negroes within our areas may also be of considerable importance.[26] Specifically we may hypothesize that the

[24] Paul C. Glick, op. cit., and David M. Heer, "The Trend of Interfaith Marriages in Canada: 1922–1957," *American Sociological Review*, 27 (April, 1962), 245–250.

[25] For a review of studies on this topic, see A. M. Katz and R. Hill, "Residential Propinquity and Marital Selection: a Review of Theory, Method and Fact," *Marriage and Family Living*, 20 (1958), 27–34.

[26] For an excellent and detailed study of patterns of Negro residential segregation in the United States, see Karl E. and Alma F. Taeuber, *Negroes in Cities*, Chicago: Aldine Publishing, 1965. For a theoretical argument relating intermarriage rates to degrees of residential segregation see James M. Beshers, *Urban Social Structure*, New York: The Free Press of Glencoe, 1962, especially Chaps. 5 to 7. For empirical data showing very strong direct rela-

greater the residential segregation of whites from Negroes within an area, the lower will be the ratios of actual to expected Negro-white marriage. Another factor which may be important in explaining areal differences in these ratios is the social status of the area's Negro community relative to that of the area's white community. We may suppose that the higher the relative status of the Negro community, the higher will be the ratio of actual to expected intermarriage.[27] A final factor which may cause variation in these ratios is the tolerance of the white community. These last three factors are presumably not independent. The degree of residential segregation may, for example, affect and be affected by the level or tolerance of the white community and the relative social status of the Negro community.

Measures of the tolerance of the white community in each of our California areas are not available. However, for the 17 metropolitan counties of California we can compute a measure of the degree to which Negroes are residentially segregated from whites, and for eight large California Standard Metropolitan Statistical Areas (consisting of a single one of our metropolitan counties or some combination of these) we can obtain a measure of the relative social class standing of the Negro community. The degree to which Negroes are residentially segregated from whites was measured by the coefficient of dissimilarity,[28] computed from 1960 census data on the number of white and Negro persons living in each census tract. This coefficient, the possible values of which vary from 0 to 100, indicates the proportion of Negroes who would have to move into a different census tract in order for the areal distribution of Negro population to be identical to the areal distribution of the white population. Table 4 shows the value of this segregation index for each of the 17 metropolitan counties in California in 1960 and the area's 1959 ratio of actual to expected Negro-white marriage for white brides and grooms. The correlation between these two variables is -0.57 ($P < .05$). Thus considerable support is given to the hypothesis that areal variation in residential segregation causes variation in Negro-white marriage proportions after controls have been instituted for the effects on intermarriage of differences in racial composition between areas.

The social status of the Negro community relative to that of the white community in each area where data were available was measured by com-

---

tionships for several cities between the degree of residential segregation of foreign-born Americans in a subarea of the city and the proportion of native Americans of foreign or mixed parentage in that subarea whose parents are both foreign-born (presumed to be a rough measure of propensity to marry within the foreign-born group), see Stanley Lieberson, *Ethnic Patterns in American Cities*, New York: The Free Press of Glencoe, 1963, pp. 156–158.

[27] For a review of studies showing the strong degree to which marriages are endogamous within social status groups, see William M. Kephart, *The Family, Society, and the Individual*, Boston: Houghton Mifflin, 1961, pp. 279–281.

[28] For technical discussions of the coefficient of dissimilarity and other segregation indices, see Otis Dudley Duncan and Beverly Duncan, "A Methodological Analysis of Segregation Indexes," *American Sociological Review*, 20 (April, 1955), 210–217; and Karl E. and Alma F. Taeuber, op. cit., pp. 195–245.

TABLE 4   Index of Residential Segregation Between Negroes and
Whites in 1960 and Ratio of Actual to Expected Negro-White
Marriage for White Brides and Grooms in 1959, for the 17
Metropolitan Counties of California

County	Index of Residential Segregation	Ratio of Actual to Expected Intermarriage
Santa Barbara	.598	.052
Solano	.625	.047
Santa Clara	.661	.045
Riverside	.687	.036
San Francisco	.702	.055
Kern	.723	.000
Sacramento	.726	.066
San Bernardino	.737	.028
Fresno	.759	.041
San Joaquin	.765	.038
Orange	.793	.029
Alameda	.794	.021
San Diego	.795	.021
San Mateo	.835	.016
Contra Costa	.852	.027
Marin	.863	.018
Los Angeles	.889	.026

puting the ratio between the proportion of employed white males in white-collar occupations and the proportion of employed Negro males in such occupations in 1960.[29] Thus a high ratio is an indicator of low relative status for Negroes and vice versa. The relevant data are shown in Table 5. The coefficient of correlation between this measure of relative status and the ratio of actual to expected intermarriage among white brides and grooms for the California SMSA's was -0.83 (P $<$ .02). This finding gives strong support to our hypothesis that variation in the relative social status of Negroes and whites provokes variation in Negro-white intermarriage proportions when the latter are controlled for the effect of differences in racial composition between areas. However, because this high correlation is based on only eight cases, further research based on a larger number of cases would be desirable.

[29] The source of data for these ratios was U.S. Bureau of the Census, *United States Census of Population: 1960*, Vol. I, Part 6 (California), Tables 74 and 78, and Vol. II, Part 1C (Nonwhite Population by Race), Table 55. Professionals, managers and proprietors except farm and clerical and sales personnel were defined as being in white-collar occupations. Ideally it would have been desirable to compute additional measures of the social status of Negroes relative to whites, such as relative educational attainment and relative income. However, comparable measures of educational attainment and of income were not available separately for the Negro and white populations of the California SMSA's from the published volumes of the 1960 Census.

TABLE 5   Ratio of the Proportion of All Employed White Males in White-Collar Occupations to the Proportion of All Employed Negro Males in White-Collar Occupations in 1960 and Ratio of Actual to Expected Negro-White Marriage for White Brides and Grooms in 1959, for 8 SMSA's in California

SMSA	Ratio of White Proportion White-Collar to Negro Proportion White-Collar	Ratio of Actual to Expected Intermarriage
Sacramento	2.15	.066
Los Angeles-Long Beach	2.45	.026
San Jose	2.62	.045
San Bernardino Riverside	2.91	.032
San Francisco Oakland	3.12	.036
San Diego	3.32	.021
Fresno	3.35	.041
Bakersfield	3.59	.000

RATIO OF ACTUAL TO EXPECTED NEGRO-WHITE MARRIAGE FOR STATES

We may also calculate the ratio of actual to expected intermarriage from the recent data for the four states of California, Hawaii, Michigan, and Nebraska and the earlier data for New York State (excluding New York City). Table 6 shows the ratio of actual to expected rates of Negro-white marriage for white and Negro brides and grooms, for white and Negro grooms, and for white and Negro brides. On examining the ratios of actual to expected interracial marriage for differences between states, we find that for both whites and Negroes the highest ratios by far are for the state of Hawaii. Far lower are the ratios for the other three states with recent data. However, the ratios for California are considerably higher than for Michigan; those for Nebraska are smaller. The ratios for New York State (excluding New York City) in the early 1920's were about as high as those for California during the last decade.

The data in Table 6, which eliminate the effect of differences in racial composition, may be compared with the data in Table 1, with no such control. Logically, the order of areas in the ratios of actual to expected intermarriage should be very much more similar to the order of areas with respect to inter-marriage proportions for the minority group than to the order of areas with respect to intermarriage proportions for the majority group. This principle is borne out in the present data. For example, according to Table 1, the inter-marriage proportions for white brides and grooms in New York State in the early 1920's are approximately one-quarter those for California in the 1950's, whereas the intermarriage proportions for Negro brides and grooms are just slightly higher. Table 6 shows the ratios of actual to expected Negro-white marriage in New York State to be almost identical to those in Cali-fornia.

As before, the causes of the rather marked differences between these four states in the ratios of actual to expected Negro-white marriage may be differences between them in Negro-white residential segregation, in the

TABLE 6 Ratios of Actual Negro-White Marriage to Proportion Expected on the Basis of Racial Distribution, for Available States and Years

State and Year	Whites			Negroes		
	Brides and Grooms	*Grooms*	*Brides*	*Brides and Grooms*	*Grooms*	*Brides*
California						
1955	.024	.010	.036	.024	.036	.011
1957	.024	.009	.039	.024	.038	.009
1958	.024	.012	.037	.024	.037	.011
1959	.029	.012	.044	.028	.044	.013
1955–59	.025	.010	.039	.025	.039	.011
Hawaii						
1956	.232	.000	.365	.229	.359	.000
1957	.333	.000	.511	.333	.513	.000
1958	.147	.143	.154	.151	.156	.142
1959	.310	.229	.350	.304	.352	.227
1960	.444	.348	.523	.436	.521	.343
1961	.426	.234	.553	.427	.554	.223
1962	.393	.114	.561	.385	.560	.110
1963	.370	.250	.457	.375	.462	.249
1964	.458	.217	.613	.454	.611	.215
1956–64	.348	.191	.467	.343	.467	.186
Michigan						
1953	.008	.005	.012	.008	.012	.004
1954	.008	.005	.012	.008	.012	.005
1955	.009	.006	.013	.009	.012	.005
1956	.010	.005	.015	.010	.014	.005
1957	.008	.001	.016	.008	.015	.002
1958	.010	.006	.015	.010	.015	.005
1959	.011	.004	.018	.011	.018	.004
1960	.011	.007	.016	.011	.015	.007
1961	.012	.006	.020	.012	.019	.005
1962	.013	.006	.021	.013	.021	.005
1963	.017	.008	.026	.017	.026	.008
1953–63	.011	.006	.017	.011	.017	.005
Nebraska						
1961	.000	.000	.000	.000	.000	.000
1962	.000	.000	.000	.000	.000	.000
1963	.003	.003	.006	.004	.005	.003
1964	.006	.003	.010	.007	.011	.003
1961–64	.003	.000	.003	.003	.004	.001
New York (excluding New York City)						
1921	.036	.009	.053	.032	.057	.007
1922	.022	.015	.036	.026	.037	.014
1923	.020	.015	.030	.022	.029	.015
1924	.026	.013	.043	.027	.042	.012
1921–24	.024	.012	.041	.026	.039	.012

relative social status of Negroes and whites, and in the tolerance of the white community. It is difficult to test these speculations. Data on white tolerance of racial intermarriage are not available for any of these states. Furthermore, suitable data on the residential segregation of Negroes from whites for areas as large as states are also lacking. Data on the ratio of the proportion of employed white males in white-collar occupations to the proportion of employed Negro males in such occupations in 1960 were available for California, Michigan, and Nebraska, but not for Hawaii. For California this ratio was 2.55, for Michigan 2.81, and for Nebraska 2.91.[30] The ranking of the three states on this ratio is inverse to their ranking on the ratio of actual to expected proportions intermarrying. Thus the hypothesis that the relative social status of Negroes affects the rate of Negro-white intermarriage is again given support.

Table 6 also reveals that the ratio of actual to expected Negro-white marriage appears to be rising in each of the four states for which we have current data. The trend can again be measured with greatest assurance in Michigan. For that state, coefficients of correlation between ratios of actual to expected intermarriage and time were computed. For white brides and grooms and for Negro brides and grooms, the coefficient of correlation between the ratios and time was +0.88 (P < .01), for white grooms +0.43, for white brides +0.93 (P < .01), for Negro grooms +0.91 (P < .01), and for Negro brides +0.51. The corresponding regression coefficients were .0007, .0002, .0012, .0012, and 0002. Thus the greatest increases in the Michigan ratios have occurred for white brides and Negro grooms.

The trend of increase in the ratios of actual to expected Negro-white marriage observed in these four states may be due in part to recent decreases in the residential segregation of Negroes and whites. Karl and Alma Taeuber show that for 64 of 109 cities in the United States the index of residential segregation between whites and non-whites was lower in 1960 than in 1950. Moreover, 35 of the 45 cities with an increasing index of segregation were in the South. Among the 64 cities in the North and West, only ten had an increase in the segregation index. For example, in the city of Detroit the segregation index (derived from city block data) decreased from 88.8 in 1950 to 84.5 in 1960.[31]

The increase in ratios of actual to expected intermarriage in these states may also be caused by decreasing divergence between the socioeconomic status of Negroes and whites. The ratio of white employed males in white-collar occupations to Negro employed males in such occupations in 1950 was computed for Michigan, California, and Nebraska. In all of these states the ratio was higher in 1950 than in 1960. In California the 1950 ratio was 2.93 compared with 2.55 in 1960; for Michigan, 3.24 compared with 2.81; and for Nebraska, 3.23 compared with 2.91.[32]

[30] The ratios for Michigan and Nebraska involve a comparison of white with nonwhite proportions since data on the occupations of Negro males were not available. However, Negroes constitute 97.3 percent of the nonwhite population in Michigan and 80.2 percent of the nonwhite population of Nebraska, with most of the remainder being American Indians.

[31] Karl E. and Alma F. Taeuber, op. cit., pp. 39–44.

[32] The data for 1950 were computed from U.S. Bureau of the Census, *Census of Population: 1950*, Vol. II, Parts 5, 22, and 27, Table 77.

Finally, the increase in ratios of actual to expected intermarriage in these states may possibly result from an increase in tolerance for such marriages. The writer was not able to find any survey data concerning attitudes toward Negro-white marriage for a year prior to 1963. However, nationwide longitudinal survey data on attitudes toward residential and school integration reveal a very substantial liberalization of opinion. For example, in 1942 only 30 percent of white persons in the United States favored white and Negro students in the same schools, but this proportion rose to 49 percent in 1956 and to 62 percent in 1963.[33] The sharp increase in the acceptance of school integration makes plausible the hypothesis that negative attitudes toward intermarriage have also softened.

IMPLICATIONS OF A RISING TREND IN NEGRO-WHITE MARRIAGE

In this paper it has been argued that Negro-white status differences will be reduced if further intermixture between Negroes and whites occurs. Racial intermarriage in the United States does appear to be increasing. Is it plausible to assume that the increase in Negro-white marriage will soon accomplish substantial racial intermixture? The answer to this is probably negative. It is hard to imagine a set of conditions under which Negro-white marriage rates would increase so rapidly as to achieve any large intermingling within the next 100 years. Thus the evident recent trend of increase in Negro-white marriage will not of itself soon bring Negroes to full equality with whites.

Nevertheless, any increase in Negro-white marriage is likely to bring Negroes nearer to equality with whites. Moreover, certain trends may be operating in interaction with Negro-white marriage to reduce the status gap between the races. For example, reductions in residential and school segregation may operate not only directly to decrease Negro-white status differences but also indirectly by increasing the frequency of Negro-white marriage. In addition, it is likely that any decreasing difference in status between Negroes and whites may increase the intermarriage rate and thus cause still further equalization.

[33] Herbert H. Hyman and Paul B. Sheatsley, "Attitudes towards Desegregation," *Scientific American*, 211 (July, 1964), 16–23.

|VI| Basic Marital Roles

Introduction to Section VI

The work of Bales and Slater at Harvard on small groups led to the proposition that small groups tend to differentiate roles, producing an instrumental leader who specializes in decision making and problem resolution and an expressive leader who specializes in maintaining the emotional well-being and cohesiveness of the group. This model has been tested on a cross-cultural sample for its applicability to the nuclear family by Morris Zelditch and found to generally, but not universally, apply. However, the test was rather crude since precise data were not available cross-culturally.

The article by Leik (17) raises some very important questions about the applicability of the role-differentiation proposition to the nuclear family such as we have in America. Social psychologists such as George Levinger have argued that one person in a marriage cannot perform the expressive function alone, for the nature of the socio-emotional role necessitates some emotional response from the other party.[1] In addition there are homekeeping tasks that are the wife's "job" and she acts as an instrumental leader to that extent. Thus, the Bales and Slater view of small-group role differentiation does not seem to fully fit the marital dyad.

Leik presents the result of a most interesting small-group experiment utilizing nine three-person family groups. He reports that the male instrumental specialization was not so obvious in interaction within his own family but was more noticeable in his interaction with members of other families involved in the experiment. Perhaps we generalize from the male occupational role, which is basically instrumental, and thereby believe that the male will be the instrumental leader in his family too. The same kind of stereotyping may lead us to

[1] Levinger, G., "Task and Social Behavior in Marriage." *Sociometry* 27 (December, 1964), 433–448.

conclude that the woman is not an instrumental leader even though she constantly resolves problems connected to child rearing. The reader should look at Rossi's article in Section VII for related comments on this point. In sum, a closer look at the "obvious" proposition concerning role differentiation in the family leads one to have serious doubts regarding its applicability.

The Rodman article (18) deals with another dimension of the marital relationship: power. There have been many studies of marital power and the interested person will soon discover the many problems of measurement, definition, and conceptualization involved. The student may wish to use the references in the Rodman article to follow up this line of inquiry. One apparent contradiction that Rodman deals with concerns the finding that higher-educated men in America have more marital power than lower-educated men but that in other countries this situation is reversed. In resolving this paradox Rodman brings in "resource" notions of power and the relevance of cultural tradition. It is just such creative thinking that is at the heart of scientific explanation. By putting forth an integrative, explanatory schema Rodman has set the stage for another social scientist to test this idea on new data, and in that way add to the amount of tested explanation available in sociology. The reader will note this element of integrative explanation in all the articles in this reader, but some articles, like Rodman's, display it more obviously than do others.

The Cuber and Harroff article (19) is taken from an impressionistic study of the marital life style of several hundred successful men. The selection is filled with intriguing classifications of marital relationships that beg for additional testing and elaboration. It should be an excellent base for discussion in class as well as a reminder of the variety of marital relationships that exist even within one segment of our population. Gilbert Bartell's research on mate exchange (in Section XII) may entice the reader to refer back to the Cuber and Harroff research and to my own comments on "swinging" in the Prologue, and to speculate on the relation of types of marriage to types of adultery. Cuber's work lays a foundation for a typology of marriage that may well aid us in understanding the varieties that are currently appearing on the American scene. Some of the articles on premarital sexuality in Section IV and some articles in the next section on parenthood will also help give perspective and substance to the changing female role as well as the changing forms of the family.

17 | Instrumentality and Emotionality in Family Interaction

ROBERT K. LEIK

Attempts to formulate theoretical principles which underlie family inter-action pose problems which have not been adequately resolved. It is usually assumed by investigators of a "small groups" orientation that the structure and consequent interaction within the nuclear family follow principles appli-cable to small groups in general. A specific instance is the task versus social-emotional differentiation of leadership, first suggested by Slater and by Bales and Slater, which now appears in increasing frequency in discussions of family interaction.[1]

It is apparent from the research literature, however, that relatively little data exist in direct support of the equivalence of families and other small groups. For example, studies of coalition relationships in family interaction do not show the same results that are obtained from ad hoc experimental groups.[2] Similarly, a recent attempt to test "some widely held beliefs about marital interaction" showed little support for nine propositions derived from general small group research.[3] Although there may be valid reasons for the discrepancies, results do not show overwhelming evidence that family inter-action coincides with theoretical expectations derived from non-family research.

The present paper will deal with one aspect of the comparability of family and non-family interaction. The particular problem to be studied is the

[1] Philip E. Slater, "Role Differentiation in Small Groups," *American Socio-logical Review*, 20 (June, 1955), 300–310, and Robert F. Bales and Philip E. Slater, "Role Differentiation in Small Decision Making Groups," Chap. V in Talcott Parsons and Robert F. Bales, eds., *Family, Socialization, and Interaction Process*, Glencoe: The Free Press, 1955. Further use of this distinction between male and female roles occurs in the following: Morris Zelditch, Jr., "Role Differentiation in the Nuclear Family: A Comparative Study," Chap. VI in Parsons and Bales, op. cit.; Fred L. Strodtbeck and Richard D. Mann, "Sex Role Differentiation in Jury Deliberations," *Sociometry*, 19 (March, 1956), 3–11; William F. Kenkel, "Influence Differentiation in Family Decision Making," *Sociology and Social Research*, 42 (September–October, 1957), 18–25; and Jerold S. Heiss, "Degree of Intimacy and Male-Female Interaction," *Sociom-etry*, 25 (June, 1962), 197–208.

[2] Fred L. Strodtbeck, "The Family as a Three Person Group," *American Sociological Review*, 19 (February, 1954), 23–29.

[3] J. R. Udry, H. A. Nelson, and R. Nelson, "An Empirical Investigation of Some Widely Held Beliefs about Marital Interaction," *Marriage and Family Living*, 23, (November, 1961), 388–390.

Revision of a paper presented to the Pacific Northwest Council on Family Relations, Tacoma, March, 1962.

Reprinted from *Sociometry*, 26, No. 2 (June, 1963), 131–145, by permission of the American Sociological Association.

importance of instrumentality, or task-oriented behavior, and of emotionality, in two respects. First, are the male role (instrumental, non-emotional) and female role (emotional, non-instrumental), which parallel the task leader and social-emotional leader, applicable to the actual interaction process within the family? Or are they merely a summary consequence of family division of labor?[4] Second, in what way do instrumentality and emotionality affect the process of reaching consensus?

CONVERGENCE IN INTERACTION PATTERNS

Although the sex roles may differ in the emphasis placed on instrumentality and emotionality, it appears reasonable to suggest that for any particular interaction sequence involving both sexes, some compromise or convergence will have to take place. In a male-female dyad, for the man to concentrate heavily on a task while the woman is primarily concerned with expressive acts would be both inefficient and frustrating. The man will have no aid on the task; the woman no return for her emotional investment. Rather, it seems more probable that for certain purposes the woman will shift to a more instrumental frame of reference, and for other purposes, the man to a more emotional frame of reference. The standard role differentiation is more a consequence of interaction *outside* the dyad. Here the male is more apt to have responsibilities calling for instrumentality, while the female is more apt to need expressive behaviors.

The family context is particularly conducive to convergence in interaction due to the relative freedom from surveillance of that interaction by other people.[5] While the family members may well be aware of and profess agreement with standard sex role differentiation, they may just as readily behave quite differently behind the closed doors of their home. Thus a man may express traditional masculine values to his fellow workers, concomitantly insisting that his wife is, and should be, properly feminine. Nevertheless he may be quite willing to show considerable emotion privately to his wife and expect her at times to be businesslike.

Once a convergent pattern is established between family members, it is reasonable to assume that that pattern will influence the behavior of the members toward each other even when under third-party surveillance. Rather than displaying "public" behavior completely in accord with a standard role, the members will compromise between their private convergence and the standard public role, retaining some of the advantages of each.

Assuming, then, a "public" acceptance of the traditional sex role differentiation, the following patterns are predicted.

[4] Although sex-role differentiation traditionally rests upon family division of labor, such as job versus child rearing, the attempt to relate this differentiation to instrumental and emotional behavior is based upon inferences from interaction data obtained in small group research, as noted above.

[5] See William J. Goode, "A Theory of Role Strain," *American Sociological Review*, 25, (August, 1960), 483–496 for a discussion of "third party" restraints on role bargaining.

1. Interaction in groups of strangers will show differentiation by sex; males will display greater instrumentality and less emotionality than will females.
2. Interaction in family groups will show little or no differentiation by sex.
3. Interaction in family groups when under surveillance of others, such as personnel conducting an experiment, will show a compromise between 1 and 2 above.

EFFECTS OF INSTRUMENTALITY AND EMOTIONALITY ON CONSENSUS

The effects of emotionality and instrumentality on the consensus seeking process depend upon the context of the interaction. If the concept of primary group is valid, family interaction occurs in a context of emotional solidarity. Members presumably are used to, and comfortable with, considerable emotionality in their interaction with each other. A comparable emotional tone among strangers, however, is apt to be embarrassing and uncomfortable, suggesting that it would not be conducive to satisfactory interaction.

Based on the above argument, it is expected that emotionality in family interaction will enhance member satisfaction, but will decrease satisfaction in stranger interaction. Because emotionality and instrumentality are in a sense complementary behaviors, the reverse relationships should hold for the effects of instrumentality on satisfaction in the two types of groups.

The relationships of degree of agreement to emotion and task orientation are less easily hypothesized. If, as has been indicated by previous small group research, efficiency in problem solving is in some degree antithetical to personal satisfaction,[6] then predictions involving agreement will be the reverse of those for satisfaction. That is, agreement in family groups should show positive relationship to instrumentality and negative relationship to emotionality, the opposite predictions being made for stranger interaction. On the other hand, if the total consensus process, involving both agreement and satisfaction, rests upon common interaction factors, then predictions for agreement should parallel those for satisfaction.

Specific hypotheses, assuming a consensus-seeking context, are:

4. Emotionality will be *positively* related to personal satisfaction in family groups and *negatively* related to personal satisfaction in stranger groups;
5. Instrumentality will be *negatively* related to personal satisfaction in family groups and *positively* related to personal satisfaction in stranger groups.

[6] Small group research suggests that task emphasis brings about a reduced popularity, implying less member satisfaction. See, for example, Slater, op. cit., and Bales and Slater, op. cit. Also, communication channel studies indicate that maximum efficiency and maximum member satisfaction are associated with contradictory systems. See Harold J. Leavitt, "Some Effects of Certain Communication Patterns on Group Performance," *The Journal of Abnormal and Social Psychology*, 46 (January, 1951), 38–50.

If satisfaction and agreement are antithetical, then:

6a. Emotionality will be *negatively* related to agreement in family groups and *positively* related to agreement in stranger groups;

7a. Instrumentality will be *positively* related to agreement in family groups and *negatively* related to agreement in stranger groups.

However, if satisfaction and agreement are common products of the same underlying factors, then:

6b. Emotionality will be *positively* related to agreement in family groups and *negatively* related to agreement in stranger groups;

7b. Instrumentality will be *negatively* related to agreement in family groups and *positively* related to agreement in stranger groups.

One further consideration is relevant. If interaction is appropriate to the context, as outlined above, then perception by each participant of the satisfaction gained by others from the interaction should be more accurate. This assertion rests upon the assumption that more appropriate interaction requires less concern on the part of the participants with the interaction itself, hence allows greater opportunity for observing the reactions of others present. As a final hypothesis, then:

8. Perception of the satisfaction of other participants is *positively* related to emotionality in the family interaction and to instrumentality in non-family interaction.

It should be apparent that, by definition, private family interaction cannot be observed. Thus Hypothesis 2 cannot be subjected to experimental test. The remainder of the paper will report a test of the other hypotheses presented above.

EXPERIMENTAL PROCEDURE

Nine families, consisting of father, mother and college-aged daughter participated in 27 experimental group discussions. All groups were triadic and all were given the problem of reaching consensus on issues of some relevance to family values or goals.[7] The first set of nine triads were homogeneous regarding both age and sex; all fathers, all mothers or all daughters. These

[7] One of the problems used was: "Two students marry while still in college, but want to complete their college education. Some persons feel the parents' financial responsibility ceases when the child marries, while others feel the parents should continue financial support. How would you solve this situation?" By careful scheduling of problems, it was possible to ensure that (1) each subject discussed each problem once and only once, and (2) problems were equally distributed among treatments to avoid contamination of results. Analysis showed no interaction between problem and either treatment or the age-sex category of the subject.

will be called the "ad hoc" groups. The second set of groups were composed of a father, a mother and a daughter, but not of the same family. Thus the age-sex structure of a family was present, but members were not united by bonds of affection or familial history. These will be called "structured" groups. Finally, the nine families met as families. Each of the 27 subjects experienced the three types of group in the same order; i.e., ad hoc, then structured, then family. Although there may be some learning involved in successive experimental sessions, there is no reason to assume that it would occur differently between the three age-sex categories.

Data were obtained by observers behind a one-way screen who recorded the source, direction, and nature of each act, and by post-experimental questionnaires. Categories of acts were derived from the Bales system, with simplification for the purposes of the specific study. Because emotion and task orientation were the major foci of this research, only these two aspects of the interaction were recorded. However, from previous use of such recording procedures, it was felt that the absolute disjunction of emotion and task orientation which is a necessary consequence of the Bales system was unrealistic and posed difficult decisions for observers. To avoid this problem, the task-nontask dichotomy was cross classified with the trichotomy of positive, neutral or negative emotion, resulting in the following six categories:[8]

(1) Positive emotion, Task-oriented
(2) Positive emotion, Non task-oriented
(3) Neutral emotion, Task-oriented
(4) Neutral emotion, Non task-oriented
(5) Negative emotion, Task-oriented
(6) Negative emotion, Non task-oriented

Six variables will be discussed in this paper, two of which are definable in terms of the six categories of acts. These are:

Instrumentality. The ratio of task-oriented acts to total acts initiated. Operationally, using n_i to indicate the frequency of acts in category i,

$$\text{instrumentality} = (n_1 + n_3 + n_5)/\sum_1^6 n_i$$

Emotionality. The ratio of emotional acts, either positive or negative, to all acts initiated. Operationally,

$$\text{emotionality} = (n_1 + n_2 + n_5 + n_6)/\sum_1^6 n_i$$

Two observers recorded each session. Reliability was measured by product-moment correlations between measurements obtained by the two

[8] Although the data show a tendency for task oriented acts to be neutral and for non-task acts to have a positive emotional content, categories 1, 4 and 5, not available in Bales' system, account for approximately one-third of the observed acts.

observers at each session. As defined above, instrumentality showed .95 reliability. Observer correlation for emotionality, however, was .78. The percentage of distribution of instrumental or emotional acts among the participants in a given session showed similar reliability: .95 for instrumentality and .77 for emotionality. For all data reported, the average of the two observer scores was used, decreasing the error implied by the rather low reliability of the emotional categories.

Three of the other four variables are definable in terms of the post-experimental questionnaire. Question 1 asked: "You may or may not have agreed with the group's decision regarding the best solution for the problem you were given. Please indicate by a check mark the degree to which you agreed or disagreed: (1) Complete agreement, (2) Agreed more than disagreed, (3) Neutral, open question, undecided, (4) Disagreed more than agreed, (5) Complete disagreement." The same question was repeated with reference to each of the other two participants in turn. Question 4 dealt with satisfaction: "You may or may not have enjoyed the group's discussion. Please indicate by a check mark the degree to which you enjoyed or were dissatisfied with the discussion: (1) Enjoyed very much, (2) Enjoyed somewhat, (3) Neutral, (4) Somewhat dissatisfied or uncomfortable, (5) Very dissatisfied or uncomfortable." As with agreement, this question was repeated with reference to the other two participants. All responses were scored inversely; i.e., "complete agreement" was scored 5, "complete disagreement" was scored 1.

Agreement. The extent to which the members of a group agreed with the decision reached. Operationally this variable consists of the sum of scores on Question 1 for the group participants.

Satisfaction. The extent to which the members of a group enjoyed the group's discussion. Operationally satisfaction consists of the sum of the scores on Question 4 for the group participants.

Accuracy of Perception; Satisfaction. The extent to which group members accurately perceived other participants' satisfaction. Absolute differences were computed between a subject's own satisfaction score and that imputed to him by each of the others. The sum of these differences constitutes perceptual error with respect to satisfaction within the group. Correlations between this sum and other variables have been reversed in sign so that the inverse of perceptual error, i.e., perceptual accuracy, will be reported.[9]

As has been recognized by investigators of empathy, there is a confounding tendency for persons to attribute to the other a similarity to self, then predict for self rather than really empathize. The concern of this study was only to determine whether the prediction of other's satisfaction, regardless of its basis in empathy or in assumed similarity, was related to the conditions of interaction.

A measure equivalent to accuracy of perception of satisfaction was computed for agreement, but showed such a close relationship with agreement itself

[9] Note that perceptual accuracy is not necessarily the same as empathy.

that no additional information was obtained. Therefore this variable has been omitted from the data to be presented.

Time to Consensus. The length of time, in minutes, which each group required to reach consensus.

RESULTS

Interaction

The ad hoc groups provide an initial check on the first hypothesis, that men will play a more instrumental, less emotional role than will women when they are interacting with strangers. Measures of instrumentality and emotionality, as defined earlier, were obtained for each session. Averages

TABLE 1 Interaction in Ad Hoc Groups: Mean Instrumentality and Emotionality by Type of Group

Type of Session	Instrumentality	Emotionality
Father sessions	70	22
Mother sessions	61	31
Daughter sessions	65	28

Acts classified as either positively or negatively emotional are represented in the "Emotional" column. The classification scheme does not make task behavior and emotional behavior mutually exclusive nor are they exhaustive. Thus the rows do not sum to 100%.

of these measures are reported in Table 1 for the three types of ad hoc sessions. Although the differences are not gross,[10] they are in the expected direction. Males, when interacting with strangers, are both more instrumental and less emotional than are either set of females.

In the structured sessions, if the stereotypic sex role is considered appropriate for family interaction, but no convergence has occurred because "real" families are not involved, the men should account for more than one third of the task behavior while each of the women provides more than one third of the emotion present. Table 2 shows that the expectation is in general fulfilled. Note that mothers tend to play an intermediate role, providing approximately their share of task-oriented behavior (not significantly less than fathers) as well as a significantly high proportion of emotion. Daughters

[10] By computing instrumentality and emotionality as averages of group measurements, then using a *t*-test, only the difference between fathers' and mothers' emotionality attains statistical significance at the .05 level. This results largely from the fact of only three father, three mother, and three daughter sessions to contribute to the means shown. If all acts initiated in all groups of a given type are combined, providing one percentage for each age-sex category, denominators exceed 1000 acts, and the differences between types of sessions are highly significant. Combining of groups in this manner seems inappropriate, however, since considerable variation between groups of a given type occurred. Data in Table 1, then, are suggestive, but not conclusive.

TABLE 2 Mean Percentage Distribution of Task and Emotional Behavior

Family Member	Structured Groups		Family Groups	
	Task Behavior	*Emotional Behavior*	*Task Behavior*	*Emotional Behavior*
Fathers	40	24	36	26
Mothers	34	41	34	32
Daughters	26	35	30	42
	100	100	100	100

Hypothesis:	Decision at .05 level:	Hypothesis:	Decision at .05 level:
Task		Task	
F > M	reject	F = M	accept
F > D	accept	F = D	accept
Emotional		Emotional	
F < M	accept	F = M	accept
F < D	accept	F = D	reject

The percentages in this table cannot be compared with those in Table 1, since Table 1 shows the proportion of all acts which were of a given type, whereas Table 2 shows the distribution of a given type of act among subjects. With each individual's proportion of the instrumental or emotional behavior in a given session treated as a single observation, means were computed across the nine fathers, nine mothers, and nine daughters. Because the scores derived from a given session must sum to unity, these means are dependent in a somewhat complex manner. To avoid three way dependency, t-tests were computed between pairs of means. Inferences drawn therefrom are subject to some qualification.

show significantly less task behavior and more emotion, as predicted. Both the ad hoc and the structured groups, then, display behavior essentially in accordance with Hypothesis 1.

Subjects in a laboratory are, of course, aware of some surveillance. According to Hypothesis 3, interaction of the family groups should be a compromise between the ad hoc pattern and an essentially equal sharing of task and emotion. Again, Table 2 shows that, regarding instrumental behavior, Hypothesis 3 is substantiated. The divergence between fathers and daughters has been cut in half, while mothers retained their "equal share" position. Although fathers had displayed significantly greater task emphasis than daughters in structured groups, no significant differences appear in family task distribution.

In the emotion sphere, results are less clear. Fathers do show a slight increase in emotion, but there is a switch between mothers and daughters, the latter remaining significantly higher than fathers in this sphere. While this switch is not directly relevant to Hypothesis 3, it implies a somewhat more complex problem concerning expressiveness in the family.

One possible difficulty with the data of Table 2 is the fact that the proportion of total group task behavior or emotional behavior initiated by an individual is partially dependent upon his overall rate of initiation. Thus a high initiator who is 50 per cent task oriented may contribute more instrumentality than a low initiator who is 75 per cent task oriented. In order to explore role differentiation further, the overall rate of initiation of each individual was used as a base line to determine whether he overemphasized or underemphasized a particular type of behavior. Two sets of ratios were computed. The numerators were, respectively, the proportion of total group task behavior initiated by the individual and the proportion of total group positive emotion[11] initiated by the individual. The denominator in both cases was the proportion of total group behavior initiated by the individual. A ratio in excess of 1.00 indicates overemphasis on the specified type of behavior, whereas a ratio less than 1.00 indicates underemphasis. All ratios have been multiplied by 100 for convenience.

TABLE 3 Task and Emotion Rates Based on Initiation Rate

| | Number of Sessions | | | |
| Family | Task Rate | | Emotion Rate | |
Member	>100	≤100	>100	≤100
Structured Groups				
Father	6	3	1	8
Mother	3	6	7	2
Daughter	3	6	7	2
	x^2 = 2.7, p > .05		x^2 = 10.8, p < .01	
Family Groups				
Father	6	3	1	8
Mother	5	4	5	4
Daughter	1	8	7	2
	x^2 = 6.3, p < .05		x^2 = 8.3, p < .05	

The ratios obtained for any three group members are interdependent only to the extent that any dichotomizing procedure requires algebraic balance around a cutting line; in this case, a ratio of 100. Thus any two members can be said to be independent, with the third dependent upon them and the relevant totals. This is precisely the "degrees of freedom" concept incorporated into x^2.

As Table 3 indicates, structured sessions show consistent, and for emotion, significant differentiation by sex, with no difference between mothers and daughters either in the task or the emotional area. Family sessions, on the other hand, show a somewhat different picture. Fathers' ratios indicate, as before, a clear task emphasis. Daughters emphasize task even less than before, with no change in emotional emphasis. Mothers provide the most interesting difference from structured sessions: in five out of nine times their ratios *exceed* 100 for both task and emotion. It appears that mothers and daughters play comparable roles with strangers. But when interaction takes place within the family, mothers "take over" a greater share of the task area, with a somewhat lessened (but still important) emotional emphasis. Concomitantly, daughters "back out" of the task sphere even more than they did in role playing sessions, producing a significant age differentiation in contrast to the sex differentiation of structured groups.

Another way of demonstrating the relationship being emphasized is to

[11] Only positive emotion has been used here for two reasons. First, it comprises the major portion of emotion, and is more reliable than total emotion. Secondly, the role differentiation being tested is meaningful only if the woman emphasizes positive emotion, not just emotion in general.

TABLE 4 Combined Factor Solutions for Three Types of Group

| | Factors | | | | | | | | |
| | I "Agreement" | | | II "Satisfaction" | | | III "Residual" | | |
Variables	Ad hoc Groups	Structured Groups	Family Groups	Ad hoc Groups	Structured Groups	Family Groups	Ad hoc Groups	Structured Groups	Family Groups
Agreement	.93	1.00	1.00						
Consensus time	−.69	−.39	−.82	.21	.30		−.57	−.40	−.25
Satisfaction		.21	.53	.69	.95	.80	.22		
Emotionality	.36	.43	−.46	.33		.82	.72	.38	.24
Instrumentality			.50		.28	−.26	−.27	.69	−.67
Perception of satisfaction		.66	.50		.63		.71	.33	.69

Loadings of less than .20 have been omitted.

combine data in Table 3 alternately by sex or by age so as to produce sets of 2×2 tables which indicate the relative importance of sex and age in the distribution of task and emotional behavior. If Q is used as an index, the association between sex and, respectively, task and emotional behavior in structured groups is .60 and .93. Age, however, is associated with type of behavior to a considerably lesser degree, the indices being .33 and .63 respectively for task and emotion. Thus sex is a notably more important variable of differentiation for structured groups.

When the same analysis is applied to family data, the association of sex with task and emotion is .60 and .80, respectively. This is similar to associations found in the structured data. Age, however, shows associations of .85 for task and .75 for emotion. Age in family sessions is a more important variable than sex for the distribution of task behavior, and nearly as important as sex for the distribution of emotion. Thus the switch in emotion between mothers and daughters shown in Table 2 becomes clearer.

In the family, apparently, mothers attempt a dual role, sharing the task sphere with their husbands, and the emotional sphere with their daughters. It can be suggested from the data presented that bridging the gap between the traditional role emphases of male and female is acceptable when the female shares the task orientation of her husband. However, at least where daughters are present, the husband does not move equally in the direction of female emotionality.

In general the present data give reason to doubt that the task leader vs. emotional leader sex differentiation provides an accurate description of the actual *interaction* of family members.

Consensus

The remaining analysis concerns the effects of instrumentality and emotionality on the consensus process. The six variables were factor analyzed for the three types of session. For each type of group, an initial centroid solution was obtained, then orthogonally rotated so that the three major factors were as nearly comparable as possible from group to group.[12] Factor I has been labeled "Agreement" to reflect the fact that agreement has the highest loading on this factor for all groups. For a similar reason, Factor II is labeled "Satisfaction." Factor III is difficult to name because loadings for no single variable or set of variables are consistent across groups. Therefore the label "Residual" is applied to indicate that the groups vary in what remains after the first two factors are extracted. Table 4 shows the loadings of the variables by type of session for each of the three factors.

Several aspects of the factor analysis are worth noting. *First*, simultaneous maximization of agreement and satisfaction poses a contradiction in all three types of group. In family groups, if the interaction is highly task oriented, agreement is greater but satisfaction diminishes somewhat. As interaction becomes more emotional (presumably subject to a point of

[12] For centroid and rotation procedures, see any standard reference on factor analysis, such as Karl J. Holzinger and Harry H. Harman, *Factor Analysis*, Chicago: University of Chicago Press, 1941.

diminishing returns) satisfaction increases greatly, but at the expense of agreement. Although this particular contradiction disappears for non-family groups, a parallel problem exists concerning the time taken to reach consensus. Whereas a short discussion is associated with agreement, a longer one is associated with satisfaction. Thus a common problem exists for each of these types of group, but for somewhat different reasons. In accordance with the earlier discussion, the first form of Hypotheses 6 and 7 should be used; i.e., Hypotheses 6a and 7a are implied by the contradiction of satisfaction and consensus.

Second, the effects of instrumentality and emotionality on family agreement and satisfaction are, as expected, quite different from the effects of those variables in ad hoc and structured groups. Considering satisfaction first, specific findings are as follows:

(1) Emotionality is moderately *positively* related to satisfaction in ad hoc groups and *not* related to satisfaction in structured groups, but is *strongly positively* related to family satisfaction. This finding supports the hypothesized effect of emotionality on family satisfaction, but does not support the expectation for stranger groups. Hypothesis 4 is thus partially validated.

(2) Instrumentality is *not* related to satisfaction in ad hoc groups, is moderately *positively* related to satisfaction in structured groups, and is moderately *negatively* related to family satisfaction. This finding in general supports Hypothesis 5.

(3) With regard to agreement, the factor analysis indicates that: Emotionality is *positively* related to agreement in non-family groups but *negatively* related to agreement in family groups. This finding directly supports Hypothesis 6a.

(4) Instrumentality is *not* related to agreement in non-family groups, but is *positively* related to family agreement. This finding in part supports Hypothesis 7a.

Clearly, both task orientation and emotion have different implications for non-family groups than they have for the family.

It should be noted that family loadings on Factor I are of considerable magnitude for all six variables. On the other hand, structured groups show little or no relationship between agreement and either satisfaction or instrumentality, and ad hoc groups display these two zero relationships and a further lack of relationship between agreement and perception of satisfaction. It appears that the process of reaching agreement is relatively explicit in stranger groups and, conversely, relatively inclusive in family groups. If this is generally valid, family consensus involves more than those facets which would be found in the laboratory study of ad hoc groups. The consensus process in family interaction, then, is a special case deserving research attention.

The implications of the time it takes to reach consensus seem to be similar for all three types of group. In each case, time is negatively related to agreement, although to varying degrees, is moderately related to satisfaction except in the family, and is negatively related to Factor III. Perhaps the strong relationship between emotion and satisfaction in family groups accounts for the reduced importance of discussion time in this instance.

The factor matrix is less useful for testing Hypothesis 8 than are the simple correlations between perception of satisfaction and instrumentality and emotionality. These correlations show that perception of satisfaction is, as hypothesized, negatively related to instrumentality in the family ($-.31$) and positively related to instrumentality in structured groups ($+.40$). Contrary to expectation, there is a small negative relationship with instrumentality in ad hoc groups ($-.13$). Findings regarding emotionality are essentially the reverse of those predicted. For family, structured, and ad hoc groups, respectively, the correlations are $-.07$, $+.47$, and $+.55$. The family correlation is sufficiently low to suggest no relationship, but this is still an unexpected result for which no adequate explanation can be offered from the present data. In all three types of group, accurate perception appears to require adequate time; the correlations with consensus time are $-.81$, $-.40$, and $-.61$.

SUMMARY

Eight hypotheses have been stated, seven of which were subjected to an exploratory test. As a consequence of the data reported, the following tentative conclusions are reached.

1. The traditional male role (instrumental, non-emotional behavior) as well as the traditional female role (emotional, non-task behavior) appear when interaction takes place among strangers. These emphases tend to disappear when subjects interact with their own families. Particularly is this true for instrumentality, because of a dual role for mothers.

2. The satisfaction of family members is positively related to emotionality and negatively related to instrumentality, as hypothesized. Conversely, instrumentality is either negatively related to or irrelevant for satisfaction in stranger interaction. Contrary to prediction, however, emotionality is, in ad hoc groups, at least, positively related to satisfaction.

3. For all types of group, agreement and satisfaction appear somewhat contradictory. Consequently, agreement in family interaction is negatively related to emotionality and positively related to instrumentality. For non-family sessions, agreement is positively related to emotionality but unrelated to instrumentality.

4. In general, the relevance of instrumentality and emotionality is quite different for family interaction than for interaction among strangers. This major finding poses new problems for the theoretical integration of family research with that based on ad hoc experimental groups. Such integration is possible only through a recognition of the fact that the context of interaction with strangers places a meaning on particular acts which is different from the meaning of those acts within the family group.

Marital Power in France, Greece, Yugoslavia, and the United States: A Cross-National Discussion

HYMAN RODMAN

The amount of cross-national research is limited, and we are therefore highly fortunate to have access to comparable data on power structure in the marital relationship for four contemporary countries. The papers by Michel,[1] Safilios-Rothschild,[2] and Burić and Zečević[3] present data on an urban French, an urban Greek, and urban Yugoslavian sample respectively, and they can all be contrasted with the data from an earlier study carried out in an urban area in the United States by Blood and Wolfe.[4] This provides an unusual opportunity to explore the comparative findings on Paris and Bordeaux, Athens, Kragujevac, and Detroit in detail. Only data collected from women are presently available.

RESOURCE THEORY AND CULTURAL CONTEXT

In presenting their data on Detroit, Blood and Wolfe found that a "theory of resources" provided the best explanation for their findings.[5] For example, the husband's mean (average) authority score generally increased with increases in his education, income, and occupational status, and these variables were conceptualized as resources which the husband brought to the marital decision-making area and which gave him greater leverage in making decisions. Similarly, the husband's decision-making powers were enhanced, according to the theory of resources, if his wife did not work and when his

[1] Andrée Michel, "Comparative Data Concerning the Interaction in French and American Families," *Journal of Marriage and the Family*, 29, No. 2 (May, 1967).

[2] Constantina Safilios-Rothschild, "A Comparison of Power Structure and Marital Satisfaction in Urban Greek and French Families," *Journal of Marriage and the Family*, 29, No. 2 (May, 1967).

[3] Olivera Burić and Andjelka Zečević, "Family Authority, Marital Satisfaction and the Social Network in Yugoslavia," *Journal of Marriage and the Family*, 29, No. 2 (May, 1967).

[4] Robert O. Blood, Jr. and Donald M. Wolfe, *Husbands and Wives*, New York: The Free Press, Macmillan, 1960, pp. 11–46. This study, as well as research carried out in Belgium by Reuben Hill, was instrumental in encouraging the comparative research in France, Greece, and Yugoslavia.

[5] Ibid.

Revised from a discussion of the papers dealing with "Substantive Reports of Cross-National Family Research," at the Sixth World Congress of Sociology, Evian, France, September, 1966.

Reprinted from the *Journal of Marriage and the Family*, 29, No. 2 (May, 1967), 320–325, by permission of the National Council of Family Relations.

wife had preschool-age children, because under these circumstances the wife was more dependent upon her husband. As stated by Blood and Wolfe:

> Having a young child creates needs for the wife which lead her to depend more on her husband for help, financial support, and making decisions. As children grow up, they shift from being burdens to being resources whom the wife draws upon in marital decision-making. They also become resources in other ways, providing emotional support which makes the wife less dependent on her husband.[6]

In general, the data on Paris and Bordeaux provided by Michel lend support to the theory of resources. But Michel also sounds a note of warning about the possible differences to be found in developing countries where occupational and educational status may play a less important, or a different role. When we compare the data on Greece and Yugoslavia with those on the United States and France, Michel's cautions are shown to be well placed. The following are the major differences:

1. In the United States and France, the husband's educational status and authority score are positively correlated. In Greece and Yugoslavia they are negatively correlated. For example, husbands at the highest educational level in the United States and France have the highest average authority score; in Greece and Yugoslavia, husbands at the highest educational level have the lowest average authority score.

2. In the United States and France, the husband's occupational status and authority score are positively correlated; in Greece and Yugoslavia they are negatively correlated.

3. In the United States and France, the husband's income and authority score are positively correlated; in Greece and Yugoslavia they are negatively correlated.

4. In Greece, the husband's authority declines steadily through the various stages of the family life cycle; in France and the United States, however, it is not the newlywed husband who has the highest authority score but the husband of the wife with preschool children.

In short, the Greek and Yugoslavian data, in their sharp contrast to the French and United States data, present a theoretical challenge and opportunity. By pursuing the opportunity, one may possibly build upon the theory of resources in order to account for a wider range of findings.

The data on Detroit pointed to the importance of "the comparative resourcefulness and competence of the two partners. . . . Once we know which partner has more education, more organizational experience, a higher status background, etc., we will know who tends to make most of the decisions."[7] From this perspective, variables such as education, income, and occupational status are resources, and the comparative amounts of such resources possessed by husband and wife are important in determining the outcome of the distribution of power. But the reversal of the relationships for the Greek and Yugoslavian data forces us to reconsider our view of education, income, and occupational status. They are not merely resource variables in a power

[6] Ibid., p. 42.
[7] Ibid., p. 37.

struggle, but are also positional variables in the social structure. The different positions of which they are indicative may involve differing patterns of social-ization and may, for example, represent a greater or lesser likelihood of learning sentiments favorable toward the equalitarian distribution of power. This is particularly true for education: the more highly educated the Greek man, as pointed out by Safilios-Rothschild, the likelier is he to grant his wife a more equalitarian status within the marital relationship.

In Greece and Yugoslavia, therefore, we are not dealing so much with resources in a power struggle, but with the learning of a new role. The more education a man has, the likelier is he to grant his wife more authority, despite a traditional patriarchal culture.[8]

One issue that is at present difficult to resolve centers around the apparent lack of fit between the official norms and the behavioral data. It appears that traditional patriarchal norms are more stressed in Greece than in France or the United States. Yet the Greek women's responses, summed across all decisions, suggest that they have more actual power than women in the United States or France. Similarly, it appears that equalitarian norms are more stressed in the United States than in France or Greece; yet the behavioral data, summed across all decisions, suggest that the United States is more patriarchal than France or Greece. See Robert O. Blood, Jr., Reuben Hill, Andrée Michel, and Constantina Safilios-Rothschild, "Comparative Analysis of Family Power Structure: Problems of Measurement and Interpreta-tion," presented at the International Seminar for Family Research, Tokyo, Japan, September, 1965.

Education may play its major role as a resource variable or as a cultural variable, depending upon the particular community or society under considera-tion. The stress placed here upon cultural differences stems from the attempt to deal simultaneously with apparently discrepant findings from four different societies. Blood and Wolfe also considered the possible influence of cultural factors in explaining the Detroit data, but found them wanting. They examined the influence of several variables that might indicate a greater acceptance of an authoritarian tradition—farm families, immigrant families, older couples, uneducated couples, and Catholic couples. But these families did not show a more patriarchal pattern of decision-making. It was after testing for the influence of such cultural factors in Detroit that Blood and Wolfe turned to the theory of comparative resources. In the present discussion we have additional data that do indicate the importance of cultural expectations. Moreover, it seems that comparative resources play an influential role in the United States because of several underlying cultural factors: (1) the emphasis upon an equalitarian ethic; (2) a high degree of flexibility about the distribution of marital power; and (3) the importance that education, occupation, and income have in defining a man's status.

[8] A number of issues must remain clouded until further data are reported. For example, we do not have data on the distribution of responses for each decision in each country; we do not have data on men's responses; we are making assumptions about norms but we do not have normative data. Further-more, in order to provide culturally equivalent decisions within each country it was not possible to use the same set of decisions. This makes it hazardous to compare the mean authority scores (summed for all decisions) of the different samples.

The French data are somewhat more difficult to interpret. The relationships between the authority score of the husband and variables such as family life cycle, husband's education, wife's employment status, and husband's income parallel the trends for the United States, but are weaker and frequently not statistically significant. It may be that lingering traditional patterns contribute toward a negative relationship between husband's educational level and husband's authority score while a developing flexible and equalitarian pattern contributes toward a positive relationship. Since these two trends tend to cancel each other out, the correlations are low. In addition, the family allowances that are paid to women provide an economic base of security for those in the lower classes, and the importance of education, occupation, and income are less stressed in defining the man's position than in the United States. These factors may also contribute toward the low correlations. It must also be remembered that there may be community and other differences within France and the other countries, so that the particular urban samples reported do not reflect all possible cultural authority patterns or family types.

To summarize, the following theoretical statement about marital power can be formulated: The balance of marital power is influenced by the interaction of (1) the comparative resources of husband and wife and (2) the cultural or subcultural expectations about the distribution of marital power. A similar statement, referring to the interaction of comparative resources and cultural expectations, can be made about the distribution of power in other areas.

EXCHANGE THEORY AND CULTURAL CONTEXT

The theory of exchange and reciprocity in social relationships has had a long history. Marcel Mauss, Howard Becker, Alvin W. Gouldner, John W. Thibaut and Harold H. Kelley, and George C. Homans, among others, have dealt with the idea of exchange and reciprocity in social interaction.[9] Heer has introduced exchange theory into the discussion of marital decision-making.[10] According to this position, the balance of power is related to the comparative value of the resources obtained within the marital relationship to the value of the resources that could be obtained in an exchange outside the marital relationship. The theory of resources proposed by Blood and

[9] Marcel Mauss, *The Gift*, translated by Ian Cunnison, New York: The Free Press, Macmillan, 1954; Howard Becker, *Man in Reciprocity*, New York: Praeger, 1956; Alvin W. Gouldner, "The Norm of Reciprocity: A Preliminary Statement," *American Sociological Review*, 25, No. 2 (April, 1960), 161–178; John W. Thibaut and Harold H. Kelley, *The Social Psychology of Groups*, New York: John Wiley, 1959; George C. Homans, *Social Behavior: Its Elementary Forms*, New York: Harcourt, Brace, 1961.

[10] David M. Heer, "The Measurement and Bases of Family Power: An Overview," *Marriage and Family Living*, 25, No. 2 (May, 1963), 133–139. See also Robert O. Blood, Jr., "The Measurement and Bases of Family Power: A Rejoinder," *Marriage and Family Living*, 25, No. 4 (November, 1963), 475–477; David M. Heer, "Reply," *Marriage and Family Living*, 25, No. 4 (November, 1963), 477–478.

Wolfe and the theory of exchange proposed by Heer are closely related. The former emphasizes the comparative resources each person brings to the marital relationship: the more resources a person has in comparison to his spouse, the more power he will have. Heer's emphasis is upon a comparison of the value of the resources obtained within the marital relationship to that obtainable outside. Since he explicitly relates this to the resources each spouse has available for exchanging, it is similar to the theory of resources. The more resources a person is contributing to the marital relationship, the more he generally stands to gain from an alternative relationship and, therefore, the more power he will be able to exercise within the marital relationship.

The important contributions by Heer and by Blood and Wolfe were based upon data for the United States and helped to illuminate that data.[11] The Greek and Yugoslavian data, however, cannot be dealt with in strictly "resource" or "exchange" terms. They add a comparative perspective to the discussion of marital power and permit a modification of earlier theoretical statements that specifically takes the cultural component into account. The theory of resources in cultural context, as elaborated here, is still highly tentative, and much remains to be done in getting measures of the strength of cultural expectations about authority or of the nature of the interaction between cultural expectations and comparative resources as they influence the distribution of power. Nevertheless, the data on the United States, France, Greece, and Yugoslavia represent an important step in the accumulation of comparative findings and provide an excellent point of departure for further work.

SITUATIONS, NORMS, AND BEHAVIOR

In an ad hoc and inductive way, a "theory of resources in cultural context" has been elaborated in order to place the findings on power structure in Detroit, Paris and Bordeaux, Athens, and Kragujevac into theoretical context. We found that the "theory of resources" was adequate for the Detroit data and somewhat less adequate for the Paris and Bordeaux data. In modifying the theory to account for the Greek and Yugoslavian data we have expanded its explanatory power. The "theory of resources in cultural context," inductively developed to account for the data from the United States, France, Greece, and Yugoslavia, requires further specification through testing on additional communities.

Now that we have developed the theory of resources in cultural context inductively, let us turn around and approach it deductively. A debate that once raged among psychologists had to do with whether behavior was an automatic reaction to stimulus influences or whether there were certain mediating processes in the organism between the stimulus and the behavior or response. A parallel debate among sociologists had to do with whether behavior was an automatic outcome of situational influences or whether there were certain

[11] For a discussion of some methodological issues in research on marital power structure and for additional references to data on the United States, see Heer, "The Measurement and Bases of Family Power: An Overview," op. cit.

mediating cultural processes that provided normative guide lines for behavior in particular environmental situations. Most psychologists realized that the naked stimulus was clothed in the prior experiential history of the organism, and in this sense the response was influenced by stimulus and organism inter-action. Most sociologists realized that the naked environmental situation was draped with normative guide lines and that behavior was influenced by the interaction between the situation and the norms. Similarly, to tie in the ad hoc theory we have developed, we might say that the naked theory of resources has to be set within a cultural context; in this way it is possible to state explicitly that decision-making behavior is influenced by the interaction be-tween resources and cultural definitions. In fact, of course, though the words and perspectives are different, the psychological S-O-R theory, the sociological theory of situation, norms, and behavior, and the theory of resources in cultural context are all getting at the same general formula for predicting behavioral outcomes. There is a stimulus or a situation; there is an organism with prior experience which may include learned cultural or normative dis-positions; and the response or behavior that ensues is influenced by these factors in interaction with each other.

A restatement of the findings in terms of the theory of behavior as a function of situation and norms summarizes several of the major arguments:

1. In the United States and France, the norms about marital decision-making have two major characteristics that are of special relevance. They tend to favor, in general, an equalitarian ethic, and they tend to be flexible about the precise degree of decision-making that should be exercised by husband or wife. As a result of this normative framework, the situation of interaction between husband and wife, including their comparative resources, comes into play and has an influence over the behavioral outcome.[12] As a result there are positive relationships between a husband's authority score and his occupation, and income.

2. In Greece and Yugoslavia the norms about marital decision-making are more patriarchal in character and less flexible. As a result, the normative guide lines place constraints upon the possible influence of situational condi-tions or resources. It is, therefore, among those groups that have learned "modern" norms regarding marital decision-making—such as groups at the higher educational levels—that there is the greatest possibility for the increased participation of women.

[12] But the fit between norms and behavior is not very good. See footnote 8. Cf., Irwin Deutscher, "Words and Deeds: Social Science and Social Policy," *Social Problems*, 13:3 (Winter, 1966), pp. 235–254; Irwin Deutscher, "Public vs. Private Opinions: The 'Real' and the 'Unreal,'" presented at the Eastern Sociological Society meetings, Philadelphia, April, 1966.

Five Kinds of Relationships

JOHN F. CUBER and PEGGY B. HARROFF

The qualitative aspects of enduring marital relationships vary enormously. The variations described to us were by no means random or clearly individualized, however. Five distinct life styles showed up repeatedly and the pairs within each of them were remarkably similar in the ways in which they lived together, found sexual expression, reared children, and made their way in the outside world.

The following classification is based on the interview materials of those people whose marriages had already lasted ten years or more and who said that they had never seriously considered divorce or separation. While 360 of the men and women had been married ten or more years to the same spouse, exclusion of those who reported that they had considered divorce reduced the number to 211. The discussion in this chapter is, then, based on 211 interviews: 107 men and 104 women.

The descriptions which our interviewees gave us took into account how they had behaved and also how they felt about their actions past and present. Examination of the important features of their lives revealed five recurring configurations of male-female life, each with a central theme—some prominent distinguishing psychological feature which gave each type its singularity. It is these preeminent characteristics which suggested the names for the relationships: the *Conflict-Habituated*, the *Devitalized*, the *Passive-Congenial*, the *Vital*, and the *Total*.

THE CONFLICT-HABITUATED

We begin with the conflict-habituated not because it is the most prevalent, but because the overt behavior patterns in it are so readily observed and because it presents some arresting contradictions. In this association there is much tension and conflict—although it is largely controlled. At worst, there is some private quarreling, nagging, and "throwing up the past" of which members of the immediate family, and more rarely close friends and relatives, have some awareness. At best, the couple is discreet and polite, genteel about it in the company of others—but after a few drinks at the cocktail party the verbal barbs begin to fly. The intermittent conflict is rarely concealed from the children, though we were often assured otherwise. "Oh, they're at it again—but they always are" says the high school son. There is private acknowledgment by both husband and wife as a rule that incompatibility is pervasive, that conflict is ever-potential, and that an atmosphere of tension permeates the togetherness.

An illustrative case concerns a physician of fifty, married for twenty-five years to the same woman, with two college-graduate children promisingly established in their own professions.

You know, it's funny; we have fought from the time we were in high school together. As I look back at it, I can't remember specific quarrels; it's more like a running guerrilla fight with intermediate periods, sometimes quite long, of pretty good fun and some damn good sex. In fact, if it hadn't been for the sex, we wouldn't have been married so quickly. Well, anyway, this has been going on ever since. . . . It's hard to know what it is we fight about most of the time. You name it and we'll fight about it. It's sometimes something I've said that she remembers differently, sometimes a decision —like what kind of car to buy or what to give the kids for Christmas. With regard to politics, and religion, and morals—oh, boy! You know, outside of the welfare of the kids—and that's just abstract—we don't really agree about anything. . . . At different times we take opposite sides—not deliberately; it just comes out that way.

Now these fights get pretty damned colorful. You called them arguments a little while ago—I have to correct you—they're brawls. There's never a bit of physical violence—at least not directed to each other—but the verbal gunfire gets pretty thick. Why, we've said things to each other that neither of us would think of saying in the hearing of anybody else. . . .

Of course we don't settle any of the issues. It's sort of a matter of principle *not* to. Because somebody would have to give in then and lose face for the next encounter. . . .

When I tell you this in this way, I feel a little foolish about it. I wouldn't tolerate such a condition in any other relationship in my life—and yet here I do and always have. . . .

No—we never have considered divorce or separation or anything so clear-cut. I realize that other people do, and I can't say that it has never occurred to either of us, but we've never considered it seriously.

A number of times there has been a crisis, like the time I was in the automobile accident, and the time she almost died in childbirth, and then I guess we really showed that we do care about each other. But as soon as the crisis is over, it's business as usual.

There is a subtle valence in these conflict-habituated relationships. It is easily missed in casual observation. So central is the necessity for channeling conflict and bridling hostility that these considerations come to preoccupy much of the interaction. Some psychiatrists have gone so far as to suggest that it is precisely the deep need to do psychological battle with one another which constitutes the cohesive factor insuring continuity of the marriage. Possibly so. But even from a surface point of view, the overt and manifest fact of habituated attention to handling tension, keeping it chained, and concealing it, is clearly seen as a dominant life force. And it can, and does for some, last for a whole lifetime.

THE DEVITALIZED

The key to the devitalized mode is the clear discrepancy between middle-aged reality and the earlier years. These people usually characterized themselves as having been "deeply in love" during the early years, as having spent a great deal of time together, having enjoyed sex, and most importantly of all, having had a close identification with one another. The present picture, with some variation from case to case, is in clear contrast—little time is spent together, sexual relationships are far less satisfying qualitatively or quantitatively, and interests and activities are not shared, at least not in the deeper and meaningful way they once were. Most of their time together now is "duty time"—entertaining together, planning and sharing activities with children, and participating in various kinds of required community responsibilities. They do as a rule retain, in addition to a genuine and mutual interest in the welfare of their children, a shared attention to their joint property and the husband's career. But even in the latter case the interest is contrasting. Despite a common dependency on his success and the benefits which flow therefrom, there is typically very little sharing of the intrinsic aspects of career—simply an acknowledgement of their mutual dependency on the fruits.

Two rather distinct subtypes of the devitalized take shape by the middle years. The following reflections of two housewives in their late forties illustrate both the common and the distinguishing features:

> Judging by the way it was when we were first married—say the first five years or so—things are pretty matter-of-fact now—even dull. They're dull between us, I mean. The children are a lot of fun, keep us pretty busy, and there are lots of outside things—you know, like Little League and the P.T.A. and the Swim Club, and even the company parties aren't always so bad. But I mean where Bob and I are concerned—if you followed us around, you'd wonder why we ever got *married.* We take each other for granted. We laugh at the same things sometimes, but we don't really laugh together—the way we used to. But, as he said to me the other night—with one or two under the belt, I think—"You know, you're still a little fun now and then." . . .
>
> Now, I don't say this to complain, not in the least. There's a cycle to life. There are things you do in high school. And different things you do in college. Then you're a young adult. And then you're middle-aged. That's where we are now. . . . I'll admit that I do yearn for the old days when sex was a big thing and going out was fun and I hung on to everything he said about his work and his ideas as if they were coming from a genius or something. But then you get the children and other responsibilities. I have the home and Bob has a tremendous burden of responsibility at the office. . . . He's completely responsible for setting up the new branch now. . . . You have to adjust to these things and we both try to gracefully. . . . Anniversaries though do sometimes remind you kind of hard. . . .

The other kind of hindsight from a woman in a devitalized relationship is much less accepting and quiescent:

I know I'm fighting it. I ought to accept that it has to be like this, but I don't like it, and I'd do almost anything to bring back the exciting way of living we had at first. Most of my friends think I'm some kind of a sentimental romantic or something—they tell me to act my age—but I do know some people—not very darn many—who are our age and even older, who still have the same kind of excitement about them and each other that we had when we were all in college. I've seen some of them at parties and other places—the way they look at each other, the little touches as they go by. One couple has grandchildren and you'd think they were honeymooners. I don't think it's just sex either—I think they are just part of each other's lives—and when I think of us and the numb way we sort of stagger through the weekly routine, I could scream. And I've even thought of doing some pretty desperate things to try to build some joy and excitement into my life. I've given up on Phil. He's too content with his balance sheets and the kids' report cards and the new house we're going to build next year. He keeps saying he has everything in life that any man could want. What do you *do*?

Regardless of the gracefulness of the acceptance, or the lack thereof, the common plight prevails: on the subjective, emotional dimension, the relationship has become a void. The original zest is gone. There is typically little overt tension or conflict, but the interplay between the pair has become apathetic, lifeless. No serious threat to the continuity of the marriage is generally acknowledged, however. It is intended, usually by both, that it continue indefinitely despite its numbness. Continuity and relative freedom from open conflict are fostered in part because of the comforts of the "habit cage." Continuity is further insured by the absence of any engaging alternative, "all things considered." It is also reinforced, sometimes rather decisively, by legal and ecclesiastical requirements and expectations. These people quickly explain that "there are other things in life" which are worthy of sustained human effort.

This kind of relationship is exceedingly common. Persons in this circumstance frequently make comparisons with other pairs they know, many of whom are similar to themselves. This fosters the comforting judgment that "marriage is like this—except for a few oddballs or pretenders who claim otherwise."

While these relationships lack visible vitality, the participants assure us that there is "something there." There are occasional periods of sharing at least something—if only memory. Even formalities can have meanings. Anniversaries can be celebrated, if a little grimly, for what they once commemorated. As one man said, "Tomorrow we are celebrating the anniversary of our anniversary." Even clearly substandard sexual expression is said by some to be better than nothing, or better than a clandestine substitute. A "good man" or a "good mother for the kids" may "with a little affection and occasional attention now and then, get you by." Many believe that the devitalized mode is the appropriate mode in which a man and woman should be content to live in the middle years and later.

THE PASSIVE-CONGENIAL

The passive-congenial mode has a great deal in common with the devital-ized, the essential difference being that the passivity which pervades the association has been there from the start. The devitalized have a more exciting set of memories; the passive-congenials give little evidence that they had ever hoped for anything much different from what they are currently experiencing.

There is therefore little suggestion of disillusionment or compulsion to make believe to anyone. Existing modes of association are comfortably ade-quate—no stronger words fit the facts as they related them to us. There is little conflict, although some admit that they tiptoe rather gingerly over and around a residue of subtle resentments and frustrations. In their better moods they remind themselves (and each other) that "there are many common interests" which they both enjoy. "We both like classical music." "We agree completely on religious and political matters." "We both love the country and our quaint exurban neighbors." "We are both lawyers."

The wife of a prominent attorney, who has been living in the passive-congenial mode for thirty years, put her description this way:

We have both always tried to be calm and sensible about major life deci-sions, to think things out thoroughly and in perspective. Len and I knew each other since high school but didn't start to date until college. When he asked me to marry him, I took a long time to decide whether he was the right man for me and I went into his family background, because I wasn't just marrying him; I was choosing a father for my children. We decided together not to get married until he was established, so that we would not have to live in dingy little apartments like some of our friends who got married right out of college. This prudence has stood us in good stead too. Life has moved ahead for us with remarkable orderliness and we are deeply grateful for the foresight we had. . . .

When the children were little, we scheduled time together with them, although since they're grown, the demands of the office are getting pretty heavy. Len brings home a bulging briefcase almost every night and more often than not the light is still on in his study after I retire. But we've got a lot to show for his devoted effort. . . .

I don't like all this discussion about sex—even in the better magazines. I hope your study will help to put it in its proper perspective. I expected to perform sex in marriage, but both before and since, I'm willing to admit that it's a much overrated activity. Now and then, perhaps it's better. I am fortunate, I guess, because my husband has never been demanding about it, before marriage or since. It's just not that important to either of us. . . .

My time is very full these days, with the chairmanship of the Cancer Drive, and the Executive Board of the (state) P.T.A. I feel a little funny about that with my children already grown, but there are the grandchildren coming along. And besides so many of my friends are in the organizations, and it's so much like a home-coming.

People make their way into the passive-congenial mode by two quite different routes—by default and by intention. Perhaps in most instances they arrive at this way of living and feeling by drift. There is so little which they have cared about deeply in each other that a passive relationship is sufficient to express it all. In other instances the passive-congenial mode is a deliberately intended arrangement for two people whose interests and creative energies are directed elsewhere than toward the pairing—into careers, or in the case of women, into children or community activities. They say they know this and want it this way. These people simply do not wish to invest their total emotional involvement and creative effort in the male-female relationship.

The passive-congenial life style fits societal needs quite well also, and this is an important consideration. The man of practical affairs, in business, government service, or the professions—quite obviously needs "to have things peaceful at home" and to have a minimum of distraction as he pursues his important work. He may feel both love and gratitude toward the wife who fits this mode.

A strong case was made for the passive-congenial by a dedicated physician:

I don't know why everyone seems to make so much about men and women and marriage. Of course, I'm married and if anything happened to my wife, I'd get married again. I think it's the proper way to live. It's convenient, orderly, and solves a lot of problems. But there are other things in life. I spent nearly ten years preparing for the practice of my profession. The biggest thing to me is the practice of that profession, to be of assistance to my patients and their families. I spend twelve hours a day at it. And I'll bet if you talked with my wife, you wouldn't get any of that "trapped housewife" stuff from her either. Now that the children are grown, she finds a lot of useful and necessary work to do in this community. She works as hard as I do.

The passive-congenial mode facilitates the achievement of other goals too. It enables people who desire a considerable amount of personal independence and freedom to realize it with a minimum of inconvenience from or to the spouse. And it certainly spares the participants in it from the need to give a great deal of personal attention to "adjusting to the spouse's needs." The passive-congenial ménage is thus a mood as well as a mode.

Our descriptions of the devitalized and the passive-congenials have been similar because these two modes are much alike in their overt characteristics. The participants' evaluations of their *present situations* are likewise largely the same—the accent on "other things," the emphasis on civic and professional responsibilities, the importance of property, children, and reputation. The essential difference lies in their diverse histories and often in their feelings of contentment with their current lives. The passive-congenials had from the start a life pattern and a set of expectations essentially consistent with what they are now experiencing. When the devitalized reflect, however, when they juxtapose history against present reality, they often see the barren gullies in their lives left by the erosions of earlier satisfactions. Some of the devitalized are resentful and disillusioned—their bitterness will appear at various points throughout this book; others, calling themselves "mature about it," have emerged with reasonable acceptance of their existing devitalized modes. Still others are clearly ambivalent, "I wish life would be more exciting, but I should have known it couldn't last. In a way, it's calm and quiet and reassuring this way, but there are times when I get very ill at ease—sometimes downright mad. Does it *have* to be like this?"

The passive-congenials do not find it necessary to speculate in this fashion. Their anticipations were realistic and perhaps even causative of their current marital situation. In any event, their passivity is not jarred when teased by memory.

THE VITAL

In extreme contrast to the three foregoing is the vital relationship. The vital pair can easily be overlooked as they move through their worlds of work, recreation, and family activities. They do the same things, publicly at least; and when talking for public consumption say the same things—they are proud of their homes, love their children, gripe about their jobs, while being quite proud of their career accomplishments. But when the close, intimate, confidential, empathic look is taken, the essence of the vital relationship becomes clear: the mates are intensely bound together psychologically in important life matters. Their sharing and their togetherness is genuine. It provides the life essence for both man and woman.

> The things we do together aren't fun intrinsically—the ecstasy comes from being *together in the doing.* Take her out of the picture and I wouldn't give a damn for the boat, the lake, or any of the fun that goes on out there.

The presence of the mate is indispensable to the feelings of satisfaction which the activity provides. The activities shared by the vital pairs may involve almost anything: hobbies, careers, community service. Anything—so long as it is closely shared.

It is hard to escape the word *vitality*—exciting mutuality of feelings and participation together in important life segments. The clue that the relationship is vital (rather than merely expressing the joint activity) derives from the feeling that it is important. An activity is flat and uninteresting if the spouse is not a part of it.

Other valued things are readily sacrificed in order to enhance life within the vital relationship.

> I cheerfully, and that's putting it mildly, passed up two good promotions because one of them would have required some traveling and the other would have taken evenings and weekend time—and that's when Pat and I *live.* The hours with her (after twenty-two years of marriage) are what I live for. You should meet her. . . .

People in the vital relationship for the most part know that they are a minority and that their life styles are incomprehensible to most of their associates.

Most of our friends think we moved out to the country for the kids; well—the kids *are* crazy about it, but the fact of the matter is, we moved out for ourselves—just to get away from all the annoyances and interferences of other people—our friends actually. We like this kind of life—where we can have almost all of our time together. . . . We've been married for over twenty years and the most enjoyable thing either of us does—well, outside of the intimate things—is to sit and talk by the hour. That's why we built that imposing fireplace—and the hi-fi here in the corner. . . . Now that Ed is getting older, that twenty-seven-mile drive morning and night from the office is a real burden, but he does it cheerfully so we can have our long uninterrupted hours together. . . . The children respect this too. They don't invade our privacy any more than they can help—the same as we vacate the living room when Ellen brings in a date, she tries not to intrude on us. . . . Being the specialized kind of lawyer he is, I can't share much in his work, but that doesn't bother either of us. The *big* part of our lives is completely mutual. . . .

Her husband's testimony validated hers. And we talked to dozens of other couples like them, too. They find their central satisfaction in the life they live with and through each other. It consumes their interest and dominates their thoughts and actions. All else is subordinate and secondary. This does not mean that people in vital relationships lose their separate identities, that they may not upon occasion be rivalrous or competitive with one another, or that conflict may not occur. They differ fundamentally from the conflict-habituated, however, in that when conflict does occur, it results from matters that are important to them, such as which college a daughter or son is to attend; it is devoid of the trivial "who said what first and when" and "I can't forget when you. . . ." A further difference is that people to whom the relationship is vital tend to settle disagreements quickly and seek to avoid conflict, whereas the conflict-habituated look forward to conflict and appear to operate by a tacit rule that no conflict is ever to be truly terminated and that the spouse must never be considered right. The two kinds of conflict are thus radically different. To confuse them is to miss an important differentiation.

THE TOTAL

The total relationship is like the vital relationship with the important addition that it is more multifaceted. The points of vital meshing are more numerous—in some cases all of the important life foci are vitally shared. In one such marriage the husband is an internationally known scientist. For thirty years his wife has been his "friend, mistress, and partner." He still goes home at noon whenever possible, at considerable inconvenience, to have a quiet lunch and spend a conversational hour or so with his wife. They refer to these conversations as "our little seminars." They feel comfortable with each other and with their four grown children. The children (now in their late twenties) say that they enjoy visits with their parents as much as they do with friends of their own age.

There is practically no pretense between persons in the total relationship or between them and the world outside. There are few areas of tension, because the items of difference which have arisen over the years have been settled as they arose. There often *were* serious differences of opinion but they were handled, sometimes by compromise, sometimes by one or the other yielding; but these outcomes were of secondary importance because the primary consideration was not who was right or who was wrong, only how the problem could be resolved without tarnishing the relationship. When faced with differences, they can and do dispose of the difficulties without losing their feeling of unity or their sense of the vitality and centrality of their relationship. This is the mainspring.

The various parts of the total relationship are reinforcing, as we learned from this consulting engineer who is frequently sent abroad by his corporation.

> She keeps my files and scrapbooks up to date. . . . I invariably take her with me to conferences around the world. Her femininity, easy charm and wit are invaluable assets to me. I know it's conventional to say that a man's wife is responsible for his success and I also know that it's often not true. But in my case I gladly acknowledge that it's not only true, but she's indispensable to me. But she'd go along with me even if there was nothing for her to do because we just enjoy each other's company—deeply. You know, the best part of a vacation is not *what* we do, but that we do it together. We plan it and reminisce about it and weave it into our work and other play all the time.

The wife's account is substantially the same except that her testimony demonstrates more clearly the genuineness of her "help."

> It seems to me that Bert exaggerates my help. It's not so much that I only want to help him; it's more that I want to do those things anyway. We do them together, even though we may not be in each other's presence at the time. I don't really know what I do for him and what I do for me.

This kind of relationship is rare, in marriage or out, but it does exist and can endure. We occasionally found relationships so total that all aspects of life were mutually shared and enthusiastically participated in. It is as if neither spouse has, or has had, a truly private existence.

The customary purpose of a classification such as this one is to facilitate understanding of similarities and differences among the cases classified. In this instance enduring marriage is the common condition. The differentiating features are the dissimilar forces which make for the integration of the pair within each of the types. It is not necessarily the purpose of a classification to make possible a clear-cut sorting of all cases into one or another of the designated categories. All cannot be so precisely pigeonholed; there often are borderline cases. Furthermore, two observers with equal access to the facts may sometimes disagree on which side of the line an unclear case should be placed. If the classification is a useful one, however, placement should *as a rule* be clear and relatively easy. The ease is only relative because making an accurate classification of a given relationship requires the possession of amounts and kinds of information which one rarely has about persons other than himself. Superficial knowledge of public or professional behavior is not enough. And even in his own case, one may, for reasons of ego, find it difficult to be totally forthright.

A further caution. The typology concerns relationships, not personalities. A clearly vital person may be living in a passive-congenial or devitalized relationship and expressing his vitality in some other aspect of his life—career being an important preoccupation for many. Or, possibly either or both of the spouses may have a vital relationship—sometimes extending over many years—with someone of the opposite sex outside of the marriage.

Nor are the five types to be interpreted as *degrees* of marital happiness or adjustment. Persons in all five are currently adjusted and most say that they are content, if not happy. Rather, the five types represent *different kinds of adjustment* and *different conceptions of marriage.* This is an important concept which must be emphasized if one is to understand the personal meanings which these people attach to the conditions of their marital experience.

Neither are the five types necessarily stages in a cycle of initial bliss and later disillusionment. Many pairings started in the passive-congenial stage; in fact, quite often people intentionally enter into a marriage for the acknowledged purpose of living this kind of relationship. To many the simple amenities of the "habit cage" are not disillusionments or even disappointments, but rather are sensible life expectations which provide an altogether comfortable and rational way of having a "home base" for their lives. And many of the conflict-habituated told of courtship histories essentially like their marriages.

While each of these types tends to persist, there *may* be movement from one type to another as circumstances and life perspectives change. This movement may go in any direction from any point, and a given couple may change categories more than once. Such changes are relatively *in*frequent, however, and the important point is that relationship types tend to persist over relatively long periods.

The fundamental nature of these contexts may be illustrated by examining the impact of some common conditions on persons in each type.

Infidelity, for example, occurs in most of the five types, the total relationship being the exception. But it occurs for quite different reasons. In the conflict-habituated it seems frequently to be only another outlet for hostility. The call girl and the woman picked up in a bar are more than just available women; they are symbols of resentment of the wife. This is not always so, but reported to us often enough to be worth noting. Infidelity among the passive-congenial, on the other hand, is typically in line with the stereotype of the middle-aged man who "strays out of sheer boredom with the uneventful, deadly prose" of his private life. And the devitalized man or woman frequently is trying for an hour or a year to recapture the lost mood. But the vital are sometimes adulterous too; some are simply emancipated—almost bohemian. To some of them sexual aggrandizement is an accepted fact of life. Frequently the infidelity is condoned by the partner and in some instances even provides an indirect (through empathy) kind of gratification. The act of infidelity in such cases is not construed as disloyalty or as a threat to continuity, but rather as a kind of basic human right which the loved one ought to be permitted to have—and which the other perhaps wants also for himself.

Divorce and separation are found in all five of the types, but the reasons, when viewed realistically and outside of the simplitudes of legalistic and ecclesiastical fiction, are highly individual and highly variable. For example, a couple may move from a vital relationship to divorce because for them the alternative of a devitalized relationship is unendurable. They can conceive of marriage only as a vital, meaningful, fulfilling, and preoccupying interaction. The "disvitality" of any other marriage form is abhorrent to them and takes on "the hypocrisy of living a public lie." We have accounts of marriages which were unquestionably vital or total for a period of years but which were dissolved. In some respects relationships of this type are more readily disrupted because these people have become adjusted to such a rich and deep sharing that evidences of breach, which a person in another type of marriage might consider quite normal, become unbearable.

I know a lot of close friendships occur between men and women married to someone else, and that they're not always adulterous. But I know Betty—and anyway, I personally believe they eventually do become so, but I can't be sure about that. Anyway, when Betty found her self-expression was furthered by longer and longer meetings and conversations with Joe, and I detected little insincerities, not serious at first, you understand, creeping into the things we did together, it was like the little leak in the great dike. It didn't take very long. We weren't melodramatic about it, but it was soon clear to both of us that we were no longer the kind of pair we once were, so why pretend. The whole thing can go to hell fast—and after almost twenty years!

Husbands in other types of relationships would probably not even have detected any disloyalty on the part of this wife. And even if they had, they would tend to conclude that "you don't break up a home just because she has a passing interest in some glamorous writer."

The divorce which occurs in the passive-congenial marriage follows a different sequence. One of the couple, typically a person capable of more vitality in his or her married life than the existing relationship provides, comes into contact with a person with whom he gradually (or suddenly) unfolds a new dimension to adult living. What he had considered to be a rational and sensible and "adult" relationship can suddenly appear in contrast to be stultifying, shallow, and an altogether disheartening way to live out the remaining years. He is left with "no conceivable alternative but to move out." Typically, he does not do so impulsively or without a more or less stubborn attempt to stifle his "romanticism" and listen to well-documented advice to the effect that he should act maturely and "leave the romantic yearning to the kids for whom it is intended." Very often he is convinced and turns his back on his "new hope"—but not always.

Whether examining marriages for the satisfactions and fulfillments they have brought or for the frustrations and pain, the overriding influence of life style—or as we have here called it, relationship type—is of the essence.

Such a viewpoint helps the observer, and probably the participant, to understand some of the apparent enigmas about men and women in marriage—why infidelities destroy some marriages and not others; why conflict plays so large a role for some couples and is so negligible for others; why some seemingly well-suited and harmoniously adjusted spouses seek divorce while others with provocations galore remain solidly together; why affections, sexual expression, recreation, almost everything observable about men and women is so radically different from pair to pair. All of these are not merely different objectively; they are perceived differently by the pairs, are differently reacted to, and differently attended to.

If nothing else, this chapter has demonstrated that realistic understanding of marital relationships requires use of concepts which are carefully based on perceptive factual knowledge. Unfortunately, the language by which relationships between men and women are conventionally expressed tends to lead toward serious and pervasive deceptions which in turn encourage erroneous inferences. Thus, we tend to assume that enduring marriage is somehow synonymous with happy marriage or at least with something comfortably called adjustment. The deception springs from lumping together such dissimilar modes of thought and action as the conflict-habituated, the passive-congenial, and the vital. To know that a marriage has endured, or for that matter has been dissolved, tells one close to nothing about the kinds of experiences, fulfillments, and frustrations which have made up the lives of the people involved. Even to know, for example, that infidelity has occured, without knowledge of circumstances, feelings, and other essences, results in an illusion of knowledge which masks far more than it describes.

To understand a given marriage, let alone what is called "marriage in general," is realistically possible only in terms of particular sets of experiences, meanings, hopes, and intentions. This chapter has described in broad outline five manifest and recurring configurations among the Significant Americans.

|VII| The Impact of Parenthood

Introduction to Section VII

The basic romantic myth in America is not in connection with boy-girl relation-ships but with parent-child relationships. Our courtship interaction is systematic and cumulative, as Broderick (5) and others[1] have shown. But our preparation for parenthood is neither systematic nor cumulative. In short, we become parents with a great deal of naivete regarding what is involved in such roles and how parenthood will affect our marital roles. This theme is well developed by Alice Rossi in the first reading (20) in this section. The reader should note that Rossi makes some interesting comments on the instrumental and expressive foci of the parenthood role, which are relevant to the readings on marital roles in Section VI. One provocative and perhaps debatable point she makes is that in parenthood women, more than men, are involved in instrumental decision-making, whereas men are more involved in the expressive, affectional aspects of parenthood. The reader may want to keep this article of Rossi's in mind when reading her article on feminism in Section XII as well as the articles on marital roles in Section VI.

One area that may experience the impact of the parenthood role is marital satisfaction. Parenthood can take so much of one's time and energy that it inter-feres with the mutual satisfaction of huband and wife. Rollins and Feldman reviewed the literature and reported a well-executed study of their own.[2] The results, as in most cases, do not unequivocally support a simple one-way answer regarding the impact of parenthood. Instead the data specify the conditions under which parenthood has an impact on marital satisfaction. Among other

---

[1] Reiss, I. L., *The Social Context of Premarital Sexual Permissiveness.* Holt, Rinehart and Winston, 1967, Chapters 7 and 9.

[2] Rollins, B. C., and H. Feldman, "Marital Satisfaction over the Family Life Cycle." *Journal of Marriage and the Family*, 32 (February, 1970), 20–28.

things, they find that such an impact is felt more by wives than by husbands. Science proceeds toward its goal of explanation via studies such as this that spell out the specific ways in which the phenomena under study operate.

By now the reader should be becoming aware of the ways in which research qualifies answers to empirical questions, and in doing so, raises new questions and the need for additional research. This specification is nowhere more apparent than in the study of working and nonworking mothers by Yarrow and her colleagues (21). They report that, in terms of impact on quality of child rearing, a mother's satisfaction with what she is doing and her educational level seem more important than whether she is working. It will pay the reader to examine carefully the tables in this article, for they embody a well-executed research design using "controls," that is, a division of the population studied into subgroups (by education, dissatisfaction with work, and so on) so that the researchers can examine the importance of such subdivisions on the phenomenon under study. The same design of "controls" can be found in many articles in this reader, but this one in particular presents it in a very useful pedagogical fashion.

In this section, as in all 12 sections, there is no intention of completely covering the area discussed. At best, I have tried to select a few provocative articles that present important thinking and research data on the area. The references in these articles, and those in whatever text the class is using, can be utilized to supplement the readings included. In this way the reader may choose which sections he or she would like to become more familiar with. This section on parenthood is one that I believe would be most rewarding to follow up with additional readings, for it is relevant to each of our lives and also quite central to sociological thinking regarding small groups, generational change, and role conflict.

Transition to Parenthood

ALICE S. ROSSI

THE PROBLEM

The central concern in this sociological analysis of parenthood will be with two closely related questions. (1) What is involved in the transition to parenthood: what must be learned and what readjustments of other role commitments must take place in order to move smoothly through the transition from a childless married state to parenthood? (2) What is the effect of parenthood on the adult: in what ways do parents, and in particular mothers, change as a result of their parental experiences?

To get a firmer conceptual handle on the problem, I shall first specify the stages in the development of the parental role and then explore several of the most salient features of the parental role by comparing it with the two other major adult social roles—the marital and work role. Throughout the discussion, special attention will be given to the social changes that have taken place during the past few decades which facilitate or complicate the transition to and the experience of parenthood among young American adults.

FROM CHILD TO PARENT: AN EXAMPLE

What is unique about this perspective on parenthood is the focus on the adult parent rather than the child. Until quite recent years, concern in the behavioral sciences with the parent-child relationship has been confined almost exclusively to the child. Whether a psychological study such as Ferreira's on the influence of the pregnant woman's attitude to maternity upon postnatal behavior of the neonate,[1] Sears and Maccoby's survey of child-rearing practices,[2] or Brody's detailed observations of mothering,[3] the long

[1] Antonio J. Ferreira, "The Pregnant Woman's Emotional Attitude and its Reflection on the Newborn," *American Journal of Orthopsychiatry*, 30 (1960), 553–561.

[2] Robert Sears, E. Maccoby, and H. Levin, *Patterns of Child-Rearing*, Evanston, Illinois: Row, Peterson, 1957.

[3] Sylvia Brody, *Patterns of Mothering: Maternal Influences During Infancy*, New York: International Universities Press, 1956.

Paper presented to the American Orthopsychiatric Association, Washington, D.C., March 22, 1967. Grateful acknowledgment is made to the National Institutes of Health, sponsor of my work under a Research Career Development Award (USPHS-K3-MH23768), and to my friend and former colleague Bernice Neugarten, at the University of Chicago, whose support and stimulation were critical in supplementing my sociological training with the human development perspective.

Reprinted from the *Journal of Marriage and the Family*, 30, No. 1 (February, 1968), 26–39, by permission of the National Council on Family Relations.

tradition of studies of maternal deprivation[4] and more recently of maternal employment,[5] the child has been the center of attention. The design of such research has assumed that, if enough were known about what parents were like and what they in fact did in rearing their children, much of the variation among children could be accounted for.[6]

The very different order of questions which emerge when the parent replaces the child as the primary focus of analytic attention can best be shown with an illustration. Let us take, as our example, the point Benedek makes that the child's need for mothering is *absolute* while the need of an adult woman to mother is *relative*.[7] From a concern for the child, this discrepancy in need leads to an analysis of the impact on the child of separation from the mother or inadequacy of mothering. Family systems that provide numerous adults to care for the young child can make up for this discrepancy in need between mother and child, which may be why ethnographic accounts give little evidence of postpartum depression following childbirth in simpler societies. Yet our family system of isolated households, increasingly distant from kinswomen to assist in mothering, requires that new mothers shoulder total responsibility for the infant precisely for that stage of the child's life when his need for mothering is far in excess of the mother's need for the child.

From the perspective of the mother, the question has therefore become: what does maternity deprive her of? Are the intrinsic gratifications of maternity sufficient to compensate for shelving or reducing a woman's involvement in non-family interests and social roles? The literature on maternal deprivation cannot answer such questions, because the concept, even in the careful specification Yarrow has given it,[8] has never meant anything but the effect on the child of various kinds of insufficient mothering. Yet what has been seen as a failure or inadequacy of individual women may in fact be a failure of the society to provide institutionalized substitutes for the extended kin to assist in the care of infants and young children. It may be

[4] Leon J. Yarrow, "Maternal Deprivation: Toward an Empirical and Conceptual Re-evaluation," *Psychological Bulletin*, 58, No. 6 (1961), 459–490.

[5] F. Ivan Nye and L. W. Hoffman, *The Employed Mother in America*, Chicago: Rand McNally, 1963; Alice S. Rossi, "Equality Between the Sexes: An Immodest Proposal," *Daedalus*, 93, No. 2 (1964), 607–652.

[6] The younger the child, the more was this the accepted view. It is only in recent years that research has paid any attention to the initiating role of the infant in the development of his attachment to maternal and other adult figures, as in Ainsworth's research which showed that infants become attached to the mother, not solely because she is instrumental in satisfying their primary visceral drives, but through a chain of behavioral interchange between the infant and the mother, thus supporting Bowlby's rejection of the secondary drive theory of the infant's ties to his mother. Mary D. Ainsworth, "Patterns of Attachment Behavior shown by the Infant in interaction with his mother," *Merrill-Palmer Quarterly*, 10, No. 1 (1964), 51–58; John Bowlby, "The nature of the child's tie to his mother," *International Journal of Psychoanalysis*, 39 (1958), 1–34.

[7] Therese Benedek, "Parenthood as a Developmental Phase," *Journal of American Psychoanalytic Association*, 7, No. 8 (1959), 389–417.

[8] Yarrow, op. cit.

that the role requirements of maternity in the American family system extract too high a price of deprivation for young adult women reared with highly diversified interests and social expectations concerning adult life. Here, as at several points in the course of this paper, familiar problems take on a new and suggestive research dimension when the focus is on the parent rather than the child.

BACKGROUND

Since it is a relatively recent development to focus on the parent side of the parent-child relationship, some preliminary attention to the emergence of this focus on parenthood is in order. Several developments in the behavioral sciences paved the way to this perspective. Of perhaps most importance have been the development of ego psychology and the problem of adaptation of Murray[9] and Hartmann,[10] the interpersonal focus of Sullivan's psychoanalytic theories,[11] and the life cycle approach to identity of Erikson.[12] These have been fundamental to the growth of the human development perspective: that personality is not a stable given but a constantly changing phenomenon, that the individual changes along the life line as he lives through critical life experiences. The transition to parenthood, or the impact of parenthood upon the adult, is part of the heightened contemporary interest in adult socialization.

A second and related development has been the growing concern of behavioral scientists with crossing levels of analysis to adequately comprehend social and individual phenomena and to build theories appropriate to a complex social system. In the past, social anthropologists focused as purely on the level of prescriptive normative variables as psychologists had concentrated on intrapsychic processes at the individual level or sociologists on social-structural and institutional variables. These are adequate, perhaps, when societies are in a stable state of equilibrium and the social sciences were at early stages of conceptual development, but they become inadequate when the societies we study are undergoing rapid social change and we have an increasing amount of individual and subgroup variance to account for.

Psychology and anthropology were the first to join theoretical forces in their concern for the connections between culture and personality. The question of how culture is transmitted across the generations and finds its manifestations in the personality structure and social roles of the individual has brought renewed research attention to the primary institutions of the family and the schools, which provide the intermediary contexts through which culture is transmitted and built into personality structure.

[9] Henry A. Murray, *Explorations in Personality*, New York: Oxford University Press, 1938.

[10] Heinz Hartmann, *Ego Psychology and the Problem of Adaptation*, New York: International Universities Press, 1958.

[11] Patrick Mullahy (ed.), *The Contributions of Harry Stack Sullivan*, New York: Hermitage House, 1952.

[12] E. Erikson, "Identity and the Life Cycle: Selected Papers," *Psychological Issues*, 1 (1959), 1–171.

It is no longer possible for a psychologist or a therapist to neglect the social environment of the individual subject or patient, nor is the "family" they are concerned with any longer confined to the family of origin, for current theory and therapy view the adult individual in the context of his current family of procreation. So too it is no longer possible for the sociologist to focus exclusively on the current family relationships of the individual. The incorporation of psychoanalytic theory into the informal, if not the formal, training of the sociologist has led to an increasing concern for the quality of relationships in the family of origin as determinants of the adult attitudes, values, and behavior which the sociologist studies.

Quite another tradition of research has led to the formulation of "normal crises of parenthood." "Crisis" research began with the studies of individuals undergoing traumatic experiences, such as that by Tyhurst on natural catastrophes,[13] Caplan on parental responses to premature births,[14] Lindemann on grief and bereavement,[15] and Janis on surgery.[16] In these studies attention was on differential response to stress—how and why individuals vary in the ease with which they coped with the stressful experience and achieved some reintegration. Sociological interest has been piqued as these studies were built upon by Rhona and Robert Rapoport's research on the honeymoon and the engagement as normal crises in the role transitions to marriage and their theoretical attempt to build a conceptual bridge between family and occupational research from a "transition task" perspective.[17] LeMasters, Dyer, and Hobbs have each conducted studies of parenthood precisely as a crisis or disruptive event in family life.[18]

I think, however, that the time is now ripe to drop the concept of "normal

[13] J. Tyhurst, "Individual Reactions to Community Disaster," *American Journal of Psychiatry*, 107 (1951), 764–769.

[14] G. Caplan, "Patterns of Parental Response to the Crisis of Premature Birth: A Preliminary Approach to Modifying the Mental Health Outcome," *Psychiatry*, 23 (1960), 365–374.

[15] E. Lindemann, "Symptomatology and Management of Acute Grief," *American Journal of Psychiatry*, 101 (1944), 141–148.

[16] Irving Janis, *Psychological Stress*, New York: John Wiley, 1958.

[17] Rhona Rapoport, "Normal Crises, Family Structure and Mental Health," *Family Process*, 2, No. 1 (1963), 68–80; Rhona Rapoport and Robert Rapoport, "New Light on the Honeymoon," *Human Relations*, 17, No. 1 (1964), 33–56; Rhona Rapoport, "The Transition from Engagement to Marriage," *Acta Sociologica*, 8, fasc. 1–2 (1964), 36–55; and Robert Rapoport and Rhona Rapoport, "Work and Family in Contemporary Society," *American Sociological Review*, 30, No. 3 (1965), 381–394.

[18] E. E. LeMasters, "Parenthood as Crisis," *Marriage and Family Living*, 19 (1957), 352–355; Everett D. Dyer, "Parenthood as Crisis: A Re-Study," *Marriage and Family Living*, 25 (1963), 196–201; and Daniel F. Hobbs, Jr., "Parenthood as Crisis: A Third Study," *Journal of Marriage and the Family*, 27, No. 3 (1963), 367–372. LeMasters and Dyer both report the first experience of parenthood involves extensive to severe crises in the lives of their young parent respondents. Hobbs's study does not show first parenthood to be a crisis experience, but this may be due to the fact that his couples have very young (seven-week-old) first babies and are therefore still experiencing the euphoric honeymoon stage of parenthood.

crises" and to speak directly, instead, of the transition to and impact of parenthood. There is an uncomfortable incongruity in speaking of any crisis as normal. If the transition is achieved and if a successful reintegration of personality or social roles occurs, then crisis is a misnomer. To confine attention to "normal crises" suggests, even if it is not logically implied, successful outcome, thus excluding from our analysis the deviant instances in which failure occurs.

Sociologists have been just as prone as psychologists to dichotomize normality and pathology. We have had one set of theories to deal with deviance, social problems, and conflict and quite another set in theoretical analyses of a normal system—whether a family or a society. In the latter case our theories seldom include categories to cover deviance, strain, dysfunction, or failure. Thus, Parsons and Bales' systems find "task-leaders" oriented to problem solution, but not instrumental leaders attempting to undercut or destroy the goal of the group, and "sociometric stars" who play a positive integrative function in cementing ties among group members, but not negatively expressive persons with hostile aims of reducing or destroying such intragroup ties.[19]

Parsons' analysis of the experience of parenthood as a step in maturation and personality growth does not allow for negative outcome. In this view either parents show little or no positive impact upon themselves of their parental role experiences, or they show a new level of maturity. Yet many women, whose interests and values made a congenial combination of wifehood and work role, may find that the addition of maternal responsibilities has the consequence of a fundamental and undesired change in both their relationships to their husbands and their involvements outside the family. Still other women, who might have kept a precarious hold on adequate functioning as adults had they *not* become parents, suffer severe retrogression with pregnancy and childbearing, because the reactivation of older unresolved

---

[19] Parsons' theoretical analysis of the family system builds directly on Bales's research on small groups. The latter are typically comprised of volunteers willing to attempt the single task put to the group. This positive orientation is most apt to yield the empirical discovery of "sociometric stars" and "task leaders," least apt to sensitize the researcher or theorist to the effect of hostile nonacceptance of the group task. Talcott Parsons and R. F. Bales, *Family, Socialization and Interaction Process*, New York: The Free Press, Macmillan, 1955.

Yet the same limited definition of the key variables is found in the important attempts by Straus to develop the theory that every social system, as every personality, requires a circumplex model with two independent axes of authority and support. His discussion and examples indicate a variable definition with limited range: support is defined as High (+) or Low (−), but "low" covers both the absence of high support and the presence of negative support; there is love or neutrality in this system, but not hate. Applied to actual families, this groups destructive mothers with low-supportive mothers, much as the non-authoritarian pole on the Authoritarian Personality Scale includes both mere non-authoritarians and vigorously anti-authoritarian personalities. Murray A. Straus, "Power and Support Structure of the Family in Relation to Socialization," *Journal of Marriage and the Family*, 26, No. 3 (1964), 318–326.

conflicts with their own mothers is not favorably resolved but in fact leads to personality deterioration[20] and the transmission of pathology to their children.[21]

Where cultural pressure is very great to assume a particular adult role, as it is for American women to bear and rear children, latent desire and psychological readiness for parenthood may often be at odds with manifest desire and actual ability to perform adequately as parents. Clinicians and therapists are aware, as perhaps many sociologists are not, that failure, hostility, and destructiveness are as much a part of the family system and the relationships among family members as success, love, and solidarity are.[22]

A conceptual system which can deal with both successful and unsuccessful role transitions, or positive and negative impact of parenthood upon adult men and women, is thus more powerful than one built to handle success but not failure or vice versa. For these reasons I have concluded that it is misleading and restrictive to perpetuate the use of the concept of "normal crisis." A more fruitful point of departure is to build upon the stage-task concepts of Erikson, viewing parenthood as a developmental stage, as Benedek[23] and Hill[24] have done, a perspective carried into the research of Raush, Goodrich, and Campbell[25] and of Rhona and Robert Rapoport[26] on adaptation to the early years of marriage and that of Cohen, Fearing et al,[27] on the adjustments involved in pregnancy.

ROLE CYCLE STAGES

A discussion of the impact of parenthood upon the parent will be assisted by two analytic devices. One is to follow a comparative approach, by asking in what basic structural ways the parental role differs from other primary adult roles. The marital and occupational roles will be used for this comparison. A second device is to specify the phases in the development of a social role. If the total life span may be said to have a cycle, each stage with its unique tasks, then by analogy a role may be said to have a cycle and each stage in that role cycle, to have its unique tasks and problems of adjustment. Four broad stages of a role cycle may be specified:

[20] Mabel Blake Cohen, "Personal Identity and Sexual Identity," *Psychiatry*, 29, No. 1 (1966), 1–14; Joseph C. Rheingold, *The Fear of Being a Woman: A Theory of Maternal Destructiveness*, New York: Grune and Stratton, 1964.

[21] Theodore Lidz, S. Fleck, and A. Cornelison, *Schizophrenia and the Family*, New York: International Universities Press, 1965; Rheingold, op. cit.

[22] Cf. the long review of studies Rheingold covers in his book on maternal destructiveness, op. cit.

[23] Benedek, op. cit.

[24] Reuben Hill and D. A. Hansen, "The Identification of a Conceptual Framework Utilized in Family Study," *Marriage and Family Living*, 22 (1960), 299–311.

[25] Harold L. Raush, W. Goodrich, and J. D. Campbell, "Adaptation to the First Years of Marriage," *Psychiatry*, 26, No. 4 (1963), 368–380.

[26] Rapoport, op. cit.

[27] Cohen, op. cit.

1. Anticipatory Stage

All major adult roles have a long history of anticipatory training for them, since parental and school socialization of children is dedicated precisely to this task of producing the kind of competent adult valued by the culture. For our present purposes, however, a narrower conception of the anticipatory stage is preferable: the engagement period in the case of the marital role, pregnancy in the case of the parental role, and the last stages of highly vocationally oriented schooling or on-the-job apprenticeship in the case of an occupational role.

2. Honeymoon Stage

This is the time period immediately following the full assumption of the adult role. The inception of this stage is more easily defined than its termination. In the case of the marital role, the honeymoon stage extends from the marriage ceremony itself through the literal honeymoon and on through an unspecified and individually varying period of time. Raush[28] has caught this stage of the marital role in his description of the "psychic honeymoon": that extended postmarital period when, through close intimacy and joint activity, the couple can explore each other's capacities and limitations. I shall arbitrarily consider the onset of pregnancy as marking the end of the honeymoon stage of the marital role. This stage of the parental role may involve an equivalent psychic honeymoon, that post-childbirth period during which, through intimacy and prolonged contact, an attachment between parent and child is laid down. There is a crucial difference, however, from the marital role in this stage. A woman knows her husband as a unique real person when she enters the honeymoon stage of marriage. A good deal of preparatory adjustment on a firm reality-base is possible during the engagement period which is not possible in the equivalent pregnancy period. Fantasy is not corrected by the reality of a specific individual child until the birth of the child. The "quickening" is psychologically of special significance to women precisely because it marks the first evidence of a real baby rather than a purely fantasized one. On this basis alone there is greater interpersonal adjustment and learning during the honeymoon stage of the parental role than of the marital role.

3. Plateau Stage

This is the protracted middle period of a role cycle during which the role is fully exercised. Depending on the specific problem under analysis, one would obviously subdivide this large plateau stage further. For my present purposes it is not necessary to do so, since my focus is on the earlier anticipatory and honeymoon stages of the parental role and the overall impact of parenthood on adults.

[28] Raush et al., op. cit.

4. Disengagement-Termination Stage

This period immediately precedes and includes the actual termination of the role. Marriage ends with the death of the spouse or, just as definitively, with separation and divorce. A unique characteristic of parental role termination is the fact that it is not clearly marked by any specific act but is an attenuated process of termination with little cultural prescription about when the authority and obligations of a parent end. Many parents, however, experience the marriage of the child as a psychological termination of the active parental role.

UNIQUE FEATURES OF PARENTAL ROLE

With this role cycle suggestion as a broader framework, we can narrow our focus to what are the unique and most salient features of the parental role. In doing so, special attention will be given to two further questions: (1) the impact of social changes over the past few decades in facilitating or complicating the transition to and experience of parenthood and (2) the new interpretations or new research suggested by the focus on the parent rather than the child.

1. Cultural Pressure to Assume the Role

On the level of cultural values, men have no freedom of choice where work is concerned: They must work to secure their status as adult men. The equivalent for women has been maternity. There is considerable pressure upon the growing girl and young woman to consider maternity necessary for a woman's fulfillment as an individual and to secure her status as an adult.[29]

This is not to say there are no fluctuations over time in the intensity of the cultural pressure to parenthood. During the depression years of the 1930's, there was more widespread awareness of the economic hardships parenthood can entail, and many demographic experts believe there was a great increase in illegal abortions during those years. Bird has discussed the dread with which a suspected pregnancy was viewed by many American women in the 1930's.[30] Quite a different set of pressures were at work during the 1950's, when the general societal tendency was toward withdrawal from active engagement with the issues of the larger society and a turning in to the gratifications of the private sphere of home and family life. Im-

[29] The greater the cultural pressure to assume a given adult social role, the greater will be the tendency for individual negative feelings toward that role to be expressed covertly. Men may complain about a given job but not about working per se, and hence their work dissatisfactions are often displaced to the non-work sphere, as psychosomatic complaints or irritation and dominance at home. An equivalent displacement for women of the ambivalence many may feel toward maternity is to dissatisfactions with the homemaker role.

[30] Caroline Bird, *The Invisible Scar*, New York: David McKay, 1966.

portant in the background were the general affluence of the period and the expanded room and ease of child rearing that go with suburban living. For the past five years, there has been a drop in the birth rate in general, fourth and higher-order births in particular. During this same period there has been increased concern and debate about women's participation in politics and work, with more women now returning to work rather than conceiving the third or fourth child.[31]

2. Inception of the Parental Role

The decision to marry and the choice of a mate are voluntary acts of individuals in our family system. Engagements are therefore consciously considered, freely entered, and freely terminated if increased familiarity decreases, rather than increases, intimacy and commitment to the choice. The inception of a pregnancy, unlike the engagement, is not always a voluntary decision, for it may be the unintended consequence of a sexual act that was recreative in intent rather than procreative. Secondly, and again unlike the engagement, the termination of a pregnancy is not socially sanctioned, as shown by current resistance to abortion-law reform.

The implication of this difference is a much higher probability of unwanted pregnancies than of unwanted marriages in our family system. Coupled with the ample clinical evidence of parental rejection and sometimes cruelty to children, it is all the more surprising that there has not been more consistent research attention to the problem of *parental satisfaction*, as there has for long been on *marital satisfaction* or *work satisfaction*. Only the extreme iceberg tip of the parental satisfaction continuum is clearly demarcated and researched, as in the growing concern with "battered babies." Cultural and psychological resistance to the image of a non-nurturant woman may afflict social scientists as well as the American public.

The timing of a first pregnancy is critical to the manner in which parental responsibilities are joined to the marital relationship. The single most important change over the past few decades is extensive and efficient contraceptive usage, since this has meant for a growing proportion of new marriages, the possibility of and increasing preference for some postponement of childbearing after marriage. When pregnancy was likely to follow shortly after marriage, the major transition point in a woman's life was marriage itself. *This transition point is increasingly the first pregnancy rather than marriage.* It is accepted and increasingly expected that women will work after marriage, while household furnishings are acquired and spouses complete their advanced training or gain a foothold in their work.[32] This provides

[31] When it is realized that a mean family size of 3.5 would double the population in 40 years, while a mean of 2.5 would yield a stable population in the same period, the social importance of withholding praise for procreative prowess is clear. At the same time, a drop in the birth rate may reduce the number of unwanted babies born, for such a drop would mean more efficient contraceptive usage and a closer correspondence between desired and attained family size.

[32] James A. Davis, *Stipends and Spouses: The Finances of American Arts and Sciences Graduate Students*, Chicago: University of Chicago Press, 1962.

an early marriage period in which the fact of a wife's employment presses for a greater egalitarian relationship between husband and wife in decision-making, commonality of experience, and sharing of household responsibilities.

The balance between individual autonomy and couple mutuality that develops during the honeymoon stage of such a marriage may be important in establishing a pattern that will later affect the quality of the parent-child relationship and the extent of sex-role segregation of duties between the parents. It is only in the context of a growing egalitarian base to the marital relationship that one could find, as Gavron has,[33] a tendency for parents to establish some barriers between themselves and their children, a marital defense against the institution of parenthood as she describes it. This may eventually replace the typical coalition in more traditional families of mother and children against husband-father. Parenthood will continue for some time to impose a degree of temporary segregation of primary responsibilities between husband and wife, but, when this takes place in the context of a previously established egalitarian relationship between the husband and wife, such role segregation may become blurred, with greater recognition of the wife's need for autonomy and the husband's role in the routines of home and child rearing.[34]

There is one further significant social change that has important implications for the changed relationship between husband and wife: the increasing departure from an old pattern of role-inception phasing in which the young person first completed his schooling, then established himself in the world of work, then married and began his family. Marriage and parenthood are increasingly taking place *before* the schooling of the husband, and often of the wife, has been completed.[35] An important reason for this trend lies in the

[33] Hannah Gavron, *The Captive Wife*, London: Routledge and Kegan Paul, 1966.

[34] The recent increase in natural childbirth, prenatal courses for expectant fathers, and greater participation of men during childbirth and postnatal care of the infant may therefore be a *consequence* of greater sharing between husband and wife when both work and jointly maintain their new households during the early months of marriage. Indeed, natural childbirth builds directly on this shifted base to the marital relationship. Goshen-Gottstein has found in an Israeli sample that women with a "traditional" orientation to marriage far exceed women with a "modern" orientation to marriage in menstrual difficulty, dislike of sexual intercourse, and pregnancy disorders and complaints such as vomiting. She argues that traditional women demand and expect little from their husbands and become demanding and narcissistic by means of their children, as shown in pregnancy by an over-exaggeration of symptoms and attention-seeking. Esther R. Goshen-Gottstein, *Marriage and First Pregnancy: Cultural Influences on Attitudes of Israeli Women*, London: Tavistock Publications, 1966. A prolonged psychic honeymoon uncomplicated by an early pregnancy, and with the new acceptance of married women's employment, may help to cement the egalitarian relationship in the marriage and reduce both the tendency to pregnancy difficulties and the need for a narcissistic focus on the children. Such a background is fruitful ground for sympathy toward and acceptance of the natural childbirth ideology.

[35] James A. Davis, *Stipends and Spouses: The Finances of American Arts and Sciences Graduate Students*, op. cit.; James A. Davis, *Great Aspirations*,

fact that, during the same decades in which the average age of physical-sexual maturation has dropped, the average amount of education which young people obtain has been on the increase. Particularly for the college and graduate or professional school population, family roles are often assumed before the degrees needed to enter careers have been obtained.

Just how long it now takes young people to complete their higher education has been investigated only recently in several longitudinal studies of college-graduate cohorts.[36] College is far less uniformly a four-year period than high school is. A full third of the college freshmen in one study had been out of high school a year or more before entering college.[37] In a large sample of college graduates in 1961, one in five were over 25 years of age at graduation.[38] Thus, financial difficulties, military service, change of career plans, and marriage itself all tend to create interruptions in the college attendance of a significant proportion of college graduates. At the graduate and professional school level, this is even more marked: the mean age of men receiving the doctorate, for example, is 32, and of women, 36.[39] It is the exception rather than the rule for men and women who seek graduate degrees to go directly from college to graduate school and remain there until they secure their degrees.[40]

The major implication of this change is that more men and women are achieving full adult status in family roles while they are still less than fully adult in status terms in the occupational system. Graduate students are, increasingly, men and women with full family responsibilities. Within the family many more husbands and fathers are still students, often quite dependent on the earnings of their wives to see them through their advanced training.[41] No matter what the couple's desires and preferences are, this fact alone presses for more egalitarian relations between husband and wife, just as the adult family status of graduate students presses for more egalitarian relations between students and faculty.

Chicago: Aldine Publishing, 1964; Eli Ginsberg, *Life Styles of Educated Women,* New York: Columbia University Press, 1966; Ginsberg, *Educated American Women: Self Portraits,* New York: Columbia University Press, 1967; National Science Foundation, *Two Years After the College Degree—Work and Further Study Patterns,* Washington, D.C.: Government Printing Office, NSF 63–26, 1963.

[36] Davis, *Great Aspirations,* op. cit.; Laure Sharp, "Graduate Study and Its Relation to Careers: The Experience of a Recent Cohort of College Graduates," *Journal of Human Resources,* 1, No. 2 (1966), pp. 41–58.

[37] James D. Cowhig and C. Nam, "Educational Status, College Plans and Occupational Status of Farm and Nonfarm Youths," U.S. Bureau of the Census Series ERS (P–27). No. 30, 1961.

[38] Davis, *Great Aspirations,* op. cit.

[39] Lindsey R. Harmon, *Profiles of Ph.D.'s in the Sciences: Summary Report on Follow-up of Doctorate Cohorts, 1935–1960,* Washington, D.C.: National Research Council, Publication 1293, 1965.

[40] Sharp, op. cit.

[41] Davis, *Stipends and Spouses, The Finances of American Arts and Sciences Graduate Students,* op. cit.

3. Irrevocability

If marriages do not work out, there is now widespread acceptance of divorce and remarriage as a solution. The same point applies to the work world: we are free to leave an unsatisfactory job and seek another. But once a pregnancy occurs, there is little possibility of undoing the commitment to parenthood implicit in conception except in the rare instance of placing children for adoption. We can have ex-spouses and ex-jobs but not ex-children. This being so, it is scarcely surprising to find marked differences between the relationship of a parent and one child and the relationship of the same parent with another child. If the culture does not permit pregnancy termination, the equivalent to giving up a child is psychological withdrawal on the part of the parent.

This taps an important area in which a focus on the parent rather than the child may contribute a new interpretive dimension to an old problem: the long history of interest, in the social sciences, in differences among children associated with their sex-birth-order position in their sibling set. Research has largely been based on data gathered about and/or from the children, and interpretations make inferences back to the "probable" quality of the child's relation to a parent and how a parent might differ in relating to a first-born compared to a last-born child. The relevant research, directed at the parents (mothers in particular), remains to be done, but at least a few examples can be suggested of the different order of interpretation that flows from a focus on the parent.

Some birth-order research stresses the influence of sibs upon other sibs, as in Koch's finding that second-born boys with an older sister are more feminine than second-born boys with an older brother.[42] A similar sib-influence interpretation is offered in the major common finding of birth-order correlates, that sociability is greater among last-borns[43] and achievement among first-borns.[44] It has been suggested that last-borns use social skills to increase acceptance by their older sibs or are more peer-oriented because they receive less adult stimulation from parents. The tendency of first-borns to greater achievement has been interpreted in a corollary way, as a reflection of early assumption of responsibility for younger sibs, greater adult stimulation during the time the oldest was the only child in the family,[45] and

[42] Orville G. Brim, "Family Structure and Sex-Role Learning by Children," *Sociometry*, 21 (1958), 1–16; H. L. Koch, "Sissiness and Tomboyishness in Relation to Sibling Characteristics," *Journal of Genetic Psychology*, 88 (1956), 231–244.

[43] Charles MacArthur, "Personalities of First and Second Children," *Psychiatry*, 19 (1956), 47–54; S. Schachter, "Birth Order and Sociometric Choice," *Journal of Abnormal and Social Psychology*, 68 (1964), 453–456.

[44] Irving Harris, *The Promised Seed*, New York: The Free Press, Macmillan, 1964; Bernard Rosen, "Family Structure and Achievement Motivation," *American Sociological Review*, 26 (1961), 574–585; Alice S. Rossi, "Naming Children in Middle-Class Families," *American Sociological Review*, 30, No. 4 (1965), 499–513; Stanley Schachter, "Birth Order, Eminence and Higher Education," *American Sociological Review*, 28 (1963), 757–768.

[45] Harris, op. cit.

the greater significance of the first-born for the larger kinship network of the family.[46]

Sociologists have shown increasing interest in structural family variables in recent years, a primary variable being family size. From Bossard's descriptive work on the large family[47] to more methodologically sophisticated work such as that by Rosen,[48] Elder and Bowerman,[49] Boocock,[50] and Nisbet,[51] the question posed is: What is the effect of growing up in a small family, compared with a large family, that is attributable to this group-size variable? Unfortunately, the theoretical point of departure for sociologists' expectations of the effect of the family-size variables is the Durkheim-Simmel tradition of the differential effect of group size or population density upon members or inhabitants.[52] In the case of the family, however, this overlooks the very important fact that family size is determined by the key figures *within* the group, i.e., the parents. To find that children in small families differ from children in large families is not simply due to the impact of group size upon individual members but to the very different involvement of the parent with the children and to relations between the parents themselves in small versus large families.

An important clue to a new interpretation can be gained by examining family size from the perspective of parental motivation toward having children. A small family is small for one of two primary reasons: either the parents wanted a small family and achieved their desired size, or they wanted a large family but were not able to attain it. In either case, there is a low probability of unwanted children. Indeed, in the latter eventuality they may take particularly great interest in the children they do have. Small families are therefore most likely to contain parents with a strong and positive orientation to each of the children they have. A large family, by contrast, is large either because the parents achieved the size they desired or because they have more children than they in fact wanted. Large families therefore have a higher probability than small families of including unwanted and unloved children. Consistent with this are Nye's finding that adolescents in small

[46] Rossi, "Naming Children in Middle-Class Families," op. cit.

[47] James H. Bossard, *Parent and Child*, Philadelphia: University of Pennsylvania Press, 1953; James H. Bossard and E. Boll, *The Large Family System*, Philadelphia: University of Pennsylvania Press, 1956.

[48] Rosen, op. cit.

[49] Glen H. J. Elder and C. Bowerman, "Family Structure and Child Rearing Patterns: The Effect of Family Size and Sex Composition on Child-Rearing Practices," *American Sociological Review*, 28 (1963), 891–905.

[50] Sarane S. Boocock, "Toward a Sociology of Learning: A Selective Review of Existing Research," *Sociology of Education*, 39, No. 1 (1966), 1–45.

[51] John Nisbet, "Family Environment and Intelligence," in *Education, Economy and Society*, ed. by Halsey et al. New York: The Free Press, Macmillan, 1961.

[52] Thus Rosen writes: "Considering the sociologist's traditional and continuing concern with group size as an independent variable (from Simmel and Durkheim to the recent experimental studies of small groups), there have been surprisingly few studies of the influence of group size upon the nature of interaction in the family," op. cit., p. 576.

families have better relations with their parents than those in large families[53] and Sears and Maccoby's finding that mothers of large families are more restrictive toward their children than mothers of small families.[54]

This also means that last-born children are more likely to be unwanted than first- or middle-born children, particularly in large families. This is consistent with what is known of abortion patterns among married women, who typically resort to abortion only when they have achieved the number of children they want or feel they can afford to have. Only a small proportion of women faced with such unwanted pregnancies actually resort to abortion. *This suggests the possibility that the last-born child's reliance on social skills may be his device for securing the attention and loving involvement of a parent less positively predisposed to him than to his older siblings.*

In developing this interpretation, rather extreme cases have been stressed. Closer to the normal range, of families in which even the last-born child was desired and planned for, there is still another element which may contribute to the greater sociability of the last-born child. Most parents are themselves aware of the greater ease with which they face the care of a third fragile newborn than the first; clearly, parental skills and confidence are greater with last-born children than with first-born children. But this does not mean that the attitude of the parent is more positive toward the care of the third child than the first. There is no necessary correlation between skills in an area and enjoyment of that area. Searls[55] found that older homemakers are *more* skillful in domestic tasks but experience *less* enjoyment of them than younger homemakers, pointing to a declining euphoria for a particular role with the passage of time. In the same way, older people rate their marriages as "very happy" less often than younger people do.[56] It is perhaps culturally and psychologically more difficult to face the possibility that women may find less enjoyment of the maternal role with the passage of time, though women themselves know the difference between the romantic expectation concerning child care and the incorporation of the first baby into the household and the more realistic expectation and sharper assessment of their own abilities to do an adequate job of mothering as they face a third confinement. Last-born children may experience not only less verbal stimulation from their parents than first-born children but also less prompt and enthusiastic response to their demands—from feeding and diaper-change as infants to requests for stories read at three or a college education at eighteen—simply because the parents experience less intense gratification from the parent role with the third child than they did with the first. The child's response to this might well be to cultivate winning, pleasing manners in early childhood that blossom as charm and sociability in later life, showing both a greater need to be loved and greater pressure to seek approval.

[53] Ivan Nye, "Adolescent-Parent Adjustment: Age, Sex, Sibling, Number, Broken Homes, and Employed Mothers as Variables," *Marriage and Family Living*, 14 (1952), 327–332.

[54] Sears et al., op. cit.

[55] Laura G. Searls, "Leisure Role Emphasis of College Graduate Homemakers," *Journal of Marriage and the Family*, 28, No. 1 (1966), 77–82.

[56] Norman Bradburn and D. Caplovitz, *Reports on Happiness*, Chicago: Aldine Publishing, 1965.

One last point may be appropriately developed at this juncture. Mention was made earlier that for many women the personal outcome of experience in the parent role is not a higher level of maturation but the negative outcome of a depressed sense of self-worth, if not actual personality deterioration. There is considerable evidence that this is more prevalent than we recognize. On a qualitative level, a close reading of the portrait of the working-class wife in Rainwater,[57] Newsom,[58] Komarovsky,[59] Gavron,[60] or Zweig[61] gives little suggestion that maternity has provided these women with opportunities for personal growth and development. So too, Cohen[62] notes with some surprise that in her sample of middle-class educated couples, as in Pavenstadt's study of lower-income women in Boston, there were more emotional difficulty and lower levels of maturation among multiparous women than primiparous women. On a more extensive sample basis, in Gurin's survey of Americans viewing their mental health,[63] as in Bradburn's reports on happiness,[64] single men are less happy and less active than single women, but among the married respondents the women are unhappier, have more problems, feel inadequate as parents, have a more negative and passive outlook on life, and show a more negative self-image. All of these characteristics increase with age among married women but show no relationship to age among men. While it may be true, as Gurin argues, that women are more introspective and hence more attuned to the psychological facets of experience than men are, this point does not account for the fact that the things which the women report are all on the negative side; few are on the positive side, indicative of euphoric sensitivity and pleasure. The possibility must be faced, and at some point researched, that women lose ground in personal development and self-esteem during the early and middle years of adulthood, whereas men gain ground in these respects during the same years. The retention of a high level of self-esteem may depend upon the adequacy of earlier preparation for major adult roles: men's training adequately prepares them for their primary adult roles in the occupational system, as it does for those women who opt to participate significantly in the work world. Training in the qualities and skills needed for family roles in contemporary society may be inadequate for both sexes, but the lowering of self-esteem occurs only among women because their primary adult roles are within the family system.

[57] Lee Rainwater, R. Coleman, and G. Handel, *Workingman's Wife*, New York: Oceana Publications, 1959.

[58] John Newsom and E. Newsom, *Infant Care in an Urban Community*, New York: International Universities Press, 1963.

[59] Mirra Komarovsky, *Blue-Collar Marriage*, New York: Random House, 1962.

[60] Gavron, op. cit.

[61] Ferdinand Zweig, *Woman's Life and Labor*, London: Camelot Press, 1952.

[62] Cohen, op. cit.

[63] Gerald Gurin, J. Veroff, and S. Feld, *Americans View Their Mental Health*, New York: Basic Books, Monograph Series No. 4, Joint Commission on Mental Illness and Health, 1960.

[64] Bradburn and Caplovitz, op. cit.

4. Preparation for Parenthood

Four factors may be given special attention on the question of what preparation American couples bring to parenthood.

(a) *Paucity of Preparation* Our educational system is dedicated to the cognitive development of the young, and our primary teaching approach is the pragmatic one of learning by doing. How much one knows and how well he can apply what he knows are the standards by which the child is judged in school, as the employee is judged at work. The child can learn by doing in such subjects as science, mathematics, art work, or shop, but not in the subjects most relevant to successful family life: sex, home maintenance, child care, interpersonal competence, and empathy. If the home is deficient in training in these areas, the child is left with no preparation for a major segment of his adult life. A doctor facing his first patient in private practice has treated numerous patients under close supervision during his internship, but probably a majority of American mothers approach maternity with no previous child-care experience beyond sporadic baby-sitting, perhaps a course in child psychology, or occasional care of younger siblings.

(b) *Limited Learning During Pregnancy* A second important point makes adjustment to parenthood potentially more stressful than marital adjustment. This is the lack of any realistic training for parenthood during the anticipatory stage of pregnancy. By contrast, during the engagement period preceding marriage, an individual has opportunities to develop the skills and make the adjustments which ease the transition to marriage. Through discussions of values and life goals, through sexual experimentation, shared social experiences as an engaged couple with friends and relatives, and planning and furnishing an apartment, the engaged couple can make considerable progress in developing mutuality in advance of the marriage itself.[65] No such headstart is possible in the case of pregnancy. What preparation exists is confined to reading, consultation with friends and parents, discussions between husband and wife, and a minor nesting phase in which a place and the equipment for a baby are prepared in the household.[66]

(c) *Abruptness of Transition* Thirdly, the birth of a child is not followed by any gradual taking on of responsibility, as in the case of a professional work role. It is as if the woman shifted from a graduate student to a full professor with little intervening apprenticeship experience of slowly increas-

[65] Rapoport, "The Transition from Engagement to Marriage," op. cit.; Raush et al., op. cit.

[66] During the period when marriage was the critical transition in the adult woman's life rather than pregnancy, a good deal of anticipatory "nesting" behavior took place from the time of conception. Now more women work through a considerable portion of the first pregnancy, and such nesting behavior as exists may be confined to a few shopping expeditions or baby showers, thus adding to the abruptness of the transition and the difficulty of adjustment following the birth of a first child.

ing responsibility. The new mother starts out immediately on 24-hour duty, with responsibility for a fragile and mysterious infant totally dependent on her care.

If marital adjustment is more difficult for very young brides than more mature ones,[67] adjustment to motherhood may be even more difficult. A woman can adapt a passive dependence on a husband and still have a successful marriage, but a young mother with strong dependency needs is in for difficulty in maternal adjustment, because the role precludes such dependency. This situation was well described in Cohen's study[68] in a case of a young wife with a background of co-ed popularity and a passive dependent relationship to her admired and admiring husband, who collapsed into restricted incapacity when faced with the responsibilities of maintaining a home and caring for a child.

(d) *Lack of Guidelines to Successful Parenthood* If the central task of parenthood is the rearing of children to become the kind of competent adults valued by the society, then an important question facing any parent is what he or she specifically can do to create such a competent adult. This is where the parent is left with few or no guidelines from the expert. Parents can readily inform themselves concerning the young infant's nutritional, clothing, and medical needs and follow the general prescription that a child needs loving physical contact and emotional support. Such advice may be sufficient to produce a healthy, happy, and well-adjusted preschooler, but adult competency is quite another matter.

In fact, the adults who do "succeed" in American society show a complex of characteristics as children that current experts in child-care would evaluate as "poor" to "bad." Biographies of leading authors and artists, as well as the more rigorous research inquiries of creativity among architects[69] or scientists,[70] do not portray childhoods with characteristics currently endorsed by mental health and child-care authorities. Indeed, there is often a predominance of tension in childhood family relations and traumatic loss rather than loving parental support, intense channeling of energy in one area of interest rather than an all-round profile of diverse interests, and social withdrawal and preference for loner activities rather than gregarious sociability. Thus, the stress in current child-rearing advice on a high level of loving

[67] Lee G. Burchinal, "Adolescent Role Deprivation and High School Marriage," *Marriage and Family Living*, 21 (1959), 378–384; Floyd M. Martinson, "Ego Deficiency as a Factor in Marriage," *American Sociological Review*, 22 (1955), 161–164; J. Joel Moss and Ruby Gingles, "The Relationship of Personality to the Incidence of Early Marriage," *Marriage and Family Living*, 21 (1959), 373–377.

[68] Cohen, op. cit.

[69] Donald W. MacKinnon, "Creativity and Images of the Self," in *The Study of Lives*, ed. by Robert W. White, New York: Atherton Press, 1963.

[70] Anne Roe, *A Psychological Study of Eminent Biologists, Psychological Monographs*, 65, No. 14 (1951), 68 pages; Anne Roe, "A Psychological Study of Physical Scientists," *Genetic Psychology Monographs*, 43 (1951), 121–239; Anne Roe, "Crucial Life Experiences in the Development of Scientists," in *Talent and Education*, ed. by E. P. Torrance, Minneapolis: University of Minnesota Press, 1960.

support but a low level of discipline or restriction on the behavior of the child—the "developmental" family type as Duvall calls it[71]—is a profile consistent with the focus on mental health, sociability, and adjustment. Yet the combination of both high support and high authority on the part of parents is most strongly related to the child's sense of responsibility, leadership quality, and achievement level, as found in Bronfenbrenner's studies[72] and that of Mussen and Distler.[73]

Brim points out[74] that we are a long way from being able to say just what parent role prescriptions have what effect on the adult characteristics of the child. We know even less about how such parental prescriptions should be changed to adapt to changed conceptions of competency in adulthood. In such an ambiguous context, the great interest parents take in school reports on their children or the pediatrician's assessment of the child's developmental progress should be seen as among the few indices parents have of how well *they* are doing as parents.

SYSTEM AND ROLE REQUIREMENTS: INSTRUMENTALITY AND INTEGRATION

Typological dichotomies and unidimensional scales have loomed large in the search by social scientists for the most economical and general principles to account for some significant portion of the complex human behavior or social organization they study. Thus, for example, the European dichotomy of *Gemeinschaft* and *Gesellschaft* became the American sociological distinction between rural and urban sociology, subfields that have outlasted their conceptual utility now that the rural environment has become urbanized and the interstices between country and city are swelling with suburban developments.

In recent years a new dichotomy has gained more acceptance in sociological circles—the Parsonian distinction between *instrumental* and *expressive*, an interesting dichotomy that is unfortunately applied in an indiscriminate way to all manner of social phenomena including the analysis of teacher role conflict, occupational choice, the contrast between the family system and the occupational system, and the primary roles or personality tendencies of men compared to women.

On a system level, for example, the "instrumental" occupational system is characterized by rationality, efficiency, rejection of tradition, and depression of interpersonal loyalty, while the "expressive" family system is characterized by nurturance, integration, tension-management, ritual, and

[71] Evelyn M. Duvall, "Conceptions of Parenthood," *American Journal of Sociology*, 52 (1946), 193–203.

[72] Urie Bronfenbrenner, "Some Familial Antecedents of Responsibility and Leadership in Adolescents," in *Studies in Leadership*, ed. by L. Petrullo and B. Bass, New York: Holt, Rinehart and Winston, 1960.

[73] Paul Mussen and L. Distler, "Masculinity, Identification and Father-Son Relationships," *Journal of Abnormal and Social Psychology*, 59 (1959), 350–356.

[74] Orville G. Brim, "The Parent-Child Relation as a Social System: I. Parent and Child Roles," *Child Development*, 28, No. 3 (1957), 343–364.

interpersonal solidarity. Applied to sex roles within the family, the husband-father emerges as the instrumental rational leader, a symbolic representative of the outside world, and the wife-mother emerges as the expressive, nurturant, affective center of the family. Such distinctions may be useful in the attempt to capture some general tendency of a system or a role, but they lead to more distortion than illumination when applied to the actual functioning of a specific system or social role or to the actual behavior of a given individual in a particular role.

Take, for example, the husband-father as the instrumental role within the family on the assumption that men are the major breadwinners and therefore carry the instrumentality associated with work into their roles within the family. To begin with, the family is not an experimental one-task small group but a complex, ongoing 24-hour entity with many tasks that must be performed. Secondly, we really know very little about how occupational roles affect the performance of family roles.[75] An aggressive courtroom lawyer or a shrewd business executive are not lawyers and businessmen at home but husbands and fathers. Unless shown to be in error, we should proceed on the assumption that behavior is role-specific. (Indeed, Brim[76] argues that even personality is role-specific.) A strict teacher may be an indulgent mother at home; a submissive wife may be a dominant mother; a dictatorial father may be an exploited and passive worker on the assembly line; or, as in some of Lidz's schizophrenic patients' families,[77] a passive dependent husband at home may be a successful dominant lawyer away from home.

There is, however, a more fundamental level to the criticism that the dichotomous usage of instrumentality and expressiveness, linked to sex and applied to intrafamily roles, leads to more distortion than illumination. The logic of my argument starts with the premise that every social system, group, or role has two primary, independent, structural axes. Whether these axes are

[75] Miller and Swanson have suggested a connection between the trend toward bureaucratic structure in the occupational world and the shift in child-rearing practices toward permissiveness and a greater stress on personal adjustment of children. Their findings are suggestive rather than definitive, however, and no hard research has subjected this question to empirical inquiry. Daniel R. Miller and G. Swanson, *The Changing American Parent*, New York: John Wiley, 1958.

The same suggestive but nondefinitive clues are to be found in von Mering's study of the contrast between professional and nonprofessional women as mothers. She shows that the professionally active woman in her mother role tends toward a greater stress on discipline rather than indulgence and has a larger number of rules with fewer choices or suggestions to the child: the emphasis is in equipping the child to cope effectively with rules and techniques of his culture. The nonprofessional mother, by contrast, has a greater value stress on insuring the child's emotional security, tending to take the role of the clinician in an attempt to diagnose the child's problems and behavior. Faye H. von Mering, "Professional and Non-Professional Women as Mothers," *Journal of Social Psychology*, 42 (1955), 21–34.

[76] Orville G. Brim, "Personality Development as Role-Learning," in *Personality Development in Children*, ed. by Ira Iscoe and Harold Stevenson, University of Texas Press, 1960.

[77] Lidz et al., op. cit.

called "authority and support," as in Straus's circumplex model,[78] or "instrumental and expressive" as by Parsons,[79] there are tasks to be performed and affective support to be given in all the cases cited. There must be discipline, rules, and division of labor in the nation-state as in the family or a business enterprise *and* there must be solidarity among the units comprising these same systems in order for the system to function adequately. *This means that the role of father, husband, wife, or mother each has these two independent dimensions of authority and support, instrumentality and expressiveness, work and love.* Little is gained by trying to stretch empirical results to fit the father role to the instrumental category, as Brim[80] has done, or the mother role to the expressive category, as Zelditch has done.[81]

In taking a next logical step from this premise, the critical issue, both theoretically and empirically, becomes gauging the *balance* between these two dimensions of the system or of the role. Roles or systems could be compared in terms of the average difference among them in the direction and extent of the discrepancy between authority and support; or individuals could be compared in terms of the variation among them in the discrepancy between the two dimensions in a given role.

An example may clarify these points. A teacher who is all loving, warm support to her students and plans many occasions to evoke integrative ties among them but who is incompetent in the exercise of authority or knowledge of the subjects she teaches would be judged by any school principal as an inadequate teacher. The same judgment of inadequacy would apply to a strict disciplinarian teacher, competent and informed about her subjects but totally lacking in any personal quality of warmth or ability to encourage integrative and cooperative responses among her students. Maximum adequacy of teacher performance requires a relatively high positive level on both of these two dimensions of the teacher role.

To claim that teachers have a basic conflict in approaching their role because they are required to be a "bisexual parent, permissive giver of love and harsh disciplinarian with a masculine intellectual grasp of the world," as Jackson and Moscovici[82] have argued, at least recognizes the two dimensions of the teacher role, though it shares the view of many sociologists that role *conflict* is inherent wherever these seeming polarities are required. Why conflict is predicted hinges on the assumed invariance of the linkage of the male to authority and the female to the expressive-integrative roles.

It is this latter assumed difference between the sexes that restricts theory-building in family sociology and produces so much puzzlement on the part of researchers into marriage and parenthood, sex-role socialization, or personality tendencies toward masculinity or femininity. Let me give one example of recent findings on this latter topic and then move on to apply the

[78] Straus, op. cit.

[79] Parsons and Bales, op. cit.

[80] Brim, "The Parent-Child Relation as a Social System: I. Parent and Child Roles," op. cit.

[81] Parsons and Bales, op. cit.

[82] Philip Jackson and F. Moscovici, "The Teacher-to-be: A Study of Embryonic Identification with a Professional Role," *School Review*, 71, No. 1 (1963), 41–65.

two-dimension concept to the parental role. Vincent[83] administered the Gough Femininity Scale along with several other scale batteries from the California Personality Inventory to several hundred college men and women. He found that women *low* on femininity were higher in the Class I scale which measures poise, ascendancy, and self-assurance, and men *high* in femininity were higher in dominance, capacity for status, and responsibility. Successful adult men in a technological society are rarely interested in racing cars, soldiering, or hunting; they are cautious, subtle, and psychologically attuned to others. So too, contemporary adult women who fear windstorms, the dark, strange places, automobile accidents, excitement, crowded parties, or practical jokes (and are therefore high on femininity in the Gough scale) will be inadequate for the task of managing an isolated household with neither men nor kinswomen close by to help them through daily crises, for the assumption of leadership roles in community organizations, or for holding down supplementary breadwinning or cakewinning jobs.

When Deutsch[84] and Escalona[85] point out that today's "neurotic" woman is not an assertive dominant person but a passive dependent one, the reason may be found in the social change in role expectations concerning competence among adult women, not that there has been a social change in the characteristics of neurotic women. In the past an assertive, dominant woman might have defined herself and been defined by her analyst as "neurotic" because she could not fill the expectations then held for adequacy among adult women. Today, it is the passive dependent woman who will be judged "neurotic" because she cannot fill adequately the expectations now set for and by her. What is really meant when we say that sex role definitions have become increasingly blurred is that men are now required to show more integrative skills than in the past, and women more instrumental skills. This incurs potential sex-role "confusion" only by the standards of the past, not by the standards of what is required for contemporary adult competence in family and work roles.

Once freed from the assumption of a single bipolar continuum of masculinity-femininity,[86] authority-integration, or even independence-depend-

[83] Clark E. Vincent, "Implications of Changes in Male-Female Role Expectations for Interpreting M-F Scores," *Journal of Marriage and the Family*, 28, No. 2 (1966), 196–199.

[84] Helene Deutsch, *The Psychology of Women: A Psychoanalytic Interpretation*, Vol. 1, New York: Grune and Stratton, 1944.

[85] Sibylle Escalona, "The Psychological Situation of Mother and Child Upon Return from the Hospital," in *Problems of Infancy and Childhood: Transactions of the Third Conference*, ed. by Milton Senn, 1949.

[86] Several authors have recently pointed out the inadequacy of social science usage of the masculinity-femininity concept. Landreth, in a study of parent-role appropriateness in giving physical care and companionship to the child, found her four-year-old subjects, particularly in New Zealand, made no simple linkage of activity to mother as opposed to father. Catherine Landreth, "Four-Year-Olds' Notions about Sex Appropriateness of Parental Care and Companionship Activities," *Merrill-Palmer Quarterly*, 9, No. 3 (1963), 175–182. She comments that in New Zealand "masculinity and femininity appear to be comfortably relegated to chromosome rather than to contrived activity" (p. 176). Lansky, in a study of the effect of the sex of the children upon the

ence,[87] one can observe increased instrumentality in a role with no implication of necessarily decreased integration, and vice versa. Thus, an increasing rationality in the care of children, the maintenance of a household, or meal planning for a family does not imply a decreasing level of integrative support associated with the wife-mother role. So, too, the increased involvement of a young father in playful encounters with his toddler carries no necessary implication of a change in the instrumental dimension of his role.

The two-dimensional approach also frees our analysis of parenthood on two other important questions. Brim has reviewed much of the research on the parent-child relationship[88] and noted the necessity of specifying not only the sex of the parent but the sex of the child and whether a given parent-child dyad is a cross-sex or same-sex pair. It is clear from his review that fathers and mothers relate differently to their sons and daughters: fathers have been found to be stricter with their sons than with their daughters, and mothers stricter with their daughters than with their sons. Thus, a two-dimensional approach to the parent role is more appropriate to what is already empirically known about the parent-child relationship.

Secondly, only on a very general overview level does a parent maintain a particular level of support and of discipline toward a given child: situational variation is an important determinant of parental response to a child. A father with a general tendency toward relatively little emotional support of his son may offer a good deal of comfort if the child is hurt. An indulgent and loving mother may show an extreme degree of discipline when the same child misbehaves. Landreth found that her four-year-olds gave more mother responses on a care item concerning food than on bath-time or bedtime care and suggests, as Brim has,[89] that "any generalizations on parent roles should be made in terms of the role activities studied."[90]

Let me illustrate the utility of the two-dimensional concept by applying it to the parental role. Clearly there are a number of expressive requirements for adequate performance in this role: spontaneity and flexibility, the ability to be tender and loving and to respond to tenderness and love from a child, to take pleasure in tactile contact and in play, and to forget one's adultness and unself-consciously respond to the sensitivities and fantasies of a child. Equally important are the instrumental requirements for adequate performance in the parental role: firmness and consistency; the ability to manage

---

parents' own sex-identification, calls for devising tests which look at masculinity and femininity as two dimensions rather than a single continuum. Leonard M. Lansky, "The Family Structure also Affects the Model: Sex-Role Identification in Parents of Preschool Children," *Merrill-Palmer Quarterly*, 10, No. 1 (1964), 39–50.

[87] Beller has already shown the value of such an approach, in a study that defined independence and dependence as two separate dimensions rather than the extremes of a bipolar continuum. He found, as hypothesized, a very *low* negative correlation between the two measures. E. K. Beller, "Exploratory Studies of Dependency," trans., *N.Y. Academy of Science*, 21 (1959), 414–426.

[88] Brim, "The Parent-Child Relation as a Social System: I. Parent and Child Roles," op. cit.

[89] Ibid.

[90] Landreth, op. cit., p. 181.

time and energy; to plan and organize activities involving the child; to teach and to train the child in body controls, motor and language skills, and knowledge of the natural and social world; and interpersonal and value discriminations.

Assuming we had empirical measures of these two dimensions of the parental role, one could then compare individual women both by their levels on each of these dimensions and by the extent to which the discrepancy in level on the two dimensions was tipped toward a high expressive or instrumental dimension. This makes no assumptions about what the balance "should" be; that remains an empirical question awaiting a test in the form of output variables—the characteristics of children we deem to be critical for their competence as adults. Indeed, I would predict that an exhaustive count of the actual components of both the marital and parental roles would show a very high proportion of instrumental components in the parental role and a low proportion in the marital role and that this is an underlying reason why maternal role adjustment is more difficult for women than marital role adjustment. It also leaves as an open, empirical question what the variance is, among fathers, in the level of expressiveness and instrumentality in their paternal role performance and how the profile of fathers compares with that of mothers.

It would not surprise many of us, of course, if women scored higher than men on the expressive dimension and men scored higher on the instrumental dimension of the parental role. Yet quite the opposite might actually result. Men spend relatively little time with their children, and it is time of a particular kind: evenings, weekends, and vacations, when the activities and mood of the family are heavily on the expressive side. Women carry the major burden of the instrumental dimension of parenting. If, as Mable Cohen[91] suggests, the rearing of American boys is inadequate on the social and sexual dimension of development and the rearing of American girls is inadequate on the personal dimension of development, then from the perspective of adequate parenthood performance, we have indeed cause to reexamine the socialization of boys and girls in families and schools. Our current practices appear adequate as preparation for occupational life for men but not women, and inadequate as preparation for family life for both sexes.

However, this is to look too far ahead. At the present, this analysis of parenthood suggests we have much to rethink and much to research before we develop policy recommendations in this area.

[91] Cohen, op. cit.

21 Child-Rearing in Families of Working and Nonworking Mothers

MARIAN RADKE YARROW, PHYLLIS SCOTT,
LOUISE DE LEEUW, and CHRISTINE HEINIG

In the history of research on child development and child rearing, social concerns have often stimulated particular areas of inquiry. An instance is the work of the 1930's and 1940's on the influences of early institutionalization upon children. Society's concerns about the impact of hospitalization, orphanage placement and the like posed empirical questions which research recast and redefined as basic problems in socialization. In similar fashion the rapidly increasing employment of mothers has currently prodded investigation of the effects of this changed mother role on the rearing of children. Judged by frequency of ocurrence in American family structure, maternal employment is a significant socialization variable: two out of five mothers of school age children were reported in the labor force in the 1957 survey.[1]

The initial questions directed to research on this problem, motivated from the social welfare concerns, were broad and atheoretical: "What happens to children whose mothers work?" The questions were framed with the strong suggestion that the working mother was a "problem," creating conditions of child neglect, juvenile delinquency, disorganized family life, etc. The studies resulting from the practical orientation produced a confusion of findings. In her review of the research literature on maternal employment, Stolz[2] suggests that the inconclusive nature of findings may be laid to the failure of investigators to specify the circumstances surrounding mothers' employment (whether in broken or intact families, motivated from economic stress or personal satisfactions in work, with young or older children, with or without good substitute care) and to the failure of investigators to include adequate control groups.

The inconclusive results can also be explained by the fact that most studies have failed to conceptualize maternal employment in terms of theoretically relevant variables. For example, inherent in the situation of a mother's work outside the home are mother-child separation, multiple mothering and changed mother-father roles, all of which are familiar variables of developmental research. It is apparent that maternal employment is not a single condition or variable of mothering; it is rather a set of conditions which may vary greatly from case to case.

[1] National Manpower Council, *Womanpower*, New York: Columbia University Press, 1957.
[2] Lois M. Stolz, Effects of Maternal Employment on Children: Evidence from Research," *Child Development*, 31 (December, 1960), 749–782.

A grant from the Elizabeth McCormick Memorial Fund to the American Association of University Women made possible the work of Miss Christine Heinig and Miss Phyllis Scott.
Reprinted from *Sociometry*, 25 (June, 1962), 122–140, by permission of the American Sociological Association.

The research questions in the present investigation are two: (1) When structural variables of the family environment (such as family class and composition, presence of mother, father, and supplemental mother figures) are controlled, do working and nonworking mothers provide different child-rearing environments? (2) Do working and nonworking mothers who differ in their attitudes and feelings about their adult roles differ in their maternal roles?

Personal variables which characterize the mother as an individual have generally been ignored in studies of child rearing. It is hypothesized that the mother's gratifications and frustrations in her other adult (nonmother) roles, her achievement needs, and her feelings of self-fulfillment influence her functioning as a mother and affect what is mediated to the child by her child-rearing practices. Since employment status may be intimately bound up with the mother's self attitudes and values, the study of employed and non-employed mothers who differ in attitudes offers an opportunity for an initial test of the more general hypothesis concerning the significance of this class of variables in socialization studies. The particular personal factors studied are those relating to the meaning of working or not working, i.e., the woman's sex role ideology, her basic preferences regarding working or not, the motivations supporting her present work status, and her motivations in her role as mother.

Choice of dependent variables was made on the basis of existing opinion and theory concerning the possible consequences of maternal employment for the rearing of children. Working is presumed to result in "deficiencies" in mothering: less dedication and less effectiveness, deviations in supervision and control of the child, exaggeration of the child's dependency needs, greater stress on achievement, altered sex role training, and decreased participation of mother with child.[3] Mothers' reports of practices and philosophies constitute the data on child rearing.

Sample

The subjects of this study are 50 employed and 50 nonemployed mothers. The classification of *working* required at least 28 hours of work per week in steady employment extending over the past year. To be classed in the *nonworking* group, the mother could not have engaged in any paid employment over the past year. Unfortunately the two groups have similar work histories: all having worked at some time. Half of the nonworking mothers had worked after marriage, before the birth of a child.

Subjects of the employed and nonemployed groups were matched in family characteristics. Families were white, intact, with a male wage earner present. There were one to four children per family, with a least one child (about whom the mother was interviewed) between four and eleven years of age.

PROCEDURES

In selecting the sample it was the objective to choose social class groups in which employment is not a traditional role for married women, but in

[3] Ibid.

which both a traditional woman's role and a changed role exist and are tolerated, and in which differing values and sentiments about women's employment are held. We wished to have groups in which working or not working is more likely to be a matter of individual choice than of dire economic necessity. Narrowing the class range should also reduce variations in child-rearing values and practices, leaving remaining variations more clearly attributable to personal maternal factors or the maternal work role. Middle and upper middle class families and upper working class families living in middle class neighborhoods were included in the sample (Groups I, II, III, IV on the Hollingshead Index of Social Position).

Family structural variations associated with maternal employment (separation of mother from child, substitute "mothers," changes in father and mother roles) were greatly reduced in range. Substitute care was primarily for the out-of-school hours, when, for the great majority, paid help or a relative (grandmother, aunt, occasionally an older sibling) cared for the children. Fathers retained wage earner roles in the homes of both groups.

The subjects were located in the Greater Washington area, in twelve public schools selected in terms of social class criteria. The location of eligible families in eight of the schools was facilitated by data on family characteristics from another study.[4] For these families, a letter, followed by a telephone call, determined willingness to cooperate in the study. For the other schools, it was necessary to canvass each home (with knowledge only of the age of the children) to enlist interest and determine eligibility. After preliminary screening on race and social class, approximately 650 families were further screened on family characteristics, using a brief set of polling-type questions. An eligible mother who did not consent to an interview after she had been informed of the nature of the study was counted as a refusal. Twenty-one per cent of the working mothers and 17 per cent of the mothers not employed did not consent to participate. Illness, imminent moving and the like, accounted for a few of the refusals. The other women indicated they preferred not to be research subjects. The social characteristics of the 100 interviewed mothers are presented in Table 1.

Interview Procedure

The subjects were interviewed in their homes. A schedule was followed as closely as was consistent with the responses of the subject. The interview dealt, in sequence, with the mother's past and present employment status, her motives for working or not working, and her attitudes concerning role differences of men and women as these relate to dependency and achievement needs and to primary responsibility to the home. Interview questions about child rearing included the kind of substitute care provided for the children in the mother's absence, mother's opinions about her own employment or nonemployment in relation to the rearing of her children, and

[4] Thomas L. Gillette, "The Working Mother: A Study of the Relationship Between Maternal Employment and Family Structure as Influenced by Social Class and Race," unpublished doctoral dissertation, University of North Carolina, 1961.

TABLE 1 Characteristics of Employed and Nonemployed Mothers

Characteristics		Working Mothers (N = 50)	Nonworking Mothers (N = 50)
Index of Social Position	I	16	13
	II	14	16
	III	8	14
	IV	12	7
Number of Children in Family	Mean	2.14	2.36
Sex of Children	Girls	27	27
	Boys	37	37
Age of Children*	9-11 years	36	38
	6-8 years	21	19
	4-5 years	7	7
Age of Mother	29-39	28	24
	40-50	22	26
Education of Mother			
Some college or college graduate		30	26
Some high school or high school graduate		20	24
Mother's Occupation			
Professional		13	—
Semiprofessional or managerial		12	—
Clerical or secretarial		19	—
Service trades		6	—

*Mothers were interviewed with regard to the children who met the criteria of the sample; i.e., keeping the age between 4 and 11 years, and having age and sex comparable in working and nonworking samples.

mother's philosophy and practices in the areas of discipline and control, dependency and independency training, warmth and involvement with the child and sex role training.

Independent Variables

Analyses of child-rearing variables were made in terms of the following group comparisons: (1) working and nonworking mothers of similar social and family circumstances, (2) working and nonworking mothers who *preferred* and those *who did not prefer* their present work or nonwork status, (3) working mothers whose *motives for working* differed, (4) nonworking mothers whose *attitudes toward the mother role* differed, and (5) working and nonworking mothers who differed in *academic achievement.*

The sixth variable of sex role ideology was not used because there was little variation among the subjects. It was reasoned in designing the study that ideology concerning masculine and feminine roles might be relevant to the mother's career choice and her functioning in the mother role. Therefore, subjects were asked how they felt about the ideological position that "woman's place is in the home," about the relative achievement needs of men and women, and about the acceptability of either sex showing dependency on the other. Responses were rated as predominantly equalitarian or traditional. Only 15 per cent of the mothers were rated traditional on two or three of the dimensions, 44 per cent were rated traditional in one dimension, and 41 per cent were traditional in none of the dimensions. The decision to work or not seems, for the vast majority of the sample, to be outside of this area of ideological consideration, in spite of a rare expression or two such as, "It is God's will that woman does what man wants."

Independent and dependent variables of child rearing are described in more detail in the presentation of the findings and in the Appendix. Group differences in child rearing were evaluated using chi squares for qualitative data and "t" tests for quantitative data. A sample of 26 interviews was coded by two raters working independently. A few codes were dropped which did not reach an arbitrary minimum of 80 per cent coder agreement. Forty-seven per cent of coded categories used in the report were between 80 per cent and 89 per cent in inter-rater agreement; 53 per cent of the coded categories were 90 per cent or above in agreement.

Dependent Variables

Several aspects of the child-rearing relationship were explored in the interview. Relative to areas of discipline and control the interviewer attempted to draw out the general tone of control in the home: how strict was the mother and how did mother and father compare on strictness? Both a direct question to the mother and a rating based on answers to all interview questions on control were obtained. Since the two scores were highly correlated, only the mother's direct statement was used in analysis. The mother was questioned about techniques of discipline used more than occasionally with her child. She was questioned in more detail about the child's display of aggressive behavior and her handling of his aggression. An over-all evaluation was made of the degree to which discipline and control seemed to be a contested issue between mother and child. The interview questions forming the basis for ratings and the nature of the rating scales are given in the Appendix for each of the dependent variables.

The nature of dependency-independency relations between mother and child is not easily tapped by interview questions. Questions were asked about the areas in which the child was granted freedom of decision and action and in which he was given responsibility, and the kinds and amount of attention and help which the child sought from his mother. The child's age was taken into consideration in judging the degree to which these factors signified dependence of child and independency training by the mother.

The mother's sensitivity, emotional satisfaction and involvement with her children and her confidence in her mother role were judged by criteria applied to the total interview or sections of questioning rather than to specific questions.

The underlying philosophy and operation of rearing were appraised in the following terms: Did the mother have clearly formulated principles regarding child rearing or did she proceed in a kind of haphazard performance of child care-taking acts as the needs arose? How did principles of rearing carry over into practice? Were the limits set for the child clear or unclear in practice?

Working might make a difference in household schedule, therefore the amount of time pressure or close scheduling was rated. Because of possible differences between working and nonworking women in attitudes toward sex roles, the mother's philosophy about the rearing of boys and girls, and the practices of the family in carrying out household duties, whether according to traditional sex-typed patterns or not, were obtained.

Finally, prior to data analysis, a model of "good" mothering was constructed which combined a set of variables of philosophy and practice. The "good" mother is described in terms of eight variables measured by the interview. (1) At a cognitive level, the "good" mother gives evidence of some formulated principles that guide her rearing practices. (2) She recognizes the importance of supporting the individual potentialities and the growing independence of the child. (3) She shows reasonable consistency between her principles and reported practices. (4) The "good" mother's practices provide clear limits for her child. (5) She establishes controls which are accepted without continuing conflict between parent and child. (6) The "good" mother shows sensitivity to the individual child's needs. (7) She has a feeling of confidence about her child rearing (though she is not necessarily without problems) and (8) she expresses warmth and emotional satisfaction in her relationship with her child. A summary score (0 to 8) of "adequacy of mothering" was derived from ratings on these eight variables.

FINDINGS

Work Status

As indicated in Table 2, the classification of mothers by whether or not they are employed is almost unrelated to child-rearing patterns. These working and nonworking mothers, who are of similar cultural background and family circumstances, are very much alike in philosophy, practices and apparent relationships with their children. In only one comparison is the difference between the groups statistically significant at the 5 per cent level. This difference is in the mother's confidence about her role as mother. Working mothers (42%) more frequently than nonworking mothers (24%) express misgivings and anxious concern about their role, often by explicit questioning and worry as to whether working is interfering with their relationships and the rearing of their children.

Absence of differences in certain of the variables is particularly interesting. The working and nonworking mothers do not express differing points of view on sex role training. About 40 per cent of the total sample present opinions of philosophy which emphasize differences in the rearing of boys and girls in such respects as handling of aggression, activity, social relationships; 40 per cent reject the idea of rearing differences; the others are uncertain. Using household responsibilities that are assigned to boys and girls as a measure of sex role typing, families of working and nonworking mothers again do not differ (40 per cent in the working group, 42 per cent in the nonworking assign tasks in terms of traditional sex roles). It may seem reasonable to expect that a working mother will have greater need to schedule time carefully and may, therefore, inject more time-tension into family routines. There is only a suggestive difference in the expected direc-

TABLE 2 Parent-Child Relationships by Work Status and Satisfaction of Mother*

Parent-Child Variables	Working vs. Nonworking Mothers			Satisfied vs. Dissatisfied	
	All Mothers	Satisfied	Dissatisfied	Working	Nonworking
Discipline					
1. Mother's strictness	—	—	—	—	—
2. Father stricter than mother	—	—	—	S < D (.05)	—
3. Disciplinary techniques	—	—	—	—	—
4. Mother's permissiveness of aggression	W < NW (.10)	—	—	—	—
5. Child's rebellious behavior	—	—	W < NW (.05)	—	—
6. Control an issue between mother and child	—	—	W < NW (.01)	S < D (.10)	S < D (.05)
Independence Training					
1. Nurturing independence	—	—	—	S < D (.10)	—
2. Household responsibilities	—	—	—	S < D (.10)	—
3. Child's dependence on mother	—	—	—	S < D (.02)	—
Emotional Relationships					
1. Sensitivity to child's needs	W < NW (.10)	W < NW (.05)	—	—	—
2. Emotional satisfaction in relationships with child	—	—	W > NW (.10)	—	S > D (.02)
3. Planned activities with child:					
by mother	—	—	—	—	—
by father	—	—	—	—	—
4. Confidence in child rearing	W < NW (.05)	—	W > NW (.10)	—	D < S (.01)
Rearing Environment					
1. Formulated principles of rearing	—	—	—	—	—
2. Clarity of limits set for child	—	—	W > NW (.10)	S < D (.05)	S > D (.05)
3. Consistency between principles and practices	—	—	—	—	S > D (.01)
4. Scheduling	W > NW (.10)	—	—	—	—
5. Traditional philosophy re sex role training	—	—	—	—	—
6. Traditional sex-typed household functions	—	—	—	—	—
7. Adequacy of mothering (summary rating)	—	W < NW (.10)	W > D (.02)	—	S > D (.01)

*The probability that an observed relationship could have occurred by chance is indicated in parentheses.

tion; pressured scheduling is prominent among 26 per cent of the working and 12 per cent of the nonworking group. Working and nonworking mothers do not differ on the summary measure of adequacy of mothering.

Role Preference

More important in differentiating mothers according to child-rearing practices than the fact of working or not working is how the work variable is combined with other maternal characteristics (Table 2). When work (or non-work) is analyzed according to whether it is a goal in itself or a means to certain goal attainments, associations with child rearing take on more mean-ingful patternings. The mothers clearly differed in their desires to work or not to work outside the home. Replies to two questions determined their classifi-cation as preferring or not preferring their present status: (1) if given the choice, would the mother want to work, and (2) how would she rank a number of alternatives involving job, marriage and children. Seventy-six per cent of the working mothers and 82 per cent of the nonworking mothers indicated preference for their present situations. The resulting four subgroups were compared in their childrearing characteristics.

The questions about these groups can be asked in two ways: (1) Do work-ing and nonworking mothers who are similarly satisfied (or dissatisfied) with present status differ in child rearing? (2) How do working mothers who prefer to work and those who do not prefer to work compare, and, likewise, how do nonworking mothers who prefer to work and those who do not prefer to work compare on child rearing?

Dissatisfaction with present role appears to contribute to mothering functions, and especially among mothers who are not employed. The sub-groups differ as follows. If mothers are in their *preferred* work or nonwork *roles*, working or not working makes little difference in their child rearing. There are only two suggestive differences: Thirty-four per cent of satisfied nonworking mothers and 11 per cent of satisfied working mothers are rated as showing high sensitivity to children's needs. There is a difference of borderline significance giving the nonworking satisfied mothers higher scores on adequacy of mothering. When *dissatisfied* working and nonworking mothers are compared, differences appear in areas of control, emotional satisfaction, confidence in child rearing and on scores on adequacy of mothering, favoring the dissatisfied working mothers. For example, 67 per cent of dissatisfied nonworking mothers and 18 per cent of dissatisfied working mothers report a more or less continuing "battle" for control between mother and child. High ratings in confidence in the mother role occur more often among the working than the nonworking dissatisfied mothers (50 per cent and 11 per cent, respectively). In the closely related measure of emotional satisfaction in relationships with the child there are similar differences favoring the working over the nonworking dissatisfied mothers. The sum of ratings shows significantly lower scores on adequacy of mothering for the dissatisfied non-working mothers than for the dissatisfied working mothers.

The same data may be examined with work status controlled. Among *working* mothers there is some support for the idea that there are more internal inconsistencies in child rearing among the dissatisfied than among the satisfied mothers. Three-fourths of the dissatisfied mothers compared with two-fifths of the satisfied mothers report clear limit-setting for the child. At the same time, however, control is more often rated a continuing issue in the family for the dissatisfied than for the satisfied mothers. More dissatisfied working mothers describe their children as dependent while at the same time tending to exert more verbal pressure toward independent behavior and to assign more responsibilities to their children than do the satisfied mothers.

Among *nonworking* mothers, several dimensions of child-rearing behavior are clearly related to role preference. Clarity in limit setting is more characteristic of the satisfied mothers (61 per cent of this group as compared with 22 per cent in the dissatisfied group). A significantly higher proportion of dissatisfied mothers show extreme inconsistency between principles and practices (57 per cent of the dissatisfied mothers as compared with 6 per cent of the satisfied mothers). Control remains a continuing "issue" between mother and child for 67 per cent of the dissatisfied and 32 per cent of the satisfied mothers. Lack of emotional satisfaction in relationships with her child is more frequent among dissatisfied than satisfied mothers (78 per cent and 35 per cent, respectively). Similarly, high confidence in the mother role, expressed in 90 per cent of the satisfied group, is rare (11%) among the dissatisfied mothers. The generally inferior mothering by the dissatisfied nonworking group is reflected in significantly lower summary scores on adequacy of mothering.

Motives for Working and Not Working

Although it is understandable that a woman's career dissatisfactions may enter into her relationships with her child, it is not so clear why this should be more the case in the nonworking than in the working group. A possible explanation may lie in understanding why the women were working or not working, regardless of their expressed preference. The mothers in this sample were working either primarily as a means of achieving certain *family and child-rearing goals* that were not available without the mother's working, or as a means of *self-fulfillment.* Mothers (52%) who spoke of family goals were interested in cultural advantages, social status, educational and health goals for the family. They included both mothers who preferred and those who did not prefer to work. Mothers (48%) who found self-fulfillment through working referred to use of their educational training, feelings of contributing to society, needing to be with people, etc. These mothers preferred to work.

Since working but preferring not to is related to valued family benefits, the situation for these reluctant working mothers does not appear to represent great frustration. Certainly one would expect these mothers to be less frustrated than women who have reason to resent the necessity for their working as a circumstance forced upon them by their husbands' failures or as a circumstance in which the work itself involves personal hardship. The absence of differences in child-rearing associated with family motivations and self-fulfillment motivation is, therefore, not surprising (Table 3).

Among nonworking women reasons for not working reflect either a *love of mothering* (48%), a *duty to mothering* (36%), or a desire for "freedom,"

TABLE 3 Parent-Child Relationships by Work Status, Motivation, and Education of Mother*

Parent-Child Variables	Family vs. Self Motives: Working Mothers Only	Love vs. Duty Motives: Non-Working Mothers Only	Working vs. Nonworking Mothers		High School vs. College Attendance	
			High School Attendance	College Attendance	Working Mothers	Nonworking Mothers
Discipline						
1. Mother's strictness	—	—	—	—	—	—
2. Father stricter than mother	F > S (.10)	—	W > NW (.05)	—	H > C (.02)	—
3. Disciplinary techniques	—	—	—	—	—	—
4. Mother's permissiveness of aggression	F > S (.10)	—	—	—	—	—
5. Child's rebellious behavior	—	L < D (.10)	W < NW (.01)	—	—	—
6. Control an issue between mother and child	—	L < D (.10)	—	—	—	—
Independence Training						
1. Nurturing independence	—	L > D (.05)	W > NW (.05)	—	—	H < C (.05)
2. Household responsibilities	—	—	W > NW (.10)	—	—	—
3. Child's dependence on mother	—	—	—	—	—	—
Emotional Relationships						
1. Sensitivity to child's needs	—	L > D (.02)	—	W < NW (.10)	H < C (.02)	H < C (.01)
2. Emotional satisfaction in relationships with child	—	L > D (.05)	—	—	—	—
3. Planned activities with child:						
by mother	—	—	—	W > NW (.10)	—	—
by father	—	—	—	W > NW (.02)	—	—
4. Confidence in child rearing	—	L > D (.02)	—	—	—	—
Rearing Environment						
1. Formulated principles of rearing	—	—	—	—	—	—
2. Clarity of limits set for child	—	—	—	W < NW (.02)	—	H < C (.05)
3. Consistency between principles and practices	—	—	—	—	—	H < C (.02)
4. Scheduling	—	—	—	—	—	—
5. Traditional philosophy re sex role training	F < S (.05)	—	—	—	—	—
6. Traditional sex-typed household functions	—	—	—	—	—	—
7. Adequacy of mothering (summary rating)	—	L > D (.05)	—	—	—	H < C (.05)

*The probability that an observed relationship could have occurred by chance is indicated in parentheses.

or an "easier" life (15%). "Freedom" is for avocations and "volunteer" work but also, on the less noble side, it is freedom regarded selfishly. As one woman said, she "had it made;" now that husband and children could get their own breakfasts and get off to work and school, the day was for herself. Because of the heterogeneity of motives in the "freedom" group, it was not used in further analyses.

Mothers classified by "love" and by "duty" express different feelings toward the mother role. The "love" mothers are oriented entirely toward mothering; the "duty" mothers speak of child rearing as a responsibility that carries with it various hardships and deprivations. The classification of "love" and "duty" in general parallels the classification of satisfied and dissatisfied nonworking mothers, although "duty" mothers appear in both the satisfied and dissatisfied groups. Differences in child rearing are similar in both classifications; the less favorable qualities appearing in the "duty" and the dissatisfied mothers.

The data on the nonworking mothers support the position that the mother's motivations and fulfillments in nonmother roles are related to her behavior in the child-rearing role. It is necessary, in a sense, first to look at maternal employment and nonemployment as dependent variables before making predictions concerning associated child-rearing variables.

Mothers' Education

If work status is ignored, college-trained and high school-trained mothers (within the class range of our sample) do not differ on child-rearing measures. But, when work status and educational level and child rearing are considered together suggestive interactions appear (Table 3). *Nonworking* college mothers and nonworking high school mothers appear to differ in more ways in child rearing than do *working* college mothers and working high school mothers. In the *nonworking* groups, college mothers are significantly more often rated high in independence training (30 per cent and 8 per cent for college and high school, respectively), in sensitivity (50% and 8%), in consistency between principles and practice (85% and 54%), and in clarity in limit setting (69% and 39%). The higher mean scores for the college mothers on "adequacy of mothering" summary score reflect the differences on the individual items. The *working* groups differ only on ratings of sensitivity to child's needs (40 per cent and 10 per cent of high school and college mothers, respectively, are rated low on sensitivity), and on the father's being the stricter parent (70 per cent and 34 per cent of high school and college groups are so rated). The data suggest that employment may be selective of certain kinds of mothers, or that working has the effect of "leveling" social class differences in child rearing. The mothers of high school background who are using working as a means of social mobility (more lessons, education, travel for family) may also be altering their child-rearing practices.

When working and nonworking mothers are compared within each educational group, it appears that families of different social class backgrounds make different types of adaptations to the mother's working. Mothers of high school background more often report the father as the stricter parent when these mothers work (70%) than when they do not work (33%).

Children are less likely to be reported as rebellious by working mothers (10%) than by nonworking mothers (46%) in the high school group. Similarly, they are more likely to be assigned a heavy load of household responsibilities (30 per cent as compared with 8 per cent). The working mothers are more likely to stress independence training (80 per cent as compared with 54 per cent). In other words, children of the working mothers with *high school* backgrounds are under firmer control and are called upon to perform with more responsibility and independence.

The picture for the college-trained group is not the same. The college working mother compared with her nonworking peers is not more likely to describe the father as the stricter parent; there is instead a tendency in the opposite direction (the father is the stricter parent in 30 per cent and 50 per cent of the working and nonworking groups, respectively). Assignment of responsibilities and nurturance of independence are not stressed by the college-trained working mothers as they are by the working mothers with high school background. (The differences, though not significant, are in the opposite direction from the high school group.)

A variable which has not shown differences in any other comparisons but which appears in the working-nonworking comparisons of college-trained women is that of planned shared time and activities with the child. In the families of college working mothers both parents apparently attempt to compensate for out-of-the-home time by planned time together with the child. Forty per cent of the college working mothers report giving planned time to the child. It is reported for 38% of the fathers. The nonworking college group have 16 per cent and 8 per cent in the comparable categories. In families of high school background there is no difference in this variable between working and nonworking groups.

Subcultural or social class analyses may be extremely important in attempting to pin down the kinds of influences that the widespread employment of mothers may have on the socialization of large populations of children. The present data suggest that rearing influences cannot be predicted across class and cultural boundaries (any more than they can be predicted across motivational differences among mothers), and that the nature of influences for different social groups will vary and will grow out of the values and needs of the particular groups.

SUMMARY AND CONCLUSIONS

Qualities of child rearing by mothers who are employed and those who are not employed outside the home have been studied. One hundred mothers of intact families, of the middle and upper middle class white urban population were interviewed. Families of working and nonworking mothers were matched on family composition and social class.

Mothers' employment status is not related to child-rearing characteristics. The data, however, support the hypothesis that mothers' fulfillments or frustrations in nonmother roles are related to child rearing. When mothers' motivations regarding working are taken into account, the nonworking mothers who are dissatisfied with not working (who want to work but, out of a feeling of "duty," do not work) show the greatest problems in child rearing. They describe more difficulties in the area of control, less emotional satisfaction in relationships with their children, and less confidence in their functioning as mothers. They have lower summary scores on "adequacy of mothering." Working mothers who prefer to work and those who do not wish to work show few group differences in child-rearing practices, probably because the working mothers (of this sample) who prefer not to work are nonetheless achieving certain valued family goals by means of their employment.

Among high school-trained mothers, differences between working and non-working mothers appear in the following areas of rearing: firmer control over children, assignment of greater responsibilities to children, and delegation of the stricter disciplinary role to the father appear more frequently in families of working than nonworking mothers. In the college-trained working and nonworking groups, these differences do not appear. The college working parents tend to compensate for time away from children by more planned, shared activities with their children than is found in the college nonworking group. The data on educational groups suggest that maternal employment brings different kinds of familial adaptations depending on the value systems of the particular cultural subgroups in which the mother is combining mother and worker roles.

The findings of the present study confirm and elaborate observations by other investigators[5] of the importance of social, familial and personal factors in determining the kind of success the mother achieves in her dual roles. The specific differences in child-rearing practices reported in the present study are perhaps less important in our conclusions (until they are replicated) than is the general pattern of significant subgroupings of mothers in relation to child rearing.

The findings of this study have relevance for studies of child rearing more generally in pointing to the interplay of rearing practices (as they are usually defined) and maternal motivations within differing subcultures. These variables need further scrutiny in studies of child-rearing antecedents of child behavior and personality.

APPENDIX

Description of Dependent Variables

Discipline 1. Mother's strictness. Mother's ratings on direct questions of how strict she regards her discipline (3 point scale).

2. Father stricter than mother. Mother's statement of relative strictness of mother and father.

[5] Ibid.; Ruth E. Hartley, "What Aspects of Child Behavior Should be Studied in Relation to Maternal Employment?" in Alberta E. Siegel, ed., *Research Issues Related to the Effects of Maternal Employment on Children*, University Park, Pennsylvania: Social Science Research Center, 1961; Lois Hoffman, "Effects of Maternal Employment on the Child," *Child Development*, 32 (March, 1961), 187–197; Alberta E. Siegel, "Characteristics of the Mother Related to the Impact of Maternal Employment or Non-employment," in Alberta E. Siegel, ed., op. cit.

3. Disciplinary techniques. Mother's reports of control techniques used: Presence or absence of physical punishment, isolation or deprivation, reasoning, commanding and scolding, manipulation by threat of loss of love or creating guilt, praise and affection, distraction. It should be noted that none of the specific techniques differentiated among groups.

4. Mother's permissiveness of aggression. Ratings based on mother's descriptions of child's "temper" and aggression—its frequency, intensity, how she handles it: "All children feel angry now and then. How about _____, would you say he (she) has a temper? How does he show it? Over what things? With whom? How often? How bad before you step in? How do you handle it? How much does he get into fights? How do you handle these?" (5 point scale)

5. Child's rebellious behavior. (Based on same questions as 4 above. 5 point scale)

6. Control an issue between mother and child. Ratings of degree of "issue," based on mother's descriptions of child's reactions to questions: "Does child find it hard to obey? What ways of handling him do you find best, if he does have difficulty? Would you say child has a temper? How does he show it? How often? How do you handle this? In what ways does child sometimes get on your nerves?" (5 point scale)

Independence Training 1. Nurturing independence. Ratings of responses to questions: "In what kinds of things do you feel you can allow your child a fair amount of freedom and in what things do you feel you should keep firm control? What regular jobs or responsibilities does he have? How important is it to you that he carry these out?" (4 point scale)

2. Household responsibilities. Ratings of same questions for quantity of jobs and responsibilities assigned. (3 point scale)

3. Child's dependence on mother. Separate ratings of reports of child's responses to separations from mother, and child's seeking help and attention from mother, "How does _____ act when you leave him with somebody else? How much help does _____ ask from you in getting things done, with homework, with ideas, dressing, or to ask for information? Do you feel this is necessary, or that he could manage without it?" (3 point scale)

Emotional Relationships 1. Sensitivity to child's needs. Overall ratings of apparent communication between mother and child, how much mother has manifested awareness of child's feelings and her response to child's feelings, how mother has indicated "adjustments" in her actions to meet needs of child, mother's recognition of individuality in her children, mother's insight into her difficulties with her child. (3 point scale)

2. Emotional satisfaction in relationships with child. Overall ratings of mother's explicit expressions of enjoyment, satisfaction, frustration, rejection as well as the indirect display of enjoyment or lack of it. (4 point scale)

3. Planned activities with child by mother and father. Description of activities with child, when and how they occur. Who initiates? Any planning ahead? (3 point scale)

4. Confidence in child rearing. Responses to question "What has child gained or lacked because of your job, or because you have stayed at home?"

Reactions to the difficulties experienced with her child with regard to control. Spontaneous expressions of "failure" and misgiving as well as of success and confidence. (3 point scale)

Rearing Environment 1. Formulated principles of rearing. Number of statements of rearing principles given spontaneously anywhere in interview, as well as evidence of formulated principles in response to questions regarding control-freedom and dependency-independency items. (3 point scale)

2. Clarity of limits set for child. Questions on giving or encouraging freedom and independence and on supporting dependence, and on handling aggression, obedience, and conformity (described under these headings). Clarity ratings are based on how explicit are the limits set for the child. (3 point scale)

3. Consistency between principles and practices. Consistency ratings compare philosophy or intention and described practices in these areas. Based on same questions as 2 above. (3 point scale)

4. Scheduling. Overall ratings of evidences of time-tension, concern about timing and schedule. (3 point scale)

5. Traditional philosophy regarding sex role training. Response to question "Do you (could you) bring up boys and girls in much the same way; or are there differences in the way they are reared?"

6. Traditional sex-typed household functions. Traditional sex typing of regular household tasks carried out or assigned to each parent and to child. (3 point scale)

7. Adequacy of mothering (summary rating). Summary ratings on eight variables; see text.

| VIII | Social Class, Race, and Family

Introduction to Section VIII

This section and those that follow tend to emphasize the interrelationships among the family system and other parts of society. The preceding sections recognized some of these relationships but stressed more the internal role relationships in the family system. We move now to show more of the causal connections with other broad societal forces. For example, the Kohn excerpt (22) is taken from his book-length report of a national study and some smaller studies of the ways in which the father's occupation shapes his values and thereby influences the values he passes down to his children. The importance of this for understanding human society cannot be overemphasized. Kohn found that lower-class occupations involve more obedience and middle-class occupations more self-reliance, and that fathers tended to pass on these specific values to their children. This means that lower-class children are taught obedience and thus are best prepared to work at lower-class occupations and least prepared to work at middle-class occupations where self-reliance is more crucial. In this fashion, limits are set on upward mobility. Note that this difference in class values parallels the difference Barry and his colleagues (3) found in the socialization of males and females in most societies. Thus, females as well as lower-class males can be seen to be at a disadvantage in the occupational world because of the emphasis in their training on obedience values. Any effort at equalization will have to take these factors into account if it is to succeed. Less discrimination will not equalize job distribution as long as some groups are less prepared for the higher-ranked jobs because of the values their parents have stressed. It is interesting to speculate on the impact of the increase in the proportion of working mothers. Will the mother's values be altered in ways that will change the values of her child? If so, will the mother with a white-collar job pass on values that counteract the values of her blue-collar husband? Kohn's initial data suggest that this will indeed be the case.

329

Family stability is generally less in the lower classes and such instability seems to interfere with occupational success.[1] Billingsley points out the importance of the family in the search for equality of the black segment of our society (23). However, he adds that strengthening the family will be most helpful if the sources of the class and caste stigmata of the blacks are attacked at the same time. It is interesting to note that Billingsley presents data for blacks and whites on the percentages of families headed by *men*. Usually this comparison is made in terms of percent of families headed by *women* and thereby stress is put on the black–white difference. Billingsley's method of presenting this data makes it clear that the majority of all subtypes of black families are headed by men. This is a more impartial way to present such information. Whatever one's values may be, the knowledge afforded in these studies should assist one in understanding the present situation of class and racial inequality.

Tallman and Marotz (24), and Rainwater (25), add some specifics to our understanding of the relations among occupation, race, and family. The Tallman and Marotz data on blue-collar families in the suburbs is quite rare. However, such data will increasingly be in demand, for the suburbs are apparently becoming more heterogeneous, and there are increasing suggestions that low-income housing be situated in the suburbs as well as in the central city areas. It is thus important to know how blue-collar life styles may be altered by a move to the suburbs. What happens to old kin ties with parents in the city and how upward mobility is affected are only two of the questions that Tallman and Marotz deal with.

One of the popular myths about blacks, and especially lower-class blacks, is that they enjoy their sexuality more than other groups. Lee Rainwater's data support the opposite conclusion. It seems that lower-class blacks are less likely to enjoy sexual relations. This was measured by both orgasm frequency and subjective feelings. Such testing of common beliefs is one important consequence of sociological research.[2] This sort of knowledge further fills out the picture of the stresses of lower-class life styles and gives some basis for understanding their higher rate of marital dissolution, which is further discussed in Section XI.

Aldous' contribution provides the reader with an overview of the relation of occupation to family roles (26). It is an excellent source of studies on this area and thus is of considerable value to one wanting to become better informed. Aldous does a skillful job of tracing the ways in which occupational demands influence the males' family-role performances. The relationship of occupation and family is one major theme of all the articles in this section of the book, and Aldous' work allows us to move closer to an understanding of the specific ways in which the occupational and family systems can succeed or fail in achieving integration. The readings in the next section also focus in part on this question.

[1] Duncan, B., and O. D. Duncan, "Family Stability and Occupational Success." *Social Problems* 16 (Winter, 1969), 273–285.

[2] See also: Rainwater, L., *Behind Ghetto Walls*. Chicago: Aldine, 1970.

22 | *Class and Conformity: An Interpretation*

MELVIN L. KOHN

Our thesis—the central conclusion of our studies—is that social class is significant for human behavior because it embodies systematically-differentiated conditions of life that profoundly affect men's views of social reality.

The essence of higher class position is the expectation that one's decisions and actions can be consequential; the essence of lower class position is the belief that one is at the mercy of forces and people beyond one's control, often, beyond one's understanding. Self-direction—acting on the basis of one's own judgment, attending to internal dynamics as well as to external consequences, being open-minded, being trustful of others, holding personally responsible moral standards—this is possible only if the actual conditions of life allow some freedom of action, some reason to feel in control of fate. Conformity—following the dictates of authority, focusing on external consequences to the exclusion of internal processes, being intolerant of nonconformity and dissent, being distrustful of others, having moral standards that strongly emphasize obedience to the letter of the law—this is the inevitable result of conditions of life that allow little freedom of action, little reason to feel in control of fate.

Self-direction, in short, requires opportunities and experiences that are much more available to people who are more favorably situated in the hierarchical order of society; conformity is the natural consequence of inadequate opportunity to be self-directed.

In interpreting the consistent relationships of class to values and orientation, it is useful to recall the many conditions that our analyses have shown to have little or no explanatory relevance. The relationship of class to parental values is not a function of parental aspirations, family structure, or—insofar as we have been able to measure them—family dynamics. The relationships of class to values and orientation in general are clearly not a function of such class-correlated dimensions of social structure as race, religion, or national background. Nor are they to be explained in terms of such facets of stratification as income and subjective class identification, or of conditions that impinge on only part of the class hierarchy, or of class origins or social mobility. Finally, the class relationships do not stem from such important (but from our point of view, tangential) aspects of occupation as the bureaucratic or entrepreneurial setting of jobs, time-pressure, job dissatisfaction, or a host of other variables. Any of these might be important for explaining the relationship of class to other social phenomena; none of them is important for explaining why class is consistently related to values and orientation.[1]

[1] It could be argued that the class relationships stem not from currently applicable structural conditions, but from historically derived cultural tradi-

Reprinted with permission from Melvin L. Kohn, *Class and Conformity: A Study of Values*, The Dorsey Press, Homewood, Ill., 1969, pp. 189–203.

By contrast, we have substantial evidence that any interpretation of the relationships of class to values and orientation must take into account the cumulative impact of education and occupational position and must recognize that occupational self-direction is importantly implicated in these relationships.

Our interpretation of these facts is that the conformist values and orientation held by people in the lower segments of the class hierarchy are a product of the limited education and constricting job conditions to which they are subject. Education is important because self-direction requires more intellectual flexibility and breadth of perspective than does conformity; tolerance of nonconformity, in particular, requires a degree of analytic ability that is difficult to achieve without formal education. But education is not all that is involved. The conformity of people at lower social class levels is in large measure a carry-over from the limitations of their occupational experiences. Men of higher class position, who have the opportunity to be self-directed in their work, want to be self-directed off the job, too, and come to think self-direction possible. Men of lower class position, who do not have the opportunity for self-direction in work, come to regard it a matter of necessity to conform to authority, both on and off the job. The job does mold the man—it can either enlarge his horizons or narrow them. The conformity of the lower social classes is only partly a result of their lack of education; it results also from the restrictive conditions of their jobs.

The Efficacy of Education

Self-directed values and orientation require that one look beyond externals, think for oneself. Education does not insure the development of these capacities, but lack of education must seriously impede their development. For most people, self-directed values and orientation require formal educational experience.

The effects of education on values and orientation are not immutable—men who are subject to occupational conditions different from those normally experienced at their educational level are likely to have somewhat different values and orientation from those of their educational peers. Nevertheless, the relationship of education to values and orientation is not greatly affected by occupational experience or by any other experiences that we have examined. The importance of education for men's values and orientation—at least under the conditions of life in the United States in the mid-1960's—is great, no matter what conditions men subsequently encounter.

Implicit in this interpretation is the assumption that the predominant direction of effect is *from* education *to* values and orientation, rather than the reverse. We do not argue that men's values have no effect on their educa-

---

tions. "Working-class culture," in this view, is derived from the historical tradition of the working class, rather than stemming from the realistic conditions of today's working class. But explanations of class culture based either on accidental origins or on past structural conditions that no longer hold sway seem to us to be insufficient. We want to know: Why does a historically derived class culture persist under present conditions?

tional attainment. Quite the contrary: It is probable that self-directed values and orientation are a powerful impetus for educational attainment. In the actual circumstances of most people's lives, though, values and orientation probably have less effect upon educational attainment than educational attainment has upon values and orientation. This is in part because critical, often irreversible, decisions about education are made in behalf of children and adolescents by parents and other adults (and thus reflect the adults' values). In larger part, it is because of the inequitable distribution of social resources. Educational opportunities—good schools, stimulating teachers—and the economic resources to take advantage of such opportunities are not equally distributed, nor are children of varying class backgrounds always treated equally even within the same school. This issue is so much at the forefront of informed public attention that it need hardly be pursued further here.

Values and orientation undoubtedly influence educational attainment, but for most people education is primarily a determinant, rather than a consequence, of self-directed values and orientation.[2]

Occupational Position and Occupational Self-Direction

In industrial society, where occupation is central to men's lives, occupational experiences that facilitate or deter the exercise of self-direction come to permeate men's views, not only of work and of their role in work, but of the world and of self. The conditions of occupational life at higher social class levels facilitate interest in the intrinsic qualities of the job, foster a view of self and society that is conducive to believing in the possibilities of rational action toward purposive goals, and promote the valuation of self-direction. The conditions of occupational life at lower social class levels limit men's view of the job primarily to the extrinsic benefits it provides, foster a narrowly circumscribed conception of self and society, and promote the positive valuation of conformity to authority. Conditions of work that foster thought and initiative tend to enlarge men's conceptions of reality, conditions of constraint tend to narrow them.

The processes by which men come to generalize from occupational to nonoccupational realities need not be althogether or even mainly rational; all that we mean to assert is that occupation markedly affects men, not that men rationally decide on values and orientations to fit the facts of their occupational experiences.[3] The essential point was made more than a third of a century ago by Waller (1932:375–376) in his classic study of teachers and teaching:

What does any occupation do to the human being who follows it? . . . We know that some occupations markedly distort the personalities of those who practice them, that there are occupational patterns to which one conforms his personality as to a Procrustean bed by lopping off superfluous

[2] The point is well illustrated by Rosenberg's (1957) study of changes in students' values during their college years.
[3] Cf. Breer and Locke, 1965, for experimental evidence on how "task experience" affects values and beliefs.

members. Teaching is by no means the only occupation which whittles its followers to convenient size and seasons them to suit its taste. The lawyer and the chorus girl soon come to be recognizable social types. One can tell a politician when one meets him on the street. Henry Adams has expanded upon the unfitness of senators for being anything but senators; occupational molding, then, affects the statesman as much as lesser men. The doctor is always the doctor, and never quite can quit his role. The salesman lives in a world of selling configurations. And what preaching most accomplishes is upon the preacher himself. Perhaps no occupation that is followed long fails to leave its stamp upon the person.

As with education, there is a question of direction of effect.[4] We have assumed—as did Waller—that the job does affect the man, that the relationship between occupational self-direction and values does not simply reflect the propensity of self-directed men to gravitate into self-directed jobs. We recognize the tendency for self-directed men to search out opportunities for occupational self-direction. Nevertheless, there are stringent limitations to men's deciding for themselves how much self-direction they will exercise in their work.

The most important limitation is that occupational choice is dependent on educational qualifications—which are greatly affected by the accidents of family background, economic circumstances, and available social resources. At any educational level, most occupational choice is among jobs of about the same degree of self-direction—men of limited educational background may perhaps choose between factory work and construction work, but neither offers much opportunity for self-direction, and jobs that do are not open to them.

Moreover, the possibilities for enlarging the sphere of self-direction by shifting to other occupations are seriously limited. Most job changes are not radical. Having completed their educations and embarked on their first jobs, few men have the chance to make any substantial change in these occupational conditions.

Furthermore, there are limits to how much men actually can mold their jobs. It is true that men placed in similar occupational positions will play their roles differently, some utilizing every opportunity for self-direction, some being altogether dependent on external direction. But there are structural limitations upon the leeway that jobs provide, and the limits are most severe at the lowest levels.

The reinforcing processes by which jobs affect values and orientation, and values and orientation reflect back on jobs, are undoubtedly more complex than we have represented. The thrust of our discussion is not that all influence is in one direction, but rather that the occupational conditions attendant on men's class positions are important in shaping their values and orientation.

[4] We intend, in our further research, to try to differentiate the effects of "occupational self-selection" from those of occupational experience. This analysis will have to take account of men's entering and leaving occupations.

Historical Trends

If our interpretation that education and occupational self-direction underlie class differences in values and orientation is valid, it suggests that a major
historical trend probably has been—and will continue to be—toward an increasingly self-directed populace.[5] It is well known that educational levels
have long been rising and are continuing to do so. What is not so well recognized is that levels of occupational self-direction have also been rising, and
almost certainly will continue to rise.

Despite the widely held belief that the industrial revolution substituted
a multitude of unskilled operations for an earlier pattern of skilled artisan-
ship, industrialization probably has increased the general level of occupational self-direction (cf. Blauner, 1966:484). Men have thought otherwise
because their images of past and present treated as typical of the times the
craftsman of preindustrial days and the assembly line worker of today. The
facts, though, are that most men in preindustrial times were agricultural
laborers, not craftsmen, and that the degradation of work on the assembly
line is far from typical of industrial occupations today. Even in automobile
plants, most men do not work on the line (cf. Walker and Guest, 1952; Chinoy,
1955). What is more important, the assembly line has never become the
dominant type of industrial organization (cf. Blauner, 1964) and is clearly not
the model for present and future industrial development.

The industrial model for the future, automation, far from extending the
assembly-line practice of dividing skilled jobs into a series of unskilled jobs,
gives mindless tasks to the machines and substitutes for mere drudgery,
newly created thinking tasks (cf. Blauner, 1964; Walker, 1957). Automation
builds on the rising levels of education of the population and markedly
increases the opportunities and requirements for occupational self-direction.
The introduction of automation comes at high social cost—ever-shrinking
employment opportunities for the less educated and the untrained. The long-
range prospect, though, is for a better educated society of men whose jobs
require substantially more judgment, thought, and initiative than did those of
any past era.

The United States and Other Industrialized Nations

Is our interpretation as applicable to other industrialized societies as
to the United States? It has been said, for example, that the family is a weak
institution in the United States, easily penetrated by the occupational system.
Perhaps occupational experiences are less relevant, and family more, in other

---

[5] Moreover, the industrialization of non-Western countries is probably
having much the same effect today. There is growing evidence from Inkeles'
(1966) research on underdeveloped countries that everywhere the movement
of peasants into industrial occupations results in changes in attitudes, values,
and beliefs (changes which Inkeles calls "modernization") that are altogether
consonant with the effects we attribute to occupational self-direction. Inkeles
sees education and occupational experience as independently contributing to
these effects.

countries. Perhaps occupational self-direction is a less critical aspect of life in societies that have a less activist ethos. Or perhaps class identification matters more and objective occupational conditions less in societies where class ideologies are more pronounced. Unfortunately, there are only limited data with which to examine these possibilities.

The most important data are those compiled by Inkeles in "Industrial Man: the Relation of Status to Experience, Perception, and Value" (1960). His thesis is that industrialization has everywhere produced comparable effects on man, manifested especially in similar relationships of class to perceptions, attitudes, and values in all industrialized countries. In support of this thesis, he has gathered evidence from a great diversity of sources and countries. For example, in the United States, Italy, West Germany, Norway, the Soviet Union, and Sweden, occupational position is consistently related to job satisfaction, with highly placed men always more satisfied. In the United States, Italy, West Germany, Norway, England, France, Australia, Mexico, and the Netherlands, there are fairly consistent relationships between class position and feelings of happiness or psychic well-being: The "better off" are in all instances happier. In 8 of 11 countries for which data on parental values exist, the lowest class (of those studied) is the most likely to value obedience. And in some seven countries, class position is positively related to men's belief in the possibility of change in human nature—which Inkeles takes as an indication of confidence that man can master his environment.

There are additional data in Inkeles' storehouse, but these are sufficient to demonstrate the validity of his assertion that class has similar effects in all industrial societies. What is lacking, as he explicitly states, is evidence that class has similar effects for the same reasons in all these countries.

To our knowledge, the only directly pertinent data are those we have reported from Turin. These data show, not only that class is related to parental values in northern Italy as in the United States, but also that occupational self-direction is as important for explaining the relationship of class to values in northern Italy as in the United States. Occupation penetrates the family in Italy, too.

Valuable as the Turin findings are, they speak only of parental values, not of values and orientation in general. Moreover, although it is invaluable to know that occupational self-direction plays as important a role in the relationship of class to parental values in Italy as in the United States, the same may not be true for non-Western societies, for non-capitalist societies, or even for these same societies under changed economic or social circumstances. Still, we have one critical bit of information (Turin), many pertinent supplementary data (primarily those provided by Inkeles), and considerable tangential evidence (the corpus of studies of social stratification in other societies)—all of which are consistent with the inference that what we have said of the United States is true for industrial societies generally.

Our best guess is that, as more is learned, we shall come to conclude that the American situation represents a perhaps extreme instance of a very general pattern. There may be minor variations on this pattern; class identification, for example, may be of greater importance in societies where class divisions are more recognized and more ideologically relevant. But we doubt that there are any sizeable industrial societies—Western or non-Western, capitalist, socialist, or communist—in which the relationship of class to conformity is much different, or in which occupational self-direction does not play a major part in this relationship.

VALUES AND BEHAVIOR

Class differences in values and orientation have far-ranging effects on behavior. That men of higher class position are more self-directed in their views of social reality and men of lower class position more conformist, means that they see—and respond to—decidedly different realities.

Granted, men do not simply act out their preconceptions: Behavior is almost always responsive to situational and institutional constraints and, even in areas of high emotional involvement, may be greatly affected by these constraints.[6] Still, there is always some (and often great) latitude for differential perception of the elements of a given situation, differential evaluation of these elements, differential choice, and differential action. The crux of the matter is elegantly summarized in W. I. Thomas' dictum, "If men define situations as real, they are real in their consequences" (Thomas and Thomas, 1928:572). Class profoundly affects men's definitions of reality and their evaluations of reality so conceived.

Our findings about parental responses to children's misbehavior are especially pertinent in illustrating how class differences in definitions of reality affect behavior. If only the external consequences of children's actions are thought to be real, parents will attend only to external consequences. If parents are oriented to children's internal dynamics, they will try to be attentive to and will respond to what they understand to be the children's motives and feelings. Neither middle- nor working-class parents necessarily follow the rationally appropriate course of action for accomplishing their goals. Nevertheless, class differences in responses to children's misbehavior can best be understood when one realizes how class differences in parental values and orientation affect parents' perceptions and evaluations of children's actions.

Since social scientists understand (and largely share) middle-class values, we find middle-class parental behavior self-evidently reasonable. But, because many of us have not had an adequate grasp of working-class values, it has been less apparent that working-class parental behavior is also reasonable. Some have asserted, for example, that working-class parents are oriented only to the present and give little thought to the effects of their actions on their children's futures. We contend, instead, that working-class parents are as concerned as are middle-class parents about their children's futures, but that social scientists have not sufficiently understood working-class-goals. Parental actions that seem, from the middle-class perspective, to be oblivious to the children's needs are, from the working-class perspective, altogether appropriate to parental goals in child rearing.

Similarly, from the point of view of middle-class values, fathers who are

[6] The evidence comes principally from one arena—race relations—but the lessons are equally applicable to other behavior. (Cf. LaPiere, 1934; Mannheim, 1941; Lohman and Reitzes, 1952; Kohn and Williams, 1956.)

not supportive of sons shirk an important responsibility. From the point of view of working-class values, there is no such paternal responsibility.

Even though the evidence in this book deals with only a limited segment of human behavior, this evidence demonstrates that values and orientation provide an important mechanism by which social structure is translated into individual actions. Admittedly, values and orientation are not the only intervening mechanism from class to behavior; in all probability, a variety of other processes reinforce the ones on which we focus. If we over-emphasize the set of processes that leads from class-determined conditions of life, to values and orientation, to behavior, it is because we deem these processes central, our data support this supposition, and previous interpretations have for the most part failed to recognize their importance.

The power of this interpretation lies in its ability to help us understand why class is important for many diverse facets of human behavior. The implications of this one fundamental class difference in values and orientation—the higher valuation of self-direction at higher class levels and of conformity at lower class levels—extend to such varied social problems as schizophrenia, the perpetuation of inequality, and political illiberalism.

In discussing these problems, we focus on the negative consequences of conformity. We do this not because we fail to see the virtue of some measure of social order or the dangers of unconstrained individualism, but because we are convinced that conformity poses far more serious problems in the United States (and throughout the industrial world). A creative, democratic society needs more self-direction—and could do with less conformity—than is evident.

Schizophrenia

Class differences in values and orientation may help clarify the problem that originally motivated this research—the relationship of class to schizophrenia. As earlier formulated, the problem revolved around the complex interrelationship of class, family, and schizophrenia; we now suggest that a more fruitful approach would be in terms of the inadequacies of a conformist orientational system for dealing with stress.

There is fairly substantial evidence that the incidence of schizophrenia is especially great at the lowest class levels.[7] It is not evident from published research reports, however, precisely which lower-class conditions of life actually are relevant to schizophrenia. There is some indication (Rogler and Hollingshead, 1965) that the great stress to which lower-class people are subjected is directly implicated. But more than stress is involved, for as Langner and Michael (1963) discovered, no matter how high the level of stress that people experience, social class continues to be correlated with the probability of mental disturbance. One implication is that people of lower class position are less prepared to deal with the stresses they encounter.

We think that the *family* is relevant to schizophernia because of its role

[7] For comprehensive reviews of the research literature on class and schizophrenia, see Kohn, 1968; Mishler and Scotch, 1963; and Roman and Trice, 1967.

in preparing children to cope with the stresses of adult life. Because lower-class families teach an orientational system that may be too gross and inflexible for critical circumstances that require subtlety and flexibility, they often fail to prepare children adequately to meet stress.

This formulation reduces the emphasis on the family as uniquely important for schizophrenia, and says instead that the family provides one institutional mechanism—perhaps, but not necessarily, the most important one—for teaching an orientational system that is conducive to schizophrenia. The crucial family processes are less a matter of role-allocation (domineering mothers, for example) than many past discussions have emphasized, and more a matter of how children are taught to perceive, to assess, and to deal with reality.[8] The orientational system that lower-class parents transmit to their children is not likely to provide a sufficient sense of the complexity of life or the analytic tools needed to cope with the dilemmas and problems men encounter. These deficiencies could be overcome by later educational and occupational experience; but often they are not, in part because people who have learned this orientational system are unlikely to want to overcome them, in larger part because circumstances probably would not be propitious even if they were.

Certainly there is a vast gap between the inadequacies of a conformist orientational system and the severe disabilities of schizophrenia. What makes the possibility of a connection seem worth taking seriously, nevertheless, is the pointed correspondence of the two phenomena. Schizophrenia is quintessentially a disorder of orientation—a severe defect in men's ability to accurately comprehend the world about them. If one looks at it clinically, it is a caricature of precisely the outstanding features of the conformist orientation—an over-simple and rigid conception of reality, fearfulness and distrust, and a lack of empathic understanding of other people's motives and feelings. One reason for the disproportionately high incidence of schizophrenia at lower social class levels may be that the disorder builds on an orientational system firmly grounded in the experiences of these social classes.

The more general implication of these speculations is that conformist values and orientation may be personally disastrous to men who are confronted with difficult circumstances that require an innovative response.

The Perpetuation of Inequality

A second implication of class differences in values and orientation is that they contribute to the perpetuation of inequality. Whether consciously or not, parents tend to impart to their children lessons derived from the conditions of life of their own social class—and thus help prepare their children for a similar class position. An obvious factor is the higher educational and occupational aspirations that parents of higher class position hold for their

[8] This is clearly consistent with the ideas of Wynne and his colleagues on cognitive processes in the families of schizophrenics, and with those of Bateson and Jackson on communication processes in such families. (Cf. Wynne, et al., 1958; Ryckoff, et al., 1959; Bateson, et al., 1956; Mishler and Waxler, 1965.)

children. Less obvious but perhaps more important: Class differences in parental values and child-rearing practices influence the development of the capacities that children someday will need for coping with problems and with conditions of change.

The conformist values and orientation of lower- and working-class parents, with their emphases on externals and consequences, often are inappropriate for training children to deal with the problems of middle-class and professional life. Conformist values and orientation are inflexible—not in the sense that people cannot learn to obey new directives, but in the sense that conformity is inadequate for meeting new situations, solving new problems—in short, for dealing with change. Whatever the defects of the self-directed orientation of the middle and upper classes, it is well adapted to meeting the new and the problematic. At its best, it teaches children to develop their analytic and their empathic abilities. These are the essentials for handling responsibility, for initiating change rather than merely reacting to it. Without such skills, horizons are severely restricted.

The family, then, functions as a mechanism for perpetuating inequality. At lower levels of the stratification order, parents are likely to be ill-equipped and often will be ill-disposed to train their children in the skills needed at higher class levels. Other social institutions—notably, formal educational institutions—can counteract this influence, but they do so to only a small extent; as the Coleman study (1966) shows, the capacity of the schools to overcome the limitations of the home is not great.

The result is that family and occupation usually reinforce each other in molding values and orientation. The influences of the family have temporal priority and have commonly been viewed as predominant in importance. Our data argue otherwise, suggesting that where there is conflict between early family experience and later occupational conditions, the latter are likely to prevail. The more important point, though, is that early family and later occupational experiences seldom conflict. No matter how dramatic the exceptions, it is usual that families prepare their offspring for the world as they know it and that the conditions of life eventually faced by the offspring are not very different from those for which they have been prepared.

Political Implications

Our data touch only lightly on political issues, but political implications are clearly evident. Conformity, as we conceive and index it, includes a strong component of intolerance of nonconformity. This conception is based on Stouffer's demonstration, in *Communism, Conformity, and Civil Liberties* (1955), that generalized conformity necessarily entails an unwillingness to permit other people to deviate from paths of established belief; conformist beliefs are necessarily anti-civil-libertarian.

Stouffer's analysis focuses on intolerance of political dissent; our analysis, particularly as embodied in the index of authoritarian conservatism, is addressed to intolerance of any behavior at odds with the dictates of authority. A self-directed orientation includes (but is not confined to) a willingness to allow others to deviate, within some broad limits, from the prescribed; a conformist orientation includes an unwillingness to permit others to step out of narrowly defined limits of what is proper and acceptable. Thus, a conformist orientation implies not only intolerance of deviant political belief, but also intolerance of any beliefs thought to be threatening to the social order—religious beliefs, ethnic and racial identifications, even beliefs about proper dress and deportment.

The political implications of conformist values and orientation extend beyond issues of civil liberties. As Lipset (1959:485) points out, people less favorably situated in the class hierarchy tend to be illiberal about many non-economic issues:

> The poorer everywhere are more liberal or leftist on [economic] issues; they favor more welfare state measures, higher wages, graduated income taxes, support of trade-unions, and other measures opposed by those of higher class position. On the other hand, when liberalism is defined in non-economic terms—so as to support, for example, civil liberties for political dissidents, civil rights for ethnic and racial minorities, inter-nationalist foreign policies, and liberal immigration legislation—the corre-lation is reversed.

Lipset cites an impressive array of evidence from several countries to support his empirical assertion that, on noneconomic issues, people of lower social class position tend to be illiberal. But he is unable to specify the deter-minants of this illiberalism, thus in effect concluding that *everything* about their conditions of life is relevant. Moreover, in choosing the intriguing term, "*working-class authoritarianism*," to describe these illiberal beliefs, he im-plies that the beliefs are an expression of authoritarian personality structure. That there are authoritarian components to the beliefs is indisputable, but to label the entire orientational system authoritarian*ism* is to explain its content in terms of the personality structures of those who endorse it.

Our data help explain working-class authoritarianism without requiring the psychodynamic assumptions of past interpretations.[9] We would contend that this illiberalism is an expression of conformist values and orientation—notably, intolerance (and perhaps fear) of nonconformity. Its explanation, we have come to think, lies not in an especially high incidence of authoritarian personality structure at lower levels of the class hierarchy, nor in "every-thing" about the conditions of life characteristic of these social classes. Rather, the explanation lies specifically in those social structural conditions that we have found to be most determinative of class differences in values and orientation: education and occupational self-direction.

The negative consequences of conformist values and orientation are of great importance, whatever their origins. Our understanding of these beliefs —and our ability as a society to change them—are increased by recognizing precisely where in the structure of society their sources lie.

[9] As Miller and Riessman (1961b) point out, psychological theories devel-oped to explain the personality structure of middle-class authoritarians are probably not valid for explaining the authoritarian beliefs of the working class.

REFERENCES

Bateson, Don D., Jay Haley Jackson, and John Weakland, "Toward a Theory of Schizophrenia," *Behavioral Science*, 1 (October, 1956), 251–264.

Blauner, Robert, "Work Satisfaction and Industrial Trends in Modern Society." In Reinhard Bendix and Seymour Martin Lipset (Eds.), *Class, Status, and Power* (2nd ed.). New York: Macmillan-Free Press, 1966, pp. 473–487.

Blauner, Robert, *Alienation and Freedom: The Factory Worker and His Industry.* Chicago: University of Chicago Press, 1964.

Breer, Paul E., and Edwin A. Locke, *Task Experience as a Source of Attitudes.* Homewood, Ill.: Dorsey Press, 1965.

Chinoy, Ely, *Automobile Workers and the American Dream.* Garden City, N.Y.: Doubleday, 1955.

Coleman, James S., Ernest Q. Campbell, Carol J. Hobson, James McPartland, Alexander M. Mood, Frederich D. Weinfeld, and Robert L. York, *Equality of Educational Opportunity.* Washington, D.C.: U.S. Government Printing Office, 1966.

Inkeles, Alex, "The Modernization of Man." In Myron Weiner (Ed.), *Modernization.* New York: Basic Books, 1966, pp. 138–150.

Inkeles, Alex, "Industrial Man: The Relation of Status to Experience, Perception, and Value." *American Journal of Sociology*, 66 (July, 1960), 1–31.

Kohn, Melvin L., "Social Class and Schizophrenia: A Critical Review." In David Rosenthal and Seymour S. Kety (Eds.), *The Transmission of Schizophrenia.* Oxford: Pergamon Press, 1968, pp. 155–173.

Kohn, Melvin L., and Robin M. Williams, Jr., "Situational Patterning in Intergroup Relations." *American Sociological Review*, 21 (April, 1956), 164–174.

Langner, Thomas S., and Stanley T. Michael, *Life Stress and Mental Health.* New York: Macmillan-Free Press, 1963.

LaPiere, Richard T., "Attitudes vs. Actions." *Social Forces*, 13 (December, 1934), 230–237.

Lipset, Seymour Martin, "Democracy and Working-Class Authoritarianism." *American Sociological Review*, 24 (August, 1959), 482–501.

Lohman, Joseph D., and Dietrich C. Reitzes, "Note on Race Relations in Mass Society." *American Journal of Sociology*, 58 (November, 1952), 240–246.

Mannheim, Karl, *Man and Society in an Age of Reconstruction.* New York: Harcourt, Brace, 1941.

Miller, S. M., and Frank Riessman, "Working Class Authoritarianism: A Critique of Lipset." *British Journal of Sociology*, 12 (September, 1961), 263–276.

Mishler, Elliot G., and Nancy E. Waxler, "Family Interaction Processes and Schizophrenia: A Review of Current Theories." *Merrill-Palmer Quarterly of Behavior and Development*, 11 (October, 1965), 269–315.

Mishler, Elliot G., and Norman A. Scotch, "Sociocultural Factors in the Epidemiology of Schizophrenia: A Review." *Psychiatry*, 26 (November, 1963), 315–351.

Rogler, Lloyd H., and August B. Hollingshead, *Trapped: Families and Schizophrenia.* New York: Wiley, 1965.

Roman, Paul M., and Harrison M. Trice, *Schizophrenia and the Poor.* Ithaca, N.Y.: State School of Industrial and Labor Relations, 1967.

Rosenberg, Morris, *Occupations and Values.* New York: Macmillan-Free Press, 1957.

Ryckoff, Irving, Juliana Day, and Lyman C. Wynne, "Maintenance of Stereo-typed Roles in the Families of Schizophrenics." *A.M.A. Archives of Psy-chiatry*, 1 (July, 1959), 93–98.

Stouffer, Samuel A., *Communism, Conformity, and Civil Liberties: A Cross-Section of the Nation Speaks Its Mind.* New York: Doubleday, 1955.

Thomas, W. I., and Dorothy S. Thomas, *The Child in America.* New York: Knopf, 1928.

Walker, Charles R., *Toward the Automatic Factory: A Case Study of Men and Machines.* New Haven: Yale University Press, 1957.

Walker, Charles R., and Robert H. Guest, *The Man on the Assembly Line.* Cambridge, Mass.: Harvard University Press, 1952.

Waller, Willard, *The Sociology of Teaching.* New York: Russell and Russell, 1932.

Wynne, Lyman C., Irving M. Ryckoff, Juliana Day, and Stanley I. Hirsch, "Pseudo-Mutuality in the Family Relations of Schizophrenics." *Psychiatry*, 22 (May, 1958), 205–220.

23 | Black Families in Perspective

ANDREW BILLINGSLEY

In a sense, the title of this book should be *Black Families in Black and White America*, a title which would reflect both the theoretical perspective and the value position being advanced here. Theoretically, we urge that the Negro family might appropriately be viewed as a social system inextricably bound up with and heavily influenced by the major institutions of the larger society. At the same time we argue that Negro families would function much more productively if the Negro experience were more adequately reflected in the dominant values and programs of the larger society.

Negro families have been mistreated, ignored, and distorted in American scholarship in part because of the absence of general theories guiding studies

From Andrew Billingsley, *Black Families in White America*, © 1968, pp. 3–15. Reprinted by permission of Prentice-Hall, Inc., Englewood Cliffs, New Jersey.

of American families. Such theoretical frameworks, we argue, might help to overcome or expose the limitations of the Anglo-European conformity type biases which still pervade most contemporary public discussions of Negro family life in this country. Unfortunately, social scientists and other students of group life, as well as the mass media, have helped to perpetuate this ignorance and distortion. This point has been made recently by Ralph Ellison,[1] when asked by a group of young Negro writers to comment on how they might more truly reflect the complexity of the human condition, using the Negro experience as a theme.

He responded that the Negro writer would never see his subject if he accepted the stereotype of the Negro family as a broken one and a matriarchy, or of Harlem as "piss in the halls and blood on the stairs." Such clichés, he went on, may have a basis in reality, but they vastly oversimplify the complexity of the Negro condition, denying " 'that something else' which makes for our strength, which makes for our endurance and our promise."

As harsh and accurate as is Ellison's view of the general treatment of Negro families, it is not a universal view, nor is the condition he describes a necessary part of the sociological perspective. A number of social scientists are beginning to approach the Negro experience with new lenses and to view it and describe it in its own right, and in much of its variation and complexity.

In this chapter, then, a particular theoretical orientation is advanced as a framework for viewing Negro families. This orientation emphasizes both the interdependence of these families with other levels of society and the variability among Negro families.

THE NEGRO FAMILY AS A SOCIAL SYSTEM

Four major concepts provide the essential elements of this perspective: (1) social system, (2) ethnic subsociety, (3) family structure, and (4) family function. Each of these major concepts refers to a stream of social science theory which has been developed and tested primarily in relation to other social phenomena than the family. The four are, however, highly compatible and suggestive for a study of Negro family life precisely because Negro families have been so conspicuously shaped by social forces in the American environment.

The concept of a social system has been elaborated most fully by Talcott Parsons and his associates and collaborators.[2] A system is an organization of units or elements united in some form of regular interaction and interdependence. The key words in this definition are *units, organization, interaction*, and *interdependence*. According to Parsons, a social system is an aggregation of persons or social roles bound together in a pattern of mutual interaction and interdependence. It has boundaries which enable us to distinguish the internal from the external environment, and it is typically im-

---

[1] Ralph Ellison, "A Very Stern Discipline," *Harper's Magazine* (March, 1967), 76–95.

[2] Talcott Parsons, *The Social System*, New York: The Free Press, 1951; and Talcott Parsons and Robert F. Bales, *Family, Socialization and Interaction Process*, New York: The Free Press, 1955.

bedded in a network of social units both larger and smaller than itself. The Negro family as a social system is diagramed in Figure 1.

Principal among the subsystems of the larger society which have a direct impact on family life are the values, the political, the economic, the educational, the health, and the communications subsystems. Negroes have been systematically excluded from active and equal participation in each of these

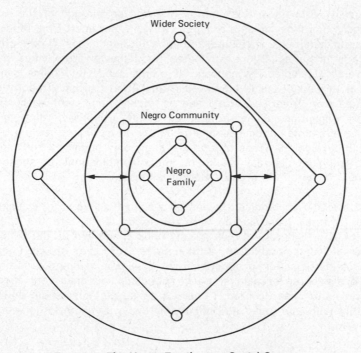

Figure 1   The Negro Family as a Social System

The Negro family is imbedded in a network of mutually interdependent relationships with the Negro community and the wider society.

The Negro family includes within itself several subsystems: that of the Husband-Wife, and those of Mother-Son, Mother-Daughter, Father-Son, Father-Daughter, Brother-Sister, Brother-Brother, Sister-Sister, and sometimes the Grandmother-Mother-Daughter subsystems, to mention only the most common.

The Negro community includes within itself a number of institutions which may also be viewed as subsystems. Prominent among these are: schools, churches, taverns, newspapers, neighborhood associations, lodges, fraternities, social clubs, age and sex peer groups, recreation associations, and small businesses, including particularly, barber shops, beauty parlors, restaurants, pool halls, funeral societies, and various organized systems of hustling.

The wider society consists of major institutions which help set the conditions for Negro family life. Chief among these are the subsystem of values, the political, economic, education, health, welfare, and communications subsystems.

major subsystems of the larger society, yet all the while have been heavily influenced by them. Another important fact is that the exclusion of Negroes from the definition and the resources of these subsystems has not been uniform.

THE NEGRO COMMUNITY AS AN ETHNIC SUBSOCIETY

In many respects in this country, as well as throughout the world, the Negro people are viewed as a group, a category, set apart from other peoples and sharing conditions, attributes, and behavior in common. On the other hand, great variations of conditions, attributes, and behavior are obvious in so large and diverse a people. The concept of ethnic subsociety helps capture the nature of this duality. It is borrowed from Milton Gordon's theoretical work *Assimilation in American Life*,[3] and is highly consistent with the social systems conception just described. An ethnic group, according to Gordon, is a relatively large configuration of people with a "shared feeling of people-hood." In our society, these groups are commonly bound by our conceptions of race, religion, national origin, or some combinations of these factors. "Common to the ethnic group," Gordon suggests,

is the social-psychological element of a special sense of both ancestral and future-oriented identification with the group. These are the "people" of my ancestors, therefore, they are my people, and will be the people of my children and their children. With members of other groups I may share political participation, occupational relationships, common civic enterprise, perhaps even an occasional warm friendship, but in a very special way, which history has decreed, I share a sense of indissoluble and intimate identity with *this* group and not *that* group within the larger society and the world.[4]

This conception of ethnic group seems to capture not only the reality of existence for the Negro people but the new sense of awareness of identity and peoplehood which is becoming increasingly legitimated in black communities throughout the country.

But if Negroes are an ethnic group bound together not only by common definition and treatment on the part of the larger society, but also by a common sense of peoplehood, they are not a uniform group. Ethnic sub-society is a concept which reflects some of the dimensions of variation within the ethnic group. The Negro community as an ethnic subsociety is diagramed in Figure 2. Gordon has stressed three social dimensions which help to capture some of the variation within ethnic groups; namely,

social class, rural or urban residence, and region of the country lived in . . . Thus a person is not simply a white Protestant, he is simultaneously

[3] Milton Gordon, *Assimilation in American Life*, New York: Oxford University Press, 1964. Future quotations from this source reprinted by permission of Oxford University Press.
[4] Gordon, op. cit., p. 29.

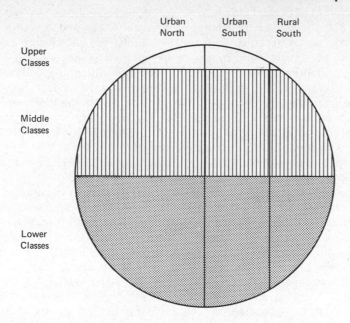

Figure 2   The Negro Community as an Ethnic Subsociety

Negro families are located variously in the social spaces created by the
intersections of social class, North-South, and urban-rural residence.
This figure is conceptual and does not reflect the exact social and geo-
graphic distribution of the Negro population. In 1966, roughly one-half
of all Negro families lived in the urban North, one-fourth in the urban
South, and still another quarter lived in the rural South. We also estimate
that roughly half of all Negro families may be considered lower class,
about 40 per cent middle class and about ten per cent upper class. If
we consider family income as an index of social class, it may be observed
that in 1966, 56 per cent of Negro families earned less than $5,000, 32
per cent earned between $5,000 and $10,000 and 12 per cent earned
over $10,000. There is a high, though by no means perfect, correlation
among income, education, and occupation of family head.

a lower-middle class white Protestant, living in a small town in the South,
or he is an upper-middle class white Catholic living in a metropolitan
area of the Northeast, or a lower-class Negro living in the rural South and
so on. . . .[5]

For our purposes, then, Negro families are not only Negroes to be compared and contrasted with white families, they may also be upper class,
middle class, or lower class, with urban or rural moorings, and with Southern
or Northern residence, and, most importantly, they may be meaningfully compared and contrasted with each other.

In modern times, social class has come to be the most powerful of

[5] Gordon, op. cit., p. 47.

these three dimensions which help to define the conditions of life for Negro families. Social class among Negroes, as among other peoples, is a complex phenomenon which explains only a part of social life. The Negro community is much more complex and highly stratified than is generally appreciated. There are, in general, three social class groupings—the upper, the middle, and the lower classes. Within each of these three major groupings, however, are additional subgroupings. About 10 per cent of Negro families may be considered upper class in the sense that they are headed by men who are highly educated (often with advanced professional degrees beyond college), who are in the high income brackets (ranging upward from $10,000 per year), who have secure and developmental occupational careers and who live in adequate and comfortable housing.

Within this upper class group, however, are two upper classes rather than one. The first and perhaps most traditional Negro upper class is composed of the "old families." These are families with long histories of privilege, achievement, and social status. They reached the top of the social status ladder by building on the head start provided in previous generations. Members of this old upper class often had parents who were middle or upper class, with higher than the Negro average in education, income, and property holdings, often dating back over several generations. These include families headed by doctors, judges, businessmen, high government officials, and the like, who got to the top over several generations. Prominent among these old families, for example, are those of the three highest Negro officials in the federal government: Senator Edward Brooke, Supreme Court Justice Thurgood Marshall, and Secretary of Housing and Urban Development Robert Weaver.

At the same time, there are other and slowly increasing numbers of Negro upper class families, headed by men who made it to the top in one generation, whose parents and grandparents before them were poor. Their achievement is based not on a long history of family status, but on ability and societal supports. Prominent among this new upper class, for example, are Mayor Richard Hatcher of Gary, Indiana, and Mayor Carl B. Stokes of Cleveland. There are, of course, more and perhaps better prototypes of these two upper classes outside the political system than within it, though the political leaders are more conspicuous at the present time.

Negro middle class families are more familiar. They account for perhaps 40 per cent of all Negro families. There are, however, three distinct groupings. There are the upper middle class families, the solid middle class, and the precarious middle class. These are distinguished by educational, income, and occupational achievement, but also by styles of family life, and by the security of their hold on middle class status.

Finally, there are the lower classes, where perhaps half of all Negro families are located. Again, however, there are several groupings, which may be distinguished by the occupational history and security of their heads as well as by education, income, and the like. Starting from the top of the lower class, then, we may identify the "working nonpoor," the "working poor," and the "nonworking poor." The first group of families is headed by men who have a stable and secure niche in the unionized industrial sector of the economy. They are likely to be semi-skilled on the basis of on-the-job experience. The largest group of lower class families, however, may be described as the working poor. Their heads work in unskilled and service occupations with marginal incomes, which often range downward from $3,000 per year. The final group of lower class families is the one about which most information appears in the literature and in the public press. Comprising about a quarter of all lower class Negro families, it is largely peopled by men and women who are unemployed or intermittently employed, supported by relatives and friends or by public welfare.

The importance of social class does not mean, as a number of social scientists still hold, that middle class Negro families have more in common with middle class white families than they do with lower class Negro families. Some liberal social reformers even hold that lower class Negro families have more in common with lower class white families than they do with middle class Negro families. Such naive analyses—on which programs are often based—are possible because of a failure to make distinctions between different types of identity people share.

The concept ethnic subsociety helps to call attention to such distinctions.

> Succinctly, then, one may say that the ethnic group is the locus of a sense of *historical identification*, while the ethclass [the intersection of ethnicity and social class] is the locus of a sense of *participational identification*. With a person of the same social class but of a different ethnic group, one shares behavioral similarities but not a sense of peoplehood. With those of the same ethnic group but of a different social class, one shares the sense of peoplehood but not behavioral similarities. The only group which meets both these criteria are people of the same ethnic group *and* social class.[6]

Although it may well be that social class divisions among Negroes are relatively less rigid or circumscribing of behavior than among other groups, they nevertheless provide a distinct basis of differentiation which helps to condition Negro family life in ways we shall consider in some detail in later sections of this book.

A Sense of Peoplehood

Middle class Negro families, then, do share certain similarities with middle class white families. They share some, though not nearly all, the privileges, opportunities, resources, and amenities of their middle class white counterparts. When, rarely, they also share neighborhoods, schools, and other common ground on a basis of sustained interaction and equality, they are also likely to share what Gordon refers to as "participational identification." They are not as likely, however, to share a common sense of peoplehood. They have very different histories, very different statuses in society, and very different levels of economic security. They consequently do not share the "historical identification" which middle class Negroes share with other middle class Negro families, including those in the lower classes. It is with other middle class Negro families, however, that these two senses of identity are combined and fortified. They are, indeed, in the same boat.

[6] Gordon, op. cit., p. 53.

While Negroes have always been aware of this historical connection with each other and with Negroes in other parts of the world, we have not always been free to recognize it, make it explicit, define it, and build on it. We have been brainwashed by the sea of whiteness which surrounds us and defines us. It was not until after World War II, when strides toward increasing freedom for Negroes were made both in this country and in Africa, that the Negro people again took up the theme, at one time advanced by Marcus Garvey, that black people have a common history, a common set of relations with the white world, and a common destiny. And it was not until twenty years later that the general society began to take note, mainly in negative terms, of this search for identity on the part of the Negro people. Now in every major community in the country, upper and middle class Negroes are turning in dozens of ways toward an explicit recognition of the common destiny shared by the Negro people. There is no important civil rights or protest activity that does not have substantial participation and leadership by the more privileged Negroes. And the country was surprised to find such substantial support among middle class Negroes for the ghetto uprisings of 1965, 1966, and 1967 in more than 100 major cities.

But again, this activity is only the surface of the iceberg. The process of identification is much more widespread than that. It reflects itself in such quiet ways as Negro families moving back into the ghetto or refusing to move out. Most communities have some form of continuing dialogue among Negroes about their common condition, destiny, and potential for change. The writings of Frantz Fanon along with those of Malcolm X and W. E. B. DuBois, particularly his *Souls of Black Folk*, frequently serve as the focus of discussion groups devoted to such dialogue. One such group in California which does not confine itself to these writings, and often produces original essays and position papers, is the Alain Locke Society. It is not an organization, has no members, dues, by-laws, or constitution. Rather, it defines itself as a Seminar. A much larger and more highly organized group is Men of Tomorrow, which recently devoted its annual retreat to the theme of the role of middle class Negroes in efforts to improve conditions of Negroes in the ghetto.

Negro physicians, social workers, teachers and other professionals are beginning to take special recognition of and special initiative on behalf of low income Negro families and children. At the University of Massachusetts, which probably has a higher proportion of Negro faculty members than most other universities, a group of Negro faculty members came together and designed a program for the recruitment and education of Negro students. A similar movement is under way at the University of California. In Berkeley, as in other cities, a group of Negro public school teachers came together and designed a special summer program for Negro children, combining a healthy amount of regular academic work with special learnings about the cultural heritage of the Negro people. The program, which had the active support of the school system and the community, was officially titled "TCB." For the general community this meant "teaching, creating, building," but for the Negro community it meant "takin' care of business."

In financial ways, too, this racial consciousness or ethnic solidarity is manifesting itself. In 1967, for the first time, a group of the wealthiest Negroes in the nation came together in New York to consider how their money, their positions in the Negro community, and their influence in the larger society might be put into more effective efforts for improving the condition of underprivileged Negroes. In Chicago, a struggling United Negro Appeal, patterned after the highly successful United Jewish Appeal, is gaining ground. Some of the larger efforts on the part of the more privileged Negroes to express their connection with the Negro experience in society were reflected in the renaissance in Negro art and drama during the three years between 1965 and 1968. Most major cities now have a least one Negro theater group where there was none before. Art galleries, book stores, Negro history courses, small business enterprises, mass meetings which deliberately exclude white people—sometimes even when whites help provide financial support—are springing up in Negro communities all over the country.

The most impressive examples of racial solidarity occurred during 1967 in the political arena. The election of Negro mayors in Cleveland and Gary was made possible only by the unprecedented collaboration of Negroes from all sectors of the community. Block voting along ethnic lines is not unusual in American politics. What is unusual about these two elections is that, for the first time, Negroes voted in larger proportions than white voters and, for the first time, Negro block voting went for a Negro instead of a white candidate for mayor. A similar effort of a Negro candidate for mayor in Memphis did not, however, meet with the same degree of ethnic solidarity present in Cleveland and Gary.

In Cleveland, for example, Mayor Stokes' margin of victory in the primary was 18,000 votes and he received only 16,000 white votes. It was solidarity among Negro voters which made this victory possible. In reality, however, many of the Negroes voted for Stokes precisely because he had an interracial campaign with important and substantial white support. Thus, white liberals, students, businessmen and the press made a major contribution to Negro ethnic solidarity and achievement working within the framework of the Negro community. The major leadership, however, came from middle class Negroes working in a new burst of collaboration with lower class Negroes.

Not all middle class Negro families are yet able or willing to see the connections they share with all other Negroes. Many still hold to the view that they are more middle class than Negro, and are still seeking to convince the white middle class of that fact. The process is fraught with what Kenneth Clark calls "fantasies" on both sides.

> A common fantasy is to deny one's own identification with the racial dilemmas: "I have no racial problem." Yet to the extent to which either the Negro or white believes this and behaves accordingly, the psychological distance between Negro and white is increased even if it may, on the surface, appear to be otherwise.[7]

It is amazing how little middle class white people know about the conditions of life and the sensibilities of the middle class Negroes with whom they are in daily contact. This is a by-product of the fantasy of denial which often

[7] Kenneth B. Clark, *Dark Ghetto*, New York: Harper and Row, 1965, p. 226.

pervades these interracial contacts. It often happens that when middle-class Negroes seek to disengage themselves from this fantasy, identifying more closely with the Negro experience, it causes a great deal of consternation among their white colleagues. Many find it possible to adjust to the new reality, while others shake their heads in disbelief, withdraw their contributions from SNCC, stop pushing for integration in their own institutions, and argue long and hard for law and order, and against "reverse segregation." It is an irreverent and irrelevant response to the situation, but wholly understandable under the circumstances. Social change is often painful, and ethnic solidarity is a powerful force for change which the country has come to accept from other ethnic groups. Its gradual but distinct and growing reawakening among Negroes has tremendous potential for disrupting old alliances and shattering old stereotypes of friend and foe alike. At the same time, however, it has even greater potential for contributing to the reconstruction of Negro family and community life and for the development of a more viable pluralistic and democratic society.

All of these recent behavioral manifestations of participational identification among Negroes indicate an intensification of those dimensions of ethnic similarity which set any people apart as a distinct subsociety. Nonetheless, there remain those dimensions of variation, such as social class, which stimulate great diversity among Negro people. It is in both these dimensions, similarity and difference, that the utility of the concept of ethnic subsociety rests as an integral part of the framework for the study of Negro family life.

TABLE 1   Negro Families with Children Headed by Men (by Family Income and Urban-Rural Residence) (1960)

	Total %	Under $3,000 %	$3,000 & Over %
All Negro families	79	64	93
Rural residence	86	82	95
Urban residence	77	53	92
All white families	94	78	97
Rural residence	96	88	98
Urban residence	93	62	96

The data in Table 1 help to clarify the relevance of the several elements of the ethnic subsociety for family structure. The table shows that each of these major variables has some impact on the structure of family life, but social class as represented by total family income is by far the major influence. Thus among Negro families as a whole, there is an important rural-urban difference, with 86 per cent of rural families with children and 77 per cent of urban families with children being headed by men. If we look at family income alone, we also note a difference with 64 per cent of families in the low income group and 93 per cent of families in the higher income group being headed by men. But among Negro families earning $3,000 or above, there is virtually no difference between rural and urban families in the proportion of male heads. Difference between ethnic groups are maintained within each subgroup, but they are diminished considerably by social class. Thus, among urban families earning $3,000 and over, for example, 92 per cent of Negro families with children and 96 per cent of white families with children were headed by men, whereas among the low income groups, these proportions were 53 per cent and 62 per cent respectively.

It is important to stress, however, that social class does not obliterate the differences between Negroes and whites, not even on so simple a dimension as the sex of the family head. There are several reasons for this. Perhaps most important is the fact that even when the two groups, Negroes and whites, are in the same income range, they do not have the same incomes. Middle class Negro families do not have the resources available to them that middle class white families do. And lower class Negro families are considerably poorer than lower class white families. Negro families earning above $3,000, for example, will have considerably lower average earnings than white families in the same range. Negro families will cluster toward the lower end of the range and white families will cluster toward the upper end. In a similar manner, levels of education, occupational security, and opportunity are not equal for middle class Negroes and whites. The same is true at the lower class levels.

Even with comparable education, however, Negroes do not have the same occupational opportunities, and even with similar occupations, they do not have the same incomes, and even if they could be equated on all these measures, they have different statuses and histories in this country. Considering all these factors, the wonder is that there is so little difference between Negroes and whites in the proportion of families with male heads. That is the phenomenon which deserves to be explained. Or perhaps neither the white-Negro difference nor the male head-female head dichotomy are sufficient for an understanding of the structure of Negro family life. It is considerably more complex and dynamic, adaptive and resilient than can be captured by such simplistic descriptions.

Another problem with the two types of family approach is that such characterization tends to treat female-headed families as if they were a Negro phenomenon, despite the fact that there were roughly four million white single-parent families and about one million Negro single-parent families in 1966.[8]

In addition, as Elizabeth Herzog has observed, such characterization tends to treat female-headed families as "nonfamilies"[9] and supports the view that the government or somebody should do something to put all Negro children into families with male heads. Furthermore, this way of characterizing family structure distorts and exaggerates the prevalence and the consequences of the "matriarchy" among Negro families. Perhaps the most important limitation of this two-way description is that it obscures rather than clarifies the range and variety of Negro family structure.

For an understanding of the structure of Negro family life, then, it seems important to take into consideration not only the sex of the family head but also the relationship of each household member to the head.

[8] U. S. Census Bureau, "Social and Economic Conditions of Negroes in the United States," *Current Population Reports*, Series P-23, No. 24 (October, 1967), p. 68.

[9] Elizabeth Herzog, "Is There a Breakdown of the Negro Family?" *Social Work*, II, No. 1 (January, 1966), 3–10.

24 Life-Style Differences Among Urban and Suburban Blue-Collar Families

IRVING TALLMAN and RAMONA MAROTZ

One of the significant trends in present day American society is the increasing migration of skilled and semiskilled manual workers to the urban fringe and into mass produced suburban developments (Lazerwitz, 1960; Dobriner, 1963:50–54; Berger, 1960; Woodbury, 1955; Taueber and Taueber, 1964). The extent to which this trend has altered generalizations about suburban life-styles has been the subject of debate in both popular and professional literature (Dobriner, 1963; Berger, 1960; Seligman, 1964).

In its simplest form, the question raised is: are working-class families who move to the suburbs substantially different in their life-styles from those who remain in the city, or conversely, are the ways of life thought to be characteristic of suburbs altered by the influx of working-class people? Underlying this debate is the broader issue of whether life-styles can be attributed primarily to cultural and subcultural factors or to ecological and residential characteristics. Writers stressing the primacy of cultural variables maintain that style of life derives less from the environs than from a set of values integral to a particular social category.[1] Those holding the ecological-residential orientation emphasize the importance of structural characteristics of the community which contribute to certain forms of interaction, and channel the flow of communication in such ways that distinctive patterns of behavior are fostered.[2]

[1] Berger (1960:13), for example, concludes that ". . . a 'way of life' is a function of such variables as age, income, occupation, education, rural-urban background, and so forth, and that this is true for suburbs as it is for any other kind of modern community." (See also Dobriner, 1963:23; Ktsanes and Reissman, 1959–60; Gans, 1967:274–295.)

[2] For example, Shevky and Bell (1955), Greer (1956; 1960), and others argue that a high ratio of single-family dwellings to multiple dwellings in a community promote home- and family-centered orientations as well as a similarity of life routines among the residents. These factors, along with a greater amount of shared open space, increase casual and informal interaction among neighbors (Fava, 1958; Dobriner, 1963:57–58). This form of interaction contributes to shared interests which, in turn, result in greater social participation both at the neighborhood and community levels (Greer, 1960). Finally, the relative isolation of the suburb is thought to account for greater depend-

This is an expanded and revised version of a paper read at the annual meeting of the Midwest Sociological Society, 1967. The research reported in this paper was supported by grants Nos. 3038 and 20–33 from the University of Minnesota Experiment Station. We are indebted to Joel Nelson, Murray Straus, and Joan Aldous for their reading and criticisms of earlier drafts of this paper.

Reprinted from *Social Forces*, 48 (March, 1970), 249–256, by permission of the University of North Carolina Press.

It is, of course, an oversimplification to depict either orientation as the singular explanation of life-style differences. There is general recognition that both locational characteristics and cultural values interact to produce the observed effects. The critical question, however, is the relative influence of these variables on life-styles. Three possibilities exist: either residence or culture has a sufficient independent effect so that, despite interaction with other relevant variables, one emerges as the prime influence on the development of life-styles; or the two variables in combination produce an effect fundamentally different from that which would be expected if either variable could function independently of the other. The primary concern of this paper is to provide data bearing on these possible outcomes.

PREVIOUS RESEARCH

The empirical studies of suburban life generally yield certain consistent results. Inhabitants in these areas are more likely than city dwellers to be younger, have larger families, and live in communities which are homogeneous in ethnicity and socioeconomic status.[3] In addition, they tend to have distinctive patterns of social relationships which are manifest principally by greater intimacy with neighbors, greater participation in community organizations, and more involvement with their nuclear families (Greer, 1960). These behaviors have also been shown to be associated with an urban middle-class style of life (Smith et al., 1954; Bell and Boat, 1957; Bell and Force, 1956; Komarovsky, 1946). Since the middle class has tended to be overrepresented in most suburban research, the relative influence of class and residence is difficult to isolate.

Parallel studies of working-class suburbs have been limited in scope and quantity. Berger's (1960) investigation of a blue-collar tract development outside of San Jose, California, seems to be the most definitive work undertaken in the United States to date. Berger interprets his data as indicating little change in class identification, upward mobility, church attendance, social participation and political orientation resulting from migration to the suburbs. Two major difficulties, however, limit the generalizability of his findings. First, the sample was composed of workers who moved en masse when their plant transferred its operations to the suburbs; this is not representative of the usual patterns of residential selection.[4] Second, no urban sample was pro-

---

ence on the immediate nuclear family, neighbors, and community (Martin, 1956; Young and Willmott, 1957:131–143).

[3] See Duncan and Reiss (1958). There is some evidence that as the suburban trend continues many of the older suburbs are becoming less homogeneous (Dobriner, 1963). Whether this tendency is characteristics, however, remains an open question (for example, Hoover and Vernon, 1959: esp. Chap. 7).

[4] On the other hand, the fact that Berger's (1960) subjects were forced to move provides a control for selective migration; a confounding factor in most attempts to assess the independent influence of location.

vided for purposes of comparison;[5] in the absence of established norms, interpretations of the findings must, therefore, remain highly speculative.

Two English investigations reach somewhat different conclusions from those advanced by Berger. Mogey (1955;1956), in a study of workers who had moved to a housing estate on the fringe of Oxford, and Willmott and Young (1960), in their study of a London suburb, report changes among working-class families in the direction of an increasing nuclear family orientation and a tendency toward middle-class identification.

Research designed to test the comparative influence of residence and social class on life-style has, with the exception of Berger's study, tended to support the ecological-residential orientation. Greer (1956), in a study of two communities in the Los Angeles metropolitan area, reports an inverse relationship between social participation and urbanization when social class and segregation are controlled. Unfortunately, class was held constant in this investigation by comparing two middle-class communities, thus leaving un-answered the question of possible modification which might occur within the working class. Tomeh (1964) reports similar results for informal group contacts. Controlling for social class and a variety of demographic variables, she found that local intimacy was more pronounced in suburban communities when compared with the inner city. Her measure of social class however, seems less than adequate for our purposes. Subjects in her sample with at least a high school education were defined as middle class and those with less than a high school education as working class. Since sizeable proportions of manual workers are also high school graduates, it is not unreasonable to wonder whether the results would have been different if occupation or some multiple indicator of class had been used.[6]

Two other problems occur in attempting to generalize from the previous research. First, although most of the studies introduced controls for demographic variables, none controlled for subjective orientations such as self-ascribed social class and mobility aspirations. If the cultural explanation is correct, these subjective orientations may be critical in accounting for residential differences in life-style. The second problem concerns the type of variables used as indicators of life-style—usually neighboring and various forms of social participation. The question raised by critics of this research is whether these variables provide sufficient evidence for making generalizations about fundamental life-style patterns. Dobriner (1963:58–59) claims that, although urban–suburban differences may occur in social relationships and home-centered activity, "as to political conversion, religious reawakenings, status climbing, attitudes toward education and basic family structure there is no evidence that the suburban situation in any way significantly modifies basic class patterns."

In brief, although previous research has provided evidence linking

[5] Berger (1960) does present data based on his respondents' retrospective experiences prior to their move to the suburbs. Aside from the issue of reliability, these data are not systematically used as a basis of comparison.

[6] For problems in overgeneralizing from the relation between education and occupation see Blau and Duncan (1967:196). See also pp. 144–145 and Figure 4.3 for evidence pertaining to occupational variance for high school graduates.

residence to formal and informal social participation, it has not conclusively accounted for other significant aspects of life-style. In addition, although there is considerable data on white-collar suburbs, the relationship between residence and working-class behavioral patterns has not been sufficiently examined. The research reported here was designed, in part, to provide some clarification of these issues.

Specifically, we shall seek answers to the following questions: *First*, do differences exist in life-styles between blue-collar families residing in the suburbs and comparable families living in the central city? *Second*, if such differences exist, are they primarily attributable to location as opposed to such cultural factors as social class identification, rural–urban upbringing, education, and mobility orientations? *Third*, if suburban–urban differences are found, to what extent are the life-style patterns (in blue-collar suburbs) comparable to those reported in white-collar suburban studies? Answers to these questions can not only provide an estimate of the primacy of residence or culture, but in addition should allow us to estimate whether blue-collar suburbs develop a unique style of life attributable to the joint effects of the two independent variables.

RESEARCH METHODS

The study was conducted by means of a structured and standardized interview with 51 couples living in a virtually homogeneous working-class tract north of the Twin Cities and 53 couples living in a central district of Minneapolis. The two areas were chosen because of their relative comparability in income, occupational status, segregation, and geographical mobility rates. Each of these variables has been found in previous research to affect residence selection and would, therefore, represent confounding sources of variation in this research.[7]

To hold constant the effects of length of residence, only families living in their homes from 9 to 18 months were accepted. Water department records and local agency publications were used to determine length of residence. Comparability in family life cycle was approximated by further restricting the sample to those families with at least one child in an elementary school. This was determined by comparing the previous list of names against the district school records. Participating families were then randomly selected from the remaining list of names. The refusal rate was approximately 15 percent for both groups. Separate interviews were con-

[7] See Rossi (1955:esp. Chap. 4) for a discussion of the influence of mobility rates. Also, Greer (1962:125–136) for a discussion of social rank and segregation as factors in residence selection. The decision to use a single urban and a single suburban tract matched on the variables described above was made to optimize analytic precision. This decision, of course, was made at the cost of having a representative sample. However, since the primary purpose of this research was to test the effects of the two critical variables, and since such a test requires controlling for the variables mentioned above, the sampling procedure used seemed the most practical. A probability sample which would allow us to control for all variables would have to be extremely large and beyond the resources available to us.

ducted with each spouse, all of whom were native born Caucasians. Upon completion of the interviewing we found that the heads of 7 suburban families and 2 urban families held white-collar jobs. These families were eliminated from the analyses.

The suburban and city samples were comparable in occupational prestige, income, and parents' occupational status. The suburban sample was relatively younger, had larger families, fewer working wives, a somewhat higher proportion of home ownership and had a higher frequency of moves since marriage. In addition, suburban husbands had slightly higher educations and were more likely to have been raised in a rural environment.[8] Each of these variables, with the exception of the last, has generally been reported as characteristic of suburban populations (Duncan and Reiss, 1958; Dobriner, 1963:19–20).

It should be noted that the area from which the city sample was selected has relatively more single-family dwellings than "super-cities" such as Boston, Chicago and New York; nevertheless, the suburban–urban differences in density are still sizeable. According to 1960 Census data, 97 percent of the homes in the suburb studied were single-family dwellings as compared to 19 percent in the central city area.[9] Since class and segregation are controlled, the research may be viewed as a partial replication of Greer's (1956) earlier investigation of two tracts in Los Angeles, except that the sample consists of representatives of the working class rather than of the middle class.

CHOICE OF LIFE-STYLE VARIABLES

The lack of constituent meaning for a concept such as "life-style" makes any set of indicators vulnerable to the criticism that they are not appropriate measures and do not tap "significant" aspects of the phenomenon. We view life-style as a broad rubric under which a number of behavioral activities and orientations can be included, each of which requires a distinctive investment of the individuals' resources of time, energy, affect or money. The behaviors investigated are not exhaustive of all possibilities but are representative of the concerns of many social scientists interested in the relationship between behavioral modes and community types.

[8] The relevant statistics for these differences are as follows: The median age for suburban men was 32.3, for urban men 38.0; for suburban women it was 30.0 as compared to 34.75 for urban women. The median number of children for suburbanites was 3.8 as compared to 3.0 for city dwellers. Sixteen percent of the suburban wives were employed whereas 33 percent of the city women held jobs. The median number of moves since marriage was 5.42 for suburbanites and 3.72 for urbanites. Eighty-two percent of the suburbanites were home owners as compared to 66 percent of those who lived in the city. Finally, 60 percent of the suburban men had a high school education or better whereas only 38 percent of the city men advanced to high school or beyond.

[9] U.S. Bureau of the Census (1962). The over-representation in our sample of city dwellers who are home owners is probably a result of controlling for family life cycle. That is, intact families with at least one child in school will more likely be home owners.

We used the following behaviors and orientations as our indicators of life-style: (a) local intimacy, (b) social participation in voluntary organizations, (c) church participation, (d) family organization, (e) subjective class identification, (f) mobility orientation, and (g) political orientation.

RESULTS

Whenever residential differences for a given life-style variable were statistically significant, test variables were introduced to check for spuriousness, possible intervening variables, and specification.[10] All of the background and demographic variables which yield suburban–urban differences were introduced as test factors.[11] Although none of the original relationships was seriously attenuated by introducing the test variable, some controls did specify conditions under which certain relationships were operable. These specifications will be discussed at appropriate points in the analyses which follow.

Local Intimacy and Social Participation

Higher rates of local intimacy and voluntary social participation have been found to be associated with both suburban residence and membership in the middle class (Greer, 1960; Smith et al., 1954; Bell and Boat, 1957; Bell and Force, 1956; Komarovsky, 1946). Using these variables as a basis for comparing blue-collar families living in the suburbs with similar families living in the central city should, therefore, provide one test of the relative influence of residence and social class.

1. Local Intimacy   Two types of indicators were used to measure local intimacy—the extent and degree of neighboring and the perception of shared interest with neighbors. The results are presented in Table 1. It can be seen that consistent and generally significant differences exist, with greater neighboring occurring in the suburbs. Similar findings occur for the indicators of shared interest although here the differences are more pronounced for husbands than for wives. Not only were the suburbanites more likely to see themselves as sharing the same interests as their neighbors but they also were more inclined to see themselves as having similar income and education. In addition, they appeared to be more sensitized to their neighbors' work and church activities. Conversely, a significantly higher proportion of city men responded to the items by claiming they had no knowledge of their neighbors' activities, income, or education. These data appear to be in accord

[10] In order to conserve space the partials will not be presented in this paper. The interested reader may obtain copies of all the partial tables for the test factors as well as comparisons based on standardizations of the test factors and the interview schedule by writing to the A.S.I.S.—National Auxiliary Publication Service, Library of Congress, Washington 25, D.C., for document number NAPS 00764.

[11] Other "subjective" variables which were introduced as test factors will be discussed later in this paper.

TABLE 1   Residence Differences on Indicators of Local Intimacy (Percent)

	Men		Women	
	Suburban (N = 45)	*Urban (N = 51)	Suburban (N = 45)	Urban (N = 51)
Neighboring Items				
Visit immediate neighbors at least once a month	69	39*	52	44
Know more than one neighbor well enough to call him by first name	78	53*	89	72*
Know more than one neighbor well enough to visit regularly	60	43*	75	51*
Wife often visits other housewives			42	25*
Other housewives often visit wife			49	24*
Shared Interest Items				
Similarity of education				
About the same	71	56	63	62
Don't know	0	22*	11	16
Similarity of income				
About the same	69	55	70	55
Don't know	7	28*	20	20
Similarity of interests				
About the same	67	35*	63	38*
Don't know	18	41*	17	38*
Type of work neighbors do				
Don't know	7	21	2	24*
Frequency that neighbors go to church				
Don't know	22	42*	24	42*

*Indicates significant residential differences by sex at beyond the 5 percent level ($\chi^2 = 3.81$, $df = 1$).

with the classic position of Simmel (1950) and Wirth (1938) that population density and close proximity produces a reserve in interpersonal contacts.[12] However, the findings probably also reflect the lack of importance of neighbors in the lives of the city men. Most of these men appear to maintain close friendship ties in other sectors of the city and were, therefore, less dependent on immediate neighbors to meet their social needs (Smith et al., 1954).

2. *Social Participation*   No significant differences were found in the initial analysis on indicators of social participation. Approximately 50 percent of both groups reported no organizational ties. This would tend to confirm other data indicating low social participation among blue-collar workers (Hausknecht, 1964; for a more general review see Scott, 1957). However, since social participation may also be a function of familiarity with the community and available voluntary groups, the findings were reexamined by dividing the suburban sample into those who had previously lived in another

[12] It is possible that this generalization holds only within metropolitan areas. Reiss (1954), for example, reports greater interpersonal contact in urban as compared to rural areas. Martin (1956) suggests that the choice of suburban residence is based, in part, on the opportunities provided for social contacts while maintaining the amenities of urban life.

TABLE 2 Residential Comparisons on Indicators of Social Participation (Percent)

	Men			Women		
	Suburban		Urban	Suburban		Urban
	City to Suburb (N = 19)	Suburb to Suburb (N = 25)	City to City (N = 51)	City to Suburb (N = 17)	Suburb to Suburb (N = 27)	City to City (N = 50)
Item						
Average time spent attending service organizations and meetings (such as P.T.A., etc.). Once a month or more	32	38	39	35	70‡§	54
Average time spent in social group activities (card clubs, bowling, etc.) in present location. One evening a week or more	26	56	22*	12	36‡	28
Often attend meetings in old location	11	20	33	18	52‡§	22†

	Suburban Men (N = 44)		Urban Men (N = 51)	Suburban Women (N = 45)		Urban Women (N = 51)
Attend church more often since move	20		4†	34		24
Importance of church since move	30		9†	29		23§

*Signifies significant differences between central city sample and suburban to suburban group by sex ($p \leqslant .05$ with chi-square test).
†Signifies significant differences by residence and sex ($p \leqslant .05$ with chi-square test).
‡Signifies significant differences between suburban migration groups by sex ($p \leqslant .05$ with chi-square test).
§Signifies significant differences between men and women within groups ($p \leqslant .05$ with chi-square test).

suburb and those who had moved from the central city. Two-fifths of the suburban sample had moved from the central city while the remaining families in the sample had moved from other suburbs or the suburban fringe. The urban sample was composed only of people with previous residence in the central city. Table 2 presents social participation comparisons for the three groups. It can be seen that women with previous suburban residence attended meetings of service organizations and participated in group recreational activities more frequently than did either of the other two groups, although the only statistically significant differences were with women who had previously lived in the city. Women who previously lived in the suburbs were also significantly more likely than the other groups to consider themselves frequent participators in their previous location. For men, the only significant differences were on participation in recreational group activities. Here men with previous suburban residence were the most frequent participators.

The evidence indicating greater social participation of suburban women as compared to their hubands is consonant with previous research in white-collar suburbs (Martin, 1956). Since the relative isolation of the suburb with its lack of rapid public transportation and toll free telephones calls tends to weaken the traditional ties of working-class women to relatives and old friends, it may make them somewhat more amenable to organizational activity. The suburban wives' greater participation in service organizations offers some confirmation for Greer's (1960) hypothesis that similarity in households creates bonds of mutual dependence as well as shared perception of common problems. This, in turn, contributes to a stronger community orientation. Inasmuch as community problems are probably more visible to wives, it is not surprising that they become more active participants.[13]

Church Participation

Research pertaining to the relationship between residence and church participation has produced inconsistent results and conflicting interpretations (Winter, 1961; Gans, 1967:264–266, suggest an increase in church attendance in suburbia; Zimmer and Hawley, 1959, present contrary evidence). The findings with regard to the influence of social class are somewhat more consistent, indicating greater church participation in the middle class than the working class (Schneider, 1964). Advocates of the cultural explanation for life-style differences have maintained that residence does not appreciably influence this aspect of social behavior and have used data pertaining to church activities as one of the bulwarks in their argument for the primacy of class and other cultural factors (Berger, 1968).

Our findings, reported in Table 2, however, indicate that residence is associated with differential rates of church activity for working-class men. A significantly higher proportion of suburban men than urban men believed that church had become more important to them and indicated that their church attendance had increased since their move.

When urban–rural background was controlled, the residential differences held only for those men who came from a farm background. Since persons with farm backgrounds usually attend church more regularly, it may be that the greater visibility of daily activities which occurs in the suburbs is experienced as added pressure to behave in a manner previously defined as appropriate (Zimmer and Hawley, 1959, for evidence pertaining to greater church participation of farm migrants; Dobriner, 1963:9–11, for discussion of visibility in suburbia). Alternatively, men with urban backgrounds may not have internalized the norm of church attendance as completely and, therefore, need not interpret visibility as a pressure to behave in this particular manner. No significant differences occurred for women on these items.

Family Organization

The single characteristic most commonly used to describe the suburban community is the centrality of the nuclear family (Bell, 1958; Dewey, 1948; Jaco and Belknap, 1953; Greer, 1956). Suburbs have been depicted as family-

[13] Unfortunately, the small number of cases resulting from dividing the suburban sample into two groups made the introduction of test variables impractical.

TABLE 3 Residential Differences in Family Orientation (Percent)

	Suburban		Urban	
	Men *(N = 45)*	*Women* *(N = 45)*	*Men* *(N = 51)*	*Women* *(N = 51)*
Differences in Movement Toward Relatives				
Item:				
Live closer to husband's relatives in new location	22	26	41*	43
Live closer to wife's relatives in new location	16	24	34*	44*
Residential and Sex Comparisons on Sources of Communication When Marital Problems Occur				
Whom talked to:				
Spouse	13	4	12	2
Friends and relatives	33	39	17	56*†
Outsiders	16	17	29	22
No one	38	39	41	20*†
Sources of Communication over 9 Problematic Situations				
Whom talked to:				
Spouse	53	64	44	64†
Friends and relatives	13	14	7	17†
Outsiders	17	9	20	11l
No one	18	13	22	8†

*Signifies significant residential differences by sex ($p < .05$ with chi-square test).
†Significant differences (between spouses) within communities computed by correlated "+" for dependent samples ($p < .05$ with two-tailed test).

centered in activities and family-oriented in values. Once again these characteristics are more frequently found in white-collar families than in blue-collar families (Cavan, 1964; Rainwater et al., 1959). In fact, several studies have suggested that the urban blue-collar family displays a high degree of role segmentation and a tendency for spouses to cling to close-knit networks of same-sex friends and relatives (Gans, 1962; Rainwater et al., 1959; Miller and Riessman, 1964). Our data on family organization seem consonant with the above findings.

Briefly the findings, which are presented in Table 3, show that urban blue-collar women were more involved with close friends and relatives than were suburban women, and perhaps as a consequence of this involvement, there was greater role segmentation in urban families.[14] The findings pertaining to involvement with friends and kin show a significantly higher proportion of urban as compared to suburban couples who felt that their move brought them closer to their relatives. In addition, the urban women were more likely to discuss their marital difficulties with close friends and relatives, whereas

[14] For discussions of role segmentation in blue-collar families see Komarovsky (1962) and Rainwater et al. (1959). See also Bott (1957:esp. Chap. 3) for a discussion of linkage between social networks and role segmentation.

a higher proportion of suburban women reported that they had no one with whom to discuss these problems. These results were modified to some extent when age and working wives were controlled. As might be expected, the results held only for nonworking wives. With regard to age, the original residence differences remained constant for women under thirty; the older women in both communities were less likely to utilize kin and close friends to discuss marital problems. At the same time, the older suburban women represented the largest group which stated it had no one to talk with when marital problems occurred. The implications of these findings will be discussed in a later section; suffice it to say at this point, that, despite some qualifications, the introduction of test variables did not attenuate the original residence differences.

In order to test for role segmentation, we compared husbands and wives in the two communities on their sources of confidants for nine problematic situations.[15] As indicated in Table 3, urban husbands differed significantly from their wives on the resources they relied upon when common family difficulties occurred. Although the differences in the suburban sample were in the same direction, they were not as pronounced and were not statistically significant.

When education was controlled, husband–wife differences in the urban sample held only for families in which the men had less than a high school education; this control did not alter the results in the suburban sample. This is in keeping with Komarovsky's (1962:155–159) findings that the less-educated urban working-class men tend to be unable to make use of confidants. While the exact temporal sequence cannot be determined from our data, it appears as if residence has a similar effect to that of education in mitigating role segmentation, probably because both variables contribute to greater spousal communication. In the case of residence this may be a consequence of isolation from friends and relatives; in the case of education it is indicative of a greater commonality of interests between spouses.

The fact that the suburban families were less apt to evidence close involvement with old friends and relatives on conjugal role segmentation suggests a shift away from the traditional working-class system of relationships, and toward a more nuclear type of family organization.[16]

[15] Subjects were asked with whom they talked in the following situations: (1) bad moods, (2) marital problems, (3) difficulty with neighbors, (4) difficulty with in-laws, (5) need for house repairs, (6) problems at work, or, for wives, problems at home, (7) difficulty with children, (8) financial problems, and (9) personal illness. Responses were coded into four categories based on whether they talked with: (1) their spouse, (2) close friends and relatives, (3) an outsider (this included neighbors, fellow workers, or professionals such as doctors, teachers, ministers, social workers, etc.), or (4) no one.

[16] The prototype of popular books fostering this image is Whyte's *The Organization Man* (1957). Bell (1958) has reported that in his middle-class sample, child and family orientations rather than career considerations were the prime motives for moving to the suburbs. Riesman (1957) considered an emphasis on pleasant environs and the good life more important to suburbanites than upward mobility. A similar position is taken by Berger (1968:esp. Chap. 2) in his report of a working-class suburb.

Social Mobility

The popular image of suburbia as inhabited by upwardly mobile strivers has been challenged by several studies (Bell, 1958; Dewey, 1948; Jaco and Belknap, 1953; Greer, 1956). Our data, however, yield significant residential differences for men on indicators of mobility. Although the majority of our respondents in both communities identify themselves as members of the working class, a greater proportion of male suburbanites as compared to city dwellers assume middle-class status. These data are shown in Table 4. Also,

TABLE 4   Residential Differences on Measures of Upward Social Mobility (Percent)

Item	Men		Women	
	Suburban (N = 45)	Urban (N = 51)	Suburban (N = 45)	Urban (N = 51)
Self-ascribed social class upper or middle	42	22*	32	24
Good chance of getting ahead in present job	50	20*	39	26
Belong to group going up in world	61	30*	63	38*
Desired social class upper or middle	89	65*	84	75

*Indicates significant statistical differences by sex at beyond the 5 percent level.

as indicated in Table 4, suburban men are more likely to consider their chances of getting ahead in their present job as very good and to view themselves as moving up in the world. Urban men, alternatively, tend to place a higher value on working-class identity as exemplified by their preference for working-class status and the tendency to want their sons to remain within this stratum.

When background variables were controlled only husband's age affected the relationships. Residence differences were attenuated for those under the age of thirty-five, but were not appreciably altered for the older group. The young men in both communities tended to view themselves as working class while, at the same time, they stated they had a good chance of moving up in the world—suggesting that they may anticipate entering the middle class at some future time. We can infer from these data that with increasing age urban men experience a gradual process of disillusionment concerning their life chances. Considering the limited mobility opportunities which exist for manual workers this disillusionment is understandable (Blau and Duncan, 1967). What is of interest is that this process does not occur for the suburban group. The differences cannot be attributed to greater job mobility among the suburbanites since the samples are comparable in occupational status and income, and controlling for education does not modify the results. One possible explanation for these findings may lie in Chinoy's (1952; 1955:83–85, 123–34) observation that older manual workers adopt certain types of material acquisitions as symbolic representations of success in order to allay the anxiety resulting from their lack of job mobility. In this case the popular image of suburbia may be used to represent upward mobility and the attainment of middle-class status. The fact that the younger men in the suburbs are less likely to consider themselves as middle class suggests that they still hope to attain this status by means of job mobility.

Political Orientation

Our final criterion of life-style was political orientation. The results of previous research on the relationship between residence and political beliefs are not sufficiently consistent to allow for easy interpretations or un-ambiguous generalizations (Wood, 1958: chap. 5, for a review of research on suburban political behavior). What is apparent, however is that the popular view of the suburb as a stronghold of Republicanism and conservatism is not supported by the data. On the other hand, the commonly held view of the traditional affiliation of the working class with the Democratic party appears to be a firmly established fact of American political life (Alford, 1963:94–122).

TABLE 5   Residence Comparisons of Political Orientation (Percent)

	Men		Women	
	Suburban	*Urban*	*Suburban*	*Urban*
Item	*(N = 44)*	*(N = 49)*	*(N = 45)*	*(N = 50)*
Party Affiliation				
Democrat	47	72*	71	63
Political Orientation				
Middle-of-the-road	62	38*	61	70

*Indicates significant statistical residential differences by sex at beyond the 5 percent level.

The findings presented in Table 5 were in accord with previous data on urban working-class political orientations. Responses among the suburbanites, however, appeared to be more in keeping with the popular view of suburban politics and did not reflect some of the previous empirical findings.

We used two measures to assess political orientation; one was re-spondents' party affiliation, the other was their self-categorization as liberal, conservative or middle-of-the-road. Again our data indicate residence differ-ences for men but not women. Almost three-quarters of the urban men considered themselves as Democrats as compared to less than half of the suburban men. In addition, the suburban men were significantly more likely to consider themselves middle-of-the-road, whereas the urbanites were in-clined to take a less ambiguous political stance by adopting the label of either liberal or conservative. When background variables were controlled the residence differences held only for those who had at least a high school education, who were over the age of thirty-five, and whose wives were not working. Again it appears that although education, age, and working wives do not account for the residential differences, they specify conditions under which the relationship between residence and political views is operative.

EFFECTS OF RESIDENCE AND CLASS

We can conclude from the data reported above that residence is asso-ciated with fundamental differences in life-styles for the working-class families in this study. Further, the results fail to support the interpretations of Berger, Gans, and Dobriner that the pervasiveness of working-class values renders residential factors virtually insignificant. The fact that none of the background or demographic variables when used as test factors appreciably altered the original relationships lends credence to these conclusions.[17] This is not to say that residence had a totally independent affect on the dependent variables. Rather, the specifications resulting from the introduction of the test variables suggest that class and class-related cultural factors interact with residence to influence some of the life-style patterns. For example, the residential differences in church interest and activity were accounted for primarily by suburban men who came from rural backgrounds. Similarly the data indicating that previous residence influenced the rate of social participation of suburban women suggests that the integration of working-class women into suburban pattern of social participation may be somewhat slower than we might expect for middle-class women.

The findings pertaining to family organization indicate a somewhat more complicated pattern. It appears that suburban residence has an effect similar to increasing age for women and better education for men in modifying traditional working-class family patterns in the direction of a more companionate-nuclear type of family organization. The greater tendency of suburban wives to express feelings of isolation, however, suggests that family nuclearization in the suburbs may be the result of the need to substitute spousal companionship for previous forms of emotional support.[18] Data reported elsewhere indicating greater couple role tension among blue-collar suburban families provide indirect support for the interpretation that this kind of forced nuclearization increases intrafamilial stress (Tallman, 1969). Apparently the greater neighboring and social participation of suburban women does not provide them with an adequate substitute for close ties with friends and relatives.

Thus, although the data from our blue-collar suburb approximate those of previous studies of white-collar suburbs with regard to neighboring, participation in voluntary associations, and family organization, there are indications that those behaviors may be qualitatively different in the two types of suburbs. These differences become even more evident when we compare our findings on mobility and political orientations with previous reports of white-collar suburbs. What seems most striking in our data is the extent to which the suburban sample approximates the *popular image* of suburbia as inhabited

[17] In order to determine more precisely the extent to which the test factors influenced the relationship between residence and the life-style variables, we standardized the effects of these variables and compared the original relationships with those resulting from the standardizations. These data are not presented here in order to conserve space; they are, however, available for the interested reader (see footnote 12). In only 3 of the 153 comparisons were the original findings reduced by as much as a third. There were no consistent reductions for any of the life-style categories standardized on a given test factor. For a description of the standardized procedure used see Rosenberg (1962).

[18] The finding that the older suburban women experienced the greatest sense of isolation is somewhat harder to account for. It may be that despite a tendency to move toward a more companionate orientation with increasing age urban women still have old patterns of relationships to fall back on in emergencies, whereas these resources are not available for suburban women.

by middle class, upwardly mobile strivers who adopt a middle-of-the-road political stance (Whyte, 1957). Paradoxically, it is just these mobility orientations which most clearly set apart our blue-collar suburb from white-collar suburbs, the latter having frequently been described as inhabited by persons with high familism and nonmobility orientations (Bell, 1958; Mowrer, 1958).

The similarity between the life-styles evidenced by the suburban men and the popular image of suburban life raises the possibility that those blue-collar men who wish to identify themselves as middle class will move to the suburbs as verification of having achieved middle-class status.[19] If this interpretation is valid then it is conceivable that many of the residential differences reported above can be accounted for by the greater mobility orientation of the suburban men. To test this possibility we reanalyzed the data controlling for class identification and perception of upward mobility. Again results did not attentuate the original residential differences on any of the life-style indicators.[20]

Controlling for social-class identification, however, did yield specifications for perceived similarity of neighbors' income and education and self-identification as liberal, conservative, or middle-of-the-road. On these three items the residential differences attenuate for men who identify themselves as middle class but remain constant for those who consider themselves working class. Apparently men with middle-class orientations were sensitized to the status attributes of their neighbors regardless of residence. A similar sensitivity to the characteristics of neighbors was found for suburban residents (see Table 1)—with the important distinction that suburbanites did not restrict their interests to just questions of income and education but included perceptions of shared interest and knowledge of the neighbors' work and church activities. This broader area of involvement suggests that the suburbanite is as concerned with his potential integration in the community as he is with status characteristics of his neighbors.

The fact that suburban–urban differences on political orientations cannot be explained by the greater middle-class identification of the suburban men suggests that residential factors play a role in the development of these views. It may be that the same factors which create greater neighboring and common interests in the suburbs also foster proximate and pragmatic political concerns, thereby mitigating the development of more absolute political orientations.[21]

Although these findings do not rule out the possibility that upwardly mobile manual workers may selectively choose to live in the suburbs, they do

[19] Chinoy (1952) suggests this is a motivating factor among automobile workers.

[20] The differences for women were weaker in the original relationships and the results using these controls were relatively inconsistent.

[21] This interpretation is not unlike Greer's (1960) notion that the basis of political participation in suburbs is shared life space and interests. See also his discussion in *The Emerging City* (1962:esp. Chap. 4). Another factor which may play a role in the lack of partisanship as well as the lack of strong commitment is the non-partisan nature of most suburban elections (Wood, 1958; Greer, 1962:141).

suggest that the life-style differences we found cannot be explained by this aspect of selective migration.[22]

CONCLUSIONS AND IMPLICATIONS

The pervasive influence of residence on the variables depicting life-style suggests that the ecology of the community has a significant, though not totally independent, effect on critical modes of behavior. Such characteristics as the ratio of single to multiple dwellings, the amount of shared common space, and relative isolation from the city appear to have as much influence on the working-class family as they do on the middle class. In fact, the isolation of the suburb may be particularly salient in the working class since it breaks up traditional patterns of close relationships with relatives and peers. This is probably more true for women than it is for men since working-class women seem to be more tied to kin than are their husbands (Rainwater et al., 1959; Komarovsky, 1962; Young and Willmott, 1957; Adams, 1968:169).

The ecological explanation does not appear to adequately account for all of the findings, however. For example, location per se does not explain the greater middle class and upwardly mobile orientation of the suburbanites. It may be that upwardly mobile workers tend to select suburban residences because they symbolize middle-class status. At the same time, our data show that mobility orientations do not significantly modify the residential differences in other aspects of life-style reported in this paper. What seems most likely is that the interaction between suburban location and upwardly mobile persons with working-class backgrounds results in a life-style which is different from that characteristic of white-collar suburbs or working-class urban areas. Should our findings be supported by more representative studies, we would expect that the blue-collar suburb, unlike its white-collar counterpart, would represent a status-conscious community with a moderately conservative bent, a moderate level of social participation, greater church attendance, and a relatively high degree of marital tension. Even where our data approximate those of white-collar suburbs (e.g., neighboring, local intimacy, social participation, and nuclear family orientations) it seems reasonable to infer that more intensive study would yield qualitative differences.

The differential effect of residence on men and women has been the subject of considerable discussion in the literature. The suburb has been described as the central domain of women, and suburban life is viewed as uniquely satisfying to their values and expressive orientations (Mowrer, 1958: 162–163; Martin, 1956). Most of the findings reported in this paper, with the exception of those referring to social participation, indicate greater residence differences for men than for women. The implications of these differences

[22] Our efforts to discover a basis for selective migration in this study did not yield sizeable residential differences. The reasons given for moving in the two communities were remarkably similar. Approximately 45 percent of the men and women in both communities stated they moved to obtain better housing or living conditions.

have been reported in some detail elsewhere (Tallman, 1969). Suffice it to say, the data indicate that the suburbs did not provide greater satisfaction for women; if anything, suburban life was viewed more positively by men. In general, the findings illustrate the importance of using both spouses in studies of this type and the dangers of assuming that a single respondent adequately represents the household.

The suburb reported here is relatively recent in origin and virtually homogeneous in class composition. In this sense it is comparable to Berger's (1968) suburb, but unlike Dobriner's (1963) description of Levittown.[23] The generalizations that can be drawn from this study are also limited by the fact that it represents only one midwest community. A definitive study of suburban life in the United States will have to provide a representative sample of communities as well as populations. Given the problems extant in defining communities it would appear that any attempt at representative sampling must be preceded by a more careful delineation of ecological and residential factors than has been characteristic of such research in the past. Our data strongly suggest that an adequate typology of communities can make a major contribution in explaining the development of divergent life-styles.

[23] For example, 42 percent of our suburban sample defined themselves as middle class as compared to 41 percent in Berger's study (1968:119).

REFERENCES

Adams, Bert N., *Kinship in an Urban Setting*, Chicago: Markham, 1968.

Alford, Robert R., *Party and Society*, Chicago: Rand McNally, 1963.

Bell, Wendell, "Social Choice, Life Styles, and Suburban Residence," in William M. Dobriner (ed.), *The Suburban Community*, New York: Putnam's, 1958, pp. 225–247.

Bell, Wendell, and Marion D. Boat, "Urban Neighborhoods and Informal Social Relations," *American Journal of Sociology*, 62 (January, 1957), 391–398.

Bell, Wendell, and Maryanne T. Force, "Urban Neighborhood Types and Participation in Formal Association," *American Sociological Review*, 21 (February, 1956), 25–34.

Berger, Bennett M., *Working Class Suburb*, Berkeley and Los Angeles: University of California Press, 1960. "Suburbia and the American Dream," in Sylvia F. Fava (ed.), *Urbanism in World Perspective*, New York: Crowell, 1968, pp. 434–444.

Blau, Peter M., and Otis Dudley Duncan, *The American Occupational Structure*, New York: John Wiley, 1967.

Bott, Elizabeth, *Family and Social Network*, London: Tavistock, 1957.

Cavan, Ruth S., "Sub-Cultural Variation and Mobility," in Harold Christensen (ed.), *Handbook of Marriage and the Family*, Chicago: Rand McNally, 1964, pp. 535–581.

Chinoy, Ely, "The Tradition of Opportunity and the Aspirations of Automobile Workers," *American Journal of Sociology*, 57 (May, 1952), 453–459. *Automobile Workers and the American Dream*, Boston: Beacon Press, 1955.

Dewey, Richard, "Peripheral Expansion in Milwaukee County," *American Journal of Sociology*, 53 (May, 1948), 414–422.

Dobriner, William M., *Class in Suburbia*, Englewood Cliffs, New Jersey: Prentice-Hall, 1963.

Duncan, Otis Dudley, and Albert J. Reiss, Jr., "Suburbs and Urban Fringe," in William M. Dobriner (ed.), *The Suburban Community*, New York: Putnam's, 1958, pp. 45–66.

Fava, Sylvia F., "Contrasts in Neighboring: New York City and Suburban County," in William M. Dobriner (ed.), *The Suburban Community*, New York: Putnam's, 1958, pp. 122–131.

Gans, Herbert J., *The Urban Villagers*, New York: Free Press, 1962. *The Levittowners*, New York: Pantheon Books, 1967.

Greer, Scott, "Urbanism Reconsidered: A Comparative Study of Local Areas in a Metropolis." *American Sociological Review*, 21 (February, 1956), 19–25. "The Social Structure and Political Process of Suburbia." *American Sociological Review*, 25 (August, 1960), 514–526. *The Emerging City*, New York: Free Press, 1962.

Hausknecht, Murray, "The Blue Collar Joiner," in Arthur B. Shostak and William Gomberg (eds.), *Blue Collar World*, Englewood Cliffs, New Jersey: Prentice-Hall, 1964, pp. 207–214.

Hoover, Edgar M., and Raymond Vernon, *Anatomy of a Metropolis*, New York: Anchor Books, 1959.

Jaco, E. Gartley, and Ivan Belknap, "Is a New Family Form Emerging in the Urban Fringe?", *American Sociological Review*, 18 (October, 1953), 551–557.

Komarovsky, Mirra, "The Voluntary Associations of Urban Dwellers," *American Sociological Review*, 11 (December, 1946), 686–698. *Blue Collar Marriage*, New York: Random House, 1962.

Ktsanes, Thomas, and Leonard Reissman, "Suburbia—New Homes for Old Values," *Social Problems*, 7 (Winter, 1959–1960), 187–195.

Lazerwitz, Bernard, "Metropolitan Residential Belts," *American Sociological Review*, 25 (April, 1960), 245–252.

Martin, Walter, "The Structuring of Social Relationships Engendered by Suburban Residence," *American Sociological Review*, 21 (August, 1956), 446–452.

Miller, S. M., and Frank Riessman, "The Working-Class Sub-Culture: A New View," in Arthur B. Shostak and William Gomberg (eds.), *Blue Collar World*, Englewood Cliffs, New Jersey: Prentice-Hall, 1964, pp. 24–36.

Mogey, J. M., "Changes in Family Life Experienced by English Workers Moving From Slums to Housing Estates," *Marriage and Family Living*, 17 (May, 1955), 123–129. *Family and Neighborhood*, London: Oxford University Press, 1956.

Mowrer, Ernest R., "The Family in Suburbia," in William M. Dobriner (ed.), *The Suburban Community*, New York: Putnam's, 1958, pp. 147–164.

Rainwater, Lee, R. P. Coleman, and Gerald Handel, *Workingman's Wife*, New York: Oceana, 1959.

Reiss, Albert J., Jr., "Rural-Urban and Status Differences in Interpersonal Contacts," *American Journal of Sociology*, 65 (September, 1954), 182–195.

Riesman, David, "The Suburban Dislocation," *Annals of the American Academy of Political and Social Science*, 314, 123–146.

Rosenberg, Morris, "Test Factor Standardization as a Method of Interpretation," *Social Forces*, 41 (October, 1962), 53–61.

Rossi, Peter H., *Why Families Move*, Glencoe, Illinois: Free Press, 1955.

Schneider, Louis, "Problems in the Sociology of Religion," in Robert E. L. Faris (ed.), *Handbook of Modern Sociology*, Chicago: Rand McNally, 1964, pp. 770–807.

Scott, J. C., "Membership and Participation in Voluntary Associations," *American Sociological Review*, 21 (June, 1957), 315–326.

Seligman, Daniel, "The New Masses," in Frederick J. Tietze and James E. McKeown (eds.), *The Changing Metropolis*, Boston: Houghton Mifflin, 1964, pp. 151–161.

Shevky, Eshrev, and Wendell Bell, *Social Area Analysis*, Stanford: Stanford University Press, 1955.

Simmel, Georg, "The Metropolis and Mental Life," in Kurt H. Wolff (trans. and ed.), *The Sociology of Georg Simmel*, Glencoe, Illinois: Free Press, 1950, pp. 409–424.

Smith, Joel, William H. Form, and Gregory P. Stone, "Local Intimacy in a Middle-Sized City," *American Journal of Sociology*, 60 (November, 1954), 276–284.

Tallman, Irving, "Working-Class Wife in Suburbia: Fulfillment or Crisis," *Journal of Marriage and the Family*, 31 (February, 1969), 65–72.

Taueber, Karl E., and Alma F. Taueber, "White Migration and Social-Economic Differences Between Cities and Suburbs," *American Sociological Review*, 29 (October, 1964), 718–729.

Tomeh, Aida K., "Informal Group Participation and Residential Patterns," *American Journal of Sociology*, 70 (July, 1964), 28–35.

U.S. Bureau of the Census, *U.S. Census of Populations and Housing: 1960 Census Tracts.* Final Report PHC (1)-93, Minneapolis-St. Paul, Minnesota, Washington, D.C.: U.S. Government Printing Office, 1962.

Whyte, William H., *The Organization Man*, New York: Anchor Books, 1957.

Willmott, Peter, and Michael Young, *Family and Class in a London Suburb*, London: Routledge and Kegan Paul, 1960.

Winter, G., *The Suburban Captivity of the Church*, New York: Doubleday, 1961.

Wirth, Louis, "Urbanism as a Way of Life," *American Journal of Sociology*, 44 (July, 1938), 1–24.

Wood, Robert C., *Suburbia, Its People and Their Politics*, Boston: Houghton Mifflin, 1958.

Woodbury, Coleman, "Suburbanization and Suburbia," *American Journal of Public Health*, 45 (1955), 1–10.

Young, Michael, and Peter Willmott, *Family and Kinship in East London*, Baltimore: Penguin Books, 1957.

Zimmer, Basil, and Amos Hawley, "Suburbanization and Church Participation," *Social Forces*, 37 (May, 1959), 348–354.

25 | *Some Aspects of Lower Class Sexual Behavior*

LEE RAINWATER

INTRODUCTION

The belief that the price of increasing affluence and sophistication (at least through the middle ranges) is loss of the ability to act and feel as a "natural man" has long been a part of the American cultural tradition. Confounded in the complex myths which express this belief are natural virtue, innocence, honesty, love, fun, sensuality and taking pleasure where and how one can find it. Natural man as hero can be constructed by any selection of these characteristics; some versions emphasize virtue and innocence, others emphasize fun, sensuality and pleasuring oneself. But to our Puritan minds natural man can also be evil; we have myths of naturalness that emphasize immorality, hatefulness, sexual avarice, promiscuity and sensual gluttony. Many of the images which Americans have, and historically have had, of the lower class can be subsumed under one or another version of natural man as good or evil. Whatever the evaluative overtones to a particular version of these myths, they add up to the fact that the lower classes (like racial and ethnic minorities, primitive peoples, Communists and others) are supposed to be gaining gratifications which more responsible middle class people give up or sharply limit to appropriate relationships (like marriage) and situations (like in bed and at night).[1] These contrasting themes of naturalness-as-good and naturalness-as-evil are really mutually reinforcing, since they support the view that "naturalness" exists and is defined by the common terms of the two themes—and *pari passu* that "unnaturalness" exists and is defined by the absence of these two themes.[2]

[1] John Dollard has analyzed some of the attitudes that white Southerners have toward Negroes, which compound both the positive and negative views of lower status naturalness. In his analysis he perhaps took somewhat too seriously the notion that lower class Negroes gain from the greater sexual freedom allowed them by the caste system (6). Allison Davis, an insufficiently appreciated pioneer in the study of lower class cultures, seems to have been similarly taken in by the myth: "In the slum, one certainly does not have a sexual partner for as many days each month as do middle class married people, but one gets and gives more satisfaction over longer periods, when he does have a sexual partner." (5, p. 33)

[2] Kai Erikson (7) in an analysis of the functions of deviance and its control in the establishment of social boundaries comments, "Every culture recognizes a certain vocabulary of contrasts which are meant to represent polar opposites on the scale of human behavior. . . . [but] when we look across the world to other cultures . . . or behind us to the historical past, it often seems that these contrasting forms are little more than minor variations on a single cultural theme."

Reprinted from the *Journal of Social Issues*, 22, No. 2 (April, 1966), 96–109, by permission of the Society for the Psychological Study of Social Issues.

An article dealing with lower class sexual behavior would be expected, then, to describe a group of happy or God-forsaken sinners who derive a great deal more sexual gratification in their society than do middle class respectables in theirs. However, the little empirical research which examines lower class sexual behavior—and, more important, lower class subjective responses to sex—tends to support quite a different view.[3] Since we have fuller comparative information on sexual relations within marriage for lower, working and middle class couples, we will examine sex within the context of marriage first.

MARITAL SEXUALITY IN THE LOWER CLASS

At all class levels, marital sexual relations provide the major source of sexual outlet for most men and women during their sexual careers. In all social classes, also, marital sexual relations are considered the preferable and most desirable outlet. Other sources of outlet are most often seen by their seekers as compensations or substitutes rather than really preferable alternatives. We start, then, with a comparison of the ways husbands and wives in the lower, working and middle classes evaluate marital sexuality, the attitudes they have toward sexual relations, and the gratifications and dissatisfactions they find in these.

The material which follows is drawn from a larger study (18, 20) which examines marital sexuality as part of the family context for family size decisions and family limitation behavior. The study is based on interviews with 409 individuals—152 couples, and 50 men and 55 women not married to each other. Thus 257 families are represented. The respondents lived in Chicago, Cincinnati or Oklahoma City and were chosen in such a way as to represent the social class range of whites from upper middle to lower-lower and Negroes at the upper-lower and lower-lower class levels.

Men and women were asked to discuss their feelings about their sexual relations in marriage, the gratifications they found, the dissatisfactions they had, the meaning of sex in their marriages and the importance it had to them and to their spouses.

One dimension emerging from the answers to all of these questions can be thought of as a continuum of interest and enjoyment in sexual relations, which ranges from very great interest and enjoyment to strong rejection. The

[3] The shift to a more jaundiced view of the happy impulse-free version of lower class sexual life is paralleled by a similar shift in the understanding of lower class delinquency. Bordua, in comparing the work of Frederick Thrasher in the 1920's with that of Walter Miller, Albert Cohen, Richard Cloward and Lloyd Ohlin, comments, "All in all, though, it does not seem like much fun any more to be a gang delinquent. Thrasher's boys enjoyed themselves being chased by the police, shooting dice, skipping school, rolling drunks. It was fun. Miller's boys do have a little fun, with their excitement focal concern, but it seems so desperate somehow. Cohen's boys and Cloward and Ohlin's boys are driven by grim economic and psychic necessity into rebellion. It seems peculiar that modern analysts have stopped assuming that 'evil' can be fun and see gang delinquency as arising only when boys are driven away from 'good.' " (1, p. 136)

range is most apparent among women, of course; men only rarely say they are indifferent to or uninterested in sexual relations, but women present the gamut of responses from "if God made anything better, He kept it to Himself," to "I would be happy if I never had to do that again; it's disgusting." On the basis of each individual's response to all of the questions about sexual relations he was classified as showing either great or mild interest and enjoyment in sex, slightly negative feelings about sex, or rejection of sexual

TABLE 1 The Lower the Social Status, the Less Interest and Enjoyment Husbands and Wives Find in Marital Sexual Relations

	Middle Class	Upper-Lower Class	Lower-Lower Class
Husbands			
Show great interest and enjoyment	78%	75%	44%
Mild interest and enjoyment	22%	25%	56%
No. of cases	(56)	(56)	(59)
Wives			
Great interest and enjoyment	50%	53%	20%
Mild interest and enjoyment	36%	16%	26%
Slightly negative toward sex	11%	27%	34%
Reject sexual relations	3%	4%	20%
No. of cases	(58)	(68)	(69)

relations. Table 1 presents the results on this variable by social class. (Since there were no differences between the upper and lower portions of the middle class, these groups were combined in the tables.) It is apparent that as one moves from higher to lower social status the proportion of men and women who show strong interest and enjoyment of sex declines. Among men the proportion showing only mild interest and enjoyment increases as one moves to the lower-lower class level. Among women the proportion who are slightly negative or rejecting in their attitudes toward sexual relations increases systematically from the middle to the upper-lower to the lower-lower class. (There is a small but consistent tendency for Negroes in the lower-lower class to show somewhat more interest in sex than similarly situated whites.)[4]

It would seem, then, that social status has a great deal to do with the extent to which couples manage in marriage to find sexual relations a valued and meaningful activity. This result is consistent with the findings of the Kinsey studies (9, 14, 15). For women the Kinsey study reports that erotic arousal from any source is less common at the lower educational levels, that fewer of these women have ever reached orgasm and that the frequency for

[4] It should be noted that the careful and detailed study of blue-collar marriages by Komarovsky (13) reports that there were no differences in sexual enjoyment between higher and lower status wives within the working class (status indicated by high school education or less than high school education). I have no explanation for this difference in findings between two studies which parallel each other in most other respects, but the readers should be aware of Komarovsky's contrary findings (see especially pp. 93–94). However, the less educated wives did view sex as more of a duty, and refused less often.

those who do is lower. For men, the pattern is less clear-cut as far as frequency goes, but it is apparent that fore-play techniques are less elaborate at the lower educational levels, most strikingly so with respect to oral techniques. In positional variations in intercourse, the lower educational levels show somewhat less versatility, but more interesting is the fact that the difference between lower and higher educational levels increases with age, because positional variations among lower status men drop away rapidly, while the decline among more educated men is much less. The same pattern characterizes nudity in marital coitus.

The lesser elaboration of the sexual relationship among lower class couples which this suggests is apparent in our qualitative data. The longer the lower class man is married, the more likely he is to express a reduced interest in an enjoyment of sexual relations with his wife, as well as indicating reduced frequency of intercourse. In the middle class, while reduced frequency is universally recognized, there is much more of a tendency to put this in the context of "the quantity has gone down, but the quality gets better and better." An examination of the very small body of literature dealing with attitudes toward and feelings about sexual relations in lower class populations in other countries suggests that this pattern is not confined to the United States (16, 19, 25, 26, 27).

Having observed that lower class husbands and wives are less likely than are middle class ones to find sexual relations gratifying, we become interested in why that should be. The major variable that seems related to this class difference concerns the quality of conjugal role relationships in the different classes. In this same study we found that middle class couples were much more likely to emphasize patterns of jointly organized activities around the home and joint activities outside the home, while working and lower class couples were much more likely to have patterns of role relationships in which there was greater emphasis on separate functioning and separate interests by husbands and wives. Following Bott (2) we have classified couples who show a fair degree of separateness in their conjugal

TABLE 2 Lower Class Couples in Highly Segregated Conjugal Role Relationships Find Less Enjoyment in Sexual Relations

	White Couples		Negro Couples	
	Intermediate Segregation*	Highly Segregated	Intermediate Segregation*	Highly Segregated
Husbands				
Great interest and enjoyment	72%	55%	90%	56%
Mild interest and enjoyment	28%	45%	10%	44%
No. of cases	(21)	(20)	(21)	(25)
Wives				
Great interest and enjoyment	64%	18%	64%	8%
Mild interest and enjoyment	4%	14%	14%	40%
Slightly negative toward sex	32%	36%	18%	32%
Reject sexual relations	—	32%	4%	20%
No. of cases	(25)	(22)	(22)	(25)

*Includes the few jointly-organized couples.

role relationships as *highly segregated*, those who show a very strong degree of joint participation and joint involvement of each in the other's activities were characterized as *jointly organized*. Those couples who fall between these two extremes we have characterized as having *intermediate segregation* of conjugal role relationships. Very few working or lower class couples show the jointly organized pattern, but there is variation in the intermediate to the highly segregated range. When the influence of this variable on sexual enjoyment and interest is examined, we find a very strong relationship.

Table 2 indicates that it is primarily among couples in highly segregated conjugal role relationships that we find wives who reject or are somewhat negative towards sexual relations. Similarly, it is primarily among couples in less segregated conjugal role relationships that we find husbands and wives who express great interest and enjoyment in sexual relations.

These results suggest that the lower value placed on sexual relations by lower class wives, and to a lesser extent by lower class husbands, can be seen as an extension of the high degree of segregation in their conjugal role relationship more generally. The couple emphasize separateness in their other activities; therefore separateness comes to be the order of the day in their sexual relationship. Since the wife's interest in sex tends to be more heavily dependent upon a sense of interpersonal closeness and gratification in her total relationship with her husband, it is very difficult for her to find gratification in sex in the context of a highly segregated role relationship.

Close and gratifying sexual relationships are difficult to achieve because the husband and wife are not accustomed to relating intimately to each other. It may well be that a close sexual relationship has no particular social function in such a system, since the role performances of husband and wife are organized on a separatist basis, and no great contribution is made by a relationship in which they might sharpen their ability for cooperation and mutual regulation. Examination of the six negative cases in our sample, that is, those in which despite a highly segregated role relationship the wife enjoys sex a great deal, indicates that this comes about when the wife is able to bring to the relationship her own highly autonomous interest in sex. To the extent that she is dependent upon her husband for stimulation, encouragement and understanding on the other hand, she seems to find frustration in sex.

Husbands whose wives do not enjoy sexual relations are not particularly comfortable about this fact and in various ways either express some guilt, or try to conceal the state of affairs from both themselves and the interviewers. However, they seem to do little to correct the situation. Husbands in segregated relationships consistently overestimate the degree of gratification that their wives find in sex. Thus, half of the men in highly segregated relationships indicated that their wives enjoyed sex more than the wives themselves indicated, compared to only twenty-one percent of the men in less segregated relationships.

Lower class men in highly segregated relationships seem to make few efforts to assist their wives in achieving sexual gratification, and place little emphasis on the importance of mutual gratification in coitus. For example, while 74% of the lower and working class husbands with intermediate relationships give some spontaneous indication that they value mutual gratification in the sexual relationship, only 35% of the husbands in segregated relationships speak of mutual gratification. It is not surprising, then, that a considerable number of wives complain about their husbands' lack of consideration. Forty percent of the wives in segregated relationships spontaneously indicate that their husbands are inconsiderate of them in connection with sexual relations, compared to only 7% of wives in intermediate relationships. Similarly, 38% of those in highly segregated relationships spontaneously indicate that they consider sex primarily as a duty, compared to only 14% of the wives in intermediate relationships.

These differences among classes, and within the lower class between couples in intermediate and highly segregated role relationships, continue to appear when the focus of inquiry is shifted from degree of enjoyment of sexual relations to the question of the psychosocial functions which people think sex serves for them. Two common themes stand out in the ways couples talk about what sex "does" for men and women. One is that sex provides "psychophysiological" relief—it gets rid of tensions, relaxes, gives physical relief ("It's like the back pressure on a car that you have to get rid of.") and provides sensual pleasure in the form of orgasm. The other theme emphasizes, instead, the social-emotional gratifications that come from closeness with the partner, a growth of love, a sense of oneness, of sharing, of giving and receiving. Almost all of the respondents who mentioned one or the other of these functions mentioned the physical aspect, but there is quite a bit of variation in whether this is mentioned by itself or in combination with social-

TABLE 3 Lower Class Couples in Highly Segregated Conjugal Role Relationships
See Only Psychophysiological Pleasure and Relief in Sexual Relations

		Lower Class	
Sexual Relations Provide:	Middle Class	Intermediate Segregation	Highly Segregated
Husbands			
Socio-emotional closeness and exchange	75%	52%	16%
Psychophysiological pleasure and relief only	25%	48%	84%
No. of cases	(56)	(40)	(31)
Wives			
Socio-emotional closeness and exchange	89%	73%	32%
Psychophysiological pleasure and relief only	11%	27%	68%
No. of cases	(46)	(33)	(22)

emotional closeness. Table 3 provides distributions by class and role relationship of the relative emphasis on these two themes.

The findings emphasize further the fact that one of the main differences between the middle class and the lower class, and within the lower class between couples in intermediate and highly segregated role relationships, has to do with the extent to which the sexual relationship is assimilated with other aspects of the on-going relationship between husband and wife. It seems very clear that in the middle class, and among those lower class couples with conjugal role relationships of intermediate segregation, the sexual relation is seen as an extension of an overall husband-wife relationship which emphasizes "togetherness," mutual involvement and give-and-take. In the lower class, among couples in highly segregated conjugal role relationships, on the other hand, the sexual relationship is isolated from aspects of the husband-wife relationship and stands in sharp contrast to these other aspects because it requires concerted cooperation on the part of the two partners. Other data showed that in a great many cases, the wife's response is to cooperate only passively, by making herself available when her husband "wants it." In a few cases the wife is able to bring her own autonomous psychophysiological needs to sexual relations and find enjoyment in them.

LOWER CLASS NON-MARITAL SEXUAL RELATIONS

We have much less systematic knowledge of lower class attitudes and customary behaviors concerning non-marital sexual relations than for marital sexual relations. We do know, however, a fair amount about the incidence of non-marital sexual relations from the Kinsey studies as this varies by social status (educational level). The considerable literature dealing with lower class adolescent peer groups also provides some insight into the place of premarital sexual relations in the peer group activities of young lower class boys and girls.

From the Kinsey studies of white males and females it seems clear that before the age of twenty both lower class boys and lower class girls are much more likely to have premarital coitus than are middle class boys and girls. However, even lower class girls are not as likely to have premarital sexual relations as are middle class boys; the overall cultural double standard seems to operate at all class levels. Further, after the age of twenty, status seems to influence premarital coitus in opposite ways for men and women. After that age middle class girls are more likely than lower class girls to have premarital relations, perhaps because the lower class girls are so quickly siphoned off into marriage, while lower class boys continue more frequently to have premarital relations.

From the Kinsey studies, we know that there are very great differences between white and Negro females in the extent to which they engage in premarital coitus. While the social class influence is the same in both groups, in the teens the level of exposure to sexual relations is on the order of three to four times higher for Negro girls than for white girls. Thus, while at age twenty only 26% of white grammar school educated girls have had premarital sexual relationships, over 80% of comparable Negro girls have.

These findings concerning premarital coitus are consistent with the impressions one gains from literature which deals with the peer group systems of white and Negro lower class adolescents and young adults (3, 4, 8, 10, 11, 19, 21, 24, 29). In the white lower class there is a great deal of emphasis on the double standard, in that white lower class boys are expected to engage in sexual relations whenever they have an opportunity, and pride themselves on their ability to have intercourse with many different girls. Making out in this fashion is turned into valuable currency within the boys' peer groups; there is much bragging and competition (leading to not a little exaggeration) among white slum boys about their sexual conquests.

The girls' position in this group is a much more complex one. White slum groups tend to grade girls rather finely according to the extent of their promiscuity, with virgins being highly valued and often protected, "one man girls" still able to retain some respect from those around them (particularly if in the end they marry the boy with whom they have had intercourse), and more promiscuous girls quickly put into the category of an "easy lay." In groups, then, although boys are constantly exposed to stimulation to engage in sexual relations, efforts are made to protect girls from such stimulation and even to conceal from them elementary facts about sex and about their future sexual roles. Mothers do not discuss sex with their daughters, and usually do not even discuss menstruation with them. The daughter is left very much on her own with only emergency attention from the mother—for example, when she is unable to cope with the trauma of onset of menses or seems to be getting too involved with boys. When women at this level assess their premarital knowledge of sex, they generally say that they were completely unprepared for sexual relations in marriage or for their first premarital experiences, that no one had ever told them much about sex and that they had only a vague idea of what was involved. There is little evidence that in this kind of white lower class subculture many girls find the idea of sexual relations particularly attractive. Although they may become involved with fantasies of romantic love, they seem to show little specific interest in sexual intercourse.

In the Negro lower class the clear-cut differences between the amount of sexual activity respectively permitted girls and boys (and men and women) that seem to obtain in the white lower class are absent. Indeed, at age fifteen, according to the Kinsey results, more grammar school educated Negro girls have experienced coitus than white boys; this is also true at the high school level. With over 60% of *grammar school* educated Negro girls having had intercourse by the age of 15, and over 80% by the age of twenty, it seems clear that within the Negro *slum* community, whatever the attitudes involved, lower class Negro girls are introduced to sexual relations early and, relative to white girls, engage much more frequently in sexual relations once they have started. There are well-established patterns of seduction within Negro slum communities which Negro boys employ. They are sharply judged by other boys and girls on their ability to employ these techniques, and boys show considerable anxiety lest they be rated low on these skills. As is well known, this higher degree of sexual activity leads to a high rate of illegitimacy.

These bare behavioral statistics might lead one to believe that among the lower class *Negroes*, at least, there is a happy acceptance of premarital sexual relations, somewhat along the line of the natural man myth discussed above. However, *close observation* of ghetto peer group activities of late adolescent and early adult Negro males and females indicates that such is not the case (4, 11). In the first place, attitudes toward sexual relations are highly competitive (among own sex peers), and heavily exploitative (toward opposite sex). Slum Negro boys typically refer to girls, including their own "girlfriends" as "that bitch" or "that whore" when they talk among themselves. Negro girls who do engage in sexual relations in response to the strong lines of the boys who "rap to" them often do not seem to find any particular gratification in sexual relations, but rather engage in sex as a test and symbol of their maturity and their ability to be in the swim of things. Over time a certain proportion of these girls do develop their own appreciation of sexual relations, and engage in them out of desire as well as for extrinsic reasons. However, it seems clear that the competitive and exploitative attitudes on both sides make sexual relations a tense and uncertain matter as far as gratification goes. In discussing marital sexuality we noted that the high degree of conjugal role segregation seems to interfere with achieving maximum gratification in sexual relations. A parallel factor seems to operate in connection with premarital relations. That is, because of the culturally defined and interpersonally sustained hostilities that exist between the sexes, it seems difficult for both boys and girls to develop a self-assured and open acceptance of sex for the pleasure it can provide, much less for a heightened sense of interpersonal closeness and mutuality. When one seeks to study the meaning and function of sexual relations in such a very complex situation as the Negro lower class community, one becomes aware of how much more subtle and ramified the issues are than can be captured in the traditional categories of sex research.

THE FUTURE OF SEX IN THE LOWER CLASS

As the working class has attained greater prosperity and a sense of greater economic stability since World War II, there seems to have been a shift from traditional working class patterns of a high degree of conjugal role segregation and reliance by husbands and wives on their same sex peer groups for emotional support and counsel. Elsewhere Handel and Rainwater (12, 13) have discussed the increasing importance of a modern working class life style which seems to be gradually replacing the traditional life style among those working class families who are in a position to partake of the "standard package" of material and social amenities which represent the common man's version of the "good American life." We have seen that among those couples who have a lesser degree of conjugal role segregation there is a much greater probability of a mutual strong interest in sexual relations and an emphasis on sexual relations as an extension of the socio-emotional closeness that is valued in husband-wife relationships. We can predict, then, that shifts in the direction of greater cooperation and solidarity based on interpenetration of family role activities in marriage will carry with them an increased intimacy in the sexual sphere. This greater mutuality is both an expression of and functional for the increased self-sufficiency of a nuclear family, in which working class husband and wife now rely less on outsiders for support and a sense of primary group membership and more on each other. In this sense a "good" sexual relation between husband and wife can be seen as one of the major strengths of the adaptable nuclear family which Clark Vincent has argued is necessary for our kind of industrial society (28).

But what of those members of the lower class who do not participate in the increasing prosperity and security which the great majority of the working class has known for the past twenty years? In recent years there has been mounting evidence that sex-related pathologies of the Negro slum ghetto community—for example, the rate of illegitimacy, venereal disease, drug encouraged prostitution (4, 17)—are increasing rather than decreasing. It seems clear that so long as the socio-economic circumstances of slum Negroes do not improve, we can expect only a worsening of a situation in which sexual relations are used for exploitative and competitive purposes. There is much less clear-cut evidence concerning white slum groups; it may well be that the rates for the same sex-related pathologies show lesser increases because the white poor are not confined to ghettos which serve to concentrate the destructive effects of poverty, but instead tend to be more widely dispersed in the interstices of more stable working class neighborhoods (24).

In short, though we see some evidence to support the notion of a "sexual renaissance" with respect to marital sexuality in the modern working class, we see no such evidence with respect to the less prosperous lower class.

SEX RESEARCH IN THE LIGHT OF LOWER CLASS SEX BEHAVIOR

It is probably not unfair to say that efforts to study sexual behavior scientifically have been plagued by an obsessive preoccupation with the terms of the larger public dialogue on the subject, and with the value conflicts and contradictions evident in that dialogue. Thus researchers who investigate sexual behavior have often been motivated by an effort to determine whether sex under particular circumstances is good or bad, or whether particular customs interfere with pleasure or are conducive to it. While these are legitimate concerns, they have tended to distract social scientists from an effort simply to understand sexual practices in their full human context. We have suggested that a close examination of lower class sexual behavior tends to disprove certain widely-held stereotypes—themselves not unknown in social scientists' own attitudes. But more important, the study of lower class sexual behavior emphasizes the importance of trying to understand that behavior *both* in the immediate context of relevant interpersonal relations (marital relations, peer group relations, etc.), and in the context of the structural position of the actors, and the stresses and strains that position engenders. Such an understanding can only come about through careful empirical research which does not take for granted supposed "facts" about the actors involved, but rather explores these interrelations empirically.

Once we have an adequate picture of the sexual behavior of individuals in a particular situation, we can begin to ask questions about the role of this sexual behavior in connection with other aspects of the individual's interpersonal relations. We can ask what the functions of particular forms of sexual behavior are for the individual and for the groups to which he belongs. More psychologically, we can ask, and not assume in advance that we know, what goals the individual seeks to effect through particular kinds of sexual behavior. It seems to me that this is the real legacy of Freud for the study of sexual behavior. Freud sought to show that sex is not simply sex, but a complex form of behavior built out of elements which extend genetically back into dim childhood history, and cross-sectionally into other vital interests which the individual seeks to maximize and protect. Just as any other applied field of social science profits from a wide application of contending theoretical paradigms, so the study of sexual behavior would profit from a more liberal application of the diverse conceptual tools at our disposal.

REFERENCES

1. Bordua, David J., "Delinquent Subcultures: Sociological Interpretations of Gang Delinquency," *The Annals of the American Academy of Political and Social Sciences*, 338 (1961), 120–136.
2. Bott, Elizabeth, *Family and Social Network*, London: Tavistock Publications, 1957.
3. Cayton, Horace R., and St. Clair Drake, *Black Metropolis*, New York: Harper and Row, 1962.
4. Clark, Kenneth, *The Dark Ghetto*, New York: Harper and Row, 1965.
5. Davis, Allison, *Social Class Influence on Learning*, Cambridge: Harvard University Press, 1952.
6. Dollard, John, *Caste and Class in a Southern Town*, New Haven: Yale University Press, 1937.
7. Erikson, Kai T., "Notes on the Sociology of Deviance," *Social Problems*, 9 (1962), 307–314.
8. Frazier, E. Franklin, *The Negro Family in the United States*, Chicago: University of Chicago Press, 1939.
9. Gebhard, Paul H., et al., *Pregnancy, Birth and Abortion*, New York: Harper and Brothers, 1958.
10. Green, Arnold W., "The Cult of Personality and Sexual Relations," *Psychiatry*, 4 (1941), 343–44.
11. Hammond, Boone, "The Contest System: A Survival Technique," Master's Honors Essay Series, Washington University, 1965.
12. Handel, Gerald and Lee Rainwater, "Persistence and Change in Working Class Life Style," in Arthur B. Shostak and William Gomberg (eds.), *Blue Collar Worlds*, Englewood Cliffs, New Jersey: Prentice-Hall, 1964, pp. 36–42.
13. Komarovsky, Mirra, *Blue Collar Marriage*, New York: Random House, 1964.
14. Kinsey, Alfred C., et al., *Sexual Behavior in the Human Male*, Philadelphia: Saunders, 1948.
15. Kinsey, Alfred C., et al., *Sexual Behavior in the Human Female*, Philadelphia: Saunders, 1953.
16. Lewis, Oscar, *Life in a Mexican Village: Tepoztlán Restudied*, Urbana, Illinois: University of Illinois Press, 1951.
17. Moynihan, Daniel P., "Employment, Income and the Ordeal of the Negro Family," *Daedalus*, 94, No. 4, (1965), 745–770.
18. Rainwater, Lee, *And The Poor Get Children*, Chicago: Quadrangle Books, 1960.
19. Rainwater, Lee, "Marital Sexuality in Four Cultures of Poverty," *Journal of Marriage and the Family*, 26 (1964), 457–466.
20. Rainwater, Lee, *Family Design: Marital Sexuality, Family Planning and Family Limitation*, Chicago: Aldine Publications, 1965.

21. Rainwater, Lee, "The Crucible of Identity: The Negro Lower Class Family," *Daedalus*, 95, No. 1, (1966), 172–216.
22. Rainwater, Lee, Richard Coleman and Gerald Handel, *Workingman's Wife: Her Personality, World and Life Style*, New York: Oceana Publications, 1959.
23. Rainwater, Lee and Gerald Handel, "Changing Family Roles in the Working Class," in Arthur B. Shostak and Wm. Gomberg, *Blue Collar Worlds*, Englewood Cliffs, New Jersey: Prentice-Hall, 1964, pp. 70–76.
24. Short, J. F., and F. L. Strodtbeck, *Group Process and Gang Delinquency*, Chicago: University of Chicago Press, 1965.
25. Slater, Eliot, and Moya Woodside, *Patterns of Marriage*, London: Cassell, 1951.
26. Spinley, B. M., *The Deprived and the Privileged*, London: Routledge and Kegan Paul, 1953.
27. Stycos, J. Mayone, *Family and Fertility in Puerto Rico*, New York: Columbia University Press, 1955.
28. Vincent, Clark, "Familia Spongia: The Adaptive Function," presented at the Annual Meeting of the National Council on Family Relations at Toronto, 1965.
29. Whyte, William F., "A Slum Sex Code," *American Journal of Sociology*, 49 (1943), 24–31.

26 | Occupational Characteristics and Males' Role Performance in the Family

JOAN ALDOUS

A great deal has been written on the differentiation of work from family roles in modern industrial societies. The general separation in time and space of family and occupational role performance is readily apparent. In addition, the formal requirements of the work group are often at variance with those of the family. Increasingly men, and women too, are playing their occupational roles in settings with bureaucratic characteristics. Here there are a number of supervisory levels. Obtaining a job and job advancement are determined by rules defining universalistic, specific standards of merit. Rules define the

The author would like to thank Judith D. Bennett and William S. Silverman for their comments on the original of this paper, which was prepared for the 1967 Groves Conference.

Reprinted from the *Journal of Marriage and the Family*, 31, No. 4 (November, 1969), 707–712, by permission of the National Council of Family Relations.

duties and privileges constituting the job, and the jobs are highly specialized. Unlike the highly formal bureaucratic organization, the family as a primary group is characterized by highly charged affective relations rather than impersonal contacts, and the vagaries of conception that may or may not follow intercourse rather than specific qualifications determine family membership. There is only one supervisory level, though parents may dispute this. Family members interact with each other while playing many roles as opposed to the segmented relationships of the factory and office. Family members for better or worse are involved in relatively lasting arrangements, while on the job their associates change because of merit promotions or seniority options. Finally, family interaction patterns develop over time in conformity to the family's version of the culture transmitted by important reference groups. This routinization of group activities is quite in contrast to the formal rule specification that provides the framework for interaction on the job.[1]

However, it can be argued that the supposed contrast between family and occupational roles is overdrawn. The whole "human relations" approach in industrial management grew out of the recognition that there existed an informal structure of communication and friendship networks that often circumvented the regimen of rules of the formal job structure.[2] Merit may be one of the requirements for getting a job or advancement, but personal impressions and contacts influence selection from those qualified, even in the most regulation-conscious bureaucracy. Sponsorship and social networks are particularly important for obtaining a position when job requirements are unclear and there is no simple measure of who qualifies, or job requirements are not too demanding so that many qualify. Once on the job, the incumbent rarely is able to remain affectively neutral toward his close associates whether behind the counter or on the assembly line. As a result, the "highly charged affective relations" found in the family are also present in the occupational world and influence what goes on there from job selection to job performance.[3]

Regardless of the extent of difference between family and work roles, they do articulate it for no other reason than that the male is an actor in both spheres. And there are other reasons. Formal organizations are eager to lessen the distance between family and job and to enlist the support of other family members as well as the huband-father. They hope thereby to encourage

[1] This discussion owes much to Eugene Litwak, *Technological Innovation and Ideal Forms of Family Structure in an Industrial Democratic Society*, paper presented before the International Seminar on Family Research, Tokyo, 1965, pp. 2–3.

[2] There is a voluminous literature on the informal structure in work groups. See among others, George C. Homans, *The Human Group*, New York: Harcourt, Brace, 1950, pp. 40–88; Hans Zetterberg, "The Secret Ranking," *Journal of Marriage and the Family*, 28 (May, 1966), 134–142; and Edward Gross, *Work and Society*, New York: Thomas Y. Crowell, 1958, pp. 222–260.

[3] It is even questionable whether family members see each other play so many more roles than do job associates. Perhaps it is the backstage, undress quality of family life that makes it appear that individuals reveal so much more of themselves in the family than they do when playing occupational roles.

the family role set to push the man toward the same goals his job supervisor is sanctioning. In this paper, however, the main focus is on the influence of the workman's role on family functioning rather than on the reciprocal effect of parental and marital functions on occupation. Structural characteristics of the occupation that affect the man's parental and marital functioning regardless of the personality of the job incumbent provide the major independent variables to be discussed. Because of the dearth of research, however, it is not possible to maintain a rigid separation between characteristics unique to a particular occupation or related occupations that affect parental and marital role functioning, and characteristics specific to a particular work setting such as a bureaucracy where persons in a number of occupations are active.

To begin with, the male's participation in the job market is essential for providing him the means for participating in the family. In our society the man's adult status depends upon his holding some kind of job. The research on unemployed men and their families in the thirties demonstrated the importance of the breadwinner role to the man's family status. Loss of a job meant his loss of power and influence on the actions of wife and children, as one of them or an outside agency succeeded him as economic support of the family.

Much the same phenomenon occurs in lower-class Negro and white families today. These families have a segregated conjugal role organization where there is a rigid division of labor in household tasks. The husband-father supplies the money for physical maintenance of the family, and the wife-mother performs housekeeping and child-care functions. When the husband is supplying an adequate income, the wife caters to his wants, overlooks his shortcomings, and is prepared to reward him for any household task or decision in which he engages. A positive reinforcement cycle of participation, reward, and further participation is set up, drawing the man into ever deepening involvement in family activities. Insufficient and unstable earnings on the other hand are associated with the man's lack of involvement in the family. The wife has less to reward him for and so provides little incentive for him to involve himself in family affairs. Thus within one working-class sample the higher the amount of income per family member, the more the husband performed household tasks and helped make family decisions.[4] Among lower-class Negro families where the matriarchal tradition is strong, unemployed men withdraw from the family not only because of their own feelings of inadequacy but at their wives' insistence. If the man is not supplying the family income, his wife often refuses to perform her wifely duties and drives him

---

[4] Joan Aldous, "Lower Class Males' Integration into Community and Family," paper presented before the Sixth World Congress of Sociology, 1966, p. 144. "The provision of needed income even enables women to overlook such unfortunate husbandly behaviors as incestuous activities. A concern about the family livelihood leads women to blame their husbands less for incestuous activities than the daughter-victims for reporting the activities to the police." The same situation occurs in brother-sister incest. "When the brother is the aggressor he usually is condemned, unless the family wholly or partly depends upon him for support." S. Kirsten Weinberg, *Incest Behavior*, New York: Citadel Press, 1955, pp. 182 and 255.

from the household.[5] Even when the man is employed, having a wife who is also employed appears to constitute a threat to his position as household head. He is less active in household affairs than his compeers whose wives are not competitors in the breadwinner role.[6] The opportunity to practice an occupation, therefore, is one community tie that enables the male to perform the role of provider, a role that for most men appears a prerequisite for their performing other family roles.

But once one goes beyond the simple dichotomy of employment and unemployment, the characteristics of the job the man holds in the occupational structure can have profound effects on his marital and parental role performance. First, there is the matter of how compatible occupational characteristics are with family participation. The *relative salience* of the job in comparison with family roles is important in this connection. If the occupation is of intrinsic interest to the man, it often competes with or even supplants the family as his major concern. Occupations that engage the man's attention at the expense of his family usually have some or all of the following qualities. The job incumbent has some autonomy in structuring its pace and schedule as well as the methods used. The occupation encompasses a variety of activities and provides a stable career line. It often requires special training, and there are sustained contacts with fellow workers, clients, or customers. Professions and positions in the higher echelons of business, highly skilled blue-collar occupations such as printing, or dangerous jobs such as mining are examples of high salience occupations.

The effect of such occupations on the man's family varies. Often the wife-mother has to assume virtually sole responsibility for the family, as the husband-father is too busy or too disinterested to supply much assistance. Particularly among the men of management as Whyte discovered, the man may co-opt the family and use it as a means of career advancement.[7] The man eliminates the autonomy of the family sphere and makes it an adjunct to his central occupational concern. He uses the family's consumption patterns and the wife's interpersonal skills in the service of his mobility strivings. Moreover, family concerns can mask occupational concerns and also permit him to escape from awkward professional commitments. The academician, for example, who finds his colleagues unexciting and his position at a dead end can suddenly discover his family's unhappiness with the climate and begin looking openly for a more satisfactory appointment. A strategic retreat into family roles disarms critics while permitting continued occupational striving.

Unfortunate, indeed, are those families where the wife's development after marriage has not kept pace with the husband's so that his family though co-opted is not useful to him. In such cases he often seeks a more com-

[5] Lee Rainwater, "Crucible of Identity: The Negro Lower-Class Family," *Daedalus*, 95 (Winter, 1966), 192.

[6] Joan Aldous, "The Restoration of the Lower-Class Male as Household Head: Support for the Moynihan Thesis," paper presented before the American Sociological Association, 1967, p. 6.

[7] William H. Whyte, Jr., "The Wives of Management," *Fortune*, 44 (October, 1951), 86–88; and William H. Whyte, Jr., "Corporation and the Wife," *Fortune*, 44 (November, 1951), 109–111.

patible partner.[8] Many of the intrinsically interesting white-collar occupations encourage change in their incumbents—change that may threaten the interpersonal "fit" of the couple. The young man preparing to enter a profession, for example, may not wish to face the long years of training in a state of celibacy. But while he is being socialized into a demanding occupational role, his wife—busy in her daily round of supporting him or attempting to cope with unplanned offspring—may not be changing as much as he. The result can be the post-Ph.D. or post-M.D. divorce. Organization man and wife may also fail to match in phase of development when the husband, at his company's behest, moves in a variety of social milieus and comes into contact with different roles, life styles, and perspectives while the wife keeps the family together. Failure of husband and wife to remain "in phase" so that their development is comparable and compatible is a constant threat to the stability of the marriages of men in management or the professions.

A dimension of the man's occupation other than its salience that affects marital and parental functioning is the *synchronization of occupational and family responsibilties*. This dimension encompasses such aspects of the job as its hours, the amount of geographical mobility it requires, and at what stage of the family life cycle the occupation makes its peak demands. Occupations having irregular hours or requiring night work, as well as those taking the man away from home for days at a time, all limit his opportunity to assist with family decisions and tasks as well as to become acquainted with his children. Afternoon shift workers, one study showed, have particular difficulty with father roles, night shift workers with marital roles.[9] Since the marital role difficulties center on such sensitive areas as sexual relationships and companionship, it is no wonder the friction between husband and wife is greater for night than day workers, though it is more pronounced for all non-day workers. Night workers develop crony cliques to supply the sociability and emotional support their families, geared to a daytime existence, are literally too asleep to provide. The man on the road may seek a compliant woman to supply the sexual comforts he is not at home to receive. It is no wonder then that Lang as far back as 1932 reported that wives of traveling salesmen and musicians were most unhappy in their marriages. Wives of bankers, physicians, corporation officials, and the owners of large businesses were less unhappy but more so than wives of teachers and accountants. Presumably the former group of husbands found their jobs more salient than their families.[10]

Where spacial synchronization and time complementarity between family and work setting seem necessary for parental and marital role performance,

---

[8] Nelson N. Foote, "Matching of Husband and Wife in Phases of Development," in *Sourcebook in Marriage and the Family*, ed. by Marvin B. Sussman, Boston: Houghton Mifflin, 1963, pp. 15–21.

[9] Paul E. Mott et al., *Shift Work: The Social, Psychological and Physical Consequences*, Ann Arbor: University of Michigan Press, 1965, pp. 111 and 146.

[10] R. O. Lang, *The Rating of Happiness in Marriage*, unpublished M.A. thesis, University of Chicago, 1932, quoted by J. Richard Udry, in *The Social Context of Marriage*, New York: Lippincott, 1966, p. 388.

synchronization of family and occupational demands can create difficulty. The peak years for child-bearing and child-rearing responsibilities for the man tend to be in the 22- to 35-year age range, but this is the same period when occupational demands are highest and most worrying. The white-collar man is trying to climb the hierarchical ladder of the bureaucracy while learning the requirements of his changing responsibilities. The blue-collar worker too may be trying out a number of different jobs because of choice or the exigencies of the job market. Young men, as a result, no matter how devoted to home and family may face difficulties in coping adequately with both job and parental responsibilities.

Wilensky has also noted the squeeze the husband-father experiences at this time between family economic needs and income rewards from the job—a squeeze that can exacerbate the marital disenchantment of the child-rearing years. Medical expenses and demands for consumer goods are high at this time, but the income peaks for white-collar men come later as does job security because of seniority for manual workers. Wives cannot eliminate the squeeze through joining the labor force because of small children at home. Job satisfaction parallels the marital satisfaction trend, recalling to our attention the reciprocal nature of the occupation-family relation. The larger the family, understandably, the longer and lower job satisfaction dips from the high of the bachelor and young married without children periods. Just as with the departure of the children there is some increase in marital satisfaction, so too does job satisfaction show some recovery in the age years of 45-54 as family economic demands diminish, job aspirations lower, and income and occupational security increase.[11]

In addition to the synchronization or the lack thereof in family and occupation careers, an additional characteristic of the job affects the men's fulfilling family responsibilities. This has to do with *overlap*—the degree of overlap in family and work settings and, often associated with the latter, overlap in the personnel of work group and family. In this country aside from the family farm and the neighborhood grocery stores where the family lives in the back or upstairs, there are few examples of this phenomenon; but in Europe even the professional has his office in a portion of his home. When this is the case, the differentiation between family and work roles that occurred because of the Industrial Revolution breaks down. Although family concerns may take second place to business matters when the family is the economic unit, at the very least the husband-father is close at hand ready to respond to family emergencies. At most, the members of his family role set also constitute the members of his occupational role set and can sanction behavior that threatens his performing essential family functions.

To this point the discussion has covered the occupational characteristics of (1) relative salience as compared with the family, (2) the degree of synchronization of family and occupational responsibilities, and (3) the degree of overlap in family and work setting and their effect on husband-father's

[11] Harold L. Wilensky, "Work Situation and Participation in Formal Associations," in *Aging and Leisure*, ed. by Robert W. Kleemeier, New York: Oxford University Press, 1961, p. 228.

family role functioning. Now it will cover the intrafamily dynamics affected by the husband-father's occupation. The Rapoports speak of the *isomorphism or similarity* of behavior patternings between occupation and family.[12] As an example, they report a finding that science-oriented technologists make more conjugal decisions on an equalitarian basis than is true among technologists concerned with equipment. They interpret the difference partly in terms of the carry-over from occupation to home of the universalistic norms underlying science.[13] Another example of isomorphism is that professionals, organization men, and others heavily concerned with interpersonal relations on the job hold high expectations of the companionship aspects of marriage. They appear to be demanding professionalization of the marital roles, perhaps in order partially to redress the balance between occupation and family. They expect high levels of competence in the performance of marital and parental roles. But the variety of roles they see as constituting the parent-spouse positions—lover, companion, housekeeper, breadwinner, teacher, and disciplinarian, to name only a few—with their contradictory requirements call for systematic training that is lacking. Therefore, though the expectations are for family roles meeting professional standards, the socialization that would enable these standards to be met is largely nonexistent. This may help explain the marriages Cuber and Harroff in their study of individuals in decision-making, policy-setting occupations designate as "conflict-habituated," "devitalized," or "passive-congenial"—terms that indicate the negative qualities of the marriage.[14]

It is in the upper middle-class group where professionals and men who manage predominate that Rainwater found husbands and wives usually have a joint conjugal role relationship. These are patterns where the couple shares activities, or either partner is willing to perform various household activities. True, these couples see themselves as concerned with activities outside the home—often separate concerns—but they expect the partner to be willing to listen and to provide support for the separate activities.[15] These are the kinds of marriages Cuber and Harroff dub "vital" as opposed to the couples with "total" relationships where each spouse is involved in the complete activity range including occupational performance of the other.[16] Husbands in such vital marriages, with their very high standards of role performance, fear the isomorphism that may exist between their occupational and family behavior. They worry that they may be too aggressive or assertive in their

[12] Robert Rapoport and Rhona Rapoport, "Work and Family in Contemporary Society," *American Sociological Review*, 30 (June, 1965), 385.

[13] Robert Rapoport and Edward O. Laumann, "Technologists in Mid-Career: Factors Affecting Patterns of Ten-Year Out Engineers and Scientists from Three Universities," in *The Impact of Space Efforts on Communities and Selected Groups*, ed. by Robert Rapoport, American Academy of Arts and Sciences, Committee on Space, cited in ibid.

[14] John F. Cuber and Peggy B. Harroff, *The Significant Americans: A Study of Sexual Behavior among the Affluent*, New York: Appleton Century, 1965, pp. 44–54.

[15] Lee Rainwater, *Family Design: Marital Sexuality, Family Size and Contraception*, Chicago: Aldine Publishing, 1965, pp. 314–317.

[16] Cuber and Harroff, op. cit., pp. 55–60.

families, personal qualities required on the job but apt to create tense relationships in the home.[17]

For most professional and managerial couples though, the power relationship between husband and wife is such as to make the marriage a "colleague" rather than a companionship type to use Gold and Slater's terminology.[18] Despite the heavy emphasis on companionship, the spouses are not equals in decision-making. There is isomorphism between occupation and family role performance. The family's status clearly rests on the husband-father's achievements and though the wife as a good colleague mobilizes special skills to aid his advancement, she makes fewer family decisions alone.[19] Husbands accustomed to having decision-making responsibilities in the office continue to make them at home. They, also, because of occupational demands engage in fewer household activities.[20]

The occupation also affects the paternal roles of professionals and executives. Aberle and Naegele found that men in these occupations have clear perceptions of the kind of sons they want and evaluate sons in terms of occupational role demands. Men expect their sons to be responsible, aggressive, show initiative, and be competent—all indicators that the boys will succeed in the middle-class occupations their fathers hold and envision for their sons. Fathers are anxious if the sons are passive, irresponsible, and overly excitable—qualities that do not augur well for the boys' future occupational accomplishments. The fathers show less concern and have fewer expectations of their daughters, who presumably will be less involved in the job market.[21]

Isomorphism also exists between the occupational and family roles of men who are in occupational roles other than those of professionals or managers. Small entrepreneurs are an example. They, of necessity, have to plan as well as to participate in the organization of their economic activity. Gold and Slater found in their sample of self-employed and workers in small businesses that white-collar wives, when they work outside the home, most often assist their husbands in the family business. Even so, the husbands retain more power in family decision-making, a power position consistent with their position in the occupational world and also consistent with their position as primary determiners of the family's social status.[22] Interestingly enough,

[17] Rainwater, *Family Design*, op. cit., p. 317.

[18] Martin Gold and Carol Slater, "Office, Factory, Store—and Family: A Study of Integration Settings," *American Sociological Review*, 23 (February, 1958), 65–66.

[19] Robert O. Blood, Jr. and Donald M. Wolfe, *Husbands and Wives: The Dynamics of Married Living*, Glencoe, Illinois: Free Press, 1960, p. 31. For a further discussion of how the comparative resources of husbands and wives affect decision-making power, see David M. Heer, "The Measurement and Bases of Family Power: An Overview," *Journal of Marriage and the Family*, 25 (May, 1963), 133–139; also Blood's "Rejoinder" and Heer's "Reply" in ibid., (November, 1963), pp. 475–478.

[20] Blood and Wolfe, op. cit., pp. 60–61.

[21] David F. Aberle and Kaspar D. Naegele, "Middle-Class Fathers' Occupational Role and Attitudes toward Children," *American Journal of Orthopsychiatry*, 22 (April, 1952), 366–378.

[22] Gold and Slater, op. cit., p. 67.

however, the farmer-entrepreneur, several recent studies have shown, seems not to set policy for the family as he does for the land.[23] In household task performance too he is much less active than urban men, which suggests the pressure of ever present occupational duties caused by the spacial overlap of occupational and family settings.[24]

The haven of the companionship family where husband and wife interact as equals is in the lower middle class. The situation here is in direct contrast to that of men in high job saliency occupations. Husbands tend to be in lower-level bureaucratic and quasi-professional jobs or in blue-collar supervisory and craftsmen level jobs of little intrinsic interest. Men, far from seeking to carry over job-related behaviors to the family, often look to their homes as havens from job monotonies and as sources of the satisfactions lacking in the occupational sphere. Husband and wife are apt to have an intermediate conjugal role organization in which both participate in child-rearing but maintain a traditional divison of labor in other areas. Social activities outside the family constitute a threat to the family-centered relation, so men worry about their tendencies to withdraw from family activities in favor of personal interests. Wives, in turn, fear their own egocentricity and also that they will by their aggressiveness deny their family-centered husbands a voice in family affairs.[25]

Yet heightened domesticity is not always associated with work alienation. Kin and cronies can provide alternate sources of emotional support and in the lower class often do. Even in the working class where men in operative type occupations have some job security and are more active in family roles than laborers and service workers in the lower-lower class, moves to the suburb that destroy social networks with relatives and peers result in increased household activity.[26]

Laborers and service workers are least involved in family tasks or decisions.[27] It is not only that these men experience enough unemployment that their wives, as noted earlier, may give them scant encouragement to participate. On their jobs they have little opportunity to associate with men in other occupations or specialities, holding different values and possessing different skills that would sharpen the role-taking abilities of these lower-class

[23] Blood and Wolfe, op. cit., p. 24; and Lee G. Burchinal and Ward A. Bauder, *Family Decision-Making and Role Patterns among Iowa Farm and Non-Farm Families*, Ames, Iowa: Agricultural and Home Economics Experiment Station Bulletin 528, June, 1964, p. 167.

[24] Blood and Wolfe, op. cit., pp. 58–59. It should be noted that Burchinal and Bauder did not find this segregated task performance among their rural couples. Burchinal and Bauder, op. cit., p. 168.

[25] Rainwater, *Family Design*, op. cit., p. 315. As with the discussion of the marital and parental relations of the top-level professional or organization man, it is difficult to separate occupational and class influences on the husband-father roles.

[26] Lee Rainwater and Gerald Handel, "Changing Family Roles in the Working Class," paper presented before the Annual Meeting of the American Sociological Association, 1963.

[27] Aldous, "Lower Class Males' Integration into Community and Family," op. cit., p. 188; Rainwater, *Family Design*, op. cit., pp. 318–321; and Blood and Wolfe, op. cit., pp. 30 and 62.

men. Many lower-class men interact with others on the basis of routinized reactions and projections of their own views.[28] Because women play different roles, lower-class men find their projecting strategy in interpersonal relations ineffective. As a consequence marital communication is limited. The job, therefore, through its limitations on security, pay, and provision of opportunities for exercising interpersonal skills offers little encouragement to the lower-class male to perform his marital and parental functions.

Thus the paper has come full cycle. The discussion began with an analysis of the economic resources which employment in some occupations gives a man—resources that supply the minimum essentials for his functioning in the family. It concludes with an analysis of how the right kind of occupation can facilitate communication skills needed for marital interaction. In both instances as in the rest of the paper's analysis, the separation of the occupation and family spheres has been demonstrated to be more myth than reality. They affect each other in many ways, and not all of them are harmful—the nepotism literature to the contrary. And this conclusion should really come as no surprise, since occupational and family roles for the overwhelming majority of men constitute first- and second-ranking life interests. The roles may not always coexist in harmony, but the dynamics arising from their conflicting as well as similar requirements provide a fruitful research area for persons in their working roles of family or occupational specialist.

[28] Herbert J. Gans, *The Urban Villagers: Group and Class in the Life of Italian-Americans*, New York: Free Press of Glencoe, 1962, p. 98.

IX Kinship in the Urban-Industrial Setting

Introduction to Section IX

Sociology is a young science but it is old enough to have witnessed the fall of several popular hypotheses. Until the 1950s it was widely believed that industrialization in the Western world had wiped out the extended family system of our ancestors and had produced the largely isolated nuclear family system of today. One article in this section documents the error of that belief (27). Furstenberg, using historical materials, points out some of the modern-day qualities of the pre-industrial family in America. In short, it appears that although industrialization may have speeded up the development of our nuclear family system, much of that system had already developed before industrialization. This was probably the case because the migrants who came here from Europe, who traveled out West, and went from rural to urban areas, largely did so as individuals or small family groups and not as three-generation extended families.

The possibility of a variety of family forms being compatible with industrialization is documented by research on the Japanese family. Wilkinson shows the importance of free family labor in the industrialization of Japan.[1] Thus, extended kin ties of some sort may be suitable at least for certain types of industrialization. Perhaps these ties will give way in time but they are still present in Japan.

Comments by Collver and others on the Indian family show the importance of the extended family in India today.[2] Widows, widowers, and orphans depend on kin ties for their very survival. It is likely that this will remain so for some time, even as India slowly industrializes. Thus, extended kin ties can under

[1] Wilkinson, T. O., "Family Structure and Industrialization in Japan." *American Sociological Review* 27 (October, 1962), 678–682.
[2] Collver, A., "The Family Cycle in India and the U.S." *American Sociological Review* 28 (February, 1963), 81–91.

such conditions be helpful to stability and to the gradual growth of industrialization. Indeed, Litwak (28) argues that extended kin ties of a modified sort are better integrated with industrialization than is the isolated nuclear family.

The message of these articles is basically that we must be more flexible in our conception of what family forms fit with industrialization and also in our concept of the causal relationship between the family and industrialization. Sociologists have tended to treat the family as simply a dependent variable in the social system—that is, as something which is shaped by other institutions. It now seems clear that the family can be an independent variable (or a cause) and indeed that it was in part just this in the growth of industrialism.

Only in the last decade or two have sociologists become aware of the great importance of kinship ties in urban centers. Before that time it was thought that the city destroyed kin ties and isolated the nuclear family from its parental kin. The prevalence of kinship ties in urban societies and, more importantly, their role in helping speed up occupational mobility, is developed by Litwak (28) using a sample of Buffalo, New York, families. Litwak points out how ties to parents not only do not hinder upward mobility but actually seem to help, and thus that extended kin ties are compatible with urban-industrial societies. Litwak's research grew out of an attempt to test some of Talcott Parsons'[3] notions concerning the integration of the isolated nuclear family with modern industrial society. Litwak's disagreement with Parsons is the type of controversy that is common in social science.

Bert Adams further delineates the way in which upward mobility relates to kinship ties (29). The Adams study is one of the most carefully done in this area of kin ties. He utilizes not only interaction frequency of kin but subjective feelings of affection and feelings of having similar values. Adams' findings show how specific aspects of kin ties are maintained despite upward mobility and thus his study bears on older theories concerning the supposed negative impact of mobility on kin ties.

[3] Parsons, T., *The Family, Socialization and Interaction Process*. New York: The Free Press, 1955, Chapter 1.

27 Industrialization and the American Family: A Look Backward

FRANK F. FURSTENBERG, JR.

The proposition that industrialization destroys traditional family structures has long been accepted by sociologists and laymen alike. In industrial societies a new kind of family, the "isolated nuclear family," has been recognized; in societies presently industrializing, the older family systems are thought to be under great strain.[1] Analysts of the American family have both assumed and asserted that the transition from an agricultural to an industrial economy is accompanied by the weakening of a family system characterized by such traits as low social and geographical mobility, high parental authority over children, marital harmony and stability, dominance of husband over wife, and close ties within the extended family. It is similarly assumed that the modern family possesses few of the characteristics of the pre-industrial family. Just as the older family pattern served the needs of a farming economy, it is frequently said that the modern family serves the needs of an industrial economy.[2]

Widespread acceptance of an ideal image of the pre-industrial family has limited empirical investigation of family change. Waller wrote some years ago: "According to the Victorian ideology, all husbands and wives lived together in perfect amity; all children loved the parents to whom they were indebted for the gift of life; and if these things were not true, they should be, and even if one knew that these things were not true he ought not mention it."[3] Few sociologists today would want to conceal unflattering truths about the family of three or four generations ago. However, certain widely

[1] Talcott Parsons discusses how the family and the economy affect each other in *Family, Socialization and Interaction Process*, Glencoe, Ill.: The Free Press, 1955, especially Chap. 1. The most forceful expression of this view was made by William F. Ogburn in his *Technology and the Changing Family*, New York: Houghton Mifflin, 1955. This view is also expressed in George C. Homans, *The Human Group*, New York: Harcourt, Brace, 1950, pp. 276–280. See also David and Vera Mace, *Marriage East and West*, Garden City, N. Y.: Dolphin Books, 1959, Chap. 1.

[2] Two excellent books on the social consequences of industrialization summarize the supposed changes in the family produced by industrialization: Harold L. Wilensky and Charles N. Lebeaux, *Industrial Society and Social Welfare*, New York: Russell Sage Foundation, 1958, pp. 67–83; and Eugene V. Schneider, *Industrial Society*, New York: McGraw-Hill, 1957, Chap. 18.

[3] *The Family: A Dynamic Interpretation*, New York: Cordon Company, 1938, p. 13.

I would like to express appreciation to Professors William J. Goode and Sigmund Diamond for commenting on an earlier draft of this paper.

Reprinted from the *American Sociological Review*, 31, No. 3 (June, 1966), 326–337, by permission of the American Sociological Association.

shared beliefs about the family of today have helped to preserve what Goode has labeled "the classical family of Western nostalgia."[4]

Goode's recent analysis of change in some of the world's major family systems suggests some general propositions that cast doubt on the traditional view of the relationship between industrialization and the family. Goode concludes: (1) there are indigenous sources of change in family systems, before industrialization takes place; (2) the relations between industrialization and family patterns are complex and still not sufficiently understood; (3) the family system itself may be an independent source of change facilitating the transition to industrialization; and (4) some apparently recent characteristics of the family may actually be very old social patterns.[5]

Each of these general propositions may be partially tested by using historical data from the United States. While this paper will touch on all four, it will concentrate on data pertaining to the fourth proposition—that certain "recent" family patterns are in fact evident in the family of a century ago. This is a particularly important theoretical point, for relatively stable family patterns would weaken the hypothesis that industrialization necessarily undermines the traditional family form. Further, it would force us to examine more carefully just which elements in the family are most responsive to changes in the economic system. A refutation of the assumption that trends in family change are well known may stimulate historians and historical sociologists to develop more precise descriptions of family systems at different period in the past and of the family's relations with other social institutions during these periods.

It is important to recognize that the sharp contrast between the pre-industrial family and the modern family has already been diminished to some extent. Recent research has brought into question the validity of the conception of the "isolated nuclear family."[6] Increasing evidence suggests that we must modify our picture of the modern family. It seems not to be nearly so isolated and nuclear as it has been portrayed by some sociologists.[7]

Thus, we may attack from two ends the view that considerable family change has occurred in the past century. On the near end, we are beginning to get a more balanced picture of what the family of today looks like. On the far end, we have less information. This paper attempts to assemble some limited but highly useful information on the family of a hundred or more years ago. This information may be used to explore certain theoretical issues con-

---

[4] William J. Goode, *World Revolution and Family Patterns*, New York: The Free Press of Glencoe, 1963, p. 6.

[5] Ibid., Chap. 1.

[6] See Marvin B. Sussman's "The Isolated Nuclear Family: Fact or Fiction" in his book of readings *Sourcebook in Marriage and the Family*, Boston: Houghton Mifflin, 1963, pp. 48–53.

[7] Marvin Sussman has done several studies on the relationship between middle-class couples and their families. See especially "The Help Pattern in the Middle-Class Family," in Sussman, *Sourcebook in Marriage and the Family*, ibid., pp. 380–385. Note the article by Gordon F. Streib in the same reader entitled "Family Patterns in Retirement." Also see Eugene Litwak, "Occupational Mobility and Extended Family Cohesion," Bobbs-Merrill Reprint Series in the Social Sciences, Sociology-177.

cerning family change. Although industrialization may have placed added strains on the family, the extent to which the industrial system affected the family has been greatly exaggerated. Further, I contend that not only did strains exist prior to industrialization, but some of these very tensions in the family may have facilitated the process of industrialization. The long-recognized effect of the economy on the family has too often obscured the converse—that the family may have important consequences for the economic system. To understand the complicated relationship between the economy and the family, we cannot simply view the family as the dependent variable in the relationship.

METHOD

The data supporting these views are drawn from the accounts of foreign travelers visting this country during the period 1800–1850.[8] Although prior to and during this period, American technical achievements were many—a canal system, the cotton gin, the steamship, a spreading rail network, etc.—the nation was almost entirely agricultural until the decade before the Civil War. In 1850 only 16 per cent of the labor force was engaged in manufacturing and construction industries, and this percentage had not greatly changed since 1820.[9] Although the country was beginning to industrialize and urbanize, over four-fifths of the population still resided in rural areas.[10] About two out of every three workers were farmers. This ratio had decreased only slightly over the previous four decades.[11] Thus, it seems safe to assert that the impact of industrialization on the American family cannot have been great prior to 1850.[12]

[8] Accounts of foreign travelers have been used in a few studies of the family. Arthur W. Calhoun made extensive use of such accounts in his three-volume study of the American family, *A Social History of the American Family*, 3 volumes, New York: Barnes and Noble, 1960, (first published 1917–1919). See also Willystine Goodsell, *A History of Marriage and the Family*, New York: Macmillan, 1939, Chap. 11. More recently, Lipset has used foreign travelers' accounts in making some observations about the early American family (Seymour Martin Lipset, *The First New Nation: The United States in Historical and Comparative Perspective*, New York: Basic Books, 1963, especially Chap. 3.)

[9] U.S. Bureau of the Census, *Historical Statistics of the United States: Colonial Times to 1957*, Washington, D.C.: U.S. Government Printing Office, 1960, Series D, 57–71. It should be noted that more change appeared in the decade between 1840–1850 than in previous decades.

[10] Ibid., Series A, 34–50.

[11] Ibid., Series D, 36–45.

[12] A limited amount of industrialization could be found in the Northeastern states prior to 1850. However, Wilensky and Lebeaux, and Schneider report that industrialization was quite confined until after the Civil War. Wilensky and Lebeaux, op. cit., p. 49; Schneider, op. cit., Chap. 4. The beginnings of an industrial economy, however, were apparent in such places as Lowell, Massachusetts. A number of travelers visited Lowell during this period and commented with great interest on the Lowell factories.

Travelers' accounts are a rich source of data on the American family in the first half of the nineteenth century.[13] Many of these accounts have both literary and historical merit, and some of the writings have become famous because of their perceptive observations on American society. While the writings of Alexis de Tocqueville, Harriet Martineau, and Frances Trollope are well known, thousands of little-known accounts were written during this period.[14] Europeans, anxious to observe what was still referred to as "the New World" became the precursors of the more systematic participant observers of today.

To what extent can we place confidence in these travelers' accounts? Do they accurately portray American society as it actually was early in the nineteenth century? Naturally, the same cautions apply in using this source of historical data as apply to any other source of data. There are several methodological qualifications about the use of travelers' accounts that should be made. While these travelers may be viewed in certain respects as sociological observers of the nineteenth century, it must be remembered that they did not possess the basic qualifications of trained sociological observers. Many of the accounts of American society lack a neutral and value-free perspective. The biases of the observers are especially evident in the area of the family. For many travelers, the family was the source of great moral concern.

Without dismissing the possibility of distortion, such moral sentiments may to a degree enhance the value of these accounts as sociological data when we can ascertain and control for such biases. Generally, liberal and conservative Europeans evaluated the American family differently, reflecting their own biases. Liberals, as one might expect, viewed the American family in a more favorable light; conservatives, in an unflattering glare.[15] The possibility of bias from political persuasion is not great, however, because most of the observations reported in this paper are common to observers of all political points of view. That travelers of very different prejudices made *similar* observations enhances the reliability and validity of these observations. Where, on the other hand, the observer's bias may have affected the

[13] There are many bibliographies of accounts of foreign travelers written during this period. Two extensive bibliographies are: Max Berger, *The British Traveler in America*, New York: Columbia University Press, 1943, and Frank Monagham, *French Travelers in the United States 1765–1932*, New York: The New York Public Library, 1953.

[14] Berger and Monagham each list many thousands of accounts and they are only partial listings for two countries.

[15] Portions of the travelers' accounts used in this study were rated by the author and an associate and placed into three categories: positive, neutral, or negative. It was found that accounts could be reliably coded. There was complete agreement in 78 per cent of the cases. Where disagreement occurred, it never involved cases where one person coded a positive evaluation and the other a negative evaluation. The traveler's general evaluation was related to his political ideology. Although this information could be obtained for only about half of the sample, it showed a distinct relationship to evaluation. All three travelers who were conservatives had a negative view of America, while only one of twelve liberals had an overall negative impression of the country.

accuracy of his accounts, I shall try to note such bias. When they do occur, these biases are more likely to be the result of the traveler's sexual status than his political status.[16]

The accounts used here do not represent a systematically selected sample of European travelers during the period. There are literally thousands of published and unpublished accounts, and a good sample of the observations of European travelers would be difficult to obtain. The sample used here is composed of forty-two accounts and selections from accounts, most of them containing extensive commentary on the family. To arrive at this sample, I examined over one hundred accounts, the majority of which made either no reference, or only an oblique reference, to family life in America.[17]

One final caution: most of the travelers base their comments on a view of the middle-class American family.[18] These travelers usually observed the family during their stay in residential hotels or during brief visits to American homes in rural areas of the country. More likely than not, these homes were middle-class. Since most of the comments and generalizations about the modern family of today also apply largely to the middle class, this limitation in the data will probably not affect the comparison adversely.

FAMILY OBSERVATIONS

Courtship and Mate Selection

To begin this discussion with the first stage in the life cycle of the family, we shall discuss some of the foreign travelers' observations on the courtship patterns of American youth. The American system of courtship and mate selection is sometimes said to be one of the consequences of the urbanized and industrialized economy in the United States.[19] Free mate selection and the "romantic-love complex" are often linked to the demands of the economic

[16] The females in the sample were inclined to view the position of married American women less favorably. They were more skeptical about the desirability of the position of women in the United States.

[17] The sample of accounts examined does not represent a systematic selection of travelers' accounts. A large proportion of the sample was located from a bibliography of Oscar Handlin, et al. (eds.), *Harvard Guide to American History*, Cambridge, Mass.: The Belknap Press, 1954, pp. 151–159, which includes a diverse selection of accounts. Handlin also edited a book of selections from travelers' accounts. This book contains some writings not listed in the *Harvard Guide*. See *This Was America*, New York: Harper and Row, 1949.

[18] Middle-class, in this context, refers to persons engaged in small business, professionals, and prosperous landowners. Travelers in the sample were more likely to comment on the habits and customs of the farmer than the farmhand.

[19] This is suggested in Harry Johnson's chapter on the family in *Sociology: A Systematic Introduction*, New York: Harcourt, Brace, 1960, Chap. 6. Parsons advocates this view in his article "Age and Sex in the Social Structure" in his *Essays in Sociological Theory*, Glencoe, Ill.: The Free Press, 1954.

system or to the weakened control by family elders in an industrialized society.[20] In fact, however, the same system of mate selection and emphasis on romantic love appear to have existed here prior to industrialization.

Although few of the travelers described the actual process of courtship in America, it is evident from their accounts that free choice of mates was the prevailing pattern as well as the social norm. Foreign visitors expressed diverse opinions on the desirability of this norm, but there was complete agreement that such a norm existed. Chevalier wrote in the 1830's that the dowry system, common in France, was almost nonexistent in the United States. He observed that American parents played only a nominal role in selecting the person their child married.[21] Parental consent was formally required, but this requirement was seldom taken very seriously. In 1842, Lowenstern wrote:

A very remarkable custom in the United States gives girls the freedom to choose a husband according to their fancy; practice does not permit either the mother or the father to interfere in this important matter.[22]

The general expectation in America was that the choice of a mate should be based on love. Some travelers were skeptical about whether love actually dictated the marriage selection. Buckingham writes, "Love, among the American people, appears to be regarded rather as an affair of the judgment, than of the heart; its expression seems to spring from a sense of duty, rather than from a sentiment of feeling."[23] A few travelers already noted that, in spite of the previously mentioned tendency of young people to spurn financial considerations in choosing a mate, there were matches that seemed to be based on material considerations. This touch of cynicism, however, occurs in only a minority of the travelers' writings. Most of the observers praised the American marriage system because it permitted young people to select mates whom they loved and with whom they could enjoy a happy marriage. Some persons, however, noted that free mate selection resulted in certain family strains. Lowenstern states that marriage between people of different social classes, a pattern sometimes asserted to be typical of an industrial society, was not uncommon.[24] Several other travelers support this view. By no means were all the comments on interclass marriages favorable.

[20] David and Vera Mace, op. cit., Chap. 5; also Robert F. Winch, *The Modern Family*, (rev. ed.), New York: Holt, Rinehart and Winston, 1963, pp. 318–320.

[21] Michael Chevalier, *Society, Manners, and Politics in the United States*, New York: Doubleday Anchor Books, 1961, p. 294. Six other travelers substantiate Chevalier's observations on the freedom of mate selection.

[22] Isidore Lowenstern, "Les Etats-Unis et La Havane: Souvenirs d'un Voyage, 1842," in Handlin, *This Was America*, op. cit., p. 183.

[23] James Silk Buckingham, *The Eastern and Western States of America*, 2 vols., London: Fisher, 1867, p. 479.

[24] Lowenstern, op. cit. James Fenimore Cooper, the American novelist, in a book on his observations of American life, notes the same pattern of interclass marriage. See his *Notions of the Americans*, Vol. I, London: Henry Colburn, 1828.

Women, it was sometimes noted with bitterness, not infrequently married beneath themselves.[25]

Another source of strain in the marriage system in the view of some travelers, was the American habit of marrying at an extremely early age. Many observers noted that there seemed to be a great pressure for young people to marry. "In view of the unlimited freedom of the unmarried woman," Moreau writes, "it is astonishing to discover the eagerness of all to be married, for marriage brings about an absolute change in the life of the girl."[26] The tendency for an early marriage and the feelings of pressure to marry may be related to the "unlimited freedom" of which Moreau speaks.

Almost half of the travelers in the sample comment on freedom given to youth before marriage. Particularly striking to the travelers was the amount of freedom given to young women. But this freedom was tempered by considerable self-restraint. Adolescents were permitted to be alone together, but they were expected to behave according to strict moral standards. In the view of at least one observer, apparently this restraint led to a pronounced lack of responsiveness. Moreau stated that a young couple could be left alone in the house together without any fear of improper behavior. In fact, ". . . sometimes on returning, the servants find them fallen asleep and the candle gone out—so cold is love in this country!"[27]

While these extraordinary feats of self-restraint may be reminiscent of the privileges of courtly love, lauded by poets but not reported by objective observers,[28] there is general consensus among the travelers that the behavior of American women, particularly of young women, was exemplary. More often, young women in America came under criticism for being cold. No doubt, the combination of the freedom granted and the strong sanctions against misbehaving have something to do with the common observation that American women lacked warmth and spontaneity. On this matter, though, there is a dissenting view. Abdy commented: "Many women, who seem cold as flint in general, give out fire enough when they find a 'blade' that suits them."[29]

The pressure to marry at an early age may have been generated by strains on the young woman. She was permitted to travel alone, to socialize with the opposite sex, and even to leave home alone for extended periods; but with this freedom went an enormous responsibility. She was expected to remain chaste, to conform to strict standards of propriety, and to respect the privileges of her freedom. The strain created by such a combination of freedom

[25] Among others, Sir Charles Lyell made this observation in his *A Second Visit to the United States of North America*, New York: Harper and Brothers, 1849.

[26] Mederic Louis Elie Moreau de Saint-Mery, "Voyage aux Etats-Unis de L'Amerique, 1793–1798," in Handlin, *This Was America*, op. cit., p. 100. Similar observations on the early marriage age were made by nine other travelers.

[27] Ibid., p. 99.

[28] Sidney Painter in his book, *French Chivalry*, Ithaca, N.Y.: Great Seal Books, 1957, presents a superb account of courtly love in mediaeval France. See especially Chap. 4.

[29] E. S. Abdy, *Journal of a Residence and Tour in the United States of North America*, Vol. I, London: John Murray, 1935, p. 74.

and moral restraint could well explain the tendency toward early marriage.[30]

Several observers note the problems that arise from early marriage. In her characteristically incisive way, Frances Trollope commented:

> They marry very young; in fact, in no rank of life do you meet with young women in that delightful period of existence between childhood and marriage, wherein, if only tolerably well spent, so much useful information is gained, and the character takes a sufficient degree of firmness to support with dignity the more important parts of wife and mother.[31]

The Pulszkys concurred with Trollope that American girls got too little opportunity to see life before they settled down to marriage.[32] It was also suggested that the rapid push toward marriage led young people to marry without knowing each other sufficiently; courtships were considered excessively casual. As one observer wrote, "Meet your girl in the morning, marry in the afternoon, and by six in the evening you are settled in your home, man and wife."[33]

To sum up, travelers perceived several strains in the American system of courtship and mate selection. Freedom of choice did not always lead to the selection of a mate on the basis of love; and it sometimes resulted in crossing of class lines and unwise marriages. The pressures toward early marriage seemed to result in inadequate preparation for marriage. These strains were observed by both critics and supporters of America alike. Their frequency and consistency suggest that they were very real problems. It is perhaps obvious to point out similarities in the criticisms of American marriages that were observed in the nineteenth century and the criticisms of American marriages today. At the time these criticisms were made, they were not thought to be related to incipient industrialization. The problems in the courtship process were regarded as the consequence of other political and economic factors, such as American ideological commitment to democracy, the opportunity for achievement in the society, and the emphasis on equality and individualism.[34]

[30] It is possible to develop a fourfold table based on the two variables of amount of moral restraint (permissiveness toward sexual expression before marriage) and degree of freedom permitted young people to associate together. I predict that marriage age will be early when freedom to associate is high and moral restraint is also high. Where freedom to associate is high and moral restraint is low, marriage age will be somewhat later. It may be even later when freedom to associate is low and moral restraint is high. It is difficult to predict how the fourth case would turn out. A study on this problem is being undertaken.

[31] Frances Trollope, *Domestic Manners of the Americans*, New York: Knopf, 1949, p. 118.

[32] Theresa and Kossuth Pulszky, "White Red Black," in Handlin, *This Was America*, op. cit.

[33] Karl T. Friesinger, "Lebende Bilder aus Amerika," Handlin, *This Was America*, op. cit., p. 254.

[34] This view is advocated by Tocqueville throughout his writings on the American family. Alexis de Tocqueville, *Democracy in America*, 2 vols., New York: Vintage Books, 1954. See especially Vol. 2, Chap. 8.

The Conjugal Relation

The aspect of married life which drew the most attention was the great loss of freedom the woman suffered when she married. As already noted, single girls were granted considerable freedom before marriage. Almost a fourth of all the travelers commented on the loss of this freedom for the woman in married life. On this situation, there are no views to the contrary. Although Tocqueville[35] and Murat[36] see the loss of this freedom as voluntary on the part of the female, other observers view it as imposed upon her. A number of writers state their belief that the American wife is neglected in favor of the single woman. She is, as one traveler put it, "laid on the shelf."[37]

Why this was so, few travelers ventured to speculate. Several travelers imply that the retirement of married women from social life gives them greater moral protection.[38] Most of the writers feel that married women suffer unnecessary discrimination. Some of our contemporary sociological notions might suggest that the women, after consenting to marry, had little left to bargain with.[39] Furthermore, there were really no alternatives open to the women which would permit them to get out of the home more often and at the same time fulfill their domestic obligations. It is also possible that the intense pressures for early marriage prohibited married women from competing with single girls for men's attentions.

The primary cause for the withdrawal of married women from social life seems to have been their demanding domestic obligations. It is commonly assumed that women were more satisfied in their domestic role a century ago, before industrialization tempted them into the job market.[40] Yet the frequent complaint that married women were "laid on the shelf" belies this picture of domestic felicity. Lacking the alternative of employment, women did not face the possibility of role conflict that the modern woman may encounter. Yet boredom and dissatisfaction with this domestic withdrawal may have encouraged women into the labor market when the possibility arose some decades later.

[35] Ibid., Chap. 10.

[36] Achille Murat, *The United States of America*, London: Effingham Wilson, 1833.

[37] Alex Macay uses this expression in *The Western World*, Vol. I, London: Richard Bentley, 1850.

[38] Grattan suggests that married women are particularly visible and thus, to a great extent, safeguarded from moral dangers. He also notes that American women do not stop flirting after they are married. Thomas Colley Grattan, *Civilized America*, 2 vols., 2nd ed., London: Bradbury and Evans, 1859.

[39] This notion of a role bargain is implicit in Willard Waller's article "The Rating and Dating Complex," *American Sociological Review*, (October, 1937), 727–734 and in his book on the family, op. cit., pp. 239–254. Goode uses the conception of a "role bargain" in "A Theory of Role Strain," *American Sociological Review*, 25 (August, 1960), 483–496.

[40] Ralph Linton, in an otherwise quite illuminating discussion of the dilemma of the modern woman, states, "Even fifty years ago the comfortably married woman looked with smug pity on the poor working girl in her drab, mannish clothes." "Women in the Family" in Marvin B. Sussman, op. cit., p. 170.

There was general consensus that American women made dutiful and affectionate wives. Lieber wrote:

> I must mention the fact, that American women make most exemplary wives and mothers, and strange, be a girl ever so coquettish—yea, even a positive flirt, who, in Europe would unavoidably make her future husband unhappy as soon as she were married, here she becomes the domestic and retired wife.[41]

The coldness that was attributed to single girls was not mentioned in the descriptions of married women. Even the most critical observers acknowledged the braveness and devotion that pioneer wives demonstrated in following their husbands into the Western wilderness.

There were a few travelers who dissented from the prevailing view that American women made good wives and mothers. A single traveler, Israel Benjamin, wrote, "The women have a characteristic, innate, and ineradicable aversion to any work and to household affairs.[42] This opinion, however, is so disparate from the vast majority of observers that it may indicate nothing more than Benjamin's generally negative attitude toward family life in America.

Although observers seemed to agree that the young women gave up an advantageous position when they married, several travelers noted that women wielded considerable power inside the home. Along with Tocqueville, these observers felt that the division of labor between husband and wife permitted the wife to have a great deal of authority over household matters.[43] One observer commented bitterly: "The reign of the women is here complete."[44] But generally, observers remarked that women deferred to their husbands' decisions in cases of disagreement. Clearly, the picture of the patriarchal household is only partially accurate. The authority of the husband was uncontested, but it seemed to be a limited authority which did not interfere with the woman's domestic power.[45] Bremer sums up the situation: "Of the American home I have seen and heard enough for me to say that women have, in general, all the rule there they wish to have. Woman is the centre and lawgiver in the home of the New World, and the American man loves that it should be so."[46]

There is a lack of consensus among the travelers on the closeness of the American family. Some observers commented that family members are united.

---

[41] Francis Lieber, *The Stranger in America*, London: Richard Bentley, 1835, p. 132.

[42] Israel Joseph Benjamin, "Drei Jahre in Amerika 1859–1862," in Handlin, *This Was America*, op. cit., p. 274.

[43] Tocqueville, op. cit.

[44] Benjamin, op. cit., p. 273.

[45] Rose Coser identifies the same pattern in the Eastern European Jewish family in her article "Authority and Structural Ambivalence in the Middle-Class Family" in the book of readings she edited, *The Family: Its Structure and Functions*, New York: St. Martin's Press, 1964, pp. 370–383.

[46] Fredrika Bremer, *The Homes of the New World*, 2 vols., New York: Harper and Brothers, 1853, p. 190.

Tocqueville interprets the close ties between husband and wife, father and sons, and between siblings as resulting from the greater equality of family members and the absence of arbitrary authority.[47]

Although Tocqueville's theory of family relations is probably sound, there was considerable opinion that family ties were not as close as in Europe. Here, the particular experiences of travelers to the United States may have created certain observational biases which cannot easily be checked. Specifically, many travelers did not observe families in their homes, but saw them in hotels and boarding houses. Families that lived in such residences were frequently engaged in business and represented the urban middle class. The observations of the urban middle class family tend to increase the appearance of similarity between the nineteenth century family and the family of today.

Most of the travelers who commented on family life in boarding houses were appalled at what they saw. Young married couples neither desired nor got privacy.[48] Young women were denied the opportunity to develop domestic skills which they would need when they moved into their own homes. Above all, boarding house life for women was exceedingly dull. Men went off to work leaving women with nothing to do. Trollope remarked that she saw the most elaborate embroidered apparel there because women had little else with which to occupy their time.[49] Several descriptions of life in the boarding house paint a dismal picture of women's pathetic attempts to occupy themselves until their husbands came home from work. A few travelers also felt the inactivity and lack of privacy endangered the wife's morals.

The claim that husbands neglected their wives for business was not restricted to accounts of boarding house life. It was one of the most frequent criticisms of American marriages. Vivid detail is supplied to give testimony to this situation. The husband left for his business early in the morning, perhaps came home for lunch, but usually did not return until late at night. This situation was frequently used to explain the dull marriages and the lack of intimacy between family members. Bishop gives a curious picture of the husband's role in the family:

> The short period which they can spend in the bosom of their families must be an enjoyment and relaxation to them; therefore, in the absence of any statements to the contrary, it is but right to suppose that they are affectionate husbands and fathers.[50]

Marryat, among others, felt that the family was disintegrating in America though he was not specific about why this was so.

[47] Tocqueville, op. cit.

[48] Boarding house life is discussed by W. E. Baxter in *America and the Americans*, London: Geo. Routhledge, 1855. Auguste Carlier associated the spread of boarding houses with the decline of domestic life in America. See his *Marriage in the United States*, Boston: De Bries, Ibarra, 1867.

[49] Trollope, op. cit.

[50] Anne Bishop, *The Englishwomen in America*, London: John Murray, 1856, p. 365.

Beyond the period of infancy there is no endearment between the parents and children; none of that sweet spirit of affection between brothers and sisters; none of those links which unite one family; of that mutual confidence; that rejoicing in each other's success; that refuge, when they are depressed or afflicted, in the bosoms of those who love us.[51]

Thus we find there is some disagreement about the closeness of the family in America at this time, despite the widespread assumption in our generation that family life then was cohesive and intimate. Perhaps the most interesting insight on this problem is offered by Chevalier, who wrote:

It may be objected that in the United States family sentiment is much weaker than it is in Europe. But we must not confound what is merely accidental and temporary with the permanent acquisitions of civilization. The temporary weakness of family sentiment was one of the necessary results of the general dispersion of individuals by which the colonization of America has been accomplished . . . As soon as they have their growth, the Yankees whose spirit now predominates in the Union quit their parents, never to return, as naturally and with as little emotion as young birds desert forever their native nests as soon as they are fledged.[52]

This statement suggests a reformulation of the common latter-day hypothesis that industrialization and urbanization weaken family cohesion. There are a number of general centrifugal forces which may weaken the family. These forces are not always accompanied by industrialization and urbanization. When, for example, the family cannot offer opportunities locally to its younger men and women that are equal to those opportunities elsewhere, we would expect that family ties will be weakened.

American morality drew praise from many of the European visitors. The American woman's self-imposed restraint was often attributed to the childhood freedom granted to her. Though a few of the travelers scoffed at the reputed moral purity of American women, the great majority of travelers who commented on morality found American women to be almost beyond reproach. Tocqueville[53] and Wyse[54] even indicate that there is less of a double standard for men than in Europe; moral restraints are binding on the males as well as the females. But Marryat counters, "To suppose there is no conjugal infidelity in the United States is to suppose that human nature is not the same everywhere."[55] Several travelers heard stories of infidelity but few actual encounters are reported. Martineau claims that disgrace is less permanent in the United States.[56]

[51] Frederick Marryat in Sydney Jackman (ed.), *A Diary in America*, New York: Knopf, 1962, p. 355.

[52] Chevalier, op. cit., p. 398.

[53] Tocqueville, op. cit.

[54] Francis Wyse, *America, Its Realities and Resources*, Vol. I, London: T. C. Newby, 1846.

[55] Marryat, op. cit., p. 431.

[56] Harriet Martineau in Seymour M. Lipset (ed.), *Society in America*, New York: Anchor Books, 1962.

Divorce

Although divorce is touched upon in the travelers' accounts, it obviously is not a matter of intense concern for most of the observers.[57] Grattan[58] and Griesinger[59] point out that a divorce is more difficult to obtain in America than in Europe. Marryat[60] and Marjoribanks[61] report just the opposite. Several observers found that divorce was increasing in this country. Wyse notes that the problem had grown to the point where divorces were said to exceed two thousand a year.[62] The fact that all the mention of divorce occurs in accounts written after 1845 suggests an increasing concern in the latter part of the century. Still, this subject was relatively neglected, and did not take on great significance until after the Civil War.

Aging

One family problem is conspicuous by its absence. This is the problem of aging. Not a single account discusses the place of old people in the society or even the position of the grandparent in the family. Indeed, the subject of the extended family is rarely, if ever, discussed. There are several possible explanations for this absence. The proportion of older persons in the population was quite small: less than 4 per cent of the population was over 60 years old.[63] Not only were there proportionally fewer old people, but they were less likely to be living in urban areas where they might be viewed as a problem to the family. In rural areas, the older person might easily live with his children. The accounts make no mention of parents living with their grown children. However, it is likely that foreign travelers, accustomed to seeing the same pattern in their own country, did not think it was worthy of notice. A careful historical study of how old people were cared for in this country would be most interesting.

Parent-Child Relations

Many travelers point out the loving care that was given to children in America. Because of early marriages and the domestic emphasis placed on the married woman's role, large families were common.[64] There was almost complete agreement that children were well taken care of in America.

[57] The intense concern with divorce does not begin until the rise of industrialization in the post-Civil War period. Then the divorce rate slowly rises, and public discussion of divorce rapidly increases. The Census did not begin to report divorce rates until after the Civil War.

[58] Grattan, op. cit.

[59] Griesinger, op. cit.

[60] Marryat, op. cit.

[61] Alexander Marjoribanks, *Travels in South and North America*, New York: Simpkin, Marshall, and Company, 1853.

[62] Wyse, op. cit.

[63] *Historical Statistics*, op. cit., Series A 71–85.

[64] Calhoun reports the frequency of large families in his study of the American family, op. cit., Vol. II, Chap. 1.

The most significant observation about American children was the permissive childrearing patterns that apparently were widespread at this time. A fifth of the sample stated that youth in America were indulged and undisciplined. Marryat put it bluntly, "Now, anyone who has been in the United States must have perceived that there is little or no parental control."[65] Many of the Europeans were shocked by the power children had over their parents, their defiance of their parents' authority, and the way the children were spoiled and pampered.

The lack of restraints on children was justified by some travelers who felt this rejection of authority was a necessary preparation for a democratic citizen. Martineau argues:

> Freedom of manners in children of which so much complaint has been made by observers . . . is a necessary fact. Till the United States ceases to be republican—the children there will continue as free and easy and as important as they are.[66]

Some observers even took delight in the spontaneity and independence shown by American children.

The above suggests that the controversy between permissive and authoritarian childrearing has not been confined to the twentieth century.[67] Also the great respect and reverence for parental authority that is generally assumed to have existed at this time is not as pervasive as the defenders of the traditional nineteenth-century family would suggest. Furthermore, the picture of the close Victorian family is not entirely supported by these accounts. Some travelers observed disharmony as well as harmony in the family, though not enough observers commented on this subject to make any conclusive statements.

Grattan, among others, comments on the enormous push for children to grow up and become independent of their families.[68] This may be part of the "business" stereotype that is present in some of these writings, but the move toward early maturity is consistent with the prevalence of early marriages. Girls over the age of 21 were considered by some as old maids, and boys, according to Marryat,[69] left home in their middle teens. This picture may be somewhat exaggerated. Yet the impression is that children were not inclined to stay in the bosom of the family for any longer than they had to. Children are frequently characterized as self-confident, independent, poised, and mature.

This contention is supported by description of the American adolescent. Freedom is the most frequent word used to describe adolescent behavior in America. However, as already noted, the freedom which existed between the sexes was tempered by considerable restraint.

[65] Marryat, op. cit., p. 351.
[66] Martineau, op. cit., p. 28. Four other travelers concur with Martineau.
[67] Miller and Swanson make a similar observation in their review of childrearing practices. Daniel R. Miller and Guy E. Swanson, *The Changing American Parent*, New York: John Wiley, Inc., 1958, pp. 8–9.
[68] Grattan, op. cit.
[69] Marryat, op. cit.

There is surprisingly little criticism of the behavior of adolescents. It is said by a few observers that there was much frivolous dancing and partying. Adolescents were not given nearly as much attention in these accounts as would be devoted to the subject today. The stress on growing up and assuming adult responsibilities seems to take precedence over what is today called "youth culture."[70]

From the little information that is reported, there appeared to be less discontinuity between the role of an adolescent and the role of an adult. This is one point where the industrialized society may have placed added strains on the family. At least there is some reason to believe that adolescence as a period of great stress had not yet been generally identified in America.

The Position of Women in Society

The final topic that emerges from the travelers' accounts is the position of women in American society. This subject has been touched upon throughout the paper. There are, however, some additional observations to be reported. Over a fourth of the travelers comment favorably on female beauty in America. Cobden describes the ladies as "petite but elegant."[71] At the same time, he notes that Boston ladies were "still deficient in preface and postcript."[72] Several writers consider the women unhealthy in appearance. It is quite interesting that so many observers find that American looks fade at an early age. Moreau expresses a common view when he writes about American women: ". . . they are charming, adorable at fifteen, dried-up at twenty-three, old at thirty-five, decrepit at forty or fifty."[73] This observation is consistent with the comments discussed earlier about the withdrawal of the older women from social life. There was probably little motivation or need for the women to keep up their appearance. In view of the strong emphasis on morality, the attractive older woman may have been viewed with a certain suspicion.

Almost all of the sample remarked that American women were treated with extraordinary deference and respect. As a matter of course, men were expected to give women any seat they desired in a public place even though someone might be sitting there and other seats be available. One traveler commented that he saw a man grab a chicken wing off another man's plate to give to a woman who had asked for it.[74] Some Europeans found this almost compulsive chivalry quite proper. To them it indicated the high esteem in which the female was held in America. Thornton wrote, "Attention and deference to women, if carried to a faulty extreme, is an error on the right side; but I deem it rather praiseworthy than faulty . . ."[75] Tocqueville

[70] Parsons, "Age and Sex in the Social Structure," op. cit.

[71] Richard Cobden in Elizabeth Hoon Cawley (ed.), *The American Diaries of Richard Cobden*, Princeton: Princeton University Press, 1952, p. 89.

[72] Ibid., p. 14.

[73] Moreau, op. cit., p. 98. Eight other travelers make the same observation.

[74] Marryat, op. cit.

[75] Major John Thornton, *Diary of a Tour Through the Northern States of the Union and Canada*, London: F. Barker, 1850, p. 110.

suggested that the respect for women was a sign of a growing equality between the sexes.[76]

Many observers do not agree with these views. They saw the respect as superficial and deceptive. The Pulszkys had an extremely sophisticated analysis of this cult of politeness:

> It appears as if the gentlemen would atone for their all-absorbing passion for business by the privilege they give to the ladies of idling time away . . . And as business is a passion with the Americans, not the means, but the very life of existence, they are most anxious to keep this department exclusively to themselves; and, well aware that there is no more infallible way to secure noninterference, than by giving the general impression that they never act for themselves, *the lady's rule* has become a current phrase, but by no means a fact in the United States.[77]

Though others do not see the degree of rationalization in the cult of politeness, there is support for the Pulszky's view. Hall [78] and Martineau[79] state that women occupy an inferior position in American society. The elaborate courtesy and deference are only substitutes for real respect.

Although several of the observers see the American woman as satisfied with her place in society and two visitors see her fulfilling a valuable function of maintaining morality in the society, others feel strongly that the woman occupies an ambiguous position. Her lower status in the society is at odds with the democratic ideology. She cannot be considered an equal to men as long as she is confined completely to the home. The single woman must give up a good deal of her freedom when she marries. This loss of freedom is not fully compensated for by the respect she gains by mothering her husband's children and supervising his household. The discontinuity in the role of a woman, is, in certain respects, similar to the conflict between career and family that exists today. It would be valuable to look at the diaries and letters of women from this period to see whether there is any indication of such a strain.

The great deference paid to women may have compensated them, in part, for this loss of standing. But many of the observers seemed to feel that the reward was not adequate compensation. It should be said, however, that some of the observers were crusaders for women's rights in Europe, and their dissatisfaction with the cult of politeness is to be expected.

Finally, it should be noted that this kind of strain, like many other strains in the family which we have pointed out, did not directly derive from emerging industrialization. No doubt, post-Civil War industrialization aggravated the ambiguous position of women in American society, but women by this time may have been ripe for emancipation from the home. Thus, we might find a convergence of social patterns rather than the often-assumed cause-and-effect relationship between industrialization and the emancipation of women.

[76] Tocqueville, op. cit.

[77] Pulszky and Pulszky, op. cit., p. 239.

[78] Captain Basil Hall, *Travels in North America in the Years 1827 and 1828*, Edinburgh: Robert Cadell, 1830.

[79] Martineau, op. cit.

CONCLUSION

The accounts of foreign travelers visiting the United States in the first half of the nineteenth century contain valuable observations on the American family. These observations suggest the following conclusions:

1. Changes in the American family since the period of industrialization have been exaggerated by some writers. The system of mate selection, the marital relationship, and parent-child relations in the pre-industrial family all show striking similarities to those in the family of today. Family strains commonly attributed to industrialization are evident to observers of the family prior to industrialization.

2. Although the American family is for the most part viewed favorably by the foreign travelers, it is in no way viewed as a tension-free, harmonious institution. Strains resulting from the voluntary choice of mates, the abrupt loss of freedom for women at marriage, women's discontent arising from total domesticity, lack of discipline of American children, the inferior position of women in American society—these were some of the common points of stress in the American family at that time.

3. It is not unlikely that some of these tensions may have eased the adaptation to an industrial society. The lack of parental restrictions on American children and the desire for women to improve their position in society and escape the demands of domestic duties may have facilitated the growth of the industrial system.

4. It should also be pointed out that certain strains in the American family which are sources of widespread concern today were not noted by foreign travelers. Few comments were directed at adolescence, old age, or divorce, perhaps indicating that at that time these areas were not sources of strain.

28 Occupational Mobility and Extended Family Cohesion

EUGENE LITWAK

It has been suggested by Talcott Parsons that there is a basic disharmony between modern democratic industrial society and extended family relations. This is in part true, he hypothesizes, because occupational mobility is anti-

Reprinted from the American Sociological Review, 25, (February, 1960), 9–21, by permission of the American Sociological Association.

thetical to extended family relations.[1] Thus he argues that the isolated nuclear family is especially functional.

The position advanced in this paper is a modification of Parsons' view. It agrees with him that the "classical"[2] extended family is antithetical to occupational mobility. However, it is suggested that a modified extended family relation is consonant with occupational mobility and more functional than the isolated nuclear family. Parsons' hypothesis tends to be valid only during periods of emerging industrialization. Because he has so clearly related his hypothesis to a more general theory of social class and organizational efficiency, the modification of his hypothesis has implications for a more general theory of industrial society.[3]

The paper is divided into two parts. The first attempts to make explicit the assumptions which underlie both the hypothesis suggested here and that made by Parsons. The second presents evidence from an empirical study dealing with the relation between occupational mobility and extended family relations.

ASSUMPTIONS SUPPORTING EXTENDED FAMILY ANOMIE

Behind the hypothesis that extended family relations are antithetical to occupational mobility lie at least two major assumptions: first, the overriding importance of "status by association," and secondly, differential socialization among various occupational strata.

Status Achievement, Occupational Mobility, and Extended Family Dissociation

It is assumed, first, that status achievement is directly and indirectly related to occupational position. The title of the occupation is itself a status symbol, or the income derived from the occupation permits the purchase of status symbols.[4] Secondly, it is assumed that status is achieved by associating with those of equal or greater occupational attainment; therefore, the nuclear family which moves up the occupational ladder would lose status if it were to retain close associations with an extended family of lower status. (Warner, in his study of "Yankee City," provides excellent illustrations of how this process works.[5]) As a consequence, it is suggested that occupa-

[1] Talcott Parsons, "Revised Analytical Approach to the Theory of Social Stratification," in R. Bendix and S. M. Lipset (eds.), *Class, Status, and Power: A Reader in Social Stratification*, Glencoe: Free Press, 1953, pp. 116 ff.

[2] The "classical extended" family is here defined in terms of geographical propinquity, occupational dependence and nepotism, a sense that extended family relations are most important, and an hierarchical authority structure based on a semi-biological criterion, i.e., the eldest male.

[3] See Parsons, op. cit.; and Talcott Parsons, "The Social Structure of the Family," in Ruth N. Anshen, ed., *The Family: Its Function and Destiny*, New York: Harper, 1949.

[4] Parsons, "Revised Analytical Approach . . . ," op. cit., p. 112.

[5] W. Lloyd Warner and Paul S. Lunt, *The Social Life of a Modern Community*, New Haven: Yale University Press, 1941, pp. 190–193.

tionally mobile individuals are likely to be status oriented and to have little extended family contact or identification.

Differential Socialization and Extended Family Dissociation

Another assumption made by those who posit the contradiction between extended family and occupational mobility is that there are extreme differences in socialization among the various occupational strata.[6] Under such an assumption, differential occupational mobility leads to different socialization experiences among members of extended families. Such differences would be sufficient to disrupt kin relations since family members would have little in common to hold them together.

These well known views are not explored in detail in the following discussion.

ASSUMPTIONS SUPPORTING EXTENDED FAMILY COHESION

The "modified extended" family is the ideal type posited in this paper. This type differs from the "classical extended" family in that it does not demand geographical propinquity, occupational involvement, or nepotism, nor does it have an hierarchical authority structure. On the other hand, it differs from the isolated nuclear family structure in that it does provide significant and continuing aid to the nuclear family. The modified extended family consists of a series of nuclear families bound together on an equalitarian basis, with a strong emphasis on these extended family bonds as an end value. In support of this family type are two assumptions which run counter to those presented above.

Status Achievement and Extended Family Cohesion

The first objection to continued viability of the extended family may be answered by pointing out that people not only achieve status by associating with others of equal or greater social rank but that they also attain it by deference from others.[7] For instance, a small businessman might achieve status by moving either to an upper-class or to a working-class neighborhood. In the first instance, his sense of status achievement derives from associat-

---

[6] For one excellent example of a study on class differences, see Herbert Hyman, "The Value System of Different Classes: A Social Psychological Contribution to the Analysis of Stratification," in *Class, Status, and Power . . . ,* pp. 426–441. For an example of different methods of communication used by various classes, see Carl I. Hovland, A. A. Lumsdaine, and F. D. Sheffield, "The Effect of Presenting 'One Side' versus 'Both Sides' in Changing Opinions on a Controversial Subject," in Wilbur Schramm, editor, *The Process and Effects of Mass Communication,* Urbana: University of Illinois Press, 1955, p. 267.

[7] Peter M. Blau does not use these concepts, but in effect makes the same distinctions in "Social Mobility and Interpersonal Relations," *American Sociological Review,* 21 (June, 1956), 290–295.

ing with those of equal or higher occupational rank, in the second from deference by his working-class neighbors.

Given this distinction, the extended family plays an especially important role for those who are upwardly mobile. Parents' energies are frequently directed toward having their children learn a trade or profession that has more prestige than their own.[8] This is completely different from the situation in which occupational colleagues often look upon upward mobility as evidence of an *arriviste*. Significantly, the family visit can be isolated from friends' visits. As a consequence, a person can achieve status by gaining deference from his family *and* by associating with friends. This is possible because in American society there is an institutional basis for keeping friendship and family visits separated, which is further encouraged by the anonymity of very large cities.

The fact that size of city plays an important role in support of the family's status function casts some doubt on a body of literature (for example, Warner's "Yankee City" studies) which suggests that extended family relations are not consonant with occupational mobility. These studies are characterized by the fact that they were made in relatively small towns which cannot be considered representative of present or future urban society. Small towns do not provide anonymity and therefore may be much more likely to encourage family dissociation among the upwardly mobile because the individuals are forced under these circumstances to choose between status by deference and status by association.

In addition to fulfilling a status function for those who are upwardly mobile there is some evidence that the extended family provides status aid to those who are either downwardly mobile or in the initial stages of their career. This status aid is frequently isolated from occupational appointment and as such does not lead to the dangers of nepotism. Sussman gives an illustration of this situation: about 70 per cent of his 97 white middle-class Protestant New Haven parents said that they gave sufficient aid to married children to influence their status position, and that if the aid were withdrawn their status position would drop.[9] What is significant about this aid is that it was rarely directed towards job advancement or appointment, but was concerned instead with the standard of living, for example, gifts for clothing, aid for house purchase, vacations, newborn babies, and during illness.[10]

[8] For one of several studies which indicate that parents have high hopes that their children will do better than they have done, see Arthur Kornhauser, "Analysis of 'Class' Structure of Contemporary American Society: Psychological Bases of Class Divisions," in G. W. Hartman and T. Newcomb, (eds.), *Industrial Conflict*, New York: Cordon, 1939, pp. 240–241.

[9] Marvin B. Sussman, "The Help Pattern in the Middle Class Family," *American Sociological Review*, 18 (February, 1953), 27.

[10] Ibid., pp. 22–28, passim. There are at least five mechanisms by which extended family structure is made consistent with the demands for occupational appointment by merit. For an analysis of these mechanisms see Eugene Litwak, *Primary Group Instruments for Social Control in Industrial Society: The Extended Family and the Neighborhood*, unpublished Ph.D. thesis, Columbia University, 1958. These may be briefly described as follows:

1. Norms of occupational appointment by merit can be inculcated even within the extended family structure.

2. Significant extended family aid can take place in non-occupational areas

Because of such considerations it is hypothesized that the extended family can and will increasingly provide aid for the mobile nuclear family without interfering with its mobility or occupational efficiency. In turn, the extended family, in providing status to mobile people, is viable.[11]

Differential Socialization, Occupational Mobility, and Extended Family Cohesion

The second objection to the claim that the extended family is viable among occupationally mobile groups—namely, that mobility leads to differential socialization—may be answered if it is hypothesized that class differ-

---

and therefore not all extended family aid need be contrary to the demands of occupational appointment by merit.

3. The professionalization of occupations has provided more objective measures of merit and therefore less reliance need be put on rules against nepotism.

4. Developed bureaucratization of occupation means that many jobs no longer belong to the individual and are therefore more difficult to hand down to relatives.

5. Rules against nepotism are costly in a mature industrial bureaucracy because they isolate the family from the occupation and play down its importance when the family in fact has a growing role in productivity. As Reinhard Bendix suggests in *Work and Authority in Industry*, New York: John Wiley, 1956, pp. 226 ff., the industrial bureaucracy in its mature state must make use of interpersonal relations as technical aspects of the job. Leadership ability, capacity to communicate with others, an inner motivation to work, all become central when the work situation means dealing with other people rather than machines. Unlike classical job attributes (engineering knowledge, accounting knowledge, mechanical skills, etc.) it is difficult if not impossible to isolate interpersonal attributes from the non-work situation. The family plays a major role in the development and continuing use of these interpersonal abilities. The large organizations, in order to increase their productivity, have found it necessary to stress a happy family life and the identification of the family with organizational goals. See William H. Whyte, Jr., *Is Anyone Listening?*, New York: Simon and Schuster, 1952, pp. 145 ff.

"Any isolation of the family from the company or any attempt to minimize the role of the family is likely to be costly to the organization since it means loss of control over a valued job skill. If it is true, as suggested in the four mechanisms above, that the dangers from the merger between family and industry have become minimized, and if it is true that the dangers of isolation have increased, then there is good reason to expect strong organizational support for family life as good per se. In this connection it would be argued that extended family relations derive benefits as well."

[11] It should be recognized that the status aid provided by the extended family is supplemental and in an absolute sense contributes far less than the occupation of the nuclear family. However, this family aid is of a psychologically crucial sort since it provides the nuclear family with the cutting edge of status advancement. As such, family support may be viewed as far more decisive by the family members than its absolute value would suggest. For an elaboration of this view see Eugene Litwak, "Geographic Mobility and Extended Family Cohesion," *American Sociological Review* (forthcoming).

ences are moderate or shrinking, but not growing larger.[12] This hypothesis is advanced because of the rise in educational standards, the development of mass media, the general rise in the standard of living, and the drop in large-

[12] It is here assumed that the extended family has not lost its functions or narrowed its scope, as suggested, for example, by William F. Ogburn in "The Changing Functions of the Family," in R. F. Winch and R. McGinnis (eds.), *Studies in Marriage and the Family*, New York: Holt, 1953, pp. 74–80. Rather what is assumed is that each area of life can be divided into those parts which have become standardized and uniform and those parts which are idiosyncratic. The development of large-scale bureaucratic organizations has meant a division of labor with the family handling the idiosyncratic and the large organization the uniform aspects of life. This is a function of the superiority of bureaucratic organizations for handling the uniform. Max Weber develops this point in *From Max Weber: Essays in Sociology*, H. H. Gerth and C. Wright Mills, (trans. and eds.), New York: Oxford, 1946, pp. 196–244. Implicit in most of the criticism of Weber's formulation is the view that the large bureaucratic organization is not as well suited as the primary group for handling the idiosyncratic: it does not have the flexibility in committing its resources nor the short lines of communication which allow for speedy action. For a review of these criticisms see Peter M. Blau, *Bureaucracy in Modern Society*, New York: Random House, 1956, pp. 61–67. The extended family is a primary group and as such will have a continuing function in most areas of life, for in all areas there are idiosyncratic as well as uniform events. Several studies provide indirect substantiation that the extended family is viable in urban society: a study in Los Angeles by Scott Greer, "Urbanism Reconsidered," *American Sociological Review*, 21 (February, 1956), 22 ff.; a study by Morris Axelrod, "Urban Structure and Social Participation," Ibid., pp. 13–18; and a study in Buffalo, by Litwak, "Geographical Mobility and Extended Family Cohesion," loc. cit., all reveal that close to 50 per cent of the respondents visited their relatives once a week or more. In addition, a fourth study in San Francisco by W. Bell and M. D. Boat, "Urban Neighborhoods and Informal Social Relations," *American Journal of Sociology*, 43 (January, 1957), 391–398, shows that close to 90 percent of the respondents name at least one relative as a close personal friend and 80 per cent say they can count on aid from their relatives if they are sick for a month or more. Finally, a study in New Haven by Sussman, op. cit., pp. 27 ff., indicates that close to 70 percent of the respondents said that if they withdrew their aid to their married children, they would suffer a significant drop in socio-economic status. All of these studies explicitly deal with middle class native Americans. In contrast, several investigations treat working-class or ethnic groups; but these also indicate certain strengths of extended family relations—see, e.g., M. Young and P. Willmot, *Family and Kinship in East London*, London: Routledge and Kegan Paul, 1957. However, these latter studies do not confirm the hypothesis presented in this paper, but rather support Parsons' hypothesis, for the most part indicating that extended family relations go hand in hand with occupational nepotism and geographical propinquity. Young and Willmot, in stressing the virtues of these classical extended family relations, do not consider their costs in terms of a democracy's industrial system. I believe that most ethnic-group and working-class studies that deal with the family are concerned with vestiges of the "classical extended" family, since the working-class groups are the last to feel the bureaucratic pressures discussed above regarding modified extended family relations. For a systematic discussion of this point, see Litwak, *Primary Group Instruments of Social Control . . .* , op. cit., pp. 12 ff.

scale immigration. Of course, there are *both* major class differences and similarities in contemporary American society.[13] In this connection, what are the comparative magnitudes of the differences and similarities? And, are differences shrinking or growing larger over time? Class similarities seem to be sufficientiy large to provide cross-class identification by extended family members and the differences appear to be shrinking.[14] The issue of shrinking class differences should not be confused with the issue of class conflict. For it is possible that class conflict may well occur between two relatively articulate groups who understand each other all too well but differ over what constitutes a fair division of the spoils.[15]

Regarding the problem of differential socialization, it shouid be noted that many of the studies which support Parsons' hypothesis use as their respondents first and second generation members of minority ethnic groups.[16] In this way, the problem of class differences is compounded by the problem of ethnic differences, often leading to an exaggeration of the former.[17]

It is maintained in this paper that among the white Americanized groups (and especially those in the middle-range occupations) upward mobility does not involve radical shifts in socialization and therefore does not constitute a real barrier to extended family communication.[18]

[13] Cf. Kornhauser, op. cit.

[14] Nelson N. Foote and Paul K. Hatt, "Social Mobility and Economic Advancement," *The American Economic Review*, 43 (May, 1953), show that the tendency since 1900 is for the entire occupational structure to become more "middle-class." For a summary of studies dealing with class differences over time, see S. M. Lipset, "American Society—Stability in the Midst of Change," unpublished paper read at the National Conference of Social Welfare, San Francisco, California, May, 1959, pp. 16–19. In this paper Lipset refers to unpublished studies as well as the following articles which indicate that class differences may be moderate or shrinking: G. Sjoberg, "Are Social Classes in America Becoming More Rigid?" *American Sociological Review*, 16 (December, 1951), 775–83; S. Goldsmith et al., "Size Distribution of Income Since the Mid-Thirties," *The Review of Economics and Statistics*, 36 (February, 1954), 26 ff.; Kurt Mayer, "Business Enterprise: Traditional Symbol of Opportunity," *British Journal of Sociology*, 4 (June, 1953), 160–180.

[15] This view tends to characterize the contemporary English Labor Party. It was also explicitly expressed by Karl Kautsky in "Terrorism and Communism," reprinted in *Man in Contemporary Society: A Source Book Prepared by the Contemporary Civilization Staff of Columbia College, Columbia University*, New York: Columbia University Press, 1956, II, pp. 549–550.

[16] E.g., Warner and Lunt, op. cit.; Walter Firey, *Land Use in Central Boston*, Cambridge: Harvard University Press, 1947, pp. 111–191, 220–225.

[17] Fred L. Stodtbeck's "Family Interaction, Values, and Achievement," in David C. McClelland et al., *Talent and Society*, Princeton: Van Nostrand, 1958, pp. 135–195 passim, points out how members of an ethnic group with a traditional extended family orientation, e.g., the Italian, are less likely to achieve success than those of an ethnic group whose values more closely match that of the dominant society, e.g., the Jewish.

[18] In this connection it should also be noted that most occupational shifts do not involve major changes in class position. See, e.g., S. M. Lipset and R. Bendix, "Social Mobility and Occupational Career Patterns II: Social Mobility," in Bendix and Lipset, op. cit., pp. 455, 457.

Occupational Power and Extended Family Cohesion

If it is granted that the extended family has important functions in contemporary society[19] and that bureaucratic pressures tend to stress the family as an end value, there should then be a positive relationship between extended family contacts and economic resources. And if it is assumed that generally persons in the stationary upper class have the greatest resources, those in the stationary manual classes the least resources, and the occupationally mobile stand between these two groups in this respect, the view presented above can be specified operationally as follows: The stationary upper class respondent will have the greatest number of extended family visits, the upwardly mobile the next greatest number, the downwardly mobile the next most, and the stationary manual the fewest number of visits.

This point of view differs from Parsons' hypothesis which argues a curvilinear relationship, with the mobile individuals having fewer extended family visits than the occupationally stable.

FINDINGS

Sample and Operational Definition of Mobility

In order to investigate empirically the alternative hypothesis, a secondary analysis was made of data gathered in Buffalo, New York, for a housing survey. The sample consisted of 920 white married women from the Buffalo urban area who had moved into a new home just prior to the time of the study (between June and October, 1952). They all had children 19 years or younger. Several kinds of sampling procedures were used which cast doubt upon the relevance of traditional statistical tests.[20] For purposes of the present discussion, however, the biases of the sampling are of great value. The population studied was predominantly middle class, and native born; as such, it is made up of persons who—according to Parsons—are most likely to bear out his hypothesis.[21]

[19] See footnote 12 above.

[20] For a detailed description of the samples see Glenn H. Beyer, Thomas Mackesey, and James E. Montgomery, *Houses Are for People: A Study of Home Buyer Motivation*, Ithaca: Cornell Housing Research Center, 1955. The sample was stratified for income, owners-renters, and house design. In addition, some groups were selected on a block cluster basis, i.e., all people on the block with children under 19, while others were selected on an area sampling basis—within income and family cycle limitations. Because of the extremely varied nature of the sample it is difficult to know what constitutes a correct statistical test. Therefore the meaningfulness of the empirical data must rest to a considerable extent on the theoretical plausibility of the discussion and its consistency with other studies. However, if the assumptions of a random area sample could be made, then all major findings are significant at the .05 level and beyond. The sign test or the Wilcoxon matched pairs signed-ranks test was used. All tests were based on signs taken from the most complex tables in which the given variables appeared, i.e., Tables 4, 5, 6, and 8.

[21] Parsons, "The Social Structure of the Family," op. cit.

Occupational mobility was ascertained by comparing the occupations of the husband and the husband's father. These occupations were first classified according to the Census Bureau's occupational scheme and were then divided into three overall classes as follows:

	Percentage of Sample in Each Group (husbands' occupations only)
1. Upper class:	
Professional, technical and kindred	25.6
Managers, officials, and proprietors	24.2
2. Middle class:	
Clerical and kindred workers	3.8
Sales workers	10.3
3. Manual class:	
Craftsmen, foremen, and kindred workers	21.6
Operatives and kindred workers	12.5
Service	1.4
	100.0 (1000)

After assigning both the husband and his father to one of these classes, four mobility categories were defined:

1. *Stationary Upper Class* All those now in the upper class whose parents were also in the upper class.

2. *Upwardly Mobile Class* All those whose parents came from a lower occupational group than that which the husband now occupies.

3. *Downwardly Mobile Class* All those whose parents came from a higher occupational group than the respondent now occupies.

4. *Stationary Manual Class* All those who are now manual workers and whose fathers were manual workers.

Eliminated from the analysis were all respondents whose fathers were farmers and all persons in the middle class whose fathers were also in the middle class—the former because of difficulty in classifying them, and the latter since there were only thirty cases (it was thought that they would only blur the analysis if they were arbitrarily classified with upper or manual groups).

Occupational Mobility and Extended Family Visits

In order to ascertain the presence or absence of extended family relationships the respondents were asked, "How often do the following people come to your house: relatives who just drop in, relatives who are invited?" With certain noted exceptions, all individuals who reported one or more visits a week were classified as having frequent family visits. Using these defini-

TABLE 1   The Occupationally Mobile Are as Likely as
Other Groups to Have Family Visits

	Percentage Receiving One or More Family Visits a Week
Stationary upper class	36 (249)[a]
Upwardly mobile class	34 (288)
Downwardly mobile class	37 (142)
Stationary manual class	39 (245)

[a]In this and the following tables, numbers in parentheses
indicate population upon which the percentage is based.

tions, initial empirical examination of the hypothesis of a negative relation
between extended family contact and occupational mobility may be undertaken. Table 1 provides no support for this hypothesis: there is almost no
difference between the mobile and non-mobile categories. If Table 1 does not
support this hypothesis, neither does it support the alternative one suggested
above. The lack of relationship, however, is due to the fact that geographic
mobility has not been taken into account. Individuals who have no relatives
in the city find it extremely difficult to visit. Since a companion paper[22] shows
that families can maintain their extended family identification despite
geographic distance, the present analysis attempts to exclude the geographic
factor and to restrict the analysis to occupational mobility. This can be accomplished partially by analyzing separately those respondents with and without

TABLE 2   Geographical Rather Than Occupational Mobility Accounts for Large Drop
in Family Visits

	Percentage Receiving One or More Family Visits a Week	
	Respondents Having Relatives in City	Respondents Not Having Relatives in City
Stationary upper class	59 (148)	2 (101)
Upwardly mobile class	51 (183)	5 (105)
Downwardly mobile class	51 (101)	0 (41)
Stationary manual class	43 (216)	10 (29)

relatives living in the city. Table 2 shows that the negative relation between
mobility and extended family contact is not substantiated even where geographic mobility is taken into account. Among the respondents with relatives
residing in the city, those in the upper class have the most visits, those in
the manual groups the fewest, and the mobile respondents an intermediate
proportion. Among those with no nearby relatives, the stationary manual
class shows the highest proportion of frequent family visits, while the other
classes report a fairly similar number of visits.

   The difference in patterns between those with and without nearby
relatives seems to be accounted for by the crudeness of the measure used
to determine how far the respondents live from their relatives. Considerable
evidence suggests that the upper-class person who has no relatives in the

[22] See footnote 11, above.

city is likely to live at a much greater distance from them than the manual worker without nearby relatives. One Census report, for example, shows that professional groups are more likely than manual workers to move greater distances.[23] Again, data in this research reveal that manual workers without relatives in the city are much more likely (21.5 per cent) to have been raised in the community under study than any other group (one per cent). In short, a lack of nearby relatives is not as apt to signify geographical mobility for manual workers as it is for other groups. Therefore such manual workers are more likely to have relatives in the immediate vicinity than other groups without nearby relatives. This probably accounts for the high proportion of manual workers without relatives in the city who have frequent family visits (as presented in Table 2).

Extreme Occupational Mobility and Extended Family Visits

The fact that the initial data do not verify the negative relation between mobility and extended family may well be accounted for by the measure of mobility, which was operationalized on an absolute rather than a relative basis. Foote and Hatt (among others) point out that the entire population has risen in occupational status during the last 60 years. As a consequence, respondents may have no psychological sense of mobility even though they are better off than their parents. To experience mobility, then, the individual must move up the social scale at a faster rate than his peers.[24] Perhaps mobility is negatively related to the extended family if relative rather than absolute mobility is taken into account.

TABLE 3 Those More Occupationally Mobile Than Their Peers Have an Intermediate Proportion of Extended Family Visits

| | Percentage Receiving One or More Visits a Week | |
	Respondents Having Relatives in City	Respondents Not Having Relatives in City
Stationary upper class	59 (148)	2 (101)
Extreme upwardly mobile[a]	59 (114)	2 (58)
Extreme downwardly mobile[a]	50 (51)	0 (12)
Stationary manual class	43 (216)	10 (29)

[a]It is assumed that those who move from manual class to upper class or *vice versa* are more mobile than most people in the country.

To investigate this question only those mobile individuals who moved from stationary manual groups to upper class groups or vice versa were considered. This constitutes a two-step move and would presumably encompass all individuals who have moved faster than their peers. Table 3 indicates that the negative relationship does not appear even where extremely mobile people are taken into account. Among those with relatives in the city the mobile individuals show no lower proportion of frequent visits.

[23] U. S. Bureau of the Census, *Sixteenth Census of the United States: 1940 Population, Internal Migration 1935 to 1940, Economic Characteristics of Migrants*, Washington: U. S. Government Printing Office, 1946, p. 9.

[24] Foote and Hatt, op. cit., pp. 370–376.

Age, Occupational Mobility, and Extended Family Visits

It is generally recognized that adequate analysis of occupational mobility requires consideration of age. For example, downward mobility means something different for persons at the beginning and at the middle of their careers. Because of the sampling procedure used in this study, more than 98 per cent of the respondents were 45 years old or younger, so that the factor of age can be examined only within a narrow limit.

TABLE 4   Occupationally Mobile Groups Have an Intermediate Proportion of Extended Family Visits Even When Age is Considered

	Wife Is 29[a] or Younger	Wife Is Older than 29
	Relatives of the Husband or Wife Living in the City	
	Percentage Receiving One or More Family Visits a Week	
Stationary upper class	61 (80)	57 (67)
Upwardly mobile class	50 (93)	52 (89)
Downwardly mobile class	47 (58)	58 (43)
Stationary manual class	44 (119)	37 (95)
	No Relatives Living in the City	
	Percentage Receiving One or More Family Visits a Month[b]	
Stationary upper class	10 (48)	18 (51)
Upwardly mobile class	18 (56)	27 (48)
Downwardly mobile class	12 (26)	0 (14)
Stationary manual class	36 (11)	33 (18)

[a]This figure was used because it is closest to the median age for the entire group.
[b]So as to have stable proportions, in the following tables a frequent visit for persons without relatives in the community is defined as above. Use of this definition does not alter the rank of any of the classes.

The population was divided at the median age of the wife (29). Table 4 shows the irrelevancy of the age factor in this study: even when this factor is considered, the negative relation between mobility and extended family still is not substantiated—the pattern of family visits is not affected.

Occupational Mobility and Extended Family Identification

Despite these findings it may be argued that family visits are not an adequate measure of family attachment and thus irrelevant to the criticism of Parsons' hypothesis. Occupationally mobile (especially upwardly mobile) persons may be in a position where family visits, although unwanted, are thrust upon them. It may be maintained that the negative relationship hypothesis merely assumes that upwardly mobile individuals are least likely to be oriented toward extended families. If it can be demonstrated that this is the case—for example, that visits tend to be thrust upon such persons—the hypothesis in large part remains viable despite the negative results reported above.

In order to investigate extended family-orientation, respondents were asked to what degree they agreed with the following statements:

1. Generally I like the whole family to spend evenings together.
2. I want a house where family members can spend time together.
3. I want a location which would make it easy for relatives to get together.
4. I want a house with enough room for our parents to feel free to move in.

Those individuals who "very strongly agreed" with the third or fourth statements[25] were defined as extended family-oriented, those who agreed with the first or second statement as nuclear family-oriented, while those who rejected all of the statements were defined as non-family-oriented. These responses form a Guttman scale pattern, with the extended family-oriented tending to agree "very strongly" with at least the first three statements, the nuclear-oriented agreeing with the first two, and the non-family-oriented not agreeing "very strongly" with any of the statements.

TABLE 5   Occupationally Mobile Groups are Moderately Identified with Their Extended Family

	Percentage Extended Family Orientation	Percentage Nuclear Family Orientation	Percentage Non-Family Orientation	Population
Stationary upper class	26	55	19	100 (247)
Upwardly mobile class	22	55	23	100 (284)
Downwardly mobile class	17	52	31	100 (147)
Stationary manual class	15	51	34	100 (242)

The data shown in Table 5 suggest that the hypothesis under criticism does not hold even for extended family identification. Upwardly mobile individuals were not less identified with their extended family than the others. Rather, the degree of extended family-orientation increased as the respondents engaged more and more in upper class occupations. This finding is consistent with the view that bureaucratic occupations (mostly upper class[26]) encourage the development of the value of the family as an end value.

[25] It should be pointed out that because of the small number who answered statement 4 positively (four per cent) almost all of the extended family-oriented were defined by statement 3. For interrelations between the items see Litwak, *Primary Group Instruments of Social Control . . .,* op. cit., pp. 43–47.

[26] In this paper and the companion paper cited in footnote 11 above, bureaucratic occupations refer to administrative and upper white-collar positions in bureaucratic organizations. Most of these people are members of the upper-class category, as a consequence of the definition of upper class used in this paper. If this category is to be used as an index of bureaucratic occupations, it must be known if those who are members of bureaucratic organizations form a sufficiently large group within the upper class to give it a

Extended Family Identification, Status Orientation, and Mobility

It could be maintained, however, that the analysis presented above does not really provide a precise test of the hypothesis that the extended family is negatively related to occupational mobility. For it could be inferred with some justification that this hypothesis only suggests that upwardly mobile persons will not be extended family-oriented only if they are status-oriented. Put somewhat differently, it could be argued that extended family-oriented individuals are unlikely to be status-oriented, especially if they are upwardly mobile.

Before investigating this point empirically, it should be noted that the term "status-oriented" is being used in the "high society" or "society news" sense. This is similar to Warner's use of "social class," and a little narrower than Weber's use of "status."[27]

In order to operationalize status-orientation, the respondents were asked to answer two types of questions: those which express a concern for "social manners," and questions which stress the importance of "social" evaluations. Again, four questions were used, two of each type. Since there were no pre-determined status positions similar to the family values (extended, nuclear, and non-family oriented) the population was divided in half to facilitate analysis.

The individual who answered positively any three of the questions listed below is considered, as a result of this procedure, to be status-oriented, while the respondent who answered only one or rejected all of them is described as having little concern for status. The following questions were asked:

1. When in public people should be extra careful of their behavior.
2. I'm uncomfortable when I am with people who have bad manners.
3. I want a house which I can be proud to have my friends see.
4. I think my house has a lot to do with my friends' opinion of me.[28]

Assuming that these questions are adequate indicators, the data presented in Table 6 show that extended family-oriented persons are more likely than those in any other category to be status-oriented. Furthermore, this

---

distinctive bureaucratic style. Data from a study by Gold and Slater indicate that 74 per cent of their respondents who match the upper-class category in this study in terms of age and occupation are members of bureaucratic organizations. See Martin Gold and Carol Slater, "Office, Factory, Store—and Family: A Study of Integration Setting," *American Sociological Review*, 23 (February, 1958), 66, 69. This would seem promising support for the assumptions made in this paper, but because of the sampling problems and the operational definitions used for bureaucratic organizations it cannot be conclusive.

[27] W. Lloyd Warner, Marchia Meeker, Kenneth Eells, *Social Class in America*, Chicago: Science Research Associates, 1949, pp. 3–46, passim; Weber, op. cit., pp. 186–187.

[28] For the interrelations between the items, see Litwak, *Primary Group Instruments of Social Control . . .*, op. cit., pp. 47–50.

TABLE 6 Extended Family Oriented Persons and Concern with Status

	Percentage Who Express a High Concern for Status		
	Extended Family Orientation	Nuclear Family Orientation	Non-Family Orientation
Stationary upper class	70 (64)	47 (136)	31 (48)
Upwardly mobile class	76 (62)	49 (157)	33 (70)
Downwardly mobile class	79 (26)	47 (75)	37 (41)
Stationary manual class	64 (50)	39 (113)	34 (80)

association holds for the upwardly mobile. Once more, these empirical findings are inconsistent with the hypothesis that mobility and family nucleation are mutually supporting.

Extended Family Relations and Occupational Power

Thus far major emphasis has been given to showing that the negative relation between occupational mobility and extended family relations does not hold under successively more specified conditions. At this point an attempt is made to demonstrate positively the validity of the alternative hypothesis advanced here. It should first be noted that the data presented in the foregoing tables indicate that extended family visits and identification increase with occupational position or occupational resources. The only exception is among those with no relatives living in the community, and this seems to be an understandable function of geographical mobility.

If, as hypothesized, occupational resources are a major element in extended family visits, there should be some distinctive differences in visiting patterns between persons with large and those with limited occupational resources. Among the former, frequent family visits are most likely to be part of a social context involving other forms of social participation since their economic resources permit a wide range of social activities. In contrast, among those individuals with limited resources family visits are likely to be isolated from other types of visits. This view is substantiated by the data presented in Table 7. Upper class persons are more likely than any others to have family visits in conjunction with neighborhood friendships and affiliation with voluntary associations. The manual class is more likely than any other class to have only family visits with minimal participation in neighborhood or voluntary associations. This combined with previous findings highlights the major role played by occupational resources in preserving extended family contact.

Joint Interaction of Family Orientation, Status Orientation, Occupational Mobility, and Extended Family Relations

The several factors which have been examined independently can now be brought together. If these factors are considered simultaneously, the negative relationship hypothesis can be restated as follows: Individuals who are least likely to have extended family visits are (a) upwardly mobile, (b) status oriented, and (c) nuclear or non-family oriented. In contrast, the hypothesis suggested in this paper can be elaborated: Individuals who are least likely to

TABLE 7   Economic Power Permits Both Familial and Other Activities[a]

	Percentage Participating in Family, Club, and Neighborhood Friendships[b]	Percentage Participating in Family and Either Club or Neighborhood Friendships[b]	Percentage Participating Only in Family Visits and No Other Activities[b]	Total Percentage Participating in Family Visits[c]
Stationary upper class	29	23	7	59 (148)
Upwardly mobile class	16	22	13	51 (183)
Downwardly mobile class	13	26	12	51 (101)
Stationary manual class	8	20	14	43 (216)

[a]This table includes only those respondents who have relatives in the city because only under such conditions can it be assumed that relatives are at an equal distance from all occupational groups.
[b]To participate in family activities means to receive family visits once a week or more; to participate in clubs signifies belonging to one or more (the closest approximation to the median number) clubs; to participate in neighborhood friendships means to know five or more (the closest approximation to the median number) neighbors well enough to call on them.
[c]Total family visits means all people whether the visit is part of a pattern of participation or a single family participation.

have family visits are (a) characterized by fewer occupational resources (stationary manual workers), (b) non-status oriented, and (c) nuclear or non-family oriented.

These hypotheses in part overlap and in part are contradictory. Table 8 permits the reader to see more clearly at what points the hypotheses run counter to one another. This table shows twelve "groups" enclosed within a dashed line. According to the view that the extended family is negatively related to mobility, two of these groups should have a lower proportion of frequent family visits than the other ten—consisting of those who are either nuclear or non-family oriented, concerned with status, and who are upwardly mobile. The hypothesis advanced in this paper leads to a different prediction: that the two groups which will have the lowest proportion of frequent family visits are nuclear or non-family oriented but *not* status oriented and, in addition, come from the *non-mobile* manual category. (Neither hypothesis can be tested by the behavior of the groups in the cells lying outside the dashed line, for both hypotheses would predict that these would have a higher proportion of frequent visits than all others.)

If the cells within the dotted lines are contrasted, then in only three out of ten possible comparisons is the negative relationship hypothesis supported, while the counter hypothesis is supported in seven out of ten instances. This may be seen more clearly if the cells are grouped into (1) those which according to the hypothesis will be the lowest, and (2) all others.[29] If this is

[29] The two "groups" which, according to Parsons' hypothesis, should contain on the average the lowest proportion of frequent family visits had respectively 55 (49) and 40 (15) per cent with frequent family visits. In contrast, the two groups suggested by the counter-hypothesis to have the lowest proportion of frequent family visits had respectively 36 (67) and 27 (52) per cent with frequent family visits. The other groups within the dashed line were averaged together and added to either of the two averages above, depending on which hypothesis was being tested.

done, then the group which would be expected to have the lowest proportion of frequent visits if there were a negative relationship between mobility and extended family, show in fact the highest proportion (54 percent as compared to 34 per cent for the rest of the population). In contrast, the group which according to the counter-hypothesis would be expected to have the lowest proportion of family visits actually reveals this pattern (30 per cent as compared to 54 per cent for the total population). In short, when the negative relationship hypothesis is specified in its most complete form it is not substantiated, while the alternative hypothesis tends to be.

TABLE 8 Upwardly Mobile, Status, and Non-Extended Family Oriented Respondents Have an Intermediate Proportion of Frequent Family Visits[a]

	Percentage Receiving One or More Family Visits a Week					
	Extended Family Oriented		Nuclear Family Oriented		Non-Family Oriented	
	High Status Concern	Low Status Concern	High Status Concern	Low Status Concern	High Status Concern	Low Status Concern
Stationary upper class	63[b]	49	74	55	56	47
Upwardly mobile class	61	75	55[c]	43	40[c]	41
Downwardly mobile class	77	33	33	64	16	29
Stationary manual class	73	60	22	36[d]	56	27[d]
Population						
Stationary upper class	35	10	35	40	9	19
Upwardly mobile class	28	8	49	51	15	32
Downwardly mobile class	13	3	24	28	13	20
Stationary manual class	26	5	41	67	23	52

[a]In this table, as in Table 7, only respondents are considered who have relatives living in the city. This avoids the extraneous consideration of geographical distance.
[b]This cell should be read as follows: 63 per cent of the 35 people who had relatives living in the city were extended family oriented, concerned with status, stationary upper class, and had visits from relatives once a week or more.
[c]According to Parsons' hypothesis, these two groups should have the lowest proportion of frequent family visits.
[d]According to the alternative hypothesis, these two groups should have the lowest proportion of frequent family visits.

DISCUSSION AND CONCLUSION

It seems quite probable that Parsons' hypothesis is applicable in the earlier stages of industrialization. In that period extended family relations were heavily influenced by the peasant farm family, which strongly incorporated the values of geographic and occupational closeness. Under such circumstances extended family relations were detrimental to occupational mobility.

In contemporary society, however, extended family relations develop from different institutional sources and as a result do not rely on geographic and occupational proximity for their viability.[30] It is suggested that these modified

[30] In comparing Italian and Jewish families in contemporary society, Strodtbeck, loc. cit., discusses shifts in extended family relations. The Italian family

extended family relations are more consonant with occupational mobility than the isolated nuclear family.

Several studies which seem to substantiate the view that the extended family is negatively related to occupational mobility suffer from the following defects: (1) they deal with small town populations which are not typical of urban development;[31] (2) they focus upon ethnic and working class groups with their passing remnants of classical extended family relations rather than developing modified extended family relations;[32] and (3) they frequently present anecdotal reports rather than systematic evidence, and therefore are more likely to concentrate on sensational family disruptions than ordinary uniformities.[33] Aside from the shortcomings of these earlier studies, there are some investigations which provide positive support for the hypothesis suggested in this paper.[34]

Yet there are some major limitations in the present inquiry which must be dealt with before the findings can be fully accepted. A more adequate sample is necessary than the present one, in which individuals on the bottom of the occupational ladder—unskilled laborers—are not adequately represented. It could well be argued that upward mobility from this group would provide evidence supporting Parsons' hypothesis. However, it should be noted that the proportion of the labor force in this category has greatly declined during the last fifty years and that unskilled workers are likely to disappear as a significant factor in urban life under the twin pressures of automation and bureaucratization. This study is also limited by the fact that there are no data on people over 45 or those without children; there might be significant differences within these two groups.[35] Even more important, additional work should be done on the indexes of extended family relation, occupational mobility, and the differentiation between bureaucratic and non-bureaucratic occupations if the hypothesis suggested in this paper is to be substantiated.

Despite these limitations, it is concluded that the hypothesis of a negative relation between occupational mobility and the extended family is not

---

structure, relatively speaking, is still defined in terms of geographical and occupational proximity. In contrast, the Jewish extended family, for historical reasons, closely resembles the family structure considered to be prototypical of contemporary urban bureaucratic life. Thus Jewish families, more than Italian, encourage mobility. Strodtbeck's interpretation of Jewish family structure seems to be largely an application of Parsons' hypothesis. Contrastingly, it is argued here that Strodtbeck's study merely establishes the fact that the Jewish extended family does not define geograpical and occupational mobility as an essential process, nor is the nuclear family defined as subordinate to the parental family. Strodtbeck neither demonstrates that the Jewish family is an isolated nuclear family nor that it does not consist of a series of nuclear families with strong equalitarian bonds through which pass much extended family aid.

[31] Warner and Lunt, op. cit.

[32] Firey, op. cit.; Young and Willmot, op. cit.

[33] Warner and Lunt, op. cit.

[34] See footnote 12 above.

[35] Litwak, "Geographical Mobility and Extended Family Mobility," loc. cit.

sufficiently established to support future research by itself. That part of Parsons' hypothesis which points to the functional inadequacy of the classical extended family is accepted, but that part which posits the isolated nuclear family as the most functional type for *contemporary* industrial society is rejected. It is hoped that the present modification and elaboration of Parsons' formulations will provide some additional understanding or raise significant questions about the relation between the family and the occupational system.[36]

[36] Litwak, *Primary Group Instruments of Social Control* . . . , op. cit., pp. 16–37. Some of the basic underlying assumptions of bureaucracy are re-examined in terms of the problems posed here.

29 Occupational Position, Mobility, and the Kin of Orientation

BERT N. ADAMS

The study of generational occupational mobility and kinship relations has produced two opposing themes as well as two variations upon them. One of the dominant positions stresses the weakening effect of mobility upon kin ties;[1] the other argues that mobility has no independent influence upon kin relations except as it promotes geographic mobility.[2]

To speak simply of "kin relations" is to overgeneralize, and this observation is the basis for two attempts to reconcile the antithetical viewpoints. Willmott and Young state that sex differences are crucial in relations with parents, mobility being detrimental to father-son interaction but not to

[1] Robert P. Stuckert, "Occupational Mobility and Family Relationships," *Social Forces*, 41 (March, 1963), 304–305; David M. Schneider and George C. Homans, "Kinship Terminology and the American Kinship System," *American Anthropologist*, 57 (December, 1955), 1207.

[2] Michael Young and Peter Willmott, *Family and Kinship in East London*, Baltimore, Md.: Penguin Books, 1964, p. 184; Eugene Litwak, "Occupational Mobility and Extended Family Cohesion," *American Sociological Review*, 25 (February, 1960), 9–21; Gordon F. Streib, "Family Patterns in Retirement," *The Journal of Social Issues*, 14 (Winter, 1958), 52.

The larger kinship study of which this is a part was supported by Public Health Service Fellowship (MH–15,571) from the National Institute of Mental Health. The author wishes to acknowledge gratefully the criticisms and suggestions of Anthony F. Costonis, Michael T. Aiken, and Howard E. Freeman on various drafts of the paper.
Reprinted from the *American Sociological Review*, 32, No. 3 (June, 1967), 364–377, by permission of the American Sociological Review.

mother-son or parent-daughter relations.[3] Bott contends that the more genealogically distant the relative, the more objective status differences determine interaction.[4] Thus, sex and degree of relationship are factors which may account for part of the discrepancy in studies of mobility and kinship.

With these distinctions in mind, the contention of this paper is that *the current occupational positions and the orientations of family members toward the dominant middle-class achievement values of our society are greater determinants of adult relations between kin of orientation than are inter-generational mobility or stability.* The orientations of the family members, we assume, are manifested during the socialization process as well as in adulthood.

The study of occupational statuses and kinship focuses on the inter-relation between economic values and kin values. On the one hand, one's occupation epitomizes the economic dimension of social existence and lies at the heart of his self-evaluation. On the other hand, the kinship tie is the prime particularistic relationship, making certain demands upon the individual simply because it exists. To the economic-achevement-oriented person, kinship is the barbaric "obligation to give affection as a duty to a particular set of persons on account of an accident of birth."[5] To those inclined to be particularistic, kinship is the refuge from an impersonal world, a positive functional relationship in urban industrial society.[6] This paper suggests that adult kin relations cannot be understood apart from the economic-achievement values impinging upon them, both during socialization and in adulthood.

We shall begin by proposing hypotheses regarding adult relations with parents and siblings, i.e., the kin of orientation, based upon the sex of the individual, the middle-class achievement motif, and the socialization process. Relations with secondary kin, i.e., aunts, uncles, cousins, grandparents and those more distant are investigated elsewhere.[7]

Relations with Parents

Hypothesis I: *Regardless of the sex or occupational position of the young adult, affection for and idealization of a middle-class father tends to be greater than when the father is working class.*

[3] Peter Willmott and Michael Young, *Family and Class in a London Suburb*, London: Routledge and Kegan Paul, 1960, p. 1967.

[4] Elizabeth Bott, *Family and Social Network*, London: Tavistock Publications, 1957, p. 147.

[5] Barrington Moore, Jr., *Political Power and Social Theory*, Cambridge, Mass.: Harvard University Press, 1958, p. 163.

[6] Raymond Firth, "Family and Kinship in Industrial Society," in Paul Halmos (ed.), *The Development of Industrial Societies*, the Sociological Review Monograph No. 8, Keele: University of Keele, 1964, p. 85. Functions performed by urban kin networks are discussed in Marvin B. Sussman and Lee Burchinal, "Kin Family Network: Unheralded Structure in Current Conceptualizations of Family Functioning," *Marriage and Family Living*, 24 (August, 1962), pp. 231–240.

[7] They are analyzed in Bert N. Adams, *Urban Kin Relations*, an unpublished monograph.

A concern of this paper is the effect of generational mobility. Thus, four basic occupational stratum and mobility categories are employed: (1) upwardly mobile and (2) downwardly mobile, or those whose parents are of one occupational level but who are themselves of the other, (3) the stable white collar, i.e., white-collar offspring of white-collar parents, and (4) the stable blue collar, i.e., blue-collar offspring of blue-collar parents.[8] Hypothesis I, restated in terms of these categories, is that downwardly-mobile and stable white-collar adults, i.e., those with middle-class fathers, are more likely to feel close to and identify with their fathers than are upwardly-mobile and stable blue-collar adults.

In American society, middle-class goals or values dominate. They are continually being interpreted to and instilled in all elements of the population by the educational system and the mass media.[9] Such goals may be accepted or altered to fit one's life situation, but they are omnipresent. The growing young person, male or female, ideally looks upon his father as a symbol of achievement or non-achievement. He likewise responds to variations in socialization according to the roles of the socializing agents, specifically the parents, and in adulthood to the outcome of the process, i.e., his own greater or lesser achievement. The blue-collar father is neither an occupational example to aspire to nor does he seem frequently to play an active role in the socialization process.[10] The middle-class father, however, is admired and

[8] A possible criticism of results based upon the simple white-collar—blue-collar division is that, as Landecker points out, we have arbitrarily dichotomized an empirical continuum. Werner Landecker, "Class Boundaries," *American Sociological Review*, 25 (December, 1960), pp. 868–877. Thus, considering those respondents who have moved from a skilled craftsman or foreman family into a clerical or other low white-collar position as upwardly mobile may in actuality be dichotomizing the similar. However, upon investigation, objective and subjective relations with parents vary but little when those who have moved two or more status categories, i.e., from a high blue-collar family into a high white-collar position, or from a low blue-collar family into any white-collar position, are compared with those who have moved from a high blue-collar family into a low white-collar position. In fact, the tendency is, if anything, to be subjectively closer to parents the *greater* one's social mobility. Willmott and Young, op. cit., pp. 160 ff, lend some support to this finding when they observe, as we have, that, regardless of whether they split their sample into two or six divisions, the same stratum effects appear.

[9] The dominance of middle-class values in United States society is stressed, among other places, in Robert K. Merton, *Social Theory and Social Structure*, Glencoe, Ill.: The Free Press, 1958 ed., pp. 136–137: "To say that the goal of monetary success is entrenched in American culture is only to say that Americans are bombarded on every side by precepts which affirm the right or, often, the duty of retaining the goal even in the face of repeated frustration. Prestigeful representatives of the society reinforce the cultural emphasis. The family, the school and the workplace . . . join to provide the intensive disciplining required. . . ."

[10] Komarovsky has reported that when a blue-collar father is admired, it is his character, not his attainment, which is appreciated; Mirra Komarovsky, *Blue-Collar Marriage*, New York: Random House, 1964, p. 253. The role of parents in socialization is described in Melvin L. Kohn and Eleanor E. Carroll, "Social Class and the Allocation of Parental Responsibilities," *Sociometry*, 23

respected by his children as embodying society's dominant achievement values. He is seen as playing a relatively active and supportive role in their socialization. This admiration and respect is likely to continue into adulthood, for socialization, aspirations, occupational achievement and adult relations with parents are ordinarily cumulative or sequential.

Hypothesis II: The current occupational status of the young adult is integrally associated with his feelings toward his mother. *If the son or daughter has achieved a middle-class position, affectional closeness to and idealization of the mother are more likely than if he or she is presently working-class.*

The mother, regardless of status, bears the major day-to-day burden of child-raising. Although the middle-class father is a role model and generally plays a positive role in socialization, the mother is nevertheless likely to receive major credit for her children's achievement or to take greater blame for their lack of achievement.

This hypothesis, it should be noted, ignores the basic role convergence of females in adulthood. Women generally have the same occupations, i.e., housewives and mothers, and are found to be little affected by occupational differentials between their husbands and fathers.[11] This may mean that the mother-daughter relationship is subjectively close regardless of the daughter's occupational status. If so, Hypothesis II will hold for sons only.

One finding of kinship studies is that working-class kin tend to be less scattered residentially than middle-class kin.[12] If the occupationally mobile—both upward and downward—incorporate characteristics of both their new stratum and their family background, they should, as a category, be between the stable white collar and stable blue collar in distance from their parents.

Hypothesis III is that *stable middle-class young adults interact with their parents least frequently and stable working-class young adults most frequently, with the occupationally mobile forming intermediate categories.*

This hypothesis draws upon Young and Willmott's contention that occupational mobility influences interaction only insofar as it signifies differential distances by status categories.[13] However, if our hypotheses are correct, we may find that despite the greater likelihood of residential separation, the stable middle classes are most likely to interact frequently with their parents when they are available or proximate. Likewise, the stable blue-collar adults,

---

(December, 1960), 391–392; and Donald Gilbert McKinley, *Social Class and Family Life*, New York: The Free Press of Glencoe, 1964, p. 116. Robert A. Ellis and W. Clayton Lane, "Structural Supports for Upward Mobility," *American Sociological Review*, 28 (October, 1963), 747, agree that the lower the father's educational level, the less the role he plays in the achievement aspirations of his offspring. One source, however, has indicated that working-class fathers may play a more active role in mobility: Joseph A. Kahl, "Educational and Occupational Aspirations of 'Common Man' Boys," *Harvard Educational Review*, 23 (May, 1953), 202–203.

[11] Willmott and Young, op. cit., pp. 167, 84.

[12] Ibid.; Adams, op. cit.; Albert K. Cohen and Harold M. Hodges, Jr., "Characteristics of the Lower-Blue-Collar-Class," *Social Problems*, 10 (Spring, 1963), 310.

[13] Young and Willmott, op. cit., p. 184.

especially males, would be least likely to utilize availability for frequent interaction.

Sibling Relations

The second relationship within the family of orientation is that between siblings. Hypothesis IV, concerning the subjective characteristics of adult sibling relations is that *affection for and idealization of one's sibling is likely to be greater if the sibling is middle class than if he or she is working class.*

Studies of siblings in the parental home have stressed rivalry, or companionship and identification, or both. Though infrequently investigated, relations between adult siblings have been characterized by the same attributes—rivalry and/or companionship.[14] One shape which sibling rivalry may take in adulthood is explicated by Form and Geschwender in their application of reference group theory to the study of job satisfaction. The more satisfied, they find, have a higher occupational status than their brothers, while the least satisfied are lower than their brothers in occupational status. Manual workers seem to use their brothers as a comparative reference point to aid them in interpreting the meaning of their own occupational position.[15]

Siblings are a durable and salient reference group, tending to be close in age and, unlike friends, being biological givens from birth.[16] Sibling relations extend into adulthood in the form of comparisons and/or identifications, influenced greatly, we suggest, by the middle-class orientation of American society. The implications of Hypothesis IV are that white-collar siblings, perceiving each other as successful, are more likely to idealize or identify with each other in adulthood than are blue-collar siblings. Occupationally disparate siblings, i.e., one white collar and one blue collar, are characterized in many cases by a non-reciprocated identification and affection of the lower status sibling toward his higher status brother or sister. That the relative occupational positions of the siblings are more crucial to the relationship than is their individual occupational mobility or stability has been supported by other studies.[17]

The general hypothesis regarding frequency of interaction between siblings is similar to that for parents.

[14] The neglect of the study of sibling relations is discussed in Donald P. Irish, "Sibling Interaction: A Neglected Aspect in Family Life Research," *Social Forces*, 42 (March, 1964), 279–288. Sources on adult sibling relations include: Phillip Garigue, "French Canadian Kinship and Urban Life," *American Anthropologist*, 58 (December, 1956), 1092; Elaine Cumming and David M. Schneider, "Sibling Solidarity: A Property of American Kinship," *American Anthropologist*, 63 (June, 1961), 498–507; William H. Form and James A. Geschwender, "Social Reference Basis of Job Satisfaction: The Case of Manual Workers," *American Sociological Review*, 27 (April, 1962), 232, 236.

[15] Form and Geschwender, loc. cit.

[16] Bott, op. cit., p. 155, notes that because kin are permanent, they are used as a basis for comparison and contrast with oneself.

[17] E. E. LeMasters, "Social Class Mobility and Family Integration," *Marriage and Family Living*, 16 (August, 1954), 229; Carson McGuire, "Conforming, Mobile, and Divergent Families," *Marriage and Family Living*, 14 (May, 1952), 110.

Hypothesis V: *Siblings who are both middle class are least likely to live near each other and to interact frequently, two working-class siblings are most likely to do so and the occupationally disparate should comprise a middle category.*

Once again, however, if the subjective hypothesis is related to interaction, the mutually blue-collar siblings should be found least likely to utilize availability, the mutually white-collar siblings most likely, and the occupationally disparate in between. The subjective factors and proximity may neutralize each other sufficiently to result in no significant differences in interaction frequency between the sex-stratum categories of siblings.

SAMPLE AND METHODOLOGY

During 1963 and 1964, interviews were administered to 799 residents of Greensboro, North Carolina, a growing, industrializing city of 150,000. A random block sampling procedure was used, with the following restrictions: all respondents are white, married, have been married only once and for twenty years or less. Limiting the investigation to young-to-middle-aged marrieds guarantees that a substantial proportion of the respondents' parents are still living while few of their own children have left home.

The sample includes 467 females and 332 males. The median age of husbands is 34.5 years, of wives 32.3 years, and the median length of marriage is ten years and ten months. According to the husband's occupation, 62 percent of the respondents are white collar and 38 percent are blue collar.[18]

The basic white-collar/blue-collar occupational dichotomy is employed in analysis of the relation between occupational status and kinship relations. Upwardly mobile are defined as those whose fathers are or were employed in a blue-collar occupation, but who are themselves, or whose husbands are, engaged in white-collar work. Within our sample are 93 upwardly mobile males and 115 females, and 26 downwardly mobile males and 38 females. Also included are 111 stable white-collar males and 160 females, and 86 stable blue-collar males and 139 females. Thirty-one respondents are either students or persons who inadequately described their own or their fathers' occupation, thus making determination of generational mobility or stability impossible.

Kin Categories

Both parents of 444 respondents are living and living together, and 697 have at least one living sibling. To maximize knowledge of siblings while holding constant neither objective nor subjective attributes, the respondents were questioned in detail about the sibling closest to them in age. In this manner 170 brother combinations were obtained, these males describing rela-

[18] The percentages of white- and blue-collar respondents differ by six from the occupational distribution for the white male population of Greensboro, which is 56 percent white collar and 44 percent blue collar. Much of the remaining six percent divergence is accounted for by the restriction of the sample to those married only once, since family breakup is more likely in the lower strata.

tions with their age-near brother. Another 324 cross-sex relationships were included, either a male discussing his sister or a female her brother. Finally, 203 relationships between sisters were included, female respondents discussing their age-near sisters. Of these sibling pairs, 76 percent are less than five years apart in age.

Dependent Variables

The analysis utilizes measures of affectional closeness, idealization or identification and frequency of interaction with parents and the age-near sibling. Affectional closeness, the first of two *subjective* factors, is ascertained by answers to the question: "How close would you say you feel to your . . . ?" The responses "quite close" and "extremely close" indicate strong feelings of positive affect. The other answers, "fairly close," "somewhat close," and "not too close," express a weaker affectional bond. Idealization or identification, the second subjective variable, is determined by answers to the following question: "Would you like to be the kind of person your . . . is?" The responses "yes, completely," and "in most ways," signify substantial idealization or identification. The answers "in some ways," "in just a few ways," and "not at all," indicate moderate-to-weak identification with the relative.

To avoid estimation, the *objective* factor of interaction frequency is based upon the actual number of times the respondent reports having seen a particular relative. The interview question is stated thus: "In the past two years (or since you moved here if less) how many times have you seen your . . . ?" The responses are then combined into "monthly or more," "more than yearly but not monthly," and "yearly or less."

RESULTS

Relations with Parents

Hypotheses I and II are, briefly, that subjective closeness to one's father in adulthood is predicated to a considerable degree upon the father's holding a middle-class position, while closeness to the mother is based more upon *one's own* achievement or maintenance of a middle-class position. Looking first at identification with one's father, Table 1 manifests significant differences as hypothesized between the two occupationally stable categories. In addition upwardly mobile females are significantly different from stable white-collar females in this regard. Downwardly mobile females also follow the hypothesized pattern somewhat but are not significantly different from those females with a blue-collar father in idealization of him.

A major divergence from Hypothesis I involves upwardly mobile males and their fathers. Affectionally, they are between the two occupationally stable categories, and in identification they approximate closely the stable middle-class males. Thus, upwardly mobile males are subjectively closer to their fathers than hypothesized, while the relations of a downwardly mobile of both sexes to their fathers are not definitive due to small numbers and non-significant statistical differences.

TABLE 1 Percent Expressing Affectional Closeness to and Idealization of Each Parent, by Sex, Occupational Stratum, and Mobility of the Young Adult (N = 444)

Sex, Occupational Stratum, and Mobility	Number of Respondents	Relations with Father		Relations with Mother	
		Affectionally Close	High in Idealization	Affectionally Close	High in Idealization
White-collar males					
Upward	(52)	54	52	60	42
Stable	(66)	65	53	62	41
Blue-collar males					
Stable	(53)	42	11	57	32
Downward	(10)	50	50	40	20
White-collar females					
Upward	(72)	58	36	83	63
Stable	(90)	71	53	83	52
Blue-collar females					
Stable	(72)	61	36	72	60
Downward	(19)	68	42	68	53

Note: Significant differences are based upon difference of proportions (Z) test: (1) Idealization of father, blue-collar males vs. other male categories, $P < .01$. (2) Affection for father, stable white-collar males vs. stable blue-collar males, $P < .01$. (3) Idealization of father, stable white-collar females vs. upwardly-mobile and stable blue-collar females, $P < .05$. (4) Stable blue-collar males, idealization of mother vs. father, $P < .05$. (5) Females with blue-collar parents, idealization of mother vs. father, $P < .01$. (6) Upwardly-mobile females, affection for mother vs. father, $P < .01$.

Percentage comparisons between the sex and stratum-mobility categories of young males in affection for and idealization of their mothers—the focus of Hypothesis II—are in the hypothesized direction, as are affectional relations between females and their mothers. However, the differences are not statistically significant. Furthermore, idealization of the mother is, somewhat surprisingly, more likely among the stable blue-collar females than among the stable white-collar. Thus, Hypothesis II is only slightly supported by the data of Table 1.

Further inspection of the Table, however, indicates that additional insight into subjective relations with parents may be gained by comparing relations with the two parents. There is significantly greater likelihood of idealization of the mother than of the father when the father is working-class, except among the upwardly mobile males. A comparison of upwardly mobile males and females in relations with parents yields several inferences regarding the socialization process. Working-class fathers often seem to be active in the socialization of upwardly mobile sons so that either or both parents influence their aspirations and later achievement. This assertion, though tentative, is supported both by the respondents' numerous retrospective comments concerning parental roles in their lives and by other research.[19] Another reasonable inference is that upwardly mobile daughters perceive their mothers as "prime movers" in their achievement, through marriage, of middle-class status. Of course, such inferences demand data beyond those provided in the present paper.

Not only is the father's working-class position accompanied by less

[19] Kahl, op. cit.; Ellis and Lane, op. cit.

likelihood of identification with him than with the mother, but, conversely, the only categories in which closer affectional ties are expressed with the father than with the mother are males with middle-class fathers. This may indicate the salience to these males of their fathers as role models.

TABLE 2 Percent Frequency of Interaction with Parents, and Physical Proximity, by Sex, Occupational Stratum, and Mobility of the Young Adults (N = 444)

Sex, Occupational Stratum, and Mobility	Number of Respondents	Respondents with Parents Living within 100 Miles	Frequency of Interaction with Parents			
			Monthly or More	*Several Times Yearly*	*Yearly or Less*	*Total*
White-collar males						
Upward	(52)	67	71	23	6	100
Stable	(66)	47	56	30	14	100
Blue-collar males						
Stable	(53)	68	74	15	11	100
Downward	(10)	90	90	10	. .	100
White-collar females						
Upward	(72)	57	61	25	14	100
Stable	(90)	52	56	39	6	101
Blue-collar females						
Stable	(72)	68	71	15	14	100
Downward	(19)	68	53	26	21	100

Note: Percentages differing from 100 are due to rounding. Significant differences based upon Z test are. (1) *respondents with parents living within 100 miles,* upwardly-mobile males vs. stable white-collar males and stable white-collar females vs. stable blue-collar females, $P < .05$; (2) *interacting monthly or more with parents,* the same two comparisons, $P < .05$.

Table 2 presents frequency of interaction between young Greensboro adults and their parents, and a comparison between residential proximity and frequent interaction. Hypothesis III, that offspring-parent interaction is most frequent among the stable working classes, least frequent among the stable middle classes, with the mobile comprising a middle category, is not borne out by Table 2. While the stable white- and blue-collar groups of each sex are significantly different in proximity and monthly interaction, the upwardly mobile males resemble the stable blue collar and the upwardly mobile females the stable white collar.[20] Apparently, upward mobile males tend to settle near their parents, whereas females migrate farther from home in the process of "marrying up." Though discussion of the small numbers of downwardly mobile is tentative, a comparison of the first two columns shows that downwardly mobile females are the only category with a lower percentage interacting monthly than living within 100 miles. The data do not appear to indicate that subjective differences in relations with parents are manifested in objective differences between physical proximity and interaction frequency.

[20] Although it should be obvious, let us note that studies of mobility and kinship may show weakening or no weakening effects, in terms of interaction, which are simply dependent upon whether the upwardly mobile are compared with others of their parents' stratum or with stable members of their own current stratum. The tendency has been to compare them with stable members of the parents' generation, with the result that upward mobility has been affirmed to have a weakening effect upon kin interaction.

In summary, a provisional finding is that downward mobility has an adverse effect upon the *subjective* relations between a young male and his parents, and upon *objective* relations between an adult daughter and her parents. That is, although residential proximity results in extremely frequent interaction between the downwardly mobile male and his parents, there are signs of subjective distance between the male and his mother. Downwardly mobile females, on the other hand, manifest less frequent interaction with their parents than residential distance would seem to suggest. Furthermore, the 355 respondents omitted from the foregoing analysis furnish negative evidence of the importance of parents in maintaining the social status of their offspring. Fifty-five percent of the downwardly mobile were excluded precisely because their parents are no longer living together; they are divorced or separated, or one or both are deceased. In no other sex and stratum-mobility category does the percentage approach fifty. Absence of one or both middle-class parents seems to make downward mobility a greater possibility.

The experience of upward mobility tends to be associated with a close relationship between both sexes and the mother, and often with a close relationship between a son and his father. Both objectively and subjectively, the upwardly mobile as a whole comprise a category between the non-mobile working and middle classes with respect to parents though much closer to the stable middle classes.[21]

Sibling Relations

Three sibling categories—brothers, cross-sex, and sisters—and four comparative occupational categories—both white collar, both blue collar, a white-collar respondent with a blue-collar sibling, and a blue-collar respondent with a white-collar sibling—result in a twelve-fold division of sibling dyads. Hypothesis IV is that subjective relations with a sibling are more likely to be close if the *sibling* is middle class than if he or she is working class. The pattern of percentage differences in Table 3, many of which are significant, strongly supports the Hypothesis. In four of six categories in which the sibling is white collar, 30 percent or more of the respondents idealize the sibling. In none of the six categories in which the sibling is blue collar is the percentage idealizing the sibling higher than 25. Likewise, in five of six categories in which the sibling is white collar, 47 percent or more of the respondents are affectionally close to the sibling. In only one of the other six categories is the percentage affectionally close to the sibling higher than 40.

While blue-collar cross-sex and sister respondents are likely to identify with a higher status sibling, the blue-collar males—contrary to the hypothesis—are less likely than any other category to identify with a white-collar brother. It seems probable that the blue-collar brother has been invidiously

[21] As we indicated in footnote 8 above, the results concerning the upwardly mobile are not accounted for by our methodology, i.e., the dividing of the sample into white-collar and blue-collar respondents. Those who have moved the greatest distance—status-wise—are the most likely to resemble the stable middle class in subjective response to their parents. Distance of movement does not explain the findings of the present study regarding the upwardly mobile.

TABLE 3   Percent Expressing Affectional Closeness to and Idealization of the Age-Near Sibling, by Sex and Occupational Stratum of Siblings (N = 655)

Sex and Occupational Stratum of Siblings	Number of Respondents	Affectionally Close to Sibling	High in Idealization of Sibling
White-collar male with white-collar brother	(72)	47	22
White-collar male with blue-collar brother	(21)	24	14
Blue-collar male with white-collar brother	(23)	26	9
Blue-collar male with blue-collar brother	(41)	37	17
White-collar respondent with white-collar cross-sex sibling	(132)	54	30
White-collar respondent with blue-collar cross-sex sibling	(57)	30	21
Blue-collar respondent with white-collar cross-sex sibling	(34)	53	41
Blue-collar respondent with blue-collar cross-sex sibling	(83)	40	25
White-collar female with white-collar sister	(90)	72	30
White-collar female with blue-collar sister	(25)	36	16
Blue-collar female with white-collar sister	(31)	61	48
Blue-collar female with blue-collar sister	(46)	50	20

Note: Significant differences based upon Z test are: (1) *affectionally close to sibling,* white-collar male with white-collar brother vs. male with brother of opposite stratum, $P < .05$; white-collar respondent with white-collar cross-sex sibling and blue-collar respondent with white-collar cross-sex sibling vs. white-collar respondent with blue-collar cross-sex sibling, $P < .01$; white-collar female with white-collar sister vs. white-collar female with blue-collar sister, $P < .01$; blue-collar female with white-collar sister vs. white-collar female with blue-collar sister, $P < .05$. (2) *idealization of sibling,* blue-collar respondent with white-collar cross-sex sibling vs. white-collar respondent with blue-collar cross-sex sibling and blue-collar female with white-collar sister vs. white-collar female with blue-collar sister, $P < .05$.

compared by himself and others with his more "successful" brother. For him the comparison produces not only dissatisfaction with his work situation, as Form and Geschwender observed, but a disidentification and affectional estrangement from the brother. The white-collar brother, receiving society's greater rewards and very likely the acclaim of his family as well, seems to find little basis upon which to identify with his lower status brother. He, too, manifests non-affection.

Identification and affection between occupationally disparate sisters and cross-sex siblings may be inferentially interpreted within the same familial framework. The closeness of the lower status to the higher status sibling may be seen as an indirect identification with a family success. More specifically, the blue-collar wife, while not necessarily seeking to deprecate her own husband, is proud of the achievement of her brother or sister who has "done so well," and she may demonstrate this by affectional closeness to and identification with the higher status sibling. The same holds for the working-class male whose brother-in-law is middle class. Although animosity toward the brother-in-law was often expressed in the interviews, this male is able to identify with success indirectly by a close relationship with his sister.

No such identification, and little likelihood of a strong affectional tie, appears in the relations of higher status cross-sex and sisters with their lower status siblings. Rather, a certain disdain is often expressed for the brother or sister who hasn't achieved, or who "could have done better." Based upon a sub-sample of 191 respondents, this rather lengthy interpretation of occupational disparity between siblings is supported both by significant percentage differences and by the fact that it contrasts with the general tendency for middle-class persons to express closer relationships with kin than working-class persons.

Because the nature of the explanation is inferential, it may be well to illustrate with comments drawn from several interviews. One young middle-class female with a working-class sister refers to the difference between herself and her brother-in-law: "He's got old-fashioned ideas. We get along, but I just have my own ideas about things." The theme of divergent ideas is echoed by another middle-class female speaking of a blue-collar brother: "We never did have much in common. Even now when we meet at our parents' home we don't spend much time together." The feeling of what one interviewer termed "contempt" in describing a middle-class respondent's attitude

TABLE 4 Percent Frequency of Interaction with the Age-Near Sibling, and Physical Proximity, by Sex and Occupational Stratum of the Two Siblings (N = 655)

Sex and Occupational Stratum of Siblings	Number of Respondents	Respondents With Sibling Living Within 100 Miles	Frequency of Interaction			
			Monthly or More	Several Times Yearly	Yearly or Less	Total
White-collar male with white-collar brother	(72)	43	43	35	22	100
Male with brother of opposite stratum[a]	(44)	57	46	23	32	101
Blue-collar male with blue-collar brother	(41)	76	46	29	24	99
White-collar respondent with white-collar cross-sex sibling	(132)	42	32	44	24	100
Respondent with cross-sex sibling of opposite stratum[a]	(91)	48	43	29	29	101
Blue-collar respondent with blue-collar cross-sex sibling	(83)	55	52	22	27	101
White-collar female with white-collar sister	(90)	46	34	48	18	100
Female with sister of opposite stratum[a]	(56)	57	54	23	23	100
Blue-collar female with blue-collar sister	(46)	67	48	26	26	100

[a]These are the siblings described in the text as occupationally disparate.
Note: Significant differences based upon Z test are: (1) *respondents with sibling living within 100 miles,* blue-collar brothers vs. white-collar brothers, P < .01; blue-collar brothers vs. males with brother of opposite stratum and males with brother of opposite stratum vs. white-collar brothers, P < .05; white-collar sisters vs. blue-collar sisters, P < .05. (2) *interacting monthly or more with sibling,* white-collar cross-sex sisters vs. blue-collar cross-sex sisters and white-collar sisters vs. females with sister of opposite stratum, P < .05.

toward her blue-collar kin is expressed by a white-collar male with a blue-collar sister: "She and I wanted to better ourselves, but then she married Ben. I think she could have done better. . . . He's a nice guy, though." The final phrase seems to indicate that "niceness" is not enough to compensate for failure to achieve in middle-class terms. Unusual insight into the non-reciprocal nature of the affectional tie between occupationally disparate sisters is found in this statement by a young middle-class female: "Her husband hasn't been what a husband should be. . . . I'm not close to her, but if you asked her she'd say I'm her favorite sister."

The admiration of one young blue-collar female for a white-collar brother is apparent in this comment: "I respect him; he's such a wonderful person. . . . He has always been the kind of person I wish I could be." A working-class female remarks: "Fred (her brother-in-law) is a good person, a good provider; he's good to his family and gives them a lovely home." She comments further: "My sister and I have had our troubles, but now we've got children of the same age." Value divergence and disdain, or respect and identification, are frequent subjective differences in the relations between occupationally disparate siblings.

Unlike the subjective aspects of a social relationship, the objective tabulating of interaction frequency is by nature reciprocal. Therefore, in considering Hypothesis V the occupationally disparate categories are combined according to the sexes of the two siblings. As for proximity, the hypothesis that mutually middle-class siblings are least likely to live near each other and mutually working-class are most likely to is borne out in all three sex categories (see Table 4). However, differential utilization of opportunity or availability virtually neutralizes distance variations between brothers, though not between cross-sex siblings and sisters. Blue-collar brothers and sisters simply do not take advantage of their greater availability, though absolute frequency is modally least between mutually middle-class sisters and cross-sex siblings.

The compartive and identificational aspects of sibling relations have been apparent in the subjective findings. However, the objective or interactional results give little indication that companionship is a dominant theme in adult sibling relations. A comparison of Tables 2 and 4 shows that over 60 percent of the young adults see their parents monthly or more, but the percentage for age-near siblings is just above 40. Even when the respondents are questioned about frequency of interaction with *any* sibling, the percentage in touch monthly is 47—considerably lower than that with parents.

Mobility or Disparity in Sibling Relations: A Justification

The justification for discussing the occupational disparity or similarity of siblings apart from the parents' occupational position has not yet been made clear. Is there not a substantial difference, it might be asked, between the relations of two white-collar siblings when their parents are middle-class and when the two siblings have been upwardly mobile?

Table 5 presents an illustrative comparison of stable white-collar and mutually upwardly mobile adults in affection for their sibling. Percentage differences dependent upon parental background, i.e., comparing the stable white collar with the upwardly mobile in relations with a sibling of the same

TABLE 5   Percent Expressing Affectional Closeness to White-Collar and Blue-Collar Siblings, for Upwardly-Mobile and Stable White-Collar Males and Females (N = 204)

Respondent's Sex, Occupational Stratum, and Mobility, and Stratum of Sibling	Affectionally Close to Brother		Affectionally Close to Sister	
	Number	*Percent*	*Number*	*Percent*
White-collar, upwardly-mobile males				
White-collar sibling	(24)	54	(22)	59
Blue-collar sibling	(18)	22	(18)	28
White-collar, stable males				
White-collar sibling	(48)	44	(35)	60
Blue-collar sibling	(3)[a]	33	(3)[a]	0
White-collar, upwardly-mobile females				
White-collar sibling	(29)	48	(30)	63
Blue-collar sibling	(21)	38	(22)	36
White-collar, stable females				
White-collar sibling	(46)	50	(60)	77
Blue-collar sibling	(15)	27	(3)[a]	33

[a]Percentages should not be figured on N's as small as these; this was done to demonstrate the basic pattern of comparisons.

Note: There are no significant differences (.05) based on divergent family background in relations with a sibling of the same sex and stratum, i.e., comparing rows one and three, two and four, five and seven, and six and eight. However, when comparisons are based upon the occupational strata of the two siblings, e.g., rows one and two, four or five percentage comparisons not involving a small N are significant at the .05 level or beyond.

status, are in no case significant. However, in four of five comparisons, controlling for family background but varying the statuses of the siblings, P < .05.[22] Although not presented in the table, similar results occur when the stable working class and downwardly mobile are compared, as well as when respondents are compared in identification with their siblings. In short, differences in subjective relations are primarily dependent upon the present occupational statuses of the siblings, not upon their family background.

DISCUSSION

Interaction Frequency as an Indicator of Kin Involvement

The value of simple interaction frequency in demonstrating the importance of parents and siblings in the life of the young adult is evident. Fifty-one percent of the *total* sample, not just those with both parents alive, interact monthly or more with a living parent or parents. Only 41 percent see *any* sibling that often. Interaction frequency also reflects, as expected, differential proximity by occupational status. However, the intricate and sometimes dramatic subjective differences in relations with parents or siblings are not manifested by this measure of involvement. The principal reasons differ for parents and siblings.

First, variations in affectional and identificational relationships with parents are not represented by differing utilization of availability due to

[22] Three categories have numbers too small to figure percentages, much less to compute a difference of proportions test of significance.

another subjective variable: kin *obligation.* Eighty-five percent of the respondents with at least one living parent insist that obligation is one motive, if not *the* motive, for keeping in touch. This author would contend that the other 15 percent, often daughters claiming enjoyment as their sole motive, also harbor a latent sense of obligation which would prevail even if their enjoyment were to diminish. The strength of obligation is seen in the fact that the interactional differences appearing in Table 2 due to differential proximity are offset by utilization of communication. How completely communication by letter and long distance telephone compensate for residential separation is apparent in that all but 39 respondents, i.e., 93 percent of those with a living parent are in some form of contact with their parent(s) at least monthly. Middle-class adults, be they upwardly mobile or stable, attempt to neutralize lack of proximity by using the means of contact at their disposal. Thus, contact obligation is an intervening variable, mitigating the effects of subjective differences in relations with parents before they are manifested in contact frequency.

Said a middle-class housewife, quoted earlier, about her blue-collar brother: "Even now when we meet at our parents' home we don't spend much time together." This comment introduces the factors which, along with moderate obligation, explain the insignificant differences in interaction with siblings despite substantial subjective variation. These related factors are *combination opportunities* and *circumstances.* The mother or "Mum," Young and Willmott state, is the major link between siblings; much of their interaction takes place at her home.[23] The parental home is often a rendezvous for offspring as well as other kin. In tabulating interaction frequency, a contact is a contact, whether or not the siblings "spend much time together." Thus, when the distance separating siblings is controlled, the data indicate that their interaction is much more frequent if one sibling lives near the parents, i.e., when there is a "combination opportunity." Furthermore, many sibling contacts are initiated by neither party but occur on ritual occasions such as holidays and birthdays, or in emergencies, such as sickness or death. Simple enumeration of these contacts does not specify the quality of the interaction.

Occupational Position, Mobility, and Kinship

The dominant theme pervading this investigation is that the *current* occupational achievements or non-achievements of two kin are more closely associated with present relationships than is their individual mobility or stability. This principle and the unmistakable influence of economic-occupational values upon the kin of orientation are best observed when these kin are considered as a network. Cleavages and solidarities occur which are most readily accountable in such terms. This is demonstrated first by means of the downwardly mobile (see Figure 1, diagram 1). Mutually downwardly mobile siblings are affectionally close while manifesting affectional distance from their parents, particularly their mothers. They are apparently drawn together by their mutual plight, while blaming their parents, or mothers, for their

[23] Young and Willmott, op. cit., p. 78.

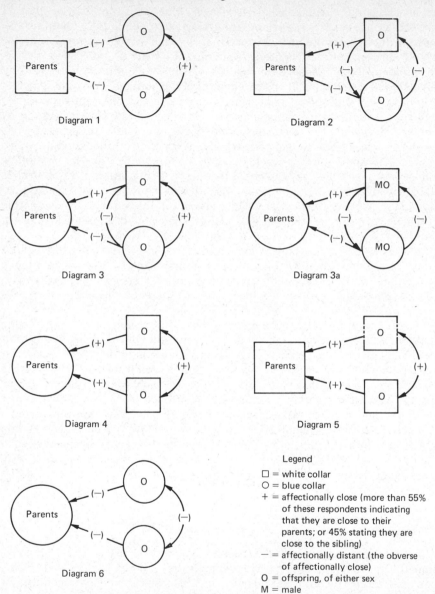

Diagram 1

Diagram 2

Diagram 3

Diagram 3a

Diagram 4

Diagram 5

Diagram 6

Legend

☐ = white collar
○ = blue collar
+ = affectionally close (more than 55% of these respondents indicating that they are close to their parents; or 45% stating they are close to the sibling)
− = affectionally distant (the obverse of affectionally close)
O = offspring, of either sex
M = male

Figure 1 Affectional Relations with the Kin of Orientation, According to Comparative Occupational Positions

"failure." When only one of the children is downwardly mobile (diagram 2), he or she is affectionally distant from parents and the sibling. Though the numbers are small, these young adults appear most likely to have attenuated kin networks, including shallow relationships with their kin of orientation.

The stable blue-collar adult whose sibling is upwardly mobile tends to identify with the sibling's achievement but may blame his parents for the fact that he was not also mobile (diagram 3). However, occupational salience and open competition prevent even such one-way identification and affection between occupationally disparate brothers (diagram 3a).

The upwardly mobile devise different solutions to the problem of integration with the kin of orientation. Mutually upwardly mobile siblings are relatively close to each other in their mutual achievement and respond positively to their parents' efforts on their behalf (diagram 4). The upward mobility of one offspring (diagram 3) results in the young adult's tending to be affectionally close to his parents but feeling little emotional attachment to his lower status sibling. Diagrams 5 and 6 indicate the typical mutual affectional responses of stable white-collar and blue-collar kin of orientation, respectively.[24]

There are variations according to the sex of the individual, especially in the role convergence and close relation of working-class daughters and their working-class mothers. However, these diagrams reveal and summarize the effect of economic-occupational values upon kin solidarity in adulthood, which characteristically override kin values in altering subjective relationships. Nevertheless, the particularistic obligation to and circumstantial contact with these immediate kin causes the quantity of contact to be maintained despite variations in both its quality and types.

CONCLUSION

We have sought to clear up some of the confusion which has surrounded the study of occupational position, mobility, and kinship in the urban United States. Not only have previous generalizations been too broad when they have ignored sex differences and degrees of relationship, but they have failed to delineate the importance of our society's middle-class values in influencing relations between the kin of orientation. Rather than individual occupational mobility or stability, primary factors include occupational and migratory histories and the resultant residential distances from specific kin, objective-subjective differences in kin relationships, the roles of parents in their children's achievement or non-achievement, and the present status of one's sibling in comparison to one's own status.

A key conclusion is that those significant others who embody, or who have led *us* to embody, the dominant societal definitions of success are more likely to be considered worthy of our affectional response. However, not all of our results are accountable in terms of economic-achievement values and their impingement upon social relations. The affectional closeness of mutually downwardly mobile siblings and the affectional distance of occupationally disparate brothers fall outside the bounds of our basic explanatory device.

[24] Komarovsky, op. cit., p. 252, refers to the tendency for less-educated husbands to be more reserved in emotional expression. In the light of our findings, it may be that the impinging of middle-class values upon the subjective aspects of kinship, particularly among males, causes these ties to be weaker among the less "successful." This may have been mistaken for a basic interpersonal reserve in response to questionnaire and interview questions. This merits further attention.

It is here that the coalition theories of Simmel, Mills, Caplow and others might be of some usefulness. Theodore Caplow, for example, finds that "sibling coalitions appear to be based on similarity of sex, age, and interest rather than on the balance of strength in the triad."[25] This and other such concepts, while beyond the scope of the present paper, would be worth pursuing in attempting to add to our understanding of the subjective findings.

In addition, two general conclusions of considerable significance have emerged in the course of the investigation. We have noted (1) that generational kin ties tend to be stronger, both objectively and subjectively, than are lateral ties, at least among young adults. Obligation and mutual concern apparently outweigh the age similarity of siblings in determining comparative involvement with parents and siblings.[26] Also obvious is (2) the fact that the social network is not spatially bound in this day of communications and high-speed transportation. The same technology which is responsible for widespread residential movement has produced the means for maintaining contact despite separation, with the result that contact with living parents is almost uniformly frequent.

The outlines of occupational position, mobility, and their relation to the kin of orientation are distinct; the inferences are in many cases tentative. Further research, particularly on downward mobility and on adult perceptions of parental roles in their socialization, is very much needed.

[25] Theodore Caplow, "Further Development of a Theory of Coalitions in the Triad," *American Journal of Sociology*, 64 (March, 1959), 493.
[26] On positive concern as a characteristic of the social relationship, see Bert N. Adams, "Interaction Theory and the Social Network," *Sociometry*, 30 (March, 1967), 64–78.

|X| Population Pressure and the Family

Introduction to Section X

One of the striking changes in the 1960s and 1970s has been the heightened public awareness of the potentially disastrous impact of the unintended consequences of human behavior. Pollution of air, land, and water has resulted from individuals and corporations satisfying their own needs without full awareness of or concern about the effect on the environment. Population growth is another good illustration of individual married couples satisfying their own felt needs, usually without awareness of any societal consequences in terms of overpopulation. Of course, overpopulation and pollution of the environment are related phenomena. As the number of people increases, so does the probability of environmental pollution. In the 1970s we are apparently starting to learn how to organize our technologies and bureaucracies so as to contain these problems.

The readings in this section offer some insight into the question of overpopulation. The 1967 article by Kingsley Davis (30) created a storm of controversy as soon as it was published. Davis' argument asserts that there is a definite limit to the effectiveness of population control by means of birth control devices. The limit he cites is that most couples around the world want three children and thus, even with full usage of birth control, they would have too many children in terms of controlling population growth. He proposes other possible avenues that would lessen the desire for children, such as de-emphasis of the mother role. The interested reader will note that Alice Rossi (in Sections VII and XII) also makes proposals concerning changing the mother role in America. Elsewhere Davis and Judith Blake[1] present a comprehensive statement of how one can intervene to affect population growth.

[1] Davis, K., and Blake, J., "Social Structure and Fertility: An Analytic Framework." *Economic Development and Cultural Change* 4 (April, 1956), 211–235.

Another major aspect of population growth concerns the ways in which marital communication patterns influence the number of children in a family. Reuben Hill and his colleagues did research in Puerto Rico that focused on the ways in which husband-and-wife communication functioned as an important variable in the use and effectiveness of contraception (31). The article points out the error of believing that contraceptive knowledge insures contraceptive usage.

It is hoped that after reading these articles the student will have a firmer grasp on the prospects and problems involved in understanding population control and the important roles that courtship, marital, and family institutions play in the overall process.

30 | *Population Policy: Will Current Programs Succeed?*

KINGSLEY DAVIS

Throughout history the growth of population has been identified with prosperity and strength. If today an increasing number of nations are seeking to curb rapid population growth by reducing their birth rates, they must be driven to do so by an urgent crisis. My purpose here is not to discuss the crisis itself but rather to assess the present and prospective measures used to meet it. Most observers are suprised by the swiftness with which concern over the population problem has turned from intellectual analysis and debate to policy and action. Such action is a welcome relief from the long opposition, or timidity, which seemed to block forever any governmental attempt to restrain population growth, but relief that "at last something is being done" is no guarantee that what is being done is adequate. On the face of it, one could hardly expect such a fundamental reorientation to be quickly and successfully implemented. I therefore propose to review the nature and (as I see them) limitations of the present policies and to suggest lines of possible improvement.

THE NATURE OF CURRENT POLICIES

With more than 30 nations now trying or planning to reduce population growth and with numerous private and international organizations helping, the degree of unanimity as to the kind of measures needed is impressive. The consensus can be summed up in the phrase "family planning." President Johnson declared in 1965 that the United States will "assist family planning programs in nations which request such help." The Prime Minister of India said a year later, "We must press forward with family planning. This is a programme of the highest importance." The Republic of Singapore created in 1966 the Singapore Family Planning and Population Board "to initiate and undertake population control programmes" (*1*).

As is well known, "family planning" is a euphemism for contraception. The family-planning approach to population limitation, therefore, concentrates on providing new and efficient contraceptives on a national basis through mass programs under public health auspices. The nature of these programs is shown by the following enthusiastic report from the Population Council (*2*):

The author is professor of sociology and director of International Population and Urban Research, University of California, Berkeley. This article is abridged from a paper presented at the annual meeting of the National Research Council, 14 March 1967.

451

No single year has seen so many forward steps in population control as 1965. Effective national programs have at last emerged, international organizations have decided to become engaged, a new contraceptive has proved its value in mass application, . . . and surveys have confirmed a popular desire for family limitation. . .

An accounting of notable events must begin with Korea and Taiwan . . . Taiwan's program is not yet two years old, and already it has inserted one IUD [intrauterine device] for every 4-6 target women (those who are not pregnant, lactating, already sterile, already using contraceptives effectively, or desirous of more children). Korea has done almost as well . . . has put 2,200 full-time workers into the field, . . . has reached operational levels for a network of IUD quotas, supply lines, local manufacture of contraceptives, training of hundreds of M.D.'s and nurses, and mass propaganda . . .

Here one can see the implication that "population control" is being achieved through the dissemination of new contraceptives, and the fact that the "target women" exclude those who want more children. One can also note the technological emphasis and the medical orientation.

What is wrong with such programs? The answer is, "Nothing at all, if they work." Whether or not they work depends on what they are expected to do as well as on how they try to do it. Let us discuss the goal first, then the means.

GOALS

Curiously, it is hard to find in the population-policy movement any explicit discussion of long-range goals. By implication the policies seem to promise a great deal. This is shown by the use of expressions like *population control* and *population planning* (as in the passages quoted above). It is also shown by the characteristic style of reasoning. Expositions of current policy usually start off by lamenting the speed and the consequences of runaway population growth. This growth, it is then stated, must be curbed—by pursuing a vigorous family-planning program. That family planning can solve the problem of population growth seems to be taken as self-evident.

For instance, the much-heralded statement by 12 heads of state, issued by Secretary-General U Thant on 10 December 1966 (a statement initiated by John D. Rockefeller III, Chairman of the Board of the Population Council), devotes half its space to discussing the harmfulness of population growth and the other half to recommending family planning (3). A more succinct example of the typical reasoning is given in the Provisional Scheme for a Nationwide Family Planning Programme in Ceylon (4):

The population of Ceylon is fast increasing. . . . [The] figures reveal that a serious situation will be created within a few years. In order to cope with it a Family Planning programme on a nationwide scale should be launched by the Government.

The promised goal—to limit population growth so as to solve population problems—is a large order. One would expect it to be carefully analyzed, but it is left imprecise and taken for granted, as is the way in which family planning will achieve it.

When the terms *population control* and *population planning* are used, as they frequently are, as synonyms for current family-planning programs, they are misleading. Technically, they would mean deliberate influence over all attributes of a population, including its age-sex structure, geographical distribution, racial composition, genetic quality, and total size. No government attempts such full control. By tacit understanding, current population policies are concerned with only the *growth* and *size* of populations. These attributes, however, result from the death rate and migration as well as from the birth rate; their control would require deliberate influence over the factors giving rise to all three determinants. Actually, current policies labeled population control do not deal with mortality and migration, but deal only with the birth input. This is why another term, *fertility control*, is frequently used to describe current policies. But, as I show below, family planning (and hence current policy) does not undertake to influence most of the determinants of human reproduction. Thus the programs should not be referred to as population control or planning, because they do not attempt to influence the factors responsible for the attributes of human populations, taken generally; nor should they be called fertility control, because they do not try to affect most of the determinants of reproductive performance.

The ambiguity does not stop here, however. When one speaks of controlling population size, any inquiring person naturally asks, What is "control"? Who is to control whom? Precisely what population size, or what rate of population growth, is to be achieved? Do the policies aim to produce a growth rate that is nil, one that is very slight, or one that is like that of the industrial nations? Unless such questions are dealt with and clarified, it is impossible to evaluate current population policies.

The actual programs seem to be aiming simply to achieve a reduction in the birth rate. Success is therefore interpreted as the accomplishment of such a reduction, on the assumption that the reduction will lessen population growth. In those rare cases where a specific demographic aim is stated, the goal is said to be a short-run decline within a given period. The Pakistan plan adopted in 1966 (*5*, p. 889) aims to reduce the birth rate from 50 to 40 per thousand by 1970; the Indian plan (*6*) aims to reduce the rate from 40 to 25 "as soon as possible"; and the Korean aim (*7*) is to cut population growth from 2.9 to 1.2 percent by 1980. A significant feature of such stated aims is the rapid population growth they would permit. Under conditions of modern mortality, a crude birth rate of 25 to 30 per thousand will represent such a multiplication of people as to make use of the term *population control* ironic. A rate of increase of 1.2 percent per year would allow South Korea's already dense population to double in less than 60 years.

One can of course defend the programs by saying that the present goals and measures are merely interim ones. A start must be made somewhere. But we do not find this answer in the population-policy literature. Such a defense, if convincing, would require a presentation of the *next* steps, and these are not considered. One suspects that the entire question of goals is instinctively left vague because thorough limitation of population growth would run counter to national and group aspirations. A consideration of hypothetical goals throws further light on the matter.

Industrialized Nations as the Model

Since current policies are confined to family planning, their maximum demographic effect would be to give the underdeveloped countries the same level of reproductive performance that the industrial nations now have. The latter, long oriented toward family planning, provide a good yardstick for determining what the availability of contraceptives can do to population growth. Indeed, they provide more than a yardstick; they are actually the model which inspired the present population policies.

What does this goal mean in practice? Among the advanced nations there is considerable diversity in the level of fertility (8). At one extreme are countries such as New Zealand, with an average gross reproduction rate (GRR) of 1.91 during the period 1960–64; at the other extreme are countries such as Hungary, with a rate of 0.91 during the same period. To a considerable extent, however, such divergencies are matters of timing. The birth rates of most industrial nations have shown, since about 1940, a wavelike movement, with no secular trend. The average level of reproduction during this long period has been high enough to give these countries, with their low mortality, an extremely rapid population growth. If this level is maintained, their population will double in just over 50 years—a rate higher than that of world population growth at any time prior to 1950, at which time the growth in numbers of human beings was already considered fantastic. The advanced nations are suffering acutely from the effects of rapid population growth in combination with the production of ever more goods per person (9). A rising share of their supposedly high per capita income, which itself draws increasingly upon the resources of the underdeveloped countries (who fall farther behind in relative economic position), is spent simply to meet the costs, and alleviate the nuisances, of the unrelenting production of more and more goods by more people. Such facts indicate that the industrial nations provide neither a suitable demographic model for the nonindustrial peoples to follow nor the leadership to plan and organize effective population-control policies for them.

Zero Population Growth as a Goal

Most discussions of the population crisis lead logically to zero population growth as the ultimate goal, because *any* growth rate, if continued, will eventually use up the earth. Yet hardly ever do arguments for population policy consider such a goal, and current policies do not dream of it. Why not? The answer is evidently that zero population growth is unacceptable to most nations and to most religious and ethnic communities. To argue for this goal would be to alienate possible support for action programs.

Goal Peculiarities Inherent in Family Planning

Turning to the actual measures taken, we see that the very use of family planning as the means for implementing population policy poses serious but unacknowledged limits on the intended reduction in fertility. The family-planning movement, clearly devoted to the improvement and dissemination of contraceptive devices, states again and again that its purpose is that of enabling couples to have the number of children they want. "The opportunity to decide the number and spacing of children is a basic human right," say the 12 heads of state in the United Nations declaration. The 1965 Turkish Law Concerning Population Planning declares (*10*):

Article 1. Population Planning means that individuals can have as many children as they wish, whenever they want to. This can be ensured through preventive measures taken against pregnancy. . . .

Logically, it does not make sense to use *family* planning to provide *national* population control or planning. The "planning" in family planning is that of each separate couple. The only control they exercise is control over the size of *their* family. Obviously, couples do not plan the size of the nation's population, any more than they plan the growth of the national income or the form of the highway network. There is no reason to expect that the millions of decisions about family size made by couples in their own interest will automatically control population for the benefit of society. On the contrary, there are good reasons to think they will not do so. At most, family planning can reduce reproduction to the extent that unwanted births exceed wanted births. In industrial countries the balance is often negative—that is, people have fewer children as a rule than they would like to have. In under-developed countries the reverse is normally true, but the elimination of unwanted births would still leave an extremely high rate of multiplication.

Actually, the family-planning movement does not pursue even the limited goals it professes. It does not fully empower couples to have only the number of offspring they want because it either condemns or disregards certain tabooed but nevertheless effective means to this goal. One of its tenets is that "there shall be freedom of choice of method so that individuals can choose in accordance with the dictates of their consciences" (*11*), but in practice this amounts to limiting the individual's choice, because the "conscience" dictating the method is usually not his but that of religious and governmental officials. Moreover, not every individual may choose: even the so-called recommended methods are ordinarily not offered to single women, or not all offered to women professing a given religious faith.

Thus, despite its emphasis on technology, current policy does not utilize all available means of contraception, much less all birth-control measures. The Indian government wasted valuable years in the early stages of its population-control program by experimenting exclusively with the "rhythm" method, long after this technique had been demonstrated to be one of the least effective. A greater limitation on means is the exclusive emphasis on contraception itself. Induced abortion, for example, is one of the surest means of controlling reproduction, and one that has been proved capable of reducing birth rates rapidly. It seems peculiarly suited to the threshold stage of a population-control program—the stage when new conditions of life first make large families disadvantageous. It was the principal factor in the halving of the Japanese birth rate, a major factor in the declines in birth rate of East-European satellite countries after legalization of abortions in the early 1950's, and an important factor in the reduction of fertility in industrializing nations from 1870 to the 1930's (*12*). Today, according to *Studies in Family Planning* (*13*), "abortion is probably the foremost method of birth control throughout Latin America." Yet this method is rejected in nearly all national and inter-national population-control programs. American foreign aid is used to help *stop* abortion (*14*). The United Nations excludes abortion from family planning, and in fact justifies the latter by presenting it as a means of combating abortion (*15*). Studies of abortion are being made in Latin America under the presumed auspices of population-control groups, not with the intention of legalizing it and thus making it safe, cheap, available, and hence more effective for population control, but with the avowed purpose of reducing it (*16*).

Although few would prefer abortion to efficient contraception (other things being equal), the fact is that both permit a woman to control the size of her family. The main drawbacks to abortion arise from its illegality. When performed, as a legal procedure, by a skilled physician, it is safer than childbirth. It does not compete with contraception but serves as a backstop when the latter fails or when contraceptive devices or information are not available. As contraception becomes customary, the incidence of abortion recedes even without its being banned. If, therefore, abortions enable women to have only the number of children they want, and if family planners do not advocate —in fact decry—legalization of abortion, they are to that extent denying the central tenet of their own movement. The irony of anti-abortionism in family-planning circles is seen particularly in hair-splitting arguments over whether or not some contraceptive agent (for example, the IUD) is in reality an abortifacient. A Mexican leader in family planning writes (*17*):

> One of the chief objectives of our program in Mexico is to prevent abortions. If we could be sure that the mode of action [of the IUD] was not interference with nidation, we could easly use the method in Mexico.

The questions of sterilization and unnatural forms of sexual intercourse usually meet with similar silent treatment or disapproval, although nobody doubts the effectiveness of these measures in avoiding conception. Sterilization has proved popular in Puerto Rico and has had some vogue in India (where the new health minister hopes to make it compulsory for those with a certain number of children), but in both these areas it has been for the most part ignored or condemned by the family-planning movement.

On the side of goals, then, we see that a family-planning orientation limits the aims of current population policy. Despite reference to "population control" and "fertility control," which presumably mean determination of demographic results by and for the nation as a whole, the movement gives control only to couples, and does this only if they use "respectable" contraceptives.

THE NEGLECT OF MOTIVATION

By sanctifying the doctrine that each woman should have the number of children she wants, and by assuming that if she has only that number this will automatically curb population growth to the necessary degree, the leaders of current policies escape the necessity of asking why women desire so many children and how this desire can be influenced (*18*, p. 41; *19*). Instead, they claim that satisfactory motivation is shown by the popular desire (shown by opinion surveys in all countries) to have the means of family limitation, and that therefore the problem is one of inventing and distributing the best possible contraceptive devices. Overlooked is the fact that a desire for availability of contraceptives is compatible with *high* fertility.

Given the best of means, there remain the questions of how many children couples want and of whether this is the requisite number from the standpoint of population size. That it is not is indicated by continued rapid population growth in industrial countries, and by the very surveys showing that people want contraception—for these show, too, that people also want numerous children.

The family planners do not ignore motivation. They are forever talking about "attitudes" and "needs." But they pose the issue in terms of the "acceptance" of birth-control devices. At the most naive level, they assume that lack of acceptance is a function of the contraceptive device itself. This reduces the motive problem to a technological question. The task of population control then becomes simply the invention of a device that *will* be acceptable (*20*). The plastic IUD is acclaimed because, once in place, it does not depend on repeated *acceptance* by the woman, and thus it "solves" the problem of motivation (*21*).

But suppose a woman does not want to use *any* contraceptive until after she has had four children. This is the type of question that is seldom raised in the family-planning literature. In that literature, wanting a specific number of children is taken as complete motivation, for it implies a wish to control the size of one's family. The problem woman, from the standpoint of family planners, is the one who wants "as many as come," or "as many as God sends." Her attitude is construed as due to ignorance and "cultural values," and the policy deemed necessary to change it is "education." No compulsion can be used, because the movement is committed to free choice, but movie strips, posters, comic books, public lectures, interviews, and discussions are in order. These supply information and supposedly change values by discounting superstitions and showing that unrestrained procreation is harmful to both mother and children. The effort is considered successful when the woman decides she wants only a certain number of children and uses an effective contraceptive.

In viewing negative attitudes toward birth control as due to ignorance, apathy, and outworn tradition, and "mass-communication" as the solution to the motivation problem (22), family planners tend to ignore the power and complexity of social life. If it were admitted that the creation and care of new human beings is socially motivated, like other forms of behavior, by being a part of the system of rewards and punishments that is built into human relationships, and thus is bound up with the individual's economic and personal interests, it would be apparent that the social structure and economy must be changed before a deliberate reduction in the birth rate can be achieved. As it is, reliance on family planning allows people to feel that "something is being done about the population problem" without the need for painful social changes.

Designation of population control as a medical or public health task leads to a similar evasion. This categorization assures popular support because it puts population policy in the hands of respected medical personnel, but, by the same token, it gives responsibility for leadership to people who think in terms of clinics and patients, of pills and IUD's, and who bring to the handling of economic and social phenomena a self-confident naiveté. The study of social organization is a technical field; an action program based on intuition is no more apt to succeed in the control of human beings than it is in the area of bacterial or viral control. Moreover, to alter a social system, by deliberate policy, so as to regulate births in accord with the demands of the collective welfare would require political power, and this is not likely to inhere in public health officials, nurses, midwives, and social workers. To entrust population policy to them is "to take action," but not dangerous "effective action."

Similarly, the Janus-faced position on birth-control technology represents an escape from the necessity, and onus, of grappling with the social and economic determinants of reproductive behavior. On the one side, the rejection or avoidance of religiously tabooed but otherwise effective means of birth prevention enables the family-planning movement to avoid official condemnation. On the other side, an intense preoccupation with contraceptive technology (apart from the tabooed means) also helps the family planners to avoid censure. By implying that the only need is the invention and distribution of effective contraceptive devices, they allay fears, on the part of religious and governmental officials, that fundamental changes in social organization are contemplated. Changes basic enough to affect motivation for having children would be changes in the structure of the family, in the position of women, and in the sexual mores. Far from proposing such radicalism, spokesmen for family planning frequently state their purpose as "protection" of the family—that is, closer observance of family norms. In addition, by concentrating on *new* and *scientific* contraceptives, the movement escapes taboos attached to old ones (the Pope will hardly authorize the condom, but may sanction the pill) and allows family planning to be regarded as a branch of medicine: over-population becomes a disease, to be treated by a pill or a coil.

We thus see that the inadequacy of current population policies with respect to motivation is inherent in their overwhelming family-planning character. Since family planning is by definition private planning, it eschews any societal control over motivation. It merely furnishes the means, and, among possible means, only the most respectable. Its leaders, in avoiding social complexities and seeking official favor, are obviously activated not solely by expediency but also by their own sentiments as members of society and by their background as persons attracted to the family-planning movement. Unacquainted for the most part with technical economics, sociology, and demography, they tend honestly and instinctively to believe that something they vaguely call population control can be achieved by making better contraceptives available.

THE EVIDENCE OF INEFFECTIVENESS

If this characterization is accurate, we can conclude that current programs will not enable a government to control population size. In countries where couples have numerous offspring that they do not want, such programs may possibly accelerate a birth-rate decline that would occur anyway, but the conditions that cause births to be wanted or unwanted are beyond the control of family planning, hence beyond the control of any nation which relies on family planning alone as its population policy.

This conclusion is confirmed by demographic facts. As I have noted above, the widespread use of family planning in industrial countries has not given their governments control over the birth rate. In backward countries today, taken as a whole, birth rates are rising, not falling; in those with population policies, there is no indication that the government is controlling the rate of reproduction. The main "successes" cited in the well-publicized policy literature are cases where a large number of contraceptives have been distributed or where the program has been accompanied by some decline in the birth rate. Popular enthusiasm for family planning is found mainly in the cities, or in advanced countries such as Japan and Taiwan, where the people would adopt contraception in any case, program or no program. It is difficult to prove that present population policies have even speeded up a lowering of the birth rate (the least that could have been expected), much less that they have provided national "fertility control."

Let us next briefly review the facts concerning the level and trend of population in underveloped nations generally, in order to understand the magnitude of the task of genuine control.

RISING BIRTH RATES IN UNDERDEVELOPED COUNTRIES

In ten Latin-American countries, between 1940 and 1959 (23), the average birth rates (age-standardized), as estimated by our research office at the University of California, rose as follows: 1940–44, 43.4 annual births per 1000 population; 1945–49, 44.6; 1950–54, 46.4; 1955–59, 47.7.

In another study made in our office, in which estimating methods derived from the theory of quasi-stable populations were used, the recent trend was found to be upward in 27 underdeveloped countries, downward in six, and unchanged in one (24). Some of the rises have been substantial, and most have occurred where the birth rate was already extremely high. For instance, the gross reproduction rate rose in Jamaica from 1.8 per thousand in 1947 to

2.7 in 1960; among the natives of Fiji, from 2.0 in 1951 to 2.4 in 1964; and in Albania, from 3.0 in the period 1950–54 to 3.4 in 1960.

The general rise in fertility in backward regions is evidently not due to failure of population-control efforts, because most of the countries either have no such effort or have programs too new to show much effect. Instead, the rise is due, ironically, to the very circumstance that brought on the population crisis in the first place—to improved health and lowered mortality. Better health increases the probability that a woman will conceive and retain the fetus to term; lowered mortality raises the proportion of babies who survive to the age of reproduction and reduces the probability of widowhood during that age (*25*). The significance of the general rise in fertility, in the context of this discussion, is that it is giving would-be population planners a harder task than many of them realize. Some of the upward pressure on birth rates is independent of what couples do about family planning, for it arises from the fact that, with lowered mortality, there are simply more couples.

UNDERDEVELOPED COUNTRIES WITH POPULATION POLICIES

In discussions of population policy there is often confusion as to which cases are relevant. Japan, for instance, has been widely praised for the effectiveness of its measures, but it is a very advanced industrial nation and, besides, its government policy had little or nothing to do with the decline in the birth rate, except unintentionally. It therefore offers no test of population policy under peasant-agrarian conditions. Another case of questionable relevance is that of Taiwan, because Taiwan is sufficiently developed to be placed in the urban-industrial class of nations. However, since Taiwan is offered as the main showpiece by the sponsors of current policies in underdeveloped areas, and since the data are excellent, it merits examination.

Taiwan is acclaimed as a showpiece because it has responded favorably to a highly organized program for distributing up-to-date contraceptives and has also had a rapidly dropping birth rate. Some observers have carelessly attributed the decline in the birth rate—from 50.0 in 1951 to 32.7 in 1965— to the family-planning campaign (*26*), but the campaign began only in 1963 and could have affected only the end of the trend. Rather, the decline represents a response to modernization similar to that made by all countries that have become industrialized (*27*). By 1950 over half of Taiwan's population was urban, and by 1964 nearly two-thirds were urban, with 29 percent of the population living in cities of 100,000 or more. The pace of economic development has been extremely rapid. Between 1951 and 1963, per capita income increased by 4.05 percent per year. Yet the island is closely packed, having 870 persons per square mile (a population density higher than that of Belgium). The combination of fast economic growth and rapid population increase in limited space has put parents of large famiiles at a relative disadvantage and has created a brisk demand for abortions and contraceptives. Thus the favorable response to the current campaign to encourage use of the IUD is not a good example of what birth-control technology can do for a genuinely backward country. In fact, when the program was started, one

TABLE 1   Decline in Taiwan's Fertility Rate, 1951 through 1966.

Year	Registered Births per 1000 Women Aged 15–49	Change in Rate (percent)*
1951	211	
1952	198	−5.6
1953	194	−2.2
1954	193	−0.5
1955	197	+2.1
1956	196	−0.4
1957	182	−7.1
1958	185	+1.3
1959	184	−0.1
1960	180	−2.5
1961	177	−1.5
1962	174	−1.5
1963	170	−2.6
1964	162	−4.9
1965	152	−6.0
1966	149	−2.1

*The percentages were calculated on unrounded figures. Source of data through 1965, *Taiwan Demographic Fact Book* (1964, 1965), for 1966, *Monthly Bulletin of Population Registration Statistics of Taiwan* (1966, 1967).

reason for expecting receptivity was that the island was already on its way to modernization and family planning (*28*).

At most, the recent family-planning campaign—which reached significant proportions only in 1964, when some 46,000 IUD's were inserted (in 1965 the number was 99,253, and in 1966, 111,242) (*29*; *30*, p. 45)—could have caused the increase observable after 1963 in the rate of decline. Between 1951 and 1963 the average drop in the birth rate per 1000 women (see Table 1) was 1.73 percent per year; in the period 1964–66 it was 4.35 percent. But one hesitates to assign all of the acceleration in decline since 1963 to the family-planning campaign. The rapid economic development has been precisely of a type likely to accelerate a drop in reproduction. The rise in manufacturing has been much greater than the rise in either agriculture or construction. The agricultural labor force has thus been squeezed, and migration to the cities has skyrocketed (*31*). Since housing has not kept pace, urban families have had to restrict reproduction in order to take advantage of career opportunities and avoid domestic inconvenience. Such conditions have historically tended to accelerate a decline in birth rate. The most rapid decline came late in the United States (1921–33) and in Japan (1947–55). A plot of the Japanese and Taiwanese birth rates (Fig. 1) shows marked similarity of the two curves, despite a difference in level. All told, one should not attribute all of the post-1963 acceleration in the decline of Taiwan's birth rate to the family-planning campaign.

The main evidence that *some* of this acceleration is due to the campaign

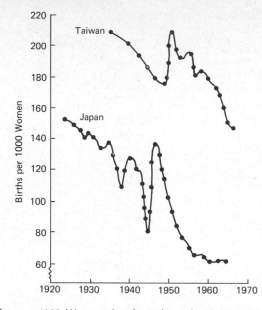

Figure 1   Births per 1000 Women Aged 15 through 49 in Japan and Taiwan.

comes from the fact that Taichung, the city in which the family-planning effort was first concentrated, showed subsequently a much faster drop in fertility than other cities (*30*, p. 69; *32*). But the campaign has not reached throughout the island. By the end of 1966, only 260,745 women had been fitted with an IUD under auspices of the campaign, whereas the women of reproductive age on the island numbered 2.86 million. Most of the reduction in fertility has therefore been a matter of individual initiative. To some extent the campaign may be simply substituting sponsored (and cheaper) services for those that would otherwise come through private and commercial channels. An island-wide survey in 1964 showed that over 150,000 women were already using the traditional Ota ring (a metallic intrauterine device popular in Japan); almost as many had been sterilized; about 40,000 were using foam tablets; some 50,000 admitted to having had at least one abortion; and many were using other methods of birth control (*30*, pp. 18, 31.)

The important question, however, is not whether the present campaign is somewhat hastening the downward trend in the birth rate but whether, even if it is, it will provide population control for the nation. Actually, the campaign is not designed to provide such control and shows no sign of doing so. It takes for granted existing reproductive goals. Its aim is "to integrate, through education and information, the idea of family limitation *within the existing attitudes, values, and goals* of the people" [*30*, p. 8 (italics mine)]. Its target is *married* women who do not want any more children; it ignores girls not yet married, and women married and wanting more children.

With such an approach, what is the maximum impact possible? It is the difference between the number of children women have been having and the number they want to have. A study in 1957 found a median figure of 3.75 for the number of children wanted by women aged 15 to 29 in Taipei, Taiwan's largest city; the corresponding figure for women from a satellite town was 3.93; for women from a fishing village, 4.90; and for women from a farming village, 5.03. Over 60 percent of the women in Taipei and over 90 percent of those in the farming village wanted 4 or more children (33). In a sample of wives aged 25 to 29 in Taichung, a city of over 300,000, Freedman and his co-workers found the average number of children wanted was 4; only 9 percent wanted less than 3, 20 percent wanted 5 or more (34). If, therefore, Taiwanese women used contraceptives that were 100-percent effective and had the number of children they desire, they would have about 4.5 each. The goal of the family-planning effort would be achieved. In the past the Taiwanese woman who married and lived through the reproductive period had, on the average, approximately 6.5 children; thus a figure of 4.5 would represent a substantial decline in fertility. Since mortality would continue to decline, the population growth rate would decline somewhat less than individual reproduction would. With 4.5 births per woman and a life expectancy of 70 years, the rate of natural increase would be close to 3 percent per year (35).

In the future, Taiwanese views concerning reproduction will doubtless change, in response to social change and economic modernization. But how far will they change? A good indication is the number of children desired by couples in an already modernized country long oriented toward family planning. In the United States in 1966, an average of 3.4 children was considered ideal by white women aged 21 or over (36). This average number of births would give Taiwan, with only a slight decrease in mortality, a long-run rate of natural increase of 1.7 percent per year and a doubling of population in 41 years.

Detailed data confirm the interpretation that Taiwanese women are in the process of shifting from a "peasant-agrarian" to an "industrial" level of reproduction. They are, in typical fashion, cutting off higher-order births at age 30 and beyond (37). Among young wives, fertility has risen, not fallen. In sum, the widely acclaimed family-planning program in Taiwan may, at most, have somewhat speeded the later phase of fertility decline which would have occurred anyway because of modernization.

Moving down the scale of modernization, to countries most in need of population control, one finds the family-planning approach even more inadequate. In South Korea, second only to Taiwan in the frequency with which it is cited as a model of current policy, a recent birth-rate decline of unknown extent is assumed by leaders to be due overwhelmingly to the government's family-planning program. However, it is just as plausible to say that the net effect of government involvement in population control has been, so far, to delay rather than hasten a decline in reproduction made inevitable by social and economic changes. Although the government is advocating vasectomies and providing IUD's and pills, it refuses to legalize abortions, despite the rapid rise in the rate of illegal abortions and despite the fact that, in a recent survey, 72 percent of the people who stated an opinion favored legalization. Also, the program is presented in the context of maternal and child health; it thus emphasizes motherhood and the family rather than alternative roles for women. Much is made of the fact that opinion surveys show an overwhelming majority of Koreans (89 percent in 1965) favoring contraception

(*38*, p. 27), but this means only that Koreans are like other people in wishing to have the means to get what they want. Unfortunately, they want sizable families: "The records indicate that the program appeals mainly to women in the 30–39 year age bracket who have four or more children, including at least two sons . . ." *38*, p. 25).

In areas less developed than Korea the degree of acceptance of contraception tends to be disappointing, especially among the rural majority. Faced with this discouragement, the leaders of current policy, instead of reexamining their assumptions, tend to redouble their effort to find a contraceptive that will appeal to the most illiterate peasant, forgetting that he wants a good-sized family. In the rural Punjab, for example, "a disturbing feature . . . is that the females start to seek advice and adopt family planning techniques at the fag end of their reproductive period" (*39*). Among 5196 women coming to rural Punjabi family-planning centers, 38 percent were over 35 years old, 67 percent over 30. These women had married early, nearly a third of them before the age of 15 (*40*); some 14 percent had eight or more *living* children when they reached the clinic, 51 percent six or more.

A survey in Tunisia showed that 68 percent of the married couples were willing to use birth-control measures, but the average number of children they considered ideal was 4.3 (*41*). The corresponding averages for a village in eastern Java, a village near New Delhi, and a village in Mysore were 4.3, 4.0, and 4.2, respectively (*42*, *43*). In the cities of these regions women are more ready to accept birth control and they want fewer children than village women do, but the number they consider desirable is still wholly unsatisfactory from the standpoint of population control. In an urban family-planning center in Tunisia, more than 600 of 900 women accepting contraceptives had four living children already (*44*). In Bangalore, a city of nearly a million at the time (1952), the number of offspring desired by married women was 3.7 on the average; by married men, 4.1 (*43*). In the metropolitan area of San Salvador (350,000 inhabitants) a 1964 survey (*45*) showed the number desired by women of reproductive age to be 3.9, and in seven other capital cities of Latin America the number ranged from 2.7 to 4.2. If women in the cities of underdeveloped countries used birth-control measures with 100-percent efficiency, they still would have enough babies to expand city populations senselessly, quite apart from the added contribution of rural-urban migration. In many of the cities the difference between actual and ideal number of children is not great; for instance, in the seven Latin-American capitals mentioned above, the ideal was 3.4 whereas the actual births per woman in the age range 35 to 39 was 3.7 (*46*). Bombay City has had birth-control clinics for many years, yet its birth rate (standardized for age, sex, and marital distribution) is still 34 per 1000 inhabitants and is tending to rise rather than fall. Although this rate is about 13 percent lower than that for India generally, it has been about that much lower since at least 1951 (*47*).

IS FAMILY PLANNING THE "FIRST STEP" IN POPULATION CONTROL?

To acknowledge that family planning does not achieve population control is not to impugn its value for other purposes. Freeing women from the need to have more children than they want is of great benefit to them and their children and to society at large. My argument is therefore directed not against family-planning programs as such but against the assumption that they are an effective means of controlling population growth.

But what difference does it make? Why not go along for awhile with family planning as an initial approach to the problem of population control? The answer is that any policy on which millions of dollars are being spent should be designed to achieve the goal it purports to achieve. If it is only a first step, it should be so labeled, and its connection with the next step (and the nature of that next step) should be carefully examined. In the present case, since no "next step" seems ever to be mentioned, the question arises, Is reliance on family planning in fact a basis for dangerous postponement of effective steps? To continue to offer a remedy as a cure long after it has been shown merely to ameliorate the disease is either quackery or wishful thinking, and it thrives most where the need is greatest. Today the desire to solve the population problem is so intense that we are all ready to embrace any "action program" that promises relief. But postponement of effective measures allows the situation to worsen.

Unfortunately, the issue is confused by a matter of semantics. "Family *planning*" and "fertility *control*" suggest that reproduction is being regulated according to some rational plan. And so it is, but only from the standpoint of the individual couple, not from that of the community. What is rational in the light of a couple's situation may be totally irrational from the standpoint of society's welfare.

The need for societal regulation of individual behavior is readily recognized in other spheres—those of explosives, dangerous drugs, public property, natural resources. But in the sphere of reproduction, complete individual initiative is generally favored even by those liberal intellectuals who, in other spheres, most favor economic and social planning. Social reformers who would not hesitate to force all owners of rental property to rent to anyone who can pay, or to force all workers in an industry to join a union, balk at any suggestion that couples be permitted to have only a certain number of offspring. Invariably they interpret societal control of reproduction as meaning direct police supervision of individual behavior. Put the word *compulsory* in front of any term describing a means of limiting births— *compulsory sterilization, compulsory abortion, compulsory contraception*— and you guarantee violent opposition. Fortunately, such direct controls need not be invoked, but conservatives and radicals alike overlook this in their blind opposition to the idea of collective determination of a society's birth rate.

That the exclusive emphasis on family planning in current population policies is not a "first step" but an escape from the real issues is suggested by two facts. (1) No country has taken the "next step." The industrialized countries have had family planning for half a century without acquiring control over either the birth rate or population increase. (2) Support and encouragement of research on population policy other than family planning is negligible. It is precisely this blocking of alternative thinking and experimentation that makes the emphasis on family planning a major obstacle to population control. The need is not to abandon family-planning programs but to put equal or greater resources into other approaches.

NEW DIRECTIONS IN POPULATION POLICY

In thinking about other approaches, one can start with known facts. In the past, all surviving societies had institutional incentives for marriage, procreation, and child care which were powerful enough to keep the birth rate equal to or in excess of a high death rate. Despite the drop in death rates during the last century and a half, the incentives tended to remain intact because the social structure (especially in regard to the family) changed little. At most, particularly in industrial societies, children became less productive and more expensive (48). In present-day agrarian societies, where the drop in death rate has been more recent, precipitate, and independent of social change (49), motivation for having children has changed little. Here, even more than in industrialized nations, the family has kept on producing abundant offspring, even though only a fraction of these children are now needed.

If excessive population growth is to be prevented, the obvious requirement is somehow to impose restraints on the family. However, because family roles are reinforced by society's system of rewards, punishments, sentiments, and norms, any proposal to demote the family is viewed as a threat by conservatives and liberals alike, and certainly by people with enough social responsibility to work for population control. One is charged with trying to "abolish" the family, but what is required is selective restructuring of the family in relation to the rest of society.

The lines of such restructuring are suggested by two existing limitations on fertility. (1) Nearly all societies succeed in drastically discouraging reproduction among unmarried women. (2) Advanced societies unintentionally reduce reproduction among married women when conditions worsen in such a way as to penalize childbearing more severely than it was penalized before. In both cases the causes are motivational and economic rather than technological.

It follows that population-control policy can de-emphasize the family in two ways: (1) by keeping present controls over illegitimate childbirth yet making the most of factors that lead people to postpone or avoid marriage, and (2) by instituting conditions that motivate those who do marry to keep their families small.

POSTPONEMENT OF MARRIAGE

Since the female reproductive span is short and generally more fecund in its first than in its second half, postponement of marriage to ages beyond 20 tends biologically to reduce births. Sociologically, it gives women time to get a better education, acquire interests unrelated to the family, and develop a cautious attitude toward pregnancy (50). Individuals who have not married by the time they are in their late twenties often do not marry at all. For these reasons, for the world as a whole, the average age at marriage for women is negatively associated with the birth rate: a rising age at marriage is a frequent cause of declining fertility during the middle phase of the demographic transition; and, in the late phase, the "baby boom" is usually associated with a return to younger marriages.

Any suggestion that age at marriage be raised as a part of population policy is usually met with the argument that "even if a law were passed, it would not be obeyed." Interestingly, this objection implies that the only way to control the age at marriage is by direct legislation, but other factors govern the actual age. Roman Catholic countries generally follow canon law in stipulating 12 years as the minimum *legal* age at which girls may marry, but the actual average age at marriage in these countries (at least in Europe) is characteristically more like 25 to 28 years. The actual age is determined, not by law, but by social and economic conditions. In agrarian societies, postponement of marriage (when postponement occurs) is apparently caused by difficulties in meeting the economic prerequisites for matrimony, as stipulated by custom and opinion. In industrial societies it is caused by housing shortages, unemployment, the requirement for overseas military service, high costs of education, and inadequacy of consumer services. Since almost no research has been devoted to the subject, it is difficult to assess the relative weight of the factors that govern the age at marriage.

ENCOURAGING LIMITATION OF BIRTHS WITHIN MARRIAGE

As a means of encouraging the limitation of reproduction within marriage, as well as postponement of marriage, a greater rewarding of nonfamilial than of familial roles would probably help. A simple way of accomplishing this would be to allow economic advantages to accrue to the single as opposed to the married individual, and to the small as opposed to the large family. For instance, the government could pay people to permit themselves to be sterilized (51); all costs of abortion could be paid by the government; a substantial fee could be charged for a marriage license; a "child-tax" (52) could be levied; and there could be a requirement that illegitimate pregnancies be aborted. Less sensationally, governments could simply reverse some existing policies that encourage childbearing. They could, for example, cease taxing single persons more than married ones; stop giving parents special tax exemptions; abandon income-tax policy that discriminates against couples when the wife works; reduce paid maternity leaves; reduce family allowances (53); stop awarding public housing on the basis of family size; stop granting fellowships and other educational aids (including special allowances for wives and children) to married students; cease outlawing abortions and sterilizations; and relax rules that allow use of harmless contraceptives only with medical permission. Some of these policy reversals would be beneficial in other than demographic respects and some would be harmful unless special precautions were taken. The aim would be to reduce the number, not the quality, of the next generation.

A closely related method of deemphasizing the family would be modification of the complementarity of the roles of men and women. Men are now able to participate in the wider world yet enjoy the satisfaction of having several children because the housework and childcare fall mainly on their wives. Women are impelled to seek this role by their idealized view of marriage and motherhood and by either the scarcity of alternative roles or the difficulty of combining them with family roles. To change this situation women could be required to work outside the home, or compelled by circumstances to do so. If, at the same time, women were paid as well as men and given equal educational and occupational opportunities, and if social life were organized around the place of work rather than around the home or neighborhood, many women would develop interests that would compete with family interests. Approximately this policy is now followed in several Communist countries, and even the less developed of these currently have extremely low birth rates (*54*).

That inclusion of women in the labor force has a negative effect on reproduction is indicated by regional comparisons (*18*, p. 1195; *55*). But in most countries the wife's employment is subordinate, economically and emotionally, to her family role, and is readily sacrificed for the latter. No society has restructured both the occupational system and the domestic establishment to the point of permanently modifying the old division of labor by sex.

In any deliberate effort to control the birth rate along these lines, a government has two powerful instruments—its command over economic planning and its authority (real or potential) over education. The first determines (as far as policy can) the economic conditions and circumstances affecting the lives of all citizens; the second provides the knowledge and attitudes necessary to implement the plans. The economic system largely determines who shall work, what can be bought, what rearing children will cost, how much individuals can spend. The schools define family roles and develop vocational and recreational interests; they could, if it were desired, redefine the sex roles, develop interests that transcend the home, and transmit realistic (as opposed to moralistic) knowledge concerning marriage, sexual behavior, and population problems. When the problem is viewed in this light, it is clear that the ministries of economics and education, not the ministry of health, should be the source of population policy.

THE DILEMMA OF POPULATION POLICY

It should now be apparent why, despite strong anxiety over runaway population growth, the actual programs purporting to control it are limited to family planning and are therefore ineffective. (1) The goal of zero, or even slight, population growth is one that nations and groups find difficult to accept. (2) The measures that would be required to implement such a goal, though not so revolutionary as a Brave New World or a Communist Utopia, nevertheless tend to offend most people reared in existing societies. As a consequence, the goal of so-called population control is implicit and vague; the method is only family planning. This method, far from de-emphasizing the family, is familistic. One of its stated goals is that of helping sterile couples to *have* children. It stresses parental aspirations and responsibilities. It goes along with most aspects of conventional morality, such as condemnation of abortion, disapproval of premarital intercourse, respect for religious teachings and cultural taboos, and obeisance to medical and clerical authority. It deflects hostility by refusing to recommend any change other than the one it stands for: availability of contraceptives.

The things that make family planning acceptable are the very things that make it ineffective for population control. By stressing the right of parents to have the number of children they want, it evades the basic question of population policy, which is how to give societies the number of children they need. By offering only the means for *couples* to control fertility, it neglects the means for societies to do so.

Because of the predominantly pro-family character of existing societies, individual interest ordinarily leads to the production of enough offspring to constitute rapid population growth under conditions of low mortality. Childless or single-child homes are considered indicative of personal failure, whereas having three to five living children gives a family a sense of continuity and substantiality (*56*).

Given the existing desire to have moderate-sized rather then small families, the only countries in which fertility has been reduced to match reduction in mortality are advanced ones temporarily experiencing worsened economic conditions. In Sweden, for instance, the net reproduction rate (NRR) has been below replacement for 34 years (1930–63), if the period is taken as a whole, but this is because of the economic depression. The average replacement rate was below unity (NRR = 0.81) for the period 1930–42, but from 1942 through 1963 it was above unity (NRR = 1.08). Hardships that seem particularly conducive to deliberate lowering of the birth rate are (in managed economies) scarcity of housing and other consumer goods despite full employment, and required high participation of women in the labor force, or (in freer economies) a great deal of unemployment and economic insecurity. When conditions are good, any nation tends to have a growing population.

It follows that, in countries where contraception is used, a realistic proposal for a government policy of lowering the birth rate reads like a catalogue of horrors: squeeze consumers through taxation and inflation; make housing very scarce by limiting construction; force wives and mothers to work outside the home to offset the inadequacy of male wages, yet provide few child-care facilities; encourage migration to the city by paying low wages in the country and providing few rural jobs; increase congestion in cities by starving the transit system; increase personal insecurity by encouraging conditions that produce unemployment and by haphazard political arrests. No government will institute such hardships simply for the purpose of controlling population growth. Clearly, therefore, the task of contemporary population policy is to develop attractive substitutes for family interests, so as to avoid having to turn to hardship as a corrective. The specific measures required for developing such substitutes are not easy to determine in the absence of research on the question.

In short, the world's population problem cannot be solved by pretense and wishful thinking. The unthinking identification of family planning with population control is an ostrich-like approach in that it permits people to hide from themselves the enormity and unconventionality of the task. There is no reason to abandon family-planning programs; contraception is a valuable technological instrument. But such programs must be supplemented with equal or greater investments in research and experimentation to determine the required socioeconomic measures.

REFERENCES AND NOTES

1. *Studies in Family Planning, No. 16* (1967).
2. Ibid., *No. 9* (1966), p. 1.
3. The statement is given in *Studies in Family Planning* (*1*, p. 1), and in *Population Bull.*, 23, 6 (1967).
4. The statement is quoted in *Studies in Family Planning* (*1*, p. 2).
5. *Hearings on S. 1676, U.S. Senate, Subcommittee on Foreign Aid Expenditures, 89th Congress, Second Session, April 7, 8, 11* (1966), pt. 4.
6. B. L. Raina, in *Family Planning and Population Programs*, B. Berelson, R. K. Anderson, O. Harkavy, G. Maier, W. P. Mauldin, S. G. Segal, (eds.), Chicago: University of Chicago Press, 1966.
7. D. Kirk, *Annals of the American Academy of Political and Social Science*, 369, (1967) 53.
8. As used by English-speaking demographers, the word *fertility* designates actual reproductive performance, not a theoretical capacity.
9. K. Davis, *Rotarian*, 94, (1959) 10; *Health Education Monographs*, 9, (1960) 2; L. Day and A. Day, *Too Many Americans*, Boston: Houghton-Mifflin, 1964; R. A. Piddington, *Limits of Mankind*, England: Wright, Bristol, 1956.
10. *Official Gazette* (15 April, 1965); quoted in *Studies in Family Planning*, *1*, p. 7.
11. J. W. Gardner, Secretary of Health, Education, and Welfare, "Memorandum to Heads of Operating Agencies," (January 1966), reproduced in *Hearings on S. 1676 (5)*, p. 783.
12. C. Tietze, *Demography*, 1, (1964) 119; *Journal of Chronic Diseases*, 18, (1964) 1161; M. Muramatsu, *Milbank Memorial Fund Quarterly*, 38, (1960) 153; K. Davis, *Population Index*, 29, (1963) 345; R. Armijo and T. Monreal, *Journal of Sex Research*, (1964) 143; Proceedings World Population Conference, Belgrade, 1965; Proceedings International Planned Parenthood Federation.
13. *Studies in Family Planning, No. 4* (1964), p. 3.
14. D. Bell (then administrator for Agency for International Development), in *Hearings on S. 1676 (5)*, p. 862.
15. *Asian Population Conference* (United Nations, New York, 1964), p. 30.
16. R. Armijo and T. Monreal, in *Components of Population Change in Latin America* (Milbank Fund, New York, 1965), p. 272; E. Rice-Wray, *American Journal of Public Health*, 54, (1964) 313.
17. E. Rice-Wray, in "Intra-Uterine Contraceptive Devices," *Excerpta Medical International Congress Series No. 54* (1962), p. 135.
18. J. Blake, in *Public Health and Population Change*, M. C. Sheps and J. C. Ridley, (eds.), Pittsburgh: University of Pittsburgh Press, 1965.
19. J. Blake and K. Davis, *American Behavioral Scientist*, 5, (1963) 24.
20. See "Panel discussion on comparative acceptability of different methods of contraception," in *Research in Family Planning*, C. V. Kiser, (ed.), Princeton: Princeton University Press, 1962, pp. 373–86.
21. "From the point of view of the woman concerned, the whole problem of continuing motivation disappears, . . . " D. Kirk, in *Population Dynamics*,

M. Muramatsu and P. A. Harper, (eds.), Baltimore: Johns Hopkins Press, 1965.

22. "For influencing family size norms, certainly the examples and statements of public figures are of great significance . . . also . . . use of mass-communication methods which help to legitimize the small-family style, to provoke conversation, and to establish a vocabulary for discussion of family planning." M. W. Freymann, in *Population Dynamics*, M. Muramatsu and P. A. Harper, (eds.), Baltimore: Johns Hopkins Press, 1965.

23. O. A. Collver, *Birth Rates in Latin America*, Berkeley, Calif.: International Population and Urban Research, 1965, pp. 27–28; the ten countries were Columbia, Costa Rica, El Salvador, Ecuador, Guatemala, Honduras, Mexico, Panamá, Peru, and Venezuela.

24. J. R. Rele, *Fertility Analysis through Extension of Stable Population Concepts*. Berkeley, Calif.: International Population and Urban Research, 1967.

25. J. C. Ridley, M. C. Sheps, J. W. Lingner, J. A. Menken, *Milbank Memorial Fund Quarterly*, 45, (1967) 77; E. Arriaga, unpublished paper.

26. "South Korea and Taiwan appear successfully to have checked population growth by the use of intrauterine contraceptive devices" [U. Borell, *Hearings on S. 1676 (5)*, p. 556].

27. K. Davis, *Population Index*, 29, (1963) 345.

28. R. Freedman, ibid., 31, (1965) 421.

29. Before 1964 the Family Planning Association had given advice to fewer than 60,000 wives in 10 years and a Pre-Pregnancy Health Program had reached some 10,000, and, in the current campaign, 3650 IUD's were inserted in 1965, in a total population of 2 1/2 million women of reproductive age. See *Studies in Family Planning, No. 19* (1967), p. 4, and R. Freedman, et al., *Population Studies*, 16, (1963) 231.

30. R. W. Gillespie, *Family Planning on Taiwan*, Taichung: Population Council, 1965.

31. During the period 1950–60 the ratio of growth of the city to growth of the noncity population was 5:3; during the period 1960–64 the ratio was 5:2; these ratios are based on data of Shaohsing Chen, *Journal Sociol. Taiwan*, 1, (1963) 74 and data in the United Nations *Demographic Yearbooks*.

32. R. Freedman, *Population Index*, 31, (1965) 434. Taichung's rate of decline in 1963–64 was roughly double the average in four other cities, whereas just prior to the campaign its rate of decline had been much less than theirs.

33. S. H. Chen, *Journal of Social Science of Taipei*, 13, (1963) 72.

34. R. Freedman et al., *Population Studies*, 16, (1963) 227; ibid., p. 232.

35. In 1964 the life expectancy at birth was already 66 years in Taiwan, as compared to 70 for the United States.

36. J. Blake, *Eugenics Quarterly*, 14, (1967) 68.

37. Women accepting IUD's in the family-planning program are typically 30 to 34 years old and have already had four children. [*Studies in Family Planning No. 19*, 1967, p. 5.]

38. Y. K. Cha, in *Family Planning and Population Programs*, B. Berelson et al., (eds.), Chicago: University of Chicago Press, 1966.

39. H. S. Ayalvi and S. S. Johl, *Journal of Family Welfare*, 12, (1965) 60.
40. Sixty percent of the women had borne their first child before age 19. Early marriage is strongly supported by public opinion. Of couples polled in the Punjab, 48 percent said that girls *should* marry before age 16, and 94 percent said they should marry before age 20 (H. S. Ayalvi and S. S. Johl, ibid., p. 57). A study of 2380 couples in 60 villages of Uttar Pradesh found that the women had consummated their marriage at an average age of 14.6 years. J. R. Rele, *Population Studies*, 15, (1962) 268.
41. J. Morsa, in *Family Planning and Population Programs*, B. Berelson et al., (eds.), Chicago: University of Chicago Press, 1966.
42. H. Gille and R. J. Pardoko, ibid., p. 515; S. N. Agarwala, *Medical Digest Bombay*, 4, (1961) 653.
43. *Mysore Population Study.* New York: United Nations, 1961, p. 140.
44. A. Daly, in *Family Planning and Population Programs*, B. Berelson et al., (eds.), Chicago: University of Chicago Press, 1966.
45. C. J. Gómez, paper presented at the World Population Conference, Belgrade, 1965.
46. C. Miro, in *Family Planning and Population Programs*, B. Berelson et al., (eds.), Chicago: University of Chicago Press, 1966.
47. *Demographic Training and Research Centre (India) Newsletter*, 20, (August, 1966) 4.
48. K. Davis, *Population Index*, 29, (1963) 345. For economic and sociological theory of motivation for having children, see J. Blake, Berkeley, Calif.: University of California, in preparation.
49. K. Davis, *American Economic Review*, 46, (1956) 305; *Scientific American*, 209, (1963) 68.
50. J. Blake, *World Population Conference, Belgrade, 1965.* New York: United Nations, 1967, Vol. 2, pp. 132–36.
51. S. Enke, *Rev. Economic Statistics*, 42, (1960) 175; ———, *Econ. Develop. Cult. Change*, 8, (1960) 339; ———, ibid., 10, (1962) 427; A. O. Krueger and L. A. Sjaastad, ibid., p. 423.
52. T. J. Samuel, *Journal of Family Welfare India*, 13, (1966) 12.
53. Sixty-two countries, including 27 in Europe, give cash payments to people for having children [U.S. Social Security Administration, *Social Security Programs Throughout the World, 1967*; Washington, D.C.: Government Printing Office, 1967, pp. xxvii–xxviii].
54. Average gross reproduction rates in the early 1960's were as follows: Hungary, 0.91; Bulgaria, 1.09; Romania, 1.15; Yugoslavia, 1.32.
55. O. A. Collver and E. Langlois, *Econ. Develop. Cult. Change*, 10, (1962) 367; J. Weeks, Berkeley, Calif.: University of California, unpublished paper.
56. Roman Catholic textbooks condemn the "small" family (one with fewer than four children) as being abnormal. J. Blake, *Population Studies*, 20, (1966) 27.
57. Judith Blake's critical readings and discussions have greatly helped in the preparation of this article.

31

The Significance of the Family in Population Research

REUBEN HILL

To place our subject in perspective, two extremes can be distinguished: the competing professional orientations and contributions of traditional demography as against family sociology. Demography, along with economics, has been considered one of the dismal sciences. Because the demographer was dealing with the questions of fate—such as marriage, birth, illness, and death —over which men traditionally have exercised little control, the traditional demographer has conceptualized man as a passive recipient—a particle—in the grip of physical, biological, and social forces. He has, accordingly, dealt with the phenomenon of reproduction in a fatalistic way, preferring to look at national trends, demographic rates, and the influence, over long periods, of changes in the economy and in the polity—in all of which the individual's behavior did not have to be accounted for. His units were large aggregates arrived at by joining together data by gross categories of the population. There were no living actors in his units.

The family sociologist has proceeded quite differently. He has taken as his unit of study the individual or the small group and has observed its behavior under different social conditions. His observations have been at the microscopic level of individual and small group actions and decisions on issues over which man does exercise some control. He sees man as initiator as well as reactor and as capable of making decisions within the context of his interpersonal relationships in the social structure.

With man's expanding control over his environment, his demographic fate—to use a term coined by the American sociologist, Kurt Back—has also begun to come under his control. The orientation and focus of the family sociologist has, accordingly, become increasingly relevant for understanding voluntary childbearing. Indeed, the man-over-nature orientation of the family sociologist gives him an advantage over the demographer whose nature-over-man fatalism has inhibited his participation in the research required for identifying the factors to be manipulated in action programs.

Each has made his contributions to population policies and programs. The demographer has contributed at the national level by the generalizations and predictions he has made about reproductive changes and their social and economic correlates. He has further undertaken cross-national studies of large magnitude to test theories about "the demographic transition" as countries have urbanized and industrialized. He has been influential in creating, staffing, and improving national systems of statistics in most of the countries of the world, treating not only vital events but all types of information useful for predicting changes in these events. The demographer's documentation of the increasing population growth in developing countries and its implications for educational and welfare goals has precipitated the formu-

Reprinted from *Family and Fertility*, William T. Liu (ed.), 1966 (pp. 3–22), by permission of the University of Notre Dame Press, Notre Dame, Indiana.

lation of explicit policies to regulate population growth. His findings have also been used in Europe to rationalize pronatalist programs of graduated family allowances to equalize the cost of child rearing and reward couples taking on the responsibility for large families. Thus, although his findings have been descriptive and nonprescriptive, they have nevertheless lent themselves to application, because they have dealt with the same aggregates utilized by policy makers and planners at the levels of national and international planning.

In contrast, the family sociologist brings the phenomenon of population growth down to the level of the decisions or nondecisions about family size. The nation's problem with population growth rate is, thereby, decomposed into the behaviors of millions of couples coping with the timing of marriage and the number of children desired. There are families which underachieve, having fewer children than they desire; families which overachieve, having more children than they desire; families which are lucky or effective in having neither more nor fewer than they desire. The family sociologist seeks to explain this relative success or failure in family size control.

When first asked by the University of Puerto Rico to undertake a study of Puerto Rico's population problem a number of years ago, the writer was intrigued by the task primarily as a means of studying family problem solving. Puerto Rico's problem appeared not so much as a population bomb exploding in the Caribbean, although that can be documented easily enough, but as hundreds of thousands of individual families failing in the first primal task of marriage, the control of family size in line with family goals.

Puerto Rico has been a good place to observe this type of family problem solving or nonsolving because its people are extremely conscious of optimum family size, uniformly preferring two or three children, yet bearing, on the average, six—a people with small-family-size goals and large-family achievements.

The problem of overachievement, moreover, was concentrated in the lower classes of the island. Our task was to discover the factors accounting for the success of some and the failure of most lower-class Puerto Ricans to contain their fertility in line with their stated goals for family size. Later, in an educational experiment, the problem took a more active form. How could those who were unsuccessful be rendered more effective in fertility planning.

The numerous studies which had been undertaken in Puerto Rico acted as a deterrent against seeking any simple solution. A family sociologist, the present writer, was to bring his own conceptual tools to bear on the problem, which had already been examined by economists, demographers, and anthropologists. One unique contribution, at the time the research was undertaken, was a view of the problem from the perspective of family heads. What did the problem of numbers look like from inside families? Our team took the position that planning the future size of the family was a function of the family itself. Government and private agency programs may suggest, advise, and facilitate, but the decision to start planning, what to do about it, and whether to continue with these actions is made by the married couple itself.

Analysis of the behavior of family units might show, therefore, why some family planning programs succeed and some fail, and how the steps in family planning are accomplished.

Finally, the challenge of this study of success in family planning was that much of what the family sociologists learned here could be used in other areas of family life. The concern of the research team was not yet primarily with the solution of the population problem in Puerto Rico and in other parts of the world. The major goal and motivation was to understand how families coped with problems. And here was one that was constantly in front of them, on the agenda all of the time. Conditions leading to effective planning of family size, it was thought, might be analogous to those which enable families to plan effectively in any field.

Let us review some of the steps that were taken to assure a family-centered study: the choice of the unit of study, the choice of an appropriate theoretical framework for formulating guiding questions and setting the limits on observations, and the construction of a schema of analytic categories encompassing the territory to be studied.

The units of observation and analysis for demographers in the general area of human fertility and its control have varied greatly—counties, states, provinces, countries, whole societies, sometimes broken down for purposes of studying differential fertility in groups stratified by income, occupation, education, and residence. Medically oriented researchers have usually focused on mothers, treating the woman as the biological unit of study, which, in turn, fits well with their conception of the problem as a special instance of maternal health.

The monumental Indianapolis study, concerned with the social and psychological factors affecting fertility, appears to have focused on wives, although they were obviously treated as reporting agents for their families. This particular group interviewed husbands, but they rarely joined these data from husbands with those obtained from wives to construct family behavior items.

At the time of the Puerto Rico study, no research team had, as yet, taken as possible units of study either reference groups or nuclear family groups. At the time of these explorations four criteria were proposed for the selection of a study and observational unit in fertility control. Working from the assumption that fertility planning was group rather than individual planning, the unit emerged as the entity of planning, choice making, and action. The unit should be capable of serving as the referent in some conceptual system or a theory if our findings were to become part of the creative theory. And the unit must be accessible for empirical observation and investigation. The unit of study should also ideally be the unit of medical and educational services in matters of fertility control.

Of the possible units considered—the individual, the marriage pair, the nuclear family group, reference groups, communities—one met all of the criteria satisfactorily, as one would expect with a family sociologist as director, the nuclear family of procreation.

Having chosen the nuclear family as a unit of study and observation, it was incumbent upon us to choose, among the many approaches to the study of the family, the conceptual framework which would most fruitfully utilize the nuclear family as a planning and decision-making association.

Seven such approaches had been developed, each with its own distinctive definition of the family, its favorite concepts, and its own body of theory.

The choice seemed to lie between the structure-functional and the symbolic interaction approaches, both of which had much to contribute to the research problem. The interactional frame of reference for studying small groups seemed most appropriate, since it lends itself especially well to analysis of the family as a planning and decision-making association. Its key concepts consist of a kit of mental tools which are uncommonly useful in the study of the dynamics of human fertility. Some of these concepts are status and interstatus relations which become the basis for authority patterns and initiative taking. The key concept of role is common to both the structure function and the interactional approach, and there are many modifications—role taking, role playing, role organization, role conceptions, process concepts, communication, consultation, conflict, compromise, and consensus. The interactional approach has been broad enough to capture and order the central processes involved in group planning and problem solving which need to be observed in a study of fertility dynamics. This is a large order, since they include among others, the processes of goal setting, choice among means, allocation of accountability and responsibiilty for actions taken, as well as built-in processes of evaluation of the successes and failures of the plan which need to be fed back as problems for a group solution and reorganization.

Finally, the interactional approach provided more than tools for observation, it provided a body of theory which can be drawn upon in the formulation of diagnostic study questions. From family interactional theory come propositions which may be used as guideposts in the quest for the social-psychological antecedents of success in family planning and control. These antecedents are different in quality from the psychological and social-economic correlates of fertility of most social demographers from the days of Indianapolis down to the present time. They pertain to the dynamic quality of interaction systems and are oriented to intergroup processes, rather than to traits, characteristics, and status categories.

Certain foci are suggested by the family interactional framework. Using it as a microscope, it is apparent that the family, if permitted, is concerned intermittently with what Robert Reed has called negative and positive control of procreation. Decisions are reached and actions agreed upon. Failures are discussed and action is taken to correct them. The process remains at the agenda level of discussion for the effective period of childbearing unless cut short by the sterilization of one, and even this would be a consequence of husband-wife interaction.

With this perception of the family as the decision-making unit of society with respect to control of the family size, the family interaction theory suggests that the family's effectiveness as a planning unit would be a function, in large part, of the efficiency of its communication system. Thus, a likely study focus suggested by the interactional conceptual framework would be the processes of communication, the factors thought to be related to communication, conditions favoring communication, and impediments to communication which thwart goal setting, discussion, consensus, and decision making. These would receive major attention. Perhaps this is enough to illustrate the large advantage in taking a family-centered view of the issues of fertility control.

Certain aspects of the family and fertility studies in Puerto Rico and Jamaica appear to have particular relevance to family planning in other countries, notably, as illustrated in Figure 1, the schema of antecedents of fertility control.

The schema is designed to show direction of relations from left to right: the most distant on the extreme left and the closest on the extreme right. What have been hypothesized as the independent, intervening, and dependent variables in the studies of the family factors in fertility control? The social setting factors (Block A) are residence, education, occupation, type of marital union, religious affiliation, and income; these are related to effective family planning, shown as Block G, by means of five intervening sets of variables, each represented by a block in the model.

The variables shown under Block B, quite a distance away from the dependent variable, Effective Family Planning, capture what might be termed the general orientation toward change. Does the individual value change, or are the traditional ways best? Does the individual value planning, or does he believe fate determines his lot in life? Does he have high aspirations for himself and his children? Does he actually strive to achieve these aspirations? In sum, this block indicates the extent to which the respondents desired to manipulate change and to which they are actually doing so.

A third crucial block of variables (Block D) is qualitatively closely related to Block B, since it reflects values and motivations to act, but is much more specific with respect to fertility control: namely, attitudes toward family size and its control; these are, therefore, placed close to Block G, Effective Family Planning. What does the individual perceive as many or few children? Does he desire many or few, or does it make little difference? If he wants few, is this desire the consequence of having many children or is it independent of such experience? When and under what conditions did he first develop a preference about family size? What are his attitudes toward limiting family size, toward methods of birth control, toward the clinics and their family planning service?

A fourth cluster, known as Block C, Information and Knowledge, involves the crucial cognitive dimension and refers to the availability of technical means for goal achievement in family size. How much does the individual know about birth control methods? What is the timing of learning about these methods? Does he know the location of the nearest dispensary, depot, or clinic? If he's either ignorant of certain methods or, as in Block D, considers them objectionable or finds the clinic unacceptable, birth control as a means of family limitation is unavailable in our sense of the term.

A fifth block, E, refers to general family organization, to the typical patterns of allocating power, responsibilities, tasks, and affection within the family. Where is the locus of power in making decisions? What is the division of tasks and responsibilities? Are the roles of husband and wife integrated or are they segregated in carrying out these responsibilities? Lee Rainwater, in a recent study, had made this the core of a typology of families: role integration and role segregation. What is the sociometric network of affectional relations, coalitions, and emotional alignment within the family? How familistic-restrictive is the family structure with respect to the wife's mobility and freedom to participate outside the home? This is what is meant by general family organization. If it is found to be related to effective fertility planning, it might also be related to other types of family planning.

Finally, consider Block F, the action potentials of the family, both with

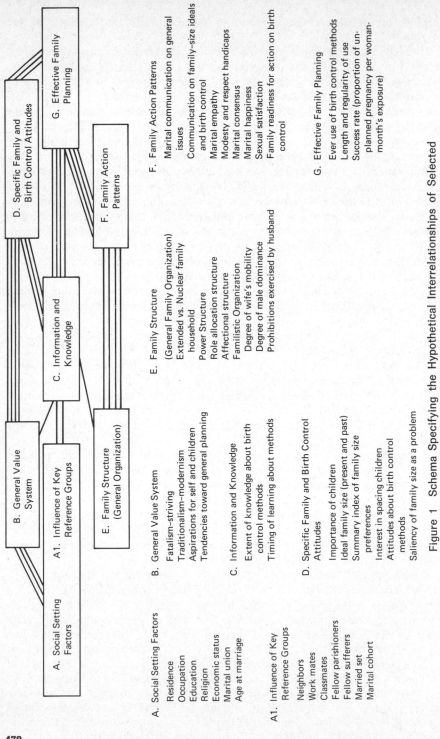

A. Social Setting Factors

Residence
Occupation
Education
Religion
Economic status
Marital union
Age at marriage

A1. Influence of Key Reference Groups

Neighbors
Work mates
Classmates
Fellow parishioners
Fellow sufferers
Married set
Marital cohort

B. General Value System

Fatalism–striving
Traditionalism–modernism
Aspirations for self and children
Tendencies toward general planning

C. Information and Knowledge

Extent of knowledge about birth control methods
Timing of learning about methods

D. Specific Family and Birth Control Attitudes

Importance of children
Ideal family size (present and past)
Summary index of family size preferences
Interest in spacing children
Attitudes about birth control methods
Saliency of family size as a problem

E. Family Structure (General Family Organization)

Extended vs. Nuclear family household
Power Structure
Role allocation structure
Affectional structure
Familistic Organization
Degree of wife's mobility
Degree of male dominance
Prohibitions exercised by husband

F. Family Action Patterns

Marital communication on general issues
Communication on family-size ideals and birth control
Marital empathy
Modesty and respect handicaps
Marital consensus
Marital happiness
Sexual satisfaction
Family readiness for action on birth control

G. Effective Family Planning

Ever use of birth control methods
Length and regularity of use
Success rate (proportion of unplanned pregnancy per woman-month's exposure)

Figure 1 Schema Specifying the Hypothetical Interrelationships of Selected Antecedent, Intervening, and Consequent Variables in Fertility

478

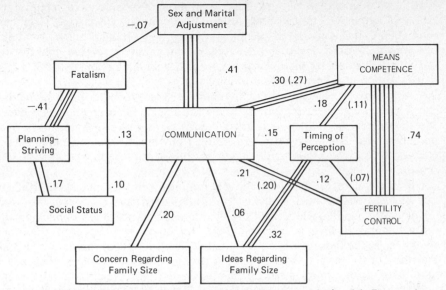

Figure 2   A Factor Analytic Model of Fertility Dynamics. *Code:* (1) Figures in parentheses are partial correlations, holding all other factors constant. All other figures are zero-order correlation coefficients. (2) The size of the correlation coefficient is approximated by the number of lines between factors; correlations less than 0.10 are not statistically significant at the 5 per cent level.

respect to coping with general problems and with respect specifically to action on family size. Is the structure of the family conducive to the implementation of joint and/or individual goals? Is there consensus on most issues in the family? Is this consensus realized? Are there barriers to communication on marital issues and on birth control? Is there agreement on initiative taking with respect to the crucial areas of family life, including sex relations and the timing of birth control use? It is within this Block F that the micro-social-psychological factors are concentrated, the degree of husband-wife communication, the ability to arrive at consensus, the phenomenon of empathy, and the general inclination toward taking action. These are among the most important variables constituting the family's action potential. A number of studies have been undertaken utilizing the major elements of this schema originated in Puerto Rico to provide guidance for data collection and analysis.

The bibliography of readings accompanying this paper identifies some of these studies. The work in Puerto Rico, Jamaica, and Haiti, and in Belgium, France, and Greece are immediate consumers and verifiers of this schema. Lee Rainwater's work on working-class families has adopted depth interview methods similar to those used in his recent book *Family Design*. The detailed findings cannot be presented here, but a factor analytic condensation of findings is given in Figure 2, based on the Puerto Rican survey phase. It is significant that communication has emerged as the "hub variable." Several of the variables which had a high zero relationship to fertility planning effectiveness show up in the factor analysis primarily by virtue of their association with communication. Thus, for example, factors of sexual and general marital adjustment, which have lost their direct association to fertility control through the factor analysis, retain their strong association with communication. The complex of planning-striving and fatalism shows a similar but weaker pattern. Ideas and concerns about family size also operate in a secondary fashion by their association with communication and the timing of perception of family size as a problem.

At this point, the presentation requires a less condensed treatment of the findings, concentrating primarily on the Puerto Rico and Jamaica data— the microscopic conditions associated with types of fertility planners. How do those who are family planners differ from those who are nonplanners? How do those who are effective planners differ from those who are accident prone?

It is possible to distinguish those families who have at least tried out one of more birth control methods from those who have not, using the terms "ever users" and "never users." With respect to the values dimension, the more couples believe in planning their life in general, the less traditional their views, the more seriously they value small families, the earlier in their marriages they feel concern about the problem, the more likely they are to have used birth control methods. Similarly, the more egalitarian the family organization, the more communication there has been between husband and wife, the more they know each other's family size desires, the more likely they are to have tried contraceptives. In short, any values which are favorable to trying family size control and any type of family organization which makes it easier to explore solutions to problems lead to the practice of birth control.

What are the differences between casual users of birth control who are short-term, irregular, and long-term regular users or persistent users? The casual user is more likely to regard the people with few children as lucky and to be, nevertheless, higher in his perception of how many is a large family. The persistent user believes more in planning in general—uses planning in his everyday affairs more frequently and is more likely to persevere in an enterprise which he has started. But more important than these beliefs, the long-range persistent user has a family geared to more protracted cooperation. Family planning is not an individual enterprise but a cooperative one. In long-range user families, there is more discussion between husband and wife, and it is less likely that the husband's mood prevails one-sidedly in decision making.

The people most likely to use birth control regularly are, thus, primarily those who can organize effectively in general. The principal factors are emphasis on planning, communication between spouses, and ability to come to a joint decision. They tend to be a well-organized family team. The casual user couple is as much or even more aware of the pressures of a growing family on resources and tries birth control methods, but it lacks the organization to follow through and pursue the goal to a successful conclusion.

Now, three distinct syndromes of family planning are identified: the "never user" whose value system, tardiness in perceiving the problem of family size, and kind of family organization are inimical to family planning; the casual user who has some motivation for controlling family size but no capacity for sustained effort; and the long-term persistent user whose ideals about planning, concern about family size, and effective family organization make him an effective user of birth control methods.

Still a fourth type of family planner has favorable attitudes toward birth control and a modern outlook but lacks the family organization to achieve the protracted cooperation so necessary to the successful use of birth control. These are families who have been sterilized—about one-sixth of Puerto Rican families. On the traditionalism-modernism continuum, the sterilized are on the modern end. The wife is permitted to work outside the home. They feel it is better to struggle against odds than to resign oneself to fate and that a child should make his own place in the world rather than follow in his father's footsteps. They believe in planning, but they actually tend to let nature take its course as far as day to day planning goes. They are, on the average, as well informed on birth control as are long-term users of birth control. It is in family organization that the sterilized appear more similar to the never users. Communication between spouses is lower; the husband tends to be dominant in most affairs, especially in reaching a decision after a disagreement. The husband is more likely to misperceive his wife's interests and ideas, and, vice versa, the wife is more likely to misunderstand and misinterpret her husband than are long-term persistent users of nonsurgical methods.

The sterilized are, thus, among the most modern in general values and most tradition-bound in family organization. Hence, if they feel the pressure of many children, it is not surprising that they use a method which does not entail any future cooperation, although it is still drastic and unconventional. This type of family reflects a set of attitudes widespread in Puerto Rico and in many other parts of the world, and it probably explains the popularity of sterilization—a one-time method—as the method of birth control.

In brief summary, we have shown that the following are important for effective planning of family size: (1) a generally modern value system, (2) definite views favoring small families, (3) sufficient information about birth control, and (4) an efficient, flexible family organization.

For successful fertility planning, the efficiency of the family must be tuned to a strong motivation. If the motivation is weak and the type of family organization is rigid or ineffective, providing a barrier to planning, planning will not occur. Here values and family organization are in negative relation to the goal. With increase in the strength of motivation arising with higher parity women, ineffectual attempts at birth control would be made. If the motivation is very strong while the family structure impedes planning, effective measures which require no planning—like sterilization or, in some countries, abortion—may result. There values are positive, but family organization is negative. In the developing countries, all three of these properties—motivation, information, and effecive family organization—are lacking in couples, particularly early in their marital careers. Ideals about family size are often not crystallized until later in the marriage. Knowledge of methods, for example, was not acquired until after the third child in Puerto Rico and Jamaica. Communication on most matters having to do with the issue of family size did not occur until late in the marriage. Couples need to share their values and their knowledge about family size control early in the marriage, but even in the United States there is a tendency to start family planning late and casually until the number desired is reached, using contraception to close a family or sterilization, as in Puerto Rico, or, as in many developing countries of Latin America, abortion. Fortunately, these features of family organization can be sufficiently changed by education and persuasion to bring about an increase in the proportion of effective planners, as we have shown in two field experiments in Puerto Rico and Jamaica.

The direct attack on the question of family organization which concentrates on widespread premarital education for marriage and parenthood, improving the competence of men and women in communication, in group problem solving, and in understanding the opposite sex, should be considered as much an integral part of a fertility planning program as the disseminating of contraceptive information and the elimination of prejudice about the use of birth control methods. Moreover, the by-product of happier families might be valuable in its own right.

With this overview of the important contributions which family structure and dynamics make in determining the success of fertility planning, let us look at the chief global irreversible decisions affecting the reproductive career and the actors involved in these decisions. The writer acknowledges the stimulation of Charles Westoff in this concept of the irreversible decision. What irreversible decisions are made over the reproductive career which affect fertility directly and who are the chief decision makers? First, there is the decision about when to marry. In closed marriage systems the parents make the decision; in open systems, the couple make it with parents participating. The second decision is how soon to have the first child. Here the couple, parents, and peers are often involved. The phenomenon of pregnancy before marriage and its consequences are detailed by Freedman and Coombs.[1] This question, how soon to have the first child, has tremendous consequences in economic achievements, ultimate family size, and family stability. Whether to use birth control methods to effect intervals between births is still a third irreversible decision: couple, parents, pastor, and medical personnel may all enter into the act. A fourth issue, what methods to use, will involve the couple, pastor, and medical personnel. When to have the second child: couple, parents, peers. How many children to have: couple, parents, peers. And, therefore, when to close a family: couple, parents, sometimes medical personnel.

Present family planning programs the world over deal with very few of these decisions. There is no work on the timing of the decision to marry, virtually no work on the timing of the first birth, very little on spacing intervals for subsequent births. The focus of action programs has been upon closing the family and upon what methods to use. Reaching women of high parity primarily late in the marriage is, as someone has said, "closing the window after the bird has flown." The argument is made that motivation is highest for high-parity women and there will be diffusion from such women to women of lower parity. This is entirely plausible but has not yet been convincingly demonstrated.

What about the decision makers reached in the worldwide family planning campaigns? In clinical programs where maternal health is the rationale in family planning, the decision maker reached is the wife, as if the decision

---

[1] Ronald Freedman and Lolagene Coombs, "Childspacing and Family Economic Position," *American Sociological Review*, 31 (October, 1966), 631–48.

were the wife's alone. And this is true in patriarchical societies as well as in societies where women are more likely to be free agents. The husband is rarely seen, as though he had no stake in the matter, whereas we know that he is the most influential referent in Puerto Rico, for example. Donald Bogue shows him to be equally influential in his Chicago studies. Moreover, in Western countries the methods most used in the past have been male methods, *coitus interruptus* and the condom, rather than female methods. This ought to be indication enough as to where the motivation is in family planning. No family planning programs have yet been aimed at couples as such, yet they are the chief decision-making unit with respect to sexual relations and birth control use. Posters all over the world invite not couples but mothers to the clinics with the admonition: "Mothers, for your children's sake and for your health, come to the clinic." Even when the poster shows the father standing by the mother, he is seen as a passive image. Parents of couples appear very rarely to be taken into account. An exception, here, is the wise-grandmother poster shown in Taiwan. The grandmother in the poster is looking across at her son and his small family of two children, saying, "Don't you wish that *your* children would be so wise," or words to that effect. It is unique. And yet, in almost all of these countries, grandmothers are especially important in decisions on when to marry and when to have the first child.

In our Puerto Rican studies, the second most important referent, after the husband, is the wife's mother. She was both the most important one and the first to suggest that maybe the couple had had enough children. Moreover, if you ask husband or wife from whom they would like to hide the fact that they are using birth control methods, they reply that it is the mother. So she serves both as the conscience, the inhibitor, and the second most important instigator in taking action.

Peer groups are just beginning to be reached, as in Chicago and Alabama where Bogue's organization of neighborhood "coffee sips" is oriented to the age peers of the couple. In India the depot holders of contraceptives indicate the peers that they feel they can influence, and they are building up their clientele through those they can influence.

Medical personnel and pastors as influentials have been largely ignored in family planning campaigns except in training programs for clinicians. The surveys show that physicians in private practice are both uninformed and obstructionists in some countries. In Morocco, there seems to be a division of labor in which the public health physicians put in the IUD's and the private physicians take them out. In that particular program the private physicians were not even invited to the National Seminar on Family Planning. The medical corps will either work for you or against you. They cannot be treated as neutral or indifferent.

In Catholic countries the clergy have been viewed as hostile to family planning, but few attempts have been made to win their cooperation, despite abundant evidence from the initiatives taken by many influential Catholic groups that this would be a profitable alliance to establish. In the Moslem countries of Turkey, Egypt, Tunisia, and Morocco the leading imams have been given authoritative statements from the theologians asserting the compatibility of family planning with the teachings of the Koran. As a consequence, there has been little evidence of obstruction from religious sources. But, in general, our programs of education and mass-communication as well as our direct contact—door to door programs—have ignored all decision makers except the "little woman." And in some countries she is the most cloistered member of the family. Now, it must be recognized that working at several decision levels with a diffuse audience of decision makers would attenuate one's messages, if carried out all at once. But experimental programs which dealt with the newly marrieds and their parents might be compared fruitfully with the somewhat stereotyped high-priority programs now monopolizing our resources.

In quick summary, what has been covered? Opening with an orientation to the contrasting stances of the demographer and the family sociologist, we indicated the contributions the latter brings to the population problem: namely, the identification of the micro-familial properties necessary before any contraceptive technology developed will be adopted and effectively used. We took account of some of the problems faced by the family sociologist in seeking to make a contribution to the body of knowledge needed for more effective fertility control. We provided a rationale for making the family the unit of study and action, and outlined the advantages of symbolic interaction as the conceptual framework for viewing the problem. We continued with a list of the micro-familial properties required, as involving high motivation, mastery of the means, and an effective family organization for taking action on family goals, all three of which appear to be lacking in families of the developing countries and in couples everywhere early in their marital careers. A schema was developed which clustered these properties into six blocks of variables which constitute the crucial explanatory variables accounting for differential fertility control effectiveness.

The findings from the Puerto Rican data, treating factors analytically, were reviewed revealing adequacy of husband-wife communication as a central explanatory factor, when all other factors were held constant, in determining success in fertility planning. From the same studies, we distinguished different types of users of contraceptive methods—the "never user," the "quitter" or "casual user," the "regular long-term user" and the sterilized—showing the propensity for general planning and acceptance of small-family-size norms, accompanied by communicativeness in spouses and egalitarian relationships. I characterized ever users as against never users, but also distinguished between casual users and long-term users. The sterilized were shown to have strong motivation, but ineffective family organization, forcing them late in the marriage to undertake a method which didn't require cooperation. A field experiment, based upon these findings, has demonstrated the feasibility of changing family ineffectiveness by education to improve fertility planning, arguing for the equal importance of such programs with information and persuasion programs designed to effect levels of knowledge and motivation.

Closing with the identification of seven irreversible fertility-related decisions and the chief decision makers involved in these decisions, we argued for making a beginning at organizing more ambitious programs of action which would increase both the number of the decision levels and number of crucial decision makers reached in social action programs.

SELECTED READINGS

Back, Kurt W., Hill, Reuben, and Stycos, J. Mayone, "The Puerto Rican Experiment in Population Control." *Human Relations*, 10 (November 1957), 315–34.

————, "The Dynamics of Family Planning." *Marriage and Family Living*, 18, No. 3 (August 1956), 196–200.

Berelson, Bernard, et al., *Family Planning and Population Programs*. Chicago: University of Chicago Press, 1966.

Blake, Judith, "Family Instability and Reproductive Behavior in Jamaica," in *Current Research in Human Fertility*. New York: Milbank Memorial Fund, 1955. Pp. 24–41.

Carisse, Colette, *Planification des Naissances en Milieu Canadien-Francais*. Montreal: Les Presses de l'Université de Montreal, 1964.

Davis, Kingsley and Blake, Judith, "Social Structure and Fertility: An Analytic Framework," *Economic Development and Cultural Change*, 4, No. 3 (April 1956), 211–35.

Girard, Alain and Henry, Louis, "Les Attitudes et la Conjoncture Demographique: Natalite, Structure Familiale et Limites de la Vie Active." *Population*, 11, No. 1 (January–March 1956), 106–41.

Hill, Reuben, Stycos, J. Mayone, and Back, Kurt W., *The Family and Population Control*. Chapel Hill: University of North Carolina Press, 1959.

————, "Family Action Potentials and Fertility Planning in Puerto Rico," in *Current Research in Human Fertility*. New York: Milbank Memorial Fund, 1955. Pp. 42–62.

————, "La Estructura de la Familia y la Fertilidad en Puerto Rico," *Revista de Ciencias Sociales*, 1, No. 1 (March 1957), 37–66.

Rainwater, Lee, *Family Design*. Chicago: Aldine, 1964.

Stanton, Howard, "Puerto Rico's Changing Families," *Transactions of the Third World Congress of Sociology*, Vol. 4. London: International Sociological Association, 1956.

Stycos, J. Mayone, *Family and Fertility in Puerto Rico: A Study of the Lower Income Group*. New York: Columbia University Press, 1955.

Stycos, J. Mayone and Back, Kurt W., *The Control of Human Fertility in Jamaica*. Ithaca: Cornell University Press, 1964.

Stycos, J. Mayone, Back, Kurt W., and Hill, Reuben, "Interpersonal Influence in Family Planning in Puerto Rico," *Transactions of the Third World Congress of Sociology*, Vol. 8. London: International Sociological Association, 1956.

|XI| Marital Dissolution

Introduction to Section XI

Every society has some means by which an individual may escape from an unsatisfying marital union. In some societies this involves covert norms sanctioning bigamy or a mistress system, whereas in others the means involve divorce or separation. The ideal of a pleasant, happy marital union is almost universally shared. Societies differ in their emphasis upon this ideal and in the ways of release when the ideal is not achieved.

The marital relationship is profoundly affected by the social setting in which it takes place. Having kin and friends who support one's values and define one as being involved in a stable marriage seems to be one key factor in producing stable marriage itself.[1] Thus, even in the most personal and intimate of marital relationships, the relationship is not simply a private or individual matter. The importance of the social and cultural setting for understanding individual behavior was also brought out in other sections, such as Sections III and IV, dealing with love and sex relationships.

The higher incidence of marital disruption of many types in the lower classes is another illustration of the power of the social setting to affect a relationship. The economic strains, the lesser overall control of life situations that prevail in the lower classes, predispose their marital relationships to higher rates of disruption. The Komarovsky chapter presents an in-depth picture of the life style of the blue-collar worker and his marriage (32). She points out the sharp male–female role separation, the presence of undeveloped communication skills, and the exclusion from community organizations, as some of the key factors in the life style of the blue-collar worker that bear upon his high rate of marital dissolution. Komarovsky is a master of the case-study method of

[1] Ackermann, C., "Affiliations: Structural Determinants of Differential Divorce Rates." *American Journal of Sociology* 69 (July, 1963), 13–20.

487

research and uses it to ádvantage in analyzing the 58 blue-collar marriages in her sample. Levinger's review of marital dissolution studies (33) fills in the picture painted by Komarovsky with an overview of such studies.

One frequent question concerning divorce revolves about the impact on the children involved. Using a carefully devised scale measuring self-esteem and a good sample of ten high schools in New York State, Morris Rosenberg attempted to find an answer to this question (34). There have been other researchers that have generally found little difference between children of divorced parents and children of intact marriages. Rosenberg finds that divorce does make a difference but that it has to be specified in terms of the mother's religion, the age of the mother, and whether she remarried, among other things. These results do not fully settle the issue but they do start us toward a qualified answer and encourage further study.

32 | Blue-Collar Marital Disorganization

MIRRA KOMAROVSKY

The theory that illuminates Glenton's problems bears little resemblance to some dominant interpretations of social ills. In contemporary sociology, social problems are generally associated with anomie or the breakdown of social norms, cultural ambiguities and institutional conflicts.[1] Relevant as these concepts are in a period of vast world changes, they may lead to an overemphasis upon consensus. Glenton's families are generally stable, respectable, and law-abiding, sharing deeply internalized and common values. Stable though they are, one-third of these marriages fail to rate our assessment of "moderately happy." In 14 per cent of the cases the marriages are "very unhappy." There is no doubt about this latter diagnosis; in these very unhappy cases all but one of the wives (and she was also wretched) voiced strong regrets about their marriages. Slightly over one-third of the marriages are rated as moderately happy. At the other extreme, slightly less than one-third are happily or very happily married. Their numerous problems will serve as a reminder that, if social ills are frequently the product of moral confusion, it does not necessarily follow that clear moral directives and consensus are synonymous with social health.

Some violations of social norms were no doubt concealed from us. Allowing for such under-reporting, the evidence nevertheless strongly suggests that deviant behavior plays only a minor role in the marriage problems of our respondents. Illegitimacy, adultery, juvenile delinquency, alcoholism, refusal on the part of the housewife and the provider to fulfill their obligations appear to be rare exceptions. The husbands are not all adequate providers but it is not for want of effort and devotion. There are many other examples, as we shall show, of failure to attain desired and culturally sanctioned goals but this failure does not generally lead to violations of legal or moral codes.

Social disorganization, however, may exist in the absence of deviant behavior.[2] The distinction between the two concepts proved its usefulness in the case of Glenton. Deviant behavior refers to violations of normative codes. Social disorganization, on the other hand, has been defined by Robert K. Merton as "inadequacies or failures in a social system of interrelated statuses and roles such that collective purposes and individual objectives of its members are less fully realized than they could be in an alternative workable system."[3] Social deviation may be one cause of disorganization but it is not the only one, and it must not be permitted to obscure the other causes.

[1] See, for example, Robert K. Merton and Robert A. Nisbet, 1961, p. 13.
[2] Ibid., pp. 697–737.
[3] Ibid., p. 720.

Reprinted from *Blue-Collar Marriage* by Mirra Komarovsky, 1967, pp. 330–347, by permission of Random House, Inc., New York.

Moreover, the distinction between the concepts of deviation and disorganization enables us to raise significant problems as to their interrelationship. For example, what are the consequences of particular kinds and degrees of deviance for the ability of specified social systems to fulfill their goals? How do other deficiencies of social systems affect the patterning of deviance?

Social disorganization in Glenton is not the result of deviant behavior, nor yet of the other conditions strongly emphasized in current theory, i.e., institutional conflict and moral dissensus. Our respondents are relatively alienated from many institutions of the community. Having few institutional ties they are consequently spared the conflicts caused by competing demands of various statuses. For example, the familiar conflict between career and family life does not plague the workingman. His emotional investment in the job is relatively slight. Irregular work shifts occasionally create problems for the family but no workingman's wife need feel jealous of her husband's job and he himself does not feel guilty because his career leaves too little time for his family. The workingman's wife does not resent her husband's career but neither does she feel that she contributes to it by social entertaining or advice. The husband cannot count on her assistance but he is protected from critical scrutiny of his performance on the job.

Though rare, competing loyalties do exist. The union, the church, and a youth group each absorbed the interests of three men to the extent that their wives felt neglected. In two of these cases the marriage is problem-ridden and the wife sensed that her husband's preoccupation is motivated by the wish to escape the unhappy home.

Conflicts in marriage are sometimes created by the outside affiliations of the wives, several of whom are more active in churches and in clubs than their husbands. One man with ten years of schooling, married to an intelligent high school graduate, active in the affairs of her church, confessed to the interviewer:

> I might not have told you but she said she already told you, that nothing in the world gets me more than coming home and finding she's not here and not knowing where she is. I get to thinking, maybe she's out gabbing with the women in the church and that gets me mad and blue. She usually comes home in the middle of church suppers and things like that to fix my meal for me. I like that a lot. I think I'm an average man. I enjoy my family. A little untidiness is O.K., but if it's there all the time, you can't take it, *especially if it's because she has outside interests* [italics ours].

Another woman, also a high school graduate, is active in the P.T.A. and in the church. The church has created the one serious problem in an otherwise happy marriage:

> He didn't want me to teach Sunday School. I cried plenty and it was a real problem in our marriage. It wasn't only the Sunday School. It grew into the teachers' meetings and afternoon services. He now feels a little more a part of it. They asked for volunteers to serve coffee during the coffee break at the church and he volunteered and had a good time talking to people. But he still doesn't like to go to church and still doesn't let me do everything I'd like to do.

Both of these men find their main gratification within the home whereas their wives are enjoying the heady wine of leadership in outside organizations. The first husband is patently dependent upon his wife. The irony of the second case is that the husband has succeeded in transforming his shy and insecure wife into a more outgoing person. She gives him full credit for this metamorphosis. But having become self-confident, she is reaching out into community activities. "He doesn't like to share me with anyone or anything" —all the more so, we might add, because he himself has no strong interest either in his work or in civic participation.

It is no accident that in both cases the wives are high school graduates. The latter exceed the less-educated women in church and club memberships. In our sample, the educated women also exceed their husbands in group memberships. The less-educated couples conform more closely than the high school graduates to the specialization of the roles posited by Talcott Parsons.[4] Among the former the husband is not merely the provider but the "secretary of state" concerned with the family's relations to the external world. But the high school wives tend to be more involved in community affairs than their husbands.

One problem caused by multiple affiliations is, however, quite prevalent. We refer to the in-law problems that are created by continued interdependence of the married couple and their parental families.

Another allegedly prevalent contemporary problem is also rare among these families. Ambiguous definitions of conjugal roles or conflicts over different conceptions of marriage cause few marital difficulties because spouses have similar cultural backgrounds. The exceptions to this consist of a few cases of religious and class intermarriages.

The intermarriage that creates the more serious strain is one in which the wife (and not the husband) has the superior class background.[5] The marriage norms of the high blue-collar worker are more egalitarian than in the lower strata and the wife who marries "up" has no difficulty in accepting this improvement in her position.

But when the high blue-collar woman marries "down," the consequences may be more stressful. A characteristic conflict of such a marriage concerns social life—especially as regards recreational activities without the children. "He likes us all to be together all the time and I'd like to leave the children home and have us do things by ourselves sometimes," said a mother of four children, a high school graduate who married "down." "Sometimes I think it's because he didn't have any education and he has nothing else to do or to think about than just relaxing at home with the T.V." The couple disagree about baby-sitters. The husband shares the frequently held attitude of low blue-collar families: "I wouldn't leave my children with a stranger." The wife, on the other hand, would prefer to pay a stranger instead of depending upon services given by relatives that she would have to repay. Social life is a bone of contention in still another way. The husband expects relatives to join in all the social entertaining but the wife considers personal congeniality on social occasions to take precedence over ties to kin. Education is another

[4] Talcott Parsons, 1955, p. 47.
[5] See Julius Roth and Robert F. Peck, 1951.

subject of disagreements in this family. The husband resents the money spent by his wife on the *Reader's Digest* and its series of abridged books. He does help the young children with their homework but frequently feels that chores around the house are more important than school work, while his wife emphasizes the latter.

The yearning for a more romantic approach to love-making was expressed by one 34-year-old high school graduate who married a rough, less-educated but benevolent patriarch. "I'd be happy if we'd just go along the road and park somewhere sometimes," she said. "What do you think you're doing?" he is likely to say, "we are too old for that kind of stuff." This is a restless, energetic woman with an inquiring mind, married to a good provider who likes his home and wants to be left alone to enjoy his comfort. She tries to stimulate and to arouse him but succeeds only in evoking a stubborn defensiveness. Their previously satisfactory sex life has been harmed by this psychological interplay. She is puzzled by his neglect of her. "It isn't that he doesn't respond, you touch him and he gets excited but he doesn't like to do that any more."

Other differences in class backgrounds of the spouses and the problems discussed so far are, to repeat, exceptional in Glenton. But these families pay a high price for their immunity to some typical ills of our time. This immunity is produced by their isolation from social mainstreams. But the shield that protects them from the disorganizing influences of social change is also a barrier against its benefits. Similarly, if they are spared the conflicting demands of various organizations they are also deprived of the advantages of social participation.

In turning now to Glenton's major problems we shall at the same time qualify the current emphasis upon institutional conflicts and the breakdown of moral consensus as the main source of social disorganization.

It is not the failure to maintain traditional social patterns but the failure to modify them that accounts for some marital problems in Glenton. In a period of rapid social change, effective socialization into traditional patterns may contribute to social disorganization.

The sharp differentiation of masculine and feminine roles and the absence of the expectation of friendship in marriage are cases in point. Even when fully accepted by both partners these cultural patterns create difficulties for each. The husband pays a price for his relative exemption from domestic duties. Irritability, the apathy, the desire for a job outside the home—these are the reactions of some women to the domestic routine unrelieved by companionship with their husbands. Mr. Daniels was not the only husband baffled by his wife's frequent depressions. He consulted a relative who told him that women are subject to fits of "neurasthenia." He could not perceive any connection between his neglect of his wife and her condition because he behaved in what was, for his group, the accepted way. Some situations create frustrations even when they do not violate any norms. The young wife who has no expectation of friendship in marriage can still feel lonely. The young husband who never expected a wife to share his interests can still experience boredom with her conversation.

The reader may cite the case of the Greens to show that marriages can be satisfying even when they are not based upon friendship. This is a fact worth noting. But such marriages require the availability of relatives and close friends. Geographical mobility tends to separate the married couples from kin and trusted friends. The Smiths are only one of several families that demonstrate the burden such separation places upon the marriage to provide the emotional support previously given by other primary groups.[6] The same lesson is implicit in the cases of the Greens and the Kings, whose satisfactory marriages depend upon functions performed for each spouse by outsiders. These older norms of marriage will become increasingly unsuitable if the following prediction by a government agency proves accurate: "Many more of our workers than in the past must have, or develop, the mobility to shift jobs. . . . Many may have to change their residence as well as their occupation."[7]

Traditional patterns have today other unfavorable consequences. Because the need for psychological intimacy could not be satisfied in marriage, some men and many more women exchange confidences with outsiders. But friendship has a dynamic of its own and cannot always be contained within the prescribed limits. Even in a marriage which is "not for friendship," the disclosure of certain matters to outsiders is taboo. Twenty-one per cent of the husbands voiced a complaint that their wives talked too much about personal matters to outsiders. The husbands were distressed to realize that their finances or marital conflicts were exposed to public view. Fewer men than women have confidants; only 7 per cent of the women have a similar grievance. The absence of the norm of friendship created certain psychological pressures to seek confidants outside of marriage. But this, in turn, resulted in violation of marital privacy.

Again, the Glenton ideal of masculinity with its emphasis upon emotional reserve and its identification of personal interchange with the feminine role resulted in what we have termed a "trained incapacity to share." Chapter 8 demonstrates the deleterious effects of these characteristics upon the ability to cope with marital conflicts and to provide emotional support for the mate. Thus, even when a couple was exposed to the ideal of the companionate marriage, this lack of interpersonal competence occasionally hindered its realization. Indeed, the intellectual acceptance of such an ideal aroused in some couples feelings of inadequacy. They knew that husbands and wives should talk to one another, but they found nothing to say. One measure of this problem is conveyed by two sets of figures. In response to one test story, 56 per cent of the wives held that something was lacking in the marriage of the couple in the story who had so little to talk about in the evenings. But as many as 44 per cent of the women, in another connection, complained that they frequently had nothing interesting to talk about with their husbands. For the husbands, the corresponding figures were 45 per cent, referring to the story, and 28 per cent, expressing a personal complaint.

The difficulties that hinder fuller realization of the ideal of companionship illustrate a familiar mode of social disorganization. Socially structured

[6] For the effect of mobility upon marriage see Elizabeth Bott, 1957; John M. Mogey, 1956; and Michael Young and Peter Willmott, 1957.

[7] Department of Labor release published in *The New York Times*, September 20, 1963.

obstacles stand in the way of attaining the newly emerging cultural goal.[8] With respect to marital communication, our data enabled us to compare the magnitude of this discrepancy between aspirations and attainment for men and women at each educational level. The older high school women experience the widest gap between their expectations, on the one hand, and the actual quality of the marriage dialogue, on the other. They are consequently more dissatisfied with marriage communication than the less-educated wives at the same stage of life, despite the fact that they actually enjoy a higher level of sharing and companionate interchange.

The reader may argue that the personal dissatisfactions described above do not constitute social disorganization. Granted that the families continue to function without the social supports or restraints required by more seriously disorganized groups. Nevertheless, since the function of companionship is an increasingly important raison d'etre of marriage, marital unhappiness by definition implies the failure of this social system to attain one of its goals, with unfavorable consequences for the fulfillment of other goals, including that of child-rearing.

The function of companionship has been frequently cited by sociologists as the distinctive feature of modern marriage. Many writers have described the evolution of the modern family with specialization in its functions.[9] The remaining functions have been variously described as affectional or expressive and child-rearing or socialization. "We have argued above," concludes one recent discussion, "that the nuclear family is specialized far over in the expressive tension-management and socialization directions."[10]

If Glenton families are at all typical of comparable classes in other communities, then for considerable segments of our population these writings are more prescriptive than descriptive. They define the appropriate functions of marriage in modern society. But the logic of the analysis does not unfortunately bring the required patterns into existence automatically. Possibly even for the unhappy third of the Glenton couples, marriage entails some satisfactions. But these men and women do not turn to one another for emotional support, and it is uncertain whether the net effect of the marriage relationship is to relieve or to increase personal tension.

Let us recapitulate our analysis. Modern marriage is called upon to fulfill new functions of friendship and emotional support, partly as a result of mobility and isolation of the couple and partly in response to new cultural expectations stimulated by the changing status of women and other trends. The fulfillment of these functions is impaired in Glenton by the persistence of some traditional values and definitions of sex roles. These operate directly in sanctioning certain behavior and indirectly, through their detrimental effects upon interpersonal competence. The relatively low educational level of Glenton respondents plays, no doubt, an independent role in retarding the development of skills and attitudes required for psychological intimacy between the sexes.

The survival of dysfunctional values and attitudes is not the only source

[8] See Robert K. Merton, 1957, pp. 162–164.
[9] William F. Ogburn, Robert M. MacIver, Ernest W. Burgess, Harvey J. Locke, and Talcott Parsons, among others.
[10] Talcott Parsons and Robert Bales, 1955, pp. 162–163.

of social disorganization in Glenton. Were the residents themselves asked to rank their difficulties, the economic situation would head the list. Their relatively low occupational and educational resources create a wide gulf between desired goals and attainments. Not only the poorest fourth of the families, but others also live from one pay envelope to the next, with no savings or insurance to cushion a possible crisis. This explains the undercurrent of anxiety which repeatedly comes to the surface in such remarks as, "He worked good last year. I hope he will this year," or "I hope we'll stay healthy." Public relief is too humiliating to contemplate for these people, and in moments of panic they are much more likely to think of their relatives as a possible source of assistance.

For the man, the economic difficulties have a special emotional significance—they undermine his self-esteem. For example, he is concerned about his parental responsibilities. Our question, "Would you like your son to follow in your line of work?" was generally answered negatively, "No, I would like him to do a lot better." But at the same time the fathers doubted their ability to provide for their children the necessary means of advancement.

The husbands experience some other characteristic strains. Their actual power in the family frequently falls short of their patriarchal aspirations. In contrast, successful professional husbands may occasionally enjoy more power in marriage than is sanctioned by their egalitarian ideals.[11] The twinges of guilt which this latter discrepancy produces are less painful than the workingman's problem. Our respondents thought that "men should have the final say-so in family decisions." However, they found themselves pitted against resourceful wives who held paid jobs prior to marriage and could hold their own in marriage. This is especially true of the women high school graduates. One young wife told the interviewer that her husband's current weekly wages were only $10.00 higher than her own pay before marriage. Even the good providers lack the halo of prestige which high achievement and high community status bestow on a successful business or professional man.

The lack of occupational and educational skills hinders the attainment of desired goals but this does not drive Glenton residents to resort to illegitimate means. Several possible explanations suggest themselves for the low rate of deviancy. In comparison with lower socio-economic groups, especially those with racial and ethnic disadvantages, these native born Protestants may feel less alienated from society and more strongly committed to its moral codes and legitimations. We have already noted, for example, that their individualistic ideology made the Glenton's poor providers deflect the blame for their low achievement from social conditions to personal failings. Moreover, the majority of Glenton's families have not given up the hope of improving their own economic position within the blue-collar class. By projecting their ambition to move out of the working class onto their children they feel that they remain true to the American norm of striving.

The relatively poor adaptation to the economic environment is, of course,

[11] See Peter Pineo, 1961, for a discussion of a middle-class sample. As this book goes to press I note that a similar observation about class differences in patterns of strain has been made by William J. Goode, 1963, p. 21.

a familiar theme in the literature on the working classes. Less familiar is the effect upon marriage of the poor utilization of the cultural, recreational and social resources of the community, also associated with this class position. The drabness of life puts a heavy burden upon the marriage relationship. Shortening of the work day, smaller families, and the withdrawal of many economic functions from the home have given these couples long evenings and weekends together. But life in general is impoverished, and marriage assumes a saliency by default. It is questionable whether any relationship can fill so great a void. Even the middle-class suburbanite, who has reputedly forsaken the world for the family nest, bristles with outside interests in comparison with out respondents. Status seeking, the elaboration of living standards, the social life, to say nothing of civic and cultural interests, fill life with tension and struggle but also with emotional involvement and rewards. The romantic ideal which decrees that each find in his mate the fulfillment of all his needs is, after all, only rarely attainable. Many marriages remain satisfying precisely because each partner can draw upon other sources of stimulation, amusement, response and accomplishment. These rewarding experiences may be shared in marriage thus nourishing the relationship. They may also compensate for whatever frustrations may be entailed in marriage. Of course, outside interests occasionally become so all-absorbing as to divest marriage of any emotional significance or they may violate the limits of cultural permissiveness as in the case of extra-marital sex. But given some psychic congeniality, the richness of life enjoyed apart from the marital relationship per se may sustain the latter and make it not merely tolerable but rewarding.

As for Glenton couples, those in their twenties still enjoy social life and other forms of recreation. The birth of children and the striving to purchase a home and to furnish it still give life a sense of movement. But many couples in their late thirties, especially among the less-educated, seem almost to have withdrawn from life. There they sit in front of the television set: "What's there to say? We both see it." "If you had two extra hours every day, how would you like to spend them?" asked the interviewer, and a man mused: "This would make the evening awfully long and tiring if you're watching T.V."

The social isolation, especially of the older men, has been repeatedly noted. We have described the relatively low involvement of the men, as compared with their wives, in the lives of their married children. Social life with friends also declines with age. Only infrequently do the men appear to enjoy emotionally significant ties with work-mates. They lack even the kind of segmented, though intense, relationships that business and professional men frequently have with co-workers.[12] If this social isolation is characteristic of working-class men of other ethnic, religious, and regional groups, it may play a role in explaining the relatively lower level of mental health in blue-collar strata as compared with the middle and upper classes.[13] In any event,

[12] See Robert Dubin, 1956, for a research finding to the effect that "only ten per cent of the . . . (surveyed) workers perceived their important primary social relationships as taking place at work." For a comparative study of a professional group, see Louis H. Orzack, 1959.

[13] Thomas S. Langner and S. T. Michael, 1963.

this social isolation, we believe, tends to strain the marriage relationship. It robs life, and therefore marriage, of stimulation and novelty and it closes outlets that might siphon off marital irritations.

We were slow to perceive the problem brought about by a drab existence and constant "togetherness," for a reason that illustrates anew how tacitly held values can distort perception. We approached the study with the image of the East London working-class marriage in mind. Will the American working-class marriage, we asked, show the same estrangement between the sexes? Do husbands and wives in Glenton, as in London, lead their separate lives in work and in leisure? The English pattern fell short of our own ideal of friendship in marriage.

Glenton families were found to differ significantly from the East London ones. Most wives know to the penny what their husbands earn, and economic decisions are made jointly. There is no lack of togetherness in the sense of time spent in each other's physical presence. Indeed, these couples probably spend more time together as a family (and probably more time together as a pair, without children, relatives, or friends) than middle-class couples with their more active social and club life. Our own moral set led us to approve these deviations from the East London patterns, and we were temporarily blinded to the problem that togetherness entailed for our respondents. We mistakenly assumed that the greater association between the spouses automatically brought about a deeper relationship than in East London.

Not all of Glenton families experience the difficulties just enumerated with equal intensity. The high school graduates on the whole, are happier in marriage than the less-educated. This is especially true in the first years of marriage. The better-educated marry later and delay child-bearing in comparison with the less-educated couples. Consequently, fewer of the former suffer from the syndrome of problems of some young couples: too many infants, parenthood too soon after marriage under difficult economic conditions and in the absence of companionship between the mates. Moreover, the high school men (perhaps because they are younger), do not include the completely defeated men whose sense of failure has such unhappy consequences for marriage.

While high school graduates also believe in the traditional division of labor between the sexes, in practice the husbands help more frequently with the care of infants and with shopping than in less-educated families. Equally significant is their fuller marital communication. They have more faith in the possibility of friendship between men and women. One young high school graduate explained why women have more need of heart-to-heart talk than men: "The husband's job is an outlet for him and her days are more routine and so she needs to sit down and feel the closeness with her husband." When depressed, this wife finds that "a good heart-to-heart talk can do a lot for her morale." A value endorsed so explicitly must surely affect behavior. In contrast, the less-educated tend to feel, as was indicated in an earlier chapter, that friendship is more likely to exist between persons of the same sex and that the principal marital ties are sexual union, mutual devotion and complementary tasks.

But the better-educated have some typical problems of their own. Status frustration is one of them. Generally, status-seeking is not a prominent drive among these families. There is an order of priorities in goals and many are preoccupied with sheer survival. Even the more prosperous families do not live with gazes fixed on their reflected image, and with the constant comparative self-appraisal allegedly so characteristic of our society. This is no "other-directed" group. Many a middle-class couple who have to cultivate the "right" people for the sake of the husband's career would envy the freedom these families enjoy to entertain only the people they like. Their social life, such as it is, is pure sociability. Nevertheless, some pressures for upward mobility do exist and some high school couples exhibit strain because their aspirations for higher status are frustrated.

We found no difference between the two educational groups in the prevalence of sexual problems or in psychological sources of marital strains. No personality tests were employed in this study, and observations about psychological factors in marital maladjustment here appear inconclusive. But some speculation is aroused by the higher proportion of hostile sons and daughters among the less-educated couples, caused apparently by a number of social factors in their early lives. An unhappy childhood and hostile parent-child relationships tend to affect adversely the marital adjustment of the individual.[14] If this excess of parent-child conflict among the less-educated is confirmed by future studies it will offer another possible explanation of their lower marital happiness.

We limited our summary to problems in marriage, brought about, directly or indirectly, by socio-economic and cultural conditions. But there is hardly a case history cited in this book which does not suggest psychological factors involved in marital strain. Sharing a home with in-laws need not necessarily create an in-law problem, but it requires, as we have seen, a closer emotional dovetailing of personalities if trouble is to be avoided. Given the same degree of congeniality, those residing in separate households will experience less strain. Given a common residence, variations in psychological factors will also produce variations in the outcome. Maintaining the fiction of her husband's supremacy in public is, for example, an accepted stratagem of a dominant wife. But this adaptation to a deviant situation is not available to some personalities. We encountered a wife whose competitiveness with her husband, more or less dormant in the privacy of the home, is aroused by the presence of an audience.

The summary of Glenton's problems was further limited to those most likely to be class-linked. The book itself illustrated many other sources of social disorganization: discontinuities in sex roles throughout the life cycle; ethical inconsistencies consequent upon social mobilty and social change, yielding unearned advantages to either husbands or wives; situational pressures giving rise to operative norms which occasionally violate the ideal code and others. Among social sources of psychological stress, our case studies revealed an interesting variety. It is well known that culture may cause stress by censuring some desired gratification or by mandating a goal difficult to attain. But social factors may affect the degree of stress also by making it more or less difficult for individuals to mask socially condemned motives. For example, the new social acceptance of working wives has not

[14] Clifford Kirkpatrick, 1963, pp. 385–386.

modified the husband's jealousy, his anxiety over the possible loss of power and other personal objections to his wife's employment. Lacking the support of public condemnation, he is robbed of acceptable rationalizations in arguing his case and must expose, to himself and to others, his "irrational" objections. Again, the well-to-do wife, whose real motive for working is the wish for power, can hardly claim that she needs to contribute to family support. The Glenton working wives, on the other hand, could plausibly rationalize less acceptable incentives in economic terms.[15]

This study did not include any middle- or upper-class respondents, and it contains no data on broad class differences in marital adjustment. Recent evidence shows that divorce rates tend to decrease with higher socio-economic and educational status. The data on marital satisfaction are consistent; satisfaction appears to go up with the rise in the class hierarchy.[16] We have no information about the rates of divorce or desertion among the general population of Glenton's Protestant blue-collar families from which we drew our respondents. Nevertheless, our comparison of the two educational categories of blue-collar families has some pertinence to the question of broad class differences in marital happiness.

Current analyses of this problem seek to ascertain the peculiarly stressful experiences of the working classes in comparison with the upper strata.[17] But it is not certain whether the extent of stress does in fact decline as one ascends the occupational or the educational ladder. The economic and occupational frustrations were indeed more prevalent among our less-educated respondents as they are, no doubt, in a comparable stratum in the society at large. But offsetting these and other difficulties of these workers is their freedom from a number of allegedly typical problems of the higher and better-educated classes. Ambiguous definitions of mutual rights and duties and the resulting ethical inconsistencies, mental conflict produced by an abundance of choices, conflicting loyalties and standards, strain produced by the sheer volume of stimuli—all these are relatively rare in Glenton. Glenton couples are also free from the self-conscious scrutiny of relationships that, some writers claim, robs marriage of its spontaneity among many highly educated persons.

Are we to assume then, ex post facto, that these problems, more prevalent among the higher classes, are somehow less disturbing than those typical of the workingman?[18]

[15] These observations suggest a new dimension to the factor of visibility in social relations. In the past it was the visibility of norms and of role-performance that was the object of discussion. Added to this now is the probability that social factors may determine the degree to which an occupant of some status can succeed in masking his motivations, or conversely, be forced to expose them.

[16] See bibliographies in William M. Kephart, 1961, and in William J. Goode, 1956 and 1963.

[17] See, for example, William J. Goode, 1956, p. 67.

[18] It is possible that the Glenton sample is too stable to be typical of working-class strata that are generally included in the class comparisons of marital adjustment. But the insulation from intellectual currents of the larger society and absence of group affiliations have been demonstrated in numerous working-class studies in other communities.

The interpretation of this problem may require a shift in emphasis. It is an open question whether life is less stressful for the higher classes. But it must surely contain richer rewards.[19] The sense of satisfaction with marriage, as with life in general, may depend not so much upon an absence of stress as upon the presence of rewards—a momentary feeling of closeness with one's mate, the occasional excitement of hope, even a fleeting triumph of achievement. True, a low level of expectations inflates the rewards of minor attainments ("I had myself a ball once when I came out two dollars over the budget that we didn't have to pay out all at once"). But even with their modest aspirations, too many Glenton couples find life drab and unrewarding.

The paradox that higher socio-economic classes may experience both more happiness and more tension in marriage is no mere conjecture. The more highly-educated respondents in one study rated their marital happiness higher than people of less education; at the same time they expressed more self-doubt and a greater sense of inadequacy.[20] Further confirmation is supplied by a recent investigation which reveals that "high marital tension or job dissatisfaction may not necessarily produce unhappiness if they are offset by a sufficient number of positive feelings."[21] The better educated, higher income groups in the same study were found to exhibit a higher level of both positive and negative feelings. The authors conclude that "men of higher socio-economic status have a higher degree of marital tension, but at the same time happier marriages . . . [than men of the lower status]."[22]

Not only is the marriage relationship of the educated middle classes—in comparison with blue-collar workers—likely to contain more positive experiences, but so does their life in general. The more abundant life provides, as noted earlier, safety valves to siphon off marital frustrations and compensations to offset them.

Life at its best is economically comfortable and rewarding, but for the great majority life is narrowly circumscribed. A spotlight outlines a small circle of ground around each family, with the relatives, a few friends, the boss and some work-mates, the tavern keeper, the church and the union. Visible also are the top movie stars, baseball players and other athletes, T. V. performers and top national office holders. But beyond that circle extends a vast darkness. These English-speaking, well-dressed, well-mannered, responsible persons do not enjoy full membership in their society. They lack even such bridges to the larger society as may be provided by membership in a women's club or a Chamber of Commerce. The union occasionally (but from what could be ascertained, only infrequently) provides such a channel of information and sense of participation.[23] Verbal and intellectual limitations curtail reflection even about the immediate environment. In the words of Beatie, the working-class rebel of *Roots:* "Ever since it began the world's bin growin' hasn't it? Things have happened, things have bin discovered,

[19] See Alex Inkeles, 1960.
[20] Gerald Gurin, et al., 1960, p. 116.
[21] Norman M. Bradburn and David Caplovitz, 1965, p. 39.
[22] Ibid., p. 41.
[23] For a similar view see Joel Seidman, "The Labor Union as an Organization" in Arthur Kornhauser, et al., 1954.

people have bin thinking and improving and inventing but what do we know about it all?"[24] Economically poorer racial and ethnic minorities are no doubt still more deprived, but this does not make the exclusion of Glenton families any less wasteful and disturbing.

This is not merely the judgment of the author. In considerable measure, this is also the respondents' self-appraisal. Why, otherwise, would a father exclaim with such feeling: "No, I want my children to go a lot farther." But for all their fervent hopes and the struggle, these parents cannot provide for their children the environment enjoyed by the average middle-class child. Unless school and society find ways to improve the life chances for all citizens, a proportion of Glenton's children will grow up to live as do their parents, on the fringes of their society.

REFERENCES

Bott, Elizabeth, *Family and Social Network*, London: Tavistock Publications, 1957.

Bradburn, Norman M., and David Caplovitz, *Reports on Happiness*, Chicago: Aldine Publishing, 1956.

Dubin, Robert, "Industrial Workers' Worlds," *Social Problems*, 3 (January, 1956), 131–142.

Goode, William J., *After Divorce*, New York: Macmillan-Free Press, 1956.

Goode, William J., *World Revolution and Family Patterns*, New York: Macmillan-Free Press, 1963.

Gurin, Gerald, et al., *Americans View Their Mental Health*, New York: Basic Books, 1960, p. 116.

Inkeles, Alex, "Industrial Man: The Relation of Status to Experience, Perception and Value," *American Journal of Sociology*, 66 (July, 1960), 1–32.

Kephart, William M., *The Family, Society and the Individual*, Boston: Houghton Mifflin, 1961.

Kirkpatrick, Clifford, *The Family as Process and Institution*, New York: Ronald Press, 1963.

Kornhauser, Arthur, Robert Dubin and A. Ross, eds., *Industrial Conflict*, New York: McGraw-Hill, 1954.

Langner, Thomas S., and S. T. Michael, *Life Stress and Mental Health*, New York: Macmillan-Free Press, 1963.

Locke, Harvey J., et al., *The Family: Analysis of Dyadic Relations*, Abstracts of the Meetings of the American Sociology Society, 1955.

Merton, Robert K., *Social Theory and Social Structure*, New York: Macmillan-Free Press, 1957.

Merton, Robert K., and Robert A. Nisbet, *Contemporary Social Problems*, New York: Harcourt, Brace and World, 1961.

Mogey, John M., *Family and Neighborhood, Two Studies in Oxford*, London: Oxford University Press, 1956.

Orzack, Louis H., "Work as a 'Central Life Interest' of Professionals," *Social Problems*, 7 (Fall, 1959), 125–132.

[24] Arnold Wesker, 1959, pp. 74–75.

Parsons, Talcott, and Robert F. Bales, *Family Socialization and Interaction Process*, New York: Macmillan-Free Press, 1955.

Pineo, Peter C., "Disenchantment in the Later Years of Marriage," *Marriage and Family Living*, 23, (February, 1961), 3–11.

Roth, Julius, and Robert F. Peck, "Social Class and Social Mobility Factors Related to Marital Adjustment," *American Sociological Review*, 16 (August, 1951), 478–487.

Waller, Willard, and Reuben Hill, *The Family*, New York: Holt, Rinehart and Winston, 1951.

Wesker, Arnold, *Roots*, Baltimore: Penguin Books, 1959.

Young, Michael, and Peter Willmott, *Family and Kinship in East London*, New York: Macmillan-Free Press, 1957.

33   Marital Cohesiveness and Dissolution: An Integrative Review

GEORGE LEVINGER

What makes a marriage "stick"? And what breaks it apart? Such questions have answers, but the answers do not yet rest on an explicit theoretical base. There is an abundance of descriptive findings and of empirical generalizations, but as yet a scarcity of conceptual construction.[1]

Consider the following instance. In a review of "willed departures" in marriage, Goode[2] has summarized a number of variables related to divorce proneness "which seem to be based on good evidence": urban background, marriage at very young ages, short acquaintanceship before marriage, short

[1] This state of affairs has not been uncommon in other areas of sociological investigation. See Hans L. Zetterberg, *On Theory and Verification in Sociology*. Totowa, N.J.: Bedminster, 1963.

[2] William J. Goode, "Family Disorganization," in *Contemporary Social Problems*, edited by Robert K. Merton and Robert A. Nisbet, New York: Harcourt, Brace, 1961, p. 425.

This paper was written in connection with research on marital relationships, supported by a grant from the Cleveland Foundation and by Grant M-4653 from the National Institute of Mental Health. The author is indebted to William J. Goode, Sidney Rosen, Steven E. Deutsch, Irving Rosow, Dorwin Cartwright, and Edwin J. Thomas for their reading of an earlier version.

Reprinted from the *Journal of Marriage and the Family*, 27 (February, 1965), 19–28, by permission of the National Council on Family Relations.

or no engagement, marital unhappiness of parents, nonattendance at church, mixed religious faith, disapproval by kin and friends of the marriage, dissimilarity of background, and different definitions by spouses of their mutual roles. Goode also notes that husband's occupation and income are inversely related to divorce proneness.[3] Other writers have shown associations between divorce proneness and childlessness,[4] low conventionality,[5] disjunctive affiliation networks,[6] and a series of other factors.[7]

It seems reasonable to seek a common conceptual base that will assist in explaining those findings. This paper presents such a conceptual frame, in which marriage is conceived as a special case of all two-person relationships. Marital cohesiveness becomes a special case of group cohesiveness in general. The findings from some major studies of divorce and of marital adjustment are interpreted according to this framework.

COHESIVENESS IN MARRIAGE

The marriage pair is a two-person group. It follows, then, that marital cohesiveness is analogous to group cohesiveness and can be defined accordingly. Group cohesiveness is "the total field of forces which act on members to remain in the group."[8] Inducements to remain in any group include the attractiveness of the group itself and the strength of the restraints against leaving it; inducements to leave a group include the attractiveness of alternative relationships and the restraints against breaking up such existing relationships. Thus the strength of the marital relationship would be a direct function of the attractions within and barriers around the marriage, and an inverse function of such attractions and barriers from other relationships.

In marriage, a spouse is attracted to his mate because of her intrinsic worth, her love, her charm, her ability to please his wants, or perhaps because she gains him external prestige or will further extrinsic goals. Barriers against a breakup emanate from other sources: the emotional, religious, and moral commitments that a partner feels toward his marriage or toward his children; the external pressures of kin and community, of the law, the church, and other associational memberships.

Thus marital strength is a function of bars as well as bonds. Yet the strength of barriers matters little if the partners' attraction is high enough.

[3] Ibid., pp. 417–418.
[4] Paul H. Jacobson, "Differentials in Divorce by Duration of Marriage and Size of Family," *American Sociological Review*, 15 (April, 1950), 235–244.
[5] Harvey J. Locke, *Predicting Adjustment in Marriage*, New York: Holt, Rinehart and Winston, 1951, 236–243.
[6] Charles Ackerman, "Affiliations: Structural Determinants of Differential Divorce Rates," *American Journal of Sociology*, 69 (July, 1963), 13–20.
[7] See also William J. Goode, *After Divorce.* Glencoe, Ill.: Free Press, 1956; Paul C. Glick, *American Families.* New York: John Wiley, 1957; Hugh Carter and Alexander Plateris, "Trends in Divorce and Family Disruption," *HEW Indicators* (September, 1963), v–xiv.
[8] Leon Festinger, Stanley Schachter, and Kurt Back, *Social Pressures in Informal Groups.* New York: Harper, 1950, p. 164.

In many marriages, the barriers have trivial importance. The spouses' close attachment precludes that either one would seriously consider breaking the relationship.

In other marriages, though, barriers have crucial importance. In the absence of positive feelings, they maintain outward signs of marital togetherness. Goode has called the latter case an "empty shell" marriage:

> . . . The atmosphere is without laughter or fun, and a sullen gloom pervades the household. Members do not discuss their problems or experiences with each other, and communication is kept to a minimum. . . . Their rationalization for avoiding a divorce is, on the part of one or both, "sacrifice for the children," "neighborhood respectability," and a religious conviction that divorce is morally wrong. . . . The hostility in such a home is great, but arguments focus on the small issues, not the large ones. Facing the latter would, of course, lead directly to separation or divorce, but the couple has decided that staying together overrides other values, including each other's happiness and the psychological health of their children.[9]

This illustration of an "empty shell" family evokes contrasting images of "full shell" and "no shell" families. To carry Goode's metaphor farther, a "full shell" marriage would be one in which not only the boundaries but also the attractions are strong for both partners; a marriage in which there is warm emotional interchange. In contrast, the "no shell" couple is in a state of dissolution; it consists of two disconnected individuals, living separate lives. In this latter instance, boundaries as well as attractions have been eroded by the events over time, until eventually alternatives to the marital state are preferred. Goode's metaphor is appropriate. It implicitly refers to two underlying continua: fullness-emptiness of attraction, and strength-weakness of boundaries.

Finally, consider the attractions and barriers outside the marriage. These are forces that pertain to relations with parents, children, lovers, friends, enemies, employers, employees, or any of a host of alternate persons. Husband or wife may be more or less attracted to any of these relationships, and he or she will have a varying sense of obligation to maintain them. Such alternate relationships can be fully compatible with the existence of a strong and stable marriage. The maintenance of relations with in-laws or employers, for example, does not necessarily conflict with the primary marital bond. However, an extreme commitment to such a relationship would interfere with the marriage; as would also, of course, a commitment to a third party that fully excludes the spouse.

COHESIVENESS AND DIVORCE

In studying marriage, high cohesiveness is far harder to detect than low cohesiveness. The privacy of the marital relationship prevents outsiders from judging how "truly happy" a particular union might be; even insiders, the

[9] Goode, "Family Disorganization," op. cit., pp. 441–442.

spouses themselves, cannot be fully aware of all the attractions and restraints that they feel.

On the other hand, the extremes of low cohesiveness eventuate in the dissolution of the relationship. If divorce is the result, it is a public index that can be studied. For this reason, it is useful to give particular consideration to research on divorce to illustrate how the present framework can be applied.

Yet consideration of such research must note the distinction between divorce and separation. In certain groups of our society, de jure separation (divorce) is a less likely occurrence than de facto residential separation. Undoubtedly, the less socially visible a couple is, the more likely it is to resort to informal procedures of separation. The less clear a family's ties to stable norms of kin and community, the less necessary it is to make a break formal. Thus desertion has been a far more common phenomenon in the lowest socioeconomic stratum than in the higher strata. This point must be remembered in interpreting findings on divorce rates.[10]

Possible Differences in the Forces Affecting the Two Partners

The term *cohesiveness* is drawn from a physical analogy. The cohesiveness of a physical bond between two nuclei in a molecule may be indicated by the amount of energy required to break it. The physical model, though, assumes homogenoity in the forces among the nuclei. A social group model of bond strength cannot assume such homogeneity. Feelings of attraction and restraint can and do vary among the members of a group.

In marriage, too, the two partners' feelings are not identical. One spouse may consider separation, while the other remains fully bound to the relationship. Nevertheless, by definition, both partners must value another alternative over that of the present marriage before both will agree to a separation. Usually, the wife is plaintiff in divorce proceedings. Nationally, the figure is about 70 per cent.[11] The preponderance of wife-initiated divorce suits results in part from cultural prescription, yet some of the author's unpublished evidence indicates that the balance of the wife's feelings is more important than the husband's as an indicator of divorce proneness.[12]

REVIEW OF FACTORS ASSOCIATED WITH DIVORCE

How do findings from actual studies illustrate the framework? Attractions that act to secure a marriage derive from love and money. The rewards that spouses receive are linked to their affection for each other, to their financial income and social position, and also to the degree that husband and wife

[10] Glick, op. cit., p. 156.
[11] Paul H. Jacobson, *American Marriage and Divorce*. New York: Rinehart, 1959, p. 119.
[12] Goode, *After Divorce*, op. cit., has pointed out that in many divorce cases, the husband has precipitated the break by providing reasons for the wife's complaint. Nevertheless, the wife's *tolerance* for the husband's normative deviation is a crucial determinant of the decision to seek a divorce.

share similar characteristics. Barriers against a breakup can be coordinated to the partners' feelings of obligation to their family, to their moral values, and to external pressures exerted on them from various sources—these are the sorts of pressures that serve to maintain the boundaries of their marriage. Finally, one can consider alternate sources of affectional and financial reward; these serve as a contrast to the internal attractions and have a potentially disruptive effect.

Table 1, together with its accompanying discussion, organizes published findings that pertain to marital cohesiveness under the three headings of attraction, barrier, and alternate attraction.

Attractions in Marriage

Esteem for Spouse It appears obvious that marital cohesiveness is positively associated with the spouses' mutual esteem and affection. Yet in what areas is esteem most apparent, and in what forms is it present or absent? Locke (24)[13] has found that spouses in happy marriages described their partners' traits in a far more positive way than did divorced persons; the former were far more likely to report the mate's traits as superior or at least equal to their own. Kelly (17) also has reported that this tendency is positively related to marital happiness. Regarding negative esteem, Goode (11), Harmsworth and Minnis (14), and Locke (24) have reported a far higher incidence of complaints about the partner among divorcees or divorce applicants than among normally adjusted spouses.

Desire for Companionship In some cultures, such as the Japanese, marriage does not promote companionship with the spouse. However, two studies of American marriages by Blood and Wolfe (4) and Kirkpatrick (20) found that desire for companionship is strongly related to marital adjustment.

Sexual Enjoyment Locke (24) has reported that happy and divorced spouses differed significantly, both in their enjoyment of actual intercourse and in their desire for it. Terman (32) found that the most adjusted couples had the highest ratio of actual/preferred frequency of sexual relations. To qualify this finding, one should note Kephart's report (18) that concern with sexual incompatibility was found primarily among divorce applicants from the higher social strata. (The present author, in an unpublished study, has obtained a similar finding.) Sexual gratification is one vital source of marital attraction, but its lack apparently is less keenly felt among spouses who have not achieved a satisfactory material standard of living.

Husband's Income In Western nations, as Goode (12) has recently pointed out, divorce rates were greater for high-income than for low-income marriages until the advent of industrialization. However, since some unspecifiable transition point during the early part of this century, divorce rates have been negatively associated with husband's income (12). It would appear

---

[13] Numerals in parentheses in this reading pertain to the references in the footnote to Table 1.

that the attractions within the marriage are lowest for the poor, and that attractions outside the marriage are relatively greater. With the reduction of legal obstacles and of economic costs of divorce, there has occurred a large increase in divorce among low-income couples.

These reasons, then, explain the inverse relation between income and divorce found in modern studies. One of the first studies to suggest this was Schroeder's (31) analysis of divorce rates in Peoria; by an ecological technique, he found a correlation of −.32 between divorce rates and average income in different districts of that city. Locke (24), in his comparison between happily married and divorced spouses, found that an income "adequate for the needs of the family" lessened the likelihood of divorce. Burgess and Cottrell (5) also found a moderate positive relationship. In contrast, neither Bernard (2) nor Terman (32) found such an association; however, their samples were probably too restricted in the range of financial income. When wide ranges of income and marital satisfaction are considered, as in studies of the entire U.S. population by the Census (34), there is a clear inverse correlation between income and divorced status, and even more between income and separated status.[14]

Home Ownership   The proportion of couples who obtain a divorce is lower for owners than for nonowners of a home. This finding is reported by Schroeder (31), by Burgess and Cottrell (5), and by Locke (24). Much of the association may be a function of family income and of length of marriage. However, even if the influence of those two variables is controlled, home ownership itself probably contributes to the stability of family life.[15] It would seem that home ownership is not only a source of attraction, but also helps to stabilize the boundaries that hold the marriage together. All else being equal, the mere fact of owning a home probably increases a couple's reluctance to dissolve their relationship.

Husband's Amount of Education   The amount of the husband's education is higher for durable than for dissolved marriages. This is indicated by data reported by Glick (10), by Monahan (28), and by U.S. Census reports (35, 36). One would speculate, *ceteris paribus*, that a wife's attraction varies with her

[14] A forthcoming paper by the author will report that income is also closely related to the outcome of *applications for divorce*, once such applications have actually been filed. This study avoids a criticism by Day, pertaining to some published studies of divorce. He points out that Census enumerations of persons currently occupying the status "divorced" have sometimes been erroneously taken to represent the *rate* of divorce itself. He suggests that ". . . socioeconomic differences in rates of remarriage or in the interval between divorce and re-marriage could seriously affect the relative sizes of these ratios." See Lincoln H. Day, "Patterns of Divorce in Australia and the United States," *American Sociological Review*, 29 (August, 1964), 509. Day's reminder, published after this paper was written, is well to bear in mind in assessing findings reviewed here.

[15] Unpublished data from the author's research indicate that homeowners are also more likely to dismiss an already filed divorce suit than are nonowners.

spouse's educational status. These findings, of course, are linked to variations in other variables, such as husband's income or prestige. His years of education undoubtedly are correlated positively with prestige, with the husband's relative superiority over his wife, and with his ability to maintain a masculine role. If the husband's education is lower than his wife's, there is more likely to be a reversal in the male-female power balance with an ensuing loss of the husband's attractiveness as her marital partner.

Husband's Occupation   Numerous studies have shown that divorce proneness is also inversely related to husband's occupational rank. Thus, Goode (11), Kephart (19), Monahan (26), and Weeks (38) have each shown that couples in which the husband's occupation ranks high have less divorce proneness than those where it ranks low. Part of this result may be attributed to the contribution of income, another part to the higher prestige of the professions and managerial occupations.

A third reason for the difference in divorce proneness among occupational groups relates to the stability of the husband's home life, as associated with his occupation. Thus Monahan (26) reported that physicians have a higher divorce rate than dentists, taxicab drivers a higher rate than truck drivers. One would hypothesize that the divorce rate of general practitioners or internists, whose home life is constantly disrupted, would be higher than that of doctors with regular working hours (e.g., pathologists, radiologists, or X-ray specialists); that it would be higher for long-haul truckers than for intracity truck drivers. High degrees of instability would tend to reduce the attractiveness of the relationship and also to erode the boundaries that contain it.

Occupational differences may also be linked to differences in susceptibility to alternate attractions. Members of certain occupations (e.g., internists, taxicab drivers, or masseurs) have a greater than average probability for extended intimate contacts with members of the opposite sex. Thus they will have a greater opportunity to explore alternate attractions that would compete with their current marital relationship. In contrast, members of other occupations (e.g., clergymen or politicians) are particularly vulnerable to externally imposed norms about boundary maintenance, which would restrain any proclivity toward divorce.[16]

[16] There are few good data to substantiate these predictions, because published divorce statistics do not generally reveal detailed occupational information. Possibly the best single source is a 1908 U.S. Census Bulletin (33), which relates occupation to divorce. Although its national returns were qualified as "incomplete and hardly acceptable," its New Jersey data for 1887–1906 covered 81.1 per cent of all husbands divorced. New Jersey husbands occupied in agricultural, mechanical, and manufacturing pursuits showed lower than average divorce rates; those in professional or personal service or in trade and transportation had a higher rate. Particularly low were farmers, agricultural laborers, blacksmiths, carpenters, clergymen, engineers, and manufacturing officials. Clearly on the high side were actors, commercial travelers, musicians, bartenders, physicians and surgeons, sailors, and barbers and hairdressers, in that order. Husbands in the high-rate occupations seem to have been highly exposed to alternate attractions.

Such additional considerations are important in weighing the impact of occupational factors in affecting marital stability. Future empirical studies may be able to distinguish among the separate influences of each of these components.

Similarity in Social Status Many studies have linked marital adjustment to similarity of religious preference—particularly Chancellor and Monahan (8), Landis (21), Monahan and Chancellor (29), Monahan and Kephart (30), and Weeks (38). Burgess and Wallin (6) noted that frequency of broken engagements was lower for same-faith couples. Hamilton (13), Kirkpatrick (20), and Williams (39) have indicated that marital attraction is positively related to similarity in education. Burgess and Cottrell (5) and Locke (24) found that it is significantly associated with age similarity, particularly when the husband is older. Blood and Wolfe (4) have found that all three kinds of similarity relate positively to marital satisfaction. Undoubtedly, these are all different aspects of status similarity. Communication between the spouses would tend to be enhanced by relative likeness on these characteristics.

Sources of Barrier Strength

Sources of barrier forces exist both inside and outside the individual. The following examples of restraints against marital dissolution include some cases where the restraints are primarily internal, others where they are mainly external, and still others where their source is difficult to locate.

Obligation to Dependent Children It is widely held that as long as there are no children involved, divorce is the couple's own affair. For that reason, one might expect that husbands and wives with children would feel a greater restraint than those without children—particularly minor children.

Early writings on divorce gave the impression that childless couples have indeed a vastly higher divorce rate,[17] but those studies neglected to adjust divorce rate by *duration* of marriage. More sophisticated analyses by Jacobson (15) and by Monahan (27) have shown that if length of marriage is controlled, the difference in separation rate between childless and childrearing couples is much smaller, but still noticeable. According to Jacobson (15), between 1928 and 1948 this disparity decreased to a ratio of less than 2:1. Even the most skeptical analysis of this difference by Monahan (27) showed some excess of divorce frequency in the childless groups.

The real question is, perhaps, what obligation do the parents *feel* toward their children? To what extent do they feel that divorce of an unattractive marriage would either damage or promote their children's well-being? If parents believe the former, then the existence of children will create barrier forces; if they believe the latter, then they would be likely to be attracted to an alternative other than the present marriage. Goode (11), for example, has

[17] E.g., Alfred Cahen, *Statistical Analysis of American Divorce*, New York: Columbia University Press, 1932; Walter F. Willcox, *Studies in American Demography*, Ithaca, N.Y.: Cornell University Press, 1940.

taken the position that, in an inevitably conflicted home, children may actually benefit from the divorce.

So far, there is no published evidence which differentiates between parents' feelings of obligation to children as *barriers* that prevent a breakup and such obligations as sources of *negative attraction* to the marriage. Until such evidence is obtained, the issue will remain unresolved.

Obligations to the Marital Bond   In a large proportion of marriages, both partners are firmly committed to respect the marital contract, and divorce is not considered as a possibility. Each partner has certain qualms against even thinking of such a thing. On the other hand, if one or both have previously experienced a divorce proceeding, then either partner would be more likely to consider divorce. Thus, the barriers against the dissolution of the present marriage would be weaker. A study by Monahan (25) has indeed shown that first marriages are more resistant to dissolution than are second or later marriages. His data were confined to population statistics and did not pertain longitudinally to particular individuals. Nevertheless, it would be hypothesized that marriages of divorcees tend to have weaker boundaries than those of first-married spouses; further evidence is needed, however, to arrive at any sound generalization.

Proscriptive Religion   It is popularly believed that Catholics are less likely to break their marriages than persons of other religious persuasions. This is only partly true. A more correct statement is that like-faith marriages in which both members are either Catholics, Jews, or reasonably strict Protestants have the lowest probability of divorce. This has been pointed out by studies of Chancellor and Monahan (8), Landis (21), and Monahan and Kephart (30). Such studies have also shown that persons of unconventional religious convictions are most prone to use divorce as a solution to their marital problems.

Joint Church Attendance   Various studies have shown that divorce proneness is inversely related to joint church attendance. Joint membership and regular attendance at church places a couple in a network of connected affiliations and exposes them to conventional values. One would assume that membership in such a net is a source of powerful external pressures. If necessary, such pressures would come into play to prevent the marriage from breaking up.

Reports by Chesser (9), Locke (24), and Schroeder (31) each indicate that, in their samples of couples, marital dissolution was less frequent among regular church attenders than among nonattenders. In his study of divorcees, Goode (11) found that (in his group of Catholics) regularity of church attendance was positively associated with duration of marriage before separation.

Primary Group Affiliation   Affiliation with a church or with other sorts of organizations is one source of barrier forces; affiliation with kinfolk is another vital source. In a recent paper, Ackerman (1) has proposed that divorce rates vary across different cultures to the extent that the culture encourages "conjunctive" as opposed to "disjunctive" affiliations with kin. Ackerman defines the former case as one where husband and wife share a common network of kinfolk and friends; in the latter, their loyalties go in different directions. One would suppose that a conjunctive net of affiliations acts to restrain marital dissolution more than a disjunctive net. Ackerman's analysis of cross-cultural data shows empirical support for this supposition.

Community Stigma   Another source of barriers against divorce is community disapproval. Such disapproval seems more characteristic of rural than of urban communities, which leads to the expectation that rural divorce rates are lower than urban ones. This expectation is borne out by 1955 Census data (37) and by 1960 Census data cited by Carter and Plateris (7). Also, studies by Schroeder (31) and by Burgess and Cottrell (5) have reported that divorced persons are less likely to be born and reared in a rural setting.[18]

Blood (3) has drawn attention to the importance of the visibility of the marriage relationship in the community where the couple lives. When both partners are known, when their behavior is observed, there are greater restraints against social transgressions such as extramarital affairs. Life in the country would seem more restrictive than that in the city; relations in the suburb more constraining than in the urban center.

In describing life in the modern suburb, Whyte has noted that it exerts a "beneficent effect on relations between husband and wife. The group is a foster family." Whyte quotes a minister as follows: "The kind of social situation you find here discourages divorce. Few people, as a rule, get divorces until they break with their groups. I think the fact that it is so hard to break with a group here has had a lot to do with keeping some marriages from going on the rocks."[19]

Legal and Economic Bars   It goes almost without saying that legal and financial considerations exert restraints against a breakup. The wide differences in divorce rates among different states can, in part, be accounted for by differences in divorce laws—as Jacobson (16) has pointed out. And, when considering differences between high- and low-income husbands, one notes that a high-income husband is likely to pay more, both absolutely and proportionately, to support his ex-wife after separation. Thus both legal and financial factors provide important restraints against going through with a divorce.

Sources of Alternate Attraction

Popularly, it might seem that alternate attractions are the chief or the only reason for broken marriages. This impression is sustained by legal fiat, which emphasizes adultery as a reason for divorce. In one state, New York, adultery is the only legal grounds for dissolving a marriage contract.*

[18] William J. Goode (personal communication) has suggested that rural divorce rates in the United States may be low only for farmers, but higher for nonowners of farms.

[19] William H. Whyte, Jr., *The Organization Man*, New York: Simon and Schuster, 1956, pp. 392–393.

* The law in New York has recently been changed. [I.L.R.]

It is logically necessary that the alternative environment be more attractive than the marital relationship, if the partners are to be willing to undergo the costs of divorce. However, it is not necessary that the attraction be "another woman" or "another man." The marital relationship itself may be so unattractive that any alternative condition—with or without another partner —is preferred.

Preferred Other Sex Partner Aside from reports on official complaints lodged with the Court, which frequently are colored to sustain the legal fiction, relatively few studies contain data about spouses' alternate attractions outside the marriage. It is difficult to inquire about this without asking the parties to a divorce action to compromise their personal and legal position vis-à-vis their spouse. Nevertheless, several published studies have reported that preference for an outside sexual partner does play a part in a significant proportion of divorce actions. The proportion may vary anywhere from 15 to 35 per cent of all cases—e.g., Goode (11), Harmsworth and Minnis (14), Kephart (18), and Locke (24). Complaints about external sexual attachments are more frequently reported by wives; but when the husband reports them in a divorce suit, they may be even more serious.[20]

Disjunctive Kin Affiliations Another source of outside attraction forces would be the loyalty toward one's kin or friends. If these ties conflict with those of the spouse, they will at the least lead to strain in the marriage. As mentioned earlier, Ackerman (1) has suggested that competing primary group affiliations are associated with divorce proneness, Locke (24) found that his "happy" couples frequently reported "a little" conflict with their own parents, i.e., (alternate) attractions to parents were at less than maximal strength. This source of marital disruption is worthy of fuller exploration in future studies of divorce.

In cases of disjunctive affiliation, one would hypothesize that the marital bond would be strengthened if the couple increases its physical and psychological distance from *both* sets of alternate affiliation groups, reducing thereby the disruptive forces. For example, partners in a heterogamous marriage that involves antagonistic in-laws would strengthen their relationship by moving away from the community where either set of parents resides. No systematic evidence to support this hypothesis can be cited, but it does coincide with informal observation.[21]

Opposing Religious Affiliations What are the effects of obligations toward alternative competing relationships? Little direct study of this question

[20] In an unpublished study by the author, a comparison was made of two groups of divorce applicants, one set of whom later dismissed the action. It was found that husbands' complaints of "infidelity" were more frequent in the divorcing group, while wives' complaints of the husband's "infidelity" were more frequent in the group of couples who dismissed their action and rejoined their marriage.

[21] E. Lowell Kelly (personal communication) has reported medical evidence from his own marriage research that substantiates this notion concerning mixed-religious marriages.

has been made. However, one bit of evidence indicates the direction in which the answer may lie.

Landis' (21) study of divorce rates in Catholic-Protestant marriages showed clearly that mixed-faith unions were less durable than same-faith marriages of Catholics or Protestants. However, Catholic-Protestant marriages were three times more likely to break up when the wife was Protestant than when the husband was Protestant.

This result is explainable by the framework as follows. Assume that both partners are attracted to their own religious group, but that the wife's feelings are stronger. Assume, also, that the children in each of these marriages are to be raised as Catholics, as is the usual agreement in Catholic-Protestant marriages. Finally, assume that the wife takes prime responsibility for child-rearing. It follows, then, that the Protestant mother is exposed to more conflict—negative attraction toward spouse's religion and disruptive pressures from own religion—than is the Protestant father. The strength of this conflict would depend on the strength of her religious identification—probably weakest in the lowest strata and strongest in the middle or higher strata. This line of reasoning has clearcut empirical derivations and may well be testable in Landis' existing data. Additional studies of this question are desirable.

Wife's Opportunity for Independent Income   One other important source of alternate attraction or repulsion lies in the possibility of the wife's separate financial maintenance. The more readily she can support herself outside the marital relationship or can be assured of such support from other means (including her ex-husband's), the more ready she would be to break the marriage.

In most cases where the husband's income is extremely low, and where the wife's earnings are a substantial proportion of family income, these conditions would seem to be met. In the upper economic strata, however, income differentials between wife and husband are large, and the wife has more reason to maintain the marriage (see Goode, 12, p. 516). In other words, wives in the lower strata appear to have less to lose and more to gain from a divorce. Economic sources of alternate attraction for the wife require further attention in research on divorce. Today, when certain forms of relief payment are contingent upon proof of the husband's nonsupport, it is particularly likely that economic factors exercise an influence on divorce proneness.[22]

Considering the wife's attraction to alternate relationships, one may also note interesting differences in divorce rates between the Eastern and Western

[22] In an article based on assumptions similar to Goode's and the present author's, Heer has recently dealt with propositions about the wife's relative power in marriage. David M. Heer, "The Measurement and Bases of Family Power: An Overview," *Marriage and Family Living*, 25 (May, 1963), 133–139. Heer writes: ". . . the greater the difference between the value to the wife of the resources contributed by her husband and the value to the wife of the resources which she might earn outside the existing marriage, the greater the power of her husband, and vice-versa" (p. 138). We would propose that in cases of *low* difference, if the husband does not readily yield power within the marriage itself, the wife is inclined instead to dissolve the marriage.

states. Both Jacobson (16) and Lichtenberger (23) have reported that the Mountain, Southwestern, and Pacific states have had high rates, while the Middle Atlantic and New England states have had low rates. Traditionally, there has been a scarcity of women in the Western states, leading to greater opportunity for remarriage and also to greater female power.

CONCLUSION

This paper introduces an elementary framework for integrating the determinants of marital durability and divorce. The framework is based on merely two components—attractions toward or repulsions from the relationship, and barriers against its dissolution. The former correspond to Lewin's concept of "driving forces," which are said to drive a person either toward a positively valent object or away from a negatively valent one.[23] The latter correspond to Lewin's concept of "restraining forces," which act to restrain a person from leaving any particular relationship or situation.[24] These components can be used to subsume a large diversity of published findings. For example, findings about the effects of both income differentials and kinship affiliation could logically be fitted within the same scheme. Marital cohesiveness was thus interpreted as a special case of group cohesiveness.

Both the limitations and the advantages of the present analysis should be noted.

Limitations

First, the scheme is based on a hypothetical conception of the attractions and barriers that affect the partners in a marriage. These influences can rarely be inferred directly from changes in overt indices. This is one reason why this paper has not attempted to examine the complex interaction effects between different sets of such influences.

Second, the concept of group cohesiveness, from which this scheme is drawn, is itself the subject of critique and reformulation.[25] Theoretically, it is difficult to define cohesiveness so that it describes under the same rubric the forces that act on both the group and the separate individuals who compose the groups.

Third, the present review of earlier studies has been illustrative rather than comprehensive. Some pertinent studies were omitted. The discussion

---

[23] Kurt Lewin, *Field Theory in Social Science*, New York: Harper, 1951, p. 259.

[24] Ibid., p. 259.

[25] For detailed discussions of conceptual and operational issues in research on group cohesiveness, see *Group Dynamics*, edited by Dorwin Cartwright and Alvin Zander, Evanston, Ill.: Row Peterson, 1960, Chap. 3; Annie Van Bergen and J. Koekebakker, "Group Cohesiveness in Laboratory Experiments," *Acta Psychologica*, 16 (1959), 81–98; Neal Gross and William Martin, "On Group Cohesiveness," *American Journal of Sociology*, 57 (May, 1952), 516–534.

was often limited to single findings of available studies that were occasionally taken out of their wider context.

Advantages

At this time, it is not intended to offer either a general theory or to present an entirely complete review. It *is* intended to understand existing studies at a more general level of abstraction. It is suggested that marriage research can fruitfully be linked to small group research, that simple general hypotheses can be derived in the beginning stages of such a linkage, and that existing evidence about marital dissolution is suitable for documenting such hypotheses.

The present approach draws on the insights of Goode and other writers on marriage and divorce. Yet it aims to go farther in several ways. First, it points to the development of a general framework, congruent with theories about all social groups. It avoids ad hoc theories about "marriage" or "family," but aims to integrate the subject with knowledge of social relationships in general.

Second, the scheme intends to deal not only with actuarial rates of divorce nor only with a particular cultural milieu. Its social-psychological concepts are, in principle, applicable to any given marriage in any society. Although marriages and societies differ in the constellation of forces that determine cohesiveness, it is assumed that these determinants ultimately will be measured and precisely described.

Third, and most important, the components of the present scheme are derived from one basic assumption about the existence of psychological and social forces. Such "forces" are hypothetical. They are not easily accessible to measurement. Yet the present statement aims to prepare for eventual measurement.

Previous attempts to explain divorce have sometimes precluded a clear operational assessment. For example, Goode recently accounted for differences in divorce rates in terms of *both* "social pressures from kinfolk and friends" and a culture-based "equalitarian ethos."[26] Yet his two concepts, kin pressures and cultural ethos, are on quite different levels of conceptualization; the former is vaguely contained in the latter. In contrast, the presently proposed framework offers an opportunity for describing the relations among such concepts. To obtain a precise estimate of the various factors which influence divorce, one would need eventually to establish some common measuring unit that would indicate the magnitude of each force.

The present interpretation does not aim at novelty, but it does attempt to prepare the ground for more advanced derivations. Consider one example of a derivation from the scheme. To increase the durability of a marriage, one can (1) increase its positive attractiveness, (2) decrease the attractiveness of alternate relationships, or (3) increase the strength of the barriers against a breakup. What would be the consequence of each of these?

Increase of marital attractions would renew the partners' interest in and affection for one another. It would further the spouses' turning toward each

[26] Goode, "Family Disorganization," op. cit., pp. 413–414.

TABLE 1   Factors Found to Differentiate between High and Low Cohesive Marriages

Sources of Attraction	Sources of Barrier Strength	Sources of Alternate Attraction
Affectional Rewards:	Feelings of Obligation:	Affectional Rewards:
Esteem for spouse[11,14,17,24*]	To dependent children[11,15,27]	Preferred alternate sex
Desire for companship[4,20]	To marital bond[25]	partner[11,14,18,24]
Sexual enjoyment[18,24,32]	Moral Proscriptions:	Disjunctive social rela-
Socio-Economic Rewards:	Proscriptive religion[8,21,30]	tions[1,24]
Husband's in-	Joint church at-	Opposing religious affilia-
come[(2),5,12,24,31,(32),34]	tendance[9,11,24,31]	tions[21]
Home ownership[5,24,31]	External Pressures:	Economic Rewards:
Husband's education[10,28,35,36]	Primary group affiliations[1]	Wife's opportunity for
Husband's occupa-	Community stigma: rural-	independent in-
tion[11,19,26,33,38]	urban[3,5,7,31,37]	come[12,16,23]
Similarity in Social Status:	Legal and economic bars[16]	
Religion[4,6,8,21,29,30,38]		
Education[4,13,20,39]		
Age[4,5,24]		

*Numerals pertain to positive findings in the corresponding references listed below. Numerals in parentheses indicate which studies reported an absence of a difference between High and Low cohesive couples.

[1]Charles Ackerman, "Affiliations: Structural Determinants of Differential Divorce Rates," *American Journal of Sociology,* 69 (July, 1963), 12-20.

[2]Jessie Bernard, "Factors in the Distribution of Success in Marriage," *American Journal of Sociology,* 40 (July, 1934), 49-60.

[3]Robert O. Blood, Jr., *Marriage,* Glencoe, Illinois: Free Press, 1962.

[4]Robert O. Blood, Jr. and Donald M. Wolfe, *Husbands and Wives,* Glencoe, Illinois: Free Press, 1960.

[5]Ernest W. Burgess and Leonard S. Cottrell, Jr., *Predicting Success or Failure in Marriage,* Englewood Cliffs, New Jersey: Prentice-Hall, 1939.

[6]Ernest W. Burgess and Paul Wallin, *Engagement and Marriage,* Philadelphia: Lippincott, 1953.

[7]Hugh Carter and Alexander Plateris, "Trends in Divorce and Family Disruption," *HEW Indicators* (September, 1963), v-xiv.

[8]Loren E. Chancellor and Thomas Monahan, "Religious Preference and Interreligious Mixtures in Marriages and Divorces in Iowa," *American Journal of Sociology,* 61 (November, 1955), 233-239.

[9]Eustace Chesser, *The Sexual, Marital, and Family Relationships of the English Woman,* New York: Roy, 1957.

[10]Paul C. Glick, *American Families,* New York: John Wiley, 1957.

[11]William J. Goode, *After Divorce,* Glencoe, Illinois: Free Press, 1956.

[12]William J. Goode, "Marital Satisfaction and Instability: A Cross-Cultural Analysis of Divorce Rates," *International Social Science Journal,* 14 No. 3 (1962), 507-526.

[13]Gilbert V. Hamilton, *A Research in Marriage,* New York: Boni, 1929.

[14]Harry C. Harmsworth and Mhyra S. Minnis, "Nonstatutory Causes of Divorce: The Lawyer's Point of View," *Marriage and Family Living,* 17 (November, 1955), 316-321.

[15]Paul H. Jacobson, "Differentials in Divorce by Duration of Marriage and Size of Family," *American Sociological Review,* 15 (April, 1950), 235-244.

other for their gratification, and would promote the mutual consummation of the marital bond.

Decrease of external attractions would lessen the distractions of the outside environment; therefore, it would encourage the spouse to look toward his partner as an object of need gratification. Yet this is only an indirect way of enhancing marital satisfaction. It is neither a necessary nor a sufficient means for creating positive consequences for the relationship.

[16]Paul H. Jacobson, *American Marriage and Divorce,* New York: Rinehart, 1959.

[17]E. Lowell Kelly, "Marital Compatability as Related to Personality Traits of Husbands and Wives as Rated by Self and Spouse," *Journal of Social Psychology,* 13 (February, 1941), 193-198.

[18]William M. Kephart, "Some Variables in Cases of Reported Sexual Maladjustment," *Marriage and Family Living,* 16 (August, 1954), 241-243.

[19]William M. Kephart, "Occupational Level and Marital Disruption," *American Sociological Review,* 20 (August, 1955), 456-465.

[20]Clifford Kirkpatrick, "Community of Interest and the Measurement of Adjustment in Marriage," *The Family,* 18 (June, 1937), 133-137.

[21]Judson T. Landis, "Marriages of Mixed and Non-Mixed Religious Faith," *American Sociological Review,* 14 (June, 1949), 401-406.

[22]Richard O. Lang, *A Study of the Degree of Happiness or Unhappiness in Marriages as Rated by Acquaintances of the Married Couples,* M.A. thesis, University of Chicago, 1932; cited in Goode (11), p. 57.

[23]J. P. Lichtenberger, *Divorce,* New York: McGraw-Hill, 1931.

[24]Harvey J. Locke, *Predicting Adjustment in Marriage: A Comparison of a Divorced and a Happily Married Group,* New York: Holt, 1951.

[25]Thomas P. Monahan, "How Stable Are Remarriages?" *American Journal of Sociology,* 58 (November, 1952), 280-288.

[26]Thomas P. Monahan, "Divorce by Occupational Level," *Marriage and Family Living,* 17 (November, 1955), 322-324.

[27]Thomas P. Monahan, "Is Childlessness Related to Family Stability?" *American Sociological Review,* 20 (August, 1955), 446-456.

[28]Thomas P. Monahan, "Educational Achievement and Family Stability," *Journal of Social Psychology,* 55 (December, 1961), 253-263.

[29]Thomas P. Monahan,and Loren E. Chancellor, "Statistical Aspects of Marriage and Divorce by Religious Denomination in Iowa," *Eugenics Quarterly,* 2 (September, 1955), 162-173.

[30]Thomas P. Monahan and William M. Kephart, "Divorce and Desertion by Religious and Mixed-Religious Groups," *American Journal of Sociology,* 59 (March, 1954), 454-465.

[31]Clarence W. Schroeder, *Divorce in a City of 100,000 Population,* Peoria, Illinois: Bradley Polytechnic Institute Library, 1939.

[32]Lewis M. Terman, *Psychological Factors in Marital Happiness,* New York: McGraw-Hill, 1938.

[33]U.S. Bureau of Census, *Marriage and Divorce: 1887-1906,* Bulletin 96, Washington, D.C.: Government Printing Office, 1908, 25-27.

[34]U.S. Bureau of Census, *U.S. Census of Population: 1950.* Vol. IV, *Special Reports,* Part 2, Chapter D, Marital Status, Washington, D.C.: Government Printing Office, 1953, Table 6, 47-48.

[35]U.S. Bureau of Census, *U.S. Census of Population: 1950.* Vol. IV, *Special Reports,* Part 5, Chap. B, Education, Washington, D.C.: Government Printing Office, 1953, Table 8, 63-64.

[36]U.S. Department of Health, Education and Welfare, *Vital Statistics—Special Reports,* 45: 12 (September 9, 1957), p. 301.

[37]U.S. Bureau of Census, *Current Population Reports,* Series 20, No. 87 (November 14, 1958), 11-12.

[38]H. Ashley Weeks, "Differential Divorce Rates by Occupations," *Social Forces,* 21 (March, 1943), 334-337.

[39]Edith W. Williams, "Factors Associated with Adjustment in Rural Marriage," Ph.D. Dissertation, Cornell University, 1938, p. 98; cited in Goode (11), p. 99.

Increase of the barriers is the least likely means of making a lasting increase in marital cohesiveness. Without an increase of internal attraction, barrier maintenance does not heighten the satisfactions that partners gain from their marriage. In the absence of adequate marital satisfaction, high barriers are likely to lead to high interpersonal conflict and tension. In fact, the very severity often found in cases of marital conflict may derive from the high restraints society places against breaking up a marriage. Yet this method of keeping a marriage together is society's usual prescription for dealing with low marital cohesiveness.

If the above points are logically correct, then they should lead to empirical investigation of marriage relationships to verify them. For example, one might study marriages with equal degrees of marital satisfaction that differ in boundary strength; under conditions of low satisfaction, lower tension would be predicted in those relationships where the barriers are relatively low. Or it is possible to conceive longitudinal studies in which indices of attraction and barrier forces depict the course of the partner's relationships. Additional illustrations can be developed.

The generality of the present scheme makes it suitable also for analyzing friendship or quasi-marriage relationships. For example, relationships that emerge during courtship and engagement can be examined in these terms. What, for instance, are the determinants of broken engagements? How do broken engagements differ from broken marriages in the constellation of factors that influence the partners? These questions can be investigated by asking what the attractions and barriers are as seen by the partners, and by developing criteria to indicate the stability or persistence of such influences.

To summarize, a conceptual framework has been outlined for integrating research on marital cohesiveness and dissolution. The concepts are the same as those employed for understanding the cohesiveness of other social groups. The strength of the marital relationship is proposed to be a direct function of hypothetical attraction and barrier forces inside the marriage, and an inverse function of such influences from alternate relationships. The scheme was then applied to a review of some major findings about divorce, and its implications were discussed.

34 | *The Broken Family and Self-Esteem*

MORRIS ROSENBERG

Thus far we have considered the relationship of various "secondary groups"—social classes, religious groups, nationality groups—to the individual's self-conception. In the present chapter, and in the two succeeding ones, we turn to one of the child's crucial primary groups—his family. What is the significance of family structure, sibling position, and parental behavior for the child's self-esteem and anxiety levels?

Among the important problems besetting modern society is that of the

Reprinted from *Society and the Adolescent Self-Image* by Morris Rosenberg, 1965, pp. 85–106, by permission of Princeton University Press, Princeton, New Jersey.

TABLE 1 Marital Status of Parents and (a)* Self-Esteem, (b)* Psychosomatic Symptoms

| Self-Esteem | Marital Status of Natural Parents | | | |
	Living Together	Divorced	Separated	Separated by Death
High	45%	38%	46%	42%
Medium	25	25	16	27
Low	29	37	38	32
Total percent	100	100	100	100
(Number)	(3871)	(268)	(146)	(402)
Number of Psychosomatic Symptoms				
Few	52%	34%	44%	45%
Intermediate	15	15	15	18
Many	33	50	40	37
Total percent	100	100	100	100
(Number)	(2670)	(169)	(104)	(270)

high frequency of marital rupture, whether expressed in divorce, separation, or separation by death. Family breakup may result from problems of the parents, but it generates problems in the child. It is a common observation that delinquency and emotional disturbance often appear among children from such broken families.

Do children from broken families differ from others in terms of self-esteem and psychosomatic symptoms of anxiety? Let us first consider self esteem. Table 1 indicates that a somewhat larger proportion of children of divorced or separated parents had low self-esteem than those whose families were intact. Children of separated parents were as likely as children of intact families to have high self-esteem, but were less likely to have medium self-esteem and more likely to have low self-esteem.[1] As a group, children whose parents had been separated by death did not differ much from those of intact families. In terms of self-esteem, marital rupture does appear to have some effect, but the differences are generally small.

Marital rupture does, however, appear to be more strongly associated with physiological symptoms of anxiety. Children of divorce, for example, are 18 percent more likely than children from intact families to report four or more psychosomatic symptoms. These results suggest the possibility that divorce, in terms of broad effects, may more conspicuously influence level of anxiety than level of self-esteem.

There is, in fact, good reason for expecting this to be the case. If one's parents are so incompatible that the marriage ends in divorce; if one's mother must struggle to make ends meet without the aid of a husband; if one must undergo the often difficult process of adjustment to a stepparent—these are conditions generating stress, tension, and anxiety but they do not

[1] In this analysis, the children of parents who have been separated at times offer responses similar to those of children from intact families and at other times offer responses similar to those of children from broken families. Because of the limited number of cases available and the inadequacy of the ancillary data, the present investigator has been unable to detect any consistent pattern in their responses.

directly challenge the worth of the child. His merit or inadequacy, his virtue or vice, have nothing to do with it.

At the same time, the child's self-esteem becomes entangled in the family rupture in various ways. On the simplest level, of course, the social stigma of divorce may produce a reputation of being strange or different and, to some extent, inferior. Secondly, it is likely that if parental disharmony prevails before the divorce then the parents may well take out their aggression on the child. They may be irritated with him, cold, sarcastic, impatient, caustic, discouraging, contemptuous, or indifferent; such behavior is almost certain to enhance the child's feeling of worthlessness. Finally, the clinical and theoretical work of Horney suggests that early fundamental anxiety in the child will tend ultimately to issue in feelings of self-contempt.[2] (Her theory is discussed later.) Perhaps the surprising thing is not that children of divorce have somewhat lower self-esteem than children from intact families, but that the differences in self-esteem are not still larger.

Do these relatively small differences thus indicate that the broken home has only a minor bearing on the self-esteem of the child? While such a conclusion is in general justified, it is at the same time misleading in the sense that it fails to specify the conditions—and we use this term broadly—under which the marital rupture occurs. Under certain conditions, as we shall see, family breakup is strongly related to self-esteem; under other conditions, it appears to make no difference at all.

Upon what does the effect of the broken family depend? It depends, first, on *who* has been divorced or widowed; it depends, second, on *when* they were divorced or widowed; and it depends, third, on *what happened after* they were divorced or widowed.

RELIGION AND DIVORCE

It is a matter of common knowledge that religious groups differ in their attitudes toward divorce. It is thus reasonable to assume that divorce in a Catholic family may represent an experience which is different in nature

[2] Karen Horney, *Neurosis and Human Growth*, New York: Norton, 1950.

TABLE 2   **Divorce and Self-Esteem and Psychosomatic Symptoms, by Religion**

	Catholics		Jews		Protestants	
Self-Esteem	*Divorced*	*Intact*	*Divorced*	*Intact*	*Divorced*	*Intact*
High	36%	44%	44%	54%	40%	44%
Medium	24	26	17	24	26	25
Low	40	30	39	21	34	32
Total percent	100	100	100	100	100	100
(Number)	(90)	(1583)	(18)	(514)	(112)	(1391)
Number of Psychosomatic Symptoms						
2 or less	27%	49%	30%	56%	42%	53%
3-5	40	36	50	34	41	35
6 or more	33	15	20	10	16	12
Total percent	100	100	100	100	100	100
(Number)	(52)	(1097)	(10)	(352)	(73)	(966)

and intensity from divorce in a Protestant family. For one thing, Catholics in our sample are less likely to be children of divorce than Protestants. In our sample, Jews are even less likely than Catholics to report divorce. It seems likely that divorce among Catholics and Jews occurs in the face of stronger group opposition than divorce among Protestants. It is thus interesting to observe that Catholic and Jewish children of divorce are more likely to have low self-esteem than Catholics and Jews from intact families, but divorce makes almost no difference among Protestant families. (Table 2) Similarly, Catholic and Jewish children of divorce are considerably more likely than their co-religionists from intact families to have many (6 or more) psychosomatic symptoms, whereas this is distinctly less true of Protestants.

The experience of divorce is thus more strongly related to signs of psychic or emotional disturbance among Catholic and Jewish children than among Protestant children. The reasons are hardly obscure. The Catholic Church, of course, rigidly proscribes divorce, and the practice is strongly opposed to the Jewish cultural tradition.

If Catholic and Jewish norms are more strictly opposed to divorce than Protestant norms, then at least three points may be considered: (1) One may perhaps assume that, on the average, the degree of parental disharmony necessary to produce divorce is greater in Catholic or Jewish than in

TABLE 3 Emotional Disturbance of Catholic-Jewish and Protestant Children Whose Familes Have Been Broken by Death

| | Catholics or Jews | | Protestants | |
	Percent	*Number*	*Percent*	*Number*
Low self-esteem	32	214	33	141
Many psychosomatic symptoms				
(more than 3)	36	144	39	97

Protestant families. If this is so, then Catholic and Jewish children of divorce have on the average probably experienced more hectic and anxiety-ridden family lives than Protestant children of divorce. (2) Since divorce in Catholic and Jewish families must be undertaken in opposition to greater social pressure, it may represent a more shocking, a more emotionally violent, experience both for the parents and for the child, thus contributing to emotional disturbance. (3) Since the Catholic and Jewish group norms are more firmly opposed to divorce, the social stigma of divorce is probably greater among Catholics and Jews than among Protestants; hence, the Catholic or Jewish child, already anxiety-ridden by the tension experienced in the home, may be reinforced in his feeling of being different, and less worthy, by the horrified reaction of members of the extended family and by neighborhood co-religionists.

But the question may be raised: Perhaps it is not divorce as such which is responsible for the results; perhaps it is due to the fact that Jewish and Catholic adolescents react more negatively to *any* family breakup.

The most obvious way to check this point is to compare Jewish and Catholic children whose families have been broken by death. While we have seen that Jewish and Catholic children of divorce manifest more emotional disturbance than Protestant children of divorce, Table 3 indicates that there is no clear difference between these groups if the families have been broken by death. It is, then, not simply family breakup in general, but divorce in particular, that is most closely associated with emotional disturbances among Catholics and Jews.

THE YOUNG DIVORCEE

Just as the significance of marital rupture depends on whose family has been broken, so does it also depend on when the marriage was dissolved. In general, our data suggest that if a woman has married early, has had a child shortly thereafter, and has been divorced a short time later, then her child will have a greater tendency to manifest emotional disturbance. If, on the other hand, both she and her child were older at the time of the marital rupture, then the child's psychological state tends to be just about normal.

While we do not have exact information on the mother's age at the time of the marital rupture, we can approximate her age in the following way: We know approximately how old the mother is now, how old the child is now, and how old the child was at the time of the divorce. Through simple calculation we can determine how long ago the divorce took place and how old the mother was at the time of the divorce.

TABLE 4   Mother's Age When Divorced and Child's Present Psychological State

Child's Present Self-Esteem	Mother's Age When Divorced		
	23 or Under	*24-31*	*32 or Over*
High	22%	39%	43%
Medium	29	22	27
Low	48	39	29
Total percent	100	100	100
(Number)	(31)	(111)	(106)
Number of Psychosomatic Symptoms			
3 or less	39%	49%	54%
4	6	13	24
5 or more	56	38	22
Total percent	100	100	100
(Number)	(18)	(69)	(68)

Table 4 indicates that if the mother was 23 years or less at the time of the divorce, then 22 percent of the children have high self-esteem; if she was between 24–31 years old, the proportion is 39 percent; and if she was 32 years or more, the proportion is 43 percent.[3] Similarly, the younger the

[3] It may be asked: Who are these people who experienced early divorce? Our data indicate that they are more likely to be urban, Catholic women. There is no indication, however, that these characteristics are responsible for the observed differences. Wherever there is a sufficient number of cases available for comparison, children whose mothers were older at the time of the divorce were more likely to have high self-esteem than children whose mothers were younger.

mother at the time of the divorce, the more frequently did the children report having many psychosomatic symptoms.

Now, as we might expect, the children of young divorcees were also very young at the time of the divorce. Specifically, seven-eighths of these children were three years or less when their mothers and fathers parted. It thus seems to be that a particular combination of life circumstances—a very young divorced mother with a very young child—is especially conducive to the development of emotional disturbance in the child.

But which factor is really crucial in these results? Is the truly decisive factor the child's age at the time of the divorce? It may be that the very young child is extremely impressionable at this time of life and that the turmoil of divorce may have a traumatic effect upon him from which he may not fully recover.

TABLE 5   Child's Age at the Time of Divorce and Present Self-Esteem

| Self-Esteem | Child's Age at Time of Divorce | | | |
	3 Years or Less	4-6 Years	7-9 Years	10 Years or More
High	33%	43%	38%	43%
Medium	28	24	21	22
Low	39	33	40	35
Total percent	100	100	100	100
(Number)	(103)	(51)	(47)	(60)

This explanation, it turns out, is not sufficient in itself. Table 5 shows that there is some tendency for children who were young at the time of the divorce to be less likely to have high self-esteem, but the differences are not very large and the trend is somewhat uneven. More to the point, however, is the question: Among all children who were three years or less at the time of the divorce, are those whose mothers were very young more likely to develop low self-esteem than those whose mothers were more mature?

TABLE 6   Mother's Age at Time of Divorce and Child's Present Self-Esteem, among Children Who Were Very Young at Time of Divorce

| Child's Present Self-Esteem | Children Who Were 3 Years or Less at Time of Divorce | | |
	Mothers 23 Years or Less at Time of Divorce	Mothers 24-31 Years at Time of Divorce	Mothers 32 Years or Over at Time of Divorce
High	26%	35%	50%
Medium	30	30	25
Low	44	35	25
Total percent	100	100	100
(Number)	(27)	(57)	(12)

Table 6 suggests that this is so. About one-fourth of the children of the very young group, one-third of the intermediate group, and one-half of the more mature group had high self-esteem. It is, then, not simply the tender age of the child which is important.

Still another factor must be considered: perhaps these results stem from the fact that these very young divorcees were also very early brides. It is possible that a girl who marries very early tends to be an unstable person or that, because of her youth, she is simply less able to deal with a home or children. It might then not be the divorce as such but the early age of marriage which is at the heart of the matter.

Since we do not know the mother's age at marriage, we must again approach the matter indirectly. Let us consider those mothers whose present age is 37 years or less. Older mothers will not be considered, since we cannot tell which of them were married early and which were married later. But we can be certain that if a woman is now 37 years or less and has a child who is a high school junior or senior (probably between 16 and 18 years old) then this woman married early; probably the majority of these women were in their late teens at the time of the marriage.

If we consider only these young mothers, we find that children's self-esteem is substantially lower if the mother has been divorced than if she has not. Among children of very young women, 53 percent of the children of divorce, but only 33 percent of the children from intact families, had low

TABLE 7   Maternal Divorce and Child's Self-Esteem among Mothers Who Are Currently Very Young

Child's Self-Esteem	Mother Currently 37 Years or Younger	
	Divorced	*Family not Broken*
High	27%	44%
Medium	20	23
Low	53	33
Total percent	100	100
(Number)	(55)	(276)

self-esteem. (Table 7) Indeed, if the woman is now young, married early, had a child soon thereafter, and was soon divorced, the children are twice as likely as average to have low self-esteem. To know that the student's mother is now very young and has been divorced is, in fact, one of the strongest

TABLE 8   Mother's and Child's Age at Time of Divorce and Child's Present Self-Esteem

Self-Esteem	At Time of Divorce		
	Mother and Child Both Relatively Young‡	*Mother and Child Both Relatively Mature‡‡*	*All Others*
High	22%	42%	41%
Medium	29	26	24
Low	48	32	35
Total percent	100	100	100
(Number)	(31)	(77)	(140)

‡Mother 23 years or less and child 6 years or less.
‡‡Mother 32 years or more and child 7 years or more.

predictors of low self-esteem. Among women with comparable careers who were not divorced, however, the child's self-esteem is practically normal.

We thus see that it is not simply a question of whether the mother has been divorced that is crucial; under certain conditions, e.g., older mothers and older children, self-esteem is fairly normal. (Table 8) Similarly, it is not a question of whether the child was very young when the marriage broke up or that the mother married very early. It is, apparently, under a special combination of circumstances—when the mother married early, quickly had a child, and shortly thereafter was divorced—that low self-esteem is especially likely to develop in the child.

When we turn from families broken by divorce to those broken by death, somewhat similar results appear, but the differences are less striking. Students whose mothers were relatively young when they were widowed are less likely to have high self-esteem and to be free of psychosomatic

TABLE 9   Mother's Age When Widowed and Child's Present Psychological State

Child's Present Self-Esteem	Mother's Age When Widowed‡		
	27 or Under	28-34 Years	40 or Over
High	23%	42%	50%
Medium	50	20	26
Low	27	38	24
Total percent	100	100	100
(Number)	(22)	(45)	(42)
Number of Psychosomatic Symptoms			
3 or less	58%	61%	73%
4	25	25	10
5 or more	17	14	17
Total percent	100	100	100
(Number)	(12)	(28)	(30)

‡In order to obtain an adequate number of cases for analysis, it has been necessary to use different age cutting points when considering divorcees and widows. The reason is that the average age of widowhood is considerably higher than the average age of divorce.

symptoms of anxiety. (Table 9) At the same time, they are not conspicuously poorly adjusted, tending, rather, to be in the intermediate category. Similarly, children of widows who are now young are less likely than others to have high self-esteem. (Table 10)

TABLE 10   Present Age of Widow and Child's Self-Esteem

Child's Self-Esteem	Mother's Present Age		
	37 or Less‡	38-47	48 or Over
High	15%	43%	48%
Medium	45	24	25
Low	40	32	27
Total percent	100	100	100
(Number)	(20)	(145)	(122)

‡The number of mothers who are 37 years or less is too small to permit comparisons of psychosomatic symptoms.

There is little doubt that early divorce or widowhood which leaves the mother with one or more very young children tends to place the mother in a difficult situation. In addition to running the house, caring for the children, etc., she is faced with serious financial problems in the absence of a husband. The mother who feels insecure, anxious, irritable, and frustrated under such circumstances is certain to affect the emotional development of her children. If the woman is older and better capable of handling these problems, the effect upon the children would in general be less deleterious than if she were younger and more likely to succumb to the strain.

One factor which might operate in favor of the young divorcee or young widow is the greater likelihood of remarriage. And, indeed, our data show that the remarriage rates of these women are relatively high. Even if these women do remarry, however, the self-esteem of their children remains relatively low. Instead of attempting to explain this finding at this point, however, let us turn to the more general question: What is the association between parental remarriage and the child's psychological and emotional development?

REMARRIAGE

Thus far we have asked: To whom does the marital breakup occur and when does it occur? The third question we wish to consider is: What happens after the divorce or death? Is the family reconstituted through remarriage or does it remain a truncated nuclear unit? Let us first consider those children whose parents had been divorced and whose mothers later remarried. (In almost all cases of divorce the children remained with the mother.) What is the association between such remarriage and the child's self-esteem?

TABLE 11   Self-Esteem of Children and Divorce and Remarriage of Mothers

Self-Esteem of Child	Parents Divorced, Mother Remarried	Parents Divorced, Mother Did not Remarry	Parents Never Divorced or Separated
High	32%	40%	46%
Medium	22	26	25
Low	46	34	28
Total percent	100	100	100
(Number)	(134)	(92)	(3533)
Number of Psychosomatic Symptoms			
2 or less	33%	41%	52%
3–4	31	39	27
5 or more	36	20	21
Total percent	100	100	100
(Number)	(86)	(49)	(2439)

Table 11 indicates that children whose mothers remarried tended to have lower self-esteem than those whose mothers did not remarry. We find that 46 percent of the children of divorce who acquired stepfathers had low self-esteem compared with 34 percent of those whose parents did not remarry.

Similar results appear when we consider psychosomatic symptoms. It is somewhat surprising to find that parental remarriage, rather than helping the psychological adjustment of the child, is associated with lower self-esteem and greater anxiety.

Now let us consider the case of parental death. As in the case of divorce, we find, the self-esteem level of children tends to be lower if their

TABLE 12   Remarriage of Widowed Parents and Child's Self-Esteem

Self-Esteem	Parent Died and Surviving Spouse . . .		Parent Never Divorced or Widowed
	Remarried	Did not Remarry	
High	34%	46%	46%
Medium	27	24	25
Low	39	30	28
Total percent	100	100	100
(Number)	(128)	(223)	(3533)

parents remarried than if they did not. Table 12 shows that if the surviving parent remarried 34 percent have high self-esteem, whereas if the parent did not remarry 46 percent of the children had high self-esteem. This latter group's self-esteem, in fact, is just as high as that of children from intact families.

But does it make a difference to the child's self-esteem whether the father has died and the mother remarried or whether the mother has died

TABLE 13   Self-Esteem of Children Whose Families Have Been Separated by Death

Self-Esteem of Child	Acquired Step-father	Acquired Step-mother	Parent Did not Remarry	Parents Never Divorced or Separated
High	36%	30%	46%	46%
Medium	28	27	24	25
Low	36	43	30	28
Total percent	100	100	100	100
(Number)	(72)	(56)	(223)	(3533)
Number of Psychosomatic Symptoms				
2 or less	39%	37%	51%	52%
3–4	39	37	29	27
5 or more	23	27	20	21
Total percent	100	100	100	100
(Number)	(45)	(41)	(148)	(2439)

and the father remarried? Table 13 suggests that self-esteem appears to be somewhat lower if the mother has died than if the father has died, although the differences are not very large. Similarly the differences in psychosomatic symptoms between those who acquired stepmothers or stepfathers is small;

if they acquired either stepparent, however, then they were clearly more likely to show more anxiety than if their parents did not remarry.

It may be noted that the negative association between remarriage and self-esteem is not simply a reflection of the age of the mother or of the child at the time the marriage was dissolved. Among mothers of equal age or children of equal age, higher self-esteem appears among children whose mothers did not remarry.

These results are surprising since, by and large, one would assume that a surrogate parent is better than no parent at all and that the restoration of an approximation to a normal family life would be better than the abnormality of having but a single parent. A father—even if he is not the biological father—can give the child someone to lean on, to depend on, to turn to for advice and support. He can reduce the sense of strangeness, of difference, which may haunt the child without a father. He can help restore the sense of "normality" which is often conducive to calm self-acceptance. Finally, he can reduce anxiety in the family by his monetary support, thus partly freeing the mother from economic burdens and cares and enabling her to devote a normal amount of time and attention to the children. One would certainly expect the child's self-esteem to respond favorably to these happy circumstances.

But let us consider the matter from another viewpoint. When the father is removed from the family, either through divorce or death, what happens to the mother and child? It is a common observation that when people are faced by a common problem or difficulty, they tend to draw more closely together. They "huddle together for warmth." Both mother and child must share the responsibilities which would ordinarily be assumed by the husband. If the child is old enough, he may be called upon to help financially. If not, his tasks around the house are likely to increase as he seeks in part to relieve his mother of the additional burdens she must face.

The broken family is thus likely to make mother and child more dependent upon one another. The mother must depend upon the child for emotional support and other kinds of help. The child is dependent on the mother for the encouragement, affection, and guidance which both a mother and father can provide. The mother's life thus comes to focus more centrally on the child; he may be a burden, but he is of supreme importance to her. The bond of mother and child is cemented by their common plight.

Then the mother remarries. Conditions of life become easier for both. The point is, however, that the mother's interest shifts, at least in part, to her new husband—to his interests, his needs, his desires. In addition, if, as is often the case, the husband has children from a previous marriage, then the mother devotes part of her attention to her stepchildren.

The child may still retain the affection of his mother, but he is no longer the exclusive center of her universe. She becomes less dependent upon him for emotional and physical support, less involved in his needs. He is now one among several in whom she is interested. To become less important to his mother is likely to diminish the child's feeling of significance.

We also noted above that, in the fatherless family, the child must often assume responsibility for tasks which are not required of a child his age. He may take pride in the fact that he can master these tasks successfully and that his mother is dependent upon his efforts. With remarriage, he is relieved of some of these burdens, for now the mother and father can share these tasks. At the same time his feeling of worth may decrease, for he can no longer take such special pride in these accomplishments. Life may be easier for him, but he may feel meaner, smaller, less significant in this new world created by his mother's remarriage.

Finally, remarriage may require a fairly fundamental readjustment on the part of the child. In the case of a family broken by death, the child may consider it a betrayal of the memory of the departed parent for the widow to remarry. It is not unusual in such cases for the child to feel resentful, if not bitter, toward both the mother and the stepfather. But even without this reaction, the child must still face the difficulty of adjusting to a new parent and perhaps new stepbrothers and stepsisters—in short, to the complex web of relationships which are involved in a new family structure. Inevitably this will contribute to his feelings of anxiety and call into question his picture of himself.

If such difficulties of adjustment do occur, then one might go one step farther to suggest that the longer the child has had a "normal" family life, i.e., the longer he has lived in an intact family, the more difficult will it be for him to adjust to the "new" family resulting from remarriage. If difficulty of adjustment is related to the child's psychological state, then we might advance the following hypothesis: the longer the child has lived in an intact family, the more adversely affected will he be by remarriage. In order to examine this question, we asked our subjects how old they were at the time their families were broken.

Let us compare those children who were 10 years or older when the marriage was dissolved with those children who were 3 years or younger.

TABLE 14   Divorce or Widowhood, Remarriage and Child's Self-Esteem, by Child's Age at Time of Family Break-up

| Self-Esteem | Child's Age at Time of Divorce or Death | | | | | |
| | 3 Years or Less | | 4-9 Years | | 10 Years or More | |
	Re-married	Not re-married	Re-married	Not re-married	Re-married	Not Re-married
High	32%	37%	33%	46%	32%	49%
Medium	32	27	19	21	27	26
Low	35	37	48	32	41	26
Total percent	100	100	100	100	100	100
(Number)	(71)	(41)	(64)	(56)	(37)	(78)

Among the older group, Table 14 shows, those who acquired stepfathers were 15 percent more likely than those who did not acquire stepfathers to have low self-esteem; among the younger group, those who acquired stepfathers were 2 percent less likely than those who did not to have low self-esteem. If the child has lived longer in an intact family, apparently, then the negative consequences of remarriage are most evident.

We have thus suggested that it is difficult for a child to adjust to a "new" family, and that the longer he has been attached to an "old" family the more difficult the adjustment and the more adverse the psychological consequences. It should be emphasized that this does not mean that children who were older at the time their families dissolved will have lower self-esteem than children who were younger; on the contrary, their self-esteem is higher. The matter may be summarized as follows: If the child was young when the family dissolved, then he will tend to have low self-esteem whether or not his mother remarried. If, on the other hand, the child was older at the time the marriage dissolved, then his self-esteem will be normal if his mother did not remarry but will be below normal if she did remarry.

Why should children who were older at the time their families broke up be more affected by parental remarriage than children who were younger? It may be that these older children remember their fathers well and remember the normal family lives they have lived throughout a good part of their childhood. In addition, the older the child is at the time of the marital break-up, the more likely it is that he has developed a relationship with his father; and, as we have observed earlier, the father-child relationship is not without importance in the emotional development of the child. It might thus be particularly difficult for older children to adjust to and accept a substitute father or mother. In addition, if the family has been broken by death, the older child may be more likely to resent the remarriage as a betrayal of the memory of the departed parent, which could make him hostile both to his natural surviving parent and to his stepparent.

DISCUSSION

If we return to our original question, "Does the broken home have an effect upon the emotional state of the child?" the best answer would seem to be "It depends." First, it depends on religion: if the child is Catholic or Jewish, there appears to be a clear effect; if the child is Protestant, there appears to be little or no effect. Second, it depends on the mother's age at the time of the marital rupture: if the mother was very young, there appears to be a clear effect; if the mother was older, there appears to be little effect. Third, it depends on remarriage: children whose mothers remarried appear to be more disturbed than those whose mothers did not remarry. The negative effect of remarriage is particularly strong among older children.

These results point to certain reasons why the broken family may be associated with emotional disturbances in the child. The greater significance of divorce among Catholics and Jews than among Protestants, for example, suggests that subcultural norms may play a role in this relationship. Similarly, the apparently more powerful effect of divorce among very young women than among older women suggests that the degree to which the parent is equipped to cope with the strain of raising a family alone may be very important. And the negative effect of parental remarriage, particularly among older children, suggests that the problem of readjustment to new family circumstances may be a significant factor. These findings suggest that the theoretical significance of a relationship may be clarified by studying the conditions under which the relationship does *not* hold as well as the conditions under which it *does* hold.

XII The Family, Change, and Deviance

Introduction to Section XII

The 1970s are a period of time when Americans are becoming increasingly aware of themselves and their society. As part of this process comes a deepened sensitivity to the problem areas of our existence and to the areas of seeming rapid change. This final section of the book is devoted to an examination of some of these areas.

There has been a great deal of talk about mate swapping and group sex in general but very little in the way of careful research has been done. Although the Bartell article cannot be assumed to describe a nationally typical mate-swapping group, it does present a sound description of group sex in the suburbs of Chicago. The high proportion of "swingers" who voted for Wallace in the 1968 Presidential election affords insight into the ability of humans to compartmentalize their beliefs. One may be quite "progressive" in one area and quite reactionary in other areas. Surely there are mate exchangers who are progressive in almost all areas, but the Bartell data make us wonder how common that is and just how such activities do get started. Is mate swapping simply a modern form of adultery that reflects our more equalitarian ethics? Is it a result of people asserting that since they know they will commit adultery at some time, they might as well accept it and do it in a more open and purposeful fashion? Does such adultery occur mostly in marriages that are unhappy or in which the degree of sharing is limited? These are but some of the fascinating questions that only future research can begin to answer. (See Cuber and Harroff [19] in Section VI for a discussion of types of marriage and see the Prologue of this reader for some thoughts on "swinging.")

The Rossi article (36) bears upon another most interesting aspect of the family in the 1970s: the women's liberation movement. Others, such as

531

Cynthia Epstein,[1] have pointed out how the more prestigious professions are male dominated and how there are mechanisms restricting any increase in female participation. The female role is heavily oriented to the home. This area of discussion relates to the Davis article in Section X, in that Davis' assertion that to lessen the importance of the mother role will help in population control has relevance to the area of occupational equality. To illustrate, if while we de-emphasize the mother role for females we emphasize the occupational role, we have the best chance of changing female status in our society. This is so because one major excuse for keeping women out of top positions is that "their place is in the home." If that attitude is altered, many occupational barriers would probably be weakened. The Barry article in Section I also ties in here, for Barry found the sharpest sex differences in those societies in which physical strength was important. Our society is not one where physical strength is crucial, and thus the chance of change toward reduced sex differences is increased. Some of the readers may have mixed feelings about such changes toward greater female occupational involvement. That is, of course, a personal value choice for each of us. But in any case one needs to understand what the situation is and here the Rossi article is of help. Rossi presents the options facing Americans today as being basically of three sorts: (1) We can stress the importance of the traditional female role in the home; (2) We can help women to have equal opportunity to do the kind of work that men do today; or (3) We can alter the basic occupational life style and family style for both men and women so as to make them more balanced and less status dominated. This last possibility stresses creativity and human fellowship rather than rationality and efficiency and it is the one Rossi favors. The reader can examine his own view and his conception of which approach is likely to dominate the last decades of this century.

The article by Simon and Gagnon (37) on homosexuality is also applicable to this question of new definitions of masculinity and femininity. One of the points made in this article is that the homosexual male typically thinks of himself as masculine. Thus, we can see how career women too can conceive of themselves as feminine despite the fact that they pursue a career that is not a culturally defined part of the feminine role. Homosexual behavior is more public now then ever before. There are increasing numbers of homosexual bars, magazines, and clubs that publicly proclaim their sexual preferences. Scientific understanding of homosexuality is in this way made easier by increased awareness and frankness.

The article by Rodman (38) constitutes a contribution to a long-standing debate within the social sciences concerning illegitimacy. Goode and Blake[2] have put forward the thesis that births out of wedlock in the Caribbean area are a form of illegitimacy. Rodman presents data and arguments that such births occur in consensual unions which are the functional equivalent of legal marriage,

[1] Epstein, C., "Encountering the Male Establishment: Sex Status Limits on Women's Careers in the Professions." *American Journal of Sociology* 75 (May, 1970), 965–982.
[2] Goode, W. J., "Illegitimacy in the Caribbean." *American Sociological Review* 25 (February, 1960), 21–30; Blake, J., *Family Structure in Jamaica*. New York: The Free Press, 1961.

and thus they are not a form of illegitimacy. My own preference is for Rodman's position. I feel that illegitimacy should be viewed as on a continuum. One can feel that legal marriage is the best way to have a child but that consensual unions are nevertheless an acceptable way. Rodman's data from Trinidad support just such a view. All societies have some conception of what conditions are not acceptable for bringing a child into the world and that in effect is what defines illegitimacy. Such conceptions can change but I would argue that all societies will arrive at some view of what are the acceptable and what are the unacceptable ways to bear a child and that these views will create a continuum of legitimacy, as Rodman suggests.

The study by Berger and his associates (39) is particularly fascinating. It is a progress report on a three-year longitudinal study of California hippie communes. The emphasis is on the family and child-rearing practices in communes and thus it is relevant to this book. It is one of the few research reports available on communal families in America. The stress in the article on what the researchers are doing is informative of research methodology. One interesting finding is the extent to which women are tied to traditional female housework in the commune. The article by Rossi indicates some of the reasons that cause women to seek changes in the female role, and yet the same "liberated" female who is willing to try communal living may be trapped in traditional female-role definitions. Similar ambivalences exist between philosophies of sexual freedom and strong feelings of sexual exclusiveness, and between desires to be economically independent and dependency on welfare payments. In many ways the "simple" commune life seems very complex. We end the presentation of readings, then, with a glimpse of one of the new contexts in which part of the American family now exists.

35 | Group Sex Among the Mid-Americans

GILBERT D. BARTELL

This paper is one in a series of special presentations for the Society for the Scientific Study of Sex, dealing with group sex. Our data were collected from a selected sample of midwestern and southwestern white, suburban and exurban couples and single individuals engaged in what they call "swinging." We contacted and interviewed approximately 350 informants during the two years of our research using data from 280 interviewees who fit into the above category.

These informants define the term "swinging" as having sexual relations (as a couple) with at least one other individual. Since more than a simple dyadic relationship exists whether the sexual activity involved takes place together or apart, the fact remains that more than two people had to enter into an agreement to have sexual experiences together. We therefore conclude that this must be considered group sex.

We were interested in the growth and development on the broad spectrum of activities associated with organized swinging but we wished to concentrate specifically upon those individuals belonging to some form of sodality or swinging organization. We attempted to ascertain to what extent American cultural patterns would be transferred to this relatively new phenomenon. Since white middle class, non-inner city people constitute the majority in the United States, and we assume they are the major actors within the cultural system, our sample is restricted to these informants.

Interviews lasted anywhere from two to eight hours. We eliminated individuals from the inner city, Blacks and Latin couples to keep our sample restricted. We did not misrepresent ourselves, but told them that we were anthropologists interested in knowing more about swinging. We did not use a tape recorder or questionnaires, as these people were frequently too frightened to even give their right names, let alone fill out questionnaires, or tape. We were also able to attend a large number of parties and large scale group sexual activities.

Our basic method of interviewing was the anthropological one of participant observer. Due to the etiquette and social mores of swinging as we

In some academic circles sex research is not considered pertinent. I therefore would very much like to thank the President of Northern Illinois University, Rhoten Smith, my anthropological colleagues, Drs. Pierre Gravel and James Gunnerson, and colleagues from other departments including sociology for their cooperation, assistance, and particularly their genuine moral support.

I wish, furthermore to acknowledge the help and assistance of Carole Dick and Nancy Frank in the preparation of this article and thank them for their effort.

Reprinted from *The Journal of Sex Research*, 6, No. 2 (May, 1970), 113–130, by permission of the Society for the Scientific Study of Sex.

shall detail below, we were able to observe and only act as though we were willing to participate.

Evidently the interest in swinging or wife swapping, mate swapping or group sex came about as the result of an article in *Mr. Magazine* in 1956. Since then it has received a great deal of attention from the semi-pornographic press. However, despite the fact that there are an estimated one to ten million people involved in mate exchange, it has received practically no attention from the scientific community. We don't have any reliable figures on how many people are involved in swinging, but a club in a midwestern city published a list with names and addresses of 3500 couples in the metropolitan area and its suburbs who are actively engaged in mate exchange.

The impetus toward swinging usually comes from the male, but it is the contention of a number of sophisticated swingers that it is often promoted by the female who lets the male take the aggressive role in suggesting that they become involved in the swapping situation. Although we have a great deal of background material on the initial introduction of the partners to group sex activity, which includes the acquiring of magazines, self-photography, discussion, and extra marital activity, we do not feel it falls within the scope of this paper.

Within the area of investigation, there are primarily four methods of acquiring similarly minded partners for sexual exchange. Most prevalent is the utilization of an advertisement in one or more of the various magazine/tabloids catering to these specialized interests. Second, an introduction to another couple at a bar, set up exclusively for this purpose or through one of the swingers sodalities. Third, personal reference from one couple to another, and fourth, personal recruitment, seduction or proselytizing.

In the first method an advertisement is placed in one of the sensational tabloids such as the *National Informer.* This might read, for example:

Athens, Georgia, marrieds. Attractive, college, married, white, want to hear from other marrieds. She, 36, 5′ 7″, 35-22-36, 135. He, 40, 6′ 2″, 190. Photo and phone a must. Discretion. Box #.

or

Florida Marrieds. Attractive, refined, professional marrieds would like to hear from similar liberal minded marrieds. Complete discretion required, and assured. Can travel Southern states. Photo and phone please. Box #.

Alternatively, the couple may respond to such an ad. This method is the least expensive and time consuming as the *National Informer* sells for 25¢ and is printed and distributed on a weekly basis. The couple has to pay for an add or a fee plus postage for their letter to be forwarded to an advertisee. Exactly the same method is used if the couple selects one of the large slick paged magazines, such as *Swinger's Life* or *Kindred Spirits.* The major difference between tabloids and slick magazines is that the magazines offer membership in a sodality and cater exclusively to swingers. Examples of such ads would be:

Baltimore, D.C., 60 mile radius, luscious, upper thirties, attractives, seeking couples, females to 40 for exotic French Culture etc. She, 35-27-35, 5' 6''. He, husky, muscular, but gentle. Let's trade pictures and telephone and addresses.

or

New Orleans, young couple, 28 and 32. She, a luscious red head, 5' 7'', 36-26-38. He, 5' 9'', 175, well built. Enjoy all cultures. Attractive couples main interest, but will consider extremely attractive single girls and men. Photo required for reply.

Please note the difference in the tenor and construction of the advertisements, remembering that the magazine sells for $3.00 per copy. Additionally these magazines offer instruction on what kinds of letters to write to attract the highest results. Initial contacts are made through letters with descriptions formulated in such a way as to stimulate the interest in making a personal contact with the other couple. These would almost universally include a nude or semi-nude photograph of the female, and sometimes, but much less frequently, a photograph of the male. These photographs are considered very important. Physical dimensions, particularly of the female, usually somewhat overly abundant in the mammary zone, are frequently included. Ages are given and usually minimized. Third, the written answer usually states that the couple is fun loving, vivacious, friendly, and extremely talented sexually. This leads, hopefully, to a telephone contact with the other couple and from there to a first meeting, which is by agreement, social in nature with no obligations to swing on the part of anyone. If successful, this first meeting leads to an invitation to swing, either open or closed (see below) or an invitation to a party. If unsuccessful, it may lead only to a referral to another couple or to some club.

The second method of meeting other couples, the bar or sodality, can be the result of reference from another couple. In a few cases, the club or bar may advertise openly in either a swinging magazine or a tabloid. These units or sodalities break down into three categories. The very common, but least imminent, is the large scale semi-annual party social, advertised in one of the national swingers magazines. The magazine advertises where the social will be held, and the cost for dinner, dance, and drinks. The organizer most commonly will be some local couple who agree to do the actual work. Usually these meetings, or socials, are held at a motel. The swingers bar is one which is open on certain nights of the week only to couples, and it is known to everyone that all couples present are either active or interested in becoming swingers. The bars can be run by either an individual who has an interest in promulgating swinging or an organizer who will contract with the bar owner offering a guarantee for the use of the bar for the particular night involved. Occasionally some interested couple or couples may institute a club which charges a membership fee and rents a hall or bar one or two nights a month at which times known swingers congregate. These clubs are frequently chartered, operating as social organizations much like ski-clubs. Inducements are offered to the members for recruiting new members. The club may, for example, sponsor "Bring another couple night," and only charge half price for entrance. A number of clubs seek to go beyond the purely sexual by organizing hay rides, beach parties and picnics. Several attempts have been made within our area to organize a group tour of swingers to the Caribbean and to Las Vegas. These efforts have not been successful. In general, swinging does not take place on the premises of these bars or clubs, but instead the couples make their alliances or organize private parties and leave the bar in groups.

A third method of meeting other compatible swingers is a simple reference from another couple. If a couple has made a few contacts either by one of the two methods mentioned above or sometimes purely by accident, they can meet a number of other couples by this reference method. A knowledgeable couple who have been swinging for some time will recommend other known swingers to the new couple. This in turn, of course, can lead to other contacts without ever having to write letters, join a club or go to a bar.

The fourth method of contacting new swingers appears with the least degree of frequency in our sample. Many swingers, either due to the zeal of the convert or personal stimulus, attempt to seduce (to convert) other couples to what they call the "swinging life." We have reports of this occasionally occurring in nudist camps or with couples that have known each other on a social basis for some time. In a few cases, couples who had been bridge partners or dance partners have mutually consented to exchange.

The neophytes coming onto the "swinging scene," as it is referred to, are faced with a number of dilemmas. They must find out, with a certain degree of care, exactly what actions are appropriate to allow them to participate in this venture which is somewhat surrounded by mystery. The various books and magazines purporting to open the door and guide the novice through the intricacies of swinging, universally exaggerate its ecstasies. In fact, what swingers do is relatively prosaic. For example, one responds to an ad with a letter. This letter gives one's interests and includes a picture. The purpose of the letter is to present oneself in such a manner as to elicit further response in the form of a telephone call. Then, usually using only first names, such as Joe and Ruth, a meeting is arranged.

This first meeting we call the Mating Dance (taken directly from ethologists). The couple goes through a patterned ritual behavior. In effect what they are doing is testing each other. If one couple is baby swingers, baby swinger meaning one who has never been involved in a swinging situation before, of necessity they must permit themselves to be seduced. This role also allows one to ask questions which the experienced couple are more than pleased to answer. In most cases this is the role we took. It is also advantageous in that you have to learn the secret vocabulary of swinging in order to interview effectively. These people do have a definite secret language, or at least they think it is secret. Terms most often used are TV (transvestite), S&M (Sado-masochist), A-C D-C (Homosexual and Heterosexual), Bi-sexual (enjoying both males and females and usually applied to women only), Ambi-sexual (the correct term, yet less frequently used for the preceding two terms), gay (homosexual or lesbian), B & D (bondage and discipline), French Culture (cunnilingus and fellatio), Roman Culture (orgies), Greek Culture (anal intercourse).

This first meeting is the equivalent of the dating coffee date or coke date. The general etiquette dictates that this first contact is without sexual involvement. Should it be decided that the foursome wants to get together they will meet later either at a motel, or at the house of one of the couples.

Once this decision to participate has been made by all four people, we arrive at the three typologies of swinging. Number one, open and closed swinging; two, open and closed large scale parties; and three, three-way parties. As defined locally, closed swinging means that the two couples exchange partners and then go off separately to a private area to engage in what amounts to straight, uncomplicated sexual intercourse. Then after an agreed upon time, all four return back to the central meeting place. Sexual behavior under these circumstances is relatively ritualized. It almost always includes fellatio, cunnilingus and coitus, with the male either dorsal or ventral. In the vast majority of cases, fellatio does not lead to orgasm. Every attempt is made by the male to bring the female to climax by cunnilingus. Climax by the male after prolonged delay occurs most frequently during coitus with the female supine.

In contrast, open swinging in a foursome means that the couples at some time during the evening, engage in sexual activity together, either in the same room, on the same bed, or as a four way participatory activity. In 75% of our cases, this will generally include the two females engaging in some form of cunnilingal activity, although in approximately 15% of the cases one of the female partners will be passive. Less than 1% of the cases reported that any male homosexual activity takes place. We have only two or three reports of males performing fellatio, and in 6 or 7 cases the male informant was passive, permitting another male to fellate him. We have no reports of anal intercourse taking place between either male or female in a swinging scene. Sometimes references are made to this fact, but we have no verification. Occasionally a foursome of the open variety may result in everyone devoting their attention to one person, three on one in effect, and again most frequently, two males and one female devoting their attention to the female. The only other variety is the so-called "daisy chain" which is alternately fellatio, cunnilingus in a circle.

The second type of swinging is the party, which can be organized in several different ways, and can be run as an open or closed party. Certain individuals are known in this area as organizers. These individuals devote a great deal of their time to the organization and promulgation of swinging activities. They may organize nothing more than social events in which people meet to make future contacts, or they may organize a party, at which sexual activity will take place. These parties are frequently held in a private home. Couples are invited by the organizer who may or may not be the owner of the home. Frequently each couple invited is asked to bring another couple who are known to be swingers. Although not always true, there is an implication that no one is required to swing. At other parties, no swinging activity takes place until after a certain time, such as 10:30. Any couple still there past 10:30 is expected to participate. In contrast to the swingers' self-image, they are not nudists and they are still relatively inhibited, hesitating to initiate any positive action. Therefore, the organizer or the host or some less patient swingers may initiate a game, the object of which, obviously, is the removal of everyone's clothing.

Parties in suburbia include evenly numbered couples only. In the area of our research, singles, male or female, are discriminated against. Blacks are universally excluded. If the party is a closed party, there are rules, very definitely established and generally reinforced by the organizer as well as other swingers. These rules may even include clothing restrictions, "baby dolls" for the women and for the men, swinger's shorts (abbreviated boxer type). Or there may be a regulation that one couple may occupy a bedroom at a time or that they may stay only so long or that no one must appear nude in the central gathering area. Most parties are "bring your own bottle" parties, although in a few cases the host supplies the liquor. Food is often prepared by the hostess, but seldom consumed. Stag films are generally not shown. Music is low key fox trot, not infrequently Glenn Miller, and lighting is definitely not psychedelic. Usually nothing more than a few red or blue light bulbs. Marijuana and speed are not permitted.

The same generalized format is true for the open party, the difference being that the party is less structured. Nudity is permitted in any part of the house and couples are free to form large groups of up to 10 or 12 people in large sexual participating masses. Voyeurism is open and not objected to by the majority of the participants. Parties generally begin around 9:00 in the evening and frequently continue until 9:00 the following morning in contrast to closed parties, which generally terminate around 1 A.M. It is not infrequent that as the party proceeds and the males become progressively more exhausted, the females continue to party without males. Open parties in suburban groups appear infrequently and when they do, they are held by the younger swingers between the ages 20 and 35, who have begun swinging in the last year and a half. Culturally this younger group resembles the older closed group with the exception that they have never been under the influence of the organizers. They have no ideas as to what is considered appropriate party behavior, as does the older group. This younger group apparently either is more innovative or is learning from the now-frequent popular writings on swinging. Some of the older swingers who are now participating in open parties state that when they began swinging they "didn't know there was any other way to do it." Although most couples state an interest in the taking of polaroid pictures during sexual exchanges, in practice, this is very infrequent. Among other reasons it points out the extreme caution and fear with which the majority of our informants react to the possibility of their identities being revealed.

The third type of swinging is in a threesome, which can hardly be called menage a trois, which implies a prolonged triadic relationship. Analysis of advertisements in swingers magazines indicates that the vast majority of swingers, whether potential or experienced, advertise for either a couple or a female. Although the majority of threesomes constitute a couple and an alternate single female, 30% of our informants indicate that they have participated as a threesome with an alternate single male. (Cross checking of informants cause our own figures to be revised upward as high as 60%.) The males report that they enjoy the voyeuristic qualities of watching their partner engaging in sexual activity with another male. Most commonly threesomes with two females include ambisexual behavior of mutual cunnilingus between the females. Although in the majority of our cases the triad is of relatively short duration, twelve couples report triadic relationships of longer duration ranging from a low of two or three weeks to a high of as long as ten years. In three of the cases the extra woman lived in the household on a more or less permanent basis. In two cases the male was a boarder, and in one case the male lived in the household for ten years, seven of which he had been involved in menage a trois.

Few other variations of sexual activity had been reported. We have in our entire sample only two reports of bondage and/or discipline. Transvestitism has never been reported. We have observed one case of bestiality. Obviously from the preceding, homosexual males are not welcome. In a few cases, three to be exact, we have reports of a lesbian participating at a large party, however she was not discriminated against. It should be noted that to accuse a woman of being "straight-gay" is considered pejorative. Clothes fetishists are uncommon. Bizarre costume is not considered proper and clothing is decidedly not "mod," but is very middle class.

THE INFORMANTS

Ninety-five percent were white. We included Latin Americans in this category as well. Of our Latin Americans, 10 individuals in all, each swung with a white partner. The predominant ethnic division was German. In fact, of all foreign born informants, Germans constituted the single largest group comprising twelve couples in our sample. We have only five black couples, none of whom live in the suburbs. The ages of our informants ranged from 18 to the mid forties for the women, and from 21 to 70 for the males. Median age for women, 28–31. For males, 29–34. All couples, based on our knowledge of certain societal factors, tended to minimize their age, except for the very young 21–30 age group. In general we believe the men gave younger ages when they were married to younger women. Age plays an extremely important role in acceptance or rejection for swinging. Although informants almost universally verbalize that age is unimportant, in reality they tend to reject couples who are more than ten years older than themselves. Invitations to parties are generally along age lines also. With the emphasis on youth in our culture today, it is important to appear young and our interviewees were reluctant to give exact ages.

Ninety per cent of the women in our sample remain in the home as housewives. We have no exact figures as to how many worked previous to marriage. In cases where this was their first marriage, they had married between the ages of 17 and 21. Several were married as young as 15 to 17. There were seventeen female teachers in our sample. Those who had advanced schooling, both males and females, had attended small colleges and junior colleges. About 25% of our males had some college. Forty to 50% of the men could be classified as salesmen of one sort or another. Our interviewees also included one M.D., one dentist, three university professors, three high school teachers, and several owners of small service-oriented businesses. A number of swingers in this group are truck drivers and some are employed in factory work. The largest professional group was lawyers. Earnings were extremely difficult to ascertain. We based our estimate on life style, houses, and occupations. The range of income extends from $6,000 to a probable high of $75,000.

Religion was seldom discussed. These people would not admit to atheism or agnosticism. They would say that they were Protestant, Catholic or Jewish. The majority are Protestant and the proportion of Jews is the same as the general population. The proportion of Catholics is a little higher. The majority did not attend church regularly.

Universally they were extremely cautious with regard to their children, about phone calls, and visits from other swinging couples. The majority of couples would not swing if their children were in the house, and some made elaborate arrangements to have children visit friends or relatives on the nights when they were entertaining. All couples took precaution that their children did not find letters from other swinging couples, pictures, or swinging magazines. We found few instances of couples merely socializing and bringing their children together, although the children might be of the same ages, and have the same interests. Only a few in our sample said that they would raise their children with the same degree of sexual libertarianism they themselves espouse, or that they would give the girls the pill at a very early age.

In interviewing these respondents, we found that they have no outside activities or interests or hobbies. In contrast, the suburbanite is usually involved in community affairs, numerous sports, and family centered activities. These people do nothing other than swing and watch television. About 10% are regular nudists and attend some nudist camps in the area during the summer. Their reading is restricted to newspapers, *occasional* news magazines and woman's magazines with the outstanding exception that 99% of the males read *Playboy.* An occasional couple owns a power boat and spends a few week ends in the summertime boating. Yet a striking contradiction is the fact that in their letters they list their interests as travel, sports, movies, dancing, going out to dinner, theater, etc. In reality they do none of these things. Therefore all conversational topics are related to swinging and swingers as well as television programs. Background is usually rural or fringe areas, not inner city.

Due to the exclusion in the midwest of singles from the swinging scene, we find that approximately ⅓ of the swinging couples interviewed admitted they were not married. However, to be included in parties and to avoid pressures and criticism from married couples, they introduced themselves as man and wife. We were unable to compile exact statistics of the frequency or cause of divorce in the swinging scene. At least one partner and sometimes both of the couple swinging currently had been married before. Frequently they have children from a previous marriage. We have only hearsay evidence that couples have broken up because of swinging. However, we feel in general that the divorce rate is about that of any comparable group of people in the country. As we have not followed up any couples who have dropped out of swinging, these findings are susceptible to change.

As much of the interviewing took place during the 1968 National Presidential Campaign, we had occasion to hear political views. Normally politics is never discussed. There were many Republicans and better than 40% of the respondents were Wallaceites (partially due to change from blue collar to white collar jobs). These people were anti-Negro. They were less antagonistic to Puerto Ricans and Mexicans. They were strongly anti-hippie, against the use of any and all drugs, and would not allow marijuana in their homes or people who use it if they had knowledge of it.

Based on overt statements in letters and advertisements, such as "whites only" and from the fact that Blacks are seldom, if ever, invited to parties, it is safe to say that a strong anti-Black prejudice exists. In social conversation antagonism, although veiled, is often expressed.

Informants overall reflect generalized white suburban attitudes as outlined in almost any beginning sociology text. Their deviation exists mainly or primarily in the area of sex. And even this has imposed upon it middle class mores and attitudes. For example, some men have been paying prostitutes to pose as their swinging partners. In the few cases in which this occurred and became general knowledge, a large outcry from both males and females was heard. The same attitudes prevail toward couples who are not married as well as singles, male or female. The reason is less the sanctity of marriage than the idea that the single individual or the prostitute has nothing to lose. They are absolutely terrified, even though they think of themselves as liberated sexually by the thought of involvement. If you swing with a couple only one time, you are obviously not very involved. It is taboo to call another man's wife or girl friend afterward, or to make dates on the side.

The consumption of alcohol, sometimes in large quantities, is perfectly permissible. Current fashions such as mini skirts and bell bottom trousers for men and beards are seldom seen except among the youngest of the swingers.

ANALYSIS

Obviously due to the nature of a short article, we have been forced to be overly restrictive in a descriptive sense. We have only touched on the highlights and those points that would be considered pertinent to the vast majority of readers of this journal. With all due respect to our readers, we should like to give a brief socio-psychological analysis of our research.

As stated originally, we were particularly interested in swinging as a cultural phenomenon. We feel convinced that it reflects very much the culture of the individuals interviewed and observed. They represent white middle class suburbia. They do not represent a high order of deviance. In fact, this is the single area of deviation from the norms of contemporary society, and there may be some question whether they really represent the acting out of an ideal image in our society rather than an attempt to be innovative. They represent an attempt to act out the cult of youth, the "in scene." They are, in their own minds, the avant garde, the leaders in a new sexual revolution. They see swinging as a "way of life." They refer, like the hippie, like the ghettoite, to the non-swinger as being "straight." In contrast to their own conceptualization of themselves, the majority of swingers are very "straight" indeed. The mores, the fears, that plague our generation are evidenced as strongly in swingers as in any other random sampling from suburbia. It has been said that our data reflect a mid-American bias, however, the O'Neills and the Smiths (personal communication) have indicated that the same phenomena can be found in suburbs in both the east and west coasts. What we find in these couples consistently is a boredom with marriage. Much of this problem stems from diffuse role expectations in the society. Americans have imposed upon themselves a number of possible roles, both ideal and real which one may assume. We believe the action of the media to be crucial in the self-perception of ideological roles. Most of the male swingers want to see themselves as—and many groups actually call themselves—international Jet Setters, the Cosmopolitans, the Travellers, the Beautiful people. Instead, they have become a consequence of suburban life. They sit in silence and look at television. The woman who feels restricted to the household environment believes she should be out doing things, be a career women, but she has her obligations. The man wants to be a swinger, and to be in on the "scene" and know "where it's really at."

Within the psycho-socio-sexual context of contemporary American culture, we would like to present those positive and negative affects of swinging for the individuals involved. Please note that we have been unable to interview more than a few dropouts from swinging. Therefore, our information is based solely on those who are participants. Our interviews with people who have discontinued swinging, about six or seven couples, reflect what we shall call the negative aspects of swinging. But first, we should like to summarize what we believe to be the positive aspects of swinging. Among these, there is an increased sexual interest in the mate or partner. All of our respondents report that due to swinging they now have a better relationship, both socially and sexually. These people are replaying a mating game. They can relive their youth and for many it is advantageous. They can get dressed up, go out together, and attempt a seduction. It is a form of togetherness that they never had before. There is the desire of each partner to reinforce in the other the idea that they are better sexually than any swinger they have encountered. There is a general increase in sexual excitation of both partners due to the possibilities of new types of sexual experiences and increase in thought and discussion of actual sexual experiences. The woman receives a great deal of positive reinforcement if she is seen as the least bit desirable. She is actively committing men to her. A fifty year old man can "make it" with a twenty-two year old girl without any legal repercussions, and his wife will be equally guilty. It must be a tremendous satisfaction. Women uniformly report that they have been able to shed sexual inhibitions that they were raised with. And our society certainly has an overabundance of sexual inhibitions, mainly because we impose different standards on different members of the society. The Raquel Welches of our world can perform in one fashion, but the good little housewife must perform in another. How does one adjust to this conflict between one's model and one's own activities? The female respondents state that one way to resolve this conflict is to swing.

The partners now share an interest, which can be explored, observed, and discussed between themselves and among their new "friends." Both partners can indulge in voyeurism at parties, and thereby utilize the learning experience in their own relationship. Due to the fact that most of these people have had few, if any, opportunities throughout their lives for actually observing or learning by observation how to act and respond to sexual stimuli, the swinging scene may be an experience which could not be provided in any other way.

Swinging may be extremely exciting inasmuch as it carries certain elements of danger. Swingers may feel very avant garde in the breaking of cultural taboos or of legal codes. There is also a certain implied danger and possibility of losing the love of one's partner; however, this is usually offset by the mutual reinforcement mentioned previously. There can be a great deal of sexual excitement provided by the stimulus of profane versus sacred love. Both partners can now become conspirators in writing and hiding advertisements and letters and evidence of the new interest from children, relatives, "straight friends," and business colleagues. We feel that one of the greatest advantages in the relationship comes from the fact that the couple may now spend more time together searching for new contacts and pursuing leads for parties, bars, and other compatible couples. They may now plan week-end trips together, vacations, etc. to other parts of the country to meet swingers. They feel that now they have broadened their social horizon, acquired new interests or hobbies as a by-product of their swinging contacts. Swingers seem to derive a great deal of satisfaction out of merely meeting and gossiping with other swingers, which gives them the dual role of also proselytizing. For the first time in many years, due to the restriction of early marriage, suburban environment, and the social and economic restraints of raising children, they may now have the opportunity to dress up, make dinner dates, plan for parties, acquire a full social calendar, and be extremely busy with telephone conversations, letter writing, picture taking. If they do prove to be a fairly "popular" couple and be in demand, they can now feel that they are both beautiful or handsome and desirable. They see themselves and each other in a new light. They may now feel that they are doing what the "in" people are doing and living up to their playboy image. Most swingers report unsatisfactory sexual relationships prior to swinging. Now, due to the necessity of operating as a pair on the swinging scene, they may find that they actually have an increase in perception, awareness and appreciation, sexual and otherwise, of each other.

One of the most important negative aspects, as we see it, is the inability to live up to one's own psycho-sexual myth and self-illusions. This is particularly disadvantageous in the case of the male. They read about sexual behavior in the outer world, and they realize they are not participating in this elaborate sexual life. Since the demise of the houses of prostitution, many early sexual contacts by males became hit and miss propositions, Boys usually begin by masturbating; to masturbate, one must fantasize (Simon and Gagnon, 1969). Most males have an elaborate fantasy world in their internalized sexual lives. One of the fantasies is that of having access to a bevy of females. He sees himself capable of satisfying any and all of them. He now goes to a party, particularly a party of the younger group, and he has all these naked women running around in front of him. He experiences the anxiety of being incapable of performing up to his own expectations. This very anxiety may defeat him. In American society, the male is expected to be a tremendous performer sexually, and he must live up to his own publicity. This is extraordinarily difficult. He may find he cannot maintain an erection, he cannot perform. He finds himself envying younger men who are physically more attractive and his anxiety and fears increase. For the woman, such self-doubts are less in evidence, although beyond a doubt all females upon initiation to the swinging scene go through a stage of comparison of their own physical appearance and sexual performance with that of the other females. Should the couple be both older and less attractive than the majority of swingers encountered, they may regard the whole swinging scene as a failure, and withdraw immediately. For those who remain, other negative aspects include sexual jealousy. The male may find after a number of parties in which his opportunity for satisfaction is limited and he sees the women around him engaging in homosexual activities and continuing to satisfy each other over and over again for the duration of the evening, he may feel, and this is verbalized, that the "women have the best time," that the swinging scene is "unfair to men." We find that less than 25% of the men "turn on" regularly at large scale open parties. In contrast to this, many men report that they "turn on" much more frequently at small scale parties or in small groups of threesomes. This is the major deterrent to the swinging situation. If one keeps experiencing failure, and continuously worries about this failure, one will keep failing. This is a complete feedback situation. In an attempt to "turn themselves on," the males push their women into having ambisexual relations with another girl. Most of them got the idea from either books or pornographic movies. Again, the male experiences disaster. Why? Sixty-five per cent of the female respondents admit to enjoying their homosexual relationships with other females and liking it to the point where they would rather "turn on" to the female than to males.

For a couple who are relatively insecure with each other and with themselves, swinging may invoke a great deal of personal jealousy. The man who finds he is occasionally rejected or easily tired physically, may resent his wife's responsiveness to other men. She, in turn, may feel that her partner is enjoying other women more or to a different degree than he enjoys her. These personal jealousies frequently erupt under the pressure of alcohol and the ensuing scene evolves into an event which makes all parties present uncomfortable if not antagonistic to the couple. This causes them to be excluded from future invitations and branded as "trouble makers."

Another less common negativism in swinging is the "bad experience." A couple may encounter another couple who have sexual "hang ups," habits, or attitudes that are repulsive or objectionable to the initiating couple. If they encounter two or three consecutive "bad" couples, they may decide that it is not worth taking the risk of such exposure.

Some of our respondents report that in the past there have been incidences of venereal disease that were introduced into a swinging group by one couple and for all concerned, this provoked a great deal of fear and embarrassment due to the legal necessity of seeking medical aid from sources that would not report to health authorities. Fear of disease is always present, and discussed frequently.

For many swingers a constant negative aspect of swinging is the perpetual hazard of discovery. To professional people and to those who work for a state or national government or for very conservative business firms, there is a strong possibility of status diminution or loss of occupational position if they were discovered. All respondents consistently insist upon all possible discretion and some go so far as to not give out addresses, correct last names, place of employment, and the majority of swingers keep unlisted telephones. The upwardly mobile feel that their "life would be ruined" if the world knew they were swingers.

Although our findings are inconclusive on this last negative aspect, we feel it is important and maybe the primary reason for the dropouts among the more sensitive intellectual group of people who enter swinging. These people seem to feel that swinging in general is much too mechanistic, that there is a loss of identity and absence of commitment and a total non-involvement that is the antithesis of sexual pleasure and satisfaction. Some explicitly say that the inconsistencies between the stated objectives and the actual performance are too great to overcome. Although a couple initially report that they want new friends, interests, and activities in addition to pure sexual contact, in reality this is not so. As proof of this we offer the fact that most couples will see another couple only once, and even on those occasions when they have relationships with the other couple, their social relationship is minimal even when their sexual relationship is maximal. In much the same light their self-image of avant-garde/sexual freedomists suffers when one considers their worries vis-á-vis jealousy.

Since many people have asked us where we think swinging is leading we should like to make some comments on our personal attitudes toward the future of the swingers. We feel that these individuals interviewed in our sample are not really benefitting themselves because the ideals that led them into swinging have not been fully realized. They may very well be acting out and getting positive reinforcement, psychologically and physically from their activities. However, their human relationships outside of the diad are not good. Their activities with other couples reflect mechanical interaction rather than an intimacy of relationships. As a cultural anthropologist one cannot doubt that this reflects the impersonalization as well as the depersonalization of human relationships in our culture. One would suppose that the next generation will carry a duality of purpose rather than a single-minded interest in sexual performance. What we would like to see is a freedom of sexuality, but one more concerned with human relationships, and that these human relationships rather than the sexual relationships become the primary goal.

REFERENCE

Simon, William, and Gagnon, John, "Psycho-sexual Development," *Transaction*, 6, No. 3, (March, 1969), 9–18.

36 Sex Equality: The Beginnings of Ideology

ALICE S. ROSSI

It should not prejudice my voice that I'm not born a man
If I say something advantageous to the present situation.
For I'm taxed too, and as a toll provide men for the nation
  While, miserable graybeards, you
  It is true
Contribute nothing of any importance whatever to our
    needs;
  But the treasure raised against the Medes,
You've squandered, and do nothing in return, save that
    you make
Our lives and persons hazardous by some imbecile mistake.
What can you answer? Now be careful, don't arouse my
    spite,
Or with my slipper I'll take you napping
  Faces slapping
  Left and right.

Aristophanes, Lysistrata, 413 B.C.

It is 2400 years since Lysistrata organized a sex strike among Athenian women in a play that masked a serious antiwar opposition beneath a thin veneer of bawdy hilarity. The play is unique in drama as a theme of women power and sex solidarity, and takes on a fresh relevance when read in this tumultuous era. Women in our day are active as students, as blacks, as workers, as war protesters, but far less often as women qua women pressing for equality with men, or actively engaging in a dialogue of what such equality should mean. Until the last few years, women power has meant only womanpower, a "resource to be tapped," as the manpower specialists puts it.

It has been a century since John Stuart Mill published his classic essay on "The Subjection of Women" in England, and the Seneca Falls Conference in New York State gave public recognition to the presence of women critical of the political and economic restrictions that barred their participation in the major institutions of American society. Thus, the time is propitious in which to examine what we mean by a goal of equality between the sexes, rather than to persist in the American penchant for tinkering with short-run "improvements in the status of women."

The major objective of this article is to examine three possible goals of equality between the sexes, while a secondary objective is to pinpoint the ways in which inequality on sex grounds differs from racial, ethnic, or religious inequality.

This article first appeared in *The Humanist*, September/October, 1969, and is reprinted by permission.

MEANING OF INEQUALITY

A group may be said to suffer from inequality if its members are restricted in access to legitimate valued positions or rewards in a society for which their ascribed status is not a relevant consideration. In our day, this is perhaps least ambiguous where the status of citizens is concerned: we do not consider race, sex, religion, or national background relevant criteria for the right to vote or to run for public office. Here we are dealing with a particular *form* of inequality—codified law—and a particular *type* of inequality —civil and political rights of an individual as a citizen. There are several other forms of inequality in addition to legal statute: corporate or organizational policies and regulations, and most importantly, those covert social pressures which restrict the aspirations or depress the motivation of individuals on the ascribed grounds of their membership in certain categories. Thus, a teacher who scoffs at a black boy or white girl who aspires to become an engineer, or a society which uniformly applies pressure on girls to avoid occupational choices in medicine and law are examples of covert pressures which bolster racial and sexual inequality. *Forms* of inequality therefore range from explicit legal statute to informal social pressure.

Type of inequality adds a second dimension: the area of life in which the inequality is evidenced. There are inequalities in the *public* sector, as citizens, employees, consumers, or students; and there are inequalities in the *private* sector as family, organization, or club members. Throughout American history, the gains made for greater racial and sexual equality have been based on constitutional protection of individual rights in the public area of inequality, as citizens, students, and workers. But precisely because of constitutional protection of privacy of home, family, and person, it is more difficult to remove inequalities rooted in the private sphere of life. Attempts to compensate for emotional and nutritional deprivation of preschool, inner-city children are through three-hour Headstart exposure to verbal stimulation and nutritious food from caring adults. We have yet to devise a means to compensate for the influences of parents who depress a daughter's aspiration to become a physician, while urging a son to aspire beyond his capacity or preference. In both instances, the tactics used tend to be compensatory devices in the public sphere (counseling and teaching in the schools, for example) to make up for or undo the effects of inequalities that persist in the family.

There is, thus, a continuum of increasing difficulty in effecting social and political change along both dimensions of inequality: by *form*, from legal statute to corporate regulation to covert and deeply imbedded social mores; by *type*, from citizenship to schooling and employment, to the private sector of family. Hence, the easiest target in removing inequality involves legal statute change or judicial interpretation of rights in the public sector, and the most difficult area involves changes in the covert social mores in family and social life. It is far easier to change laws which presently penalize women as workers, students, or citizens than it will be to effect social changes in family life and higher education which depress the aspirations and motivations of women.

An example of this last point can be seen in higher education. Few graduate schools discriminate against women applicants, but there are widespread subtle pressures once women are registered as students in graduate departments—from both faculty and male peers. In one graduate department of sociology, women represent a full third of the students, and, hence, the faculty cannot be charged with discriminatory practices toward the admission of women students. On the other hand, it was not uncommon in that department to hear faculty members characterize a woman graduate student who showed strong commitment and independence as an "unfeminine bitch," and others who were quiet and unassertive as "lacking ambition"—women who will "never amount to much." Since it is difficult to be simultaneously independent and ambitious, but conventionally feminine and dependent, it would appear that the informal rules prevent many women from winning the game, although they are accepted as players.

Discrimination against women in hiring or promotion may be barred by statute and corporate policy, but this does not magically stimulate any great movement of women up the occupational status ladder. Progress on the legal front must be accompanied by compensatory tactics to free girls and women from the covert depression of their motivations and aspirations through ridicule and double-bind pressures to be contradictory things.

UNIQUE CHARACTERISTICS OF SEX INEQUALITY

Many women find an easy empathy with the plight of the poor, the black, and minority religious groups—not from any innate feminine intuition, but simply because a subordinate group is sensitive to both unintended and intentional debasement or discrimination where another subordinate group is concerned. Women know from personal experience what it is like to be "put down" by men, and can therefore understand what it is to be "put down" as a black by whites. But there are also fundamental differences between sex as a category of social inequality and the categories of race, religion, or ethnicity. I shall discuss three of the most important differences.

Category Size and Residence

In the case of race, religion, and ethnicity, we are literally dealing with minority groups in the American population, whether Mexican, Indian, Jewish, Catholic, or black. This is not the case for sex, since women are actually a numerical majority in the population.

While the potential is present for numerical strength to press for the removal of inequalities, this is counterbalanced by other ways in which women are prevented from effectively utilizing their numerical strength. The Irish, the Italians, and the Jews in an earlier period, and blacks in more recent history, have been able to exert political pressure for representation and legislative change because residential concentration gave them voter strength in large urban centers. By contrast, women are for the most part *evenly distributed throughout the population.* Women can exert political pressure in segmental roles as consumers, workers, New Yorkers, or the aged; but not as a cohesive political group based on sex solidarity. It is inconceivable that a political organization of blacks would avoid the "race" issue, yet the League of Women Voters does precisely this when it takes pride in avoiding "women's" issues.

Early Sex-Role Socialization

Age and sex are the earliest social categories an individual learns. The differentiation between mother and father, or parent and child, is learned at a tender, formative stage of life, and consequently, we carry into adulthood a set of age and sex role expectations that are extremely resistant to change. Not only do girls learn to accept authority from the older generation and from men, but they learn this lesson in intense, intimate relationships. By the time they reach adulthood, women are well socialized to seek and to find gratification in an intimate dependence on men, and in responsible authority over children. They may be dominant and affirmative mothers with their own children, or as teachers in classrooms, but pliant and submissive as wives.

Sex role expectations tend to remain a stubborn part of our impulse lives. This is often not visible among young men and women until they become parents. Many young people are egalitarian peers in school, courtship, and early marriage. With the birth of a child, deeper layers of their personalities come into play. Since there is little or no formal education for parenthood in our society, only a thin veneer of Spock-reading hides the acting out of old parental models that have been observed and internalized in childhood, triggering a regression to traditional sex roles that gradually spreads from the parental role to the marriage and self-definition of both sexes.

As a result of early sex-role socialization, there is bound to be a lag between political and economic emancipation of women and the inner adjustment to equality of both men and women. Even in radical political movements, women have often had to caucus and fight for their acceptance as equal peers to men. Without such efforts on their own behalf, women are as likely to be "girl-Friday" assistants in a radical movement espousing class and racial equality as they are in a business corporation, a labor union, or a conservative political party.

Pressures Against Sex Solidarity

Racial, ethnic, and religious conflict can reach an acute stage of political strife in the movement for equality, without affecting the solidarity of the families of blacks, whites, Jews, or gentiles. Such strife may, in fact, increase the solidarity of these family units. A "we versus them" dichotomy does not cut into family units in the case of race, religion, or ethnicity as it does in the case of sex. Since women typically live in greater intimacy with men than they do with other women, there is potential conflict within family units when women press hard for sex equality. Their demands are on predominantly male legislators and employers in the public domain—husbands and fathers in the private sector. A married black woman can affiliate with an activist civil rights group with no implicit threat to her marriage. For a married woman to affiliate with an activist women's rights group might very well trigger tension in her marriage. While there is probably no limit to the proportion of blacks who might actively fight racial discrimination, a large proportion of married women have not combated sex discrimination. Many of them fear conflict with men, or benefit in terms of a comfortable high status in exchange for economic dependence upon their husbands. There are many more women in the middle class who benefit from sex inequality than there are blacks in the middle class who benefit from racial inequality.

The size of a women's rights movement has, therefore, been responsive to the proportion of "unattached" women in a population. An excess of females over males, a late age at marriage, postponement of childbearing, a high divorce rate, a low remarriage rate, and greater longevity for women, all increase the number of unattached women in a society, and therefore increase the potential for sex-equality activism. The hard core of activists in past suffrage and feminist movements were women without marital and family ties: exwives, nonwives, or childless wives, whose need to support themselves triggered their concern for equal rights to vote, to work, and to advance in their work. The lull in the women's rights movement in the 1950's was related to the fact that this same decade saw the lowest age at marriage and the highest proportion of the population married in all of our history.

Since 1960, the age at marriage has moved up; the birth rate is down to what it was in the late 1930's; the divorce rate is up among couples married a long time, and more married women are in the labor force than ever before. These are all relevant contributors to the renascence of women's rights activism in the mid-1960's. The presence of older and married women in women's rights organizations (like the National Organization for Women) is also responsible for a broadening of the range of issues that concern women activists—from the civil, political, and economic concerns they share with feminists of an earlier day, to a host of changes affecting family roles: repeal of abortion laws, revision of divorce laws, community provision of child-care facilities, equal treatment under Social Security in old age, and a debunking of the clinging-vine or tempting-Eve image of married women that pervades the American mass media.

The point remains, however, that movement toward sex equality is restricted by the fact that our most intimate human relation is the heterosexual one of marriage. This places a major brake on the development of sex solidarity among women, a brake that is not present in other social inequalities, since marriage tends to be endogamous with respect to class, race, and religion.

MODELS OF EQUALITY

Courses in social stratification, minority groups, prejudice, and discrimination have been traditional fare in sociological curriculum for a long time. Many sociologists studied immigrants and their children and puzzled about the eventual shape of a society that underwent so massive an injection of diverse cultures. From these writings, we can extract three potential models that will be useful in sketching the alternate goals not only for the relations between ethnic groups, but for those of race and sex as well.

Three such models may be briefly defined, and then each in turn explored in somewhat greater detail:

Pluralist Model

This model anticipates a society in which marked racial, religious, and ethnic differences are retained and valued for their diversity, yielding a heterogeneous society in which it is hoped cultural strength is increased by the diverse strands making up the whole society.

Assimilation Model

This model anticipates a society in which the minority groups are gradually absorbed into the mainstream by losing their distinguishing characteristics and acquiring the language, occupational skills, and life style of the majority of the host culture.

Hybrid Model

This model anticipates a society in which there is change in both the ascendant group and the minority groups—a "melting-pot" hybrid requiring changes not only in blacks and Jews and women, but white male Protestants as well.

PLURALIST MODEL OF EQUALITY

It is dubious whether any society has ever been truly pluralist in the sense that all groups which comprise it are on an equal footing of status, power, or rewards. Pluralism often disguises a social system in which one group dominates—the upper classes (white Anglo-Saxon Protestants)—and minority ethnic, religious, or racial groups are confined to the lower classes. The upper classes may ceremonially invoke the country's cultural heterogeneity, and delight in ethnic food, art, and music, but exclude the ethnic members themselves from their professions, country clubs, and neighborhoods. Bagels and lox for breakfast, soul food for lunch, and lasagna for dinner; but no Jews, blacks, or Italians on the professional and neighborhood turf! Pluralism has been a congenial model for the race segregationist as well, rationalizing the confinement of blacks to unskilled labor, segregated schools, and neighborhoods.

In the case of sex, the pluralist model posits the necessity of traditional sex role differentiation between the sexes on the grounds of fundamental physiological and hence social differences between the sexes. This is the perspective subscribed to by most behavioral scientists, clinical psychologists, and psychoanalysts, despite the fact that the women they have studied and analyzed are the products of a society that systematically *produces* such sex differences through childrearing and schooling practices. There is no way of allocating observed sex differences to innate physiology or to socio-cultural conditioning.

Freudian theory has contributed to the assumption of innate sex differences on which recent scholars in psychology and sociology have built their case for the necessity of social role and status differentiation between the sexes. Freud codified the belief that men get more pleasure than women from sex in his theory of the sexual development of the female: the transition from an early stage in which girls experience the clitoris as the leading erogenous zone of their bodies to a mature stage in which vaginal orgasm provides the woman with her major sexual pleasure. Women who did not make this transition were then viewed as sexually "anaesthetic" and "psychosexually immature." Psychological theory often seems sterner and more resistant to change than the people to which it is applied. It is incredible that the Freudian theory of female sexuality was retained for decades despite thousands of hours of intimate therapeutic data from women, only recently showing signs of weakening under the impact of research conducted by Masters and Johnson and reported in their *Human Sexual Response*, that there is no anatomical difference between clitoral and vaginal orgasm.

Implicit in both psychological theory of sex differences and the Freudian, vaginal-orgasm theory was a basic assumption that women should be exclusively dependent on men for their sexual pleasure, hiding from view the realization that masturbation may be different from, but not necessarily less gratifying sexually than, sexual intercourse. Much the same function has been served by the strong pressures to disassociate sex from maternity. Physicians have long known that nursing is associated with uterine contractions and have noted that male babies often have erections while nursing, but no one has suggested that the starry-eyed contentment of a nursing mother is a blend of genital as well as maternal pleasure. The cultural insistence upon separating sex from maternity, as the insistence that vaginal orgasm is the only "normal satisfaction" of a mature woman, serves the function of preventing women from seeing that they can find pleasure and fulfillment from themselves, other women, and their children and do not have to depend exclusively upon men for such gratification.

Coupled with this is the further assumption, peculiar to American society, that childrearing is the exclusive responsibility of the parents themselves, and not a community responsibility to assure every child a healthy physical and social development (as it is, for example, in East European countries, Israel, and Sweden). This belief keeps women tied closely to the home for the most vigorous years of their adulthood. The "new" look to a woman's life span, now institutionalized by over 100 centers for continuing education for women in the United States, does nothing to alter this basic assumption, but merely adapts to our lengthened life span. Women are urged to withdraw from outside obligations during the childbearing and rearing years and to return for further training and participation in the labor force when children reach an appropriate mature age. The consequences of such late return to active work away from the home are lower incomes, work at levels below the ability of the women, and withdrawal for the very years all studies show to be the peaks of creativity in work, their twenties and thirties.

Why does American society persist in maintaining erroneous myths concerning female sexuality, contrary to research evidence, as it does in urging women to believe their children's development requires their daily attendance upon them, again contrary to research evidence? I believe the answer lies in the economic demand that men work at persistent levels of high efficiency and creativity. To free men to do this requires a social arrangement in which the family system serves as the shock-absorbing handmaiden of the occupational system. The stimulation of women's desires for an affluent style of life and a bountiful maternity—to be eager and persistent consumers of goods and producers of babies—serves the function of adding continual pressure on men to be high earners. The combination of pronatalist values and aspirations for a high standard of living has the effect of both releasing and requiring men to give heavy psychic and time investment to their jobs, and requiring women to devote their primary efforts and commitments to homemaking. As a result, the broad sweep of many an American woman's life span is caught by the transitions from Bill's daughter to John's wife to Johnny's mother and Billy's grandmother.

Behind the veneer of modern emancipation is a woman isolated in an apartment or suburban home, exclusively responsible for the care of young children, dependent on her husband for income, misled to believe that sex gratification is only possible via a vaginal orgasm simultaneous with male ejaculation, and urged to buy more and more clothes and household possessions, which she then takes more time but little pleasure in maintaining. Complementing the life of the woman in the pluralist model of sex roles, the American male is prodded to seek success and achievement in a competitive job world at the emotional cost of limited time or psychic energy for his marriage or his children, tempted by the same consumption-stimulating media and promises of easy credit, expected to uproot his family if a move is "good for his career," and ridiculed if he seeks to participate more extensively in home and child care as "unmanly."

The odds are heavily stacked against the pluralist model of society as a goal in terms of which racial, ethnic, or sex equality can be achieved.

ASSIMILATION MODEL OF EQUALITY

This model anticipates that with time, the minority groups will be gradually absorbed into the mainstream of society by losing their distinguishing characteristics, acquiring the language, educational attainment, and occupational skills of the majority host culture. Concern for inequality along ethnic or racial lines is concentrated on the political, educational, and economic institutions of society. Little sociological interest or political concern is shown once men in the minority group are distributed throughout the occupational system in roughly the same proportion as mainstream males.

Feminist ideology is but one variant of the assimilation model, calling upon women to seek their place with men in the political and occupational world in sufficient numbers to eventually show a 50–50 distribution by sex in the prestigious occupations and political organizations of the society. The federal government has served as a pacesetter for the economy in urging the appointment and promotion of competent women to the highest civil service posts and encouraging private employers to follow the federal example by facilitating the movement of women into executive posts.

The feminist-assimilation model has an implicit fallacy, however. No amount of entreaty will yield an equitable distribution of women and men in the top strata of business and professional occupations, for the simple reason that the life men have led in these strata has been possible only because their own wives were leading traditional lives as homemakers, doing double parent and household duty, and carrying the major burden of civic responsibilities. If it were not for their wives in the background, successful men in American society would have to be single or childless. This is why so many professional women complain privately that what they most need in life is a "wife"!

The assimilation model also makes an assumption that the institutional structure of American society developed over decades by predominantly white Protestant males, constitutes the best of all possible worlds. Whether the call is to blacks or to women to join white men in the mainstream of American society, both racial integration and feminist ideology accept the structure of American society as it now exists. The assimilation model rejects the psychological theses of innate racial or sex differences implicit in most versions of the pluralist model, but it accepts the social institutions formed by the ascendant group. This is precisely the assumption numerous blacks, women, and members of the younger generation have recently been questioning and rejecting.

HYBRID MODEL OF EQUALITY

The hybrid model of equality rejects both traditional psychological assumptions and the institutional structure we have inherited. It anticipates a society in which the lives of men and of whites will be different, not only women and blacks. In fact, it might be that this hybrid model would involve greater change in the role of men than of women, because institutional changes it would require involve a restructuring to bring the world of jobs and politics closer to the fulfillment of individual human needs for both creativity and fellowship. From this point of view, the values many young men and women subscribe to today are congenial to the hybrid model of equality: the desire for a more meaningful sense of community and a greater depth to personal relations across class, sex, and racial lines; a stress on human fellowship and individual scope for creativity rather than merely rationality and efficiency in our bureaucracies; heightened interst in the humanities and the social sciences from an articulated value base; and a social responsibility commitment to medicine and law rather than a thirst for status and high income. These are all demands for social change by the younger generation in our time that are closer to the values and interests women have held than they are to the values and interests of men. They represent an ardent "no" to the image of society projected by the new crop of male technitronic futurists—a machine- and consumption-oriented society that rewards technological prowess in a "plasticWasp9-5america."

Because women have tended to play the passive, adaptive role in the past, they have not been prominent as social and political critics of American institutions. In fact, the traditional roles of women confined them to the most conservative institutions of the society: the family, the public schools, and the church. Women deviant enough to seek greater equality with men in professional, business, and academic life have tended to share the values of their masculine colleagues, while professional women who did not share these values have been quiet, either because they distrusted their own critical bent as a vestige of unwanted "womanliness," or because they feared exclusion from the masculine turf they have precariously established themselves on.

But there is a new groundswell in American society, which is a hopeful sign of a movement toward the hybrid model briefly sketched here. One finds it in women's liberation groups across the country, particularly on the university campus. I would predict, for example, that these young women, unlike their professional older sisters, will not bemoan the fact that academic women have been less "productive" than men, but will be critical of the criteria used to assess academic productivity. Up to now these criteria have been such things as "number of publications," "number of professional organization memberships," and "number of offices held in professional organizations." The new breed of women will ask, as many young students are now demanding, that the quality of teaching, the degree of colleagueship with students, the extent of service to both an academic institution and its surrounding community, become part of the criteria on which the productivity of an academic man or woman is evaluated. No one has conducted research on academic productivity with this enlarged net of criteria, and it is a moot point whether men would show greater productivity than women if such criteria were applied. Though it will be a difficult road, with all the money and prestige pulling in the opposite direction, this thrust on the part of the young, together with like-minded older humanist scholars and critics, creative artists, and natural and behavioral scientists, has the potential of developing oases of health and sanity in many educational, welfare, and cultural institutions of American society.

CONCLUSION

A *pluralist* model of social equality is implicitly a conservative goal, a descriptive model that accepts what exists at a given point in time as desirable and good. The *assimilation* model is implicitly a liberal goal, a Horatio Alger model that accepts the present structure of society as stable and desirable, and urges minority groups to accept the values and goals of the dominant group within that system as their own. The *hybrid* model is a radical goal which rejects the present structure of society and seeks instead a new breed of men and women and a new vision of the future. Applied to the role of women, these models may be illustrated in a summary fashion as follows: the pluralist model says the woman's nurturance finds its best expression in maternity; the assimilation model says women must be motivated to seek professional careers in medicine similar to those pursued now by men; the hybrid model says, rather, that the structure of medicine can be changed so that more women will be attracted to medical careers, and male physicians will be able to live more balanced, less difficult and status-dominated lives.

An analysis of sex equality goals may start with the reality of contemporary life, but soon requires an imaginative leap to a new conception of what a future good society should be. With the hybrid model of equality one envisages a future in which family, community, and play are valued on a par with politics and work for both sexes, for all the races, and for all social classes and nations which comprise the human family. We are on the brink not of the "end" of ideology, but its "beginning."

37 Homosexuality: The Formulation of a Sociological Perspective

WILLIAM SIMON and JOHN H. GAGNON

The study of homosexuality today, except for a few rare and relatively recent examples, suffers from two major defects: it is ruled by a simplistic and homogeneous view of the psychological and social contents of the category "homosexual," and at the same time it is nearly exclusively interested in the most difficult and least rewarding of all questions, that of etiology. While some small exceptions are allowed for adolescent homosexual experimentation, the person with a major to nearly exclusive sexual interest in persons of the same sex is perceived as belonging to a uniform category whose adult behavior is a necessary outcome and, in a sense, reenactment of certain early and determining experiences. This is the prevailing image of the homosexual and the substantive concern of the literature in psychiatry and psychology today.[1]

In addition to the fact that sexual contact with persons of the same sex, even if over the age of consent, is against the law in 49 of the 50 states, the homosexual labors under another burden that is commonly the lot of the deviant in any society.[2] The process of labeling and stigmatizing behavior not

[1] Irving Bieber et al., *Homosexuality, A Psychoanalytic Study*, New York: Basic Books, 1962.

[2] Sex law reform occurred in the State of Illinois as part of a general reform of the criminal code in 1961. For the manner in which the law's reform was translated for police officials, see Claude Sowle, *A Concise Explanation of the Illinois Criminal Code of 1961*, Chicago: B. Smith, 1961.

A revised version of a paper presented at the 61st annual meetings of the American Sociological Association in Miami, August–September 1966. This research was supported in part by USPHS MH grants No. 07742 and No. 12535.

Reprinted from *Journal of Health and Social Behavior*, 8, No. 3, (September, 1967), 177–185, by permission of the publishers.

only facilitates the work of legal agencies in creating a bounded category of deviant actors such as the "normal burglar" and the "normal child molester" as suggested by Sudnow, but it also creates an image of large classes of deviant actors all operating from the same motivations and for the same etiological reasons.[3] The homosexual, like most significantly labeled persons (whether the label be positive or negative), has *all* of his acts interpreted through the framework of his homosexuality. Thus the creative activity of the playwright or painter who happens to be homosexual is interpreted in terms of his homosexuality rather than in terms of the artistic rules and conventions of the particular art form in which he works. The plays of the dramatist are scanned for the Albertine Ploy and the painter's paintings for an excessive or deficient use of phallic imagery or vaginal teeth.

It is this nearly obsessive concern with the ultimate causes of adult conditions that has played a major role in structuring our concerns about beliefs and attitudes toward the homosexual. Whatever the specific elements that make up an etiological theory, the search for etiology has its own consequences for research methodology and the construction of theories about behavior. In the case of homosexuality, if one moves beyond those explanations of homosexual behavior that are rooted in constitutional or biological characteristics—that is, something in the genes or in the hormonal system— one is left with etiological explanations located in the structure of the family and its malfunctions.[4] The most compelling of these theories are grounded ultimately in Freudian psychology, where the roots of this as well as the rest of human character structure is to be found in the pathological relationships between parents and their children.[5]

As a consequence of our preliminary work and the work of others, such as

[3] David Sudnow, "Normal Crimes," *Social Problems*, 12 (Winter, 1965), 255–276.

[4] A. C. Kinsey, "Criteria for the Hormonal Explanation of the Homosexual," *The Journal of Clinical Endocrinology*, 1 (May, 1941), 424–428; F. J. Kallman, "Comparative Twin Study on the Genetic Aspects of Male Homosexuality," *Journal of Nervous and Mental Disorders*, 115 (1952), 283–298; F. J. Kallman, "Genetic Aspects of Sex Determination and Sexual Maturation Potentials in Man," in George Winokur (ed.), *Determinants of Human Sexual Behavior*, Springfield: Charles C Thomas, 1963, pp. 5–18; and John Money, "Factors in the Genesis of Homosexuality," George Winokur (ed.), *Determinants of Human Sexual Behavior*, Springfield: Charles C Thomas, 1963, pp. 19–43.

[5] The work of Bieber op. cit. is the most recent of these analytic explorations, the central finding of which is that in a highly selected group of male homosexuals there was a larger proportion of males who had mothers who could be described as close-binding and intimate and fathers who were detached and hostile. The argument proceeds that the mother has selected this child for special overprotection and seductive care. In the process of childrearing, sexual interest is both elicited and then blocked by punishing its behavioral manifestations. As a result of the mother's special ties to the child, the father is alienated from familial interaction, is hostile to the child, and fails to become a source of masculine attachment.

Regardless of the rather engaging and persuasive character of the theory, there are substantial complications. It assumes that there is a necessary relationship between the development of masculinity and femininity and heterosexuality and homosexuality. There is the assumption that homosexuals

Hooker, Reiss, Leznoff and Westley, Achilles, and Schofield,[6] we would like to propose some alternative considerations in terms of the complexity of the life cycle of the homosexual, the roles that mark various stages of this cycle, and the kinds of forces, both sexual and nonsexual, that impinge on this individual actor. It is our current feeling that the problem of finding out how

---

play sexual roles that are explicitly modeled upon those of the heterosexual and that these roles are well-defined and widespread. This confusion of the dimensions of sexual object choice and masculinity and femininity is based on two complementary errors. The first is that the very physical sexual activities of the homosexual are often characterized as passive (to be read feminine) or active (to be read masculine) and that these physical activities are read as direct homologues of the complex matters of masculinity and femininity. The second source of the confusion lies in the two situations in which homosexuality can be most easily observed. One is the prison, where the characteristics of homosexuality do tend to model themselves more closely on the patterns of heterosexuality in the outside community, but where the sources and the character of behavior are in the service of different ends. The second situation is that of public homosexuality characterized by the flaunted female gesture which has become stereotypic of homosexuality. This is not to say that such beliefs about the nature of homosexuality on the part of the heterosexual majority do not influence the homosexual's behavior; however, just because stereotypes are held does not mean that they play a role in the etiology of the behavior that they purport to explain.

Another major problem that exists for etiological theories of homosexuality based on family structure is the difficulty one finds in all theories that depend on the individual's memories of his childhood and that call upon him for hearsay evidence not only about himself, but about his parents. We live in a post-Freudian world and the vocabulary of motives of the most psychologically illiterate is replete with the concepts of repression, inhibition, the oedipus complex, and castration fears. The rhetoric of psychoanalysis permeates the culture as a result of a process that might best be called the democratization of mental health. One of the lessons of existentialism is that our biographies are not fixed quantities but are subject to revision, elision, and other forms of subtle editing based on our place in the life cycle, our audience, and the mask that we are currently wearing. Indeed, for many persons the rehearsed past and the real past become so intermixed that there is only the present. Recent research in childrearing practices suggests that two years after the major events of childrearing, weaning, and toilet training mothers fail to recall accurately their previous conduct and hence sound a good deal like Dr. Spock. An important footnote here is that persons do not always edit the past to improve their image in the conventional sense. Often the patient in psychotherapy works very hard to bring out more and more self-denigrating materials to assure the therapist that he, the patient, is really working hard and searching for his true motives.

[6] Evelyn Hooker, "The Homosexual Community," James C. Palmer and Michael J. Goldstein (eds.), *Perspectives in Psychopathology*, New York: Oxford University Press, 1966, pp. 354–364; Albert J. Reiss, "The Social Integration of Queers and Peers," *Social Problems*, 9 (Fall, 1961), 102–120; M. Leznoff and W. A. Westley, "The Homosexual Community," *Social Problems*, 3 (April, 1956), 257–263; N. Achilles, "The Development of the Homosexual Bar as an Institution," in J. H. Gagnon and W. Simon (eds.), *Sexual Deviance*, New York: Harper and Row, 1967; and Michael Schofield, *Sociological Aspects of Homosexuality*, Boston: Little Brown, 1965.

people become homosexual requires an adequate theory of how they become heterosexual; that is, one cannot explain homosexuality in one way and leave heterosexuality as a large residual category labeled "all other." Indeed, the explanation of homosexuality in this sense may await the explanation of the larger and more modal category of adjustment.

Further, from a sociological point of view, what the original causes were may not even be very important for the patterns of homosexuality observed in a society. Much as the medical student who comes to medicine for many reasons, and for whom the homogeneous character of professional behavior arises from the experiences of medical school rather than from the root causes of his occupational choice, the patterns of adult homosexuality are consequent upon the social structures and values that surround the homosexual after he becomes, or conceives of himself as, homosexual rather than upon original and ultimate causes.[7]

What we are suggesting here is that we have allowed the homosexual's sexual object choice to dominate and control our imagery of him and have let this aspect of his total life experience appear to determine all his products, concerns, and activities. This prepossessing concern on the part of nonhomosexuals with the purely sexual aspect of the homosexual's life is something we would not allow to occur if we were interested in the heterosexual. However, the mere presence of sexual deviation seems to give the sexual content of life an overwhelming significance. Homosexuals, moreover, vary profoundly in the degree to which their homosexual commitment and its facilitation becomes the organizing principle of their lives. Involved here is a complex outcome that is less likely to be explained by originating circumstances than by the consequences of the establishment of the commitment itself.

Even with the relatively recent shift in the normative framework available for considering homosexuality—that is, from a rhetoric of sin to a rhetoric of mental health—the preponderance of the sexual factor is evident. The change itself may have major significance in the ways homosexual persons are dealt with; at the same time, however, the mental health rhetoric seems equally wide of the mark in understanding homosexuality. One advance, however, is that in place of a language of optimum man which characterized both the moral and the early mental health writings, we find a growing literature concerned with the psychological characteristics necessary for a person to survive in some manner within specific social systems and social situations.[8] In this post-Freudian world, major psychic wounds are increasingly

[7] Howard S. Becker, "Change in Adult Life," *Sociometry*, 27 (March, 1964), pp. 40–53.

Howard S. Becker, Blanche Geer and Everett C. Hughes, *Boys in White: Student Culture in the Medical School*, Chicago: University of Chicago Press, 1961.

[8] Marie Jahoda, "Toward a Social Psychology of Mental Health" in Arnold M. Rose (ed.), *Mental Health and Mental Disorder*, New York: Norton, 1955, pp. 556–577.

F. C. Redlich, "The Concept of Health in Psychiatry," in A. H. Leighton, J. A. Clausen and R. N. Wilson, *Explorations in Social Psychiatry*, New York: Basic Books, 1957, pp. 138–164.

viewed as par for the human condition and, as one major psychiatric theore-
tician observes, few survive the relationship with their parents without such
wounding.[9] The problem becomes then, whether these wounds become exposed to social situations that render them either too costly to the individual
or to the surrounding community. Accompanying this trend toward a recon-
ceptualization of mental health has been a scaling-down of the goals set for
men; instead of exceedingly vague and somewhat utopian goals, we tend to
ask more pragmatic questions: Is the individual self-supporting? Does he
manage to conduct his affairs without the intervention of the police or the
growing number of mental health authorities? Does he have adequate sources
of social support? A positively-balanced and adequately-developed repertoire
for gratification? Has he learned to accept himself? These are questions we
are learning to ask of nearly all men, but among the exceptions is found the
homosexual. In practically all cases, the presence of homosexuality is seen
as prima facie evidence of major psychopathology. When the heterosexual
meets these minimal definitions of mental health, he is exculpated; the
homosexual—no matter how good his adjustment in nonsexual areas of life
—remains suspect.

TABLE 1 Reported Incidence of Social Difficulties by Education and Exclusivity of
Homosexual Commitment

	High School		College	
	Exclusive Homosexual	Mixed Homosexual and Heterosexual	Exclusive Homosexual	Mixed Homosexual and Heterosexual
	%	%	%	%
Trouble with:				
Police	31	22	24	17
Family of origin	25	16	19	11
Occupation	10	8	7	8
(N)	(83)	(83)	(283)	(101)

Recent tabulations drawn from a group of 550 white males with extensive
histories of homosexuality, interviewed outside institutions by Kinsey and his
associates, suggest that most homosexuals cope fairly well, and even
particularly well, when we consider the stigmatized and in fact criminal
nature of their sexual interest.[10] Of this group, between 75 and 80 per cent
reported having had no trouble with the police, the proportion varying by the
exclusivity of their homosexual commitment and their educational attainment (see Table 1). Following this same pattern, trouble with their families
of origin tended to occur in a joint relationship with level of education and
degree of homosexual commitment, with the less educated and the more
homosexual reporting a greater incidence of difficulties. Only about 10 per

[9] Lawrence Kubie, "Social Forces and the Neurotic Process," in A. H.
Leighton, J. A. Clausen and R. N. Wilson, Explorations in Social Psychiatry,
New York: Basic Books, 1957, pp. 77–104.
[10] Extensive homosexuality is here defined as a minimum of 51 or more
times and/or contact with 21 or more males.

cent of the group reported trouble at work and less than five per cent at school as a result of their homosexuality. Of those who had military experience, only one fifth reported difficulties in that milieu. In the military, possibly more than in civilian life, homosexuality is a difficulty that obliterates all other evaluations made of the person.

We do not wish to say that homosexual life does not contain a great potential for demoralization, despair, and self-hatred. To the contrary, as in most deviant careers, there remains the potential for a significant escalation of individual psychopathology. This potential is suggested by some other aspects of these same data. About one half of these males reported that 60 per cent or more of their sexual partners were persons with whom they had sex only one time. Between 10 and 20 per cent report that they often picked up their sexual partners in public terminals, and an even larger proportion reported similar contacts in other public or semipublic locations. Between a quarter and a third reported having been robbed by a sexual partner, with a

TABLE 2 Selected Negative Aspects of a Homosexual Career by Education and Exclusivity of Homosexual Commitment

| | High School | | College | |
	Exclusive Homosexual	Mixed Homosexual and Heterosexual	Exclusive Homosexual	Mixed Homosexual and Heterosexual
	%	%	%	%
Proportion with 60% or more of sexual partners with whom had sex only once	49	43	51	45
Often pick up partners in public terminals	19	18	17	7
Ever been rolled	37	26	34	29
Ever been blackmailed	16	6	12	15
(N)	(83)	(83)	(283)	(101)

larger proportion characteristically having exclusively homosexual histories. Finally, between 10 and 15 percent reported having been blackmailed because of their homosexuality (see Table 2).

There were further indicators of alienation and difficulty in the findings. For two fifths of the respondents the longest homosexual affair lasted less than one year, and for about one quarter kissing occurred in one third or less of their sexual contacts. In addition, about 30 per cent reported never having had sex in their own homes. Accumulatively, such conditions add up to the two fifths of these men who indicated some serious feelings of regret about being homosexual, giving such reasons as fear of social disapproval or rejection, inability to experience a conventional family life, feelings of guilt or shame, or fear of potential trouble with the law. These figures require a more detailed analysis, and there are also uncertainties about sample bias that must be considered. However, it is our feeling that these proportions would not be substantially changed, given a more complete exploration of these factors. These data, then, suggest a depersonalized character, a driven or compulsive quality of the sexual activity of many homosexuals, which cannot be reckoned as anything but extremely costly to them.

Obviously, the satisfaction of a homosexual commitment—like most forms of deviance—makes social adjustment more problematic that it might be for members of a conventional population. What is important to understand is that consequences of these sexual practices are not necessarily direct functions of the nature of such practices. It is necessary to move away from an obsessive concern with the sexuality of the individual, and attempt to see the homosexual in terms of the broader attachments that he must make to live in the world around him. Like the heterosexual, the homosexual must come to terms with the problems that are attendant upon being a member of society: he must find a place to work, learn to live with or without his family, be involved or apathetic in political life, find a group of friends to talk to and live with, fill his leisure time usefully or frivolously, handle all of the common and uncommon problems of impulse control and personal gratification, and in some manner socialize his sexual interests.

There is a seldom-noticed diversity to be found in the life cycle of the homosexual, both in terms of solving general human problems and in terms of the particular characteristics of the life cycle itself. Not only are there as many ways of being homosexual as there are of being heterosexual, but the individual homosexual, in the course of his every-day life, encounters as many choices and as many crises as the heterosexual. It is much too easy to allow the label, once applied, to suggest that the complexities of role transition and identity crises are easily attributable to, or are a crucial exemplification of, some previously existing etiological defect.

An example of this is in the phase of homosexuality called "coming out," which is that point in time when there is self-recognition by the individual of his identity as a homosexual and the first major exploration of the homosexual community. At this point in time the removal of inhibiting doubts frequently releases a great deal of sexual energy. Sexual contacts during this period are often pursued nearly indiscriminately and with greater vigor than caution. This is very close to that period in the life of the heterosexual called the "honeymoon," when coitus is legitimate and is pursued with a substantial amount of energy. This high rate of marital coitus, however, declines as demands are made on the young couple to take their place in the framework of the larger social system. In these same terms, during the homosexual "honeymoon" many individuals begin to learn ways of acting out a homosexual object choice that involve homosexual gratification, but that are not necessarily directly sexual and do not involve the genitalia.

It is during this period that many homosexuals go through a crisis of femininity; that is, they "act out" in relatively public places in a somewhat effeminate manner; and some, in a transitory fashion, wear female clothing, known in the homosexual argot as "going in drag." During this period one of the major confirming aspects of masculinity—that is, nonsexual reinforcement by females of masculine status—has been abandoned, and it is not surprising that the very core of masculine identity should not be seriously questioned. This crisis is partially structured by the already existing homosexual culture in which persons already in the crisis stage become models for those who are newer to their homosexual commitment. A few males retain this pseudo-feminine commitment, a few others emerge masquerading as female prostitutes to males, and still others pursue careers as female impersonators. This adjustment might be more widely adapted if feminine behavior by men— except in sharply delimited occupational roles—was not negatively sanctioned. Thus the tendency is for this kind of behavior to be a transitional experiment for most homosexuals, an experiment that leaves vestiges of "camp" behavior, but traces more often expressive of the character of the cultural life of the homosexual community than of some overriding need of individual homosexuals. Since this period of personal disorganization and identity problems is at the same time highly visible to the broader community, this femininity is enlisted as evidence for theories of homosexuality that see, as a central component in its etiology, the failure of sexual identification. The homosexual at this point of his life cycle is more likely to be in psychotherapy, and this is often construed as evidence for a theory which is supported by a missampling of the ways of being homosexual.

Another life cycle crisis that the homosexual shares with the heterosexual in this youth-oriented society is the crisis of aging. While American society places an inordinate positive emphasis on youth, the homosexual community, by and large, places a still greater emphasis on this fleeting characteristic. In general, the homosexual has fewer resources with which to meet this crisis. For the heterosexual there are his children whose careers assure a sense of the future and a wife whose sexual availability cushions the shock of declining sexual attractiveness. In addition, the crisis of aging comes later to the heterosexual, at an age when his sexual powers have declined and expectations concerning his sexuality are considerably lower. The management of aging by the homosexual is not well understood, but there are, at this point in his life, a series of behavioral manifestations (symptoms) attendant to this dramatic transition that are misread as global aspects of homosexuality. Here, as with "coming out," it is important to note that most homosexuals, even with fewer resources than their heterosexual counterparts, manage to weather the period with relative success.

A central concern underlying these options and the management of a homosexual career is the presence and complexity of a homosexual community, which serves most simply for some persons as a sexual market place, but for others as the locus of friendships, opportunities, recreation, and expansion of the base of social life. Such a community is filled with both formal and informal institutions for meeting others and for following, to the degree the individual wants, a homosexual life style. Minimally, the community provides a source of social support, for it is one of the few places where the homosexual may get positive validation of his own self-image. Though the community often provides more feminine or "camp" behavior than some individuals might desire, in a major sense "camp" behavior may well be an expression of aggregate community characteristics without an equal commitment to this behavior on the part of its members. Further, "camp" behavior may also be seen as a form of interpersonal communication characteristic of intracommunity behavior and significantly altered for most during interaction with the larger society. The community serves as a way of mediating sexuality by providing a situation in which one can know and evaluate peers and, in a significant sense, convert sexual behavior into sexual conduct.[11] Insofar as the community provides these relationships for the individual homosexual, it allows for the dilution of sexual drives by providing social gratification in ways that are not directly sexual. Consequently, the homosexual wth access to the community is more protected from impulsive sexual "acting out" than the homosexual who has only his own fear and knowledge of the society's prohibitions to mediate his sexual impulses.

It should be pointed out that in contrast to ethnic and occupational subcultures the homosexual community, as well as other deviant subcommunities, has very limited content.[12] This derives from the fact that the community members often have only their sexual commitment in common. Thus, while the community may reduce the problems of access to sexual partners and reduce guilt by providing a structure of shared values, often the shared value structure is far too narrow to transcend other areas of value disagreement. The college-trained professional and the bus boy, the WASP and the Negro slum dweller, may meet in sexual congress, but the similarity of their sexual interests does not eliminate larger social and cultural barriers.[13] The important fact is that the homosexual community is in itself an impoverished cultural unit. This impoverishment, however, may be only partially limiting, since it constrains most members to participate in it on a limited basis, reducing their anxiety and conflicts in the sexual sphere and increasing the quality of their performance in other aspects of social life.

Earlier we briefly listed some of the general problems that the homosexual—in common with the heterosexual—must face; these included earning a living, maintaining a residence, relations with family, and so on. At this point we might consider some of these in greater detail.

First there is the most basic problem of all: earning a living. Initially, the variables that apply to all labor force participants generally apply to homosexuals also. In addition there are the special conditions imposed by the deviant definition of the homosexual commitment. What is important is that the occupational activity of homosexuals represents a fairly broad range.

[11] Ernest W. Burgess makes this useful distinction in his article, "The Sociologic Theory of Psychosexual Behavior," in Paul H. Hoch and Joseph Zubin (eds.), *Psychosexual Development in Health and Disease*, New York: Grune and Stratton, 1949, pp. 227–243. Burgess says, "Accurately speaking the various forms of sexual outlet for man are not behavior, they are conduct. Conduct is behavior as prescribed or evaluated by the group. It is not simply external observable behavior, but behavior that expresses a norm or evaluation."

[12] For descriptions of the content of other deviant subcultures see, Harold Finestone, "Cats Kicks and Color," *Social Problems*, 5 (July, 1957), 3–13.

Howard S. Becker, *The Outsiders*, New York: The Free Press, 1963.

James H. Bryan, "Apprenticeships in Prostitution," *Social Problems*, 12 (Winter, 1965), 278–297.

[13] The homosexual community does provide for an easing of strain by training essentially lower class types in middle class life styles and even middle class occupational roles to a greater extent than most people realize. In contrast, for those for whom homosexuality becomes the salient organizing experience of their lives there may be a concomitant downward mobility as their ties with commitments to systems of roles that are larger than the homosexual community decrease.

The differences in occupational activity can be conceptualized along a number of dimensions, some of which would be conventional concerns of occupational sociology, while others would reflect the special situation of the homosexual. For example, one element is the degree of occupational involvement, that is, the degree to which occupational activity, or activity ancillary to it, is defined as intrinsically gratifying. This would obviously vary from professional to ribbon clerk to factory laborer. A corollary to this is the degree to which the world of work penetrates other aspects of life. In terms of influence upon a homosexual career, occupational involvement very likely plays a constraining role during the acting-out phase associated with "coming out," as well as serving as an alternative source of investment during the "crisis of aging." Another aspect bears directly upon the issue of the consequences of having one's deviant commitment exposed. For some occupational roles disclosure would clearly be a disaster—the school teacher, the minister, and the politician, to mention just three. There are other occupations where the disclosure or assumption of homosexual interests is either of little consequence or—though relatively rare—has a positive consequence. It should be evident that the crucial question of anxiety and depersonalization in the condict of sexual activity can be linked to this variable in a rather direct way.

A second series of questions could deal with the effects of a deviant sexual commitment upon occupational activity itself. In some cases the effect may be extremely negative, since the pursuit of homosexual interests may generate irresponsibility and irregularity. Some part of this might flow from what we associate with bachelorhood generally: detachment from conventional families and, in terms of sex, constant striving for what is essentially regularized in marriage. Illustrations of these behaviors include too many late nights out, too much drinking in too many taverns, and unevenness in emotional condition. On the other hand, several positive effects can be observed. Detachment from the demands of domestic life not only frees one for greater dedication to the pursuit of sexual goals, but also for greater dedication to work. Also, the ability of some jobs to facilitate homosexual activity—such as certain marginal, low-paying, white-collar jobs—serves as compensation for low pay or limited opportunity for advancement. There may be few simple or consistent patterns emerging from this type of consideration, yet the overdetermination of the sexual element in the study of the homosexual rests in our prior reluctance to consider these questions which are both complex and pedestrian.

Similarly, just as most homosexuals have to earn a living, so must they come to terms with their immediate families. There is no substantial evidence to suggest that the proportion of homosexuals for whom relatives are significant persons differs from that of heterosexuals. The important differences rest in the way the relationships are managed and, again, the consequences they have for other aspects of life. Here also one could expect considerable variation containing patterns of rejection, continuing involvement without knowledge, ritualistically suppressed knowledge, and knowledge and acceptance. This becomes more complex because several patterns may be operative at the same time with different members of one's family constellation. Here again it is not unreasonable to assume a considerable degree of variation in the course of managing a homosexual commitment as this kind of factor varies. Yet the literature is almost totally without reference to this relationship. Curiously, in the psychiatric literature—where mother and father play crucial roles in the formation of a homosexual commitment—they tend to be significant by their absence in considerations of how homosexual careers are managed.

This order of discussion could be extended into a large number of areas. Let us consider just one more: religion. As a variable, religion (as both an identification and a quality of religiosity) manifests no indication that it plays an important role in the generation of homosexual commitments. However, it clearly does, or can, play a significant role in the management of that commitment. Here, as in other spheres of life, we must be prepared to deal with complex, interactive relations rather than fixed, static ones. Crucial to the homosexual's ability to "accept himself" is his ability to bring his own homosexuality within a sense of the moral order as it is projected by the institutions surrounding him as well as his own vision of this order. It may be that the issue of including homosexuality within a religious definition is the way the question should be framed only part of the time, and for only part of a homosexual population. At other times and for other homosexuals, to frame the question in terms of bringing religiosity within the homosexual definition might be more appropriate. The need for damnation (that rare sense of being genuinely evil) and the need for redemption (a sense of potentially being returned to the community in good standing) can be expected to vary, given different stages of the life cycle, different styles of being homosexual, and varying environments for enactment of the homosexual commitment. And our sense of the relation suggests that, more than asking about the homosexual's religious orientation and how it expresses his homosexuality, we must also learn to ask how his homosexuality expresses his commitment to the religious.

The aims, then, of a sociological approach to homosexuality are to begin to define the factors—both individual and situational—that predispose a homosexual to follow one homosexual path as against others; to spell out the contingencies that will shape the career that has been embarked upon; and to trace out the patterns of living in both their pedestrian and their seemingly exotic aspects. Only then will we begin to understand the homosexual. This pursuit must inevitably bring us—though from a particular angle —to those complex matrices wherein most human behavior is fashioned.

38 | Illegitimacy in the Caribbean Social Structure: A Reconsideration

HYMAN RODMAN

Much theoretical and empirical controversy has centered upon the family in the Caribbean area. One controversial question concerns the values of members of the lower classes in Caribbean societies regarding non-legal marital unions[1] and the illegitimate children born to these unions.[2] There is general agreement on the high rates of illegitimacy and non-legal unions to be found in Caribbean societies, but there is disagreement on whether these patterns of behavior are normative or deviant with respect to the value system of the lower class. It is an intriguing question because, if these patterns are normative, then they are very much at odds with the dominant values of the society, and if these patterns are deviant, then the behavioral patterns within the lower class are very much at odds with the normative patterns. As a result, the Caribbean data have an important bearing upon certain theoretical formulations, and most especially upon the general questions of the development of "deviant" subcultures and the correspondence between behavioral patterns and normative patterns.

Some researchers have taken the position that within the lower class the

[1] The term, "non-legal marital unions," is used in this paper to refer only to those unions in which the man and the woman are cohabiting. The controversy in the Caribbean data centers on this union, called variously by researchers common-law marriage, concubinage, and consensual union. See Hyman Rodman, "On Understanding Lower-Class Behaviour," *Social and Economic Studies*, 8 (December, 1959), 445.

[2] Judith Blake, "Family Instability and Reproductive Behavior in Jamaica," *Current Research in Human Fertility*, Milbank Memorial Fund, New York, 1955, pp. 24–41; Lloyd Braithwaite, "Sociology and Demographic Research in the British Caribbean," *Social and Economic Studies*, 6 (December, 1957), 541–550; Judith Blake, "A Reply to Mr. Braithwaite," *Social and Economic Studies*, 7 (1958), 234–237; Judith Blake, *Family Structure in Jamaica*, New York: Free Press of Glencoe, 1961; William J. Goode, "Illegitimacy in the Caribbean Social Structure," *American Sociological Review*, 25 (February, 1960), 21–30; Hyman Rodman, "The Lower-Class Value Stretch," *Social Forces*, 42 (December, 1963), 205–215.

Patricia G. Voydanoff has contributed to this paper as a research assistant and as a critical reader of an earlier draft. In addition, Lloyd Rogler, Constantina Safilios-Rothschild, and John S. Watson have made a number of helpful suggestions, although I have not followed their advice at all points. The research and analysis were supported in part by NIMH grant No. MH 08249–01, and by research grants from the Research Institute for the Study of Man and the Welfare Administration, Department of Health, Education, and Welfare, Washington, D.C.

Reprinted from *American Sociological Review*, 31, (October, 1966), 673–683, by permission of the American Sociological Association.

non-legal marital union and the resulting illegitimate children are the norma-tive patterns, and marriage is rejected or disliked.[3] Blake[4] and Goode[5] have taken the position that the non-legal marital union and the resulting ille-gitimate children are deviant patterns, and that marriage and legitimate childbirth are normative. In two earlier papers[6] I have suggested that these positions are both only partly correct, and that, as many researchers have recognized,[7] both marriage and the non-legal marital union are normative. The dominant pattern within the lower class can best be described as a "lower-class value stretch"—the normative pattern within the lower class has been stretched so that, in addition to subscribing to the middle-class ideals of marriage and legitimate children, they have also come to subscribe to the pattern of non-legal unions and "illegitimate" children.[8] In this paper I shall present new evidence supporting the position that the value stretch is the dominant lower-class response.

A Review of Goode's Position

In an influential paper Goode reconsidered a number of publications on Caribbean family structure as they bear on the question of the normative status of non-legal marital unions and illegitimacy.[9] The predominant con-clusion of the researchers was that non-legal unions and the resulting ille-gitimate children are normative. However, Goode points to statements in the writings of these same researchers which are supposed to demonstrate that, despite their conclusions that non-legal marital unions and the resulting illegitimate children are normative, they are in actual fact deviant.

Most of the statements that are singled out by Goode[10] are of the follow-ing kind—statements to the effect that: (1) non-legal unions and illegitimacy are considered deviant by individuals who are not members of the lower class; (2) the girl in her parents' house who becomes illegitimately pregnant is punished by her parents; (3) non-legal unions are not as stable as legal marriages; (4) most adults eventually do marry; and (5) marriage is pre-ferred to the non-legal union. Yet none of these statements constitutes evi-dence that the non-legal marital union and the illegitimacy resulting there-from are considered to be deviant within the lower class.

The first three points need little comment. Obviously, if we are specific-ally concerned with values of members of the lower class, knowledge about the values of other classes is not directly relevant. If we are concerned with the non-legal union and the resulting illegitimate children, knowledge about

[3] T. S. Simey, *Welfare and Planning in the West Indies*, Oxford: Clarendon Press, 1946, p. 183.

[4] Judith Blake, *Family Structure in Jamaica*, op. cit.

[5] William J. Goode, op. cit.

[6] Hyman Rodman, "The Lower-Class Value Stretch," op. cit.; Hyman Rod-man, "On Understanding Lower-Class Behaviour," op. cit.

[7] Lloyd Braithwaite, op. cit.; Raymond T. Smith, *The Negro Family in British Guiana*, London: Routledge and Kegan Paul, 1956.

[8] Hyman Rodman, "The Lower-Class Value Stretch," op. cit.

[9] William J. Goode, op. cit.

[10] William J. Goode, op. cit., pp. 24–26.

attitudes toward illegitimate children who are not conceived within a non-legal union is not directly relevant. And finally, the argument that non-legal unions are less stable than legal marriages does not give us information about the normative status of the non-legal union.

What about the implications of the fact that most adults eventually marry? In Goode's words, "as individuals move through the life cycle, an increasing proportion are actually married, a phenomenon which would be inexplicable if the consensual unions were backed by a set of alternative norms."[11] But consensual or non-legal marital unions are backed by a set of alternative norms, and the explanation for the increasing proportion of married individuals in the older age groups is a simple one. As I have pointed out in an earlier paper, "Legal marriage and a non-legal union are not in opposition, but are, rather, two different types of acceptable marital patterns among the lower classes of the West Indies. . . . This is not to say that these two patterns are equally valued, nor that there are no regularities with respect to when one or the other pattern will be followed."[12] The fluidity of marital relationships that is symbolized by the non-legal marital union makes it possible for lower-class individuals to adapt to the economic uncertainties they face. The lower-class man's occupational and economic problems make it difficult for him to play the breadwinner role with ease; the non-legal marital union provides a flexible relationship within which a marital exchange is possible without the legal bonds of marriage.[13] It is in the later age groups, after a non-legal marital union has stood the test of time, that a marriage may be entered into in order to safeguard the legal rights of the wife and the children to the man's inheritance. Consequently there is good reason for the rising proportion of individuals who are married in the older age groups,[14] even though the non-legal marital union is normative and fulfills important functions within the lower class.

Preferential versus Normative Structure

Perhaps the major defect in the arguments by Goode and Blake is the failure to distinguish between preferential and normative structure. They commit the fallacy of transforming preferential information into normative information. Information is presented that marriage is "preferred" to the non-legal union, that marriage is the "ideal," that marriage is "superior." This is used to bolster the conclusion that marriage alone is normative and that the non-legal union is deviant. For example, Blake asked the following question in Jamaica: "In general, for people in your position, do you think it is better

[11] Ibid., p. 24.
[12] Hyman Rodman, "On Understanding Lower-Class Behaviour," op. cit., pp. 448–449.
[13] Hyman Rodman, "Marital Relationships in a Trinidad Village," *Marriage and Family Living*, 23 (May, 1961), 166–170.
[14] A related paper is being prepared to provide further documentation of the reasons presented here for the rising proportion of married individuals in the older age groups.

to marry or just to live with a man (woman)?"[15] She reports that 83 per cent of the men and 83 per cent of the women "choose marriage unreservedly." On the basis of other unspecified questions in the interview she modifies the figure for women so that she can be conservative in her conclusion:

74 per cent of the women and 83 per cent of the men unreservedly choose marriage and are consistent in this point of view throughout. The remaining 26 per cent among the women and 17 per cent among the men are ambivalent toward marriage (i.e., choose it with reservations or elsewhere give evidence of ambivalence) with the exception of 3 women and 2 men who are negative.[16]

These data show a strong preference for marriage, but they do not permit the conclusion that "legal marriage is the only true union,"[17] and they tell us very little about the normative status of the non-legal union.

Marriage may very well be the ideal pattern, or the preferred pattern; but to say that the non-legal union is deviant because marriage is preferred is clearly fallacious. It is also possible for the non-legal union to be normative, although less preferred than marriage.

Methodology

There is a basic methodological problem underlying Blake's analysis—she did not ask any questions that would enable her to assess the normative status of the non-legal union.[18] Similarly, in Goode's review of the research literature, he was limited to the statements made by various researchers. His contribution was to single out the apparently confusing statements made about non-legal unions and illegitimacy—some to the effect that they were cultural alternatives to marriage, some that they were preferred to marriage, some that they were less preferred than marriage, and some that they were negatively sanctioned. But there has been no consistent research effort to explore the normative status of the non-legal union and of illegitimacy, and Blake's and Goode's error of considering these behavioral patterns to be deviant is therefore understandable; it is also a bold error, flying in the face of many researchers who have carried out detailed field observations in the Caribbean area.

The controversy was sharply drawn with the publication of Goode's paper in 1960 and Blake's book in 1961. More adequate data on the normative

[15] One could quarrel with the wording here. "For people in your position," coming from a middle-class interviewer, has a patronizing sound, and is perhaps not the best way of getting valid responses. Even more significant is the use of the word "just"—surely a possible indication to the respondent of which response is considered to be more socially desirable by the interviewer.

[16] Judith Blake, *Family Structure in Jamaica*, op. cit., pp. 118–119.

[17] Ibid., p. 122.

[18] This is not meant as a criticism of Blake's entire book. On the contrary, I gave it a generally favorable review in the *Canadian Journal of Economics and Political Science*, 28 (November, 1962), 622–623.

TABLE 1 Per Cent Favorable to Living (Non-Legal Unions) by Sex and Class[a]

Question	Sex	Upper-Lower Class	Lower-Lower Class	Total
1. Is it all right for a man and woman to live together in order to get to know each other's ways before they decide to marry?	Female Male	38 (8) 75 (20)	73 (40) 98 (47)	81 (115)
2. Is it better for a man and woman who are very poor to get married, or is it better for them to live together common-law?	Female Male	0 (17) 15 (34)	16 (57) 37 (57)	21 (165)
3. Do you think that (1) living common-law is better than marriage, (2) that marriage is better than living common-law, or (3) that they both come as the same?	Female Male	12 (17) 31 (36)	19 (57) 38 (57)	28 (167)
4. Do you think that living common-law is a sin or not a sin?	Female Male	24 (17) 61 (36)	36 (56) 63 (60)	50 (169)
5. A man and woman are thinking of getting married: (a) One person says they should marry right away, without having sexual intercourse before marriage. (b) Another says they should have sexual intercourse before marriage in order to get to know each other's ways. Which do you think is better? (If b) How should they get to know each other—by friending or by living common-law?	Female Male	6 (16) 21 (33)	27 (51) 44 (50)	29 (150)
6. Some people are talking about marriage and living common-law. (a) One person says that only *living* is good and that marriage is wrong. (b) Another says that only marriage is good and that *living* is wrong. (c) Another says that marriage is better but that *living* is also good. (d) Another says that *living* is better but that marriage is also good.	Female Male	41 (17) 63 (35)	58 (55) 83 (58)	66 (165)
Favorable to *living* on a majority of the questions answered.	Female Male	18 (17) 45 (36)	28 (57) 65 (59)	43 (169)

Note: Bases of percentages are shown in parentheses. The first question was not added until after some of the interviews had been done. Other variations in N are due to cases in which the information was not ascertained.

[a]Since we do not have a random sample, the use of significance tests is questionable; the discussion in the text is based upon the consistency of the percentage differences. For those prepared to overlook the limitations of our sample, the following results are based upon a 2 X 2 X 2 chi-square test: sex differences in response are significant at the 0.10 level on all six questions; class differences are significant on all questions except (3) and (4); the sex-class interaction is not significant for any of the six questions, while the combined effect of sex and class is significant for all six questions. For a description of the statistical tests used, see J. P. Sutcliffe, "A General Method of Analysis of Frequency Data for Multiple Classification Designs," *Psychological Bulletin,* 54 (March, 1957), 134-137; Hubert M. Blalock, *Social Statistics,* New York: McGraw-Hill, 1960, p. 239.

nature of the non-legal union within the lower class were needed in order to resolve certain questions. On my third field trip to Trinidad, in 1962, I attempted to collect some of the needed normative data. An initial attempt to collect data from respondents in randomly selected households proved unwise because I was asking highly personal questions, including questions about a person's "marital career." It took only one day of interviewing to demonstrate that respondents were troubled by the presence of others in the household while they were answering the questions. As a result, it was deemed necessary to conduct the interviews in complete privacy.

Through the cooperation of various employers, labor unions, and the Trinidad and Tobago Government, it was possible to arrange for private interviews with employees at their place of work. The total sample consists of 97 men and 79 women. Of this number, 8 men and 6 women were interviewed in the Unemployment Exchange, and 28 men and 19 women were interviewed from a remote village where the author had done previous field work. As a result of our procedure, we do not have a random sample, and must reserve judgment on the representativeness of the sample; our findings must be taken as tentative. On the other hand, our data are possibly more valid because they are not contaminated by the presence of third parties.[19]

General Findings

A series of questions was asked of the respondents about marriage and non-legal unions (called *living*, in Trinidad). These questions are shown in Table I in the order in which they were asked. (Other questions were interspersed.) For the total sample, from 21 per cent to 81 per cent are "favorable" to the *living* relationship. Forty-three per cent replied favorably to *living* on a majority of the questions they answered; 25 per cent replied favorably on all questions or on all questions but one.

Even though all six questions are getting at the "favorableness" of the respondents to the non-legal union, the great range in the percentages who reply favorably should not come as a surprise. The questions asked were deliberately worded differently, in order to get some idea of the conditions under which a favorable reply is more likely to be given. The most striking result is the distinction between responses to "preferential" questions and to "normative" questions. Questions 1, 4, and 6 are normative— they are getting information about the normative nature of the non-legal union. Questions 2, 3, and 5 are preferential—they are merely getting information on whether marriage or *living* is preferred. It turns out that the three highest percentages favorable to living (81%, 66% and 50%) are given in

[19] Although there is very little information available on the interaction effect of respondent characteristics, interviewer characteristics, and interviewing procedures upon the nature of the research information obtained, a tendency for responses to be biased in the direction of what is considered socially desirable has been noted. It is therefore likely that the figures which were obtained in this study by middle-class interviewers minimize the normative acceptance of non-legal marital unions. Cf. Carol H. Weiss, "Interviewing Low Income Respondents: A Preliminary View," paper presented at the American Association of Public Opinion Research meetings, May, 1966.

response to the three normative questions, and the three lowest percentages (21%, 28% and 29%) are given in response to the three preferential questions. The predominant response within this lower-class sample is clearly and dramatically that marriage is preferred to the non-legal union, but that the non-legal union is normative. Our results for Trinidad are roughly in accord with Blake's results for Jamaica (cited above); she found approximately 20 per cent of her lower-class respondents "favorable" to the non-legal union on a preferential question.

The same pattern of responses—marriage is preferred, but *living* is norma-

TABLE 2 Percentage Distribution Summarizing Responses to Three "Preference" Questions, by Sex and Class

	Males		Females		
Response Pattern	Upper-Lower Class	Lower-Lower Class	Upper-Lower Class	Lower-Lower Class	Total
Prefer marriage on all questions	55	30	82	50	47
Prefer marriage on 2 of 3 questions	24	21	12	32	25
Prefer marriage on 1 of 2 questions	6	9	0	6	6
Prefer marriage on 1 of 3 questions	6	19	6	9	12
Prefer marriage on no questions	9	21	0	3	10
Total	100	100	100	100	100
Number of cases	33	57	17	56	163

TABLE 3 Percentage Distribution Summarizing Responses to Three "Normative" Questions, by Sex and Class

	Males		Females		
Response Pattern	Upper-Lower Class	Lower-Lower Class	Upper-Lower Class	Lower-Lower Class	Total
Living is normative on all questions	48	61	18	31	44
Living is normative on 2 of 3 questions	14	19	6	14	15
Living is normative on 1 of 2 questions	9	7	17	7	8
Living is normative on 1 of 3 questions	3	10	6	18	11
Living is normative on no questions	26	3	53	30	22
Total	100	100	100	100	100
Number of cases	35	59	17	59	168

tive—is shown in Tables 2 and 3. In these tables the information is presented separately for the three normative questions and for the three preferential questions. (In a number of cases we have information on only two of the questions.) Once again the distinction between the preferential questions and the normative questions is fundamental. Looking at the percentages for the total sample, marriage tends to be "favored" on the preferential questions. On the normative questions *living* tends to be "favored." These data document the fact that it is erroneous to use responses to preferential questions to make inferences about norms. They put the controversy about the Caribbean family in perspective by permitting us to clarify the nature of the normative structure among the lower classes of the Caribbean area.

THE LOWER-CLASS VALUE STRETCH

As suggested in an earlier paper, the lower-class value stretch is a response of members of the lower class to a situation in which circumstances make it difficult or impossible for them to behave in accordance with the dominant values of an open-class society.[20] The following is an elaboration of the assumptions and hypothesized relationships that enter into the theory of the lower-class value stretch.[21]

(1) In an open-class society the possibility of mobility is open to all.

(2) The values of the dominant social classes (including the possibility of mobility for all) are promulgated to all members of the society.

(3) Members of the lower classes have difficulty in behaving in accordance with some of the dominant values because of inadequate resources.

(4) Members of the lower classes therefore show more "deviance" from some of the dominant values.

(5) As a result, in order to minimize negative sanctions, members of the lower classes are less committed to some of the dominant values than other members of society.

(6) Furthermore, some members of the lower classes develop alternative values that are more in accord with their circumstances, so that their actual behavior is likelier to be rewarded. What is deviant from the point of view of the dominant values is normative from the point of view of the alternative values.

(7) The development of alternative values is a continuing process; some lower-class members are socialized into accepting them from childhood, others come to accept them later in life, while others never accept them.

(8) The major form taken by the system of values that thus develops in the lower class is the "lower-class value stretch":

By the value stretch I mean that the lower-class person, without abandoning the general values of the society, develops an alternative set of values. Without abandoning the values of marriage and legitimate childbirth he stretches these values so that a non-legal union and legally illegitimate children are also desirable. The result is that the members of the lower class, in many areas, have a wider range of values than others within the society. They share the general values of the society with members of other classes, but in addition they have stretched these values, or developed alternative values, which help them to adjust to their deprived circumstances.[22]

[20] Hyman Rodman, "The Lower-Class Value Stretch," op. cit. This paper was based upon field observations in Trinidad, an extensive review of data on levels of aspiration, and brief reviews of data on the Caribbean and on delinquency.

[21] This formulation has been influenced by George C. Homans, "Bringing Men Back In," *American Sociological Review*, 29 (December, 1964), 809–818.

[22] Hyman Rodman, "The Lower-Class Value Stretch," op. cit., p. 209. Alternatives to the lower-class value stretch response would be a response in which the lower-class individual retains the dominant values without

The above assumptions and implied relationships are not new, but they make explicit what has remained largely implicit in the literature—that the value stretch is an important response within the lower classes. It is possible to develop a large number of specific hypotheses to test various portions of the theory of the lower-class value stretch.[23] Hypothesized relationships that stem from points (1)–(4) above are numerous. Are there differences in the rates of mobility in different types of societies? To what extent are the dominant values of society internalized in different segments of that society? Do the rates of "deviance" vary by social class status? These questions have all been phrased as hypotheses and explored in the literature. But the questions that are suggested by points (5)–(8) are relatively new, and have been little explored. In order to formulate testable hypotheses it is necessary to specify which of the dominant values are not in accord with lower-class circumstances, and which alternative values are more in accord with such circumstances. Since tests of the theory depend upon a specification of the relevant values, it is necessary to be explicit about the grounds on which the specified values are or are not in accord with lower-class circumstances. In this paper marriage is specified as a value which is not in accord with lower-class circumstances because it is a legally binding relationship, whereas the lower-class male is frequently unemployed, underemployed, and in poorly paid employment, and accordingly finds it difficult to fulfill his economic obligations within a legally binding relationship. The non-legal marital union is specified as a value which is in accord with lower-class circumstances, in that it provides the partners with a flexible behavioral pattern that may permit them to adapt to such circumstances.[24] As a result, we would expect that the lower the status of a person, the more likely is he to be affected by these value changes. Similarly, since it is the man who is most immediately and directly affected by lower-class occupational circumstances (given the assumption that the man should be the family's breadwinner),[25] we would expect that men are more likely to be affected than women. The following four hypotheses are to be tested:

(1) Social class status is inversely related to the normative acceptance of non-legal marital unions.

(2) Social class status is inversely related to the "value stretch," i.e., to the acceptance of both legal marriage and the non-legal marital union.

(3) Lower-class men show more normative acceptance of non-legal marital unions than do lower-class women.

---

developing any other values, abandons the dominant values and subscribes to a new set of values, or abandons all commitment to values of any kind in a particular area. Since commitment to a value is a matter of degree it is often difficult to determine whether or not a person is committed to a particular value.

[23] Robert R. Bell, "Lower Class Negro Mothers' Aspirations for Their Children," *Social Forces*, 43 (May, 1965), 493–500.

[24] For further elaboration of these points see Hyman Rodman, "Marital Relationships in a Trinidad Village," op. cit.

[25] Hyman Rodman and Constantina Safilios-Rothschild, "Business and the American Family," in Ivar Berg, ed., *The Business of America*, New York: Harcourt, Brace and World, in press.

(4) Lower-class men stretch their values to accept both legal marriage and the non-legal marital union more than do lower-class women.

Hypothesis 1

Although the present study concentrated upon the lower class, it was nevertheless possible to divide the sample into a lower-lower-class group and an upper-lower-class group.[26] A comparison of these two groups indicates that on every normative question in Table 1 (Questions 1, 4, and 6), for males and for females, the lower-lower-class group shows a higher percentage of favorable responses to *living* than the upper-lower-class group. Similarly, the summary information on the three normative questions in Table 3 indicates that *living* is accepted as normative within the lower-lower-class group to a greater extent than within the upper-lower-class group. Among males, 80 per cent within the lower-lower-class group reply that *living* is normative on a majority of the questions, in contrast to 62 per cent within the upper-lower-class group. For females, the comparable figures are 45 per cent and 24 per cent. The hypothesis is therefore validated for this sample on a limited domain of status categories. Comparison with middle-class groups would undoubtedly show even more pronounced value differences.[27]

It can also be seen that the lower-lower-class group gives a higher percentage of favorable responses, both for males and for females, on the three preferential questions. This suggests that there may be an inverse relationship of social class status not only with the normative acceptance, but also with the preferential acceptance, of certain deviant patterns. The latter hypothesis needs to be tested on independent data.

Hypothesis 2

Question 6, in Table 1, was specifically formulated to get information on the lower-class value stretch. A breakdown of the answers to that question

[26] Social-class position was determined on the basis of occupation, education and income data, by adapting Hollingshead's technique to the Trinidad material, and using income in some borderline cases (August B. Hollingshead, "Two Factor Index of Social Position," mimeographed, 1957). The upper-lower class consists predominantly of skilled workers, and of semi-skilled workers with comparatively high educational or income levels. The lower-lower class consists of semi-skilled workers with comparatively low levels of education and income, and unskilled workers, private household and service workers. The paper therefore does not deal with social classes as clearly demarcated groups in which the members share an awareness of their collective interests, but with social categories in which the members share a roughly similar position in a status hierarchy. No attempt has been made to determine "category" boundaries on the basis of interaction patterns, or to determine the degree to which there may be an awareness of shared interests. Cf. Dennis Wrong, "Social Inequality without Social Stratification," *Canadian Review of Sociology and Anthropology*, 1 (February, 1964), 5–16.

[27] Nine middle-class respondents were uniformly unfavorable to the non-legal union on all questions. Because of the small number of middle-class respondents, the data on them are not reported.

TABLE 4   Percentage Distribution of Responses to "Value Stretch" Question, by Sex and Class

Responses to "Value Stretch" Question	Males		Females		
	Upper-Lower Class	Lower-Lower Class	Upper-Lower Class	Lower-Lower Class	Total
Marriage is good and *living* is wrong	37	17	59	42	34
Marriage is better but *living* is also good	49	48	41	53	49
Living is good and marriage is wrong	0	0	0	0	0
Living is better but marriage is also good	3	12	0	5	7
No difference	11	23	0	0	10
Total	100	100	100	100	100
Number of cases	35	58	17	55	165

Note: See Table 1, question 6 for "value-stretch" question.

is provided in Table 4. An alternative to the value stretch would be the rejection of some dominant value and the acceptance of an alternative value ("*Living* is good and marriage is wrong."). Not a single respondent selected this alternative. Another alternative to the value stretch would be the acceptance of some dominant value and the rejection of an alternative value ("Marriage is good and *living* is wrong."). In the total sample, 34 per cent gave this response, suggesting that it is an important response within the lower classes. A value stretch response [Marriage (*living*) is better but *living* (marriage) is also good"; or the spontaneously mentioned "no difference"] was given by 66 per cent of the respondents in the total sample. Most of these responses, as we would expect from the discussion about the normative and preferential data, indicate that "marriage is better but *living* is also good." In other words, the data lend strong support to the existence of the value stretch as the predominant lower-class response.

What about the inverse relationship between social class status and the value stretch response? In Table 4 (cf. Table 1) we see that 83 per cent of the lower-lower-class men, as compared with 63 per cent of the upper-lower-class men give a "stretch" response, while 58 per cent of lower-lower-class women, as compared with 41 per cent of upper-lower-class women give this response. Thus, for both men and women, the lower-lower-class group shows a higher proportion of value stretch responses; the data from this sample validate the hypothesis on a limited domain of status categories.

Hypothesis 3

In response to all of the normative questions in Table 1, as well as to all of the preferential questions, men are more favorable to the non-legal marital union than women, and this holds within both class groups. In addition, in Table 3, we see that men are much more likely than women to state that the non-legal marital union is normative on all questions answered, or on 2 of the 3 questions answered, and this also holds within both class groups. Within the lower-lower-class group, 80 per cent of the men, compared with 45 per cent of the women, accept the non-legal marital union on a majority of the normative questions. Within the upper-lower-class group the figures are 62 per cent for men and 24 per cent for women. Hypothesis 3 is therefore validated—lower-class men do show more normative acceptance of non-legal marital unions than lower-class women.

Hypothesis 4

The data on the value stretch and alternative responses are presented in Table 4 (cf. Table 1, Question 6). It can be seen that men stretch their values to accept both legal marriage and the non-legal marital union to a greater extent than women. This is the case within both class groups. In the lower-lower-class group, the value stretch response is given by 83 per cent of the men and 58 per cent of the women. In the upper-lower class group the comparable percentages are 63 and 41. These are the percentages that replied "marriage is better but *living* is also good," "*living* is better but marriage is also good," or "no difference." The hypothesis is therefore validated for this sample. The value stretch response, however, is not the predominant response of upper-lower-class females in this sample: 42 per cent of the lower-lower-class women and 59 per cent of the upper-lower-class women accept marriage and reject the non-legal marital union.

Further Points of Controversy

Although many of the statements marshalled by Goode from Caribbean researchers to support the argument that the non-legal marital union lacked normative status were easily disposed of, this is not so for all of them. Perhaps the strongest support for Goode's argument is the data that he cites from Hatt's study:

Two-thirds of both men and women in a national sample of Puerto Rico said that a consensual union is a bad life for a man, and over 80 per cent of the respondents made the same assertion for women. Perhaps a more penetrating test of the normative status of the consensual union may be found in the attitudes expressed about a *daughter* entering a consensual union; only 7.4 per cent of the men and 5.5 per cent of the women admitted that this arrangement would either be "all right" or that "it's up to her; doesn't matter."[28]

Hatt presents the data as normative, and they appear to be normative. It therefore seems that the non-legal union in Puerto Rico is preponderantly considered to be deviant. For our purposes, however, several qualifications must be emphasized: (1) These data are from a national sample, and not from a lower-class sample; (2) Within this national sample several factors have biased the data collected toward groups of higher socioeconomic status;[29] (3) A close examination of the questions that were asked suggests that we must have strong reservations about the presumed "normative" status of the data. A translation of one of the questions into English, and the results,

[28] William J. Goode, op. cit., p. 26.
[29] Paul K. Hatt, *Backgrounds of Human Fertility in Puerto Rico*, Princeton, N. J.: Princeton University Press, 1952, pp. 11–17, 20–22.

TABLE 5   Percentage Distribution of Responses to a Question Concerning Attitudes Toward Consensual Unions for Men, by Sex: Puerto Rico

Responses	Males	Females
Which of the following statements expresses your feelings best?		
1. To live with a woman is the best possible life for man. *(To live with a woman without marriage is the best possible life for a man.)*	3.05	2.64
2. It is a good life for man.	12.75	16.62
3. It does not matter.	16.33	12.57
4. It is a bad life for a man. *(It is not a good life for a man.)*	46.37	45.01
5. It is a very bad life for a man.	21.14	22.91
6. Other answers.	0.36	0.24
Total	100.00	99.99
Number of cases	6,187	7,085

Source: Paul K. Hatt, op. cit., p. 61.

are given in Table 5. It is accurate to conclude from these data, as Goode did, that "two-thirds of both men and women in a national sample of Puerto Rico said that a consensual union is a bad life for a man." However, my more exact translation of portions of Hatt's question, given in italics in the table, raises some questions. In part (1), "to live with a woman without marriage" is not the same as "to live with a woman."[30] In part (4), "a bad life" is not the same as "not a good life." Both of these differences are likely to inflate the reported percentages that consider a "consensual union" to be "bad." More important, however, the initial instructions and part (1) put the whole question into a preferential context. As a result, each normative condition which follows part (1) is colored by this preferential context, and we simply do not know to what extent the respondents' replies are a reflection of the normative status of the non-legal union or of its preferential status in relation to marriage.

Finally, a word of caution regarding generalizations about "the Caribbean area." Data have been presented on Trinidad, and they have been contrasted with Blake's data on Jamaica, Hatt's data on Puerto Rico, and Goode's general discussion of the data on some ten different territorial or national units within the Caribbean area. Since there may very well be value differences that stem from independent variables such as nationality or community type, it remains to be seen whether the relationships validated in this study stand up once other independent variables are introduced into the analysis.

THEORETICAL CONSIDERATIONS

It has been seen that both sex and social class are related to the normative acceptance of certain alternatives to the dominant values, and more

[30] It should be noted that the Spanish phrase used in this question, *vivir con un hombre sin casarse*, is unlike the phrase used on p. 495, Question 32, dealing with matrimonial status—*viviendo juntos* (*unión consensual*). The former phrase places the "consensual union" in a comparatively bad light, and is therefore likelier to invite responses that are unfavorable to such a union. See ibid., pp. 60–63, 495–497.

generally that sex and social class are related to a value stretch response. Specifically, an inverse relationship has been shown between social class status and the normative acceptance of both the non-legal marital union and marriage. In addition, males were shown to have a greater normative accept-ance of both the non-legal marital union and marriage than females.

Why should there be such relationships? Perhaps the factor that under-lies these relationships is "vulnerability to environmental circumstances." Since the defining attributes that have been used in this paper for social class are occupation, education, and income, members of the lower class are, by definition, low in occupational status, educational status, and income. They have limited economic resources and therefore face greater difficulty in maintaining a marriage relationship. In this sense they are more vulnerable to environmental circumstances, and are likelier to stretch their values. More-over, within the lower class, if the woman plays the traditional role of house-wife, and if the man is expected to be the breadwinner, the major impact of lower-class circumstances falls upon the man. The woman's ability to perform the role of housewife is not as much affected by lower-class membership as is the man's ability to perform the role of breadwinner. In this sense, lower-class men are more vulnerable to environmental circumstances than lower-class women, and they are more likely to stretch their values. If environ-mental circumstances make performance in accordance with certain dominant values difficult or impossible, then behavior is less likely to be in accordance with these values; commitment to these dominant values is likely to be less-ened; alternative values more in accordance with lower-class circumstances are likelier to develop; and we are more likely to find a value stretch.

Several other suggestions immediately come to mind. One is that the existence of the value stretch should show up in other areas where per-formance in accordance with the dominant values is difficult, such as the area of occupational, income, and educational values. [31] In addition, there may be other independent variables besides social class status and sex that reflect differences in "vulnerability to environmental circumstances," and thus per-mit further tests of the general relationship.

While there has been agreement about the nature of the behavioral pat-terns in the Carribean—high rates of non-legal marital unions and illegitimacy —there has not been agreement about the normative patterns. The data pre-sented on a sample of lower-class respondents in Trinidad offer strong sup-port for one aspect of the theory of the lower-class value stretch: that many members of the lower class share the dominant values and have also stretched these values and developed a set of values unique to themselves.

The data presented in this paper indicate that we do not merely have "deviation from the norm" in the lower classes,[32] but also a stretched system of norms in which the non-legal union is normative. Furthermore, we do not merely have a "lowering of both punishment for deviation and reward for conformity"[33] but also a situation in which the non-legal union is considered to be normative and is positively evaluated (even though it is less preferred

[31] Hyman Rodman, "The Lower-Class Value Stretch," op. cit., pp. 210–212.
[32] William J. Goode, op. cit., p. 30.
[33] Ibid.

than marriage). Perhaps there is a historical sequence for the development of the lower-class value stretch, such that the kind of situation that Goode describes is an interim step on the way to the development of the value stretch. At any rate, the present data for Trinidad clearly point to the value stretch as a major response.

In sum, those who suggest that members of the lower class reject the dominant values and develop alternative values seem from our data to be wrong. Those who suggest that members of the lower class share the dominant values and reject alternative values, also seem to be wrong (although they are documenting an important lower-class pattern). The question about the values that are held in the lower classes is a complex one. In part this reflects the complexity of the social-class structure itself, for we are not dealing with the values of any clearly demarcated group but rather with categories of people who vary on attributes such as occupation, education, and income. The behavioral experiences of these people are not homogeneous; since they are not members of a demarcated group they do not directly exchange solutions to life's problems and share the same values. Nevertheless, the circumstances that are shared toward the lower levels of the class structure do seem to produce certain similarities of behavior and values. Most significantly, it has been shown that the lower one goes in the class structure, where the vulnerability to environmental circumstances is greater, the more likely one is to find stretched values.

39 | *Child-Rearing Practices of the Communal Family*

BENNETT BERGER, BRUCE HACKETT, SHERRI CAVAN, GILBERT ZICKLER, MERVYN MILLAR, MARILYN NOBLE, SUSAN THEIMAN, RICHARD FARRELL, and BENJAMIN ROSENBLUTH

During the first eight months of our study of child rearing in communal families, we have done the following:

1. Located and maintained residence of at least a month in seven communes in northern California.
2. Visited and studied less intensively at least a dozen other communes.

From Bennett Berger, et al., "Child-Rearing Practices of the Communal Family," excerpts from a progress report to the National Institute of Mental Health, Grant No. 1-RO1-MH 16570-O1A1-SP to Scientific Analysis Corporation, San Francisco. References cited in the original have been deleted. Reprinted by permission of the authors.

3. Held many research-group seminars on clarifying the major research problem in operational terms and on other basic issues of theory and method.
4. Initiated a community study of a small rural town in the heart of a dense cluster of rural communes to study the impact of the influx of "hippies" on local institutions.
5. Attended two major conferences on subjects related to our study: the nature of drug subcultures and the development of "free schools."
6. Studied the "underground press" up close by placing one of our staff members (a former newsman) on the Berkeley *Barb*, where he rose from reporter to managing editor (during the illness of the editor and publisher). A separate report will be made of this study.
7. Conducted a small sample survey of attitudes toward communal living.
8. Compiled and examined a substantial bibliography.

A major focus of the research is on the nature of community-building: on the creation of institutions capable of sustaining and carrying the subculture of hippies and thus providing for the socialization of children. Our initial decision was to study these developments primarily—or at least at the outset—in rural or quasi-rural settings rather than looking at urban networks of hippies. Our rationale was simple: the relative absence of or insulation from "straight" institutions provided by land ownership or rental would permit fuller institutional implementation of hippie ideology in rural areas. Our desire was to gain information and make observations from relatively "pure" communal settings, even if problems of access to data were thus enlarged—as they were. It also meant that we clearly undersampled certain types of communes, for example, the "political" communes which are primarily urban and "crash pads" which serve primarily "drifting" hippies who have not (yet) made a genuine commitment to communal living.

Once this research decision was made, it became necessary to determine what, for the purposes of the study, constituted a commune. We decided against paying great initial attention to crash pads and similar urban places where turnover is high, anticipation of future needs minimal, and a conscious "family" orientation absent. In order to eliminate the less stable living arrangements that have proliferated within the hip scene, our minimum definition of a working commune was at least five adults and at least two children sharing resources and facilities in a common household or domestic establishment, and having been together for at least six months.

Our initial access to existing communes came from two sources primarily. On our research team are two part-time employees of the Haight-Ashbury Medical Clinic. They were able to supply us with very valuable information concerning the character and location of several communes, and they enabled us to make initial contacts. The other source was through our own "regular" assistants who had either done previous commune research or who utilized previous personal contacts with a wide variety of hippies in the Bay Area to locate other communes. Other sources included underground publications, advertisements, bulletin boards, and other scholars doing research in related fields.

In order to gain and maintain access to these communes, special strategies were sometimes necessary to meet the exigencies of each different situation. Access has been a recurrent problem because there are no self-evident reasons why communes should allow themselves to be studied, to say nothing of actually welcoming researchers. In one commune with a substantial number of school-age children, we were able to gain access through a research assistant who happens to have a teaching credential. Although her own research commitment was made clear, she was allowed in to observe the commune in "exchange" for teaching services she is performing. Access to the Berkeley *Barb* was gained through its owner who is an old acquaintance of the project director and through the presence among our assistants of an experienced newsman. In another case we gained access to a commune on the "coattails" of a Medical Clinic team whose good reputation in the hip commune brushed off on us through our association with them. In every case but one, however, our research intent was made clear to the hippies, and misrepresentation or incognito roles avoided. This would have been impossible without the *personal* qualities of our staff who have been able to elicit apparent trust and acceptance from people normally quite skeptical (to put the matter mildly) of the aims of researchers. This "up-front" posture of the research staff enabled us to participate fully in the ongoing life of the communes for long periods without being subject to the sanctions possible against unwanted or ambiguously identified guests or transients. Once inside the communal settlements as participant observers, it was possible to obtain other leads and introductions to other communal settlements by conversations with people there and by visitors who happened by from other communes. The one exception to our candid identity as researchers is the staff member doing the community study of a small town with an influx of large numbers of hippies—most of whom are not living in communal families. She is living and participating in town life in the incognito role of a writer doing a book on children's lore.

During these early months we have been continually concerned with "clearing" our credentials as participant observers within the communes themselves. We knew that the project was being widely discussed both in the hip community and in scholarly circles concerned with related matters, and that communes (fresh from their disastrous experience of the Haight-Ashbury community with researchers and journalists) were formulating very guarded attitudes toward "research" before we ever arrived in their presence. And we worried lest our federal sponsorship create levels of anxiety—even paranoia—too high to overcome. We had continually to face the question of "Why is NIMH interested in supporting a study of us?" We have devoted great care to answering this and similar questions, and by this time our skills at allaying such anxieties have grown enormously. But the problem may be expected to recur continually as we enlarge our samples, and the anxieties rise and fall depending to a considerable extent on a commune's relations with the "straight" institutional world (Has there been a pot bust recently? Have FBI men been around looking for draft evaders? Have county health and housing code officials been harassing them lately?), so that our acceptance may never be completely unreserved or established without question. But so far this issue has not obstructed our work. Actually, the successful confrontation of it has helped to establish our trustworthiness.

We have at the same time helped validate our credientials by exercising great discretion in maintaining confidences and in limiting access to our seminars and now-voluminous field notes. And our staff is under instructions to politely turn away all requests (there have been several) from newspaper and television journalists for interviews, which, we feel, cannot do the research any good now, and may do it great harm. While in the field, we have taken great care not to be "intrusive"—notes are taken only in private or after the fact, children are not "interviewed," and access to "private" quarters of nuclear family units (a very important part of the research) is not sought before it happens "naturally." As our assistants move back and forth between their research sites and our seminars, their skills at observing and at retaining information and their ability to systematize their observations have increased greatly, so that our seminars have developed into highly rewarding settings for comparative analysis. . . .

As we emphasized in our research proposal, this has been a period for generating basic ideas and hypotheses, rather than for testing hypotheses already extant in the literature. The following section presents examples of some of our initial observations and of some of the ideas that our preliminary findings and observations have generated.

We have organized this brief discussion of our preliminary findings under four headings: child rearing itself, and three related matters which are both relevant to the viability of all communes (hence relevant to child rearing) and depending upon which child rearing itself is likely to vary somewhat. At this point in the research, these four headings are to some extent arbitrary; they have been selected as convenient ways of presenting in an organized manner illustrations of the kinds of observations we have been making, and the problems of commune viability they reveal. All our conclusions thus far must, of course, be regarded as tentative and subject to further study, particularly with respect to their impact upon the children of the communes.

CHILD REARING AND THE FAMILY

At the outset it must be recognized that such "child rearing" that goes on in communes is in general highly deliberate and self-conscious (hence the quotation marks) because commune members themselves, having rejected much of their own upbringing and having faced (indeed, continually facing) the problem of "getting their heads together," are generally painfully aware of the lasting impact of childhood socialization.

The children of the communes are raised in a variety of family settings. Most of the communes regard themselves as extended families, not only consciously using the term but in one case actually adopting a common surname. And a typical mode of trying to settle disputes among children is through the appeal by adults to the children's sense of kinship, that is, "Janey is your sister, don't abuse her." But over and above the commune-as-family, a variety of nuclear units exist—everything from legally married spouses-plus-their-children, to unmarried couples with and without children, to couples in which the male partner is not the father of the female's child, and even to one case in which the female partner is not the mother of the male's child. We mention this because the character of the nuclear unit seems to affect the intensity of the obligation of "parents" toward "their" children in ways we intend to study more closely. Whereas our studies thus far indicate a rejection of the commonly held stereotype of communes as places of random and unrestricted sexual promiscuity, the *ways* in which couples pair off, the stability of such liaisons, and the consequences of them remain to be intensively investigated. Some general observations, however, can be made at this point in the research. We have, for example, seen a range of variation in child-family relations from an emphasis on the solidarity of the traditional nuclear unit within the communal family to the practice of regarding the child as "belonging" to the commune as a whole—with each adult member sharing responsibility for the child's welfare and upbringing. At this point, however, we have not yet determined whether this is a structural variation in different *types* of communes or a sequential (or developmental) change that occurs as the child becomes less physically dependent on its mother. While infants are nursing they are, of course, literally connected to their mothers and to that extent dependent. But at the same time that there seem to be informal consensuses that biological mothers are primarily responsible for their nursing infants, there is also general agreement that mothers need to "get away" now and then (although how frequently and for what lengths "now and then" may be is a source of argument), and infants left around the communal house will be looked after by the adults there regardless of whether "arrangements" have been made. The situation with older children is more ambiguous still. One observation was made of an argument between the mother of a four-year-old girl and an adult-male commune member (neither the father of the child nor the mother's "old man") who was holding the child on his lap at the dinner table feeding her. The man was berating the mother for interfering with him and the child "doing a dinner thing" together—suggesting that the "mother" in this instance had no special rights over her child.

This ambiguity about the relationship of a child to its parents and to the commune is manifest also in the ritual celebration of childbirth common to many communes. On the one hand, the entire commune is frequently present at the birth (including the children), chanting and offering encouragement in other ways to the mother in labor. On the other hand, the father of the child is encouraged to assist directly in delivery, his actual participation in the birth of his own child being assumed to symbolically establish paternal connection far more profoundly than the impersonal, antiseptic practices of hospitals. This emphasis on "natural" childbirth is significant to communards not only for the obvious ideological rejection of the idea of childbirth as an "illness" requiring doctors and hospitals; far more important, it seems to us, is the significance for the identity of the child and the commune. For when "officials" are not present at the birth, the child "belongs" to the family rather than to the State whose certified representatives preside at hospital births. Or so it seems to seem to the communards. In one instance, the childbirth was not only ritually celebrated by the entire extended family, but a photographic record made of the entire process and an invocational poem in praise of life composed by the father. The father and the photographer are presently engaged in publishing the poem and the photographs as a book which they intend to distribute free to interested communes and others.

Within the range of nuclear family types, stability and fidelity among couples is encouraged as a general pattern in the relatively durable (two to three years) communes we have studied most closely. Although a biological father may be absent in many of these nuclear units, and although children may refer to having had many "fathers," nuclear units generally have a male figure (father) who is *regarded as stable*, even if he and the mother have been together only a short time and are still working out the degree of their commitment to each other. In spite of the approval of couple stability and fidelity as a general pattern, there is a negative attitude toward the idea of sexual property. At the same time, the possibility of sexual freedom may threaten the affectional stability of nuclear units. We have seen instances in which couples remain "together" in spite of the fact that each may occasionally have sexual relations with another—the general feeling being that if one spouse wants to, it's better that he (or she) satisfies that want than if he (or she) doesn't. Exclusive sexual access is, however, a norm that runs deep, and its violation (in spite of ideology) may cause deep tensions. These matters are difficult to study closely because they are generally legitimate areas of privacy in communal life, and we will get more deeply into them the longer our assistants remain with a particular commune, and when we begin formal interviewing next year. These observations have been made in the communes we have studied ourselves, which are mostly quite stable and with a conscious "family" orientation. We have, however, *heard* of other communes in which sexual liaisons and nuclear units are not much less stable, but in which the notion of "incest" among the extended kin group is encouraged. In one group we heard about, several men had sexual relations with a woman during her fertile period so that no one could be sure who the father of the expected child was. We expect to make further efforts to locate some of these "deviant" (from our present perspective) communes.

Parents of communal children face a persistent dilemma regarding discipline and guidance. Their dominant ideology is to let the child "do his own thing," to allow maximum expression of his "individuality" and "creativity." But in implementing their beliefs in the natural creativity of children and their (the children's) rights to choose the activities they want, communal parents find it necessary to circumvent their own ideology to some extent in order to handle necessary discipline, to encourage conformity to valued practices in communes (such as meditation in yoga-based—and other—communes), and to guide the children toward parental goals—goals that intensify the dilemma by including the generally accepted objective of raising the child to be free to "do his own thing." But life has a habit of resolving everything, even dilemmas, and the communards cope with their problem in ad hoc ways every day, sometimes preferring to impale themselves on their dilemma rather than applying severe sanctions to recalcitrant children as a matter of principle, and sometimes making efforts toward creating a model of child rearing which encourages the child's desire to "do his own thing," even if such socialization undermines the sources of recruitment to the commune's next generation. Most communes, it seems at this point, if faced with a choice between training the next generation of communards and training children to be free, would opt for the latter. In the terminology of the communes, there are strong pressures on adults not "to lay their own heavy trip" on the children, and only light pressures toward conformity are exercised, as exemplified by the appeal to kinship in settling aggression among children, or by refusal of a father to forcibly take an adult's smoking pipe away from his sixteen-month-old son, who insisted upon smoking it, and would not give it up even after he was coughing on the smoke. The father applied only the gentlest pressure, under the apparent assumption that the child would willingly give it up after a little while (an assumption that turned out to be correct). We are currently paying special attention to the ways in which accommodations occur between the day-to-day pressures of child rearing and what the communards believe with respect to children. The universality of the problem and the highly conscious attempt to cope with it, makes this one of the most fascinating dimensions of the study, and of enormous potential importance.

ECONOMIC SUPPORT

Members of communes also face a dilemma with respect to economic activities. On the one hand they ideally seek economic self-sufficiency either at the communal level, the tribal (several communes with specially close relations) level, or the regional level (communes tend to cluster regionally). On the other hand, welfare continues to be a principal source of income in most of the communes we studied. The communes tend to be aware of this dilemma but to have no solution for it, and a common topic of discussion at commune meetings is what they will do when "the Man" ceases to support them through welfare. A related dilemma is the desire for subcultural exclusiveness in all economic arrangements, but a reluctance to engage in the kinds of regular commerce which might provide the economic strength they need eventually to achieve the institutional completeness they envision. An example of this is the refusal by the two men producing the book on the baby's birth to accept the several offers they have had from commercial publishers; they prefer instead to go through the difficult process of raising the necessary funds from sources within the subculture, and do the publishing (and the distribution) themselves.

In general, intercommunal or tribal bartering, subsistence farming, and small craft industries do not provide sufficient funds for necessary expenses (machinery, foods, utilities, mortgage, or rent payments) so that they are forced to continue relying on welfare, benefactors, and occasional windfalls from commune members (generous parents, inheritances, etc.). Pressures are also thereby generated to seek economic arrangements with institutions outside the subculture, thus creating other problems for communes. First of all, it contradicts some of their major objectives—about fleeing polluted cities, about engaging in alienated work—and threatens their hope of "living off the land" in harmony with nature. There are no visible solutions to this problem.

Moreover, even when commune members have specially salable skills as craftsmen, too great an involvement in his skills is likely to be regarded as an individual's "side trip," not *directly* connected with the solidarity of the commune-as-family. This suggests that *some* work is regarded as more central to the collective welfare of the commune than others (for example, gardening, knowledge of care of domestic animals, plumbing and electrical skills, and so on), and problems develop when a craftsman is so "into" his craft or art that it begins to be perceived by others as distracting from the "family trip," which is the major goal of communal living.

This distrust of "side trips" exists alongside of the aim of most communes to reestablish work as a kind of "holy" or natural activity through which the worker may experience personal growth, satisfaction, and serenity. This is most clear in the tender care and religious feeling with which gardens are sometimes decorated with religious objects. In addition, there is much talk, sometimes in quasi-religious terms, about how the crops are growing. People with "green thumbs" may be heard observing that it's not a good idea for many people to be in the garden at the same time because "too many vibes freak out the plants."

Although communards tend to work hard (subsistence farming is hard work, and the insight that a hard life produces the severity of mien common in communes is contradicted only by the frequent and recurrent festive atmosphere, particularly after family dinners), work tends not to be organized except for those tasks that require regularity (preparation of meals, care of animals). Other work is regarded as a "trip" which, if someone is into it, he will ask for help on if he needs or wants it. But most of the work is not scheduled, there are no deadlines, and with few exceptions the "need" for something to be done does not take precedence over the desire or willingness of people to do it.

Communes are not places likely to be praised by serious women liberationists, since women seem to fall naturally into doing most of the traditional "women's work." But this is less a matter of traditionalism than of natural functionality and available skill. If a woman is in possession of special skills, she will generally not spend a great deal of time in the kitchen or milking goats. If she isn't, she's likely to cook rather than haul lumber or do other heavy work which men are better equipped for.

LEADERSHIP AND AUTHORITY

In the communes we have observed there is a general tendency to have no formal provisions for leadership roles. Nevertheless, in most communes, individuals assume positions of commune-wide influence and leadership, the basis for which and the occasion of which varied from commune to commune. In some, the oldest members had an age-based influence, while in others masters of ideology (or religious practice) central to the commune's self-image maintained a higher status. Seniority of commune membership was another characteristic of influential members, and still another was commitment to communal goals as measured by the amount of communal work one did. On the whole, however, leadership fluctuates among several "strong" figures in a given commune depending on what they call the "flow of energy."

Leadership of whatever sort tends to correlate with a talent for serene rhetoric enabling the leader to appeal to the sense of love and fraternity in resolving intracommunal disputes or hostilities, and these talents are often exercised at family meetings where grievances will be aired and disputes over policy discussed.

Decisions affecting the welfare of the community as a whole (such as admission of new members, child welfare, health and hygiene, relations with outsiders) seemed to us to require commune-wide acceptance (at least the withholding of opposition). When meetings are called they are generally in response to particular issues and events. Meetings can be serious, solidarity-shaking occurrences because there is a presumed consensus about issues affecting the routine maintenance of social organization, gaps in which can easily be revealed in the meetings.

There is one other source of leadership which has ambiguous status. Where one person either owns the land or a substantial piece of it, he or she is likely to be prominent by virtue of this fact. But ownership by itself is not regarded as a *legitimate* source of authority, and, in the cases we know of, ownership is correlated either with age, seniority, or commitment. But that individual ownership may be a problem is indicated by the high value placed upon communal or other collective ownership of the land. In any case, we have seen no instances of the kind of leadership that has become notorious through the publicity given to the "Manson Family."

RECRUITMENT

As participant observers we have investigated communal recruitment processes from practical as well as theoretical perspectives. In practical terms, we have sought to identify the processes by which prospective members gain information about and access to communes, and the processes by which prospective membership becomes full membership. By identifying these processes we have also helped to solve our own very practical problems of finding the subjects of our research and of becoming participant observers in the communes. In theoretical terms we have tried to identify types of communes in terms of the active or passive character of their recruitment practices and the population from which they draw their membership.

Those who are seeking communal living arrangements tend to use the same sources we ourselves have used in locating the places we studied: friends, public meetings or benefits presented by communes, crash pads or more stable communal houses in the Bay Area, "underground" information media, and "hip" establishments such as health-food stores, cafes, boutiques, free clinics, and random conversations with "street people" and hitchhikers. First contacts with rural communes tend to be with the "open" places, whose very openness have gained them wide publicity since all are welcome, including journalists who write about them: most prominently places like Wheeler's Ranch and Morningstar. The communes we have studied most closely are primarily "closed" communes, open only to members, to guests invited by members, and for short periods to visitors only if their motives are legitimate or if they otherwise pass the scrutiny of the group.

From a more theoretical perspective, we have recognized that implicit in all recruitment practices is the commune's image of the "ideal" member, a model toward which the already established communes strive. But this image, along with the activity or passivity of recruitment, varies in terms of what Zablocki has called "consensus" or "solidarity" types of communes. Consensus communes are those which are organized around a common religious or ideological (including political) creed which gives the commune its *raison d'etre* and provides a basis for cohesion. Such communes tend to actively recruit new members by advertising the creed and its promise of a new life, and by inviting adherence at least for a trial period. There is often a fee or regular payments of one kind or another involved. For obvious reasons these are the communes for which there is much publicity and to which access is easiest—although our investigations indicate the emergence of a new creedal type of commune in which general dedication to communal living constitutes the creed and in which recruitment has become selective in terms of the skills that the commune needs at the moment to make it more viable.

Access to communes with passive recruitment policies is far more difficult, and is what we have spent most of our time studying. These are the communes Zablocki calls "solidarity" communes, ones in which cohesion is provided by friendship or similar nonconsensual ties, and whose emphasis is on individual and family development rather than on conversion experiences of a basically religious sort. Such groups typically feel that they already have enough or more people than the land can support, and discussion is common on whether and how to acquire more land (to support more people) and whether to admit to membership people who want to join—for example, guests who may have been living at the commune for some time without actually being members of the family.

Communes of this type not only do not actively seek new members but may carefully guard their anonymity and value their insulation from publicity. At the same time they tend to be seriously concerned with the influx of young people into rural areas looking for communal living arrangements, and though they may be unable or unwilling to accommodate these people themselves, they are much concerned with the spread of the communal movement and encourage the development of new communes and the acquisition of additional land to sustain them. A recurrent question to our researchers, for example, is why we don't spend our money to start new communes.

We are currently using this typology and developing others in order to pay closer attention to their impact on the children. One of the first things one learns from field experience with communes is that it is very difficult to make general statements that are true of "communes"; and most of our subsequent findings and assertions will be carefully limited to types of communes.

METHODOLOGICAL ISSUES AND NEW DIRECTIONS

Our research design presumes the existence of communes as relatively distinct or discrete entities; it presumes as well the existence of communards with identifiable personal histories or biographies, the understanding of which helps to explain the communard's present situation. The design also assumes the value of gathering information on life in the commune primarily from the commune itself—that is, from observation and interviewing done primarily "on location." It also tends—though this is hardly a necessity—to deemphasize the "historical" quality of daily life. We are inclined to be more interested in "types" of communes and commune experiences than we are in the "stages of growth" of communards, particular communes, or the commune movement as a whole. Finally, we presume a relatively insignificant impact of the study or the individual researcher on the research site. These are not our only assumptions, of course, but they are important ones that have caused some repeated difficulty and should be discussed briefly here.

The assumption that communes can be studied as relatively discrete entities raises the traditional "unit of analysis" question common to most sociology and perhaps the study of socialization most particularly. Studies focusing initially on communities, families, institutions, or similar entities have a tendency to expand their focus as forces generating behavior within the unit being studied are traced to "outside" institutions. Thus our own field work made it apparent early in the study that many communes are integral to larger "tribes" or regional associations and raised the question to what extent these larger networks are the source of ideas or practices that bear directly or indirectly on socialization. Evidence that they are important in this regard raises the question whether we wish to focus primarily on the family or primarily on socialization—these overlap considerably, of course, but are not the same. A rigorously psychological or psychiatric orientation might incline us to limit the focus to the basics of parent- or adult-child interaction, but our view has been that the child may realistically "belong" to more than this primordial association and his growth substantially altered or conditioned by this fact. In practice, we are trying to avoid having to choose between narrower and broader foci; we are examining parent-child interaction in detail, but one of our research assistants is studying the lives of commune children not only within the commune but especially in their interaction with (and comparison to) the lives of children from the larger "straight" community, and another research assistant is studying the commune network in what amounts to an entire county.

In a similar vein, we are moving to include within our research the study of relations between communes and the often substantial panoply of officials with whom they have regular contact, including especially police, welfare, health, and school officials. Government agencies are a rich source of information about commune developments; more importantly, perhaps, the views of officials regarding these developments not only condition the development and implementation of public policy but often have a more direct impact on the behavior of communards. It is especially significant, too, that the "intervention of the state" seems so often to follow or be legitimated by official concern for the welfare or treatment of children—concerns that run directly parallel to our research interests.

This is, of course, especially the case with schools—public agencies of socialization. We have, accordingly, begun to examine in some greater detail a number of the many "free schools" that have recently been springing up in profusion in California and elsewhere. In many respects, examining how communes handle the "school problem" may be one of the best strategies for studying communal child rearing in general; as at least minimally formal and quasi-public institutions, they are relatively open to study—they straddle, as it were, the fence that stands between the commune and the larger society. It may be, too, that having to face the issue of what to do with the school-age children—in terms of their education—typically forces communes to begin formulating child-rearing strategies and ideas with a dedication that can be foregone (relatively and formally) as long as most of the children are not yet old enough for school in conventional terms. Interestingly, too, it has seemed to us that only recently, in the past year or two, have the second-generation school-age communards begun to be a significant population within the larger population of the communes.

The latter point is an example of the kind of information that is probably important but tends to be lost by our tendency, in drafting the original research design, to deemphasize the importance of history or stages of development. Significantly, communards typically do not move into or raise their children in "established" settlements—indeed, the creation of the settlement is one of the dominant themes of commune life. This means, however, that many behaviors might better be related to stages of development than to basic commune or family "types." The development of quasi-"professional" child care, for example, may not be absent in communes: it may come faster in communes that are based on creedal commitments rather than friendship alone, but it may owe its existence primarily to the demographic fact of an enlarging school-age population. This is probably the single most important reason why a longitudinal design is important, and led us to the decision to sample not only communes themselves, but the times at which we visited them over the three-year period of the study.

Another methodological issue of some importance to our study is the problem of gathering "biographical" information. Our design calls for the study of communards over three generations; biographies, however, are not highly visible (except, perhaps, those of the third generation) and information on them must thus be gathered through semistructured interviews. This is a difficult feat; communards are often very reserved about offering information of any kind to social scientists and, in our experience, exceptionally reticent about offering information regarding personal histories. At the outset this seemed to us simply to reflect the fact that building relationships of trust takes time, that biographical details would come naturally as our research team became accepted in the communes. A somewhat more subtle and perhaps more interesting possibility has been suggested, however—that there exists on the communes and perhaps among hippies in general a kind of taboo on "biography." Discourse on one's personal history is rare; the meaning of this, if it turns out to be as distinctive as it now seems, is as yet obscure to us, but it may serve to heighten participation in and commitment to the present setting, just as religious conversion often involves the idea of rebirth and the attempt to diminish the importance of the past. It may, too, make it easy to *leave* the present setting, since one has not selectively reconstructed his past so that it "points to" the decision to join a commune. In either case, however, biographical information may be either very hard to come by or very distorted in its presentation. One consultant has suggested that we attempt to do individual in-depth case histories of particular communards—that if we make our biographical work a more distinctive set of events, it may be more acceptable to the subjects. This is a possibility, but it may also be necessary to at least supplement our study of the three generations within particular families with small sample survey (interview) studies of separate adult and youth populations. One pilot study of this sort has already been undertaken— a study of attitudes toward communes and interest in communal living among approximately 300 students at the University of California at Davis; this study is currently approaching the analysis stage.

One final methodological concern deserves mention, namely, the degree to which our field work may operate to alter the situation being studied and hence "contaminate" the data to a greater or lesser degree. In general, our field workers have been accepted into their research sites—after some initial difficulties—to a gratifying degree, and have had no significant sense that the communards were "performing" for them. Such performing, however, is difficult to detect, and it is altogether reasonable to expect that communards being studied will behave more like ideal communards than would otherwise be the case. Moreover, in at least one case discussion of whether or not to admit a sociologist to the commune triggered the elaboration of an extensive set of rules regarding the treatment of outsiders—sociologists, guests, and visitors—that probably "defined" the commune to a greater degree than had previously been the case. In another situation, inquiries about schooling for the children appeared to have stimulated a considerable degree of semiformal "schooling" activity. The research team has been working to increase its sensitivity to issues of this sort and to develop appropriate strategies for handling them, including the use of "unobtrusive measures," interviews with ex-communards and commune visitors, use of field workers with different interests and perspectives in the same site, and, above all, comparison of the apparent consequences of approaching communes in different ways. In any case, we have no reason to believe at the present that the "up-front" identity of our staff as participant-observer researchers has "contaminated" the data in ways that compromise our efforts. And our sensitivity to the possibilities of this may in fact produce important methodological insights for future field work of this sort.

Epilogue: Themes, Theory, and Research

The student has now examined the articles in this book and my comments about them. I will not detain the reader very long but I do want to point briefly to certain common themes, interrelations, and implications for sociology that are present in these readings.

BASIC THEMES

1. Note that we began the book with my article on the theme of the universality of the family and ended the book with articles on the question of the universal meaning of illegitimacy and the new communal family. In short, sociology is not simply the study of narrowly delinated empirical areas in one society. It is also the study of very broad theoretical questions concerning the nature of human existence in terms of the essential features of human society. With our increased awareness of change, such an emphasis on essentials is very relevant. If one is interested in change, he must know what limits there are in terms of the universal requirements of human societies. Such limits in terms of mate selection, legitimation of offspring, and nurturance of the newborn are of first importance in the understanding of social change in the family system.

2. To some extent the question of male–female roles also cuts across the book. The early sections deal with articles on male–female role differences in childhood by Barry, Heilbrun, and others. The middle section of the book (Section VI) picked up this theme in terms of instrumental and expressive roles in marriage and the final section of the book points to family and occupational limits on female equality. Here too the fundamental issue of male and

female role differences is pervasive in many of the selections and raises some of the key issues in any explanation of the American family system. What is the range of alterable qualities that exist in both males and females? Which of Rossi's three approaches to female and male roles is most likely to occur? What impact will there be on our type of marital system from such role changes? These are but a few of the many fascinating questions that are raised by several of the readings on this theme.

3. The emotional involvement of husbands and wives and of courting couples is discussed in many of the articles, starting with those on premarital love in Section III and on sex in Section IV and following into the articles on marital dissolution in Section XI. Here again is a major theme that requires elaboration. Primary relationships (face-to-face, durable and intimate relationships) are the backbone of a social system and the family system offers the best perspective for viewing such relationships. Despite all the writing on divorce, separation, and general marital alienation, remarkably little is known about the process by which people increase or decrease their determination to stay together. I have called such determination to stay together "dyadic commitment" and, together with several colleagues, I plan to research this area carefully in a longitudinal study of newly married couples. The same should be done regarding dyodic commitment in courtship. Such studies would help us learn the basic nature of the formation and dissolution of dyads of all sorts, from short friendships to life-long matings.

4. Another key theme found in these articles is that concerned with the fit of the family system within the broad sociocultural context. This is discussed in articles by Leik (17) and Rodman (18) in Section VI, as well as in the articles in Section VIII dealing with occupational involvement. Clearly, one cannot understand the family system without understanding these strands that weave it into the social fabric. One of the most important points to arise from this area is that concerning the impact of parental occupational values on children, which can either help or hinder their upward mobility. With increased female occupational participation another force for change has been added to our social system. The communal family presents still another blending of occupation and family. The future shape of our society can be grasped much more clearly if we understand this key relationship between the family and occupational systems.

THE VALUE OF THE SOCIOLOGICAL APPROACH TO THE FAMILY

The four broad themes we have mentioned that permeate this reader afford some indication of the basic integrity and coherence of the sociology of the family, although they do not exhaust all the themes one could abstract from these readings. The articles that embody these four themes, which I have divided up into twelve major subdivisions, show the breadth of the family area of study. The integration of these twelve subject divisions by four themes and by other explanatory concepts I have discussed in my introductions, makes the study of the family *manageable*. But what makes the study *valuable* is that it is an essential prerequisite for both personal and scientific understanding of the current scene in America. If one is to understand what is happening to our courtship, marriage, and family institutions, then one must read research studies such as these. No one person's experience is representative and broad enough to enable him to understand and generalize about the entire society.

To understand how Americans carry out the universal functions of mate selection, legitimation, and nurturance of the newborn, one needs data from key research projects. But one needs more than that—one needs explanations. I have tried to stress in my choice of articles, and in my comments upon them, the essential quality of doing more than simply reporting percentages of what is going on. What we need to do is to develop theory—that is, to develop *explanations* of what is going on. Virtually every article in this reader does that. Some do more explaining than others and some do it better, but all the authors do more than simply report statistics. I have tried in my commentaries to raise the key questions that theory must answer and, on occasion, to offer some explanations of my own.

Finally, it is important that we gather our data with some sophistication and utilize the best methods and samples, so that we do not waste our energies trying to explain petty, unreliable, and unrepresentative research findings. I chose the studies in this reader partly on the basis of how well their authors had executed their research designs. I have occasionally made comments on the fact that a study used a probability sample of the country, or had carefully checked its findings in various subgroups of the sample, or had developed some other important area of methodology.

My basic reason for talking about theory and method is to alert the reader to the importance of being evaluative in his reading even of these carefully selected articles. The only way one can assess the various research reports intelligently is to have some fundamental ideas about what is good theory and good methodology. I believe this book will help in developing those ideas. If we want more than emotional responses to the key issues of our time, then we must support careful social-scientific research into the nature of human society. If we are to be intelligent consumers of research, then we must develop our critical faculties and examine closely the quality of the theoretical and methodological contributions of a research report. I believe one outcome of courses in sociology, in the family and in other subfields, is development of these critical faculties. I have tried to present these readings in a fashion that would arouse the curiosity of the reader about the sociology of the family area. If I have succeeded to some degree in this endeavor then my work in putting together this anthology has been worthwhile.